Managing Sport Facilities

Gil Fried, JD

University of New Haven

HUMAN KINETICS

Library of Congress Cataloging-in-Publication Data

Fried, Gil, 1965-
  Managing sport facilities / Gil Fried.
      p. cm.
  Includes bibliographical references and index.
  ISBN 0-7360-4483-3 (hard cover)
  1. Sports facilities--Management--Textbooks. I. Title.
  GV401.F75 2005
  725'.8043--dc22

                              2004030046

ISBN-10: 0-7360-4483-3
ISBN-13: 978-0-7360-4483-7

The Web addresses cited in this text were current as of September 29, 2004, unless otherwise noted.

Acquisitions Editor: Myles Schrag; **Developmental Editor:** D.K. Bihler; **Managing Editor:** Amanda S. Ewing; **Assistant Editor:** Amanda M. Eastin; **Copyeditor:** Joyce Sexton; **Proofreader:** Pam Johnson; **Indexer:** Susan Danzi Hernandez; **Permission Manager:** Dalene Reeder; **Graphic Designer:** Nancy Rasmus; **Graphic Artist:** Dawn Sills; **Photo Manager:** Kelly Huff; **Cover Designer:** Keith Blomberg; **Photographer (cover):** © Dale Garvey; **Art Manager:** Kelly Hendren; **Illustrator:** Kathleen Boudreau-Fuoss; **Printer:** Edwards Brothers

Printed in the United States of America   10 9 8 7 6 5 4 3 2

Human Kinetics
Web site: www.HumanKinetics.com

United States: Human Kinetics
P.O. Box 5076
Champaign, IL 61825-5076
800-747-4457
e-mail: humank@hkusa.com

Canada: Human Kinetics
475 Devonshire Road Unit 100
Windsor, ON N8Y 2L5
800-465-7301 (in Canada only)
e-mail: orders@hkcanada.com

Europe: Human Kinetics
107 Bradford Road
Stanningley
Leeds LS28 6AT, United Kingdom
+44 (0) 113 255 5665
e-mail: hk@hkeurope.com

Australia: Human Kinetics
57A Price Avenue
Lower Mitcham, South Australia 5062
08 8277 1555
e-mail: liaw@hkaustralia.com

New Zealand: Human Kinetics
Division of Sports Distributors NZ Ltd.
P.O. Box 300 226 Albany
North Shore City
Auckland
0064 9 448 1207
e-mail: info@humankinetics.co.nz

To all the men and women who keep our
public assembly facilities running

Contents

PART IV Facility Administration

PART V Event and Activity Management

Preface

Almost all of us have fond memories of a sport-related experience. The experience might entail our first game as a spectator, our first request for a ballplayer's autograph, or even eating our first hotdog. We may look back at having wonderful seats to watch a game, catching a foul ball in the stands, or attending a game with a special promotional giveaway. Whatever the experience, more than likely a sport facility was involved.

When people think about large sport facilities they often focus on how to navigate through crowds and traffic in the shortest possible amount of time. Others might think about the sights, sounds, and smells that made an event memorable. Still others might have negative thoughts based on a professional team's threats to move if not given a new facility. For smaller facilities such as health clubs, people might think about convenience and the breadth of services available.

For those managing sport facilities, the facility experience is vastly different. Indeed, very few people realize what an enormous undertaking it is to develop and operate these facilities. For example, how much toilet paper needs to be ordered for 1,000 bathroom stalls? How many hotdogs need to be ordered if 70,000 fans will be attending a game? What happens when the facility's water pressure is interrupted? What if a major generator breaks during a sporting event? What if a storm or an environmental disaster damages (or destroys) the playing field? How do you promote a rock concert one day and a monster truck pull the next? How do you change over a facility from an ice hockey surface to a basketball surface in just three hours without ruining the ice? How do you handle disorderly or rowdy fans and customers? How do you hire and manage a part-time staff of possibly 600 ushers, concessionaires, ticket takers, and security personnel? What happens when a facility runs into financial hardships? These are just some of the questions that a facility manager has to face

on a daily basis. This book was written to help highlight the broad array of responsibilities faced by facility managers.

The Purpose of This Book

The question this book addresses is how to effectively manage a sport facility. The book focuses on sport facilities. However, much of the subject matter is also applicable to any number of public assembly facilities, including music theaters, auditoriums, convention centers, and high school and college arenas and stadiums. Public facilities can also include bowling alleys, health clubs, sports-plexes, park and recreation facilities, and numerous other natural and man-made environments.

Written for students in sport and facility management, as well as professionals already working in the field, the text provides a comprehensive knowledge base. An introductory-level discussion is provided for those who have never before studied sport facility management (FM). Thus, after reading this book, beginning students will have a solid grasp of the fundamental skills in FM and will have the knowledge base to apply those skills in the real world. In-depth explanation, real-world examples, and detailed assessment of various FM issues are also provided to expand understanding and spur knowledge application for industry professionals. Some of the FM concerns discussed in this text are preventive maintenance, facility planning, event administration, box office management, house and grounds management, systems management, marketing, finance, and personnel administration.

It should be noted that every facility and its management structure is different. Some facilities rely on an owner to make all decisions, from designing the building and obtaining funds to removing the trash every day. Other facilities, primarily larger ones, have multiple individuals serving in different capacities and may have a financial consultant developing the funding strategy, a construction manager working during construction, a facility manager handling bookings, and an outside contracting company providing security and concession services.

The comprehensive overview offered by this book currently is not available from other texts. Most FM books focus on safety, marketing, construction, or event management. They fail to combine these important disciplines into one comprehensive text and rarely cover important topics such as the history of sport facilities, the types of systems within a building, and the ways in which buildings are actually built and managed. This text covers FM for a sport facility in a comprehensive manner that includes both educational references and professional industry insight.

The need for a comprehensive sport FM text has been highlighted over the past several years with the push to build new, large, high-technology sport facilities that are more complex to operate and manage than in the past. Similarly, fitness, recreation, and sport facilities have fueled significant career opportunities that present unique issues such as how to develop a facility business plan including feasibility studies; what finance vehicle is most effective for raising necessary capital; how to control costs through preventive maintenance; how to schedule and book event dates; and how to market luxury and premium seating to maximize revenue. Through reading and understanding this text, a current or future sport facility manager will be in a better position to respond effectively to new challenges.

How This Text Is Organized

After presenting an overview of sport facilities through the ages, the text focuses on what is involved in FM and on the manager's primary responsibility, getting employees at the facility to accomplish their job. The text then walks the reader through the basics from developing a facility through running a facility. It then turns to issues involved in running programs and personnel. Lastly, the text examines what is required to produce a high-quality event at a sport facility. The book is organized into five parts.

Part I of the book is an introduction to the sport facility industry. A brief historical perspective helps highlight how sport facilities have evolved over the years. Chapter 2 then addresses the role of the facility manager and the various concerns faced by facility managers. Since facility managers must accomplish goals primarily through employees, chapter 3 deals with the art of effective managerial communication and leadership.

Part II analyzes the complex process of deciding to build and finance a facility. Various topics such as the validity of feasibility studies, how to select a site, and how to handle environmental impact issues are discussed. This part of the text continues with an in-depth analysis of the initial facility business planning process, a discussion of how to obtain financial and political support, and an examination of the various types of facilities and fields that can be built. This part highlights the facility building process, including analysis of how to develop a site plan to maximize the available resources. Part II ends with a thorough analysis of the construction process to build a facility.

After a facility is built, it has to be operated. Part III covers the operations side of facilities (both internal and external) and such topics as maintenance and housekeeping. Systems management is then covered, with emphasis on major systems such as facility infrastructure, HVAC (heating, ventilation, and air conditioning), energy management, waste management, and all exterior systems.

Part IV analyzes the FM process by looking at some of the critical administrative areas that a facility manager supervises. This part covers some of the nuts and bolts associated with FM, such as marketing, finance, legal issues, human resource administration, and the entire administrative process.

Part V provides an in-depth analysis of managing all the activities that occur within the facility. Once a facility is up and running, is in good shape, and has qualified personnel, what are the steps required to make money? Event administration is the primary focus of this part of the text. Topics include booking, scheduling, box office management, event safety, guest services, food and beverage management, and all the issues encountered when the event is planned, run, and then concluded.

How to Use This Text

Besides the educational material contained within the discussions of the various topics, the text is organized to clearly convey concepts through several strategies. Each chapter lists specific objectives and includes a chapter overview. Each chapter also has a chapter summary and several discussion questions and activities. Among the most important elements in each chapter are sections titled "Facility Focus" and "Behind the Scenes." The facility focus sections provide information about particular facilities, including important facts and strategies used by the facility to succeed. The "Behind the Scenes" material presents unique concerns and strategies that can make a facility manager more successful. All these elements combine to help weave the material into a full and coherent picture of the subject.

Acknowledgments

I would like to thank my wife and kids for the time and patience they have shown over the past couple years as this book was finished. Writing a book takes a lot of effort, and those around me had to understand and appreciate the long hours and the time away from the family. My parents were always there to listen to my thoughts and ideas, and I love them and appreciate everything that they have done for me over the years.

I would like to extend a special thank you to the entire School of Business at the University of New Haven for their assistance throughout the project. Special accolades go to my dean, Julian Schuster, Department Chairperson Abbas Nadim, and my close colleague, mentor, and friend, Allen Sack, who is an inspiration in terms of his dedication and love of teaching sport management.

The entire Human Kinetics staff has been phenomenal through both the good and the bad times. Amy Clocksin has been a great acquisitions editor to work with on the past couple books. D.K. Bihler was a good source of direction for the text. Unfortunately, she passed away during the editing of this book, and we will all miss her dedication to this project. Myles Schrag and Amanda Ewing came in and provided valuable advice and assistance to help get the book finished. The entire production staff at HK was instrumental in this, and I really appreciated their help.

I want to extend a very special thanks to my contributing editor, Frank Russo, Jr. Frank has been both a colleague and friend for many years. I am humbled by the breadth of his knowledge and also by his eagerness to share that knowledge with me and my students. In addition, Frank has been instrumental in furthering the body of knowledge for the International Association of Assembly Managers (IAAM), and I want to give credit to the IAAM for all their work on spreading knowledge for facility managers.

Lastly, I would like to thank the folks at Carolina Academic Press for allowing me to use the sexual harassment policy from my employment law book and the facility risk audit from *Safe at First*, also published by Carolina Academic Press.

PART I

Introduction to Sport Facility Management

History of Sport and Public Assembly Facilities

After completing this chapter you will be able to do the following:

- Understand how the Greeks and Romans used sport facilities for political and cultural ends
- Have a historical understanding of how sport facilities have changed to accommodate changes in sport and spectating demands
- Identify how sport facilities have evolved from multiuse to single-use facilities
- Appreciate the history behind several major sport facilities
- Understand how facility trends that developed in the United States were adopted in the late 20th century in international construction projects
- Understand how and why politics will continue to influence sport facilities in the future

How many sport facilities exist in the world? This is a difficult question. The answer depends on your definition of a **sport facility**. Arenas or stadiums, YMCAs, and bowling alleys can all be classified as sport facilities. Typically excluded from the definition of a sport facility are natural areas such as lakefront property where people might engage in water-related sports. Also excluded from the traditional definition are open recreational areas such as golf courses. While a golf course is a self-contained sport facility, some might categorize it as a recreational facility that can be torn down quickly to be replaced by a business park. Thus, permanency could be a factor in defining a sport facility. However, any facility can be torn down and replaced by a business park. Over the past 20 years, numerous stadiums and arenas have been torn down and turned into parking lots. Therefore, permanency might not be as important as other factors, such as being enclosed, being able to control conduct in the facility, or having room for participants and spectators. For purposes of this text, a sport facility is defined as any enclosed facility where sports are played. The enclosure can be either natural or man-made. However, the enclosure has to be complete so that the facility is self-contained.

Another equally important term is **public assembly facility (PAF).** Public assembly facilities include sport facilities as well as other entertainment or non-entertainment facilities where large groups of people can gather. Typical examples of PAFs are arenas, stadiums, theaters, and convention centers. All these types of facilities can host sport-related events. This text utilizes the term *PAF* as well as the term *sport facility.*

From ancient times to the present, sport facilities have been the hallmark or focal point of many cultures. Sport facilities have changed, but the changes are not as dramatic as they might seem. The ancient Greeks and Romans utilized their sport facilities to placate people, help train athletes, entertain fans, and achieve political agendas. Present-day Olympic stadiums serve the same purpose. This chapter presents information on ancient through modern facilities, focusing on how facilities have evolved and what might have led to this evolution. Facilities were initially publicly funded to provide entertainment and promote religious and political goals. In brief, facilities have gone through a transformation process such that they still often focus on entertainment but also promote financial objectives as much as political goals. The Greeks and Romans mastered the art of the **multiuse facility**—facilities used for numerous types of events from chariot races to mock naval battles. Similar facilities were built in the 1960s and 1970s to host baseball and football games, but these facilities became extinct with the single-use outdoor facility boom of the 1990s. Indoor arenas, however, still host multiple events and can switch from a setup for one event to a completely different setup in just a couple of hours.

After outlining how facilities have changed over time, this chapter examines several professional and collegiate facilities to show the variety of facilities that exist today. Discussion then turns to future trends such as international facility issues, the growth of Olympic facilities, and the ways in which politics will continue to affect sport facilities in the future.

Facilities in Ancient Times

In order to appreciate current and future issues involved in sport facility management, it is critical to understand how far the industry has progressed since ancient times. However, a review of some facts associated with Greek and Roman sport facilities suggests that we are still using some of the ancient strategies.

Greece

In ancient Greece, sports were a form of worship. Olympia was one of the oldest religious centers in the Greek world. Because of its religious history, Olympia was a natural site for the origin of the Olympic Games. The Games were part spectacle and part religious ceremony. The Greeks undertook a major religious festival honoring Zeus, and the festival held at Olympia was the biggest event in the world at that time ("Real Story," 2002).

Olympic Facilities

People came from near and far to participate in and watch the games at Olympia. The throngs of people needed a place to gather—in other words, they needed a PAF. The original Olympic stadium, built in Olympia in 776 B.C., was an extension of an already existing religious sanctuary dedicated to Zeus. Combining the sanctuary and other buildings added over time, the facility formed the first known **sport complex,** complete with altars, a hostel for visitors built in the fourth century B.C., training facilities for wrestlers and boxers, a gymnasium with a covered running track, and of course the facility called the Stadia where the actual events took place ("Real Story," 2002).

The Stadia was shaped like a U built into the hillside, with massive sloping embankments on each side of the U that served as seating. On the fourth side, the natural slope of the hill was also used for seating. Athletes and umpires came into the Stadia through their own entrance. There were multiple vaulted entrances for spectators. The chief judges and a priestess sat in special stone seats. According to some, all women except for the priestess were banned as spectators. Others believe that only unmarried women were welcome to enter the stadium ("Real Story," 2002).

Inside the Stadia the track was about 230 yards (210 meters) long and 35 yards (32 meters) wide. It was separated from the sloping embankments by a low stone parapet beside which ran an open stone water channel with basins at intervals. There was enough space for 20 people to run at one time. There was also enough space for cart races and chariot races ("Real Story," 2002). Sources show some discrepancy as to what games were held in the Olympic stadium and when they were held. Some evidence suggests that Olympic Games date back to a time before the actual stadium was built. In fact, various open fields and areas were used for religious sanctuaries. It would seem logical that games were held in these places as part of the religious ceremonies.

Some historians argue that a foot race of one stadium length was initially the only competition held in the new stadium at Olympia. Others say that even in the beginning, the Olympic competitions consisted of a wide variety of sports that are still represented in modern-day Olympic competitions. There is widespread agreement that by classical times, 18 different contests were held, including boxing, wrestling, horse races, the pentathlon, and other running events.

In addition to athletic events there were religious ceremonies that included sacrifices, speeches by well-known philosophers, poetry recitals, singers, parades, banquets, and victory celebrations. Merchants, craftsmen, and food vendors sold their wares. And, of course, no large gathering would be complete without gamblers, con men, prostitutes, and pimps ("Real Story," 2002). Though considered large even by today's standards, the original Olympic stadium could not have begun to accommodate current numbers of athletes and spectators. The Atlanta Olympic Games in 1996 attracted 10,700 athletes from 197 countries. There

Ancient Olympia Stadium, built in Olympia, Greece, in 776 B.C., is a stark contrast to the Olympic stadium from the 2004 Athens Summer Olympic Games.

were over 2 million live spectators and as many as 3.5 billion television viewers ("Context," 2002). These numbers will probably continue to increase in future Olympics. All-time records were set when 202 countries and 11,099 athletes participated in 28 sports and 296 events in the 2004 Olympics in Greece (Athens 2004, 2004).

Information on basic comfort and hygiene in ancient facilities is difficult to come by, which may indicate that there were no rest rooms. However, 50,000 to 60,000 visitors slept outside the stadium, under the stars, so there must have been some accommodations. Wealthy people and members of official delegations erected elaborate tents and pavilions. Water was carted from springs a half-mile away. Water was critical and probably fostered the first concession sales since the stadium was uncomfortable, dusty, and hot.

Similar to the situation with Madison Square Garden (see later in this chapter), the stadium at Olympia did not remain in its original location. At about the middle of the fourth century B.C., the stadium was moved 90 yards (82 meters) east and a little to the north of its original location. Although it moved, it retained its connection to the sanctuary via the Krypte. The Krypte was a covered entrance that ran through the embankment. This was the entrance through which athletes and umpires entered the stadium. Just as it is today, location was important in the choice of a stadium site. Olympia was convenient to reach by ship. Athletes and spectators traveled from Greek colonies as far away as modern-day Spain, the Black Sea, and Egypt.

The stadium at Olympia was not the only stadium in Greece. The Olympic Stadium in Athens was built in 331 B.C. and held 50,000 spectators. Like many older modern facilities, it has gone through major renovations, beginning with a reconstruction in A.D. 160. However, it lay dormant for centuries, since in A.D. 393. Emperor Theodosius abolished the Games for being "too pagan" ("History," 2004a). This facility was used to host the 1896 Olympic Games.

Hippodromes and Theaters

Other PAFs developed by the Greeks included theaters and hippodromes. Greek theaters had three main parts. The scene or skene was a painted backdrop. The orchestra was a circular area in front of the scene. The actors performed on a narrow raised

Delphi stadium, built in the fifth century B.C., was used extensively during the Pythian and Panhellenic games for athletic events and for music festivals.

© Sergio Piumatti

platform in front of the scene called the logeion. Lastly, there was the koilon for seating. The koilon was originally built from wood and later from stone. It was semicircular and was built around the orchestra. The koilon was divided into two sections, called diazoma, which included upper and lower seating tiers. Special seats were reserved for officials and priests. Examples of Greek stadiums can be seen in Epidauros (where the stadium was built about 330 B.C.), Argos, and Delphi. These theaters seated 14,000, 20,000, and 5,000, respectively ("Epidauro," 2002).

Many hippodromes were built around Greece. These facilities were for horse races as well as chariot races. They were originally open fields lined with raised banks of earth. There was no seating—spectators stood for the races. Eventually these rudimentary facilities evolved into huge stone facilities seating tens or even hundreds of thousands of spectators. The hippodrome in Olympia lay south of the stadium in the open valley of the Alpheus. No trace of it has been found.

Rome

The Roman Empire followed the Greek Empire as the dominant culture of its time. The Romans loved their sports, and the leaders leveraged this interest into a means to control their subjects for days on end. Some events lasted for several days, with spectators eating and drinking themselves beyond traditional limits. It was hoped that the excited and tired subjects who had spent all their money would eventually return to their homes and not complain about the leadership since they had experienced such a wonderful event. In order to help effectuate these plans, the leaders needed large facilities such as the Coliseum and Circus Maximus.

Coliseum

As Roman civilization rose, the need for PAFs rose with it. Most notable was the Coliseum with its spectacles and gladiators (Blickstein, 1995). The Romans built their stadiums based on past Greek structures. In some cases, as with the amphitheaters, Rome simply renovated or rebuilt old Greek structures.

The Coliseum was originally named the Flavian Amphitheater after the emperors who built it: Vespasian and Titus, both of the Flavian family. Construction began around A.D. 70 and took about 10 years to complete. When it was done, the Coliseum stood 160 feet (48 meters) high with four stories of windows, arches, and columns. Each of the three exterior floors consisted of 80 arches. The facility could hold up to 50,000 spectators ("History," 2002). Visitors climbed sloping ramps to their seats. Seating was according to gender and social class. Women and the poor stood or sat on wooden benches in the fourth tier of seating. The reserved luxury seats were marble, and their bases were inscribed with the names of the senators and knights who occupied them. Vestal virgins, religious officials, soldiers, civilians, and boys with their tutors all had special seating sections. The emperor had a special box for himself and his family.

The Roman Coliseum is a classic example of a multiuse facility.

© AP/World Wide Photos

It is estimated that 50,000 people could enter the arena and be seated in about 15 minutes, owing to the ticketing system developed by the Romans. Before an event a spectator would pick up a ticket, often made from pottery shards. Each ticket had a number that corresponded to one of the 78 entrance archways, which all had numbers above them. Tickets also had levels and seat numbers. Similar ticketing systems are used to this day ("History," 2002).

The Coliseum embodied much of the technology of its time. Enormous colored awnings made of canvas could be stretched overhead to prevent the hot sun from making spectators uncomfortable. These awnings, called velarium, were attached to rigs operated by sailors who were hired solely for this purpose. The wooden floor contained lifts, pulleys, and at least 24 giant trap doors. The Coliseum also had subterranean chambers where the gladiators, as well as the animals, were kept prior to performances. A hand-operated elevator was used to raise animals from the basement up to the arena floor. The underground chambers could be flooded with water and the stadium then used to stage mock naval battles. Over time this activity damaged the flooring and was thus discontinued ("History," 2002).

Circus Maximus

In addition to the Coliseum and other Roman amphitheaters, the Romans had the circus. The circus was the Roman version of a racetrack. It was the setting for chariot races and other events, both equestrian and non-equestrian. The most famous Roman circus was the Circus Maximus, built to emulate the Greek hippodrome and considered one of the architectural wonders of the ancient world. Constructed of wood in the sixth century B.C., it was destroyed by fire twice and also was subject to flooding. On at least two occasions the stands collapsed, killing many people. Eventually the Circus Maximus was rebuilt of stone and masonry ("Amphitheater," 2002).

Historians have estimated the seating capacity of the Circus as ranging from 150,000 to over 300,000. It is assumed that the number of spectators surpassed seating capacity and that many observers stood for the duration of the events. Unlike what happened in other Roman PAFs, men and women could sit together at the Circus. The Circus also had skyboxes and reserved seating for the emperor, senators, knights, judges, a prize-awarding jury, and the financial backers for the various races ("Circus Maximus," 2002). The track was a third of a mile (0.5 kilometers) long and 150 yards (137 meters) wide. It was covered with earth and then a layer of sand. The sand allowed chariots to hold the track. It also protected the horses from injury and allowed water to drain off. Like today's racetracks, the track was a large oval.

Admission to the Circus Maximus was free; however, it was still a revenue center. Concession stands sold fast food and snacks. Spectators could rent a seat cushion if they did not bring their own from home. In his book *Roman People*, Robert B. Kebric describes the Circus as a four-story facility with a maze of shops, rooms, stairways, and arcades. Thousands of people moved about the large corridors throughout the facility. In the facility, vendors sold their wares, which included refreshments and souvenirs. There were also a plethora of prostitutes, gamblers, pickpockets, girl watchers, and drunks (Kebric, 2000).

Facilities From the Middle Ages to the 1800s

Most sports and games of medieval times were less organized than today's sports. The sports also involved more "folksy" types of activities that highlighted the skills of the local citizenry. One of the popular sports during this time was "folk football," which was a wild and rough attempt at organized attacking of other people. The more common events included such activities as hunting, falconry, and tracking with hunting dogs. These events did not require a set facility and often were conducted in hunting grounds or forests.

Medieval events that were most suited to such settings included jousting and archery matches. Jousting was probably the best-known sport of the times, especially for the upper class. The common folk were more accustomed to archery matches, which often pitted one town against another. The lower class was allowed to participate in other simultaneous events such as running, jumping, cudgeling, and wrestling. These matches often involved large feasts, which included a large amount of alcohol. The abundance of alcohol and lewd conduct was one reason the Church stepped in to try to stop these events. In fact, religion played a major role in sport for many years.

In addition to the Greeks and Romans, the Chinese, Japanese, North American Indians, and other groups developed various sports around religion. The Christian Emperor Theodosius stopped the Olympic Games because he felt they were pagan rites. However, in the Middle Ages the Church supported horse races and tournaments as long as the events honored the Virgin Mary (Aurandt, 2002). The Church and the government sometimes encouraged and at other times banned sport. In fact, in England during the 14th century, working people who were caught playing football or tennis (played with a pig's bladder or leather stuffed with rags) were imprisoned for up to six years. The upper class and clergy were not subject to such punishment (Aurandt, 2002).

Because of the lack of support by the clergy and government, the Middle Ages were not the high point for PAFs. In fact, PAFs went into decline at the end of the Roman Empire when the Church outlawed theaters. Ironically, though, it was the Church that kept theater alive through seasonal festivals, which took on a dramatic form to help better illustrate the religious connotations to illiterate congregants. Because the authorities were concerned about touring companies carrying the plague or about civil unrest caused by drunken spectators, theaters did not prosper ("Greek Theater," 2002). While theaters eventually grew out of and thrived after the Roman and Greek periods, sport facilities were hard to find. In fact, research has shown very few sport facilities except for informal areas established for such events as horse races, hunts, and other outdoor, open-air, events that did not necessarily require any fixed seating areas. Thus, while cricket and tennis were to become popular in the United States, there is no record of any public facilities for these sports until the end of the 19th century (Manchester, 1931).

In the 19th century, most restrictions against sport were lifted; and one of the first facilities built in the United States was Union Course, constructed in New York in 1825. The horse racing facility included stands, a clubhouse, and a balcony. It was very popular—over 60,000 spectators attended one race (Manchester, 1931). Baseball started gaining popularity in the 1850s, and facility management rules were initially developed in the 1870s. The first three major rules for the National League had to do with banning alcohol from the parks, removing the betting booths from the field entrances, and removing gamblers from the stands (Manchester, 1931).

Facility Management From Ancient to Modern Times

While facilities have changed significantly over the years, it is interesting that their management and operations have remained somewhat stable. Just as there were different classes of seating in the Coliseum, amphitheaters, and the Circus Maximus, we have different classes of seating today. Just as in earlier eras important people had reserved seats in advantageous positions, we have club seats and luxury suites today.

The "behind-the-scenes" workings of an event are often beyond the knowledge of average facility patrons. Security, stagehands, and medical services are just a few examples of behind-the-scenes support services. In ancient times there were also staff members whose job it was to keep things running smoothly. At the Coliseum, sailors were employed to work the enormous colored awnings used to shelter spectators from the hot sun. Archers took stations on catwalks above the crowd. They were there to shoot rowdy fans, resistant participants, or animals that presented a threat to the audience.

Regardless of the type of entertainment offered by large public venues, many of the managerial concerns have stayed the same. Some of the considerations that have remained consistent over the centuries include the following:

- Controlling and moving large numbers of people
- Managing rowdy or violent crowds
- Maintaining flexibility in multiuse venues (e.g., gladiators and mock naval battles; basketball and ice shows)
- Providing security and protection for VIPs
- Controlling the types of petty crime that are inherent with large gatherings of people
- Keeping facilities clean and operational
- Navigating the politics associated with getting appropriate funding for publicly owned facilities

Of course there have been changes in the PAF industry over the years. A few modern-day concerns that did not trouble managers in ancient times are these:

- Providing amenities for the press such as interview rooms and press boxes with Internet access
- Setting up TV camera platforms and TV cable hookups
- Selling advertising space and naming rights
- Providing batting cages and other practice areas
- Providing athletic training rooms
- Utilizing heating, ventilation, and air conditioning (HVAC) systems
- Complying with environmental, zoning, accessibility, and other legal issues

These differences have evolved over many years. The evolution has been led by the change in sport facility owners and providers. Initially the government and churches were behind PAFs. However, with the increased money found in sport in the 19th and 20th centuries, private providers built or ran PAFs as profit ventures, even if public funds had been used to build the facility. Numerous changes have been spearheaded by managers trying to generate the greatest revenue stream possible from the facilities. One example is the shift of concession sales from peanuts and Cracker Jack to sushi and five-star cuisine.

Evolution of Professional and Collegiate Facilities

The modern era for sport facilities started in the late 1880s, with several additional booms occurring in the 1960s to 1970s and the 1990s. The first ballpark, Union Grounds in Brooklyn, New York, was built in 1862. Union Grounds and other ballparks of that time were generally made of wood and often did not have outfield fences; instead there was a barrier at the end of the property to prevent freeloaders (Schlossberg, 1983). Horse-drawn carriages and, later, cars were allowed to pull into the outfield so that people could watch the game from their vehicles. Other spectators were allowed to sit on backless planks of wood. The last game to be played in such a stadium before the concrete-and-steel stadiums became the norm was a game at Robison Field in St. Louis on June 6, 1920. The Philadelphia Nationals built their Baker Bowl in 1887 and opened the season to an attendance of 14,500 fans. The Bowl cost $80,000 to build, which 90 years later was the average yearly salary for a Major League Baseball player (Schlossberg, 1983). The first fireproof stadiums built of concrete and steel opened in 1909, with

The 1908 Olympics were held at London's White City Stadium. The stadium held 150,000 spectators.

Philadelphia's Shibe Park and Pittsburgh's Forbes Field (Blickstein, 1995).

The sport facility revival was also fueled by the Olympic Games. For the first modern Olympic Games in 1896, Greece built a stadium that sat 66,000 fans. Large stadiums were built for subsequent Olympics such as London's White City Stadium, built in 1908; and the Los Angeles Memorial Coliseum, originally built in 1923, was subsequently enlarged for the 1932 and 1984 Olympic Games (Blickstein, 1995).

Intercollegiate sport also helped further the development of sport facilities in the United States. In 1912, Yale was the first university to build a large football only stadium. This facility had wood planks that sat 18,000, and in 1916 was expanded to seat 33,000 fans. Yale's perennial nemesis Harvard jumped on the bandwagon earlier in 1904 when it built the first steel- and concrete-reinforced stadium in America, which seated 23,000 fans. In response, Yale spent $235,000 building a steel and concrete stadium that could seat 50,000 fans (Blickstein, 1995). Yale also built one of the oldest active baseball stadiums, which is used by the university's baseball team and a minor league professional baseball team (see the Facility Focus in chapter 9). Most professional baseball teams now play in more modern facilities, but some older

Table 1.1 Oldest Active Baseball Stadiums

Facility	Opened	Capacity	Cost to build
Fenway Park	1912	36,298	$650,000
Wrigley Field	1914	38,902	$250,000
Yankee Stadium	1924	57,545	$2,500,000

From Ballparks.com, 2002.

ballparks are still being used. Table 1.1 lists the oldest baseball facilities that are still being utilized at the start of the 21st century.

While some teams have played for numerous years at the same facility, only two recent expansion teams, the Tampa Bay Devil Rays and the Arizona Diamondbacks, have been in the same stadium since their inception. Sometimes the facility journey undertaken by a team is as significant as the way the team has evolved, as in the case of the Cincinnati Reds. Table 1.2 highlights the various names the team has used and the facilities they have played in over the years. It should be noted that Crosley Field in Cincinnati hosted the first lighted night baseball game in the majors in 1935.

While professional baseball teams have moved over the years, moving is usually not an option for college and university teams and facilities. Most colleges do not move, especially well-established colleges that are housed on large campuses. These schools often have had facilities for numerous years on campus and have continually expanded the facilities to meet attendance demands. Table 1.3 lists the opening dates and seating capacities of football stadiums in the Big Ten Conference.

Table 1.2   Cincinnati Reds Stadium Odyssey

Year	Stadium	Team name
1876-1879	Avenue Grounds	Cincinnati Red Stockings
1880	Bank Street Grounds	Same
1881	Did not play	
1882-1883	Bank Street Grounds	Same
1884-1889	League Park	Same
1890-1901	League Park	Cincinnati Reds
1902-1911	Palace of the Fans	Same
1912-1933	Redlands Field	Same
1934-1952	Crosley Field	Same
1953-1958	Crosley Field	Cincinnati Redlegs
1959-1970	Crosley Field	Cincinnati Reds
1970-1996	Riverfront Stadium	Same
1997-2002	Cynergy Field (name changed)	Same
2003	Great American Ball Park	Same

Table 1.3   Big Ten Football Stadium Seating Capacity in 1990s

Facility, university	Opened	Capacity
Camp Randall Stadium, Wisconsin	1917	76,129
Ohio Stadium, Ohio	1922	101,568
Memorial Stadium, Illinois	1923	70,904
Ross-Ade Stadium, Purdue	1924	67,861
Ryan Field, Northwestern	1926	49,256
Michigan Stadium, Michigan	1927	107,501
Kinnick Stadium, Iowa	1929	70,397
Spartan Stadium, Michigan State	1957	72,027
Memorial Stadium, Indiana	1960	52,354
Beaver Stadium, Penn State	1960	106,537
Medrodome, Minnesota	1982	64,035

As shown in table 1.3, teams that have traditionally been national powerhouses (e.g., Penn State, Michigan, Ohio State University) have the highest seating capacities to maximize their revenue potential. These facilities have often undertaken significant renovations to expand their seating bowls over the years. In contrast, teams that have traditionally not been as strong (e.g., Northwestern) have not expanded their facilities since the market demand for tickets has not dictated such an expansion (even if tickets are scarce in the years when the school does very well). Such a decision can impact opposing teams; gate receipts are usually shared, and if the venue is too small, this will eventually hurt other teams in the conference.

While collegiate facilities have remained relatively constant with some updating, professional sport facilities have changed significantly. The 1960s saw a trend to build multiuse facilities to save money. However, in the 1990s there was a push for single-use and more intimate stadiums, as well as larger arenas with more luxury seating options. During the building boom between 1987 and 2002, 84 new stadiums and arenas were built (with another seven under construction), often under the threat of current teams moving to a new city if a facility was not built. Six NFL teams switched cities between 1980 and 2002; two NBA teams switched between 2000 and 2002; and three NHL teams moved in the 1990s (Ellis, 2002). Table 1.4 shows the various major professional leagues

in the United States, the number of teams in the leagues, the number of new facilities built, and the number of facilities planned as of 2004.

As of 2001, only Minnesota, Miami, Oakland, and San Diego still had football and baseball tenants in the same stadium, and Miami and San Diego were hoping to have separate facilities in the near future ("NFL Stadium Financing," 2001). While the threat of a team leaving a given city can help fuel a push to build a new facility, other factors include strong economic trends (as witnessed in the 1990s), new marketing trends (such as the luxury suite and naming right trends of the 1990s), special event needs such as Olympics or the World Cup, and technological innovations such as retractable roofs or domed stadiums. For example, the first domed stadium ever built was the Astrodome in Houston, Texas, completed in 1965. Nine additional domes were built in the 1970s, including the Silverdome, Kingdome, and Superdome. In the 1980s only seven domes were built. In the 1990s, 12 domes were built ("Domed Stadiums," 2002). Between 2000 and 2002, seven domed stadiums were constructed. These numbers indicate that domes are still being designed to help eliminate one of the biggest marketing disasters that can befall a facility—inclement weather.

One of the biggest advances over the past 40 years has been the transition to more privately financed and built facilities. Government entities are the most common owners/operators of sport facilities. In socialized countries such as Great Britain and Canada, numerous sport facilities are owned and managed by government entities. In the United States there are also a significant number of government facilities. There are 92,000 public schools in the United States. Almost every public school has a multipurpose room, gymnasium, or playing field (or more than one of these). In addition, there are thousands of park and recreation departments, most having several facilities and fields.

During the 1990s, as is typical in strong economic periods, government-owned sport facilities were being built across the United States. This does not usually represent a problem. However, just building a facility does not end the financial and managerial responsibility of operating the facility. When the economic environment soured in the early 2000s, state and local government units began to get strapped for cash. To reduce budget problems, government facilities started to

Table 1.4 New Stadium and Arena Construction Since the 1980s

League	Number of teams	Number of new facilities	Number of proposed facilities
Major League Baseball	30	18	7
National Basketball Association	29	26	2
National Football League	32	21	7
National Hockey League	30	23	1

Adapted from Ballparks.com, 2004.

12

reduce staff, cut maintenance budgets, or reduce hours—or they closed outright.

Many elections are held each year throughout the United States to determine whether or not a sport, recreation, or educational institution should be built and whether public funds should be used to build a facility. Numerous stadium and arena projects have ended in court for a determination as to whether political expediency excluded voters from the funding process. A judge in Memphis ruled that public money could not be used to build the Vancouver Grizzlies a new $250 million arena without a public vote ("Judge Rules," 2001). In contrast, residents in Arizona hosted a mock "Boston Tea Party" protest after their elected supervisors approved a countywide quarter-cent sales tax hike to help finance the Bank One Ballpark. The citizens were not necessarily opposed to the stadium or to allocating more taxes to the project; they just wanted a say in the process (Pitzl, 1996).

The political fight is not just over government subsidies; it is also over whether a facility should be built. For example, more than 90 civic organizations ganged up against the Washington Redskins' planned new stadium in Landover, Maryland. The group sued to overturn a zoning change that would have allowed the team to build the stadium at the preferred site ("Stadium Suit," 1996). The stadium was eventually built at another location.

Government officials have a fiduciary obligation (obligation to act truthfully and honestly)

to protect their constituents, the people who voted them into power. A conflict arises when a politician promotes building a facility that might benefit some individuals but can cause harm to others. This concern has reared its ugly head on numerous occasions. For example, a San Diego council member was forced to resign her seat and pled guilty to two misdemeanors for allegedly taking gifts from the San Diego Padres ownership. Although the gifts were legal, the council member did not report the gifts as required and did not excuse herself from council votes regarding the Padres' ballpark ("Padres' Park," 2001).

Before the 1990s, there were very few large privately owned facilities. The most well-known private facilities are Lambeau Field for the Green Bay Packers and Dodger Stadium in Los Angeles. The next big wave of privately owned facilities was ushered in by Joe Robbie, who built Joe Robbie Stadium in Miami for the Dolphins. Since the 1990s a number of privately financed facilities have been built, and an even larger number of facilities have been built with a blend of public and private funds.

Individuals who privately finance and manage sport facilities often do so as a profit-generating business enterprise. Thus, while a government-owned facility might not be as "bottom line" oriented (may focus more on service than revenue), a private facility does not have that luxury. Any money saved at a private facility results in greater profits. Thus, the managerial perspective required to run a private facility is significantly different from that for a public facility.

The major difference between private and public facilities is that a private facility can operate at a loss without a significant outcry from the owners and taxpayers. However, a privately financed facility can operate only for a limited time with negative returns. The push for profits with private facilities is hard to fulfill with a baseball or football stadium because of the limited number of events (around 90 games a year for baseball; around 10 play dates a year for football). Even with several concerts a year, there is not enough traffic and spending to generate a strong return. In contrast, a facility manager can generate a much better return for a private owner of an arena utilized for basketball and hockey. In these arenas there may be 300+ event days a year, which represents a greater chance to generate a positive return on the owner's investment.

© Steve Ryan

Lambeau Field, home of the Green Bay Packers, is one of a few privately owned facilities. Originally constructed in 1957, the stadium now has a capacity of more than 60,000.

Facility Focus

This section highlights some of the premiere public and private facilities in the United States and Canada, along with a recently constructed arena and one of the largest multiuse sport facilities in the world. These sample facilities were chosen because of their name recognition or because they were recently constructed, renovated, or closed and represent an opportunity to explore current trends. In each of the remaining chapters of this book, other noteworthy facilities are featured in "Facility Focus." This is an opportunity to get a glimpse of the wide variety of facilities that exist, their unique features, and the multitude of functions and issues that their managers must handle.

Facility Focus: Madison Square Garden

© AP/World Wide Photos

Madison Square Garden in New York, known as the "World's Most Famous Arena," includes a 5,600-seat theater, a 20,000-seat arena, a 40,000-square-foot (3,716-square-meter) expo center, two restaurants, and 89 club suites. This enormous facility had its humble beginnings as an abandoned railroad shed at 26th Street and Madison Avenue. P.T. Barnum purchased the shed in 1874 and replaced it with a roofless structure that he named Barnum's Monster Classical and Geological Hippodrome. Some of the early events featured were chariot races, waltzing elephants, and fire eaters ("New York Landmarks," 2002).

Here are a few interesting facts about Madison Square Garden:

- The facility has more than 1,000,000 square feet (92,900 square meters) of space.
- It hosts more than 600 events each year.
- It hosts more than 4 million visitors each year.
- The roof is 404 feet (123 meters) wide and 64 feet (19.5 meters) high.
- The facility is located right on top of Pennsylvania Station, which serves as both a subway and a train station (Schoenberg, 2001).

The first Garden was demolished in 1889. In its place, a $2 million extravaganza was built and opened in 1890. Then in 1925, the officers of the New York Life Insurance Company, which held the land mortgage, decided to build the company headquarters there. Madison Square Garden moved to Eighth Avenue to the site of the former city trolley car barns, where it stayed until 1968. The current Madison Square Garden is located directly above Pennsylvania Station on 34th Street. Construction of the new facility began in 1963; its concrete foundation was poured in 1964. The building cost $116 million to construct ("New York Landmarks," 2002).

Over the years the arena has hosted dogs and cats, elephants and athletes, award shows, musical artists, superstars, and even Big Bird. Currently it is the home of the New York Knicks, the Rangers, and the Liberty. The Westminster Kennel Club Dog Show, the National Horse Show, and Ringling Bros. and Barnum & Bailey circus are regular events. One of the famous fights between Muhammad Ali and Joe Frazier took place at the Garden in 1971. Paul Simon, the Grateful Dead, and Elton John are just a few of the musical acts that have passed through the Garden's doors over the years. Madison Square Garden is a prime example of a successful multipurpose PAF (Schoenberg, 2001).

© AP/World Wide Photos

In 1931 Conn Smythe, then manager of the Toronto Maple Leafs, built Maple Leaf Gardens in Toronto. This 16,000-seat multi-purpose facility was to host the Maple Leafs for the next 68 years. During that time it also hosted a wide variety of concerts by such performers as Duke Ellington, Elvis Presley, the Beatles, Pearl Jam, and Rush.

The following are interesting facts about Maple Leaf Gardens:

- It took 1,200 construction workers five months and 12 days to build the yellow brick-faced structure.
- The Gardens was built for $1.5 million.
- It had 16,000 seats and 85 box seats.
- Construction costs were minimized as a result of agreements made with labor unions to provide the workers with Maple Leaf Gardens stock in place of a portion of their earnings.
- The building materials included 750,000 bricks; 77,500 bags of cement; and 70 tons of sand.
- The 350- by 282-foot (106- by 86-meter) building extended 13 stories (44 yards or 40 meters) above street level.
- Opening night seat prices ranged from $0.95 to $2.75 ("Maple Leaf Gardens," 2002).

The Gardens was financed in a unique manner. The land was purchased for $350,000 from a major backer. In order to help reduce construction costs, Smythe entered into an agreement with the unions stipulating that those working on the project would receive Gardens stock in exchange for a wage reduction of 20% ("Maple Leaf Gardens," 2002). Since the facility was built during a depression, material costs were between 20% and 30% lower than pre-depression costs due to low demand.

As part of an attempt to provide a sport complex, the Gardens originally included a six-lane bowling alley, a billiards room, and a gymnasium. These areas were transformed over the years into carpenter and electrician workshops and storage areas. The ice surface was 85 by 200 feet (26 by 61 meters), and it remained in place from late August to the end of the hockey season. During non-hockey events, sheets of plywood covered the ice, and the staging and chairs were placed on top.

In 1999 the Maple Leafs left the Maple Leaf Gardens to move five blocks away to the state-of-the-art $265 million Air Canada Centre with its Bose sound system and plush surroundings. Concert promoters cleared out of the Gardens shortly thereafter. Faced with a future of minor concert and sport bookings such as lacrosse and junior hockey games, Maple Leaf Sports and Entertainment Ltd. put the facility up for sale.

Courtesy of the Arena at Harbor Yard.

The arena at Harbor Yard, completed in the fall of 2001, is home to the American Hockey League's Bridgeport Sound Tigers, an affiliate of the NHL's New York Islanders, and the Metro Atlantic Athletic Conference's Fairfield University men's and women's basketball teams. The arena is equipped to accommodate 8,500 people for hockey games and 9,000 people for basketball games. The facility has five locker rooms, seven permanent concession stands, 13 loge suites, 20 portable kiosks, 14 women's and 13 men's rooms, 33 executive suites, 1,300 club seats, 40,000 light bulbs, 10,600 gallons of water (needed to create the ice rink), 6,000 pieces of structural steel, and 4,754 cubic yards (3,635 cubic meters) of concrete, and took 721 days to construct (Elsberry, 2001). The construction cost breakdown for the project is shown in table 1.5. Based on the 196,300 square feet (18,237 square meters) in the facility, the cost per square foot was $262.29, and the final construction price was $56,278,684. The original schematic budget was just under $37 million, and the estimated construction price was only slightly more than $39 million (Kasper Group, 2001).

The main seating area is all on one level, divided into 20 sections, providing the spectator with up-close views of all the action. The Arena boasts fixed scoreboards and live-action replay video boards at either end, giving it a clean design, an open feel, and unparalleled sight lines. Executive suites, situated on the Arena's perimeter, are private suites that include such amenities as VIP club lounge membership, season tickets for all Sound Tiger and Fairfield University men's and women's basketball games, full concierge service, wide-cushioned seats, storage closets, private rest rooms, private entrance, TV monitors with full cable service, and local telephone service. The large, theater-style club seats, located in three sections just below the executive suites, offer the spectator terrific views of all the action.

Table 1.5 Harbor Yard Construction Costs

Category	Cost ($)	Cost/foot² ($)	% of total
General insurance and bond issuance costs	3,379,423	15.75	6.77
Additional general requirements	408,057	1.90	0.82
Site work	4,322,600	20.15	8.66
Concrete	4,855,785	22.63	9.72
Masonry	3,238,681	15.09	6.49
Metals	6,949,401	32.39	13.92
Wood and plastics	586,766	2.73	1.18
Thermal and moisture protection	2,260,087	10.53	4.53
Doors and windows	1,194,967	5.57	2.39
Finishes (paint, carpeting, etc.)	3,721,601	17.34	7.45
Equipment	15,175	0.07	0.03
Furnishings including retractable seating	1,640,662	7.65	3.29
Conveying systems (elevators, escalators)	350,445	1.63	0.70
Fire protection	815,850	3.80	1.63
Plumbing	2,623,075	12.22	5.25
Heating, ventilation, and air conditioning	6,911,690	32.21	13.84
Refrigeration	771,925	3.60	1.55
Electrical	5,885,993	27.43	11.79
Construction management fee	2,410,383	11.23	4.83
Construction contingency	(1,777,304)	(8.28)	-3.56
Owner's contingency	408,422	1.90	0.82
Furniture, fixtures, and equipment allowance	5,305,000	24.72	10.62
Total cost	56,278,684	262.29	

From Kasper Group, 2001.

Players have their own entrance into the building, giving them privacy and the ability to enter and exit without disrupting or being disrupted by other events. The Arena also has an exclusive fitness center for players and five locker rooms that allow scheduling of men's and women's doubleheaders. Members of the media are also treated to state-of-the-art facilities including a fully equipped media area, interview room, and green room.

Facility Focus: Yale University Sport Facilities

Courtesy of Bill O'Brien.

Yale University has numerous athletic facilities, including

- Yale Bowl, which was opened in 1914 for the Yale-Harvard football game;
- Coxe Cage, home to Yale's men's and women's indoor track teams;
- Yale Tennis Center, a tennis complex that includes 22 outdoor Deco Turf II courts, 5 outdoor clay courts, and 4 indoor Deco Turf II courts;
- David S. Ingalls Rink, a whale-shaped rink used by Yale hockey since 1959;
- Colonel Lanman Center, a 57,000-square foot (17,374-square meter) facility used for basketball and recreation activities; and
- The Adrian C. "Ace" Israel Fitness Center, a 27,000-square foot (8,230-square meter) facility with hundreds of training machines and free weight areas.

However, one of the gems of Yale University is the world-famous Payne Whitney Gymnasium (PWG)—the world's largest indoor sport facility. Nine and one-half stories high with a total of 12 acres of floor space, the facility was constructed in 1932. PWG is currently undergoing a $100 million long-term upgrade. During this phased renovation the building will remain open for use, creating significant logistical and scheduling concerns for the facility managers. The facility was initially built for the needs of 3,500 students but currently serves the needs of over 10,000 students and another 12,000 university employees.

The first floor contains a sports medicine center and indoor rowing area. There are other areas for basketball, gymnastics, volleyball, and swimming/diving. The second floor contains the Kiphuth Trophy Room, which was constructed with hand-carved wood and features trophies and memorabilia dating back to 1842. The other floors have gyms, offices, and rooms for such activities as dancing and wrestling. Among PWG's current facilities are a 3,100-seat amphitheater, an exhibition pool, 26 squash courts, racquetball courts, rowing tanks, and basketball and volleyball courts.

The Future of Sport Facilities

As noted earlier in the chapter, Greek and Roman facilities were the precursors of modern PAFs. However, other civilizations, from the Far East to South America, also contributed to the spread of sport facilities. For example, the Mayans (A.D. 300-A.D. 1200) and the Aztecs (A.D. 1500-A.D. 1200) played ball games in stone courts; nobles could sit inside to observe the competition, and all other spectators had to listen to the event from the outside (Leonard, 1974).

From ancient times to the present, the basic structure of such facilities remained essentially unchanged until the last 40 years. Tremendous changes over the past 40 years include such innovations as domed stadiums, stadiums with retractable roofs, and structures that can rotate on tracks to change from a large arena to an intimate performing arts stage. While the United States has been the leader in terms of the breadth and diversity of new stadiums and arenas in the past 30 years, the facility construction boom that hit North America in the 1990s has started to spread internationally. The greatest growth at the start of the 21st century occurred in Japan and Greece. Japan went on a massive soccer stadium building binge to host the 2002 World Cup with cohost Korea. The largest of the stadiums is International Stadium in Yokohama, which can seat 71,416 and cost $526.32 million to build. A total of 20 facilities were built at a cost of $4.64 billion ("Kick-off for 2002," 2001). It is estimated that Korea spent an additional $1.7 billion on facilities, while France spent $1.5 billion on facilities for the 1998 World Cup. These numbers not only help highlight the magnitude of international facility growth; they also show how expensive stadiums are to build and indicate the price escalation that is attributable to the desire to have domed or movable/adjustable facilities and other expensive innovations.

This cost aspect is also seen in Olympic Games facilities. Athens mounted a tremendous construction effort to prepare for the 2004 Olympic Games. The Olympic Stadium had to be refurbished and renovated. As of May 2001, a large percentage of the 23 facilities required to host the Games had yet to be built ("Athens' Challenge," 2001). The International Olympic Committee was concerned about the completion of the facilities and voiced a strong warning to Greece to hasten their construction efforts. The Games budget was estimated to be $1.7 billion, with a large percentage of these funds dedicated to sport facilities, but grew to over $11.6 billion (Varouhalkis, 2004). In contrast, constructing all the facilities necessary for the Australian Olympics in 2000 cost over $3 billion. The required buildings included 110,000-seat Stadium Australia; 20,000-seat Sydney SuperDome; the Sydney International Athletic Centre; and several other aquatic, sailing, and shooting facilities (Jackson and Menser, 2000).

China is scheduled to host the 2008 Olympic Games. The expected cost for completing all the required facilities is estimated at $3.4 billion. It is estimated that 37 stadiums and arenas will be either built or renovated for the Games. In addition, another $1.94 billion is to be spent on ancillary facilities such as the Olympic Village, press center, and broadcasting center ("Beijing to Spend," 2002). One of the issues for these Games (and all past and future Olympics) is how to utilize the facilities after the Olympics have ended. Nobody wants the facilities to become "white elephants," but obviously there are significant financial issues associated with running facilities. For example, the Calgary Olympics in 1988 generated a $150 million profit, but the lasting legacy has been the facilities, which are still actively utilized. The Olympic Oval is one of the fastest speed skating tracks in the world and is used as a training center (Sibold, 2002).

These Olympic examples highlight a major push for future sport facilities. While there will always be a demand for health clubs and school/community sport facilities, most countries or communities cannot afford to spend hundreds of millions of dollars for new state-of-the-art facilities. Thus, older facilities that might be condemned in richer countries need to be kept open in poorer countries. Even wealthier countries will have a mix of old and newer facilities. A typical sport facility is designed to last 50 years. It is possible for 50-year-old facilities to be in great shape and for those that are only 10 years old to be in poor shape. Political, financial, equipment, personnel, and other factors can help explain why some facilities are in good shape and others are in poor shape. There can also be a blend of facilities such as on a college campus (like Yale University) that has some very old and some modern facilities.

While poorer countries may not be able to afford building new PAFs, richer countries must carefully evaluate any efforts to modify or build facilities. Any new construction effort may necessitate compliance with requirements that can significantly affect building budgets and even the ability to build or renovate. One of the key concerns with building Olympic dream facilities is accessibility. In Greek and Roman times, disabled persons who could not enter a facility would be out of luck; now a disabled person can sue to get into a facility. Immediately after the Olympic Games, the Paralympics are held. These Games for the disabled use the same facilities as the Olympics, which must accommodate the needs of the disabled. Thus, handicapped access and other services need to be considered in construction. This concern was evidenced in the Atlanta Olympic Games in 1996, six years after the Americans with Disabilities Act (ADA) was passed. The ADA requires facilities and programs to accommodate the needs of the disabled whenever practicable. All new construction projects in the United States are required to comply with this law, which is one reason the Atlanta Olympics were viewed as the most accessible Games held to date (Beasley, 1997).

Trends That Will Affect Future Facilities

As noted earlier, political and religious concerns helped foster construction of the Roman Coliseum and Circus Maximus. The idea was that if citizens were busy enjoying sport and other events, they might be more content and not try to overthrow the government. Modern facilities are often built with the same political goals in mind. Most voters would be hard-pressed to find an elected official who wants to be known as the politician that lost a professional team. Elected officials often go out of their way to provide any assistance possible to attract or retain a professional team. Debacles involving poor political planning are numerous. Examples from the 1990s include the following:

• Cincinnati officials did not reveal the true cost of their new stadiums until after the election ended; they then raised the estimated price for the football and baseball stadiums approximately $100 million each, just one day after the voters approved the construction (Fried, Shapiro, and Deshriver, 2003).

• Tampa officials bought the argument raised by the Tampa Bay Buccaneers' owner that

he needed a new stadium because he was losing money in his old facility, but never checked to confirm the veracity of his statement (Fried, Shapiro, and Deshriver, 2003).

• Texas officials negotiated a contract with the Texas Motor Speedway that exempted the Speedway from property tax requirements, which cost the local school district over $21 million a year and prompted the schools to sue (Fried, Shapiro, and Deshriver, 2003).

• Houston voters agreed to build a downtown baseball stadium even though an advisory group recommended a different site. Elected officials along with a wealthy businessman and his company, which hoped to cash in on a downtown site, spearheaded the site change. The businessman was Kenneth Lay, and the company was the now-bankrupt Enron.

These examples highlight why there have been significant battles after almost every vote to build a stadium or arena for the primary benefit of a private business owner. While some facilities are financed entirely with private funds, most are built with a majority of public funds. Public funds are utilized because of the perceived benefit that a stadium (and its major tenant team) will provide the city or region. The true benefit is hard to quantify, but arguments on both sides are possible regarding whether or not a stadium or arena provides a benefit, or whether people are willing to invest several dollars a month in extra taxes in order to be able to talk about the local team around the water cooler at work. However, while public funding was a popular trend in the 1990s, a poor economy at the start of the 21st century has curtailed some projects. Other projects have faced the voters' wrath, and there are also projects such as the proposed new stadium for the New York Jets that will contain a significant private contribution to the total proposed construction cost. The team has indicated that it would contribute $800 million to the estimated $1.5 billion price tag for a new facility (Heyman, 2003).

Chapter 4 provides a more detailed analysis of political issues. However, it is necessary to acknowledge the political issue here because PAFs have for centuries been closely tied with politics. Any effort to analyze PAFs without examining the political influences associated with how facilities are built, funded, and maintained fails to recognize the historical social significance these facilities have had. Political entities do not just build facilities to placate the masses. Every issue, from bond issuance and tax abatements through safety inspection and zoning/nuisance debates, intertwines the facility and various government entities. These and other overlaps are discussed throughout this book. But it is important to understand from the beginning that without government support (or we could say the support of "the public"), sport facilities as we have them today would not exist.

Other trends besides political shifts include technological and sport-related changes. Technological innovations range from new rigging systems (to support large weights such as scoreboards) to stadium fields on rollers (to allow the use of natural grass in a domed stadium; in favorable weather conditions the grass can be rolled outside).

Sport-related changes can be seen with new sports. Extreme sports are changing numerous sport and recreational facilities. Skateboard parks are being built in record numbers to help keep kids off city buildings and out of dangerous locations. Other facilities that are not traditionally considered sport facilities, such as bridges, can become havens for base jumpers and other extreme sport enthusiasts; and such usage can generate significant liability and safety trends that facility managers need to carefully consider and act upon.

Summary

Sport facilities have undergone significant changes over time, especially over the past two centuries. The Greeks and Romans intertwined politics and religion to build large PAFs to placate the masses. These types of facilities have evolved over the years into architectural and mechanical marvels. Today's PAFs serve as economic catalysts for growth to promote economic, geopolitical, and local political ends. While this chapter gave more attention to larger facilities, smaller facilities have also undergone changes that have made them more marketable and economically viable. This growth will undoubtedly continue in the future, and the same trends seen in the growth of facilities in the United States will feature more prominently around the world.

DISCUSSION QUESTIONS AND ACTIVITIES

1. What do you think current facility managers have learned from their predecessors?

2. What similarities and differences can you see between Madison Square Garden and Maple Leaf Gardens?

3. Take a tour of your university athletic fields and athletic facilities. What similarities and differences can you see between these and the facilities at Yale University?

4. Why did the Romans build stadiums?

5. Why did modern universities build major sport and recreation complexes on campuses?

6. Why do cities build stadiums and arenas for professional sport teams with public money?

Facility Management

After completing this chapter you will be able to do the following:

- Understand what facility management is and what the facility manager's role is
- Appreciate the complex blend of duties required to manage a facility
- Appreciate the consumer orientation required to effectively run a facility
- Appreciate the impact that external entities have on a facility

Facility management involves significant dedication on the part of the facility manager to present events that have value and to present these events in the most attractive, most convenient, and safest environment possible. Facilities have so many components requiring management that the failure of any one can spell disaster. Imagine a fire sprinkler system turning on in an arena and flooding the floor. Imagine 20,000 people in an arena without any air conditioning. Patrons would be irate and the facility would suffer significant negative publicity and economic damages. Thus, much responsibility rests on a facility manager's shoulders to make sure that a facility is operating correctly.

This chapter starts with a critical analysis of facility management and the role that the facility manager plays in achieving the facility's goals and objectives. The facility manager has numerous duties that are significantly affected by the facility size and ownership structure. The chapter also introduces facility and personnel management issues.

Facility managers do not operate in a vacuum. They are influenced by numerous parties, from the lead tenants to government entities or private companies. A facility manager's most important **constituents** are the customers and employees. In addition, facility managers must report to numerous other **stakeholders.** Stakeholders range from the politicians who authorized funds to help build the facility to the independent parties who provide facility management outsourcing services. The last part of this chapter highlights managerial functions, specifically planning, organizing, implementing, and controlling the facility and those working in the facility.

What Is Facility Management?

Managing sport and public assembly facilities (PAFs) is often referred to as facility management, and the people who perform the tasks/duties are called facility managers. Facility management can also refer to managing any other type of facility, from an office building to a hospital or an entire university with hundreds of buildings. **Facility management** entails a broad array of disciplines including, but not limited to, planning; designing; leasing; space planning; project management; capital management; construction management; property management; facility marketing; building and operation management; and real estate acquisition, planning, and disposal (Teicholz and Noferi, 2002). Facility managers for larger facilities often have to spend more time marketing, developing ancillary income streams (concessions, catering, merchandising), and booking and scheduling events, especially if there is no anchor tenant. Differences between sport facilities may be due to size or ownership structure. That is, a high school or college sport facility may not have to make money every day the facility is open, but a stadium or arena will normally not open on a given day unless there is an event that will generate enough revenue to cover all costs.

A significant focus for facility management is to make sure an existing facility runs smoothly and is safe for its intended purpose. Facility management often focuses on the hardware required for smooth operation of the facility. Are parking lots ready for 10,000 cars? Are the bleachers, walkways, elevators, escalators, and other facility components operating safely? Managers have to coordinate maintenance and renovation schedules to make sure that existing facilities do not deteriorate from abuse or from failure to properly maintain them. However, facility management can also apply to building a new facility. A facility manager may be called upon by a university to help design and manage the construction process of a new gym with the help of architects, designers, contractors, and numerous other parties.

Managers may have to design and launch a new facility, but this process may occur only once in a manager's professional career. Thus, a facility manager needs to focus more on actual building operations to meet the facility's service-oriented goals. The facility's goals often focus on filling the facility's time and space opportunities and conducting events in a safe and client service-oriented fashion. Facility management also entails the art of coordinating the physical workplace with the people and entities that will use the workplace. In essence, facility management blends a wide variety of disciplines, from architecture and engineering to business and behavioral science, to optimize how a facility and its users interact and optimize the use of the facility. In summary, facility management entails every aspect of making sure a building is operating efficiently in terms of safety, revenue production, tenant satisfaction, and preventive maintenance.

Facility management is not an easy job. With diverse responsibilities and obligations, a facility manager must have many highly specific skills. Facility managers also need a significant amount of time to complete their tasks. The facility manager is often the first person to arrive on the job each day and the last to leave. In many facilities the facility manager has to be present on game nights and may be present on weekends. But, though the job may at times seem thankless and unusually time-consuming, putting on well-received events in the facility can be a tremendous reward.

The Facility Manager

A facility manager is the person responsible for coordinating all the employees and entities involved in the facility to ensure that they work on behalf of the facility and help meet its short- and long-term goals and objectives. Many people are in fact facility managers in their daily lives and do not realize it. The person who is the "head" of a household is really a facility manager. That person needs to purchase the house, pay the mortgage, paint the rooms, install new equipment such as air conditioners, maintain existing systems such as the roof, manage facility "subletting" as in determining who is going to get which room, interact with government entities to pay taxes, and employ tradespeople such as plumbers and electricians.

The term facility manager is often used in the context of general facilities such as office buildings, but most of the same duties and responsibilities also apply to sport facility managers. Facility managers for big and small buildings face the same types of concerns daily. A facility manager's role is affected by the facility size and the workforce available to the manager. In a small facility, the facility owner may be the manager and can be responsible for opening and closing the facility as well as painting the walls and cleaning the rest rooms. A facility manager for a large facility may have several hundred full- and part-time employees handling everything, from cleanup crews to ushers and ticket takers. Because of the diverse duties each facility manager faces, facility management can be considered both an art and a science.

Specific duties need to be undertaken in order to ensure that a building can be opened for a planned event. From making sure there are enough hotdogs to monitoring indoor air quality, facility management has many facets. Managing all these tasks can appear to be onerous. Smaller facilities often rely upon one individual to undertake all facility management activities, from building repairs to cleaning of the bathrooms. In many instances, a smaller facility has only one person who serves as the owner, manager, custodian, and secretary. The manager of a small health club has to find an appropriate location to build or must lease an existing structure (chapter 4). Part of the location identification process focuses on choosing the proper area (chapter 5), sales/marketing opportunities in the area (chapter 10), and financing options (chapter 11). Managers must work with outside vendors and government entities to secure necessary permits and complete any needed construction or renovations. The facility manager may have to design the facility, choose appropriate color and material schemes, and purchase/install all necessary fitness and office equipment (chapters 5-8). Once the facility is completed the manager will need to maintain it (chapter 9), make sure the facility is operating within the law and in accordance with contracts (chapter 13), and then focus on planning for future needs and marketing to increase income streams. Smaller facilities that start to grow will often need to add employees, and then the facility manager must apply basic human resource skills (chapter 12) to appropriately manage the employees. All these tasks often fall in the lap of one person, which makes the facility manager's job difficult and time-consuming. The job is even more difficult when the facility needs constant

For smaller facilities, a facility manager can be in charge of organizing events and staff, as well as cleaning and maintaining the facility.

attention, forcing the manager to spend time on keeping the facility clean and running rather than on generating revenue.

Larger facilities may have several different crews responsible for different functions such as ticketing, marketing, game operations, mechanicals, and janitorial responsibilities. Thus, facility management for larger facilities involves orchestrating the work of employees and volunteers to help accomplish the facility's goals. Since a PAF is dedicated to attracting events that will generate either income or indirect economic activity (ripple effect; see chapter 4), PAF managers must always examine the facility's best use and determine what events will produce the most positive outcome to the bottom line consistent with the facility's mission. A manager for a larger facility has some duties similar to those of a small-facility manager, such as marketing and financial management. However, a manager for a small facility normally has to blend other responsibilities with facility management. Thus, the general manager of a minor league baseball team may have to sell tickets, groom the field, move furniture, and undertake tasks involving both team and facility management, since typically the budget does not allow the hiring of others. In contrast, a manager for a large facility typically has a staff that can undertake marketing, maintenance, renovations, and numerous other functions. This gives the manager the opportunity to work on broader issues such as long-term planning, developing strong constituent relations, and making sure the right employees are doing the various jobs.

Even though the duties undertaken in facility management may be fluid and can change according to the facility size, a facility manager has some well-defined expectations. According to the International Facility Management Association, facility managers are critical for implementing any facility management plan and need to understand and appreciate several distinct functions:

- Planning, both long- and short-term
- Financial forecasting
- Property acquisition and disposal
- Specifying work responsibility and space
  ...on
- ...tural and engineering planning and
  ...ment

- Managing all phases of construction and renovation work
- Managing maintenance systems and protocols
- Managing all operations from administrative functions to security protocols ("What Is FM," 2002)

Numerous activities occupy a facility manager's time:

- The facility manager needs to plan all facility activities, control schedules, manage contracts, develop work standards, and evaluate both employees and external contractors.
- Managers need to hire and organize all personnel, develop work schedules, and implement appropriate policies and procedures.
- Facility managers need to develop short-, intermediate-, and long-term plans with a strong focus on financial ramifications for each option.
- The facility manager needs to develop an inventory of available space and manage that space by allocating space as needed and obtaining additional space for future growth.
- A facility manager needs to have a strong appreciation and understanding of building design/planning, architectural design, engineering design, code/zoning compliance, construction costs, and building systems and their maintenance needs.
- Workplace planning and design entails procuring and managing furniture and equipment for such areas as concessions, locker rooms, and press box.
- Facility managers need to focus significant effort on budgeting, accounting, and economic forecasting.
- Managers need to be involved in managing construction projects or moving from one area or facility to another.
- A facility manager will need to spend significant time on operations, maintenance, and repairs. These activities can include exterior maintenance of the building and aspects such as trash and pest control.

25

- Since 9/11, facility managers have been forced to deal with security and life safety concerns to a much greater extent than ever before.
- Lastly, managers have to supervise general administrative departments such as food service or a mail room (Cotts and Lee, 1992).

Although these functions are numerous, the primary function and the overriding concern for any facility manager should be employee and patron safety. After safety, legality is the next most important concern for facility managers (Cotts and Lee, 1992). When surveyed in 1988 about the most frequent managerial activities, facility managers indicated that maintenance absorbed the greatest amount of their time (17%), followed by space management (14%), interior design (11%), and budgeting and forecasting (9%) (Cotts and Lee, 1992). It could be assumed that managing people and human resources and administrative responsibilities consumed a large portion of the remaining 49%. A newer survey would probably show that facility managers are now spending more time on security, air quality, compliance with laws such as the Americans with Disabilities Act, and workplace violence issues.

In a recent study conducted by the International Association of Assembly Managers ("IAAM Membership," 2002), 576 respondents indicated the areas that they felt needed to be researched to assist practitioners in the facility management field. These areas, listed from the highest to lowest need for research, are as follows:

- Legal
- Human resources
- Technology
- Marketing
- Financial
- Operations
- Management

Not every manager is an expert in each area. However, working with competent employees, receiving training from good mentors, working with management teams, and getting direction from an educated board can help managers effectively balance their various roles.

The various roles highlighted show that managers first and foremost must manage the various stakeholders associated with the facility. This means that before a manager can open a facility's doors, or even plan to build a new facility, he or she must understand who will use the facility. Constituent analysis helps define who the manager must interact with to positively affect the facility's long-term success.

Constituents

Many people put their trust in a manager. Employees come to work assuming that the facility will not be dangerous. Customers attend an event assuming that the event will go on as scheduled, will be safe, and will provide an enjoyable entertainment experience. Companies may be willing to put their name on a building for millions of dollars assuming that the facility management team will not undertake any action that will diminish the sponsorship value. Government entities may allow the facility's doors to open for an event since they trust that the facility managers will follow all applicable laws.

Because of the large number of individuals who rely on each other to ensure a successful facility, a facility manager needs to constantly balance his or her interests with the interests of all other constituents. This balancing act can be difficult. Furthermore, it is impossible to develop a facility's goals, objectives, and mission without understanding the constituents who affect the facility.

A facility leader serves three constituents:

- **Customers**—promoters, tenants, ticket buyers, and those attending the events
- **Internal constituents**—boards/owners, employees, and coworkers
- **External constituents**—bankers, politicians, the media, executives, and others who can influence the facility

Customers

The primary responsibility for a facility manager is to make sure that people can attend events within the facility in a safe and secure manner. Customers, fans, and ticket buyers can be demanding. Customers want the food they want, the way they like it, at the best location, and at the lowest price. It is impossible to deliver exactly what each customer wants when there are thousands of customers. A VIP may receive personal attention in a luxury box because that is one of the amenities the facility manager can ensure for a box. It is much more difficult to provide such a high level of service to a section seating several hundred people. However, this goes to one of the critical skills for a manager—providing the highest level of service possible given the strengths and weaknesses inherent in the facility and its personnel. If there is not enough money to hire additional employees but the manager makes every effort to provide quality service, the customers will hopefully see the effort and will be happier even though they are not getting everything they want.

Promoters want the facility to be clean and ready for setting up a show. If a facility is regularly late opening, is in poor condition, provides poor employees, and lacks amenities such as loading docks and storage areas, promoters will shy away from working with the facility, which will then affect its reputation. The facility management industry is small enough that a poor reputation will make it impossible for a facility to meet its goals, objectives, and mission.

Tenants can range from professional teams to personal trainers leasing space at a gym. Each tenant has a different bargaining position with the facility manager. An anchor or primary tenant has precedence over lesser tenants. Thus, a facility manager has to respond differently to an NBA team, which typically would be the primary tenant, than to second-tier tenants such as an NHL, AFL, or Women's National Basketball Association team or any smaller shows that may use the arena.

Internal Constituents

Internal constituents can include employees, independent contractors working for the facility, investors in the facility, board of directors overseeing the facility, and even government officials if the facility is a government facility. Each group has a vested interest in the facility, so all groups may push the facility manager to better the facility since this would benefit everyone. The facility manager will be called upon by superiors to make sure that the facility follows its mission and meets its goals. The facility manager must also focus on motivating internal constituents to work as hard as possible to make sure the facility is successful.

Through various managerial techniques such as motivation strategies or strong leadership skills, a facility manager can motivate even the staunchest internal opponents to work toward the facility's success. For example, a board member overseeing the facility may have a negative disposition toward the facility and may have voted against every single budget. The facility manager can take the board member to an event and show him or her the types of people who come to events. Through such exposure the board member may have a more positive feeling about the facility.

Certain decisions, such as the decision to accept a sponsorship agreement, can lead to internal strife, which a facility manager needs to prevent. For example, the University of North Dakota completed construction in 2001 of the Ralph Engelstad Arena, which featured 11,400 leather seats, a brass ceiling, Italian chandeliers in the lobby, and other fancy amenities. The facility was not the center of controversy; rather, the controversy centered on the individual who donated $50 million to build it. In a *Sports Illustrated* article the university appeared to receive a black eye for accepting money from someone who threw parties on Hitler's birthday and who had persuaded the university to reinstate its old Indian-head logo and Fighting Sioux nickname. The gift sparked protests on campus about the "death" of the university's integrity (Dohrmann, 2001). A manager can have a hard time managing a facility if employees do not want to be associated with the facility and if students start boycotting the facility.

External Constituents

Facility managers must interact with a wide variety of entities. Aside from customers and employees, the two most important categories of parties that interact with facilities and their managers are government entities and private entities. The facility manager must reach beyond the facility to those who can exert influence on the facility. This marketing effort may be focused on gaining clout for future funds, legal or crisis management, financial security, or promoting long-term growth. For example, a facility manager may wine and dine a businessperson to help attract a future event. At another time the facility manager may need to meet with government officials concerned about the temperature at which food in the facility is cooked.

Facility Focus: Ralph Engelstad Arena

Bill Alkofer Photography

The Ralph Engelstad Arena and its funding were controversial from the beginning, but no one can attack the elegance and detail of this $100+ million facility. The 400,000-square-foot (37,160-square-meter) facility has a marble entryway and granite concourse floors (rather than concrete floors as at most facilities); all seats are made of cherry wood and leather; and there is a 10,000-square-foot (930-square-meter) weight room with an underwater treadmill. The facility features 48 luxury suites and two large club rooms with the longest freestanding bar in the state of North Dakota. The suites include 10-person mini-suites, 18-person midsize suites, and 28-person full-size suites ("Ralph Engelstad Arena," 2004).

The arena has not tried to distance itself from its namesake, even with the controversy publicized in *Sports Illustrated*. In 2003 the arena issued a four-coin commemorative set highlighting the facility's first years. The Fighting Sioux Indian-head logo appeared on the front, and the back showed various images, including that of Mr. Engelstad on the 2002 coin (the year of his death). The four coins sold for $79, and 1,000 sets were minted. A different version of the coins was also minted to be used as currency within the facility (Dodds, 2003).

Numerous government entities interact with sport facilities. Everything from zoning to taxes and health code compliance requires government involvement. Besides regulating facilities, the government often owns sport-related facilities. One of the most frequent challenges faced by facility managers when dealing with the government is the almost constant change in laws that affect a sport facility. For example, the Houston Astrodome is a Harris County-owned facility. As such, any regulations passed affecting county facilities affect the Astrodome. The county administrators decided in the mid-1990s to assist handicapped citizens and passed a rule allowing persons with a handicap placard to park without charge at county facilities. While the intent behind the regulations was noble, the application was not smooth. When people discovered that the handicap placard holders could park for free, many persons who were not handicapped borrowed and used the placards. Besides losing parking revenue, the Astrodome faced another possible problem, as those who were truly disabled had fewer parking spaces. A manager must abide by the requirements of external constituents, with the potential impact affecting other constituents. A disgruntled disabled fan deprived of a parking space will not find solace in a manager's explanation that nothing can be done since others passed the law and the facility must live with the regulation. Numerous government regulations affect sport facilities, and chapter 13 covers these influences in greater detail.

Besides government-based constituents, numerous external vendors can affect a facility. A facility manager needs to establish cordial relationships with a number of external people or companies that may be able to provide a benefit in the future. A private company can become a ticket purchaser in the future. A private company can also provide items such as office supplies and toilet paper and concession items. A facility manager needs to develop harmonious relationships with these providers to ensure the consistent flow of needed supplies, especially when thousands of hotdogs, hamburgers, and cans of beer, for example, are sold at every event and new deliveries will be needed for another event several hours later.

Thus, to deal effectively with a wide variety of constituents, a facility manager needs to focus on marketing efforts to keep attracting customers, utilize appropriate leadership and managerial skills to galvanize internal constituents, and promote strong relationships with government and private entities that can affect the facility's overall performance.

Managerial Functions

According to one model, there are four primary functions of management: planning, organizing, implementing, and controlling (Bridges and Roquemore, 1996). Others categorize the primary functions of management as planning, organizing, leading, and evaluating (Chelladurai, 1985). Within each of these functions are numerous subcategories. For example, under planning, a typical manager may engage in activities such as scheduling, evaluating, hiring, problem solving, auditing, interpreting, budgeting, and communicating.

Before addressing the four primary functions, it is important to consider the facility's **mission** (see the sample mission statement below). It is impossible to plan without knowing what is to be accomplished. The mission statement states the end result envisioned by the facility's owner and encompasses the goals and objectives critical for the facility's success. The mission statement provides the roadmap for the facility. If the mission statement indicates that the facility should be open for free use by the public, then the goals will center on attracting users, and the manager will plan strategies to accomplish that goal. Every facility will have a different mission statement to guide its path, and that mission statement can change every couple of years based on internal or external variables. Traditionally, the people at the highest level of a facility—whether owners, elected officials, or board members—help determine the facility's mission with some input from

---

Sample Mission Statement for a University Intramural Facility

The Intramural and Sports Club Program (ISCP) joins in a partnership with the university to improve the quality of student life on campus and to provide valuable recreational opportunities for students, faculty, staff, their families, and the greater community.

The ISCP will utilize the following principles to help fulfill its mission:

- Provide diversity in programs to meet the constantly changing needs/interests of users
- Maintain safe and clean facilities to enhance the user experience
- Adhere to green building technology and principles to help conserve energy and avoid waste
- Provide adequate facility access to ensure an opportunity for everyone to participate in desired activities

stakeholders such as the public, management, and employees.

Innumerable mission statements have been written for sport teams, organizations, leagues, and so on; but very few such statements focus on or even mention the facility and how the facility needs to be managed. The reason is that a facility is not the main focus of any sport business. At the same time, though, without the facility there could not be a sport business. A health club, for example, may have as its mission statement the need to provide quality service to members to help them live a happy and healthy life. This mission statement will hopefully help the health club become successful, but there is no mention of the facility. However, without a clean and attractive facility it will be impossible to attract and retain members. In order to highlight the facility and its importance, managers need to specifically mention the facility in the mission statement. Thus, the mission statement serves as a planning tool to help a facility manager accomplish the other managerial functions.

Planning

Planning focuses on setting goals and objectives and then developing the plan to reach those goals and objectives. Planning involves developing both short- and long-term goals and is a constant challenge produced by changing circumstances. In essence, planning can be summarized as deciding in advance what to do, when to do it, and how to do it. Another way to phrase this is that planning is a blueprint for the future. Planning forces those who control a facility to examine the internal and external environment as a means to hold events that will maximize the goals set for the facility.

Planning is difficult because it is associated with change. Most people do not like a lot of change in their lives. Through planning, one may determine that little change is needed if the goals and objectives stay the same. Nevertheless, planning needs to be conducted on a regular basis since internal and external conditions change and goals and objectives can quickly become obsolete. Planning is also beneficial in that it can reduce organizational conflict since all those involved will know what they are all working to achieve. Planning also can help eliminate overlapping or wasteful activities. If a manager plans effectively, he or she may be able to identify areas where employees are overlapping

work and be able to assign employees to more productive activities (Davis, 1994). It should be noted that poor planning is often the primary cause for failure, whether in the classroom or the board room.

While the facility leaders develop the mission statement, managers often have the flexibility to develop plans that help the facility accomplish its mission. Planning can be broken down into categories such as strategic, operational, single-use operational, standing operational, and functional. **Strategic plans** are designed to help achieve the highest-level goals and objectives for the facility; that is why they are often called master plans. **Operational plans** are more detailed and are used to help carry out the strategic plans. Operational plans can include single-use operational plans that may apply to a one-time event such as hosting the Olympics; standing operational plans are set plans for doing everything from ordering paper to how to issue a refund to a patron. **Functional plans** focus on what operational plans are designed to accomplish; marketing plans and safety plans are examples (Bridges and Roquemore, 1996). Another type of plan is a contingency plan that can be used if one of the other plans fails and the facility has to pursue another strategy.

Plans are often synthesized into organizational guidelines. Guidelines are often referred to as "red tape," but they represent how any activity needs to be accomplished so the plan can work. For example, a facility may have a standing operational plan for ordering chairs. If a chair breaks, an employee is required to report the break to a maintenance employee. That employee decides whether or not the chair can be fixed; if not, he or she may need to complete a damage report and then a requisition form to purchase another chair. Some think of this type of process as a headache, but the guidelines are in place to prevent overspending on new equipment and to allow for repairing equipment if at all possible. The guidelines help save money and provide specific steps to help accomplish the facility's goals.

Goals and Objectives

What is a goal? We have often heard that a coach wants to have a winning season. Is a winning season a goal? The answer for some people is yes. For others, the goal may be to have a good time. While the mission statement focuses on the overall direction a facility wants to pursue, the goals are more refined. A facility's goal could be to have 20 sellouts or to host 10 major conferences a year. It is impossible to list all potential goals, since all facilities and all constituents associated with the facility will have their own goals. This does not mean that the goals are inconsistent. An employee may have a goal to sell 100 beers a game. A customer may have a goal to enjoy the event, and part of that process includes drinking beer. If the customer buys a beer, then both the customer and the employee are working to reach their respective goals.

Sample goals for a health club could include the following:

- Maintain a 95% retention rate for current members
- Attract 100 new members every year
- Offer five new classes each year
- Minimize the number of customer complaints to five per week

Each one of the goals is measurable, which is critical for analysis. If a club has a goal to have happy customers, then there must be a means to measure that happiness or the club will never know if it reached the goal. Thus, many facilities conduct yearly surveys to see what the patrons think. If a patron's feeling can be expressed as a number, then patron reaction can be evaluated and used to create a standard for future growth.

Some commentators feel that there is very little difference between goals and objectives (Bridges and Roquemore, 1996). **Strategic goals** are set by the highest-level managers and are introduced to affect and empower the overall facility for the long run. Strategic goals often focus on broader aspects such as market share, profitability, industry leader position, or changes in the facility. **Tactical goals** are often introduced by midlevel managers and focus on what needs to be accomplished to reach the strategic goal. Operational goals are set by low-level managers and are more short-term, referring, for example, to what can be done to reach the tactical goals (Bridges and Roquemore, 1996). To incorporate these concepts into an example, a health club may have a strategic goal to become the largest health club in the market. The tactical goals could be to increase membership by 10% each year and to minimize nonrenewals by 50%. The operational goals could be to attract new members by introducing new programs such as discount packages or new workout opportunities.

The operational goals are often more accurately called **objectives.** Whereas the goal is a specific directive, an objective focuses on how to reach a goal. In our example of the employee and the customer regarding the beer transaction, the employee's objectives could be to carry the best-tasting beer, have the coldest beer possible, and sell at the lowest possible price to reach the goal of selling 100 beers. Goals will never be reached if there are no concrete means to reach the goals.

While managers can develop objectives, the most effective technique is to get employees involved in the process. Noted management guru Peter Drucker coined the term **management by objective (MBO)** in 1954; the MBO theory focused on developing realistic, achievable, and motivating objectives through management's developing the objectives with employee input (Davis, 1994). This process is designed to turn facility goals and objectives into group and individual goals and objectives. Thus, objectives should not be developed in a vacuum and are more effective when there is institutional buy-in.

It is worthwhile noting that although goals and objectives are well known, some businesses do not use them and instead use policies and procedures. Policies are the most general guidelines that should be flexible and give basic direction to managers and employees. Procedures are a series of job tasks or steps that employees need to take in a preestablished manner to achieve the end results. For example, a policy might be that each new customer has to pay at least $40 a month for gym membership. The procedures might indicate what an employee can say to a prospective customer to avoid making fraudulent statements or getting the customer upset.

Short-Term Planning

A facility manager plans every day. Who will be using the facility? Does the facility have insurance? What type of crowd will be there? Are all the systems operating? Are there enough employees to work the event? Will the weather affect either the facility or the event? These are all questions that may not be answered until the event day. However, through proper planning the manager will know what options exist depending on the circumstances that develop.

Short-term plans typically cover less than one year and focus on activities that may have a sense of emergency. A facility may have a short-term plan that a given event should be sold out to help accomplish the facility's mission. Besides short-term plans, midterm plans can be used that may extend for several years. These plans need to be flexible enough to respond to environmental changes and at the same time concrete enough to provide directions to employees who are charged with implementing the plan.

Long-Term Planning

The facility manager, or a designated employee, needs to focus on the future and determine what events or services will maximize revenue generation and the facility's long-term goals. Often a facility books events several years in the future. For example, if a facility manager knows that a competing facility is being built 40 miles away, he or she may enter into long-term contracts with several traveling shows and circuses to prevent them from going to the new arena for a number of years.

Long-term plans need to focus on long-term projections, which can be influenced by political, geographical, and economic trends. Most people have plans that they regard as fairly realistic; they probably realize there is little likelihood they will win an Olympic gold medal or marry a wealthy celebrity. However, such "pie in the sky" plans are essential to determine where a facility should try to reach. There is no reason a facility cannot shoot for being the best facility in the area. This is the beauty of long-term planning: It allows managers to think creatively about the future and develop innovative strategies.

Business Plans

Besides short- and long-term plans, **business plans** need to be developed. The business plan examines the product, marketing, legal, financial, and general business outlook for a facility. Every facility needs to develop a business plan that may cover individual events through yearly business cycles. Each event can face financial hardship if patrons do not show or if too much is spent on marketing. That is why a budget (such as a pro forma budget) is a critical part of any business plan. Business plans for building facilities are

Facility managers need to keep on top of trends and publications so that they can make better decisions for both short- and long-term planning.

covered in chapter 4, and those for hosting events at a facility are discussed in chapter 14.

Business plans rely on forecasting what can happen when business decisions are made. Forecasting, a critical component in planning, can be accomplished only with good information. This is why it is imperative for a manager to acquire reliable information from whatever sources are available. Colleagues, employees, friends, newspapers, television stations, magazines, and other sources are essential elements in effective planning as they all provide input that can help influence the decision-making process. Information can be critical when planning an event for a facility. Necessary information may include data on facility availability, competing events/facilities, weather conditions, **building load capacity**, current economic conditions, demographic breakdown of expected fans, and numerous other variables specific to a facility or event.

Organizing

Organizing, the second function of facility managers, refers to a blend of human resource management and leadership. One of the most difficult tasks for a manager is to assign the right person with the right skills and interests to a given job. The fact that someone's job description specifies certain tasks does not make that individual the best person to do a particular job. A manager must recognize this and understand the skills that each employee brings to the facility. If it is necessary to rotate jobs or change job descriptions, then the manager must be able to do so even if this means that employees might not support their new roles. While some employees might learn to like or appreciate their new position, others might forever complain about the changes. If this process is not undertaken, either other employees or the manager will be forced to carry the extra load created because an employee performs inadequate or incorrect work.

In addition to assigning the right person to a task, managers need to ensure that proper resources are provided to employees. Talented employees have little value if they are not given the proper tools and resources. Someone who is a great ticket seller cannot sell tickets if he or she cannot check a computer system to see what tickets are available.

Besides creating specific job descriptions, defining job qualifications, providing resources, and identifying appropriate responsibilities, a manager must specify and adhere to organizational relationships. Every business has a set of organizational relationships, often depicted in an **organizational flowchart** (see figure 2.1). The flowchart shows who reports to whom and what the lines of managerial/supervisory responsibility are. But while the organizational chart may place one employee above another, thus giving the upper-level employee the right to manage the lower-level employee, there still may not be a leadership relationship. In other words, the organizational chart does not guarantee a following or dedication; it merely represents a hierarchical order of responsibility and obligations.

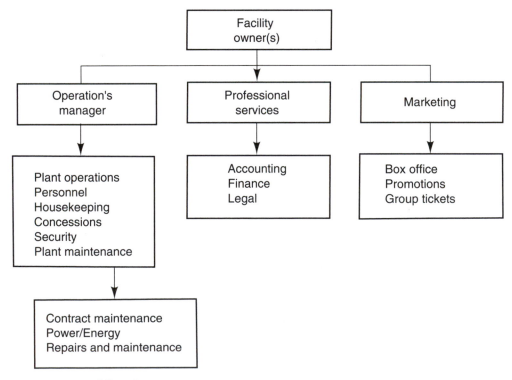

Figure 2.1   Organizational flowchart.

Reprinted from F. Borsenik and A. Stutts, 1997, The management of maintenance and engineering systems in the hospitality industry, 4th ed. (New York, NY: John Wiley & Sons, Inc.).

Behind the Scenes: A Day in the Life of Victor Dellaripa, Jr.

Courtesy of MSG-CT.

Victor Dellaripa, Jr. has been in facility management for 23 years. He held positions with the Hartford Civic Center (pictured here) for 15 years and served as the facility manager for both Western Connecticut State University's O'Neil Center and the New Haven Fieldhouse. In 2004 Mr. Dellaripa moved from his facility manager position at the Fieldhouse to a higher managerial position. Mr. Dellaripa identified the various activities he engaged in on two dates while he worked at the Fieldhouse—one an event date and one a non-event date. The Fieldhouse is completely indoors except for the parking lot. Thus Mr. Dellaripa is not responsible for grass fields, which require significant attention to weather conditions to aid in determining mowing and watering schedules.

Non-Event Date

Time	Activity
8:00 a.m.	Walk to office using different routes to check for any problems
8:30 a.m.	Review phone messages and return calls, check with night supervisor to determine status of evening changeover and cleaning
10:00 a.m.	Weekly staff meeting to discuss pre- and post-event information with representatives from all departments
11:00 a.m.	Advance the show (discuss the specific event times and dates, ticket prices, seating manifest, staffing needs, security needs, etc.) with future game or team promoters with a focus on maintaining the integrity of the event and the facility. (These discussions are then written down into production notes that are discussed with staff members and become the event's "bible.")
1:00 p.m.	Lunch
2:00 p.m.	Weekly meeting with facility tenants to analyze complaints or problems; issues covered in such meetings focus on financial consolidation, capital projects, business outlook, tenant concerns, cleanliness, etc.
3:00 p.m.	Call promoters and facilities in other states to analyze potential events that could generate additional revenue for the facility and negotiate potential contracts
6:00 p.m.	If lucky, get to go home

(continued)

(continued)

Event Date (Night Event)

Time	Activity
5:00 a.m.	Arrive with the trucks to set up the facility and help with the back of the house crew to examine rigging, stage, sound system, etc.
8 a.m.-12:00 p.m.	After the facility is set, shower and get dressed in a suit to work with the front of the house staff on customer relations, ticket sales, etc.
6:00 p.m.	Security meeting to discuss specific procedures
6:30 p.m.	Open doors to allow for security searches and work with those in the back of the house such as stagehands, facility workers, caterers, and custodians to make sure the work is being done correctly and safely
8-9:00 p.m.	During the event, head to the administrative offices to sit in on the settlement process (paying the bills and totaling the revenue) to help resolve any issues with the stagehand bill or staffing costs
10-11:00 p.m.	Work with the night crew to get the load out (set removal) started, which can take several hours, and then prepare the facility for the next day
2:00 a.m.	Go home—many show promoters, especially for rock concerts, want to see the same face before and after an event

Implementing

Implementing refers to executing goals and objectives with the appropriate personnel. Plans have no value in the absence of a structured system for executing them. In implementing, the manager is in some ways like the conductor of an orchestra. Available to the conductor are people, money, constituents, legal opportunities, and other resources for meeting the facility's mission. However, all these elements cannot just be thrown into a blender to create "success soup." Each element needs to be carefully measured and added with the proper motivation to direct the facility.

Controlling

The last managerial function is controlling. Controlling involves evaluating the results for individuals who report to the manager and providing appropriate feedback, whether positive or negative. Controlling is a monitoring process to ensure that the facility is accomplishing its mission and goals. At the same time, the manager needs to monitor whether employees are following their job descriptions and reaching their individual employee goals. The process is designed to either strengthen good conduct or correct inappropriate conduct. Correction is easier to accomplish when objective evaluation criteria exist. Problems often occur in the employee evaluation process when subjectivity enters into the analysis. Will an employee be reprimanded because he or she failed to meet one of 10 goals or because of some interpersonal factor?

Summary

Facility management is hard to define. Many aspects of managing focus on the facility and on making sure that the facility is safe and is well designed, constructed, and maintained. Among other issues that face a facility are legal, finance, marketing, and human resource concerns. Lastly, facility management entails working with various individuals and groups to ensure that all the elements fit together. A facility in optimal condition will not be a good facility if employees do not take pride in working there and making sure the facility is running correctly. In contrast, a facility in poor condition can still attract people if management makes a strong enough effort.

Through working with both internal and external constituents, facility managers can develop a platform from which they can run a facility. Constituents help management determine the appropriate, goals, objectives, and mission so that the facility can plan for the future. The plan becomes a blueprint for organizing and implementing successful strategies that lead to positive results.

DISCUSSION QUESTIONS AND ACTIVITIES

1. What is planning, and how would you go about planning for a new or existing facility?

2. If you were hired as the new manager of a public fitness facility in a small community, what are some of the goals and objectives you would try to develop? What would the goals and objectives be if you were the facility manager of a large stadium used by a professional baseball team?

3. Analyze the voting results from several stadium elections to see what issues affected the vote. Identify how those issues can affect planning.

4. Read a management book or article and critique its application to the facility management area. What can you take from the book or article to apply in the facility management context?

Management Theory and Practice

THREE

CHAPTER OBJECTIVES

After completing this chapter you will be able to do the following:

- Understand how facility management differs from personnel management
- Identify and apply appropriate managerial and leadership strategies
- Appreciate the need for ethical facility management
- Understand the impact that various facility owners have on the management process
- Appreciate how outsourcing can help a facility run more efficiently

Chapter 2 dealt with the diverse duties a facility manager faces. From finance and marketing concerns one day to maintenance and legal concerns the next, a manager has to work around numerous obstacles. A manager for a small facility needs to wear many hats and often has little help in the process unless he or she hires new employees or brings in external contractors. However, a manager for a larger facility such as a stadium or arena needs to work with and through numerous employees.

Facility management focuses on managing equipment and structures to make sure they are working correctly, but also on a totally different type of task—managing people. Equipment that needs to be repaired is fixed and will hopefully run smoothly in the future or will be replaced. In contrast, employees have emotions, feelings, moods, desires, and complex personalities. It is fairly straightforward to manage a piece of equipment and make sure it operates effectively. Managing a staff that may number in the hundreds is much more difficult. Thus, facility managers need to focus on their most important skill, which is using management theory and practice to help a facility reach its goals and objectives. As noted in chapter 2, a manager can be compared to an orchestra conductor. A manager who focuses only on facility systems and infrastructure can be likened to a conductor who makes sure all the musical instruments are in good shape. However, the musical instruments cannot play themselves; playing requires musicians. Managers need to conduct not only the instruments, but also the musicians.

Facility managers have a specific role in making sure all their employees perform their work in an appropriate manner. This chapter explores various management-related theories, strategies, and leadership concerns associated with a manager's effectiveness and also provides specific strategies to help manage the people in a facility. Special attention is given to working with employees and contractors and the particular leadership concerns that arise in working with these groups.

Management Theory

Management is defined as the achievement of predetermined objectives (based on goals or missions) while working through others such as employees and contractors (Bridges and Roquemore, 1996). The difference between facility management and **personnel management** is that facility management involves the use of equipment or buildings to help achieve the facility's mission and personnel management focuses on how people can help reach the facility's goals. Thus, the fact that someone is an expert in heating, ventilation, and air conditioning (HVAC) systems or in negotiating stadium lease agreements does not mean that the individual can manage people. But while facility management and personnel management are significantly different, in fact they are integrated because equipment in a facility cannot operate without people. Even a computer maintenance management system (see chapter 9) cannot run a facility's maintenance process, but requires a computer operator, programmer, technician, and people to do repair work. Management theory helps a manager determine how to efficiently synthesize equipment and people. Important figures in the development of management theory are described on pages 41-42.

Management trends are constantly evolving and changing. They also are contingent on other variables such as economic conditions. A facility manager has more difficulty finding employees and providing appropriate motivational strategies during good economic times than during tougher times since employees have many other work options. In contrast, during hard economic times, people may be scouring for jobs and take whatever is available. Employee management is one of the most difficult components of a facility manager's job. The dynamics imposed by dead-end positions, inadequate budgets, hiring freezes, union disputes, the requirement to use student employees (in effect at certain college facilities), and the burdens of working with full-time employees who may have wholly contradictory motivational issues and crazy work schedules makes human resource management a major headache. Human resource-related concerns are highlighted in chapter 12. The fact that a manager needs to work with existing employees who may not be motivated gives managers one of their biggest challenges and opportunities. That is why motivation and leadership are so important in implementing any management theory. Nevertheless, although a manager needs to learn how to motivate people, being able to motivate does not turn a manager into a leader. A leader is a manager who has the ability to motivate with fewer tricks or gimmicks.

Motivation is just one component in the management process and involves both implementing and controlling. Motivation comprises three basic elements:

- Motivating the person
- The job of motivator
- The environment as a motivating force

By understanding the interrelationships among these elements, a manager can better succeed at getting the most out of employees. For example, it is important to know what has motivated someone to work as a janitor for a facility for 10 years when the job is not exciting or rewarding. Is the reason that the employee has no other employment option? If that is the case, fear may be a motivator because the person will not want to lose the job—but this type of motivator could also result in leadership problems in the future. In contrast, if the janitor likes the people he or she works with, the manager could throw more staff parties or allow coworkers to take their breaks at the same time.

Getting the most out of employees becomes more critical in a technological era. For example, computers are changing the way individuals perform their work. Tasks that used to take a great deal of time may take seconds with new technologies. Instead of the need to take manual temperature and humidity readings for a gym, for example, a computer associated with an energy management system can take the readings and automatically adjust all the HVAC equipment to maintain the most cost-efficient and comfortable levels. But while computers can provide significant value, they can also represent a management dilemma. Some employees may refuse to work with computers, or a union can fight automation efforts that may save money but cost union jobs. Thus, one of the important motivational tasks focuses on helping employees embrace computer technology. This is an even greater task for new managers in the field who have grown up with computers and now have to manage people who have been doing their jobs for 20 years without computers.

Frederick Taylor

When trying to decide how to properly manage people in a facility, managers often focus on past theories and research to help determine the best managerial techniques. Frederick Taylor (1856-1915) is considered the father of modern management theory through utilization of scientific testing to improve productivity. Taylor is known for his time and motion studies, which examined how an employee was performing a task and what steps could be taken to improve efficiency or reduce the potential for injuries (Bridges and Roquemore, 1996). Taylor focused on examining how to increase physical output, decrease unit costs, reduce employee fatigue and injuries, and eventually increase wages through increasing profits. However, he is best known for utilizing scientific principles that required employers to set standards and measure performance to see if it met the standards.

G. Elton Mayo

Taylor's work evolved in the early part of the century with G. Elton Mayo's research on the Hawthorne effect. The study was undertaken at Western Electric's Hawthorne Works near Chicago. Workers were exposed to different levels of light in a controlled environment to determine what impact the light had on them. The results showed that every change of light had a positive impact and that at each level the workers performed better because they knew they were being treated differently and reveled in the added attention. The implications raised by the results are that managers need to consider personal feelings, morale, self-esteem, and employee relationships. Thus the discipline of behavioral science in management was born.

Abraham Maslow and Max Weber

Management theory progressed through the 1940s with such great management scholars as Abraham Maslow and Max Weber (Weber studied how bureaucracies worked). **Maslow's hierarchy of needs** was created (figure 3.1; see chapter 12 to examine employee motivation). While many management students learn to memorize the elements, they often lose sight of simple application. The hierarchy of needs highlights what factors will motivate an individual to achieve a higher goal. In order for a manager to properly motivate an employee, the manager needs to know what is important for that individual employee. Individuals need some form of motivation to excel. People who are primarily concerned with their paycheck will want to do their job to survive. A fancy title or a nice office will not be as strong a motivator as receiving better pay or benefits. Those who are financially secure may want something more to motivate them to produce better work, such as a better parking spot for being named employee of the month. The most senior executives will need something more than a plaque to motivate them. Stock options representing ownership interest in the company could be a motivator for such an executive. Again, ownership interest or a better parking space will not necessarily motivate someone who is just trying to work enough to meet financial needs. Using Maslow's theory for current facility employees, a manager would not try to motivate a janitor with a fancy title when the janitor is at the "safety level" and is more interested in cash. Cash would be the best motivator. In contrast, a high-level manager would probably thrive with the prospect of a higher job title, which can move the person up to the "self-actualization" level.

Frederick Herzberg

Frederick Herzberg developed his theories of hygiene and motivator factors in the 1950s. According to Herzberg, a manager needs to eliminate dissatisfaction by improving hygiene factors (such as increasing salaries) and to increase motivators through adding responsibilities, providing more meaningful work, providing greater autonomy, and providing job feedback.

(continued)

(continued)

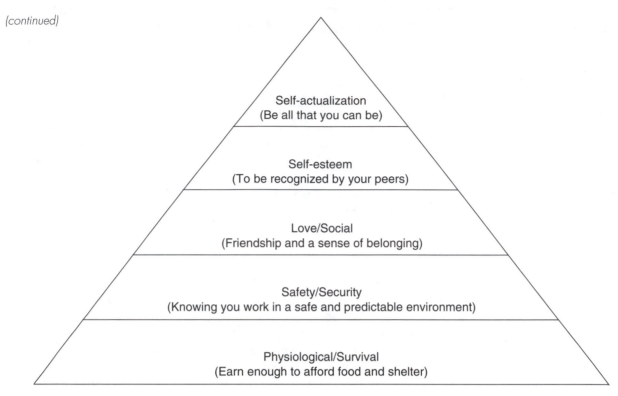

Figure 3.1 Maslow's hierarchy of needs.

Adapted, with permission, from Francis J. Bridges and Libby L. Roquemore, *Management for Athletic/Sport Administration*, fourth edition, 2004 (Decatur, GA: ESM Books), p. 259.

Victor Vroom

Victor Vroom published his **expectancy theory of motivation** in 1964. This theory requires the manager to choose the option that will result in the outcome employees want. Basically, an employee places a value on a reward and will do what is required to get that reward. Thus, if the facility manager has told the sales team that the person who sells the most tickets in November wins a cruise, the manager knows that the cruise is a motivator to some employees who will seriously compete to win the prize.

Gemba Kaizen

The joint interaction of employees and management was the hallmark of the Japanese style of management in the 1970s and 1980s. Management and front-line employees can work effectively only if there is a proper communication channel, with each party being on the same communication level. The Japanese concept of **Gemba Kaizen** refers to knowing what goes on in the workplace at the point of production. Gemba Kaizen analysis includes eight steps:

1. Selecting a project
2. Understanding the facility's current situation and goals/objectives
3. Analyzing all available data to determine how to reach the goals/objectives
4. Establishing appropriate countermeasures to avoid failure
5. Implementing the countermeasures
6. Analyzing the impact of the countermeasures
7. Developing standards for handling the same issue in the future in the same manner
8. Reviewing the process to determine if there are better solutions or choices (Elbo, 2000).

Computer-Aided Facility Management

The acronym CAFM (for **computer-aided facility management**) originated in the 1970s, but at that time referred to space and asset management systems that also contained a rough computer-aided drafting (CAD) component (Teicholz and Noferi, 2002). **Computer-aided drafting** systems are utilized in the design of facilities and allow a facility to be planned and moved around on the screen without having to make a new set of blueprints each time an element is changed. Over the years, CAFM has developed to include any technology platform that assists a facility manager in running a facility. Computer-aided facility management and the systems integrated within it such as HVAC systems are covered in greater detail in chapter 7. There are six primary areas in which CAFM has been applied (Teicholz and Noferi, 2002):

• Space and asset management focuses on occupancy information, space planning, asset management, and move management. Asset management focuses on how to use the real estate, buildings, and equipment in the most effective manner, along with the need to buy, repair, or sell current and future assets. In space planning, one examines how much additional space may be required. If the current occupant utilizes 100 square feet (9.3 square meters) per employee and there are 100 employees, then the utilized facility space is 10,000 square feet (930 square meters) (100 square feet × 100 employees). If it is anticipated that the workforce will grow 10% in the next year, the occupant will need 11,000 square feet (1,022 square meters) to house the current employees and the anticipated 10 additional employees. This information can be a useful tool for assuring that each employee has sufficient space, which will help in motivation.

• A CAD system is used to plan and design the floor plan for the facility to optimize flow and function. For example, if inventory can be moved to a more accessible location, this might save employee time and potential wear and tear on a facility. The CAD system does not deal with numbers or strategies, but rather with drawings such as floor plans.

• **Capital planning** and facility condition assessment tracks the condition of the facility and equipment to improve operation, maintenance,

and management. Employees utilizing such a system are able to make sure that the workplace is safe by quickly tracking hazardous and other conditions that may need to be addressed. Employees may be more highly motivated if they have a say in how the workplace will evolve to meet their needs for safety and future growth.

• Maintenance and operation, often referred to as computerized maintenance management systems (CMMS), tracks any asset or equipment that needs to be fixed or any situation in which maintenance personnel need to be more effectively utilized.

• Real estate and property management helps track all the space and how it is being purchased, leased, managed, and disposed of. While asset management programs may cover these issues, some programs separate these areas if the facility is part of a very large bundle of properties and there are large numbers of acres and buildings.

• Catch-all application is used to streamline the entire facility management process or integrate

© Human Kinetics

Facility managers and staff must know how to use computers in order to effectively manage facilities and support services within the facility.

43

some of the previously listed components. However, the larger the system, the more difficulty some employees may have in operating the system.

The CAFM system is just one example of the changing dynamics of facility management and its impact on employees. Numerous "old-guard" employees will attempt to resist change whether it relates to computers, new ticketing procedures, new ground maintenance procedures, or any other unfamiliar strategy discussed in this text. That is why managers need to learn how to motivate and encourage employees to embrace change, even if this is difficult at first.

Strategies

If there is no one best way to manage a facility, and if new technologies such as CAFM are helping to make facility management easier, then obviously there are other strategies and techniques that have helped managers over the years. Such strategies represent fundamental management trends that have been utilized over time and are as appropriate today as they were when first identified.

It is often the little things a manager does on a day-to-day basis that represent great strategies to motivate others or may represent leadership in its truest sense. For example, some managers achieve success through being friendly. Not merely superficially nice, they show genuine compassion and understanding. These managers may know the name of every person in the facility and address each employee personally. Other similar behaviors include writing personalized thank-you notes, remembering secretaries on their birthdays and Secretary's Day, always being on time and prepared for meetings (see page 45), and showing compassion when someone is sick or injured. While these strategies may not represent structured managerial theories, they are concrete steps a manager can take to get employees to work well.

The One-Minute Manager

Of the many managerial strategies and theories that have evolved over the years, the idea of the one-minute manager is among the best known. This simple managerial strategy is explained in one of the most popular management books of all time, *The One Minute Manager* by Kenneth Blanchard and Spenser Johnson. The authors advocated very

proactive management, but in the most efficient manner possible (Blanchard and Johnson, 1986). The book argues for one-minute goal setting and performance standards that need to be expressed in 250 words or less. Two copies of the standards are made—one for the employee and the other for the manager. The employee needs to have appropriate authority and latitude to complete the work indicated in the standard.

The manager is supposed to monitor the employee's work through detailed reports. However, the work needs to be completed by the employee alone rather than the manager. Based on whether the employee is doing well or poorly, management responds appropriately, immediately, sincerely, and consistently. In one-minute praising, the manager looks the employee in the eye and tells him or her exactly what was done correctly and how the manager feels about the work. If the praise is delayed, insincere, or random, then the employee may think that the manager is being sarcastic or ungrateful, or is giving false praise. With the one-minute reprimand, the manager looks the employee in the eye and explains what the employee did wrong and why the manager may feel angry, frustrated, or annoyed about it. The manager needs to be specific and not just lash out. It is not the employee that is criticized, but the negative behavior. The success of the one-minute system stems from the existence of predefined expectations for each employee, making objective analysis possible. These expectations need to be communicated effectively, and such communication efforts occur daily in the form of meetings.

While the one-minute manager is just one strategy that can be used, several key issues arise in its implementation that relate to numerous other managerial strategies. First, communication is critical for a manager. Goals need to be written and communicated; employee performance needs to be reviewed (often through communication with colleagues, customers, letters of praise, etc.); the review results need to be communicated to the employee; and the entire process needs to be recorded in the employee's file. Thus, communication is critical to effective management of subordinates, no matter which strategy is used.

Time Management

Time management is another highly important skill for a manager. Some managers seem to be always putting out fires while rushing from one concern to another. Executives are known to arrive early in the morning and leave late at night. Facility managers must make sure that the facility is ready for each day that it is open, and with a heavily used building a facility manager can easily work 60 hours a week. Thus, any strategy that can help save time means more time to do other activities or accomplish additional work. Computers, Palm Pilots, and day planners can all be used to remember key tasks, times, and dates. Through streamlining meetings, managers can save time.

Meetings

No matter what strategy or technique is used, such as the one-minute manager, facility managers spend much of their time in meetings. Meetings are held daily to discuss everything from budgets to upcoming events and security issues. Many managers also would say that meetings are often ineffective. Thus it becomes important to know how to make meetings more productive.

Meetings should be held on a consistent date each month or week, at the same time (preferably early in the morning before the regular workday begins), and should be held earlier in the week rather than later (Conrad, 2000). The following are additional meeting pointers:

- Always be on time.
- Start and end meetings at specified times.
- Control the meeting; do not allow interruptions (e.g., ask attendees to turn off cell phones and pagers).
- Create a meeting agenda and distribute it to all the attendees before the meeting.
- Insist that attendees come prepared.
- Before a meeting, talk to those who try to control meetings to let them know how the meeting will work and that it is important for them to comply with the agenda and with time restrictions.
- Encourage quiet people to participate. For example, ask for each individual's opinion.

Facility managers need to know how to run effective meetings, regardless if the meetings are held in formal meeting rooms or at a table set up in a gym.

- Get everyone's feedback before making a final decision (this will prevent "yes" men and women from simply agreeing with the decision).
- Give specific assignments with dates they are due.
- Keep meetings friendly by bringing food or small gifts.
- Once in a while, invite a guest speaker (e.g., for specific training, motivation).

Through effectively running meetings a manager can develop a reputation as an efficient person. Employees are more motivated when managers give them a clear and concise charge. Whether through gestures such as calling employees by their names, through established managerial strategies, or through meetings, managers have numerous options not just for getting the job done, but for leading employees. Each facility takes on the management style of the facility manager. Each facility also takes on the characteristics of the facility leader, who may or may not be the facility manager.

Leadership

What makes a good leader? There have been celebrated leaders throughout history, from Moses and Jesus to Gandhi and Martin Luther King. Every leader has had his or her own unique style and technique. The leader needs to be an activist for the facility and needs to be the voice for quality, safety, ethics, consistency, and compassion. In other words, the facility manager's leadership style is the spark that can make the facility succeed or fail. A facility manager can get employees to be more effective by using motivational tools such as more money. This does not necessarily make the manager a good leader. A good leader may be able to motivate employees through means other than more money or other techniques to "buy" respect and compliance—that is, through devotion or a sense of respect, for example. Thus, one can view leadership as a way of properly motivating employees through a combination of traditional or nontraditional techniques.

Almost every facility has a veteran employee who has been there for over 20 years. This individual may be a manager, but even if he or she does not intend to become a leader, the person may possess leadership authority based on years of experience or technical expertise. However, the longtime employee can also be someone without any ambition who criticizes the facility management at every turn but does nothing to make the facility better. Leaders are traditionally good at speaking and communicating, cost conscious, decisive, good at multitasking, very outgoing, action oriented, and able to deal with all types of people and problems with a level head (Cotts and Lee, 1992).

Leaders also have one critically important skill that sets them apart from others. Leaders hire well. This means that a leader can see potential in less experienced employees and can tell when they have the capabilities to become great. Besides hiring well, a leader can groom others well and train them to be future leaders. In fact, some leaders feel that their best legacy is to train others to lead. A leader also should be good at working on a "team" and should not be afraid to delegate. There is no "right" way to become an effective leader. However, the tools required of a good leader include being able to identify and communicate a shared value with others, developing and embracing a team concept, choosing the right players on the team to assume key roles that maximize their skills and potential inputs, motivating team members with appropriate incentives, working with team members

What makes a good manager? What makes a good leader? Are these qualities always the same?

to achieve their predetermined goals, and being willing to work with team members to share risks as well as rewards.

Successfully Leading

The leader and the manager can be intertwined within the same person. Some managers have gained leadership positions through years of service, and new leaders can also become great managers. There is a significant distinction between a leader or manager who has been established for a long time and someone who was recently hired from the outside. It is more difficult for a leader to delegate duties when the leader does not know the employees well. A new leader must prove his or her abilities, even if he or she was an internationally acclaimed facility leader in a prior position. Steps that a new leader should take include the following:

- Immediately assess the facility through an internal and external SWOT (strengths, weaknesses, opportunities, and threats) analysis. The SWOT analysis is covered in greater detail in chapter 4.
- Implement change by starting small and then expanding as time progresses.
- Explain all changes to the staff.
- Take a pay cut to show that financial issues are important and that everyone needs to make a sacrifice to help the facility in the long run.
- Take charge and make a change if something does not work.
- Make a major decision with definite cost reductions and then publicize the results. This will show an intention to make the facility better. Another way to follow this strategy is to allow employees to recommend changes and share in the cost reductions.
- Undertake very visible projects such as repainting bathrooms and concession areas, which shows a desire to make the work environment better.
- Take a lead in developing appropriate short- and long-term budgets and plans.
- Review and manage all existing service/supply contracts to see if services are at a high standard. If they are not acceptable, facilitate change, as this will show employees a willingness to make changes (Cotts and Lee, 1992).

If these strategies are successful, employees may embrace the changes and the leader who implemented them. Even a poor decision can make a manager a great leader if the manager takes personal responsibility for the decision while identifying and correcting the problem.

Being a successful businessperson or manager does not make a person a good leader. Almost everyone has worked for a boss who was a great manager but a poor leader. A manager may be able to motivate employees to reach sales goals, but it may be that not every employee in that department will respect or consider the manager his or her leader. The employees reach their goals because they want to keep their jobs, but they may not strive to reach a higher level because they do not feel they are being led to greater success. Conversely, many people have worked with great leaders who were poor bosses. Employees may love a manager who leads them, but if the manager cannot properly plan or organize resources so that employees can reach their goals, he or she is not an effective manager. In the sales example, a good leader can inspire employees to make numerous cold calls to sell tickets, but if the leader does not provide employees with proper ticketing equipment and supplies they will not be able to finalize the sales and achieve their goals.

Leadership by Example

Leaders can be effective managers, and vice versa, by doing employees' jobs just as well as the employees do. If a facility manager has worked up from the janitorial ranks to the position of crew chief and finally to the position of an assistant manager, most employees will respect the person because of his or her work "in the trenches." If someone fresh out of college obtains the same managerial position, lower-level workers may perceive the person differently. Until the manager has proven him- or herself and shown the requisite knowledge for performing the job, he or she will be eyed with suspicion.

If the manager has had prior experience and can gain the trust of lower-level employees by pitching in to clean toilets, working a changeover shift, or selling hotdogs, then he or she can lead by example. Leading by example also focuses on ethical behavior.

Ethics

Every facility manager has to have the ethical underpinnings to be honest in all his or her dealings. Some booking agents are sleazy and unscrupulous. This does not mean that a facility manager needs to stoop to that level. A reputation is one of the most valuable assets a person will ever have. If another party is not acting ethically, the manager can rise above the mediocrity and act in an impeccable manner.

Ethical behavior means identifying what conduct is right and wrong and then choosing to take the right path. The question becomes, what is right? The fact that the law allows a manager to act in a certain way does not mean that the action is ethically correct. For example, a facility manager has to comply with the Americans with Disabilities Act (ADA) requiring facilities to provide reasonable accommodations to the disabled (see chapter 13). It is possible for a facility manager to comply with the law but for a disabled patron to still be unable to enjoy the event. Is it ethical to take the position that the manager has acted within the law, or should the manager go beyond the letter of the law to make sure that the patron can in fact equally enjoy all benefits other patrons receive? This example suggests that ethical conduct requires a blending of legal and moral obligations. The same issue also relates to employees covered under the ADA.

As another example, suppose that a boxing match is scheduled at a facility. The match is secured by a contract. If one of the parties does not show, he or she is breaching the contract and the facility can recover damages. But should the facility be allowed to sue if the fight is canceled and the facility loses money? Would the answer change if the boxer had lost a very close family member and wanted to attend the funeral, or if the event was canceled due to a snowstorm? Under each option, the manager knows that others will be looking at the decision that is made and at its future impact. Numerous issues will come before a manager, and the actions taken will help determine what type of leader the individual may be.

Due to the large number of people who rely on each other to ensure a successful facility, facility managers need to constantly balance their interests and ethical underpinnings against the interests of all other constituents. This balancing act can be very difficult but also represents an opportunity to utilize integrity to advance while still protecting constituents. At times, managers may determine that the best answer to a problem is to bring in an expert who can more effectively complete the desired work.

Outsourcing

Good leaders and managers know what they can and cannot accomplish. Managers cannot do everything, and if there is an area they are not strong in or if they want to focus on their key competencies, they can outsource their work. Thus, some facility owners do not want to manage the facility at all, but do want to run the events in the facility. They may outsource all facility management operations to a company specialized in facility management.

Many management companies provide services to both private and public facilities. These for-profit companies attempt to provide optimal services at a reasonable price to maximize revenue. The owner of a facility, whether private or public, may hire a third company to run the facility as a means to reduce costs or a means of allowing the facility management to focus on their key responsibility—producing successful events in the facility—rather than worrying about the HVAC system, for example. Managers also can hire outside companies to complete very specific tasks such as janitorial, brewing fresh coffee, or photocopying. The facility management services offered by an **outsourcing** company can include

- facility analysis and assessment to make sure that the facility is running smoothly and tenants are satisfied,
- energy usage analysis to determine where energy conservation measures can be taken to reduce costs,
- HVAC and energy management to more effectively maintain and operate HVAC equipment,
- construction/renovation management so the owner does not have to hire contractors and tradespeople,
- preventive maintenance through developing corrective maintenance plans or installing a CMMS,

Behind the Scenes: Problem Solving

© Human Kinetics

There is no "right" way to manage any part of a business. The same holds true for facility management. Assume that you are the manager of a large stadium that has a unionized workforce. One of your janitors cannot read. While this may not appear to be a problem, the employee works with some hazardous materials and needs to be able to read the Occupational Safety and Health Administration (OSHA)-mandated Materials Safety Data Sheets. The employee admits that he cannot read, but says that he has been doing fine for over 20 years and will not change now. He also brings the union into the dispute. The union raises concerns under the collective bargaining agreement, which prevents you from punishing a person without just cause, and also raises the potential of an ADA violation. How would you resolve such a dispute? What steps do you need to take to protect patrons, other employees, this particular employee, the facility, the union, and all other affected parties?

As it turned out when a situation similar to this actually occurred, the facility manager worked with the union to provide a remedial reading program for the employee. The employee was able to take the classes during normal work hours while he was still under the clock and getting paid. Everyone agreed that if he were able to correct his reading problem and thus provide for his own safety and the safety of others, he could return to his position without any difficulty. However, management and the union also agreed that if he did not improve his reading he could be terminated because then he would represent a threat of harm to himself and others, including other union members. This example shows how facility managers need to resolve conflicts and generate unique solutions for various problems. It also suggests that legal and ethical issues come into play every day. The manager could have terminated the worker and then fought with the union over various grievances before possibly proceeding to a court battle. The ethical decision helped save all parties headaches and costs.

- budget and pro forma analysis to make sure the facility is operating within a budget and not spending too much money, and

- housekeeping and environmental services to ensure that the facility is clean and to prevent illegal waste dumping or the use of environmentally unfriendly cleaning agents.

Private management companies are generally more focused on the bottom line compared with facility managers. Some contracts require a management company to reduce costs. Outsourcing is often obtained through a competitive bidding process, which means that various companies are competing against one another to win a contract. This in turn means that the competitors are trying to win the contract by offering their services at the lowest price while still trying to maintain the highest level of safety and cleanliness. Management companies typically offer the following advantages:

- Increased operating efficiency through buying in bulk or having one expert who can focus on reducing costs

- Increased continuity, since a management company often keeps tenants happier, which reduces the loss of tenants who may leave if dissatisfied

- Fast reaction time in response to problems and opportunities, as outsourcing firms often utilize CAFM systems to make a facility more efficient, which can help solve problems or reduce costs

- Professional marketing and group sales support

- Performance-based compensation for key management employees, which is negotiated in the contract so that the facility will know the long-term goals of the management company

- A more efficient procurement process for goods and services, since a management company cannot only negotiate the best price but can also establish distribution systems to quickly deliver goods and services

- Ability to take risks using past experience at other facilities as a guide to help change facilities

- Ability to invest in a facility, as outsourcing contracts often require the management company to install new equipment and help upgrade the facility

Pros

Cities, counties, universities, and other facility owners hire privatized facility management for numerous reasons such as the following:

- Network of managed facilities—creates event booking leverage (i.e., more events, better deals). If a management company runs 10 facilities in a given state it can significantly increase its bargaining power to attract events because it can package the tour at multiple facilities. If each facility negotiated its own contract, some events might not be scheduled because there are not enough facilities interested in meeting the demand or schedule.

- Increased corporate support (professional staff)—results in more comprehensive management, oversight, and on-site assistance. Professional facility managers who often manage outsourced facilities have greater access to facility experts within their company and do not need to chase after tradespeople such as plumbers, technicians, and electricians.

- Reduced stress, time, and budget implications for other governmental or university departments since they can focus on their key strengths rather than on running a facility. For example, a physical education department may have to teach classes and manage a facility. With someone else managing the facility, the instructors can focus on their teaching.

- A private management company is often the most effective means for a city, county, or university to balance competing departmental interests, since all facilities are treated the same and athletics will hopefully not receive preferential treatment over the science or math building.

- More effective negotiation and renegotiation of labor agreements through the ability to focus workers on their specialty and to give them specific responsibilities that can be negotiated into their labor contracts.

- Facility staff will have greater opportunities for professional growth since staff can focus on their expertise rather than trying to wear multiple hats, which often occurs when budgets are tight.

- Increased contacts and knowledge, resulting in more ideas and better problem solving.

- Shared database and industry research.

Cons

While there are numerous advantages to outsourcing facility management, some facility owners and managers are not so receptive to private management. Some facility owners want to be "hands-on" and want their own employees to manage the facility. In fact, this is typically the case for smaller facilities. It is primarily the largest facilities or larger groups of buildings that are outsourced. Outsourcing has disadvantages including the following:

- Expense: Expenses include an obligation to pay a fixed monthly management fee plus incentives.

- Control: In some cases, facility owners are better off relying upon their own management expertise.

- Loyalty: Some facility owners fear a turnover of loyalty to the private management company if employees may be fired or reassigned or if tenants are forced to leave.

Behind the Scenes: Deciding Whether to Outsource

Many schools are now outsourcing various services to either save money or provide expertise that is not available in-house. Some of the most common outsourced services are transportation, vending, security services, HVAC maintenance, computer services, and facility management. The primary benefits envisioned by the schools that utilize outsourcing are efficiency and cost reduction. One study showed that a typical CMMS could reduce operational cost for a school by 20% to 30%.

This analysis was put to the test at two different school districts in Connecticut averaging over 1 million square feet (92,900 square meters) in multiple buildings. One district managed its system in-house while the other outsourced its facility management operations to a company called OR&L Facility Management. According to data from several years (1998-2001), the total facility management cost for managerial staff per square foot, including salaries, was $0.62 for the in-house program and $0.81 per square foot at the OR&L-managed facility. Thus, the salaries appeared higher, but additional numbers quickly turned the tables in favor of outsourcing. For example, the mechanical/HVAC costs were reduced from $0.98 to $0.48 per square foot. Another major drop in cost involved housekeeping, environmental, and custodial, which decreased from $1.66 to $1.05 per square foot. The total analyzed cost for the in-house program was $3.52 per square foot. In contrast, the outsourcing costs were just $2.71 per square foot, a savings of $0.81 per square foot. Thus, outsourcing saved over $800,000 annually (OR&L, 2003).

- Responsibility: Private management companies are sometimes put in the position of aggressively pursuing the "bottom line" at the expense of owner goals, objectives, desires, and external responsibilities.

- Incentive fee-driven cost cutting that would lead to long-term cost increases. If a management company is forced to lower costs, it may spend less on service, which in the long run will damage equipment and create more expensive problems in the future.

- Excessive turnover of the general manager due to opportunities at other network facilities. If a management company installs a general manager for the property, that person can develop a great reputation and save money, but may be switched by the management company to a different property that needs managerial help.

As the pros and cons of outsourcing suggest, a manager can use external assistance to help solve problems and as some problems are solved, other problems can arise. In general, though, the outsourcing of services has been a very positive step in facility management since it allows owners/managers to focus on their key competencies and lets professional facility managers take charge of the facility and reach certain service and quality levels.

Private Management Companies

There are a number of larger facility management companies serving the sport facility market. Aramark is one of the largest facility service companies in the world. As of 2000, Aramark managed over 45 professional sport facilities, 30 convention centers, and over 25 amphitheaters serving more than 75 million people annually. Sport facilities managed by Aramark include Wrigley Field, MCI Center, Staples Center, Conseco Fieldhouse, and Veterans Stadium ("Aramark Acquires," 2000). Aramark also has an ownership position in SMG, which manages almost 100 stadiums, arenas, convention centers, and theaters around the world ("SMG, Leisure Management," 2000).

Global Spectrum began operations in January 2000 and quickly acquired over 30 facility management contracts. Global Spectrum actually began in 1994 as Globe Facility Services, which was acquired by Comcast-Spectacor in January 2000. Global Spectrum differs from other facility management companies in that its parent company, Comcast, owns the First Union Center and Spectrum (Philadelphia, Pennsylvania) and also the Philadelphia Flyers and the Philadelphia 76ers.

Although there are a number of larger facility management companies serving the sport facility market, smaller companies are also starting to get involved. One such company is OR&L, which has several divisions including commercial real estate

Facility Focus: Staples Center

Photo courtesy of AEG.

The Staples Center is one of the crown jewels in Phil Anschutz's sports empire. Mr. Anschutz has quickly become one of the most powerful sport moguls by owning five Major League Soccer teams, a stake in the Staples Center, ownership interests in the Los Angeles Lakers and Kings, and interests in several European hockey teams and facilities. He also built the Home Depot Field. These entities are structured under Anschutz Entertainment Group (AEG), which has significant development plans for the Los Angeles market. AEG is proposing a $1 billion entertainment center near Staples Center with a 1,500 room hotel, a smaller luxury hotel, and a 7,000 seat arena which could serve as home for the Emmy Awards. The development is a continuation of the $7 billion growth in investment in Los Angeles spurred on by the Staples Center (Orlov, 2004).

The following facts give a picture of the Staples Center in Los Angeles, which is home to two NBA teams and one NHL team.

- Built: 1997-1999 (total construction time was 18 months, and a penalty in the contract provided for a $50,000 per day fine for every day the project went past the 18-month time line)
- Cost: $375 million
- Basketball seating: 20,000
- Hockey seating: 18,118
- Luxury suites: 160
- Party suites: 32
- Club seats: 2,500
- Concession stands: 23
- Total square footage: 900,000 (83,610 square meters)
- Elevators: 10
- Escalators: 11
- Rest rooms: 55
- Locker rooms: 12
- Watts of audio amplification: 125,500
- Feet of fiber optic cable: 148,000 (45,110 meters)
- Tons of structural steel: 2,500
- Cubic yards of concrete: 73,000 (55,810 cubic meters)
- Miles of data/telephone cables: 14 (22.5 kilometers)
- Square yards of carpeting: 32,500 (27,175 square meters)
- Square feet of terrazzo tile: 81,000 (7,525 square meters)
- Square feet of drywall: 2,865,000 (266,170 square meters)
- Feet of broadcast production cable: 3,800,000 (1,158,240 meters)

From "Staples Center by the numbers," 2000, *Facility Manager*, 27.

sales, construction management, and facility management. The facility management services offered by OR&L Facility Management include

- HVAC and energy management,
- construction/renovation management,
- corrective and preventive maintenance plans,
- computerized maintenance management systems,
- emergency management systems (EMS),
- security and crisis management,
- budget and pro forma analysis,
- housekeeping and environmental services, and
- various consulting projects from feasibility analysis to economic impact studies (*Introduction*, 2001).

Ancillary Service Providers

The number of companies that provide services to facilities is almost endless. It would be impossible to list all the companies that provide services apart from facility management. These companies deal with food products, fire suppression, crowd management, concession management, architectural design, engineering design, insurance, uniforms, cleaning, janitorial, and countless others. A manager needs to select these companies, monitor them, and terminate relationships with them when necessary. A security company can provide several hundred people to work a stadium event. Facility managers do not necessarily need to manage these employees, as the security company is responsible for hiring, training, managing, and firing the security personnel. However, the facility manager needs to monitor and track the security service provider to make sure that the personnel are doing their job, the contract is not being violated, and patrons are happy with the service.

Besides for-profit businesses, many other types of organizations have an impact on the field and assist facility managers. Whether membership organizations or organizations that develop standards, these entities can help shape an entire industry. A membership organization such as the ones mentioned next provides numerous educational resources, includes a network of fellow managers that can offer advice, and is able to help establish industry benchmark standards that can be used to study whether a facility is operating effectively. One specialized association is the Sportsplex Operators and Developers Association (SODA), which is a 300+-member education association focused on outdoor and indoor sport facilities offering such sports as softball, soccer, and flag football. SODA sells numerous specialized books and case studies, holds yearly educational conferences, and has developed a purchasing pool to allow smaller facility managers the opportunity to buy products such as grass seed or softballs at discount prices.

Larger associations include the Stadium Managers Association (SMA), the International Association of Assembly Managers (IAAM), and the International Facility Managers Association (IFMA). The IAAM is the largest association focused on arenas, stadiums, concert halls, convention centers, and related PAFs. It offers several specialized conferences each year on topics such as stadium management and crowd management. The IAAM has both student and faculty memberships and has several university chapters.

Summary

Facility managers must manage facilities and the people who are in them. While facilities cannot be motivated or fired, employees can, and that is why facility managers have to spend a significant amount of time managing employees. No facility can operate without employees; a beautiful new facility with employees who are poorly trained, skilled, and motivated will quickly become a disaster.

Besides managing employees, facility managers have to become leaders or retain leaders who can motivate personnel to provide the highest level of service quality. Leadership entails making tough decisions, and one of the more difficult decisions may be whether to use an outsourcing company rather than existing personnel. Whether current employees are not doing a good job or costs are too high, sometimes a facility owner or manager needs to make a tough decision to focus on core competencies and retain an outside company to provide services.

Managing people is an art and an acquired skill. Not everyone is comfortable with managing others. However, leaders need to be found in every facility to take charge and ensure that work is done. By combining current employees and industry professionals, along with using information from industry associations, a manager can increase his or her skills and comfort level in managing and leading others, and the result will hopefully be a better facility and work environment for everyone.

DISCUSSION QUESTIONS AND ACTIVITIES

1. Define management and then leadership, and then explain the difference between the two.

2. How would you motivate employees if they do not respect you as a leader?

3. Do you have the managerial strength to fire a friend who has not performed up to expectations but has not done anything wrong?

4. Read a management book and critique it for application to the facility management area. What can you take from the book to apply in the facility management context?

5. Why would any facility want to hire a facility management company?

PART II

Facility Development

FOUR

Facility Planning

CHAPTER OBJECTIVES

After completing this chapter you will be able to do the following:

- Understand the principles of planning a facility
- Appreciate the need to continuously plan for existing facilities
- Develop a thorough understanding of how to plan for a new facility
- Compare the various types of sport facilities as an aid to finalizing options that arise in the planning process
- Appreciate that some of the data utilized to justify building new facilities will be uncertain or biased, and try to verify all data
- Develop an understanding of the entire facility business plan process and the components necessary to gain appropriate approval

Planning is the process of determining a facility's future direction. Facility management is not conducted using a fortune-teller gazing into a crystal ball. Facility management occurs through proper planning and then execution of the plan. This chapter deals with the planning process and its importance for facility managers.

As discussed in chapter 2, planning is a fundamental skill required by all managers. Managers must plan for capital improvements, staffing needs, crowd dynamics, emergencies, and booking and scheduling (including breaks for scheduled and unscheduled maintenance).

Whether developing goals and objectives or planning new marketing techniques, any facility manager finds that planning occupies a significant amount of time. The planning process is most evident in facility management, which involves planning for each event, all repairs, ticket-selling strategies, facility renovations, and all new construction. Thus, planning can originate as a result of short-term needs or a long-term vision. There are numerous planning demands for a large stadium or arena and different issues for a high school facility. Since these demands are so different, it would be impossible to cover all issues for each facility. Thus, this chapter covers general planning issues.

The chapter addresses the steps in the planning process, with a detailed examination of planning for existing facilities and planning for future facilities. Special attention focuses on the steps involved in the planning process for a new facility. Additional discussion centers on facilities in Houston, Texas, and New Haven, Connecticut. We examine the types of facilities that exist, how to conduct a feasibility study, how to determine the best site selection, and how to develop an appropriate facility plan that can be used to convince the voters or lenders to support the project. A critical component of this plan is the financing element. How will the new facility be financed, and where will the money come from for continued operations and maintenance?

Fundamentals of Planning

Planning can help make an otherwise unworkable deal work. For example, Clark College in Vancouver needed some extra classroom space for sports medicine and sport management classes and worked out a deal to help construct a 5,000-seat baseball stadium to be shared with a professional baseball team. Both entities would receive something of value through looking outside the box to solve a problem (Hewitt, 1998). Thus, planning needs to examine unique potential solutions to problems that could be present for multiple parties and their multiple needs.

There is no one correct method to plan. Nevertheless, a facility cannot exist without planning. Some facilities lie vacant due to incorrect planning, while other facilities have too many events and demands on facility time due to poor planning. Thus, **planning** is the process of determining the appropriate allocation of precious resources to ensure facility success. The failure to properly plan will not necessarily lead to failure of a facility. However, it can lead to significant hardship that may take years to overcome or may never be overcome.

Planning can be accomplished through numerous means. The most productive planning technique is to utilize a group of people. The group can include a broad range of individuals, from facility users and community members to lawyers, architects, and engineers. These people are collectively referred to by some as "a gang in a room" (AGIR). This technique contrasts sharply with the authoritarian technique whereby one person decides everything. While the latter technique is frequently used in smaller buildings, this does not make it correct—a group can always provide additional insight to help improve the accuracy of projections. The process in which one person makes all the decisions is often called OMOM ("one man on a mountain") (Borsenik and Stutts, 1997). The OMOM process is also seen in a top-down management system in which all those under the leader are afraid to challenge the leader, and push a project through no matter how bad they think it is.

Two types of planning are critical for facilities: planning for existing facilities and planning for future facilities.

Planning for Existing Facilities

A manager may be hired to help develop a facility from the very beginning conceptual stages, since a manager may be able to identify concerns or opportunities during the planning process. Some facility managers specifically take a job managing a yet-to-be-built facility because they want the challenge or the opportunity to be part of something new and exciting—and it can be very exciting to work on a building from the design phase all the way through to obtaining the **occupancy permit.** But while most facility managers never plan for more than one new facility during their career, managers of an existing facility always need to plan for the next day, month, and year.

Planning for an existing facility entails examining the current uses and future potential uses. For some facilities this process can be fairly simple. Managers of a single-use facility such as an ice rink know what events will be held in the future and how to plan for those events. Such planning includes coordinating maintenance schedules and personnel; monitoring electricity usage to keep the ice frozen; scheduling daily events, special events, and games; coordinating concession purchases and sales; and dealing with numerous other concerns associated with various facets of the facility and its ancillary areas (bathrooms, parking lots, etc.). Fiscal planning is often the most important planning concern. In an ice rink, a breakdown of the Zamboni can generate five-figure expenses within minutes. If the facility only has $5,000 in the bank and no credit, how can it handle such emergencies? Through planning the facility hopefully has analyzed existing systems and maintenance needs to project future capital requirements.

Money, Personnel, and Scheduling

Money is needed to run a facility. After a given sum of money has been raised to construct a facility, there obviously needs to be enough money to keep it running. This concern is often raised at planning meetings when a facility is being proposed, but is not as frequently addressed later. At schools, for example, often the primary concern is providing appropriate funding for teachers or charging students a fee for participating in sport so that there is money for transportation, coaches, or uniforms. Facility-related costs are frequently an afterthought. It is not uncommon to walk into a gymnasium and see nonfunctioning lights. Is the school waiting for more lights to go out so that it is worthwhile bringing in a hoisting unit, or does the school simply lack funds to replace the lights?

Personnel is another major concern in planning for existing facilities. Are there enough employees to operate the facility? The hours that the facility will be open and the events that will be held help dictate the number of people that will be required for facility operation. The planning process will also help determine where employees may be needed and what skills will be needed.

Another major issue in the planning process is facility scheduling. If the facility has 20 scheduled events for a week, how will all the events work together without causing problems? Scheduling may raise equity issues also. Will all the basketball games be played at night? If so, is this fair to the minor sports such as volleyball or badminton? Could such a schedule be seen as discriminatory, particularly if the volleyball players are all women? Furthermore, would it matter what participant numbers are expected for each event? These types of questions require careful consideration.

These examples help suggest how important planning is for an existing facility. The planning processes required for the future of an existing facility are similar to planning for a new facility. Background data (internal and external) need to be obtained and compared with facility policies and procedures. All this information is crafted into a document, the plan, that helps drive the facility into the future.

Space Management

Space management refers to future growth needs and the proper allocation of time and space for bookings, which are the best means to maximize revenue generation. A facility may be large enough to support current needs, but what if new activities are added and there is no additional room?

Management might need to lease (rent) additional space so there will be enough space for all activities. **Move management** may require analyzing where in a building individuals or equipment can be moved to free up space. However, space planning requires a more significant effort to provide for the future. The failure to plan can result in unnecessary moves and relocating expenses, the need to rent additional space, underutilization of existing space, and related situations that not only waste money but can also demoralize those who must pay the price for poor space management.

Facility managers normally plan based on standard allocations such as the square footage required for each staff member multiplied by the number of staff members. If each marketing employee requires 100 square feet (9.3 square meters) and there are currently 10 marketing employees, then the office space for marketing, not including corridors or other common areas, needs to be at least 1,000 square feet (93 square meters). If the office area is only 1,000 square feet, what would happen if a new employee was hired? Another 100 square feet would be needed. Through space planning, a facility manager creates space for future growth through such means as redesigning existing space or leasing additional space with the idea that personnel can grow into a facility.

Other space planning concerns include swing space and growth space. **Swing space** is any space that is available during renovations, alterations, or realignment. A corner of the gym used to store equipment during renovation of a room is an example of swing space. **Growth space** is space contiguous to currently utilized space that allows a business to expand without undertaking any additional construction or leasing (Cotts and Lee, 1992). Large businesses require 2% to 3% growth space, and smaller businesses require 5% to 7% growth space. Growth space is based on historical growth data or anticipated future growth if new programs or activities are planned. Thus, growth space planning requires significant managerial input.

Facilities often face problems when administrators plan for growth and do not tell the facility managers about the plans. In one facility, the school administrators planned for a nature trail with a crushed gravel walkway. The facility administrator was not asked about facility-related concerns and was not consulted during the entire process until the construction began. At this point he rushed to raise concerns such as the lack of toilets to service the area, the lack of electricity, the need to ensure compliance with the Americans with Disabilities Act, and other problems relating to the growth space. These last-minute concerns cost the school a significant amount of time and money. This situation probably could have been avoided through proper planning. Issues that should be examined by the facility and business managers include the amount of available space, the type of space available, the overall condition, architectural limitations, and the ability to interact with other business units.

Planning for Future Facilities

Future facilities raise numerous concerns such as where to build, what to build, and how to pay for the facility. Only through effective planning can a facility be developed that meets the greatest current needs, anticipates future needs, and causes the least amount of harm. For example, facilities today need to be planned with an eye toward media exposure, demographics, property size, planned events, and the "sellability" of commercial rights such as naming rights and personal seat licenses (PSLs). A list of planning questions that one should ask when considering the construction of a new sport facility is shown on page 61.

This planning process starts with an analysis of existing internal and external constituents. The internal constituents are the people who will use the facility, such as athletes, students, or spectators. The external constituents are stakeholders outside the facility such as government leaders, alumni, donors, and others who have an interest in the facility but are outside the traditional facility planning process. A politician may approve funds that can help construct the facility, and he or she may eventually use the facility. However, this person is still considered an external constituent since he or she is not a primary user. People who are a potential internal constituent because they might at one time use the facility are distinguished from people for whom the facility is planned and who may use the facility every week.

How should a group, whether public or private, plan for a new facility? Steps include the following:

- Conducting a feasibility study
- Developing a potential budget
- Organizing various planning committees
- Setting realistic goals and objectives
- Researching the political and financial marketplace
- Trying to bring aboard the right people before the project even starts

Other useful planning strategies include garnering community support, creating a planning committee, conducting a needs assessment, and identifying comparable facilities.

Community Support

If any public funds will be used, the planning process requires community involvement in order to generate the community "buy-in." Any effort to reach out to the public requires the facility planners to be honest. People should not be invited to meetings if they will not be allowed to provide meaningful input that will be used. If people attend the meetings and are ignored, the process will generate more negativity than would be the case if it had never been undertaken. Although the community meeting should be very formal, it must also be fun and engaging to help bring people to meetings in the future. Numerous community boards fail because the meetings are not productive, are boring, and are a waste of everyone's time. This process can also be enhanced if the board members are focused on the public good rather than individual agendas.

Often the most important part of gaining community support is convincing the public about the need for the facility. Through utilizing common sense and allies, facility planners can win some opponents over. Some opponents may need incentives, which can be identified through negotiations. Others will always be opponents. But planners should never burn bridges, even if there is posturing: People who are major opponents today may change their tune years down the road, for example when they have grandchildren who want to use the facility. Thus it is important to take care when dealing with opponents in the planning process.

Some opponents will use the strategy known as NIMBY ("not in my backyard"). According to this position, the facility is worthwhile and is needed, but should be built someplace else. For example, citizens frequently are in favor of jails but do not want one built in their town. And although some

Typical Planning Questions for a New Sport Facility

Will the facility be an integral part of the organization?

Does the facility take into account current and future needs?

Is the facility planned for maximum usage?

Is the facility centrally located and are there existing transportation routes such as roads?

Is adequate parking available?

Are utilities available such as electricity, sewage, water, and gas?

Will the facility comply with all local, state, and national standards?

Has the soil been tested for any contamination?

Has the title been searched to make sure there are no claims against the property such as liens?

Will the facility be constructed with cost reduction, environmental concerns, and reduced maintenance costs as top priorities?

Can the space be maximized—for example, can the rooftop be used for additional recreational activities?

Has safety been highlighted throughout the planning process?

Has system engineering been analyzed to reduce electrical and maintenance costs?

Are locker rooms planned with sloped floors so water can drain effectively?

Have surface choices been analyzed to lower maintenance costs and reduce the threat of dust, allergens, and other airborne material?

Is the facility planned with adequate buffer room between activity areas?

Will the ceiling height be sufficient to support all intended uses?

Is the facility designed with enough usable storage areas?

Will the facility meet all lighting, sound, and related usage standards?

Will the facility utilize security systems such as closed-circuit television (CCTV), card scanners, or special locks?

Have broadcasting issues been taken into consideration if there may be broadcasts in the future?

Are the needs of the media, such as a press box, being considered?

Are scorekeeping and timekeeping needs being considered?

Will the facility need specialized equipment such as backboard systems, floor plates, wall hangers, ceiling attachments, and other specialty items?

Will specialized rooms be needed for such activities as ticket sales or laundry?

Will personal transportation (vertical, horizontal) be installed?

Will the facility accommodate the needs of the disabled, and how will it accomplish this goal?

Will the facility utilize general or reserved admissions, and what type of seating options will be available?

What risk management steps have been taken to avoid both minor and serious threats?

How many bathrooms will be available, and will there be options for men, women, children, and families?

Is there enough room for people to mingle?

How many concessions stands will be built and where will they be positioned?

From "Details, details," 1985.

die-hard sport fans would love to see a stadium within walking distance of their home, other fans do not want the traffic and noise associated with having a stadium in their "backyard." At other extremes are supporters who want the facility no matter where it is built and their opposites, the BANANA opponents. BANANA stands for "build absolutely nothing anywhere near anything." These individuals oppose building a facility because of a reluctance to spend public funds, a dislike of sport, or countless other reasons. Regardless of the reason for support or opposition, a facility planner needs to understand and appreciate opponents and respect their right to disagree.

It is also crucial for planners to be forthright from the very beginning. If those involved in the planning process feel that they have been heard and that their concerns have been addressed they will be more likely to be supporters rather than detractors. Fairfield University in Connecticut was sued by four neighbors over playing fields equipped with sound systems. The neighbors claimed that the sound was too loud and that lights from the fields allowed them to read the newspaper in their houses at night without any of their own lights on (Tepfer, 1999). If these neighbors had been involved in the planning process, and had been informed about the systems being installed and the times they would be used, the lawsuit could possibly have been averted. At the same time, though, it is important to note that even if everyone is involved in the planning process and every view has been raised, there will always be disgruntled individuals who will challenge the plans for a facility.

Some community facility planning boards travel to visit other facilities to compare and contrast various features. This is an active planning component that can generate enthusiasm among participants because they learn more about their purposes and the importance of their analysis in shaping the facility. However, voters and supporters may be resentful if too many trips are taken or if the trips are used as political payoff. Special care should be taken to choose committee members who will represent their constituents in an honest and forthright manner.

Creating a Planning Committee

It may seem relatively easy to create a committee to help plan for the future facility; the difficulty lies

in determining who should be on the committee. The appointment process is often very political, and leaving out key constituents can lead to significant trouble for a planned facility. The process is designed to elicit critical assistance, not develop enemies. A typical committee to plan for a college recreation center might include the following representatives (Greusel, 1992):

- Administration (student life, development, finance, provost, student activities, public relations, and even the president)
- Athletic department (administration, coaches, trainers, student-athletes, alumni athletes)
- Faculty (faculty users, faculty senate, physical education faculty, staff members)
- Recreation staff (intramural staff, club sport staff, student participants)
- Students (traditional, dorm residents, commuters, evening, undergraduate, graduate, international, minority, and disabled students along with student government)
- Off-campus constituents (alumni, booster clubs, university foundation members, local government officials, neighbors, local nonprofit organizations, high schools, athletic organizations)

Part of establishing a planning committee is choosing one or more leaders to lead the meetings. Leaders must get everyone to cooperate and work toward the same goals. Part of this task requires the leader to focus the participants on ideas rather than personalities. Sometimes people have great ideas but the ideas are not heard over personality clashes or turf and ego battles.

One of the leader's responsibilities is to foster compromise. Areas in which compromise can be successful include space, time, programs, and quality (Greusel, 1992). For example, marble may be the material of choice for a part of a facility but it is expensive. A compromise is to use a special finish that looks like marble but costs significantly less. Compromises take place throughout the planning process. However, it should be noted that those who can override the planning process also shepherd in numerous changes. Thus, the committee might decide on a particular material only to have the mayor override the decision. This happens commonly in some projects and can lead to exasperation of the board members.

Behind the Scenes: The Houston Stadium Issue

The planning process in Houston started with the recognition of a need for a new ballpark, sparked by the NFL Houston Oilers' leaving for a new football stadium in Nashville. The Oilers had asked for a new stadium in Houston, but there was little public or government support for the idea. This rebuff was partially blamed on the owner, who had a contemptuous relationship with the fans and politicians even though the team contributed significantly to the local economy. On the basis of this loss, the city did not want to lose the Houston Astros baseball team.

Houston's mayor and county judge established a committee to examine possible sites for a new baseball field. The committee was composed of various community, business, and industry leaders, including corporate leaders, judges, elected officials, and even university professors (among them the author of this book). The committee returned three major conclusions:

1. The economic value of major sports in Houston was significant to the point that they deserved some level of public support.

2. Professional sports added significant qualitative values to the community.

3. An active program to support developing professional and amateur sports could add significant value to Houston ("Shaping Houston's Sports Future," 1996).

The committee concluded that the Astrodome, built in the 1960s and opened in 1965, was too small at 60,000 seats for football, but too large in comparison to the intimate baseball stadiums being built in the 1990s.

The preferred plan raised by the committee entailed a $200 million renovation of the Astrodome to be used for football, a $250 million baseball stadium next to the Astrodome, and $175 million for a downtown basketball/hockey arena. However, the arena was not to be examined in the same bill as the baseball stadium. It was felt that if the two were lumped together it would be too difficult to get voter approval. The proposal was to locate the baseball stadium in the Astrodome area rather than downtown because this option would help buttress the local economy, would reduce the risk that the rodeo would be the only event taking place in the area, and would reduce costs by $20 to $25 million (in comparison to costs for a downtown stadium) since the land was free and infrastructure was already in place. Other reasons were that a large parking lot already existed on the premises and fans were accustomed to traveling there ("Shaping Houston's Sports Future," 1996).

In anticipation of the need to fund the facility with tax-backed bonds, the county had to obtain voter approval for the proposed stadium. In a poll of 650 likely voters, citizens were asked if they supported a new ballpark, and they agreed as long as no new property or sales taxes were to be used. Among the potential voters, 49% felt that the ballpark should be built near the currently existing Astrodome while only 31% felt it should be built downtown—where it eventually was built (Stinebaker, 1996). Despite the benefits just described and public sentiment, and contrary to the committee's conclusions, the political and business leaders decided to build the ballpark downtown. The major leader promoting this effort was Kenneth Lay, the chairman and CEO of the now-bankrupt Enron Corporation.

The Union Station ballpark was built under the assumption that the Astros would contribute 32% of the construction costs, which was a greater contribution than that provided by owners at several other projects: Camden Yards (10%), Coors Field (24%), Ballpark-Arlington (26%), Jacobs Field (30%), and Bank One Ballpark (32%) ("Advantage: Houston Taxpayers," 1996). Such comparisons were part of the effort to sway the public to support the ballpark. The battle was hard fought, and the proponents went so far as to have Mr. Lay write a major editorial piece in support of the vote with the assistance of the Reverend William Lawson, pastor of Wheeler Avenue Baptist Church, which may be the largest church in Houston (Lay and Lawson, 1996). The vote for Proposition 1 was very close, with only 16,000 votes separating the supporters from the opponents. The vote

(continued)

(continued)

Here's the ballot.
No property taxes.
That's the law.

Actual ballot

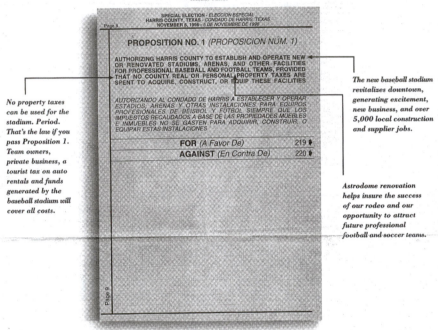

No property taxes
can be used for the
stadium. Period.
That's the law if you
pass Proposition 1.
Team owners,
private business, a
tourist tax on auto
rentals and funds
generated by the
baseball stadium will
cover all costs.

The new baseball stadium
revitalizes downtown,
generating excitement,
new business, and over
5,000 local construction
and supplier jobs.

Astrodome renovation
helps insure the success
of our rodeo and our
opportunity to attract
future professional
football and soccer teams.

Houston Chronicle

Morales agrees proposition for stadium can't use property taxes

PROPOSITION 1
Yes!

was partially split along racial and economic lines. Only 46.2% to 50.3% of Caucasians voted in favor of the stadium while 68.1% to 69.2% of African-Americans voted for the stadium (Williams, 1996).

Later, Enron agreed to pay $100 million for the naming rights to the ballpark for 30 years (Williams, 1999). Enron would possibly be able to earn as much as $200 million over the 30 years through managing the ballpark's energy services and all mechanical and electrical equipment. Enron fought with a competitor, Reliant Energy, over which company would lay pipes under downtown streets to deliver cold water for temperature control of the buildings. Reliant Energy's subsidiary had initially bid $8.73 million while Enron had bid $12.7 million for the rights to provide the stadium with chilled water (Williams, 1998). With the subsequent demise of Enron, the Astros removed Enron's name from the ballpark, which is now called Minute Maid Field.

Even with significant planning and compromise, there is no guarantee that elements from the planning process cannot go wrong, as shown in the Houston example. In fact, a number of facilities have been tarnished when similar naming debacles have occurred. Some were built with naming rights contracts as one of the revenue-generating sources to secure bonds. A facility may be sponsored by a very reputable business, but the situation changes if the business is sold, goes bankrupt, or becomes embroiled in a controversy. The TWA Dome in St. Louis changed its name to the Edward Jones Dome and lost the goodwill generated by the stadium name recognition when the airline went bankrupt.

Naming rights changes normally cannot be planned for by the facility planning committee and attorneys except through an exit clause in the naming rights contract. First Union Center in Philadelphia faced a name change when Wachovia Bank took over First Union Bank. With more bankruptcies and mergers/acquisitions, there will probably continue to be changes that a committee cannot anticipate when planning a facility. But committees cannot focus only on sponsors when trying to avoid problems in the planning process; it is not only corporations that can generate negative publicity. In Bridgeport, Connecticut, the mayor was convicted on numerous racketeering and corruption charges, some of them stemming from deals regarding the design and construction of a baseball park and arena ("Ganim," 2003). Even though the facilities are operating well and were running fine before the convictions, the conviction created a negative perception of the facility and of the integrity of the planning process.

These types of concerns should be examined throughout the planning process, as biased individuals can disrupt or destroy the project by trying to advance their own agenda or poor choices. Thus, strong managerial skills need to be exercised by leaders to prevent the committee from being hijacked. One can give direction by assigning subcommittees very specific tasks, called charges, such as researching sites. Having been organized and given its charge, the committee must critically analyze what type of facility is needed.

Needs Assessment

As shown in the Houston example, the planning process for a new baseball stadium started with a needs assessment made by the planning committee. The assessment was that they did not want to lose another professional sport franchise and felt that professional sports were a major benefit to the Houston community and economy. The **needs assessment** can be based on internal demand as highlighted by future facility users or by industry-driven needs. Industry-driven needs can be based on various factors, from competing institutions to market forces.

The market-driven needs assessment can be based on industry data showing whether or not a current facility meets industry standards. A 1999 survey examined college fitness centers and determined the average types, size, and amenities. The survey results showed, for example, that the average college fitness center had increased 10% to 20% between 1994 and 1999. Furthermore, during the same period, the number of recreation directors reporting that they needed to share facilities with athletics or physical education decreased from 80% to 56%. Thus, more collegiate fitness centers were being built across the United States and were often being dedicated exclusively to student fitness needs (Patton, 1999). This type of information can be critical in the needs assessment area if one of the primary concerns for a fitness facility is to help recruit more students. If prospective students are comparing various colleges, one of the considerations that may tip the scale is the availability of a recreation center. If a college wanted to stay competitive, it would need to build such a facility.

Demographics-based, market-driven concerns can focus on age, nationality, religion, race, and gender. Some facilities have thrived by catering to specific clientele. Some churches are building health clubs for their current and future members as a way to distinguish themselves and recruit. Curves for women and other health clubs are designed to reach a particular market segment in need of such facilities.

Facility users' gender is an important consideration. If a college is 75% female, more equipment or program space should be set aside for women's activities versus male-oriented equipment or activities chosen strictly on the basis of their overall popularity. Table 4.1 lists preferred fitness equipment based on a gender survey. Such data are crucial for determining space needs and proposed activities for a given facility. On the basis of these data, and unless internal surveys suggest otherwise, a new fitness center that expects to serve equal numbers of men and women would probably emphasize treadmills and bikes to please the largest number of users. Knowing what the internal and external constituents want helps to identify the type of facility to be built.

Table 4.1 Preferred Equipment by Gender

Choice	Men	Women
1st	Free weights	Treadmills
2nd	Bikes	Steppers
3rd	Treadmills	Elliptical trainers
4th	Steppers	Bikes

From Patton, 1999.

Types of Facilities

There are countless types of sport facilities, from empty fields to $800 million stadiums. Some sport facilities are easy to distinguish. Stadiums and arenas are obviously sport facilities if their primary tenants are professional teams. Other facilities, like civic centers and multipurpose venues, are blended-use facilities in that they are used for sport but also for numerous other types of events. Another category includes facilities that are used primarily for other activities but also sometimes for sport. Recreational areas such as open fields or beaches may not traditionally be considered sport facilities, but at various times serve as such. Knowledge of the broad array of facility types can help planners determine the best facility (or facilities) to serve the constituents.

Stadiums

Stadiums are large facilities designed to house certain field sports such as football, baseball, soccer, lacrosse, rugby, and track and field. Stadiums may seat less than 100 spectators or over 100,000. Professional baseball stadiums often hold between 40,000 and 50,000 people; football stadiums often hold between 50,000 and 60,000. All stadiums need a relatively flat surface for play. Almost all fields are built with a crown to assist in water runoff. The crown, a raised section in the middle of the field that a person at ground level can see at the end of a gradual incline, helps reduce the accumulation of water on the field through use of gravity. Sport stadiums also have additional commonalities such as spectator seating, locker rooms, parking lots, concession stands, press boxes, and TV/audio sound rooms. These areas vary based on facility size. Thus, a small high school football stadium may have a stand on top of the press box for filming a game. A college or professional stadium may have several rooms for the same purpose.

Structurally, stadiums are now built exclusively with steel and concrete. In the 1900s, the first stadiums were built with wood, and often burned down. Chapter 1 included discussion of the stone coliseums—they are still around today, though they may not be in the best shape. Today, stadiums are primarily built for safety and fan convenience.

Arenas

Arenas differ from stadiums in their capacity to host more types of events and in that they are protected from the elements. Arenas are fixed-seating facilities that can hold from several hundred to over 30,000 spectators. Professional sport arenas typically hold between 12,000 and 20,000 fans. Similar to stadiums, larger arenas typically have locker rooms, storage areas, press boxes, and concession stands. One of the key elements of an arena is an open floor plan for basketball or hockey. This means that various techniques need to be used in the design process to support the weight of a roof and possibly a scoreboard without any middle support columns.

An arena can host sport events, concerts, circuses, family shows, conventions, and a multitude of other events to increase profits. In fact, most economists argue that a single-use stadium such as a football-only stadium has very limited financial return. During the 10 to 15 event days at a stadium, a lot of money can be made; but the low number of event days puts a limit on total profitability. In contrast, an arena may generate 200+ event days a year, which provides opportunities to earn more total revenue per year than is the case for stadiums.

Arenas can be constructed with an ice surface for skating or hockey. These systems are very complex and beyond the scope of this text. Ice floors require miles of piping and wires to transfer brine or other solutions to the floor subsurface. Numerous layers of water are sprayed and frozen to build an appropriate surface. The efforts required to prepare an ice surface are detailed and complex. Significant planning is needed when one is designing such an arena. For example, most arenas require a large number of mounting plates in the floor to help hoist the tons of equipment needed for events. Circuses can use over 100 tons of hanging equipment, and the mounting plates help lift all this weight and serve as tie-down spots. The plates need to be installed before installing an ice-making system since drilling any holes can rupture underlying pipes.

Gyms

Some gyms are health clubs that have floor space for aerobics. Other gyms are mini-arenas with a complete basketball court and space for other indoor activities. Today, more than ever, gyms are sprouting up all over the country due to their adaptability. A gym can be used for basketball, volleyball, badminton, dancing, aerobics, floor exercises, indoor games, and other activities. "Multipurpose" is the key to the modern gym. Through technical innovations, improvements in floor surfacing, and other modern amenities, gyms can now be quickly converted from basketball to volleyball and badminton and then to indoor soccer, lacrosse, or dance classes. Gyms are often equipped with multipurpose activity courts (MACs); there are currently several hundred such facilities in the United States at various levels (Popke, 2001). The MAC surfaces often include hardwood, synthetic sheet goods, poured urethane, interlocking plastic tiles, and similar flooring elements that can be used for various sports. These types of courts have been installed in facilities measuring 65 by 165 feet (19.8 by 50 meters), as well as in facilities as large as the 104- by 185-foot (31.7- by 56-meter) facility at the University of California-Santa Barbara (Popke, 2001).

Community Sport Centers

Community sport facilities can be anything from a pool to a health club, a bowling alley, or an enclosed field. Several different types of facilities are highlighted later in the chapter. Public parks and schools are considered the most frequently built and managed community facilities. Other community facilities include YMCAs, community recreation centers, and sport facilities built by homeowner associations. Pools are often a major component within community-based sport facilities. As with ice skating/hockey surfaces, pools are highly complex and beyond the scope of this text. Pool construction itself may be simple, but the heating, pumping, and chemical filtration systems are not. Many individuals and companies are experts in these systems and are able to help develop and manage pools.

Sportsplexes

A **sportsplex** is a multisport facility that may include indoor or outdoor spaces or a combination of the two. Sportsplexes can be owned by a public entity or a private entity, partnership, or

Facility Focus: New Haven City-Wide Field House

Courtesy of the New Haven City-Wide Field House.

The New Haven City-Wide Field House is a large gym with an indoor track, weight room, space for a portable full-size basketball court, concession areas, locker rooms, and other amenities to serve several public high schools in New Haven, Connecticut. Some interesting facts about this facility are the following:

- The 219-yard (200-meter) indoor track is housed in a 360- by 160-foot (110- by 48.8-meter) building frame.

- The precast wall systems were built in Quebec, Canada, and trucked to New Haven.
- There are 58,900 square feet (5,472 square meters) of sport surfaces.
- The entire facility is 102,000 square feet (9,476 square meters).
- The school district considered a Mondo system (rolls of synthetic surfacing), but utilized a liquid applied surface costing $350,000, which has no seams but is harder to clean.
- Approximately $4.5 million was spent on steel, with 160-foot-long (48.8 meters) trusses, weighing 45 tons, having to be cut in half to be transported and then welded back together in New Haven.
- The total construction costs were estimated at between $250 and $260 per square foot.
- The heating, ventilation, and air conditioning system utilizes two air-handling systems the size of trucks that are mounted on the roof. When the heat index reaches 100 and the air cannot be cooled, participants need to be sent home; also if the facility temperature is at 0 and no heat is available, the participants are sent home.
- The seating capacity is 2,500 and includes both fixed and portable seating. The portable seating is rolled out with hydraulic lifts that are transported on movable surfaces so the weight of the lift and seats does not harm the floor.

corporation. Typically sportsplexes have softball fields, soccer fields (both indoor and outdoor), roller–hockey rinks, basketball courts, volleyball courts, and various other recreational facilities or a combination of these.

According to the Sportsplex Operators and Developers Association (SODA) site newsletter, the average sportsplex lies on 47.9 acres of land (SODA, 1993). About 43% of these facilities have 25 to 35 acres, the most popular size range. The average sportsplex has 6.5 softball fields, and the majority of the fields have lights. The average facility is in operation nine months of the year and has been in existence for eight years. Volleyball is the second most popular sport played at SODA facilities, and soccer is being played more frequently (SODA, 1993).

Domes

Domed stadiums have had a major impact on sport facility development since the 1960s. The Astrodome, which was built in 1964, was the first domed stadium. The Astrodome ushered in the building of other dome facilities in cities such as New Orleans, Seattle, Minneapolis, Indianapolis, and Detroit.

One of the major reasons for creating domed stadiums was to ensure that games would take place. Cities with unfavorable climates could remove the weather factor by playing indoors. Tickets holders would not need to worry about whether the game would go on. Also, bad weather could deter fans from attending games, hurting ticket sales. Another important reason for building a dome was the ability to hold a variety of events year-round. Domes can host numerous events—the Superdome in Louisiana, for example, hosts New Orleans Saints football games, Tulane University football games, the Nokia Sugar Bowl, and the Bayou Classic and has been the scene of five Super Bowls and three National Collegiate Athletic Association "Final Fours." However, with the development of retractable-roof stadiums the fixed-domed stadium has decreased in popularity.

One of the major disadvantages of domed stadiums is that they do not work perfectly for every event. The Seattle Kingdome had a configuration that was not optimal for either football or baseball. For baseball, 50% of the seats were in the outfield. Also, when the weather was nice, fans would not be able to enjoy the game with Mother Nature. This concern helped foster retractable-roof stadiums in the 1990s. The Toronto Skydome, which opened in 1988, was the first stadium capable of opening and closing its roof. Since then, retractable-roof stadiums have been built in cities such as Houston, Seattle, and Milwaukee. Their popularity has increased because many teams no longer wish to share facilities and want a stadium built for their specific sport. The Astrodome, which now has no professional sport team tenant, can still hold events and create revenue in other areas. Across the street from the Astrodome is the new Reliant Stadium, home of the Houston Texans, which has a retractable-roof system.

Domes are being built more frequently for facilities other than stadiums. More facilities are utilizing fabric domes to increase their revenues and operating seasons. Domes are being installed over pools, tennis courts, and synthetic fields. Domes fall into four categories:

- Solid construction involving glass, metal, or wood and sometimes built on movable tracks

- Air-supported structures in which fabric is kept in place by air blowers and possibly cables
- Frame-supported structures in which fabric is stretched over an aluminum or steel frame (the frame can be either permanent or removable)
- Construction involving tensile-membrane fabric stretched over masts, similar to the construction of circus tents (Cohen, 2001)

Fabric structures are inexpensive compared with solid structures. A typical frame-supported structure can cost about 30% to 50% less than a conventional solid structure; an air-supported structure can be built for as little as 10% of the cost for a solid structure (Cohen, 2001). Thus, with about a $1 million investment a dome can be raised where a conventional building would have cost $10 million. However, while the construction costs are lower, the operating costs (such as air conditioning and heating) are significantly greater. Extra expense is also required to remove snow, prevent deflations during storms, and provide adequate lighting. Thus, fabric-based domes are not necessarily the right solution if the facility is meant to last 20 to 30 years. However, if the facility is designed to provide a large field without any support beams, an air-supported structure may be the best solution.

The various designs discussed here need to be considered in the planning process to help determine appropriate design issues. Although geographic issues with proposed sites will affect a facility's design, a rough design needs to be considered based on similar projects. An experienced architect can help design a practical and economical building. However, care should clearly be taken to make sure the designer has developed similar facilities in the past.

Other Facilities

There are countless types of facilities that can be used for recreational purposes. Often facilities were not intended for sport-related purposes but have evolved into such facilities. For example, wilderness areas can be used for fishing, hunting, backpacking, camping, and other recreational purposes. The front facade of a courthouse can become the best local skateboarding hangout. Other facilities are specifically designed for sport-related activities. These facilities can range from golf courses to water parks. The facilities highlighted in this text include sport complexes and fabric domes.

Some communities prefer to package recreational and sport needs in one location. A community sport complex can be very large and can include an anchor facility (arena or stadium) as well as ancillary facilities such as golf courses, playing fields, pools, playgrounds, and other sport/recreational amenities. Such facilities can often take advantage of a common parking area or common concession stands. Sport complexes are gaining popularity as a means to leverage a location, parking, or other amenities while offering the greatest variety of sport facilities. The Yale University facilities highlighted in chapter 1 provide a good example of such sport campuses. Numerous youth sport complexes exist that may have several baseball fields, soccer fields, or a combination of various sport fields. These facilities are often similar to sportsplexes, but may be connected with schools or park and recreation facilities.

Urban sport environments present unique challenges since it is harder in cities to find usable space. This has helped spawn unique facility types such as rooftop facilities. Green roofing refers to planting grass, shrubs, and trees on rooftops to help absorb heat and water while producing attractive areas for birds and for humans to relax in. Another benefit of green roofs is the opportunity to play golf. Some green roofs on company buildings include putting greens for use by employees at lunchtime. This setup is similar to that of facilities such as Chelsea Pier in New York, a 30-acre sport village, which is an entire recreation center built on top of a water treatment plant. A roof-based system consists of a waterproof membrane, vapor barriers, thermal insulation, flashings, and a system to both retain and drain water ("Miniature Golf," 2002).

No matter what type of facility is being considered, it is essential to develop a facility plan and determine its viability through a feasibility study.

Feasibility Studies

When the needs assessments has been completed, the next step in the process is typically a **feasibility study** to see if the needs can be met and at what cost. The feasibility study is not developed just to raise funds, but rather to identify strengths and weaknesses in the planning process. Questions typically asked are what legal challenges exist, whether the right administrative team is in place, what the facility will be used for during dead time periods, how future expenses will be covered after the facility is completed, and what site options are the best. The inputs required for a feasibility study are outlined on the top of page 71, and the outputs obtained from a feasibility study are presented on the bottom of page 71.

The purpose of the feasibility study is to answer the following questions and provide research information about the project to help make a financial decision:

1. Can the project be accomplished?
2. Will the project be suitable and successful?
3. Is the project logical? (Farmer, Mulrooney, and Ammon, 1996)

The feasibility study focuses on various concerns from demographic makeup to competitors in the marketplace. A traditional strengths, weaknesses, opportunities, and threats (SWOT) analysis is often a cornerstone for a feasibility study. A **SWOT analysis** attempts to weight the various positive and negative factors that can affect the proposed plan. Strengths can include inexpensive land, favorable borrowing terms, and strong community support. Weaknesses could include contaminated land, high property taxes, and poor managerial foresight. Opportunities could include new leagues, a young active population, and new technologies or fads. Threats could include significant competition, a lack of trained leaders, and economic downturns. If there are major threats such as a competitor opening a facility at the same time, such information needs to be analyzed, or the facility may be doomed due to poor research and planning.

A key component of any feasibility study is the financing section. Voters, constituents, proponents, and opponents want to know how much public money will be spent on a project and where those funds will come from. It may be that a public recreation area is built by the citizenry, a major donor has given the land, and a foundation has paid for the renovations and construction. However, the public coffers may be tapped for the operational and maintenance costs. In contrast, a private fitness center needs to specify all the anticipated revenue sources and expenses in the business plan and pro forma statements.

Input Required for a Feasibility Study

1. Prospective owner's financial data
   a. Balance sheet or statement of net worth
   b. Business experience
   c. Present cash position
   d. Any sport-related experience—that is, have any managers previously owned a club or managed a team
2. Prospective site locations
   a. Type of ownership to be obtained/present status of selected site
   b. General topography of selected site
   c. Present improvements, including utilities
   d. Current zoning of site
   e. Population within 20-minute drive of site
   f. Proximity to other sport facilities
   g. Neighboring businesses and/or residences
   h. Metropolitan map and demographics
3. Present local competition
   a. Present number of facilities and/or teams, by sport, in the largest adjacent sport programs
   b. Cost breakdown of all neighboring programs
   c. Number of competitors that have closed/opened in the past couple years and the reasons why
   d. Name, address, and phone numbers of directors of all sport-related teams, facilities, leagues, organizations
   e. Number and description of all similar facilities within a 20-minute drive
   f. Listing of typical services and amenities offered by sport facilities in the general area of the proposed site including officials, awards programs, team incentives, and the like
   g. Breakdown of percentage of youth versus adult programs by sport currently in area and any other relevant demographic breakdowns that can highlight market potential

Output Obtained From a Feasibility Study

1. General industry conditions that are favorable and unfavorable for the proposed facility
2. Statistical and systemic experience of three to five other similar facilities, including critical analysis of the strengths and weaknesses of these facilities as compared to the proposed facility
3. The recommended facility size and scope
4. How many employees will be needed to operate the facility
5. The development costs
6. The operating costs for the first five years
7. The projected revenues for the first five years
8. How the facility will affect the local community
9. Components of the local community that will provide positive and negative impacts to the facility
10. The main facility users and what additional users the facility could attract
11. Data that can help the facility obtain necessary financing
12. Specific indications of what data were not obtained and why they were not obtained so the study could be qualified (Day, 1992)

Tables 4.2 and 4.3 indicate where potential financing sources can be found to finance a stadium or arena. It is important to separate pre-opening expenses and post-occupancy revenue

Table 4.2 Preconstruction Revenue

Revenue source	Type of revenue
Owner	Direct contribution
Users	Personal seat licenses Ticket deposits Club/Suite leases Parking outsourcing contracts Concession outsourcing contracts Naming rights details Taxes (such as sales or ticket surcharge tax)
Targeted public	Sales taxes Car rental taxes Hotel taxes Sin taxes (liquor and cigarettes)
General public	Sales taxes Property taxes Utility taxes General public obligations

From Harris County Sports Facility Public Advisory Committee, 1996.

Table 4.3 Ongoing Operating Revenue

Revenue source	Type of revenue
Owner	Direct contribution
Users	Personal seat licenses Ticket deposits Club/Suite leases Parking revenue Concession revenue Naming rights revenue Ongoing taxes (such as sales or ticket surcharge tax)
Targeted public	Sales taxes Car rental taxes Hotel taxes Sin taxes (liquor and cigarettes)
General public	General taxes for road and other improvements

From Harris County Sports Facility Public Advisory Committee, 1996.

and expenses, since some revenues and expenses are a one-time occurrence while other expenses reoccur annually. Also, some facilities sell their contractually obligated revenue, such as naming rights contracts and luxury suite leases, to generate immediate funds to help build a facility. The problem with such an approach is that it can deplete the facility of future operating revenue that will be needed to pay for operating expenses such as maintenance.

Throughout the planning process, data are gathered on the feasibility of a given plan, site, or facility. The data must be unbiased and must address legitimate issues. Just having numbers will not seal a deal. On the other hand, having appropriate numbers that answer critical questions can help diffuse numerous attacks. Thus, data need to be reliable. Although some feasibility studies make wild assumptions not backed by hard facts, effective planning requires the use of accurate data.

Preliminary Phase

Determining the feasibility of a major project is normally a two-phase process composed of a preliminary phase and an expanded phase. The purpose of the preliminary feasibility study is to summarize the initial findings. Frequently the study is based on one visit to the proposed site, a cursory review of background materials, and preliminary financial and building program examples provided by the owners.

Additional information may become necessary, depending upon the scope of the study. For example, in the case of a new arena, the first phase of the study may include previously discussed elements as well as a preliminary market demand analysis for potential events, preliminary testing of potential demand for premium seating (private suites and club seating) and sponsorships, and a rough estimate of operating expenses to determine if there is sufficient economic merit to pursue the project.

Study Size and Comprehensiveness As with any major building project, the size and comprehensiveness of the feasibility study depend on the size and scope of the project. There are no set requirements for the size or depth of the analysis. Studies may range from a few pages to several hundred pages. A preliminary study for the University of Houston's proposed student recreation center was

42 pages in length, while the preliminary study for Minute Maid Stadium was several hundred pages.

Regardless of the proposed sport facility's size, essentials of a preliminary feasibility study are as follows:

- Site feasibility (based on a preliminary visit)
- User-usage feasibility (based on brief background provided by owners)
- Design feasibility (based on conceptual design and plans)
- Financial feasibility (based on preliminary financial information provided by owners)

Cost and Time Required   Much like the size and depth of the study, the cost and time requirements vary. According to University of Houston officials, the preliminary study cost approximately $30,000. The feasibility study for Minute Maid Stadium cost approximately $3.3 million (Rynd, 1998). Of that amount, approximately $1 million was allotted for the preliminary study.

Expanded Phase

After the feasibility study comes the all-important (and often all political) economic impact analysis. The political reality of both feasibility and economic impact analyses is that they are usually undertaken to justify a position that either a sport organization or elected officials have adopted or are proposing (Howard and Crompton, 1995). Frequently the goal of "independent" studies is not to find the truth, but rather to legitimize the project that the sponsoring group wants to develop; these studies can seldom be more than position papers for proponents or opponents of a particular project.

Economic impact is defined as the net economic change in a host community that results from spending attributed to a sport event or facility (Howard and Crompton, 1995). Economic impact studies typically examine direct impact (the first round of spending effect), indirect impact (the ripple effect of additional rounds of spending), and induced impact (further ripple effect resulting from spending by employees of impacted businesses).

What is the economic impact of a sport facility? For a large stadium or arena with a professional sport team, the impact is felt through direct spending, indirect beneficiaries, and increased salaries for those only tangentially related to the facility. Thus, every event and facility generates some impact, ranging from customers' spending on tickets to the facility buying hotdogs from a local distributor.

The following is a sample of results from an economic impact report for an event at a motor speedway. The economic impact was based on several assumptions, including the following:

- Projected attendance was 130,000 fans.
- Approximately 45% of the fans were to travel from more than 150 miles (240 kilometers) away and stay overnight, while the remaining 55% were local or regional fans.
- Approximately 80% of the overnight stays were to be double occupancy.
- The estimated travel expenditures were based on a US Travel Data study.

Based on these assumptions the projected economic impact was $8,881,700 and was calculated as follows:

Local fans: 36,000 spending $22 each = $792,000

Regional fans: 40,000 spending $44 each = $1,760,000

Double-occupancy main guests: 23,400 × $151 each = $3,533,400

Secondary guests: 23,400 × $44 each = $1,029,600

Single occupancy: 11,700 guests × $151 each = $1,766,700

Total $8,881,700

From Charlotte Motor Speedway, 1994.

Additional Elements

All economic impact studies include a **ripple effect**. The ripple effect represents the spread of money through the economy. This concept of a ripple effect in an economy is termed a multiplier by economists (Andelman, 1992). Commonly used multipliers are sales, income, and employment. The multipliers are derived from input–output tables that disaggregate an economy into industries and examine the flow of goods and services among the affected industries.

These data need to be carefully scrutinized for accuracy. Sometimes additional expenditures are left out of the equation, such as media expenditures when a large number of press members are attending an event. On the other hand, economic impact studies often overstate simple issues such as how many people who may be staying overnight are in fact sharing a room. For some events, it is not uncommon for four or more people to occupy a room designed for two. If this fact is not considered in the initial estimate, the estimate will be overinflated. This is one reason a number of studies have concluded that large sport facilities do not produce the economic benefits projected in the economic impact studies (Johnson and Sack, 1996).

Other concerns with economic impact studies include **redirected spending,** which refers to money that would have been spent on other entertainment in the same area, such as spending at a local movie theater rather than at the ballpark; **displacement,** which refers to a portion of hotel rooms that would have been full whether or not the event took place; and **induced effects,** which refer to the multiplier effect and visitor spending being recirculated in the community (Schumacher, 2001). These concerns are not necessarily bad, but they need to be analyzed in the feasibility study in order for the study to be taken seriously. It should also be noted that in some cases the data are not as important as in others. For example, even if the economic impact section of the feasibility study shows very little prospect for return, a city may still pursue building a large stadium or arena to achieve "major league" status, revitalize a city, develop a positive image, or serve political agendas (or achieve a combination of these) (Schumacher, 2001). Thus ego and civic pride often are the driving forces behind a new facility rather than significant economic impact (Day, 1992).

Other areas examined in the expanded feasibility study include, but are not limited to, the following:

- Private financing (equity, corporate bonds, letters of credit, limited partnerships, public offerings, lease/purchase)
- Government financing (government obligation bonds, revenue bonds, special districts, certificates of participation, grants, redevelopment districts)
- Hybrid financing (private equity/government bonds, public land/private improvements)
- Operating assumptions (income, expense, payroll, general and administrative, per cap estimates, usage estimates, break-even analysis, stabilized levels, normal capacity)
- Business plan (pre-opening, opening, and executive summary)

Site Planning

Site selection and design are covered in detail in chapter 5. However, site selection needs to be critically addressed in the planning process because of the impact that a site may have on the success of a project. Most feasibility studies examine at least one site for a proposed facility. It is important to examine site issues at this point in the process because a plan will be worthless if the land is too expensive, for example, and if the economic assumptions will not work.

A site also needs to be analyzed for legal and governmental concerns. For example, if a stadium is planned for a parcel near an airport, federal officials may need to be contacted to make sure that the facility will not interfere with the line or height of flight to and from the airport. Environmental issues are another concern.

Some states have specific guidelines for sport facilities that can affect the sites to be potentially presented to the public. For example, Massachusetts has specific school standards requiring that a school with more than 12 classrooms have a separate gymnasium with at least two teaching stations, each measuring a minimum of 3,000 square feet (280 square meters). Gymnasiums at the secondary level require two stations, but each station must be at least 6,200 to 7,500 square feet (575-700 square meters) ("Education Laws," 2002).

Besides local and governmental concerns, a potential site can involve significant community concerns. The NIMBY argument can doom a project even if the project satisfies all the feasibility concerns and promises to be very successful. If the facility replaces an existing facility loved by the local population, the plan may be sunk if the citizens go to the federal government and obtain historical designation, which would prevent tearing down the old facility. This is only one option. The citizens can also petition for reconsideration, start a letter-writing campaign, hold fund-raisers to buy the property and preserve it, or use a host of other strategies. That is why it is critical to develop a selling plan to generate support and hopefully avoid detractors. It is impossible to get rid of all detractors; they will be present in every project. However, it is possible to dampen their influence or even win a large percentage over to support the facility.

When examining potential sites, numerous sources of information can be useful. Data can come from the following sources:

- Federal and state agencies such as the U.S. Geological Survey, Army Corps of Engineers, regional land planning studies

- Information from city and county authorities, such as zoning maps, property tax records, and planning abstracts

- Public records such as mortgage history, liens, leases, and easements

- Site-specific issues such as blueprints or building permits

- Interviews with current or former owners, real estate appraisers, and planning consultants (Cotts and Lee, 1992)

Developing and Selling the Future Plan

All the data obtained through numerous studies will not necessarily influence the right people. Those who are in support of the proposed facility will not necessarily require convincing. However, additional data can reinforce their decision and provide them with information to buttress their positions. Those opposed to the facility may be willing to change their minds if the right data are presented to address their needs or concerns. The information is most important for those who are sitting on the fence and can be convinced that the project is in fact worthwhile. Those that need convincing can range from voters and politicians to people who will be asked to underwrite the bonds used to finance the stadium or arena. Smaller facilities can also utilize the data to support or reject initial notions about the success of a given facility.

Selling the plan for a proposed facility can take many forms. Conventional campaigns such as advertising on billboards and the newspapers are traditionally undertaken. However, support can also be generated through word of mouth, letter-writing campaigns, asking individuals to serve on committees or assume honorary posts, holding public meetings, and bringing athletes to community events to generate support. Gathering support is a very sensitive process. Some individuals may be willing to vocally support a new facility, but normally the opponents are much louder than the proponents. It is critical to examine means to interest people in the project without alienating opponents. Chapter 5 discusses this fine line in greater detail.

Business Plan for a Facility

If economic impact numbers are simply plugged into a press release, most readers do not know how to interpret them. If the data are properly presented through the business plan for a facility or through a similar document, the planning process is often more successful than when the feasibility report is utilized by itself. Similarly, if no feasibility study is used, the business plan may be the only comprehensive planning tool that a prospective facility manager undertakes.

Once the basic background information is gathered, an initial business plan for a facility needs to be developed. This process is designed to solidify the entire facility planning process from theoretical, practical, financial, and managerial perspectives. By acquiring additional information on the site and on construction and operations costs, management can develop a more detailed business plan that will be required by anyone considering funding the facility. Thus, even though elements not yet discussed in this book are required for a business plan, it is important to consider business plans as part of the planning process. The business plan is the roadmap that incorporates ideas for the facility into a formal document for others to examine.

The business plan serves multiple purposes such as helping allocate resources and setting realistic goals and objectives. It also establishes standards for measuring feasibility and operates as a benchmark for future activity. Whenever a facility veers from its course, the plan can help the manager make decisions to get the facility back on the right track. Of course, no matter how well

---

Top Ten Greatest Project Pitfalls

1. Lack of proper preparation: failing to have a mission/goal, failing to involve professionals in the process, and failing to have all the t's crossed and i's dotted

2. Failing to follow a well-defined and established process: failing to have the right team in place to shepherd the facility through the planning and construction process

3. No time: most projects take about three years to complete (2-3 months to assemble the project team; 3-4 months for the feasibility study; 2-3 months to bring a public project to a vote; 6-8 months to design; 12-18 months to construct; 12-18 months to prepare for a facility's opening)

4. No funds: failing to garner public support or public partnerships

5. Failing to involve the public in the process: failing to involve special interests and stakeholders

6. Poor site selection: failing to establish defendable criteria for site evaluation

7. Failing to overcome opponents: failing to determine why there would be opposition and failing to develop answers to each potential attack

8. Failing to receive final approval: not receiving necessary support

9. Failing to have preestablished operating plans: not planning for staff, programs, financial needs, risk management, facility policies, and facility maintenance needs

10. Failing to deliver: from promising too much to failing to meet the public's expectations

---

From Ballard and King, 2002.

the business plan is prepared, it cannot guarantee reaching the destination safely. The top 10 greatest project pitfalls are listed above.

Starting a facility without a well-thought-out business plan is like traveling into unknown territory without a map. If prepared with care, the business plan or roadmap will not only indicate the route to follow to reach goals, but will also highlight hurdles that may be encountered along the way. Creating an effective business plan involves seven steps:

1. Determine and define the business opportunity. A facility is a living entity that will grow and change. Therefore people starting a sport facility need to take the time to determine exactly what type of facility they want and what they want the facility to become as an extension of themselves.

2. Make an operational plan. This covers geographic location, facilities and their improvement, production, layout, and key strategies and planning plus certain areas of administration, depending upon the facility. The operational plan highlights

how the facility will be managed. It specifies, for example, when grass will be planted, what type of grass it will be, how it will be watered, how the soil will be compacted, what type of crowning will be used, what aeration technique will be used, and what fertilizer will be used.

3. Create a marketing plan. For good reason, market analysis is often considered the most important activity an entrepreneur can engage in before a business start-up. This analysis teaches the person not only a great deal about the marketplace and prospective competitors, but also much about the prospects for success. The marketing plan specifies how the facility will be marketed toward teams, events, tournaments, and other revenue-producing activities from arcade games to concession items. It is as critical to properly budget for the marketing of a facility as it is to budget for building the facility. Failing to develop a sufficient budget and marketing plan will doom even the best-designed building. The days of "If we build it they will come" are long gone given the multitude of events and other activities drawing our time and resources.

4. Develop a business structure. Will the business operate as a sole proprietorship, with a partner or partners, or under the corporate/LLC (limited liability corporation) form? Each of these forms has certain advantages and disadvantages. This part of the business plan specifies who is involved in the planning process or if a "management team" is being formed that will help launch the facility and then remain in place. Frequently people reach this step and only then receive legal advice that the project cannot be completed due to zoning or other legal restrictions. That is why it is advisable to have an attorney and an accountant on the management team during the organizational planning step. A developer needs to obtain input from others before progressing and to heed their advice.

5. Define your resources. This part of the plan focuses on resources that will be used, ranging from political ties to financial resources. The impact of any recent legislation affecting the facility needs to be noted.

6. Work up a financial plan. The financial plan will also serve as an operating plan for the financial management of the facility. This will be the final test of the viability of the overall business plan. Whereas the budget helps track the future direction of the facility, the financial plan dictates whether the budget is realistic, what steps will be needed to obtain funding, and exactly how much money will be needed.

7. Complete the business plan. After all the preceding elements have been completed and if the decision is to go forward with the facility, then all the plans need to be coordinated and reviewed for fine-tuning purposes. Nevertheless, just completing the business plan does not finish the job because the business plan is worthless unless it is acted upon.

Financing the Facility

Chapter 11 discusses financing in greater detail. Still, it is imperative that the planning process include analysis and confirmation of the financial viability of a proposed facility. The facility planner needs to determine whether to purchase, build, or lease. This analysis examines the cost of capital, lease terms, purchase price, the cost and

political ramifications associated with borrowing money, and any political ramifications associated with owning versus leasing. While a project may not make sound economic sense, some facilities are built to accomplish political goals. If a business or municipality builds a facility to appear progressive, obtain a competitive advantage, or meet some other ulterior objective, the fact that the facility is a loss leader may not be as big a concern for the politicians. If a facility has been built for purely political motives, the planning process most likely failed to critically examine costs and expenses. If the facility has not been properly planned, political opponents can attack the financing scheme or revenue sources. Thus, financial planning is critical even in politically motivated projects.

The financial ramifications also affect final selection of the site and the design. Chapter 5 addresses various site-related issues from political ramifications to hostile neighbors. It is imperative to base any decision about a facility being built on a combination of variables, and among these the financial concerns should be the most carefully analyzed.

Summary

Planning for a new facility is the process of examining what type of facility will meet a given need or objective and working out the justification for building or leasing the facility. The types of facilities that can be built are limited by people's imaginations, the laws of physics (whether or not a design can hold the weight of the roof, for example), political constraints, laws and regulations, and the amount of money available.

Besides determining what facility to build or lease, a facility planner needs to justify the need for the facility. Not many buildings are built in the absence of some need. The planning process for a specific facility should examine the rationale for building the facility based on solid empirical numbers rather than hunches. If the financial numbers from a feasibility study indicate that a project is not viable, then the project should not be undertaken. However, if the planning process indicates success, then the next step is to finalize the site selection and facility design.

DISCUSSION QUESTIONS AND ACTIVITIES

1. Why is planning important for an existing facility?

2. Why is planning essential for a future facility?

3. Research one of the recently built stadiums or arenas to see what planning was undertaken and how long the planning process took.

4. Design a business plan for a martial arts studio to be built or leased in your town.

5. Develop a strategic plan for facilities on your campus to help them grow over the next two years and then over the next five years.

Facility Site and Design

FIVE

CHAPTER OBJECTIVES

After completing this chapter you will be able to do the following:

- Understand the importance of location in choosing the proper site
- Analyze the various components that need to be considered when choosing a sport facility site
- Analyze the various external issues affecting a proposed facility site
- Understand specific components within a facility such as locker rooms and concession areas
- Appreciate the layout needed for an effective floorplan

Sport facilities are traditionally designed to last 50 years. The design process takes into consideration elements such as regional temperature, average snowfall totals, water concerns (humidity, sea salt/mist, etc.), seismic movement, wind-related concerns, and other environmental issues. The natural concerns are in addition to human issues such as fan violence, vandalism, and crowds. The planning process requires a critical analysis of all these elements to help determine the most appropriate type of facility to build.

While a number of technical characteristics are involved in deciding what type of facility to construct, the process offers numerous opportunities for creativity. A gym does not need to be a rectangular cement building. Planners can choose colors that brighten the facility, blend with other buildings, or blend into the surrounding landscape. Tile, glass, wood, and other materials can be chosen that enhance a given design or form a type of facility that has never been attempted before. Various roofing systems can be added to help reduce costs and provide optimal lighting. Facilities are limited by three basic constraints: money, site configuration, and the creativity of everyone involved in the planning process.

Chapter 4 discussed the steps in facility planning, which includes completing a needs assessment and feasibility study. The next steps are determining the site and designing the facility. The first part of this chapter examines some of the broader concerns with site location and its impact on the proposed facility. The chapter concludes with an analysis of site selection and design, including the various facility components that must be designed and their effect on the decision to build a given facility.

Site Location

Site location is one of the most important considerations in the planning of any sport facility. "The literature on sports and entertainment facilities has focused primarily upon financing, economic impacts, and intangible benefits associated with constructing a new facility. The ubiquitous and controversial 'economic multiplier' and the intangible economic and cultural benefits have remained at the core of the sports facility literature throughout its development in the past 20 years. However, facility location has often been overlooked" (Chapin, 1997). Even a high-quality complex cannot succeed if the population for which it is designed does not use it, does not know where it is located, or refuses to travel to the site. Deciding on the right site requires analyzing numerous issues (see figure 5.1). Acquisition methods, cost considerations, and environmental constraints are just some of the factors. There are also political, community, and accessibility issues.

Private organizations that are considering building will have different goals from the entities involved in a public facility. The private facility is built normally to generate a profit. In contrast, a publicly funded facility is built to meet community needs. All facilities must be revenue generators to survive, but the private facility must generate a profit. Public ownership can have many drawbacks, such as limited funds, bureaucratic management, and the need to obtain voter approval on new funding initiatives. Other problems include the need to utilize the competitive bidding process, which can lead to the least expensive but not necessarily the most qualified contractor. Political agendas and conflicting egos of political leaders can also hamper negotiations and make the process almost unbearable (Chapin, 1997). Even with these problems, the ability to tap public land and public coffers is a tremendous benefit and can be a great opportunity.

Private entities may want to work with government entities because of the eminent domain power held by government units. **Eminent domain** allows a government entity to seize private property and use it for the public good after compensating the owner for its fair market value. If a private facility developer wants a piece of land but cannot convince the landowner to sell, the facility has to be canceled or has to be built around the unobtainable lot. A facility can also be a hostage to a landowner who demands a huge payoff. The situation is different if a government entity is involved or if the private entity enlists governmental help. In this case it may be possible to seize the property for the public good and then use it for the facility.

Site Planning

Whether a public or a private facility is to be built, site planning begins with the appointment of a site committee or one individual to find the right site. Typically a site committee is organized and then meets to discuss the goals of the facility. While one person can certainly find a site, a single individual will not likely appreciate every concern or issue that might arise. That said, some very successful facilities have been built with one person spearheading the entire process.

Next, committee members develop a site mission statement. The mission statement will drive the options available for the most appropriate sites. The mission statement might focus on choosing a site that minimizes the negative impact on natural resources or that leverages the relationships between various government and nongovernment entities. After writing the mission statement, the site committee develops goals and objectives. The goal, for example, might be to purchase a facility within a half mile of a major freeway. A site objective might be to purchase a site with over 3 acres for under $300,000. Appropriate tactics for such a goal might be driving around the area and determining

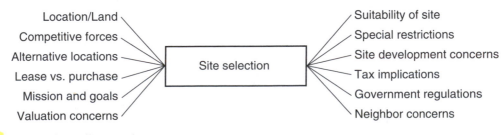

Location/Land
Competitive forces
Alternative locations
Lease vs. purchase
Mission and goals
Valuation concerns

Site selection

Suitability of site
Special restrictions
Site development concerns
Tax implications
Government regulations
Neighbor concerns

Figure 5.1 Issues that affect site location.

Hypothetical SWOT Analysis for a Sportsplex

Strengths

Convenient location

Cheap land

City willing to work with owners

Weaknesses

Bad neighborhoods surrounding property

Needs extensive infrastructure repair

Limited funds

Opportunities

There are more softball players in the area who are not being served

Local schools may want to use facility

Parks department needs more space

Threats

Parks department wants to build its own fields

A competing facility 20 miles (32 kilometers) away is starting to advertise in the area

which properties have at least 3 acres, contacting the assessor's office to find out the assessed value, and contacting property owners to see if they are interested in selling. Other tactics might include contacting a real estate broker or determining which property owners are in default on their mortgages or property taxes. The goals and objectives will affect various site options. For example, if the facility will need an external water source for irrigation, then being located near a water source such as a lake or river might be an important goal or priority. Analysis of the proposed facility leads to a better understanding of facility site needs.

In site planning, a SWOT analysis (introduced in chapter 3) can be particularly helpful. As detailed in chapter 4, the SWOT analysis encompasses strengths, weaknesses, opportunities, and threats. A hypothetical SWOT analysis for a sportsplex is shown above. The SWOT analysis, coupled with the strategies and objectives, is synthesized into an action plan, which will help determine how much land is needed.

Size

There is no formula for determining the size of the parcel required. Whatever type of analysis is used, extra room needs to be considered for future growth and for handling problems that might arise in the construction process. If there is not enough

room and the construction process uncovers problems, the land may not be usable. The appropriate site size is contingent on the sports that will be played in the location. Table 5.1 provides dimensions for the playing areas for fields and gyms.

Once the specifics of a site are determined, a search committee is formed to look for an area that meets the land size requirements, keeping in mind the facility's goals and objectives as well as preliminary design concerns. All potential sites should be reviewed closely with respect to the following questions:

- What are the surrounding businesses?
- What is the residential neighborhood status within a 5-mile (8-kilometer) radius?
- Will resident neighbors and community welcome or object to the facility?
- How can the area benefit from the intended facility?
- Are the proper utilities in place (gas, electric, sewer, water, phone)?
- What, if any, are the zoning restrictions?
- How will nighttime lighting and noise influence the surrounding area?
- Is extra parking already in place?
- Will the sale of alcohol be met with resistance?

Table 5.1 Playing Field Dimensions

Activity	Indoor/ Outdoor	Play area		Safety space		Total area	
		Width	Length	Width	Length	Width	Length
Badminton	Indoor	20.0	44.0	6.0	8.0	32.0	60.0
Basketball							
Junior high instructional	Indoor	42.0	74.0	6.0	8.0	54.0	90.0
Junior high interscholastic	Indoor	50.0	84.0	6.0	8.0	62.0	100.0
Senior high interscholastic	Indoor	50.0	84.0	6.0	8.0	62.0	100.0
Senior high instructional	Indoor	45.0	74.0	6.0	8.0	57.0	90.0
Neighborhood elementary school	Indoor	42.0	74.0	6.0	8.0	54.0	90.0
Community junior high school	Indoor	50.0	84.0	6.0	8.0	62.0	100.0
Community senior high school	Indoor	50.0	84.0	6.0	8.0	62.0	100.0
Boccie	Indoor	18.0	62.0	3.0	9.0	24.0	80.0
Fencing							
Competitive	Indoor	6.0	40.0	3.0	6.0	12.0	52.0
Instructional	Indoor	3.0	30.0	2.0	6.0	7.0	42.0
Field hockey	Outdoor	180.0	300.0	15.0	15.0	210.0	330.0
Football	Outdoor	160.0	330.0	15.0	30.0	190.0	390.0
Lacrosse							
Boys	Outdoor	180.0	330.0	18.0	15.0	216.0	360.0
Girls	Outdoor	210.0	300.0	13.0	30.0	236.0	360.0
Rifle	Indoor	5.0	50.0	6.0	20.0	17.0	90.0
Shuffleboard	Indoor	6.0	52.0	6.0	2.0	18.0	56.0
Soccer							
Outdoor*	Outdoor	225.0	360.0	5.0	–	235.0	360.0
Indoor*	Indoor	82.0	137.8	–	–	82.0	137.8
Squash							
Singles, hard ball	Indoor	18.5	32.0	–	–	18.5	32.0
Doubles, hard ball	Indoor	25.0	45.0	–	–	25.0	45.0
Tennis							
Deck (doubles)	Indoor	18.0	40.0	4.0	5.0	26.0	50.0
Hand	Indoor	16.0	40.0	4.5	10.0	25.0	60.0
Lawn (singles)	Indoor	27.0	78.0	12.0	21.0	51.0	120.0
Lawn (doubles)	Indoor	36.0	78.0	12.0	21.0	60.0	120.0
Paddle (singles)	Indoor	16.0	44.0	6.0	8.0	28.0	60.0
Paddle (doubles)	Indoor	20.0	44.0	6.0	8.0	32.0	60.0
Table	Indoor	9.0	31.0	–	–	9.0	31.0
Volleyball							
Competitive and adult	Indoor	30.0	60.0	6.0	6.0	42.0	72.0
Junior high school	Indoor	30.0	50.0	6.0	6.0	42.0	62.0
Water polo	Indoor	65.6	98.4	–	–	65.6	98.4
Wrestling	Indoor	28.0 diameter		5.0 diameter		33.0 diameter	

Notes: All dimensions are shown in feet. * Represents the dimensions of the largest recommended playing field; some fields, given limited space and resources, can be smaller in size.

From Planning Areas and Facilities for Health, Physical Education, and Recreation Court and Field Diagram Guide

How the committee answers these and similar questions will influence the final site chosen for the facility. One important decision is whether to communicate potential site locations before the land is purchased. Any tipping of the hand concerning a potential site can have a significant impact on the land's price. Thus, until the land has been purchased, the plan should be communicated only to a small audience.

Potential Sites

Once having located several sites, the facility developer must determine which route to take to acquire the site. In any real estate investment the purchaser should always have more than one prospective location. If the first choice is inadequate, for whatever reason, the developer will have another option. Another reason to have more than one property in mind is leverage. If the facility developer can make the seller think he or she is competing with another potential landowner, the seller may be more willing to negotiate a more favorable price.

When examining potential sites, a facility developer needs to sell the project. Although it is important to have several locations under consideration, a developer will eventually have to focus on one primary site in order to obtain necessary approval and support. Even for small facilities, surrounding businesses or residents can become the greatest supporters or opponents of a proposed site, and their response can either help finalize a site or doom the site before the facility can be built.

Promoting the Positive

Communicating the plan includes letting the surrounding businesses know exactly how the facility will enhance the area. The idea of attracting customers to an area may greatly influence local business owners but can possibly anger residents. The local government authorities should be informed if they are not already part of the committee. It is important to get the support of the local leaders to increase perception of the site's positive aspects. Government officials welcome the opportunity to say that they were part of a new facility. Getting positive government officials involved early will only enhance the facility's success.

The community will also need to be informed about the project and about how the facility will improve the area. Surrounding neighborhoods and organizations will want only what is in their best interest, not necessarily what is best for the community as a whole. Showing the community the positive aspects of the project and getting the community's support are critical. The following are examples of positive community influences:

- Increasing property values
- Lowering crime rates among youth groups by keeping kids off the streets
- Allowing the community better access to recreational events
- Additional tax revenues from out-of-town teams competing in tournaments
- Additional spending in surrounding areas resulting from increased traffic
- Increasing civic pride of the neighborhood around the facility
- Enhancing the city's reputation to help attract new businesses and residents

While such positive influences are possible from any project, a facility can also reduce property values, increase crime rates, and reduce recreational choices. Every facility project needs to be critically examined to determine what true positive and negative impacts may occur over time. A nice new facility can be an economic engine or can become an unused eyesore.

Once communities, politicians, and others are notified, the next step is getting their input. Local leaders such as church officials, neighborhood board of directors, and other community leaders will want to have input into the new facility during the entire process. Careful attention needs to be paid to the information provided by the community leaders. Including these people on the organization committee or on an advisory board can alleviate some concerns. The public will probably wish to have major input in the facility's design, for example the exterior color or the size. However, some individuals can also be troublemakers who can make the process more difficult. Such individuals may demand numerous changes or modifications that could make a proposed facility impractical.

Handling Opposition

Once the public knows about the proposed site, opposition to the project is bound to arise. Normally, the opposition is much more vocal and organized than is the support for a project. After the opposition has been identified, their concerns should be addressed quickly and thoroughly. The more rapidly the facility developer can help influence the opposition, the better chance the project will have of being realized. Restating the positive influences mentioned earlier and emphasizing how the opposition can benefit will hopefully change the opinions of some. Being able to change the opinion of any member of the opposition will greatly enhance the facility's creditability. The opposition's arguments will also bring up issues not initially considered. Thus, having an open forum to discuss a proposed site or facility can produce valuable benefits.

Opponents should not be ignored or scorned, as they can be a positive tool for facility growth. Addressing their concerns can be the most challenging part of site selection. For example, if religious leaders are doubtful about game scheduling on Sundays, the committee might inform them that all Sunday games will be played after 2:00 p.m. This will allow participants to go to church in the morning. A site close to a church can be chosen to reduce travel time, or the facility can be opened for church league participants.

Finally, several managerial issues should also be considered when sites are being explored. Secrecy is a major concern from a political, financial, and competitive perspective. Political squabbling can follow any potential site, and such squabbles can be minimized if no specific site is identified until the very end. On the flip side, if homeowners or businesses are affected, they can rebel if they have not been part of the process from the very beginning. Financially, if landowners know that a facility is being planned and that their land is being considered, they will try to raise the selling price. Lastly, competitors who know that a new facility is being planned may purchase the land to stifle competition.

The analysis discussed so far is appropriate for private facilities. However, most public sport or recreation facilities are built on public land that is already owned or is being acquired through eminent domain. Since such land may be in unique areas, sport facilities are often customized or adapted to fit the surroundings. Public land that lies in a flood plain might still be used for sport fields most of the year. Nevertheless, though site selection issues may be minimized if the public owns the land, they do not disappear. Some issues can be resolved quickly—zoning, for example, since the government can modify the zoning for the public benefit. However, irate neighbors can still pose a problem. If the lights from a new field will spill over into a neighborhood, the residents will be up in arms regardless of whether the facility is public or private. Thus, for public facilities, significant effort needs to be expended to avoid the same problems that befall private facilities.

Site Considerations

Every potential site must be analyzed for unique concerns, from cost to environmental factors. For example, will the landowner be unwilling to sell the land no matter how much the facility developer is willing to pay? On the other hand, if the public is involved, what political ramifications might there be if the city took the property through eminent domain, even if it paid the prevailing market value?

Other important criteria to examine about potential sites are applicable laws or jurisdictional regulations. Even if price is not an object, if the site is not properly zoned or if the municipality does not allow certain structures, the site will not be an option unless the laws change. For example, state laws may dictate what size facility is required for a school. Thus, even if price or zoning were not issues, the ability of the site to accommodate the needed building size would need to be determined before proceeding.

Alaska, for example, has specific regulations governing school pools. The regulations allow state reimbursement for building expenses if the pool is used for an instructional program or as an emergency water storage facility within a fire suppression system. However, funding is not available to combine the two features, even though such a strategy would not be difficult to accommodate. The regulations cover details such as competitive pool size, which must be at least 75 by 30 feet (23 by 9.1 meters) in order to handle 30 students per class and 720 students per year in swim-related classes. Beginning swimmers, under the guidelines, must have at least 100 square feet (9.3 square meters) each, and intermediate and advanced swimmers must have at least 120 square feet (11 square meters) each ("Swimming Pool Guidelines," 1997).

There are countless other issues that affect a potential site. In order to successfully plan and describe a multipurpose facility, the committee must include a detailed plan of what the facility will entail, what sports will be offered, what amenities will be offered, and what the community can expect from the new facility. Other issues include the following:

- Area size and availability (both funds to purchase and willingness to sell)
- Appropriate historical information records showing, for example, whether the land was used as an Indian burial ground or used for storing chemicals
- Legal issues such as accessibility, convenience, parking, safety, and adaptability
- Orientation of the playing fields
- Government (federal, state, and local) regulations
- Time allotted for development (Farmer, Mulrooney, and Ammon, 1996)

Location, zoning, user needs, community impact, and land features are also important site considerations. These are discussed next.

Location

When it comes to land options, three factors can make or break a facility: location, location, and location. The facility developers must ensure that the location is suitable for the type of facility or business being planned. For example, someone who is planning to build a large recreation complex should probably not look into investing in a piece of land that is a wildlife sanctuary, a wetland, or a flood plain. Choosing a site entails doing some intense research but also requires common sense. A developer who plans a facility that will cover 4 acres should not buy 4.5 acres, as there will not be enough room for parking or expansion. It is important always to allow room for adequate parking and it might be important to purchase additional land for future expansion. It is key to a successful investment to locate an area that generates proper exposure, has good vehicular access, comes at a reasonable cost for site development, and meets government restrictions or zoning laws.

Zoning

A site should be zoned so that commercial recreation is a compatible use. This saves the additional step of changing the **zoning** or acquiring a **variance**. Since recreation is a broad term as used in zoning regulations, it is often possible to "slip the project through" in many zoning classifications. Industrial and manufacturing zoning usually accommodates commercial recreation. Business and commercial zoning is generally too expensive for consideration. Residential zoning is not recommended because of the fights that can erupt with neighbors. There is a split regarding open space and agricultural zoning that can be resolved only on a case-by-case basis. Zoning issues can also affect liquor-related policies and procedures.

Lighting and noise from a potential site can also raise zoning concerns. The most important aspect related to lighting and noise is the effect on the neighborhoods around the facility. Most cities and neighborhoods have restrictions against intrusive lighting and disturbing noise. Light and noise issues could relate to the type of events that will be held in the facility, the time of day and days of the week events will be held, and the type of crowd that will be attending the various events. While these issues can be resolved through negotiations with neighbors, it is often easier to approach elected officials and try to change the zoning classification for a given site. Zoning concerns, though, are not the only regulatory concerns that may affect a site.

Apart from local or regional guidelines, laws such as the Americans with Disabilities Act (ADA) pose further restrictions for a proposed site. Critical consideration of ADA issues needs to be part of the design process (chapter 13 deals in detail with ADA issues). If participants or spectators will need to travel over rough terrain to get to the facility, it may be inaccessible and thus possibly violate the law.

User Needs

After the analysis of government regulations, the next step is to characterize the potential users. The first question to ask is who the typical facility users will be and what their needs are. Future facility users typically want to know the following:

- Size of facility
- Proximity to major transportation routes
- Hours of operations
- What events will be held
- The cost of building and using the facility

The second question is what groups will be able to effectively utilize the facility. It may be envisioned that local community organizations, charity groups, service organizations, and schools and professional teams will be permitted to use a facility, but what if people in these groups cannot reach the site? If a facility is planned for use by a school, will children be able to walk or will a bus be used? Who will have priority for use? Will schools always have first priority, or will the facility be reserved on a first-come, first-served basis?

The third question has to do with what the community wants from the site. If the site has historical value or is part of a natural habitat, the community may fight vigorously to prevent its use. Projects have been delayed or scrapped because local citizens succeeded in getting an area designated as a historical site or as an environmentally protected area.

Community Impact

Another important consideration is the facility's potential economic impact. Specifically, are there intangible benefits or cultural benefits associated with the site? The economic effect of a new facility could include new enterprises in the area and increase local land values due to increased traffic flow (i.e., local businesses will increase tax revenue and offer more employment opportunities). Negative aspects of the site may include lights, noise, or traffic in residential areas. Indeed, the failure to properly consider these impacts is often the most costly blunder from a public relations and legal perspective.

Land and Environmental Considerations

So far the site considerations have centered on external issues from government concerns to community impact. But the focus will always come back to the land. Whether because of location or geographic limitations, if the land option is not appropriate, the site should not be pursued. Other features to review regarding the site may include the following:

- Detailed geography (soil, subsoil, vegetation)
- Population composite (demographics of area)

- Constituency representation (political clout)
- Flood area (drainage, runoff)
- Climate, precipitation, winds, natural disaster strikes (i.e., hurricane paths, tornadoes, earthquakes, floods, etc.)
- Capital improvement plan maps (illustrating current and planned projects by council district)
- Enterprise zone ownership and land use maps
- Acreage (adequacy for buildings, parking, picnic areas, etc.)
- Additional acreage for expansion
- Shape (acute angles or odd shapes are possible wasted space)
- Topography (level terrain, steep slopes)
- Zoning regulations (permit requirements, parking, setbacks, etc.)
- Access (from principal roads, local streets, truck or bus access)
- Security considerations

It is very difficult to obtain approval for all environmental and off-site challenges without having outside cooperation. Facility developers must do their homework and legwork by checking and rechecking all issues when considering each site option. No single site will meet all the requirements for any facility developer. However, once all the affected parties are contacted and all the requirements finalized, it is much easier to select the best site options.

Several impact studies are required for every potential site. These studies must be completed before any work begins. The developer must find out if any of the grounds are hallowed (e.g., Indian burial grounds). Other types of sensitive sites include cemeteries and sites of archeological finds or digs. Some sensitive sites can be uncovered through a review of old newspaper articles or interviews of local residents. Contamination is another potential issue. If there was a gas station or a manufacturing plant on the site in the past, then it is likely that the site was contaminated.

Soil Testing

When surveying the land, soil testing is important because it will reveal what is beneath the soil.

Soil testing helps determine whether the land has been polluted or used as a waste dump. In one example, a wealthy philanthropist offered to give a private school some land for new school grounds. The land was located next to old railroad tracks and had been used for dumping over the years. The school conducted soil testing to see if there were any potential hazards to which the children could be exposed. Based on this heightened duty to protect children, the school paid more than $140,000 to test the soil and then had a second test conducted when some results were inconclusive. In the end the land was shown to be contaminated with everything from heavy metals to cyanide and oil. The costs to clean the soil were potentially so high that the school gave the land back to the donor.

Another issue related to soil testing is what surface will be best suited for the facility. If the surface will be grass, for example, the ground needs to be tested to ensure that it can support grass. In many instances the type of grass used (see chapter 8) can be adapted to the present soil. However, some facilities are looking to use a specific type of grass, and in these cases the soil must be examined for compatibility with that type of grass.

Finally, soil treatment may also be a major concern. If the playing surface requires chemicals (e.g., football, baseball, and soccer fields), the chemicals need to be tested for their effectiveness in various climates, as well as their environmental friendliness. The primary concern is any kind of runoff into rivers or drainage into other properties. If there is a potential for chemical runoff from the proposed site to another property, this could mean potential litigation or future cleanup concerns.

Core Drilling

It is important to understand the kind of foundation the facility will be built on; therefore, an engineering firm is needed to conduct **core drilling,** that is to test whether the foundation is sand, clay, dirt, or rock. A rock foundation will raise the excavation costs significantly due to blasting or other major work. Clay varies in consistency and is affected by wetness. Clay can be very sticky, messy, and difficult to work with in constructing a building or developing a field. Another important consideration is whether or not the land is at sea level. Water may become a problem if the foundation has to be set deep in the ground. The ground

around and under the foundation can be saturated and therefore difficult and expensive to work with. In this situation, equipment must be brought in to pump out the water, adding to the cost. Thus, what may have seemed a good deal on cheap land could turn into a major expense. Common sense suggests that if the price is too good, there must be a reason.

Grading

Every site needs to be graded, or leveled and prepared for construction. This can include removing dirt, rocks, trees, and other vegetation. **Grading** can also include disposing of wood, concrete, metal, or other building materials left on the site. Additional grading may be necessary if the site is located along a river or other body of water. Most grading deals with moving dirt. The type of soil and the amount being moved determine most grading costs.

Because grading can be costly, the facility builder needs to get bids. Prices vary depending on the type and quantity of material being moved. Soil is easier to move than other types of material such as rocks or trees. Grading costs are determined by the cubic yard. The cost to move (and possibly replace) dirt, plus equipment, labor, and trucks, can exceed $25 per cubic yard; but the cost does not necessarily end there. A survey team is needed because the area to be graded needs to be precisely measured. If significant grading costs are anticipated or additional expenses are involved, the site could turn out to be too expensive.

Wetlands and Endangered Species

With any construction project there will be consultation with and approval from federal/state governments. The site must not be on any protected land. Some wetlands are federally or state protected, as well as some trees, especially older trees. Animals that have been placed on the endangered species list can pose a problem. Thus, if there are protected oak trees that also serve as the nesting grounds for protected owls, there is almost no chance that a variance will be given to remove the trees. However, if there is little threat to an endangered species or to protected land, the government will probably give a variance. As part of the site analysis process the facility developer must retain an environmentalist to examine the site and determine what wildlife will be affected. The time of the year at which the site is examined has an impact on protected migratory animals that may use the site in certain seasons and not others. If the habitat survey is conducted at different times during different seasons, any potential impact on migratory animals can be minimized.

Accessibility

Does the prospective site have access roads to handle the future traffic? If yes, will it be able to handle the traffic flow? Could the current roads handle the exiting traffic without causing major delays for other motorists? Will the facility be located next to a highway or will individuals need to travel on back roads to get to the facility? Will access roads go through neighborhoods where parking and noise could become major issues? Will stop signs or stop lights need to be installed, and if so, how far apart will they be placed? Regardless of the answers to such questions, the next question concerns who will build the needed roadways and how much they will cost. The state department of transportation will probably be involved in significant road analysis and construction issues. Thus, it is important to get local officials, residents, and state officials involved in any thoroughfare planning process. It should be noted that while infrastructure issues are covered in this analysis,

there may be a number of non-infrastructure access concerns such as the need for police and traffic patrols for any new roads. Such elements can be significant because a facility may have to pay thousands of dollars for off-duty police to help with traffic flow and pedestrian crossing.

Road access is not the only access-related factor. Buses may need to reach the facility, and large trucks deliver items and remove trash. Such vehicles may be able to travel only on certain roads. Parking areas need to be developed for such vehicles, and entry/exit bays may need to be developed in the facility to allow vehicles to load and unload. Some facilities also have a helicopter pad to allow for arriving dignitaries and emergency transportation flights.

Utilities

Site utilities are a major concern, as the cost of bringing utilities to a remote site may be prohibitive. Where the sewage waste will go and where the utilities will come from are just two of the issues that need to be addressed. Water usage must be considered for sprinklers, fire protection, and building use (e.g., bathrooms). Storm drainage, energy sources, telephone lines, and solid waste disposal are all factors. Economic factors such as

Construction and renovation to a facility can affect surrounding traffic areas and make parking lots inaccessible.

© AP/World Wide Photos

acquisition costs, taxes, financing, and development costs should also be considered for all utilities (Farmer, Mulrooney, and Ammon, 1996). The primary utility concerns include gas and electricity, phone, and cable/satellite.

With respect to electricity and gas, if the complex is built in an open area as the Houston Astrodome was 40 years ago, supply lines will need to be run to the site. The most important question is how an enormous arena will be cooled. If electricity will be used to power the cooling system, the facility will need a tremendous amount of power. Water can be used as a coolant for some facilities. Pumping cold water through the hot water radiating system reduces the cost of cooling a building compared with traditional air conditioning systems. Facility developers who will be relying on city or municipal services should make sure that the city is able to generate the amount of power needed, or that the extra energy can be purchased on the open market or produced through options such as solar cells, fuel cells, or wind-generated devices.

Issues of capacity and load capabilities also apply to telephone and cable systems. Will new phone lines be added? If so, will they be above ground or possibly fiber optic cables buried underground? Cable may be very expensive if it has to go through rock. Satellite data and image delivery is gaining in popularity, and the wiring and delivery costs are lower as long as the receiving dish can be positioned appropriately.

Water, Drainage, and Sewer

When working with water and sewer provisions, it is extremely important to know if a city has the capacity to serve the facility's needs. The following factors must be considered:

- Is there water on the site?
- Is there an existing well?
- Will water be brought in and removed through city or municipal delivery systems?
- Will the facility need to build its own water and sewer systems (e.g., septic system, drain fields)?

If water will be transported or additional lines need to be built, the project will become more expensive. That is why some facilities build their own sewer tank and wastewater treatment plants

on-site or utilize recycled water. Water concerns also are prominent when it comes to irrigation or a sprinkler system for the playing surface. Where will the water come from? How much will it cost? These questions help determine which grass type should be used.

Besides water delivery, a site must be able to deal with water drainage and retention. The site slope must be just right to allow the proper drainage so that water does not remain standing, and when the water leaves the area it should collect in either a man-made or a natural basin. The next problem is how to get the water out of the basin. Some water will evaporate, and some will soak into the ground. The remaining water will need to be pumped out and placed elsewhere. This is extremely important in areas that get an abundant amount of rain. In an outdoor stadium or even one with a retractable roof, mosquitoes will not only affect the fans, but may also affect the athletes. If the mosquitoes are bad enough, the city may have trouble attracting quality athletes to come and play. Fans and customers can also become upset if they have to walk through puddles to get where they want to go.

After examining all the potential land and environmental concerns, the facility developer is almost ready to make some final decisions. The following suggestions can help narrow the list of potential sites:

- Physical examination of proposed sites
- Feasibility studies (see chapter 4) specifically developed for the potential sites (facts including development trends, conditions, and populations)
- Site information, including site surveys, soil testing, erosion analysis, surface water resources, wetland issues, groundwater, precipitation, climate, open areas, utilities, existing buildings and roads, projected roads, residential areas, commercial and industrial developments, easements, right-of-ways, and zoning restrictions
- Meetings with local leaders, citizen committees, and other groups
- Analysis of recreational, aesthetic, and engineering features
- Most importantly, the cost of each option and what the facility developer can afford

Site Cost

Obviously care needs to be taken in buying and developing land to ensure the best possible deal for the amount of money spent. If facility developers cannot afford a piece of land, they cannot buy it. Two important questions are involved in cost consideration: How much will the land cost and who will pay for it? If the public owns the land, then the decision may not be as difficult, even for a private facility developer. Many facilities, from professional baseball stadiums to local gyms, are built with a blend of public and private cooperation, land, and perhaps financial assistance.

No matter who pays for the land, there needs to be enough money available to keep the facility operating. Facility operations can assist in paying off a facility's debt service, but this is not advisable. For a successful project, there needs to be enough money not only for building, but also for operation. If all operational revenue goes to debt service, rather than maintenance and growth, the facility will fail.

Affordability

The most important question facility developers can ask themselves is "What can I afford?" When it comes to determining land value, there are three different valuation methods: the cost approach, the direct sales approach, and the income approach. The cost approach determines value by adding the value of any improvements to the value of the vacant land when purchased. If the land was purchased for $1 million and $500,000 in improvements were made, then the land should be valued at $1.5 million. The direct sales comparison approach analyzes similar properties in the area that have sold recently. If three properties in the area sold for $20,000 an acre, then the property in question should be worth around $20,000 an acre. In the income approach, land value is based on the present value of future benefits of property-generated income (Fisher and Martin, 1994). This approach requires analyzing future income streams and then determining the present value of those streams.

After determining the property's value, developers must decide if the price is within their limits. It is not wise to settle for a tract that is cheaper due to its size. It is normally better to give up some of the location benefits in order to obtain the right amount of land. At the same time, though, it is important to remember "location, location, location"; and if the large parcel is too far away from customers it may not be the ideal choice.

Taxes

If a private developer is buying land he or she must also consider what taxes will have to be paid. Taxes are charged based on a percentage of the property's assessed value. Government agencies have created incentives through the granting of tax credits, depreciation deductions, and property tax reductions to encourage developing and rehabilitating certain properties. The value of such incentives is deemed non-realty interest (Fisher and Martin, 1994). Negotiating with government officials before buying a property is crucial to lower property taxes. If government leaders really want a facility, they may waive significant tax obligations, and this can make a project economically feasible.

Hookup and Development Fees

Hookup and development fees may be charged by the municipality to bring municipal utilities to the site. Usually sport facilities are proposed in areas that are already hooked into public works operations, but even then the facility developer will incur additional hookup costs. When developing land that is not tied into public works systems, the facility developer will face significant additional costs to bring gas, sewer, water, electricity, and phone service to the property.

Other Fees

Other fees may include land clearing costs and even surveying costs. These costs are incurred in all projects, but their extent varies. For example, a site may include swampland or a high water table, requiring drainage, and also forest land that needs to be cleared. These costs can be significant. However, every challenge can also represent a potential opportunity. One way to ease the financial burden of land clearing is to have a logging company come in and clear-cut the land for timber. Of course this would be an option only with heavily wooded property and if a logging company is interested in buying the trees.

Buying Versus Leasing

Facility developers must often push their financial resources to purchase a site, clear the land, lay a foundation, build a shell, complete the interior, equip the facility, and then open the facility for business. This is clearly a long process with numerous expenses. The only means to avoid these start-up costs is to renovate and utilize an existing facility instead of buying. An existing facility often has appropriate government approval (zoning), parking areas, HVAC equipment, and other options that significantly reduce the price in comparison to the price of a new building. While the developer loses some of the glamour associated with building a new facility and the flexibility to build exactly what is needed, the cost savings can be substantial. At the same time one should note that although an existing facility is often cheaper to start with, the renovation costs for some projects are so large that it is often more worthwhile to build a customized facility.

To help make a sound financial decision it is important to use a buy–lease analysis. In this approach, the net present value of the cash outflow associated with the lease option is compared with that for the buy option. The option with the lower present value is preferred (Cotts and Lee, 1992). This means that the current value of the cost of building is compared with the cost of leasing a facility, and the project that costs less from the beginning (assuming all other factors are the same) is chosen. The following two alternatives help highlight the analysis required to compare projects:

- Alternative 1: signing a five-year lease, with annual payment of $7 million each year, for a facility that can be occupied without any major modifications
- Alternative 2: buying a building for $20 million and spending another $6 million modifying the building, which after five years would have a salvage value of $8 million

Yearly projections for the two options are shown in tables 5.2 and 5.3.

Leasing the facility would cost the facility developer $17.52 million over five years. In contrast, purchasing, renovating, and then salvaging after five years would cost $15.58 million. There is a risk when buying in that the price of the property (salvage value) could drop or increase significantly. On the other hand, when leasing it may be difficult to find another viable facility option after five years, or the new lease obligations may be significantly higher. These issues need to be explored when one is trying to determine whether to purchase or lease.

For a first-time facility developer, leasing may be the only option due to capital restraints. Yet even major corporations utilize leasing methods to tackle expansion and short-term needs. Leases can have the drawback that the owner may limit renovations or uses of the building. Ultimately, if a leased project fails, developers may lose more money than if they owned the land outright. This happens since the developer might have lease payment obligations and will have no assets when the lease period ends.

Table 5.2 Yearly Projections for Alternative 1

Action	Year					
	0	1	2	3	4	5
Lease obligation	−7	−7	−7	−7	−7	
Tax shield	2.8	2.8	2.8	2.8	2.8	
Net cash flow	−4.2	−4.2	−4.2	−4.2	−4.2	
Discounted cash flow	−4.2	−3.82	−3.47	−3.16	−2.87	
Cumulative facility cost	−4.2	−8.02	−11.49	−14.65	−17.52	−17.52

Shown in millions ($).

Table 5.3   Yearly Projections for Alternative 2

Action	Year					
	0	1	2	3	4	5
Purchase of building	−20					
Renovations	−6					
Depreciation	−3.6	−3.6	−3.6	−3.6	−3.6	−3.6
Tax shield	1.44	1.44	1.44	1.44	1.44	1.44
Salvage value						8
Net cash flow	−26	1.44	1.44	1.44	1.44	9.44
Discounted cash flow	−26	1.31	1.19	1.08	.98	5.86
Cumulative facility costs	−26	−24.69	−23.50	−22.42	−21.44	−15.58

Shown in millions ($).

A lease allows predictability of rental costs, but only minimal control. The landlord controls issues such as renting adjoining space to competing businesses and can prevent certain activities not expressly covered in the lease. These policies can make the facility less attractive for the facility developer. To avoid such problems, a lease agreement needs to cover the concerns that could potentially arise during the lease term. The following are some of the key clauses that should be included in a lease:

- The parties to the lease and what the facility will be used for
- Description of the leased property
- Commencement date and length of time of the lease
- Payment amount or method of calculating rent
- Responsibility for expenses: property taxes, insurance, utilities, janitorial and maintenance, and management
- Method of handling delinquent payments
- Alteration or improvement restrictions
- Restrictions on the operation of the tenant's business or subsequent assignment/subleasing
- Use of common areas and facilities
- Indemnification of landlord and insurance requirements

- Remedies in the event of total or partial destruction
- Rights in the event of condemnation
- Right of entry
- Early-termination penalties
- Arbitration provisions for resolving disputes
- Statement that the lease represents the entire agreement
- Future options in the lease
- Subordination and partial invalidity of the lease
- Compensation if the government takes the land (eminent domain) (Fisher and Martin, 1994)

The other option when it comes to obtaining a location is buying the land. One major advantage of purchasing the land is that if all else fails, the developer may walk away from the project with land that could be sold.

Site Selection

As explained so far in this chapter, before a final site can be chosen a committee must look at all variables. Once the potential sites have been narrowed to a manageable list of "final" sites, each must be inspected one last time. Various factors go into making a final decision:

Behind the Scenes: Dallas Mavericks' Failed Proposal

The entire planning and construction process is obviously complex. The following example is from a planned, but failed, initiative to build an arena in Lewiston, Texas, for the Dallas Mavericks and Stars. Prior to American Airlines Center being built in Dallas, the Mavericks and the Stars were looking for a new home. They looked both in and outside Dallas. One proposal was the city of Lewiston in an adjoining county. The voters in Lewiston narrowly defeated a bill that would have authorized the selling of bonds to build the proposed arena. The initiative involved more than 87 steps before the facility would even open its doors. These steps primarily related to financing and feasibility, but also dealt with construction issues.

1. Do financial and political groundwork for creating new state law necessary to levy taxes
2. Call election for half-cent sales tax
3. Hold election day for half-cent sales tax
4. Hold half-cent bond closing with the release of bond proceeds
5. Hire political consulting firm
6. Hire public relations firm
7. Call general obligation bond (GOB) election for county residents
8. Hold GOB election
9. Release GOB bond proceeds
10. Develop complete financing package
11. Negotiate and determine the arena ownership structure
12. Negotiate with all parties for ownership contract
13. Develop memorandum of understanding highlighting key contractual terms
14. Develop terms and conditions for three categories: anchor tenant, concessions, and sponsorship
15. Develop terms under which the anchor tenant will be bound to stay in the facility
16. Research and finalize potential sponsors
17. Research and finalize agreement with concessionaire if food service is being outsourced
18. Retain consultants to help in securing additional sponsors
19. Research and finalize list of potential facility management providers
20. Retain consultants to research potential facility management companies
21. Research luxury marketing and suites sales, including having staggered expiration dates to maximize revenue
22. Analyze potential patrons/purchasers of luxury suites
23. Obtain commitment for 75% of luxury suites before progressing further with project
24. Analyze potential patrons/purchasers for premium seating
25. Obtain commitment for 75% of premium seats before progressing further with project
26. Analyze various companies that will be asked to provide long-term services to the arena
27. Research all necessary equipment and fixtures such as concession stands
28. Send request for financing to commercial banks and institutional investors
29. Obtain binding letters of financing that provide the terms for borrowing money
30. Test the debt instruments to determine interest
31. Test any potential equity instruments to gauge interest

(continued)

32. Obtain bond opinion letter from attorney indicating that conditions of bond indenture comply with all applicable laws
33. Escrow closing of bonds and release funds to start construction
34. While financing is being pursued, examine site needs
35. Undertake a detailed survey of all potential final sites
36. Conduct geotechnical engineering of subsurface at final site(s)
37. Conduct environmental and wetlands analysis
38. Conduct Phase I feasibility study to determine market demand for events, sponsorship, etc.
39. Conduct Phase II feasibility study examining premium seat market
40. Conduct Phase II feasibility study examining financial projections
41. Undertake an economic impact report for the direct, indirect, and induced spending impact of the new arena
42. Undertake a traffic study to see what impact the arena will have on local and regional traffic
43. Close on the site and purchase the land
44-58. Undertake various steps with the state legislature and department of transportation to build a highway bypass for the arena
59. Conduct design phase involving architectural, structural, mechanical, electrical, interiors, acoustic, civil, planning, landscaping, codes compliance, elevators, lighting, roofing, rigging, and related professional services
60. Use order of magnitude package to clarify the project's scope—a preliminary pricing tool
61. Receive estimates from initial engineering analysis followed by the first round of value engineering
62. Architect prepares schematic design
63. Developers undertake value engineering to reduce costs
64. Architect prepares design documents
65. Developers undertake value engineering to reduce costs
66. Architect prepares construction documents
67. Developers undertake value engineering to reduce costs
68. Build suite mock-ups to simulate how the suites will look and help sell suites
69. Work with architect to hire appropriate consultants such as construction managers
70. Hire a graphic designer to prepare signs and graphic images of the new facility
71. Ensure that the architect works with the developer throughout the construction process
72. Begin physical construction
73. Solicit bids for construction and award the contract to the best builder/contractor
74. Undertake site preparation such as clearing and grubbing
75. Set foundation and slab-on-grade such as drilled piers
76. Pour concrete structure such as columns and decks
77. Install precast seating such as precast stair treads and risers
78. Build roof structure

79. Build enclosures such as masonry and glass
80. Build interior partitions with masonry and drywall
81. Install finishes such as carpentry, painting, floor coverings
82. Place fixed and movable seating
83. Finish all suites
84. Finish concession fit-outs for all cooking and service equipment
85. Finish building parking garage
86. Reach substantial completion of project and complete punch list
87. Obtain occupancy permit (Lewiston, 1995)

- Review of feasibility studies (economic and political impact) as covered in chapter 4
- Permits (lease, license, or letter) and whether they can be obtained
- Site information (from environmental issues to historical concerns such as burial grounds)
- Regulations (building codes, health ordinances, and other concerns that may make a proposed site unusable)
- Community involvement—is there a significant amount of opposition?
- Affordability and decision whether the facility should be purchased or leased
- Easements—will the neighbors have the right to go across the property?
- Zoning (cluster, flood plain, open space) issues and whether the facility can be classified as business use only or as commercial and residential
- Restrictive covenants that may limit who can purchase the land or use it for certain purposes
- Aesthetic value of the site and whether there are any beautiful views, trees, or waterways that may affect the site's use
- Recreational opportunities such as whether the site can be used for indoor and outdoor facilities

No single variable makes one site better than another. A good analogy has to do with the purchase of a residence. While one spouse may want more space in a house, the other may want a nice neighborhood or beautifully manicured lawns. One family member may want a certain type of bathroom while others may want energy-efficient appliances. With so many variables, it is difficult to develop a consensus that forces a lot of people to compromise on their final choice. The factors on the preceding list are some of the compromise elements that those on the planning committee may have to consider.

Finally, the benefits and costs for each site are compared and the final site is selected. Often site selection comes down to a "gut" decision. Site selection can be finalized due to a hunch or just a feeling, but only after a thorough review. If one has done all the analysis before making this gut decision, then there is no problem with using this technique: There may be two equally attractive options, and a final decision will need to be made on instinct or intuition.

Facility Design

Once a site has been selected, facility design is the next step. The design may incorporate elements of the site; Camden Yards in Baltimore, for example, incorporated brick warehouses as part of the design. A recent phenomenon has been to design open-air stadiums to incorporate a view; stadiums in Denver and Pittsburgh have views of the downtown skyline. No one design can be used as a cookie cutter for other facilities. Even recreation centers have different facility designs based on numerous considerations such as the following:

- Off-site nuisances (e.g., rivers, sewage treatment plants, industries)
- Safety factors (roads, buffer zones, sight lines, emergency access)
- Proper drainage for turf and hard-surface areas (flood zone area)
- Fencing and planting to serve as separation of areas
- Placement of service building for safety, control, and supervision (access for vehicles)
- Layout of walkways for safe and efficient circulation (must meet ADA requirements)
- Lighting of fields, courts, and general areas
- Cost of maintenance (preventive and corrective)
- Provision of first aid facilities, equipment, and supplies
- Taking advantage of existing topographic features, trees, and vegetation
- Accessibility and use of the site for the aging and disabled
- Use of durable and vandal-proof materials and equipment

The facility developer will also have to determine how all the building elements will fit together into the facility. This part of the design process allows for significant creativity, within the budget. A facility planning committee can develop numerous ideas and communicate these ideas to the architects and engineers. However, at some point the words need to be transformed into drawings that will hopefully adequately portray the desired results. Architects can help highlight the possible results through scale models and blueprints. A **scale model** is a miniature version of what the facility will look like. Construction documents, which include **blueprints** and written specifications, also show what the facility will look like.

The facility design begins with a **site plan** that includes a number of separate drawings—the master site plan, grading plan, irrigation plan, landscape plan, traffic flow plan, and fencing plan. Additional plans include the building plan; floor plan; construction drawing; lighting plan; and specifications for all irrigation, lighting, fencing,

Scale models, such as this one of the Seoul World Cup Stadium, show in 3-D fashion what a facility will look like.

recreation area (playground) equipment, buildings, and regular facility equipment.

The master site plan gives an overall view of how the finished facility will look on the site. The grading plan shows how the site will be leveled, where dirt will be moved, and what trees or natural areas will not be touched. The irrigation plan shows where sprinkler systems will be placed. The landscaping plan shows how shrubs, flowers, artwork, and even fake streams may be located and incorporated into an overall landscaping strategy. The traffic flow plan indicates where cars will park and how roads will be designed to ease congestion and speed entry into and exit from the facility. The fencing plan indicates how natural boundaries and man-made fences will be incorporated to secure the property in the most aesthetic manner possible. The other plans all help show how different elements

Facility Focus: American Airlines Center

© American Airlines Center

The American Airlines Center, home of the NHL Dallas Stars and the NBA Dallas Mavericks, is a fan friendly complex utilizing the very latest technology. The American Airlines Center revolutionized sport building systems, especially in terms of new technologies. Wrightson, Johnson, Haddon & Williams was responsible for acoustics and noise control recommendations, design of the building's sound reinforcement system, design of all video systems including distributed television, the broadcast cable system, design of the low-voltage cable system, and the scoreboard/replay systems. The ceiling of the American Airlines Center is lined with acoustical tiles, nylon swags, and large, flat plane surfaces. Nylon swags absorb sound during concerts, and the planes direct fan noise back to the playing surface for sporting events. The ceilings and walls are covered with perforated vinyl and metal, giving sound a place to escape.

Video was also pushed to new levels. In January 2001, American Airlines Center awarded a $7.9 million digital signage package to Daktronics, Inc. The deal, which was one of the largest and most sophisticated in the world for a sport venue, provided an integrated scoring, video, and information display system. The unique scoreboard, which hangs 35 feet (10.7 meters) above the playing surface, has eight sides and is 25 feet tall by 49 feet wide by 49 feet deep (7.6 by 15 by 15 meters). It weighs 80,000 pounds (36,300 kilograms) and took eight cables to raise. Daktronics ProStar VideoPlus LED technology is incorporated in the scoreboard, which is a 68-billion pixels color display system capable of showing video, animation, and graphics. Additional displays are located throughout the facility, including one continuous ring of full-color digital advertising technology that circles the entire inside of the arena on the platinum-level facade. The American Airlines Center is the first venue to use HDTV wide screens throughout. The facility is also the first building to incorporate three major displays: the scoreboard, the end zone displays, and the 360° ring around the club level.

"The technology allows us to sell every item to every seat," said Martin Woodall, the Mavericks' representative on arena issues. "No other building does this" (Wrightson, Johnson, Haddon, and Williams, 2004).

Here are some key facts about the American Airlines Center (Mooradian, 2001):

- 19,200 seats for basketball
- 18,500 seats for hockey
- 20,021 seating capacity for concerts
- 1,600 club seats
- 2,000 platinum seats
- Over 500 accessible seats
- 142 suites ranging in price from $150,000 to $300,000 per season
- 840,000 square feet (78,000 square meters)
- 24 ticket windows
- 12 escalators, 10 elevators
- 550 televisions throughout the facility
- 280 men's room urinals and 96 stalls
- 337 women's room stalls

http://www.sportsvenue-technology.com/projects/american_airlines/

Wrightson, Johnson, Haddon & Williams, http://www.wjhw.com/aac.html

http://www.americanairlinescenter.com/index.cfm/FuseAction/Page/PageID/73/ArticleID/86

of the facility will fit together to produce the best design for accomplishing the facility's objectives safely and cost-effectively.

Building Systems

Components within any facility include exterior enclosures from walls to roofs, windows, doors, and other elements such as skylights. The interior can include **vertical space dividers** such as walls and partitions, **horizontal space dividers** such as floors and ceilings, plumbing systems, HVAC systems, fire protection subsystems, electrical networks, communication systems, security systems, and **furniture, fixtures, and equipment (FFE)**. The numerous systems in a sport facility are covered in greater detail in chapter 7. However, it is important to note here that buildings, especially the technology-driven buildings of today, are not just a collection of walls. They are often as complex as the human body. There are miles of cables running throughout a building along with wood, steel, ductwork, and glass work, among many other components. All these materials present design and construction challenges (construction is covered in the next chapter) that need to be analyzed during the planning process. For example, while a glass wall may appear attractive, the potential energy loss and cleaning costs may make such an option less attractive than a brick wall requiring very little maintenance and conserving a significant amount of energy.

Ancillary Facilities

One of the important considerations in the design process involves ancillary facilities. It is one thing to say that a gym will be built but another to specify what ancillary rooms or areas will be built around the gym. Those involved in the planning process will undoubtedly generate numerous ideas; and if the budget allows, many ideas will be incorporated when the facility is being designed since it is cheaper to build in the extra areas than to add them at a later date. Some of these adjacent areas are locker rooms, coaches' offices, training rooms, exercise areas, media rooms, bathrooms, storage areas, and equipment rooms.

One of the key factors in accurately determining the price for a structure is the details of the elements within the structure. For example, what size should the locker room be? How many lockers should be installed? How many toilets and shower stalls should be included? Each element costs money and needs to be examined before the construction process starts. The design process also affects the price (e.g., tile walls vs. marble walls).

Locker Rooms

Determining the number of lockers and total space needed for a changing room is not an arbitrary exercise. The most efficient way of allocating space for a changing room is by means of two simple formulas. The first formula, used to determine the optimal number of lockers, is a function of the number of people using the changing room and the number of storage lockers in each unit. (A locker unit is used because most lockers are not sold individually, but rather in units of 10, 20, or more lockers.) It is calculated as follows:

number of lockers needed = people using the changing room + 10% of people using the changing room ÷ number of storage lockers in each unit

Once the optimal number of lockers has been determined, the area needed for the changing room is determined. According to the second formula, the total amount of space a participant should have around a locker is 14 square feet (1.3 square meters). This could mean a 2- by 7-foot (0.6- by 2.1-meter) section or some other permutation that allows people to stretch and move around while getting dressed and using the space (Gabrielsen and Miles, 1958).

Concessions

Concessions are a major revenue generator, so concession areas need to be built with money in mind. A sink placed too far away from a preparation area could be a health code violation, but it also would mean that employees need to spend more time preparing food, which means lost income. Similarly, concession areas need to be designed to help sell the most items possible in the shortest time period. Thus, concession areas often have a large number of point-of-purchase locations so orders can be processed quickly and lines are minimal. The optimal number of purchase processing locations can be calculated using a formula similar to that for lockers and based on the latest industry research. Chapter 16 covers the concession area in greater detail.

Other Areas

Calculations similar to those for lockers and concession stands can be made for other facility components. One industry consultant recommends 8.5 to 10.5 gross square feet (0.8-1 square meter) per student as a base number for a recreational center. This number can be higher in small residential colleges where the students will use the center more frequently than on large urban campuses, whose students may be members of other clubs. Additional space needs to be added to the base number for employees (1-1.5 gross square feet [0.09-0.14 square meters] per employee) and alumni/community members (5-7.5 gross square feet [0.46-0.70 square meters] per alumnus/community member) (Brailsford and Noyes, 2000).

Space concerns are also important in the design of office space, as people do not like small offices that may be hard to move around in. However, some offices can be built into gym walls that have glass windows so that employees who supervise the gym can see into the gym. In fact, many facilities have unique internal areas. At The Ohio State University, among several other places, dorms have been built into the football stadium to maximize space usage.

Bathrooms need to be carefully planned, since larger facilities may have thousands of people using the bathrooms at the same time. Women traditionally take longer to use bathrooms, so larger public assembly facilities often have more women's stalls than men's. Also, empirical data and personal observations show that men use fewer sinks for washing their hands than women. Such data need to be used to help design bathrooms with appropriate fixtures.

Sport facilities also have numerous attributes not found in typical office buildings, such as family bathrooms, luxury suites, bleachers, and audiovisual rooms. Some of the often overlooked adjacent areas that need to be planned in a sport facility are shipping and receiving (loading docks, storage, access to dumpsters, proximity to users/freight elevators), security (operations center, guard post, access to storage equipment), mail distribution room, and food service (access to refrigeration/cooking equipment, vending locations, loading docks) (Cotts and Lee, 1992).

Layout

Regardless of the amenities or rooms being considered, all ideas need to be highlighted in the initial layout. Ancillary areas need to be included in the initial drafts since structural issues may be associated with these areas that can affect the facility. For example, the wiring, soundproofing, and viewing perch of a sound booth need to be developed with careful foresight. Architects often try to identify all the usable areas for the facility and then develop a way to link all these areas. They frequently use **common space** such as a foyer or an atrium from which usable spaces can be accessed. Areas can be linked by hallways, which are also a common space. Some areas in the facility will be dedicated to specific uses such as stairways, elevators, janitor closets, and storage closets.

Some of the additional concerns that architects analyze are the following:

- Path of travel and distance an athlete would have to walk from one area to another such as from a locker room to a training room
- Noise from one area that can affect another area
- Security concerns between different areas
- The availability of storage rooms and janitorial closets
- Government regulations such as Occupational Safety and Health Administration requirements that may affect placement
- Environmental surround concerns such as rooms requiring windows or a view (Walker and Stotlar, 1997)

Blueprints

No matter what elements are eventually decided upon by the facility developer, these concepts, elements, thoughts, and concerns will eventually need to be documented. It is best for an architect to have been involved with the facility planning process from the beginning. If not, all the ideas need to be boiled down to a written description showing how all the elements fit together. During this process, ideas may be scrapped or modified, and a site may even be ruled unfeasible due to design constraints. This process often entails multiple rounds in which changes and more changes are tinkered with to reach a final decision. It is best to have any changes identified and incorporated at this point in the process to reduce costly alterations when construction begins. When this review process is completed, a final set of drawings will emerge that is called the blueprints.

Blueprints are so named because the diagrams were initially made with white lines on a blue background (today the diagrams have blue or black lines on off-white paper, making it easier to write comments and notations). Many diagrams are drawn for any given project, from broad depictions showing the building envelope to detailed mechanical drawings showing where all the plumbing components will be located. The plan view is a bird's-eye view from the top down of how the facility will look. In contrast, an elevated view is a view from "street level" showing what the outside walls will look like. The detail view drawings are designed to show internal elements such as individual rooms or stairways in detail. A sectional view is a detailed view of how a horizontal or vertical element will look when cut in half. This could be a drawing of metal work or insulation inserted into a wall to provide appropriate reinforcement. This cutaway view in the sectional prints is used by the construction crews to construct building units pursuant to necessary strength or building code requirements. The mechanical view highlights the mechanical and electrical systems within the planned building. Lastly, the plot and survey lines show the boundaries of the property on which the building will be constructed (Borsenik and Stutts, 1997).

Summary

This chapter has focused on identifying the best possible site for building a sport facility. While it is impossible to have a perfect location, a number of locations might be very good for an intended project. Each site needs to be evaluated based on variables such as size, cost, location, zoning concerns, and community impact.

With very strict state and federal laws affecting land use, some facility sites may not be appropriate due to environmental concerns. Through testing, it is to be hoped that a site with minimal cleanup needs can be identified. Sites also can be chosen based on the expenses for elements associated with making the site usable, such as access to water, roads, and utilities, which can be expensive additions to any proposed site. After these variables are considered, each site needs to be evaluated based on the anticipated cost for completing the project on that particular site. After this analysis has been completed, a site is chosen and a facility designed. The next chapter covers how the facility is actually built.

DISCUSSION QUESTIONS AND ACTIVITIES

1. What would make the best facility site for a stadium?

2. What would make the best facility site for an arena, and is it different from a site that would be great for a stadium?

3. What concerns arise with government entities and proposed facility sites?

4. Examine a newly built facility and research issues that arose in choosing that site. Be sure to examine political, legal, and financial hurdles that may have been encountered.

5. What are some arguments to make to convince local businesses and residents to support a planned arena or stadium in their community?

Facility Construction

After completing this chapter you will be able to do the following:

- Appreciate how plans for building a structure are finalized
- Understand the public bidding process often used to construct new facilities
- Appreciate the elements involved in the construction process
- Understand how to calculate construction costs
- Know how to complete the construction process

There are two primary ways to build a sport facility. The first is to determine how much money might be available for the project and then to fit the facility into the budget. Thus, if a school bond issue raises $2 million for a gymnasium, the school will have to make sure that the facility is constructed for less than this figure because it will still be necessary to purchase "furnishings" (chairs; special bleachers; basketball hoops; and other furniture, fixtures, and equipment). If the school does not have any other funds to dedicate to the construction process, then the options are very limited.

The other option, referred to as the **planned approach,** entails examining what is specifically needed and then developing an ideal facility within rough cost constraints. After a basic analysis has been completed, a detailed cost estimate can be developed. When all the component prices are roughly established, a facility developer can start eliminating items that have a low priority or are not feasible economically in order to fall within the potential budgetary constraints. This process is often referred to as value-based engineering. Unlike other approaches that are more reactionary and often produce a facility that is less than desired, the planned approach strives to utilize management prioritizations to allocate funds in a rational manner. This text emphasizes the planned approach of researching all potential options and then developing a comprehensive building plan.

Although budgeting should have been analyzed in both the planning and design processes, costs are still a major issue in the construction process. Change orders, material discrepancies, union disputes, delays in material delivery, budget overruns—there are literally hundreds of cost concerns that can cause price fluctuation.

Assuming a reasonably stable budget, this chapter focuses on the process of building a sport facility. The chapter starts by analyzing site preparation procedures through the construction planning and pre-construction phases, and then moves on to the foundation, frame, and roofing. The last sections cover project costs and completing the facility.

The facility construction process involves various elements decided through the planning and site selection processes. No one builds anything, whether a bookcase or a house, without detailed advanced planning, deciding on the right size, and obtaining the right materials. The following phases help put the construction process in the proper context with issues previously discussed and those covered later in the text.

Programming Phase

- Deciding what to build
- Examining space, cost, and other criteria
- Deciding what events will be held at the facility including capacity and amenities issues
- Deciding the number and location of food and beverage preparation and sales areas
- Finalizing support areas that will be needed

Design Phase

- Design the facility with architects
- Schematic drawings and cost estimates
- Design development with details such as heating, ventilation, and air conditioning (HVAC) systems
- Reviewing and verifying the documents
- Operational review to ensure that systems will operate as intended
- Construction documents
- Legal documents
- Bidding documents

Construction Phase

- Contract award after checking references and qualifications of all parties
- Construction schedule through substantial completion of the facility.
- Construction process and change orders
- Inspection process

Occupancy Phase

- Finishing, including completing punch lists
- Occupancy permit
- Facility maintenance and renovations

Construction Planning

Chapter 4 covered some of the planning issues that affect the facility. However, once the facility design, style, and site are chosen, there are still several steps that need to be taken before construction actually begins. During the construction planning phase, the first question is who is going to build the facility. There are several issues to examine when deciding on the final builder, such as reputation, the final cost, and the construction contract.

Builders

Every project, including public facilities, has an owner. Owners can build the facility themselves if they have the resources. A government entity that has a public works department may have all the construction personnel already on the payroll to build a facility. This can save time and money in comparison to the situation with other owners who must hire each trades group needed. Private owners may have a designated builder that has worked with them in the past and is willing to build the sport facility. However, the primary step to be taken by a facility owner is to interview several builders, obtain several price quotes, and then select the builder. Owners who do not want to be involved in the process can hire a consultant, construction manager, or contractor to manage the building process. An **owner's representative** is the middle person between the owner and those who will build the facility, such as the architects, construction managers, and contractors.

Public projects are significantly different from owner-constructed facilities. In the latter case the owners can choose whomever they wish to design and build the facility; almost all public projects must go through the bid process. The bid process may come into play in the planning process as various architectural, consulting, or design companies are examined.

Project Bids

One of the first elements within the bidding process is the **request for qualifications (RFQ)**. The RFQ is designed to determine which companies meet the minimum requirements for building the facility. This does not mean that a given company will do the building but rather which companies will move on to the next round in which financial and other variables are analyzed. Most states require by law that professional services be procured based on qualifications, not necessarily price. Normally RFQs are developed to determine the best company to help develop the master plan; consulting projects such as feasibility studies or soil testing; architectural, engineering, or design services; construction management; or facility management.

Builder Criteria

While there is no one correct list of expected experience or skills for any company responding to an RFQ, RFP, or RFB, the following are some basic concerns:

- Length of company existence (to determine staying power if something goes wrong)
- Relevant project experience
- Expertise and experience of engineering staff
- Experience with other companies already working with the facility planners
- Past experience working for the municipality
- Staff experience on similar projects
- State or other required licensure
- Existence of required elements such as insurance or local office
- Technical competence
- Letters of recommendation
- Past record of coming within budget
- Past experience with problems and how they were resolved

Typically RFQs are published in the legal sections of the newspaper to provide appropriate public notice. The RFQs also contain written descriptions mailed to past contractors with the municipality; these letters contain a project summary, a detailed analysis of services being requested, detailed explanation of the expected deliverables, and possible submission requirements or selection criteria. Potentially interested companies are often invited to attend a "walk-through" in which they can examine a potential facility or site.

Besides the cost to advertise an RFQ, the bid package itself can be expensive. It can cost $300 to print the documents (specifications/drawings) for a typical bid set. Bidders are often asked to put down a deposit that covers the printing costs; they will obtain a refund after a winner is chosen. Regardless of what process is used, the expense needs to be considered, or a reprographic business needs to be consulted to make copies for any potential bidders. The bidder may have to pick up other costs with no guarantee that the bidder will ever get any contracts. It is not uncommon for a company to submit numerous bids and qualifications during a year and receive only a limited number of actual projects, if any.

Besides RFQs, there are **requests for proposals (RFPs)** and **requests for bids (RFBs)**, which are basically the same. Both request particular action;

for example, the RFP can ask a company how it would propose solving a problem or what price it would charge to build the facility. Sometimes an RFQ produces a list of several qualified companies and those qualified companies receive an RFB and are asked to bid on a project. Criteria for determining who might get the bid are listed above.

Contracts

The individual or business that wins the bid or is awarded the contract normally meets with the facility developer to finalize a contract and all the associated terms. Each entity involved has to understand its role in the construction process. Facility developers often feel an entitlement that they can do what they want with the facility when it is being built. However, any efforts on their part to change the facility design during the construction process often result in large time delays and increased costs.

To help deal with this concern, specific contractual relationships need to be developed. The options available are listed next. The advantages and disadvantages of some of the options are outlined in table 6.1.

- Paying a lump sum for the construction
- Paying a set cost plus a fixed fee to the contractor as its profit

- Hiring a construction manager or general contractor to serve on the developer's behalf and giving that person the financial authority to complete a project
- Hiring a construction company to complete the project for a guaranteed maximum price
- Entering into a **turnkey contract** in which a construction company builds the facility with very little input from the future owner; when the construction is completed the construction company turns the keys of the new building over to the new owner
- Entering into a **design/build contract,** which is similar to the turnkey process with the exception that the owner rather than the builder provides the land and may control the schedule and budget (Bentil, 1989)

The construction manager/general contractor (CM/GC) needs to become involved in the very earliest phases of the construction process—most frequently, in a private facility, during the planning process. As the party responsible for final construction and for hiring the subcontractors, the CM/GC can collaborate more effectively with all other parties including the developer and architect. The

CM/GC also can help with reducing budgeting and scheduling restraints since the CM/GC is involved from the beginning and represents the developer. The CM/GC is also a facilitator to ensure that the design, schedule, cost, and "buildability" issues are working smoothly.

One of the requirements in starting the construction process is often some form of guarantee that the work will be completed. While contracts provide some form of protection, they are valueless if the construction company goes out of business or has multiple shell companies to hide its money. One step that can be taken to avoid this problem is to have construction bonds or insurance that pays the facility owner if the builder or general contractor fails to perform. In one example in Connecticut, a city hired a pool builder to build the city pool. As part of the construction bid requirement, the builder was required to post a $950,000 bond. The project faced significant delays and cost increases. The contractor blamed the delays and cost increases on the rocks found on the site. On the basis of the delays, the town council voted that the contractor was in default. Such a step was required in order to start the process required to collect on the performance bond (Gannon, 2002).

Table 6.1 Advantages and Disadvantages of Various Construction Options

Construction option	Advantages	Disadvantages
Lump sum	Fixed price Owner in control of quality/operation and management (O&M) A single responsible contractor	Lengthy process Numerous revisions over time Impact of cost escalation most severe Contractor and owner/designer not necessarily working together
Construction management	Impact of price escalation reduced Construction management works as owner's agent Owner in control of quality/O&M Design construction time reduced	Total cost not known until construction started Extra costs when modifications made
Guaranteed max price	Complete plans can be finished later Maximum price known from start Owner in control of quality/O&M Design construction time reduced	Any changes increase costs Contractor and owner/designer not necessarily working together High contractor's profit margin
Turnkey	Complete plans not necessary Price fixed at start Design construction time reduced	Hard for owner to make changes Contractor and owner/designer not necessarily working together Less say on quality/O&M High contractor's profit margin

From Cotts and Lee, 1992.

Behind the Scenes: Constructing a Baseball or Softball Field

It is important to hire an experienced general contractor and architect. Any contractor who has ever moved dirt says that he or she is capable of following a grading plan and constructing fields. Potential architects will also claim that a field is a minor project for them. However, there are many nuances to the grading plan, irrigation system, and other systems that directly affect the facility's quality for years to come. Anyone interested in building a baseball/softball field should ask potential general contractors and architects for references concerning fields that they have actually built and then question the maintenance person for that facility.

Various Field Layouts and Various Sports

The standard and accepted softball infield is a "skinned" surface. Attempts at using a grass surface have generally been ill advised. A dirt surface is easier to maintain and holds up better under the extensive use a field receives. The actual mix of dirt is dependent on the facility's location. Various clay–sand mixes can be purchased, but over the long term the field will end up with indigenous materials of some sort. The facility developer should choose "clean" material, free from rocks and small pebbles, and then properly apply and maintain it. A properly maintained clay–sand mix will result in a first-class infield.

Drainage is a major consideration in the construction of infields. It is important that the infields be crowned to induce drainage, but more importantly a regular schedule of infield dragging patterns should be maintained so that material is not constantly being dragged off but rather returned to the infield. It is also important that the problem areas around home plate and the bases be properly maintained and dragged in a pattern consistent with the rest of the infield.

A second issue that is rarely addressed is the cut of the infield dirt. The cut is the distance of the radius around the pitcher's rubber at which the outfield grass starts. Baseball and softball have gone to a livelier ball and the bases have been moved back. Although some sanctioning now recommends a 65-foot (19.8-meter) radius to the grass cut, some facility developers recommend a minimum of a 75-foot (23-meter) cut. This solves a maintenance problem, decreases the cost of the irrigation system and maintenance, and provides some additional flexibility for women's events.

Field Maintenance

Outfields should be made of grass and require a proper irrigation system. The major maintenance issue is that of wear in the areas where the outfielders, particularly the left fielders, play. The extent of the problem is determined by the design, quality of maintenance, and amount of use. In some cases it is simply impossible to avoid the occurrence of these spots, and annual resodding over these areas must be scheduled. This is particularly true for wet fields. Drainage is again an issue, since wet spots are the spots most easily damaged. A 3% grade should be constructed through the turf areas to move the water away from the field. The irrigation system should be properly monitored to prevent man-induced wet spots due to overuse. Also critical is constant aeration of the worn areas to prevent soil compaction problems.

A second construction consideration is warning tracks. Lawsuits have been filed against complexes without warning tracks after players have run into fences. In addition to the safety factor, warning tracks have some very practical cost-saving effects. They cut down on the cost of the irrigation system and maintenance of turf, provide access for the occasional vehicle that must cut across the field, are easily maintained, and add prestige to the complex. The material used on the warning tracks need not be as closely scrutinized as that used in the infields. A crushed rock mix that will absorb water is most appropriate. The critical concern is again a maintenance issue—keeping the warning track and infield substances separate so that the infields are not contaminated with the warning track substance. Warning tracks are generally constructed using the same material as dirt parking lots and walkways since this option is inexpensive.

(continued)

(continued)

Dimensions

The outfield fence must be a minimum 300-foot (91-meter) radius from home plate, and all side fencing must be a minimum of 20 to 25 feet (6-7.6 meters) from the foul lines. It is recommended that in complexes of more than one field, all fields be identical in dimension. Facilities should also be constructed with a north–south orientation so that the third base line is on the north side of the field. This helps minimize the sun glare for players.

Irrigation

Effective turf maintenance requires proper watering, fertilizing, aerating, and mowing. Of these elements, water is the most critical. The type of irrigation system is determined by the facility's climate; however, all facilities require some sort of automatic irrigation system. The sprinkler systems with smaller heads are safer and better suited for the playing surface than systems with large heads. Skimping on the irrigation system can be a serious error.

Some options that can be included in the irrigation system are an automatic clock, a computer monitor, and a sensor system. The automatic clock is not really an option as it is an integral part of the irrigation system; any system without a clock is inadequate. The clock should provide watering in the various cycles during the hours the fields are not in use. The size of each station can be determined by the professional who designs the irrigation system. It is of course vital that the complete watering cycle be accomplished within 8 to 12 hours so as not to interfere with games.

A sensor system is very cost-effective in areas where irrigating can be expensive. A sensor system shuts off a station when it determines that the root system has received adequate water. These systems can cost around $3,000 per field and result in a highly efficient use of water. A sensor-based system can produce a 30% to 50% reduction in water consumption. It also eliminates overwatering and the accompanying maintenance problems.

A final consideration for the irrigation system is to install couplers within the dirt portion of the infields, located so hoses can water down the dirt in the infield and then be removed for play. The most common maintenance problem in the dirt areas is lack of water. Couplers or faucets allow the field maintenance staff to bring a hose to the center of the field and water the infield.

Preconstruction Phase

Besides finalizing the builder and any contractual issues such as construction bonds or liquidated damages clauses to penalize a builder that does not finish construction on time, several additional steps need to be taken before actual construction begins. For example, preconstruction meetings are held to make sure that the architect/engineer, owner representative, contractors, and other parties are all "on the same page." Does each party have all necessary resources and personnel to complete its tasks, especially if these may be needed in a sequential manner? No project runs without glitches. However, some glitches are more expensive than others. If a roofing crew is supposed to begin installing the roof starting on July 1 but the trusses are not completed on that date, the crew could be waiting around for weeks, all having to be paid. The workers must be available because if they move to a different job there is no guarantee they will be available when the trusses are finally up—delaying the project even more and incurring even more expenses. Thus, all the parties including project managers, superintendents, engineers, architects, laborers, carpenters, subcontractors, material suppliers, equipment suppliers, consultants such as surveyors, professionals such as lawyers, and even city or municipal building inspectors need to work together on a set schedule.

Documentation

Also important in this phase is making sure that all the proper documentation is available to all parties. The preconstruction documents that are needed, in addition to the construction contract, include what are commonly referred to as contract drawings. Among these are the following:

- Site drawings, which provide information on the geographic location, how the project contours to the land, any roads and parking lots, and where current and future utilities will be placed
- Architectural drawings, which show the floor plans from the lowest to the highest floor
- Structural drawings, which show all the supporting systems such as foundations, columns, floor systems, roof systems, and other elements depicted in great detail (such as where pieces should be welded together and how)
- Plumbing drawings, which depict the water distribution system from piping to fixtures
- Mechanical drawings, which provide information about the HVAC system, for example the location of ductwork and where heating and air conditioning units will be placed
- Electrical drawings, which show the electrical and electronic demands for the building and placement of electrical and electronic fixtures (Bentil, 1989)

Once all the documents and parties are ready, the construction process can begin. The first step is site preparation.

Site Preparation

Building contractors cannot just start building on a site. They first need to establish a field office and then build an access road for equipment and materials to reach the site. Next the rough grade of the site needs to be evaluated. This may entail removing existing buildings, utilities, vegetation, and other impediments to construction. The process of removing tree stumps, bushes, and other undergrowth is called **grubbing** and is normally accomplished fairly quickly with a bulldozer. Existing buildings can be more complicated. Tearing down some old stadiums has required a significant amount of explosives. Other facilities may have asbestos or other hazardous components that may require care, money, and time to abate.

Soil boring is then undertaken to determine if the soil is suitable for the proposed foundation. Core drilling, covered in chapter 5, can include testing of the subsoil strength. However, testing for contaminants or rocks often does not go as deep as strength testing needs to go to determine how deeply cement pylons may have to be sunk

to ensure a strong support. Through the boring process, a contractor can determine the presence of rock, organic materials, or a water table that can affect the foundation. After the clear surface for the site is exposed, earthwork operations begin. Earthwork includes stripping the existing topsoil, mass excavation or filling (site grading), building excavation, and backfill (Bentil, 1989). Typically, the first 4 to 6 inches (10 to 15 centimeters) of a site is removed, unless a facility existed on the same site in the past, because it is not a suitable base upon which to build a foundation. The area that needs to be cleared is the **building area,** which is defined as 5 feet (1.5 meters) beyond the limits of the proposed structure.

Normally the ground is not flat but has dips, valleys, hills, mounds, and other irregularities. A topographic survey of the site will show all these contours and help the contractor determine what areas need to be lowered or filled so that the site will be properly graded for supporting the foundation. The grading plan was discussed in chapter 5. Rough grading is the initial movement of clay, earth, gravel, or sand; fine grading is the smoothing of the site to a finished surface. If a hole needs to be dug to support the foundation, or for a basement, garage, elevator shaft, or substories for a structure, the contractor will need to excavate the site.

The contractor can utilize machine excavation (trenching machines, bulldozers, and excavators) or hand excavation. During the excavation process the contractor may run into water and then will need to engage in dewatering, or extracting water. Water can be removed through pumping the water out directly, pumping the water from one pit to another, draining the water to a lower elevation, or installing a permanent pumping system (Bentil, 1989).

After the site is at the appropriate level, the soil is chemically treated to prevent insects such as termites. Utilities are also added at this point, and some of the basic landscaping may also be completed at this time.

Construction Elements

Building a facility is similar to putting together a jigsaw puzzle. Most people put a puzzle together by looking at the picture on the box to see what it should look like. They then sort the pieces with edges and put the frame together. After the frame is in place the inside can be completed. Similarly, the construction process for a PAF typically starts with examining the plans, building a foundation for a solid structure, creating the external shell, and then completing the interior. The construction process must include examination of the material used for the facility's base, the exterior components, and then the interior elements.

Foundation Materials

Before examining the foundation, it is important to understand the basic construction material that will be used throughout the construction process. Wood is one of the materials most commonly used since it can be easily shaped or cut to size. Wood is typically used for joists, columns, posts, beams, and trusses. If the wood is laminated, which provides greater strength, it can also be used for rigid frames, arches, vaults, and other areas requiring significant strength. Most lumber is categorized by size—for example, 2 by 4 inches (5 to 10 centimeters) and 4 by 4 inches—and grade, which refers to its quality.

Concrete is one of the most frequently seen construction materials because it is not flammable, is highly versatile, and is relatively inexpensive. Cement (or Portland cement) is made of silica, lime, slag, flute dust, and alumina. These ingredients are mixed, heated, cooled, and pulverized, and then the powder is sold either in bulk or in bags. Combining cement with water, sand, gravel, crushed stone, and other inert items makes concrete. Concrete is rated by its strength after it has been allowed to cure (harden) for a 28-day period. Concrete that will be exposed to freezing elements, such as in sidewalks, needs to have a strength of about 4,000 psi (pounds per square inch). Stronger concrete can reach a strength of 19,000 psi (Bentil, 1989). Since concrete can suffer from tension and shear, reinforced steel is often placed in designated locations to strengthen it. Concrete can be cast in place (poured on the spot) or precast (formed at a different location and then trucked to the spot where it will be erected), or can take the form of masonry such as concrete block, which is used for load-bearing walls. Similar to concrete blocks, walls can be made of bricks, stones, rocks, and other inert hard compounds.

Structural steel is often used to frame a building. Steel can lose strength over time due to corrosion or when exposed to severe heat, as evidenced in the 9/11 tragedy. Steel is produced from three basic materials: iron, ore, and limestone. Steel is often used to help carry the vertical and horizontal loads of the structure to the foundation. Steel columns can support elevated concrete slabs on higher floors because of the strength that steel possesses.

Substructure and Load

Once the types of materials are known, it is easier to appreciate the various elements that make up the structure's lowest levels. The level at and below ground level is called the **substructure.** The substructure helps transfer the **structural load** from a building into soil or rocks for the safest base possible. The substructure is typically composed of a slab-on-grade and a foundation. (The process is called slab-on-grade if a concrete floor placed directly on the ground can support the structure.) The slab of concrete is poured over a polyethylene sheet (commonly called Visqueen), which is laid over crushed gravel/stone to prevent moisture from penetrating the concrete and getting into the structure. The slab is usually reinforced with steel-wire mesh to provide additional strength

The foundation transfers the building weight (load) to the earth below. Several types of load need to be carried. Dead load refers to the total weight of the entire building including frame, walls, floors, roof, and foundation. Live load includes all the people, furnishings, equipment, and elements such as rain or snow on the roof. The live and dead loads are carried down to the foundation through columns. The columns can be set in either a shallow or a deep foundation. A shallow foundation utilizes "footers" to transfer the load to the earth below the foundation. However, if the earth below the foundation is not strong enough, a deep foundation may be used. A deep foundation transfers the load deep into the ground to bedrock if the subgrade surface is not strong enough. This deep transfer is completed utilizing piles sunk into the ground; the piles are made of timber, concrete, or steel (Bentil, 1989). To ensure that the piles provide a stronger base, they are often driven into the ground in clusters and then capped.

Superstructure

The previous section dealt with the ground level and everything underneath that supports the structure. The **superstructure** is everything above the substructure and includes the framing, columns, beams, and trusses. Framing can be made with steel, concrete, wood, or masonry. The various materials can be formed at another location and then set, bolted, welded, or connected on-site. Concrete is often poured in liquid form to be cured and finalized in place. Cast-in-place concrete requires significant planning for formwork, which consists of creating the molds used to contain the poured concrete. Formwork is the critical component for holding poured concrete in its intended shape and can amount to about one-third of the cost of the overall concrete work. Table 6.2 lists the cost percentage breakdown of various components within a complete concrete-framed building.

Exterior Components

In addition to the frame, the **support** is also an integral component of the construction process. The support is also referred to as the exterior closure, building skin, or envelope. This element, which is often the most expensive, not only serves as an external barrier to the elements but can also serve as a structural element such as a load-bearing wall.

The exterior can be made of wood, cement, metal, or other materials, often covered by a waterproofing material and then with an external material that can be seen from outside the facility. This outside "skin" of a building is frequently called the exterior fascia or external facing. The exterior fascia can be made of glass, brick, steel, plastic, masonry, wood, or other elements. These elements, or combinations thereof, are held in place with a metal frame. The frame can be precast or built on

the spot; fascia can be built around a frame or can be hoisted into place from precast segments. No matter what method or material is used, all fascia needs to be weatherproof and must provide some degree of insulation to minimize energy usage. Other exterior components that must be built include the roof, turf, and watering system.

Roofing

A roof is not as expensive as might be assumed. However, a problem with a roof, such as a leak, can cause extensive damage to the building and items within the building. There are three types of roof: pitched, flat, and dome. A pitched roof is built at a slope to facilitate drainage and the melting of snow. A flat roof has a minimal slope (from 1/8- to 1/2-inch [0.32- to 1.3-centimeter] drop per foot of run) to drains. A dome can be used to provide greater clearance for internal activities while also ideally allowing water and snow to drain more effectively. However, a number of sport domes and traditional roofs have collapsed due to wind, the weight of excess snow, or both. Roofing is covered in greater detail in chapter 7 as one of the primary building systems.

A roof is typically supported through a truss system of wood or steel angles connected together to increase strength. These frames support the roof, but also serve as a support mechanism for such items as scoreboard, speakers, lights, and other rigging. These support systems are even more important in basketball/hockey facilities that use a large-span roof since there cannot be any center support beams. In other facilities where a center support column can be used, the weight load potential for the roof can significantly increase.

Table 6.2 Cost Percentage Breakdown of a Concrete Framed Building

Component	Percentage
Form labor to make the concrete mold	28
Concrete	24
Reinforcing steel materials	19
Placing labor	11
Reinforced steel labor	11
Form material	7

From Bentil, 1989.

© Human Kinetics

Pitched roofs are ideal for facilities in areas that receive high amounts of rain and snow. The shape of the roof helps facilitate drainage and the melting of snow.

These facilities often can support heavy weights on the roof such as HVAC systems. Such weights cannot be sustained by most open-span roofs.

At the same time the roofing system is being installed, internal construction can begin. The substructure, superstructure, exterior fascia, and roof need to be mostly completed before internal work begins to prevent weather damage to internal components.

Turf

One of the important decisions for any facility is whether to have natural turf fields or artificial turf, often called Astroturf. A new system that reduces rug burn and is softer on ankles is the FieldTurf in-filled system, which utilizes a loosely laid mixture of recycled rubber granules and sand within a fiber mat consisting of 2.5-inch-long (6.4 centimeters) polyethylene blended fiber imitation grass blades. The mat rests on a compacted subgrade of free-draining rock and an underground drainage system (Korcek, 2001). (The subgrade is the surface underneath the mat.) For FieldTurf the underneath structure consists of stones (normally 1-2 inches [2.5-5 centimeters] in size) compacted down so they do not move, but also spaced so that water can filter down to the drainage system. Some claimed that Astroturf, which traditionally had a subgrade made of cement with padding on top, contributed to ankle strains (Korcek, 2001). The subgrade is critical for more than just safety reasons. A well-designed subgrade can help drain a field, allowing teams to play even in bad weather conditions. The FieldTurf system can drain 10 inches (25 centimeters) of rain from a field in an hour.

While the author is not out to promote any one product, the FieldTurf system has been increasing in popularity since the late 1990s; the average cost per square foot is $7 using the in-filled system versus $16.50 per square foot for synthetic fields (Korcek, 2001). In one project, Northern Illinois University changed from synthetic top in-filled and installed 94,720 square feet (8,800 square meters) of the in-filled type of synthetic grass (in 5-yard-wide sections [4.5 meters]). The project also used 370 tons of silica sand and 90 tons of granular rubber, which came from recycled tires (Korcek, 2001). Savings from such systems include time and expense savings because yard marker lines do not have to be painted. Synthetic grass can come already painted, and the paint does not wash away, which can save numerous hours of repainting.

Watering System

As mentioned in chapter 2, most facility managers who have grass or turf fields need to pay careful attention to weather reports. Rain can be the saving grace for a dry field, but too much rain can lead to puddles and excessively fast drainage with failure of the water to soak into the ground. Too little rain requires the facility manager to spend significant time and money making sure that the surface is watered at the right time. Since one never knows when it might or might not rain, a water delivery system must be installed to supplement the drainage system in each field. The steps for installing a watering system are as follows:

- Clear the area
- Grade the area
- Select necessary pipes
- Install watering system

Artificial turf or natural grass? The debate continues.

- Add grass (select type of grass and method of planting according to type of soil, events, and weather conditions)

Other External Components

Other external components that should be examined include areas such as parking lots, roads, lights, security cameras, fences, billboards, outdoor rest rooms, and a host of external amenities that can be added to a facility. Some facilities have external buildings such as maintenance sheds or garages to store vehicles. External systems are covered in greater detail in chapter 7.

Interior Components

The primary internal components include partitions, millwork, doors and hardware, building systems, and furniture and finishings. Partitions may be either movable or permanent. A locker room may have permanent partitions between the visitors' and home locker rooms. An example of a movable partition is a gym divider that can be raised to create a large gym space or lowered to create distinct playing areas. Partitions can also serve as firewalls or load-bearing walls.

Millwork refers to wood, plastic, or metal components with customized finishes. The term originated from the milling process that converted soft woods into such items as molding and trim. Over the years new processes have been developed to make millwork from other materials. Examples of millwork include door frames, coving, handrails, shelving, and similar components that add a distinctive look and feel to a building.

Doors, frames, and hardware refers to metal or wood doors hung on wood or metal frames using hinges. There are numerous variations, from revolving doors to turnstiles, that affect how people get into and out of a facility. Whether wood or hollow metal, doors typically carry a label with either a letter or an hour rating (such as 3 hours), which is the fire rating for the door. Table 6.3 lists the hour ratings for fire doors.

In addition to completion of all internal components, systems must be integrated throughout the building. Systems include HVAC, electrical, communication (sound, computer, telephone), plumbing, and fire suppression (covered in more depth in chapter 7). Each system requires wires, pipes, ducts, and other components that need to be installed before the walls, ceiling, and floors are put in place. Many facilities are built with drop ceilings on each floor. These ceilings are in fact like false closets. They create a space between the ceiling of one floor and the floor above. Within the space a significant amount of wiring and piping can be installed for easy access and changes. Drop

Table 6.3 Fire Door Ratings and Requirements

Hour (rating)	Usage	Maximum glass area in door
3 hours (A)	Doors between buildings	No glass allowed
1 1/2 hours (B, D)	Doors to vertical passageways (stairs) Doors subject to severe fire exposure	100 in.² (645 cm²)
1/2 hour (C, E)	Corridor doors and room partitions Doors subject to moderate exposure	1,296 in.² (0.8 m²) for C 720 in.² (0.5 m²) for E
1/2 hours or 1/3 hour	Fire doors primarily for smoke control	No limit

Letters by fire rating hour is the rating letter which appears on a door. A door with a plate bearing a large 'C' would have a 1/2 hour fire rating.

From Bentil, 1989.

ceilings often have a metal grid with light fixtures and fireproof acoustical title.

Furniture and Finishings

Finishings include such items as paint and wallpaper, ceiling tiles, flooring, and artwork on the walls. Wall finishes include paint and wallpaper and other coverings. Ceilings can also be finished; many facilities use fire-retardant acoustical sprays that both protect against fires and help bounce sounds back to the floor. Flooring can be hardwood, tile, ceramic, or commercial carpeting. Flooring choices are often based on cost and maintenance criteria. However, usage also dictates finishing needs, since areas such as showers require tile or other types of water-resistant surfaces on the walls and floor. Artwork can also be classified as a finishing because it enhances the ambiance of the facility. Sport facilities often have a significant amount of sport memorabilia on the walls that may need protection from deterioration or theft. Finishing also refers to drapes, mirrors, light fixtures, and numerous other elements that make the facility more pleasant.

In older facilities, materials may have stayed the same color as when they were made. For example, concrete areas typically stay gray. Now, the number of options is almost limitless; for example, dyes can be added to cement, and cement adhesion paint can transform any dull area into a bright environment.

The furniture and finishings component of facility construction is often one of the most innovative aspects of building a new facility. There are almost infinite options for everything from stadium seats to chairs or benches in a locker room. Furniture includes all the various items installed within the facility that make it functional. For a locker room, the furniture can range from dressing booths and television sets to entertainment systems and Jacuzzi tubs.

Furniture, fixtures, and equipment is commonly referred to as FFE in the facility management industry. In a large stadium or arena, FFE could refer to everything from the scoreboard and sound system to photocopiers and Zambonis. Smaller facilities have an equal number of FFE elements, from free-weight machines in a gym to the juice dispenser at the health bar. Typically each item in a facility that is not physically attached to the property or that can easily be removed is put into the category of FFE.

Seating

One issue that needs careful consideration in the design of a facility is the fanny of the customer. Similar to the situation with airline seats over the years, stadium seats have been shrinking as facility designers and managers try to squeeze more people into the stands. In Europe, seats are designed with a minimum of 29.53 inches (750 millimeters); the recommended minimum is 29.9 inches (760 millimeters). The typical seat in the United States is 33 inches (840 millimeters) wide. However, at some colleges the width per seat is as little as 17 to 19 inches (432-483 millimeters). While this may appear too narrow, airlines regularly use 17- to 18-inch (432- to 457-millimeter) seats. In the New York subways, width per seat was 16.5 inches (419 millimeters) in 1907, increased to 17.25 inches (438 millimeters) in 1927, and settled at 17.6 inches (447 millimeters) in 1971.

The seat growth trend in part reflects the increase in the girth of the average size person. Today, in fact, double-wide seats are designed for fans who are obese. This is not just for convenience (since the customer can be charged for two seats), but also possibly a requirement to comply with the Americans with Disabilities Act (ADA). The seat size numbers are increasing for the general public as well. The old seats for the Indiana Pacers' arena were 18 inches (432 millimeters). However, the new Conseco Fieldhouse has a minimum seat width of 21 inches (533 millimeters) (Jorgensen, 2001). The size of seats and benches affects issues such as capacity, aisle width, egress, and emergency evacuations.

© Ron Hoskins

Conseco Fieldhouse in Indianapolis, Indiana, has seats with a minimum width of 21 inches. While this wider seating does provide more comfort to spectators, it also limits the number of seats the facility can hold.

Flooring

Flooring can include carpet, resilient flooring (vinyl tiles), composite flooring, wood flooring, and stone. Flooring can make a significant difference in sport facilities. For example, the system used to support the wood floor in a basketball gym can take many forms with different levels of support, or resiliency. A high school basketball court has a significantly different substructure from a professional basketball court based on the weight load and physical demands placed on the floor.

According to the Maple Flooring Manufacturers Association, approximately 70% of all sport floors installed in the United States each year are made with maple (Kronish, 2002). Maple is utilized because it is durable, long lasting, flexible, easy to maintain, and very attractive. A well-maintained maple floor could last 70 to 100 years. The famous parquet floor in the old Boston Gardens exemplified the beauty and durability of wood flooring. However, wood flooring has different degrees of quality. First grade lumber is almost defect free and the most expensive. Most colleges and professional teams play exclusively on first grade floors. After first grade are second grade (better grade) and third grade. Third grade, the least expensive, is the quality grade most frequently used by schools on a tight budget.

One of the most important decisions in installing a wood floor is uniform stability. Uniform stability ensures uniform ball bounce, faster play, and longer durability. This is more important than higher shock-absorbency levels. The floor system should also have a well-engineered subfloor system that does not compromise stability. One method is to use padding underneath the subfloor. In fact, under wood floors there are often several levels of padding and shock-absorbent systems that allow the floor to give. Point-elastic surfaces restrict the impact underfoot to the point of contact, whereas with area-elastic surfaces an impact can be felt up to 20 inches (51 centimeters) away (Viklund, 1995). Specific differences in climate and performance expectations can also dictate which wood floor will work best in any given gym.

Synthetic floors are utilized if wood flooring is not the preferred choice for expense reasons or if the facility will have multipurpose uses unsuitable for wood. There are three types of synthetic floors. Poured urethane is embedded with rubber granules to meet resilience needs. The urethane is poured onto a concrete substrate and can last almost 40 years if it is properly maintained (damp mopping and use of some industrial cleaners) and resurfaced every 10 years. The maintenance requirements for such floors are less than for wood floors, which may need to be resurfaced every year if used extensively (Kronish, 2002). Rolled and sheet goods are various types of synthetic surfaces that are purchased in large rolls or sheets and are applied directly on top of cement or other subflooring. These floors typically do not last as long as urethane, but they are simple to clean and come in a variety of colors. The last category of synthetic floors is modular polypropylene tiles. These plastic-based tiles are resistant to water, more difficult to damage, and very easy to install and repair. However, they do not provide the same resiliency and do not have the same look as some of the other synthetic floor systems.

The steps of the floor selection process include the following:

- Determine which room or space the floor will cover
- Prioritize which sports and activities will use the room
- Determine whether the floor should be area-elastic or point-elastic
- Review the performance criteria for the various floor types being considered
- Test floor options and compare costs
- Review potential warranties
- Compare the life-cycle costs for the various floor options
- Conduct activities on floors installed in other facilities
- Make the final decision
- Hire individuals who have previously installed the type of floor selected (Viklund, 1995)

One of the keys for a synthetic floor is having an appropriate concrete subfloor in which no curing agents have been used and in which the variation is no more than 1/8 inch (0.32 centimeters) for every 10 feet (3 meters). The slab should have a hard steel-troweled finish and should be adequately waterproofed ("More than Just a Gym Floor," n.d.).

The issues involving flooring can be complex. From shock absorption and deformation to surface friction or rolling loads, there are many concerns that are typically beyond the scope of knowledge and experience of most beginning facility managers. That is why it is beneficial to use an expert who understands both wood and synthetic floors to help choose the right materials.

Special Considerations

Numerous special considerations arise in building a sport facility. The uniqueness associated with each facility makes sport facilities harder to design and build than some other types of facilities. Everything from energy conservation to drainage for artificial turf fields must be considered. The following sections cover a few of the more common special concerns.

Restoration and Renovation

No analysis of the construction process would be complete without consideration of the **restoration** or **renovation** process. Because of the cost of some sport facilities or their historic importance, the decision may be to renovate rather than build a new facility. Renovations can be almost as expensive as construction, and restorations can cost more than a facility originally cost to build. The renovations and restorations of historic Soldier Field in Chicago cost approximately $606 million ("Make No Small Plans," 2003). This amount is significantly greater than the initial cost of building the stadium in the 1920s, which was $13 million ("Make No Small Plans," 2003).

Renovations are often undertaken on college campuses, where building a new stadium or arena may be cost prohibitive and the nostalgia evoked by an old facility would make any effort to demolish a stadium futile and politically suicidal in the eyes of alumni and major givers. For example, the Ross-Ade Stadium on the Purdue University campus was built in the 1920s and has been renovated four times. A new renovation project undertaken in 2001 focused on increasing traffic flow on concourses and concession areas while maintaining the historical importance and feel. These concourses were very narrow because they were obstructed by an old steel-frame renovation of the upper stands using cross-bracing beams. With the aid of architects and structural engineers it was possible to remove most of the bracing to increase room and at the same time avoid compromising the structural integrity (White and Slade, 2001).

One concern with renovations is that initial construction may have complied with existing rules and laws but renovations need to comply with current building codes and laws. At Purdue, the stadium was built without analysis of the lateral sway load, since this was not a requirement at the time. The need for renovations to comply with building codes can open a Pandora's box. In fact, some facilities do not undertake any renovations because they may create more problems than solutions. This can occur, for example, when renovations affect asbestos-covered materials and the costs for required asbestos removal (abatement) are more than the total value of the anticipated renovation project. Another concern entails grandfathering of existing facilities under certain laws such as the ADA. Existing buildings do not need to undertake renovations for the purpose of complying with the ADA or with some other codes or laws. However, any new renovations or additions must comply with such laws.

The decision whether to renovate/restore or build a new facility is based on various factors, among them a building's having historical designation and protection or having a unique place in a community's history. The process requires examining the potential costs and the various political ramifications associated with the work. Before any work is undertaken it is critical to examine various systems, from life safety and fire systems to structural specifications and mechanical and electrical systems. It may not make sense to spend a lot of money on the outside of a facility when the inside is worthless because of incompatible electrical systems or because insulation or fire protection will be too expensive to modify. Thus, the process of restoring/renovating a facility requires more planning than that of designing a new facility. The following are some of the issues that need to be covered:

- Is information available on maintaining existing systems?
- Are there health concerns such as asbestos or lead paint?
- What impact will the work have on existing tenants?
- Are parts still available, or will items need to be hand or machine made?

Facility Focus: Renovating Soldier Field

© AP/World Wide Photos

Soldier Field, home of the Chicago Bears of the NFL, opened in 1924. The facility has had a rich tradition, with a panoramic view of Lake Michigan and perimeter columns that made it a landmark in Chicago. However, as an older facility it had problems that were hard to overcome, such as poor sight lines for viewing the game, uncomfortable seats, and not enough bathrooms. The stadium underwent numerous renovations, the largest occurring in 1979 when new lights were installed along with artificial turf and upgrades to locker rooms, seats, and sight lines. More rest rooms and concession stands were added several years later. Several years after those renovations, the artificial turf was removed and replaced with a natural grass surface. At the same time, 116 skyboxes were installed, increasing the seating capacity to 67,000 fans by the end of the 1980s (Ryan, 2004).

Even with all these changes, the facility was not ideal, and the Bears wanted a new stadium. Thus, in 2001 the decision was made to build a new stadium inside the old stadium. Instead of tearing down the old stadium, as has occurred with many new football and baseball stadiums, Soldier Field's facade was barely touched. The inside received a significant makeover, with the architects creating a sleek metal oval-shaped stadium inside and above the older rectangular stadium. The $606 million project, completed in 2003, has two times as many rest rooms and four times as many concession stands as before. The Bears paid $200 million of the renovation costs and covered cost overruns totaling almost $50 million. Surprisingly, the new stadium lost seats and now sits only 61,500 fans, making Soldier Field one of the smallest stadiums in the NFL. There are 133 luxury suites that can sit 16 people each. Below the suites is a 100,000-square-foot (9,300-square-meter) club that opens directly into an underground parking lot (Ryan, 2004).

The renovation project was not without controversy. After a year of being open, broadcasters were still making fun of the stadium's new shape and fans did not appreciate the blend of the old and the new. While typical renovation projects are not as extensive as the process at Soldier Field, this example helps highlight that facilities may go through many renovations until some point in time when they need to be gutted or torn down to build a new facility.

- Is there time available (restorations often take longer than building a new facility)?
- Are there qualified workers who can help on the project?
- Is a lot of money available for when things go wrong and unexpected scenarios arise?

Conservation

Whether the issue is conserving energy or recycling building products, conservation has become a major concern for new facilities. A key concern with new facilities is their ability to minimize waste. From reducing the amount of wasted energy to building with sustainable materials, constructing more efficient facilities is a sound and correct decision. American buildings consume 30% of the nation's total energy and 60% of all electricity used (McCarron, 2001). The process of creating energy-efficient buildings is called **green design**. Green designing should be analyzed in the facility planning process and in the actual design process discussed in chapters 4 and 5. However, even if a building is designed with conservation in mind, the facility may not accomplish this goal if it is not constructed properly.

The best-designed building will not work well if the materials are not efficient or not properly connected to reduce air loss. Green design considers the building design, site, region, building envelope, construction materials, building systems, and other variables. Through **life-cycle costing** of materials or initial costs, maintenance costs, and finally replacement costs, a facility or its components can be examined to determine if they are operating efficiently and conserving energy. While green facilities typically cost more to build, in the long run their maintenance and energy usage costs more than make up for the higher starting price (McCarron, 2001). Facilities being built to comply with the LEED (Leadership in Energy and Environmental Design) criteria cost 5% to 10% more than other buildings. LEED takes into consideration a facility's site, water, energy, air, and materials. It is hoped that LEED compliant facilities will be environmentally friendly and, in the long run, reduce facility operational costs.

All the LEED variables affect the construction process. For example, the site criterion is affected by local environmental conditions. If care is to be taken to avoid harm to adjoining land, the construc-

tion process may need to be significantly altered. Chapter 7 highlights the money-saving options in various lighting systems. If energy-efficient lighting systems are installed from the beginning, subsequent costs to convert a system can be eliminated and energy efficiency can be reached right away. Additional building considerations include co-generation. Co-generation involves analyzing the combined heat and power produced at a power plant. Most power plants convert only 35% of the fuel into electrical energy. An additional 8% of the electricity is lost during transmission, and the rest of the energy produced during the conversion process is heat energy released into the environment (McCarron, 2001). A green facility would be designed so that the power plant is near a pool or other area that could use the heat energy to reduce heating costs. If the plant is closer to the area that will use the electricity, then less electricity will be lost in the transmission process.

Building materials play a major role in energy conservation. Insulation and vapor barriers help reduce HVAC needs, but do not address air circulation since air is trapped in a building. Exterior color can also have a significant impact. Facilities in the south are often built with light-colored or reflective materials to reflect heat, which reduces cooling demands during the summer. Walls can also be designed to collect sunlight during the winter and then re-radiate the heat throughout a facility. But while numerous materials are available for constructing a building and many are now made with recycled products, there can be potential health concerns. Chapter 7 highlights some of the air quality issues that can occur with any facility, including green facilities.

Project Costs

Cost-based concerns are numerous, and costs often drive the entire construction process. To help complete a project with the lowest potential costs, facilities often utilize **value-based engineering**. Value-based engineering can be combined with value construction to see where money can be saved. Value-based engineering needs can be addressed at all points during the design and construction process. The developer should always remind the site supervisor or general contractor that cost is a major concern that must be strictly monitored.

The costs of new buildings or facilities differ on the basis of many variables. Generally speaking, there are six standard budget items for a new building:

1. Preliminary costs
   - Acquisition of site
   - Site decontamination
   - Site development
   - Legal fees
   - Cost of bond issue
   - Promotion and publicity
   - Preliminary architect fees for preparation of preliminary plans
   - Consultant fees (legal, tax, bonds, polling, political, etc.)
2. Architectural fees
   - Preparation of architectural and engineering plans (working plans)
   - Supervision of construction
   - Engineering requirements
3. Construction costs
   - Building contract and subcontracts
   - Supervision costs
   - Building permits
4. Furniture, fixtures, and equipment (up to 15% of the total budget)
   - Building
   - Outdoor play areas
5. Insurance costs to pay the facility developer if the construction company fails to complete the project
6. Contingencies (usually 10% of the total cost)—may include more money for paint, new toilet seats not included in the initial budget, and countless other last-minute additions or changes to the original design budget (Gabrielsen and Miles, 1958)

This breakdown of costs associated with the construction process was written over 40 years ago; however numerous cost elements have stayed the same over the years. Costs are often examined today in terms of whether they are direct or indirect costs. This categorization is somewhat misleading because all costs end up being direct costs in that the facility developer will have to pay them. Tradi-tional **direct costs** include labor, materials, equipment, and subcontractor costs. **Indirect costs** typically include profit, home office expenses, printing costs, and other such expenses. Costs that are often overlooked include strikes by laborers, escalating costs associated with inflation and litigation delays, and weather-related delays.

Cost Variables

When constructing a facility, it is necessary to examine variables that can affect project costs. Every construction project faces changes before and during the construction process. When a facility is being designed, cost considerations can help dictate whether to use tile or marble as flooring. During the construction process, the builders often run into trouble when unexpected issues arise. For example, a chosen window design might no longer be available, so a more expensive alternative is required to complete the project on time. Each change costs money, but some changes can be less expensive if less expensive material can be used. Cost variables apart from those relating to design and construction include the following:

- Access to market and distribution centers and the cost to penetrate a market
- Cost of transporting and purchasing supplies
- Site-related costs
- Relocation and moving expenses
- Interest expenses on borrowed funds
- Environmental costs
- Prevailing wage rate for laborers and skilled craftsmen
- Costs related to various taxing authorities that get involved
- Costs related to various government authorities such as building inspectors and their requirements (Cotts and Lee, 1992)

An additional variable affecting cost is quality. The higher the quality of items used, the higher the price. For example, the typical cost for a wood basketball floor is between $6.70 per square foot for a low-quality floor and $15 per square foot for an NBA-quality floor. Between these two extremes, most facilities try to get the best bang for their

Table 6.4 Average Square Foot Costs for Indoor Floor Systems

Type	Average cost per square foot
Single sleeper hardwood floor system	$7.50-$9.00
Panel hardwood floor system	$9.00-$10.00
Anchored hardwood floor system	$12.00-$14.00
Interlocking polypropylene tiles	$4.75-$5.75
PVC sheet goods with foam backing	$6.00-$7.00
Rubber sheet goods	$6.00-$7.00
Full-pour polyurethane	$5.75-$6.75
Sandwich system	$5.75-$5.75
Panel system subfloor with synthetic top	$9.00-$13.00
Anchored system subfloor with synthetic top	$11.00-$15.00

limited dollars. Table 6.4 shows average flooring costs per square foot.

Quality can also be seen in almost every facet of the construction process. Skilled artisans can be brought in to complete the fine woodwork that can be very attractive, and expensive. Machine-finished woodwork may not be as attractive, but can be significantly less expensive and still be safe. Paint can also vary based on quality and cost. An interior paint designed to last for 10 years will be cheaper than a paint designed to last for 20 years. While the initial cost for the cheaper paint may make it an attractive option, the costs to repaint down the road should convince any facility builder to go with the better paint to avoid higher future maintenance costs.

Construction and Other Costs

Construction costs can be calculated in several different ways. The most accurate cost analysis always occurs after a facility has been built and all the costs have been tabulated. However, this does not help those on a fixed budget. Banks, lenders, and investors need to know the cost of a project before it begins. Several techniques exist to estimate the potential cost for a building. The three primary methods are the end-product units method, the ratio method, and the physical dimensions method.

The end-product units method is used when enough historical data are available to compare the proposed building with previously built facilities. Thus, if other gyms were recently built in a given region for $1.5 to $3.0 million, one could assume that a new gym would fall into the same range.

The ratio method is used for facilities with extensive equipment needs. The equipment costs are so high that their cost is multiplied by a ratio based on historical data to help determine the potential completed cost.

The physical dimensions method examines components being included in the facility and then adds the square-foot values of those components to determine a potential price. One service that compiles such data is Means Building Construction Cost Data. Someone building a 20,000-square-foot gym could look at the data and see that similar gyms have been built for $98.80 per square foot, which translates to approximately $2 million as the estimated cost to build the new gym.

An excellent resource for calculating construction costs is *RSMeans Square Foot Costs*. These books have information on the costs required to construct various facilities. From 1990 to 2001, a typical 20,000-square-foot (1,860-square-meter) gymnasium increased in cost from $69.55 to $98.80 per square foot. Some of the largest changes include the following:

Commercial/Industrial/Institutional Information for a Gymnasium

The mean square foot calculations for a gymnasium are highlighted below. The first table highlights three different external facades and the cost to build each type of building based on the building's square foot area. The second table highlights additional costs for elements such as bleachers, backboards, and lockers. The third table highlights how the total building costs in the first table are calculated based on building a 20,000-square-foot reinforced concrete block gym with laminated wood arches.

Cost Per Square Foot of Floor Area

Exterior wall	Square foot area	12,000	16,000	20,000	25,000	30,000	35,000	40,000	45,000	50,000
	Linear feet perimeter	440	520	600	700	708	780	841	910	979
Reinforced concrete block	Laminated wood arches	105.20	101.20	98.80	86.90	93.95	92.85	91.85	91.20	90.65
	Rigid steel frame	103.85	99.85	97.40	95.55	92.60	91.50	90.50	89.85	98.30
Face brick with concrete block back-up	Laminated wood arches	122.55	116.60	113.00	110.15	105.15	103.40	101.80	100.75	99.95
	Rigid steel frame	121.20	115.20	111.60	108.75	103.75	102.05	100.45	99.40	98.55
Metal sandwich panels	Laminated wood arches	101.60	98.00	95.85	94.15	91.65	90.65	89.75	89.20	88.75
	Rigid steel frame	100.25	96.65	94.45	92.75	90.25	89.30	88.40	87.85	87.35
Perimeter adjustment, add or delete	Per 100 linear feet	4.45	3.35	2.65	2.15	1.80	1.50	1.35	1.20	1.05
Story height adjustment, add or delete	Per 1 ft	.65	.55	.50	.45	.40	.35	.35	.35	.35

Basement—not applicable

The above costs were calculated using the basic specifications shown in the third table. These costs should be adjusted where necessary for design alternatives and owner's requirements. Reported completed project costs, for this type of structure, range from $46.30 to $139.00 per square foot.

(continued)

(continued)

Common Additives

Description	Unit	$ Cost	Description	Unit	$ Cost
Bleachers: telescoping, manual			Lockers, steel, single tier, 60 in. or 72 in.	Opening	125-220
To 15 tier	Seat	79-109	2 tier, 60 in. or 72 in. total	Opening	70-119
16-20 tier	Seat	160-195	5 tier, box lockers	Opening	40-60
21-30 tier	Seat	170-205	Locker bench, laminated maple top only	Linear feet	18.05
For power operation, add	Seat	30-48	Pedestals, steel pipe	Each	58
Gym divider curtain, mesh top			Sound system		
Manual roll-up	Square foot	9.25	Amplifier, 250 watts	Each	1650
Gym mats			Speaker, ceiling or wall	Each	145
2 in. naugahyde covered	Square foot	3.45	Trumpet	Each	271
2 in. nylon	Square foot	5.10	Emergency lighting, 25 watt, battery operated		
1 1/2 in. wall pads	Square foot	6.70	Lead battery	Each	289
1 in. wrestling mats	Square foot	4.62	Nickel cadmium	Each	655
Scoreboard					
Basketball, one side	Each	2750-17,300			
Basketball backstop					
Wall mounted, 6 in. extended, fixed	Each	1625-2125			
Swing up, wall mounted	Each	1825-2750			

Model Costs Calculated for a One-Story Building With 25-Foot Story Height and 20,000 Square Feet of Floor Area

			Unit	Unit cost	Cost per square foot	% of subtotal
1.0 Foundations						
.1	Footings and foundations	Poured concrete, strip and spread footings, and 4 in. foundation wall	Square foot ground	2.71	2.71	
.4	Piles and caissons	N/A	–	–	–	5.1%
.9	Excavation and backfill	Site preparation for slab and trench for foundation wall and footing	Square foot ground	1.08	1.08	
2.0 Substructure						
.1	Slab on grade	4 ft. reinforced concrete with vapor barrier and granular base	Square foot slab	3.32	3.32	4.5%
.2	Special substructures	N/A	–	–	–	

		Unit	Unit cost	Cost per square foot	% of subtotal
3.0 Superstructure					
.1	Columns and beams	N/A	–	–	–	
.4	Structural walls	N/A	–	–	–	18.3%
.5	Elevated floors	N/A	–	–	–	
.7	Roof	Wood deck on laminated wood arches	Square foot ground	13.51	13.51	
.9	Stairs	N/A	–	–	–	
4.0 Exterior Closure					
.1	Walls	Reinforced concrete block (end walls included) *90% of wall*	Square foot wall	8.61	5.81	
.5	Exterior wall finishes	N/A	–	–	–	11.4%
.6	Doors	Aluminum and glass, hollow metal, steel overhead	Each	1061	.32	
.7	Windows and glazed walls	Metal horizontal *10% of wall* pivoted	Each	302	2.27	
5.0 Roofing					
.1	Roof coverings	Ethylene propylene diene monomer (EPDM), 60 mils, fully adhered	Square foot ground	1.80	1.80	
.7	Insulation	Polyisocyanurate	–	1.14	1.17	4.0%
.8	Openings and specialities	N/A	–	–	–	
6.0 Interior Construction					
.1	Partitions	Concrete block, toilet partitions *50 square foot floor/linear feet partition*	Square foot partition	7.20	1.44	
.4	Interior doors	Single leaf hollow metal *500 square feet floor/door*	Each	534	1.07	
.5	Wall finishes	50% paint, 50% ceramic tile	Square foot surface	3.33	1.33	21.0%
.6	Floor finishes	90% hardwood, 10% ceramic tile	Square foot floor	9.72	9.72	
.7	Ceiling finishes	Mineral fiber tile on concealed zee bars *15% of area*	Square foot ceiling	3.63	.54	
.9	Interior surface/ exterior wall	Paint *90% of wall*	Square foot wall	2.12	1.43	

(continued)

(continued)

			Unit	Unit cost	Cost per square foot	% of subtotal
7.0 Conveying						
.1	Elevators	N/A	–	–	–	
.2	Special conveyors	N/A	–	–	–	0.0%
8.0 Mechanical						
.1	Plumbing	Toilet and service fixtures, supply and drainage *1 fixture/515 square feet floor*	Each	3182	6.18	
.2	Fire protection	Wet pipe sprinkler system	Square foot floor	1.69	1.69	23.2%
.3	Heating	Included in 8.4	–	–	–	
.4	Cooling	Single zone rooftop unit, gas heating, electric cooling	Square foot floor	9.26	9.26	
.5	Special systems	N/A	–	–	–	
9.0 Electrical						
.1	Service and distri-bution	400 ampere service, panel board and feeders	Square foot floor	.66	.66	
.2	Lighting and power	Fluorescent fixtures, receptacles, switches, A.C., and miscellaneous power	Square foot floor	5.99	5.99	11.0%
.4	Special electrical	Alarm systems, sound system, and emergency lighting	Square foot floor	1.45	1.45	
11.0 Special Construction						
.1	Specialties	Bleachers, sauna, weight room	Square foot floor	1.1	1.11	1.5%
12.0 Site Work						
.1	Earthwork	N/A	–	–	–	
.3	Utilities	N/A	–	–	–	0.0%
.5	Roads and park-ing	N/A	–	–	–	
.7	Site improvements	N/A	–	–	–	
			Subtotal	73.86		100%
		Contractor fees (general requirements: 10%; overhead: 5%; profit: 10%)	25%	18.47		
		Architect fees	7%	6.47		
			Total building cost	98.80		

Total Project Cost Estimation Form

1. Probable construction cost $30,000,000 _____

2. Design-related cost $3,000,000 _____

    Multiply line 1 by 0.1

3. Furniture, fixtures, and equipment $3,000,000 _____

    Multiply line 2 by 0.05 (normal), 0.1 (above average), or 0.15 (extensive)

4. Subtotal $36,000,000 _____

    Add lines 1,2 and 3

5. Contingencies $5,400,000 _____

    Multiply line 4 by 0.15

6. Total project costs $41,400,000 _____

    Add lines 4 and 5 (does not include financing, land acquisition, or other special costs)

- The cost per bleacher seat increased from $67-$78 in 1990 to $170-$205 in 2001.
- A swing-up, wall-mounted basketball backstop increased from $1,575-$2,350 per backboard to $1,825-$2,750.
- A wood deck roof increased from $10.76 to $13.51 per square foot.
- Floor finishing increased from $7.65 to $9.72 per square foot.
- The cost of paint more than doubled, from $0.71 to $1.43 per square foot.
- Plumbing increased from $4.15 to $6.80 per square foot.
- Cost of a single-zone rooftop unit, gas heating, and electric cooling system increased from $7.46 to $9.26 per square foot.
- Lighting and power-related construction increased from $4.01 to $5.99.

Some prices also declined. The cost per square foot of Naugahyde-covered gym mats decreased from $4.07 to $3.45. Some costs stayed the same:

For example, architect fees have stayed the same at 7% of the total construction costs, and contractors' fees have stayed the same at 15% (Balboni, 2001).

Construction-related expenses should include not only the cost for the facility itself but also all furniture, fixtures, and equipment. Design and start-up and move-in expenses such as the following should also be estimated:

- Freight, storage, delivery, and setup
- Office supplies, cleaning supplies, and day-to-day materials
- Maintenance supplies
- Advertising and communication costs
- Facility insurance
- A sinking fund for the replacement of building components that wear out

In an analysis of the total construction costs, a worksheet can help determine what the real costs may be for a given facility. A sample project is highlighted above. The hypothetical project

Common Pitfalls When Building a Facility

- Not contracting with an experienced sport architect or engineering (A-E) firm
- Not letting the designers know all the facts
- Allowing the A-E firm to interview and hire consultants
- Hiring a contractor who has never built a facility in the given market
- Failing to establish a hard budget
- Approving changes before they can be evaluated and costed
- Not monitoring work done by subcontractors
- Failing to have regular planning and progress meetings
- Failing to define requirements for documentation including punch lists
- Allowing politicians to get involved in the construction process
- Failing to have proper training before taking over the facility
- Failing to budget enough for contingencies

From Cotts and Lee, 1992.

is a $30 million arena. The $30 million project quickly escalates to a $41 million project when the design-related costs, FFE, and contingencies are added. This analysis helps highlight how certain projects can quickly get out of hand and why constant financial vigilance is required to avoid cost overruns.

Completion and Analysis

After the facility is constructed, it is not necessarily finished. A pre-final inspection is conducted with the general contractor, architects/engineers, owner, and possibly others to examine the quality of the construction. Any deficiencies are recorded on a **punch list.** A punch list can record small matters, such as a gap in a door or window frame or torn carpeting, that need to be addressed before the owner will take ownership of the building. After all these problems are corrected, a final inspection is completed. The architect/engineer accepts the project as final on behalf of the owner, and then the contractor submits a request for final payment.

Thereafter, the project needs to be finalized. This happens when as-built drawings and any operating and maintenance manuals are obtained, along with affidavits showing that all amounts

have been paid and there are no builder's liens against the property (Bentil, 1989).

This is when the project's overall success and cost can be analyzed. Whether or not a project was successful is largely subjective and is determined by many factors, including intermediate scheduling and completion dates, procedures, accidents or mistakes along the way, and of course the end result. The most common pitfalls of building a new facility are listed above.

Cost analysis is much more objective. Actual project costs can be assessed in terms of the budget, industry norms, and comparable facilities. While no two facilities are the same, some comparisons can be very beneficial. Table 6.5 presents the costs for two different sportsplexes.

These comparisons show that some facilities can be significantly more expensive than others based on a number of variables. The Illinois facility spent over $300,000 more on its design for three fields as compared to the six-field Arizona facility. The Illinois facility was significantly more expensive in terms of shrubs and trees, lighting, site mobilization, snack bars, and development fees. The Arizona facility was more expensive when it came to having to spend $100,000 to drill wells in the desert to help water the fields and for an administrative building.

Table 6.5 Cost Comparisons for Two Sportsplexes

Description	Six-field complex in Arizona		Three-field complex in Illinois	
	Actual cost	Average per field cost	Actual cost	Average per field cost
Engineering/Architectural plans	40,000	6,666.67	350,000	116,666.67
Site mobilization	140	23.33	122,938	40,979.33
Site grading and prep	65,480	10,913.33	166,367	55,455.67
Storm drains	0	0	71,632	23,877.33
Sewers	19,036	3,172.67	14,860	4,953.33
Water system	45,000	17,000.00	14,894	4,964.67
Underground cable	6,000	1,000.00	10,000	3,333.33
Well costs	100,000	16,667.67	5,000	1,667.67
Topsoil	6,000	1,000.00	24,000	8,000.00
Sod and soil	59,000	11,500.00	139,445	46,481.67
Shrubs/Trees	23,230	3,871.67	298,000	99,333.33
Path/Walls	66,100	11,016.67	72,000	24,000.00
Warning tracks	5,015	835.83	12,000	4,000
Area lighting	21,201	3,533.50	131,000	43,666.67
Sports lighting	185,000	30,833.33	220,000	73,333.33
Parking paving	101,450	16,908.33	100,000	33,333.33
Fencing	57,900	9,650.00	65,000	21,666.67
Scoreboards	15,000	2,500.00	22,000	7,333.33
Batting cages	48,890	8,148.33	63,775	21,268.33
Tot lot	27,785	4,630.83	62,542	20,247.33
Volleyball court	20,403	3,400.50	27,551	9,183.67
Basketball courts	0	0	88,223	29,407.67
Picnic area	11,772	1,962.00	5,000	1,666.67
Entryway	4,000	666.67	10,000	3,333.33
Snack bars	290,150	48,358.33	446,150	148,716.67
Trash enclosures	4,700	783.33	4,000	1,333.33
Maintenance shed	14,215	2,369.17	66,500	22,166.67
Admin building	300,000	50,000.00	13,750	4,583.33
BBQ area	25,000	4,166.67	3,000	1,000.00
Fees and permits	103	17.17	8,900	2,966.67
General conditions	10,950	1,825.00	109,000	36,333.33
Maintenance equipment	35,000	5,833.33	22,500	7,500.00
Concession equipment	65,000	10,833.33	40,000	13,333.33
Park furnishings	3,000	500.00	8,000	2,666.67
Computers	0	0	10,000	3,333.33
Video security/PA	17,000	2,833.33	6,000	2,000.00
Bleachers	10,600	1,766.67	20,000	6,666.67
Signage	2,900	483.33	6,000	2,000.00
Inventory and supplies	22,000	3,666.67	8,000	2,666.67

(continued)

Table 6.5 *(continued)*

Description	Six-field complex in Arizona		Three-field complex in Illinois	
	Actual cost	Average per field cost	Actual cost	Average per field cost
Pre-opening expenses	16,000	2,666.67	20,000	6,666.67
Legal/Accounting	8,500	1,416.67	30,000	10,000.00
Feasibility study	3,800	633.33	25,000	8,333.33
Development fees	144,600	24,100.00	225,000	75,000.00
Totals	$1,641,920	$273,653.33	$3,168,027	$1,056,009

Reprinted, by permission, from G. Fried, S.J. Shapiro, and T.D. DeShriver, 2003, *Sport finance* (Champaign, IL: Human Kinetics), 110.

Summary

For anyone who has seen a building go up from a flat piece of land, the experience can be moving. The creation process is more intense if someone has invested a significant amount of time and energy in designing the facility and obtaining necessary funding. The construction process is easier when it is possible simply to contact a construction company and have the company build a facility from plans. However, most larger facilities need to follow the bid process, which should lead to a competitive contract and a lower total price.

After a contract is entered into with a general contractor or another entity responsible for building the facility, the site needs to be prepared. Once the site is cleared, the foundation can be laid, followed by the substructure, superstructure, roof, flooring, FFE, and landscaping. Numerous issues arise throughout the construction process, often focusing on cost and quality. The element that completes a project is covered in the next chapter—systems that are installed within a facility.

DISCUSSION QUESTIONS AND ACTIVITIES

1. What material would you use to build a facility if you were concerned only with appearance (as opposed to price)?

2. Where can money be saved in construction of a facility?

3. Should a facility be built with a lot of glass windows? What are the pluses and minuses?

4. Travel to a construction site and observe what construction phase the facility is going through. Pay careful attention to the types of equipment and materials being used along with the number of people working at the site.

5. Develop a project completion timeline highlighting all the various steps seen from the time a facility is first conceived until the construction process is completed.

PART III

Facility Systems and Operations

SEVEN

Facility Systems

CHAPTER OBJECTIVES

After completing this chapter you will be able to do the following:

- Understand some of the ways in which the systems in a facility interact
- Appreciate the issues associated with heating, ventilation, and air conditioning systems
- Have knowledge about the importance of air quality and how it is maintained
- Characterize the energy systems used in a facility
- Know how the plumbing system delivers and extracts water
- Appreciate the various internal and external systems that help a facility function

Chapter 6 covered the building envelope and the process of building a facility, including all the necessary components. These components can encompass all the electrical wiring, fire suppression piping, phone and data lines, plumbing systems, the roof, the parking lot, and the all-important **heating, ventilation, and air conditioning (HVAC)** system.

The post-World War II era radically changed buildings. For example, more exterior glass, lighter construction, non-opening windows, and an emphasis on interior comforts changed the way facilities were managed (Carlson and DiGiandomenico, 1992). These new buildings required HVAC systems to ensure compliance with new ventilation codes and to provide a comfortable work environment.

This chapter critically examines the systems within a building—how they operate and strategies for maximizing their effectiveness. The first and foremost system within a building is the HVAC system. The HVAC system cannot operate without all the appropriate ductwork, electrical supply, and associated hardware. But even if all the mechanical elements are present, if the HVAC system is too noisy it can interrupt an event. Concert goers listening to an orchestra play a quiet piece in a quiet theater do not appreciate suddenly hearing the air conditioning system come on and begin to rattle.

Other systems covered in this chapter include lighting, plumbing, internal systems, and external systems. These systems are the soul of the building, and no building can work unless these systems are functioning properly. If the plumbing system malfunctions, spectators will be upset about the toilets or the lack of water. If a fire suppression system is not functioning, scores of deaths could be the result. Parking, an external system, allows people access to a facility, and can also be a source of revenue.

It should be noted that building automation systems have revolutionized the way systems operate. Systems can be programmed to turn on and off based on variables from the light level to the time or the number of people in a room. Furthermore, security systems based on an identification card, the iris of the eye, the voice, or thumbprints cannot work without a computer to analyze the information and compare it to information in a database. Older systems relied on information cards to track maintenance records. Now computer programs provide records for energy audits, material inventory, maintenance management programs, scheduling software, and numerous other applications. Thus, it is important to remember that the systems discussed in this chapter need to interact with an automated processing system to function effectively and maximize value while minimizing expenses.

Heating, Ventilation, and Air Conditioning

You have probably sat in your dorm room or apartment sweating on a hot summer day. You open the window to let air in, but there is no breeze and the room is still hot. You turn on the air conditioner, which cools the air. The air conditioner is a form of an HVAC system. An HVAC system is needed in every building since the building is designed to keep inside air inside and outside air outside, unless someone wants to interchange the air by opening a window or door. Otherwise, a building is designed to be "closed." But while it is nice to keep warm air inside during winter and warm air out during summer, this is difficult because of building structures (such as high ceilings that trap heat near the roof) or building materials that do not effectively prevent air and temperature transfer. Thus, electronic systems from vents to hot-water registers to air conditioners are used to keep a room or building at the desired temperature, move air around, and regulate the humidity level.

Air needs to be moved in and out of every building. One area that requires significant ventilation is the kitchen. Kitchen appliances such as deep fryers, ovens, and broilers produce a significant amount of heat that needs to be vented out of the area. In a facility, if the venting system can be run underneath seating areas, then some of the radiant heat can help warm the building. Incidentally, if the system is designed correctly, the smells from the kitchen can be pumped through the facility to help generate interest in purchasing food.

The HVAC system can contain numerous components, and each component needs to be critically analyzed to determine if changes or modifications are needed. An HVAC system typically accounts for 20% to 25% of a new facility's cost. Thus, significant time and effort need to be spent on maintaining the system so it operates effectively.

Heating

A building heating system utilizes an energy conversion process to create usable heat and a control system to distribute the heat. If conventional fuels such as coal, oil, or natural gas are used, the facility needs a heat plant to process the fuel into heat. Other heating options, such as city steam, do not require a heat plant. The fuel is transformed through a heat transference system to steam, warm air, or hot water that is pumped through the facility to generate heat.

Once the heat is generated in a heat plant, it is transferred to the building. One transference option is a warm-air transference system in which the warm air is pumped by means of ductwork through the same distribution system utilized by the air conditioning system. Hot-water transference systems utilize baseboard heaters or convectors, which are like car radiators. When cold air hits the tubes filled with hot water, the cooler air is warmed, thus warming the room. Steam-heating transference systems are similar to hot-water systems, but steam is pumped through the pipes rather than hot water. Steam systems utilize radiators that are similar to the convectors for hot water but are exposed directly to the air in the room; convectors normally are covered to prevent burns.

Once the fuel is transferred to heat and the heat is transferred to the proper location, a heat control network dictates where the heat will actually go. The heat control network is usually governed by a thermostat, which measures the temperature and

Temperature Impact on Facility Users

Age: Older patrons prefer warmer temperatures compared to younger patrons.

Gender: Women prefer warmer climates than men.

Activity level: Those engaged in working activities prefer cooler temperatures versus those who are just sitting, who prefer warmer temperatures.

From Borsenik and Stutts, 1997.

its location and compares these results to predetermined temperature settings. Computers are also being utilized to monitor room temperature and provide more efficient heat distribution.

Cooling

The most popular cooling system is a vapor compression system. The heart and soul of this system is the refrigerant, which starts absorbing heat when it boils. Besides a refrigerant, the vapor compression system requires an evaporator, a compressor, a condenser, and an expansion device. These elements are typically integrated into one or two units. However, such a system is classified not as an air conditioning system but as an air chilling system. Other air chilling systems operate similarly to heat radiator systems except that cold water is pumped to radiators and the surrounding hot air is chilled. No matter what system is used, the intent is to reach an ideal air temperature.

Some people prefer a hot environment while others like it cooler (facts about temperature impact on facility users are shown above). The HVAC system should be designed to automatically maintain an appropriate temperature and humidity level. Most people consider 64.4° to 77° F (18°-25° C) a comfortable and pleasant temperature, and 30% to 60% is the preferred humidity level (Immig and Rish, 1997). The ideal range is a warm environment between 65° and 75° F (18.3°-23.9° C); the American College of Sports Medicine (ACSM, 1992) recommends a temperature range of 68° to 72° F (20°-22.2° C). These numbers are not standards, just recommended ideals.

Another major concept that affects air conditioning is humidity. A high relative humidity means that the amount of moisture in the air is high. Humidity is especially important in sport as it affects the amount of heat produced by an athlete and the ability of air to absorb moisture from the body. If the humidity level is over 80%, the ability of air to absorb moisture from the body is reduced and an athlete will sweat more. That is why people tend to sweat much more when competing in humid summer air than when they work out at the same intensity in lower humidity. The ACSM recommends a humidity level below 60%, but this level is very hard to achieve even in some air-conditioned buildings.

Cooling effectiveness is influenced by the occupant **heat load.** The heat load is affected by two factors—the number of people in a facility and their activity. If a large number of people are jumping around and producing heat, the air conditioning system must work harder to compensate for the added heat they are generating. In addition to occupants, appliances such as stoves also produce a heat load.

Ventilation

It is estimated that people in industrialized countries on average spend 70% to 90% of their time indoors (Immig and Rish, 1997). Ventilation helps produce better air quality by extracting older air and replacing it with new air. The ACSM recommends 8 to 12 **air exchanges** per hour in a gymnasium, which can be accomplished with several large ceiling fans. Most facilities utilize multiple intake and exhaust locations to circulate the air appropriately. For example, a central ventilation system for a building draws from every corner of a room and possibly returns the air from a center location.

Behind the Scenes: Calculating Air Exchange

© Human Kinetics

The ACSM recommends 8 to 12 air exchanges per hour in a gymnasium. To calculate the appropriate ventilation rate, the volume of space (length × height × width) needs to be determined. This number then can be compared with the amount of air handled by the air exchange medium such as exhaust fans. If an exhaust fan can pump out 20,000 cubic feet (570 cubic meters) per minute (cfm), it can achieve an air exchange every six minutes in a 120,000-cubic-foot (3,400-cubic-meter) building. This can be extrapolated to 10 air exchanges per hour. Another way to calculate the ventilation rate is to use the room floor area. Some building codes require 0.5 to 12 cubic feet (0.014-0.3 cubic meters) of air per minute per square foot of floor space. A third method depends on the number of people using a building (900 to 1,200 cubic feet [25-34 cubic meters] of air per hour for each occupant is the standard according to the American Society of Heating, Refrigeration, and Air Conditioning) (Borsenik and Stutts, 1997).

A large arena may not need the recommended number of air exchanges per hour when very few people are present. However, if there are 20,000 people in the building, numerous air exchanges are needed to keep the air from being stuffy. This is especially true if many persons are smoking (now prohibited in many states) or if a lot of carbon monoxide is being produced (e.g., by Zambonis in hockey; in fumes pumped out by monster trucks). Assume that a room can hold 100 people and that the ventilation rate is 10 cubic feet (0.3 cubic meters) per minute per person. Multiplying the number of people by the ventilation rate (100 people × 10 cubic feet) produces the preferred ventilation rate of 1,000 cubic feet (28 cubic meters) per minute for the room. The following calculation from an actual gym helps highlight the process of calculating appropriate air exchanges.

The gym, located in the South (where heat and humidity are high), measures 102 by 72 by 23 feet (31 by 22 by 7 meters). Thus it measures 7,344 linear feet (2,240 meters) and 168,912 cubic feet (4,780 cubic meters). The gym has four roof vents, each with a cfm rating of 17,000. Calculating for eight air exchanges per hour, the numbers are as follows: 168,912 × 8 exchanges per hour = 1,351,296 cubic feet (38,264 cubic meters) that need to be exchanged per hour / 60 minutes in an hour = 22,521.6 cfm. This standard can be met easily if two fans are on. Calculating for 12 air exchanges per hour, the numbers are as follows: 168,912 × 12 exchanges per hour = 2,026,944 / 60 minutes = 33,782.4.6 cfm. This standard can be met if two fans are on (34,000 cfm) and is greatly exceeded when all four fans are on (68,000 cfm). Thus, the ACSM-recommended air exchange ratio can be met if two ceiling exhaust fans are used and can be increased even more if all four fans are operating.

Air Quality

Air quality has various meanings. Some people prefer the term "air environment" as a broader term that includes air, temperature, humidity, and ventilation rate. However, these factors do not necessarily affect air quality. External air quality cannot be managed the same way as indoor air quality. Thus, if a stadium is 1 mile from a dump, it may be safe on some days, but on windy days the smell may be horrendous. Air quality can be influenced by the following:

- Smells (which can be caused by any of the following)
- Chemicals (volatile organic compounds, pesticides, cigarette smoke, carbon monoxide, and nitrogen dioxide)
- Biological elements (molds, fungi, microorganisms, and dust mites)
- Physical components/pollutants (dust, radiation, radon, respirable particles, electromagnetic fields) (Immig and Rish, 1997)

A variety of factors can also influence indoor air quality (IAQ), which refers to the nature of air that affects the health and well-being of a facility's occupants:

- External variables including climate, water infiltration, and ventilation and infiltration of outdoor air
- Building- and HVAC-related factors such as building design; structural materials; and HVAC design, operations, and materials
- Internal variables such as interior design, building materials (paints, sealants, adhesives, carpets, etc.), furnishings, equipment, occupant activities, pest management, cleaning agents, and any internal construction or renovation (Immig and Rish, 1997)

Air quality is such a major issue that the Sydney Olympic facilities used a 56-page document specifying IAQ guidelines that was developed by a group called Green Games Watch 2000. These were some of the recommendations:

- Indoor air quality needs to be considered in all facility design.
- Operating manuals should be developed for all facilities to help maintain good IAQ.

- Facilities should use foliage plants with known capacity to absorb indoor air pollutants.
- Air quality should be managed through selecting building materials that do not emit harmful levels of pollutants, can be easily cleaned with benign cleaners, do not emit harmful levels of radiation, and are resistant to microorganisms such as bacteria, mold, and dust mites.
- Construction should be completed with sufficient time to have the new buildings dissipate any volatile constituents (Immig and Rish, 1997).

One of the greatest concerns about IAQ involves ice arenas. The arenas themselves are not the biggest problem, even though new "airtight" buildings minimize the amount of passive ventilation in a building and temperatures are kept lower to reduce the cooling costs. The problem is with the resurfacers (often called Zambonis). In a study of 19 rinks, those with propane- and gas-powered resurfacers showed a much greater likelihood of having a dangerous level of nitrogen dioxide. At one rink the level was 4,000 parts per billion, which was 36 times the recommended maximum exposure ("Breath of Not-So-Fresh Air," 1999). Three states, Massachusetts, Minnesota, and Rhode Island, have standard air quality requirements for ice rinks. Electric resurfacers produce much less nitrogen dioxide but cost about $20,000 more than other resurfacers.

Chemicals in the air are nothing new for sport facilities. Casinos are known for pumping fresh

Though entertaining to watch, Zambonis can produce dangerously high levels of nitrogen dioxide or carbon monoxide.

air or pure oxygen in to keep people awake. Some sport facilities take the opposite approach when they anticipate rowdy crowds. Thus, at a monster truck pull or motocross event where the crowd could be rowdy, an arena may slow down the ventilation to keep the carbon monoxide levels high, which makes the fans sleepier and more lethargic and thus lowers risk. During concerts the same technique can be used to recirculate the existing air rather than bringing in new air so that the marijuana smoke filters throughout the building. This has the effect of mellowing the crowd and can also help increase food sales. Any such strategies need to be used with caution to avoid violating Occupational Safety and Health Administration or other standards and causing illness. These steps are also affected by new laws that are being passed regarding smoking in public places and the ways in which a facility needs to respond when fans smoke. Thus, ventilation can involve numerous legal and ethical issues.

As stated earlier, buildings have been built to be "closed." To reduce the loss of hot air, buildings have been designed to limit the amount of natural or passive ventilation. This reduces the air exchanges that occur naturally and makes it necessary to increase the number of air exchanges to ventilate the building. To improve air quality, maximizing air ventilation is more important than maximizing air circulation (Immig and Rish, 1997).

While there is no magic recipe for improving IAQ, strategies include building with the right materials, removing harmful materials or restricting access to harmful areas, limiting the use of certain pesticides, installing localized exhaust systems, and diluting the environment through more aggressive ventilation (Immig and Rish, 1997).

Air Temperature

The "ideal" temperature, if there can be an ideal temperature, was established in the 1970s at 72° to 75° F (22.2°-23.9° C). However, as energy costs have risen, the ideal building temperature has declined to 68° F (20° C). Is there an ideal temperature for sport facilities? Some people like to work out in a cooler environment, while spectators might leave if a gym or stadium is too cold. As mentioned earlier, most people consider 64.4° to 77° F (18°-25° C) a comfortable and pleasant temperature (Immig and Rish, 1997).

Energy Systems

Energy, especially electric energy, is indispensable for sport facilities with all their lights, cooking equipment, electronic scoreboards, and so on. Approximately 67% of the energy used in larger office buildings is electrical energy (Carlson and DiGiandomenico, 1992). Large sport facilities typically consume the same amount of energy during game days with use of all the electronic devices, though they use much less electricity when the facility is not putting on an event. Of the total amount of electricity used in a typical building, 40% is used by the cooling system, 33% for lighting, and 12% for heating. By analyzing where and how energy is utilized, a facility can take specific steps to reduce expenses. For example, alternate cooling and air movement strategies need to be implemented to reduce HVAC costs. Furthermore, while lighting costs account for 33% of a building's electrical costs, most buildings are unoccupied 72% of the time (Carlson and DiGiandomenico, 1992).

A watt is a measure of electrical energy used. Higher-watt appliances utilize more energy than lower-watt appliances. Electricity is billed in kilowatt-hours (a kilowatt is 1,000 watts), which represents the energy consumption rate. Thus, a room with five 200-watt light fixtures turned on is using 1,000 watt-hours, which equals 1 kilowatt-hour.

Backup generators are critical for life safety systems in a sport facility. With possibly over 100,000 people in a public assembly facility, what happens if the power goes out? Backup energy is required for lighting and sound systems so exit instructions can be broadcast over loudspeakers or on the scoreboard. A backup generator may also be required to maintain the HVAC systems to keep ventilating the building or remove harmful smoke from certain areas.

Lighting

What impact does poor lighting have on people? In sport, lighting is crucial for seeing the action on the field during a night game, seeing the action on the ice or court in an arena, or seeing weights being lifted. Facility managers need to be concerned with both indoor and outdoor lighting. For sport facilities, **ambient lighting,** or atmosphere lighting, refers to actual sunlight. In other words, both indoor and outdoor facilities utilize ambient

Foot-Candle Requirements at Various Sport Surfaces

These are the recommended numbers when a system is installed:

Baseball	50-150 foot-candles in the infield; 30-100 foot-candles in the outfield
Basketball	60-100 foot-candles
Football	50-100 foot-candles
Hockey	40-80 foot-candles from youth to college competition
Soccer	50-75 foot-candles
Softball	30-50 foot-candles in the infield; 20-30 foot-candles in the outfield
Swimming pool	50-100 foot-candles
Tennis	40-70 foot-candles
Track	50 foot-candles

From Fried, 1999.

lighting. The Houston Astrodome, for example, was originally built with glass panes in the dome to allow sun into the facility to help the grass grow. However, the glare from the sun made it very difficult to field balls, which led management to paint the glass and install Astroturf.

Before detailing the specific types of lighting at facilities, some general explanation of lighting terminology is in order. A lamp refers to any source of light, whether a candle, flashlight, torch, or spotlight. The output produced by any lamp is measured as lumens. A lumen is a quantity of light and represents the amount of light energy that strikes a specific distance from the light source. If 1 lumen falls a distance 1 foot (0.3 meters) from the light source (called a standard candle), the light intensity is called 1 foot-candle of light intensity. The further one moves away from the light source, the larger the area that the lumens are spread over, so light intensity decreases. **Light intensity** is measured by the foot-candles at the playing surface (Borsenik and Stutts, 1997). Foot-candle requirements for various sport surfaces are highlighted above. These numbers are the recommended numbers when a system is installed; changes can occur as a result of wind movement and burned-out lamps, for example, which requires facility managers to be vigilant with light maintenance.

Indoor Lighting

Lighting can be provided by various means, such as windows that let in natural ambient light, gas lanterns, and light bulbs. Light sources can be placed in different locations from the ceiling to the floor. The exact location depends on style and how strong the light needs to be. The optimal light strength and direction also depend on the particular activity. For example, badminton is best played with darker-colored walls to help with seeing the shuttlecock. However, play can be enhanced either through the use of indirect lights all over the court or through strategic placement of direct lights around the court's outer boundaries to help prevent losing shuttles in the light.

Direct lighting is light that is directed downward from a fixture. **Indirect lighting** from ceiling fixtures focuses the light against the ceiling so that 90% of the light energy is reflected back to the floor from the ceiling. In contrast, **diffuse lighting** reflects only 40% to 60% of the light energy back from the ceiling to the ground, and semi-direct lighting reflects 60% to 90% of the light back to the floor. Semi-indirect lighting bounces back only 10% to 40% of the light from the ceiling to the floor, with the remaining percentage being direct light to the ground (Borsenik and Stutts, 1997).

The key to any indoor lighting system is to have the proper light, directed at the proper spots, and replaced at regular intervals. Table 7.1 shows differences between three types of indoor systems and the impact associated with direct versus indirect lighting.

The fact that a system is cheaper to install does not mean that the system will be less expensive in the long run. Incandescent lamps typically last for 1,000 hours. If such a lamp is in an office and the office light is on 10 hours per day, four days

135

Table 7.1 Direct Versus Indirect Lighting Systems

Category	Systems		
	Direct	Inverted high bay	Asymmetric indirect
Wattage	400	1,000	1,000
Number of fixtures	40	20	20
Cost to install (estimate)	$13,920	$10,600	$30,000
Energy use* (kilowatts/year)	92,160	115,200	115,200
Annual energy cost	$3,926	$4,907	$4,907

* Based on lights being on 16 hours a day, seven days a week for 12 months.
From Brooks and Martinez, 2002.

a week, for an average of 4.33 weeks per month, the light will be on 173 ($10 \times 4 \times 4.33$) hours a month. By dividing the expected life by the hours per month ($1,000 / 173$), one can determine that a typical incandescent lamp in that office will last 5.8 months (Borsenik and Stutts, 1997). A fluorescent lamp typically lasts for about 6,000 hours. Knowing the lamp's life expectancy is especially critical for lamps above a gym floor that may be 30 feet (9 meters) in the air. In order to change the lamps the facility must rent or buy an expensive hoist system.

Rigging

Indoor lighting is normally suspended from the ceiling. Lights, scoreboards, and sound systems cannot merely be attached to the roof or substructure. The entire system utilized to suspend items from a facility's roof is called **rigging**. The key variable for rigging is the load capacity. Load capacity refers to how much weight the system can support. For example, a given beam may be able to support 5,000 pounds (2,270 kilograms) at its center point or 10,000 pounds (4,535 kilograms) across its whole length. Besides weight loads, riggers need to understand weight limits, forces, geometry, the strength of rigging equipment, safety concerns, and dynamic loading (Donovan, 1994). All these aspects are associated with one overriding concern: safety. Rigging strength can be significantly reduced by age, wear, heat, fatigue, chemical exposure, and the impact force can play on the rigging gear (Donovan, 1994). On the basis of these dynamics, the rigging can help determine what lighting system may be installed in a facility.

External Lighting

In 1883, General Electric installed open-face lights across a minor league field and created what some consider the first night ball game (Steinbach, 2001b). Others claim that the first night game took place in 1924 and that the first professional night game was held in 1935 at Crosley Field in Cincinnati (Lindstrom, 1993). Lighting an athletic facility is not as simple as mounting high-powered lights on towering posts and aiming them at the surface. There are various factors to weigh when one considers lighting in terms of the actual light, the structures, and the electrical devices needed.

Quantity and Quality

An effective indoor and outdoor sport lighting system is measured by both the quantity and the quality of the lights. The proper quantity, or level, of lights differs according to the level of play, and is measured according to initial and maintained foot-candles (Rogers, 1994). Initial foot-candles relates to the amount of light produced with a new system; maintained foot-candles is the light level in an older system that has been running for a while.

The quality of lighting is measured by the uniformity or evenness of light on the field. Poor light uniformity poses a threat to player safety and often detracts from spectator enjoyment. Lighting that is uneven causes the movement of players from light areas to dark areas to appear as if it is changing speeds, making the action hard to follow (Rogers, 1994).

Besides cost, one of the biggest problems with any external lighting system has to do with light leaving the intended area through glare, trespass, and sky glow (Steinbach, 2001a). **Glare** refers to light that is hard on the viewer's eyes. Glare can also be defined as a point of very bright light. This problem can come from too much light or uneven light on a field. **Trespass** involves light that was intended to go into one area but also enters into another area. Trespass is often referred to as spill (light is spilling from the intended area). The last term, sky glow, represents light that is directed or reflected upward and is wasted in space. Sky glow can be seen as an orange haze over a city when one is flying in a plane at night. These problems can be minimized with fixed visors, internal louvers, soft lighting systems, and faceted reflectors.

Structural Considerations

The two structural components of an outdoor lighting system are the luminaire assemblies and the poles. The luminaire assembly, which consists of the lamps, reflectors, ballast mounting, crossarm, and mounting hardware, should be engineered as a single integral unit. The unit is installed and positioned by field aiming, which entails creating a grid on the playing surface with strings and flags and then targeting each light fixture to a point on the grid. After all the alignments are completed, light levels are measured and workers lock each light into place.

The poles used for a lighting system can be made of wood, concrete, or steel. Wood poles are the least expensive to purchase and install but have high maintenance costs due to warping and twisting from exposure to the elements. Concrete poles are less expensive than steel poles and can be buried directly into the ground. Concrete poles are often found on the coast, where sea salt can cause extensive damage to steel. Steel poles have a long life, cost little to maintain, and are aesthetically pleasing. New steel poles are being developed that can be raised and lowered by means of a motorized mechanism. This process can reduce costs by making it cheaper to replace lamps, and the poles can be lowered before a major storm.

Energy Usage

One of the key elements to managing any system within a facility is tracking usage and expenses. If certain systems cost more to operate than they should, they should be replaced. A refrigerator that runs continually can cost several hundred dollars more per year than a cycling unit. The largest energy expense for any facility, 50% of total energy cost, originates from the kitchen. The greatest single energy use within a kitchen comes from cooking, followed by equipment and lighting (Borsenik and Stutts, 1997).

An **energy audit** examines where energy usage and energy losses are coming from. Assume that a facility uses 1,000 bulbs that are 100 watts each. The energy consumption from these lights will be 100,000 watts (100 $\times$ 1,000). The audit can help identify the cost associated with such energy usage and then be used to propose acceptable alternatives. If the facility could use 75-watt bulbs in place of the 100-watt bulbs with no appreciable difference in lighting, there could be a significant savings. The 75-watt bulbs would produce 75,000 watts of energy consumption, which is a 25% reduction in energy expenses. Furthermore, it might be feasible to reduce the hours used from 10 to 7 hours per day, which would also represent a significant savings (30%).

Energy Conservation

After the audit, an energy program needs to be developed. The first phase entails trying to establish a specific goal. For example, a facility manager could plan to reduce energy consumption 10%. If the facility has a zoned HVAC system, the temperature setting in unoccupied offices could be reduced to 55° F (12.8° C) during the heating season and allowed to reach 85° F (29.4° C) during the cooling season (Borsenik and Stutts, 1997). Another usage strategy is to limit water consumption by guests. Rest rooms in stadiums and arenas often have built-in sensors on toilets, urinals, and faucets to reduce the total amount of water used. Other energy reduction strategies include replacing windows and caulking; installing time clock and motion detection systems to automatically open and close appliances; installing load-cycling systems that monitor electrical usage and turn devices on and off in a cyclical manner to save energy and reduce costs; and using a computer energy control system that can cycle loads, control demand, and reduce total energy consumption.

It should be noted that some energy conservation ideas cannot be implemented. For example, the water temperature cannot be reduced in dishwashing units if the minimum temperature to ensure killing germs is already set by a government agency.

Facility Focus: Bryant College Energy Savings

Courtesy of Bryant University Sports Information.

Savings can be substantial for certain renovation projects, but long-term financial analysis needs to be performed. Some modifications can reduce energy consumption by $1,000 annually; but if it costs $100,000 to make the modification, then the project should not be undertaken. The following is an example of a successful renovation project that saved significant energy consumption and costs. The parking lot at Bryant College in Rhode Island used 32 mercury vapor fixtures, 400 watts each, mounted on eight 30-foot (9-meter) poles. Because of the poor lighting in the location, there were five auto accidents annually and a dozen break-ins. The school replaced the lights with eight 1,000-watt high-pressure sodium fixtures. The new fixtures cut the operating and maintenance costs by 45%, which saved the college $3,000 annually. Just as important as the cost savings, the parking lot became safer and this saved the college $6,000 annually in claims payouts. Thus, a $12,000 investment in new fixtures paid for itself in about 16 months (Sanders, 1998).

Plumbing

Plumbing systems help transport water and waste from one area to another. Plumbing systems are critical in sport facilities for rest rooms, kitchens, and showering areas. The first question to raise with plumbing systems concerns the amount of water pressure necessary to lift water to the highest plumbing fixture. If drinking fountains are on the fifth floor of a stadium, there needs to be enough pressure for the water to rise from below street level to the fifth floor. Otherwise the fixture will not work. If there is not enough water pressure, a water-circulating pump must be used to get the water to reach the fifth floor.

The plumbing system is highly technical. For example, if one pipe is feeding five toilets, 35 gallons per minute (GPM) of water pressure is needed, which would require a 1.5-inch (3.8-centimeter) feeder pipe. If the facility has 20 toilets all connected to the same pipe, the pipe has to be 2 inches (5 centimeters) (Borsenik and Stutts, 1997).

Wastewater Systems

Within the miles of plumbing in a large stadium or arena, a large proportion is for water that is going to fixtures for waste removal. Maintenance concerns include inspections of the traps and vents. A trap is a U-shaped pipe under a fixture that contains a certain amount of water; its purpose is to allow water to drain from the fixture but prevent sewer gases from entering the building. Vents allow air to circulate within the drainage system to prevent wastes from coming up through the traps. Besides making sure traps and vents operate effectively, facilities must make every effort to prevent clogging of toilets, which is a major concern and a turnoff for customers. The toilets need to be inspected on a regular basis; maintenance workers should have access to augers, rods, and snakes so that they can unclog a toilet quickly.

In addition to removing wastewater to sewer systems, water recycling can be used to remove wastewater, especially during drought conditions. Thus, it may be possible to recycle shower water for use in watering plants. In addition to its uses for drinking, showering, and food preparation, water is required for other systems that may not ever be used, such as fire suppression systems.

Fire Suppression Systems

Most people do not think about fire safety as a plumbing issue. However, putting out fires effectively requires more than fire extinguishers and axes. Some compound must be delivered to the fire location, and these compounds are transported through plumbing systems. The average financial loss in a facility ravaged by fire without a sprinkler system is $2.2 million versus only $0.4 million for buildings with sprinklers ("Understanding the Hazard," 2000). Furthermore, a fire causing over $1 million in damages occurs every 31 days for facilities without sprinklers versus 152 days for facilities with sprinklers. While these numbers are impressive, the cost to obtain such protection is only $1.5 to $3 per square foot.

There have been a number of sport facility fires over the years; some have killed over 100 fans (*Society of Fire Protection Engineers*, 2002). Fire risks have decreased as a result of facility construction techniques. At the turn of the century, most baseball stadiums were destroyed by fire since they were made of wood. With the modern concrete structures (which are not a fuel for fire), it is harder for a fire to thrive but still possible. In the 9/11 tragedy, the twin towers, primarily made of concrete and steel, were still burning several weeks after the attacks.

The first step in fire prevention entails developing strategies that minimize the potential for fires. That involves asking the following questions:

- Does the facility comply with all appropriate codes and industry standards?
- Are the various fire-alert and suppression systems adequate?

- Are hazardous chemicals or compounds isolated?
- Are there safe escape routes and exits?
- Are employees trained in responding to various fires?
- Are there annual fire suppression tests?
- Have the fire and carbon monoxide alarms been tested in the prior three months?

Another step is to determine where there are potential fire hazards. Most fires originate in the kitchen area, from cooked food or hot cooking appliances. Fires can also start in equipment rooms where torches may be used to repair or improve equipment (e.g., waxing hockey sticks) or in places where combustible material like old boxes is stored, such as the bottom of stairwells. In fact, one of the deadliest fires of all time in a sport stadium occurred when trash that had been accumulating for years caught on fire at a soccer game. On May 11, 1985, at Bradford's soccer stadium in England, 56 fans burned to death and 200 were injured when fire engulfed the grandstands ("Sport Disasters," 2003). The 10 most frequent causes of fire are listed below.

Armed with a good understanding of the potential hazards, facility managers can start the process of developing fire prevention strategies. These strategies can entail facility-related steps such as properly housing flammable liquids and combustible materials and training employees

Ten Most Frequent Causes of Fire

Activity	Percent of fires caused
Electrical problems	26.1
Hot work	19.9
Hot surface/radiant heat	11
Arson/incendiary	10.5
Exposure from off-site hazards	5.4
Smoking	5.1
Spontaneous ignition	4.2
Friction	4.1
Overheating of equipment	3.4
Burner flame	1.8

on the proper response to fires. One of the most important steps in fire prevention training is conducting mock drills. If a facility is housing 15,000 for an event, the facility manager needs to conduct large-scale fire simulation exercises to effectively train employees and give local emergency officials the chance to learn about the facility.

The next step is to have proper alarm systems. A fixed-temperature detector identifies when the temperature around the alarm is at a predetermined point and then signals an alarm or triggers a suppression system. A rate-of-temperature-rise detector is triggered when the temperature increases a preset amount in a given time period (such as 15° F in 30 seconds). Some alarms are designed to identify smoke rather than heat. Besides having the proper alarm/detection devices, it is essential that devices be placed in the right areas and then maintained. A typical smoke detector unit covers 900 square feet (84 square meters) and should not be more than 35 feet (10.6 meters) from the next detector. Detectors also should not be placed in high-humidity areas or where there is excessive air current (Borsenik and Stutts, 1997). Other options include flame detector alarm systems and manual pull alarms. Regardless of the system used, fire codes require all such devices and control systems (fire panel) to be inspected and tested yearly. Once an audit has been conducted and the proper alarm system developed, a fire suppression system must be installed.

The following are the types of fire suppression systems that can be used in a facility.

- Wet-pipe sprinkler systems are always filled with water that is ready to flow onto a fire when the sprinkler head is triggered.

- Dry-pipe sprinkler systems are used in cold weather where water freezing is a problem. In these systems the pipes are filled with air, which is released when the sprinkler is triggered. The released air triggers a valve that releases water into the pipes.

- Deluge sprinkler systems are similar to dry-pipe systems in that there is no water in any of the pipes. However, all the sprinkler heads are open; and if there is a fire, the system triggers a flow of water out of all the sprinklers. These systems can cause significant water damage, since a typical sprinkler set at 15 pounds (6.8 kilograms) per square inch will distribute 22 gallons per minute (which can cover a 16-foot [4.9-meter] radius).

- Pre-action systems utilize a timed delay to allow putting a fire out with suppression agents before the water flows into the dry-pipe system. This system is used in areas such as computer rooms or accounting offices where water can cause substantial damage.

- Misting/Fogging systems suppress a fire by spraying a mist from the sprinkler.

- Standpipe/Hose systems are required in addition to sprinkler systems. These large pipes, often seen on the outside of large buildings, are like fire hydrants. A fire department can attach fire hoses to these pipes and start pumping water.

- Chemical systems use carbon dioxide, Halon replacement, and dry chemicals instead of water. These systems are critical for handling class B (flammable liquid) and class C (electrical) fires. Dry chemicals can cause significant damage to electrical connectors, so such a system is appropriate around a kitchen, but not a computer room (Borsenik and Stutts, 1997).

A last concern about fire is the fact that often the smoke from a fire causes more harm than the fire itself. The building should be designed to funnel smoke outside, and all building codes related to fire suppression must be properly followed (e.g., separation of elevator lobbies from corridors).

Laundry System

Every facility produces laundry. High school, college, and professional teams need to wash towels, jerseys, physical education apparel, and other items almost daily. Health clubs that offer towels to their members may have their own laundering system or may outsource to a private company for all laundry work. The proper laundering of athletic apparel depends on having a functional laundry room, maintaining the laundry room, and maintaining the equipment.

The equipment needs for a laundering facility vary depending on the amount of apparel that requires laundering. High schools and small colleges generally require only one or two 50-pound (22.7-kilogram) washers and 75-pound (34-kilogram) dryers, while larger universities require as many as 10 of each (Mundt, 1997). Laundry facilities should use microprocessor-controlled washing machines that allow the user to specify fabric-appropriate cycles, spin speed, and water extraction levels. It should be noted that some facilities forgo having a laundry system by utilizing linen rental services, commercial laundries, or even disposable linens.

Interior Systems

Interior systems can range from carpeting and floor tiling to video and audio systems. These systems are designed to enhance the overall facility experience. If seats are not comfortable a fan will not want to come back. If carpeting is not provided between a locker room and a pool, patrons may have to walk on cold and possibly slippery tiles and may not be as comfortable. This section focuses on some of the important systems that are often overlooked: audiovisual and sound-related systems, broadcasting data networks, and personal transportation systems.

Audiovisual Systems

Fans would not appreciate going to a game where they could not see the scoreboard. Health club members would not appreciate an aerobics room where the music was too loud. One of the most visible components of any audiovisual system is the scoreboard. Scoreboards started out as manual communication devices with people moving the numbers by hand. The electronic age has produced magnificent scoreboards costing millions of dollars and providing a plethora of sights and sounds.

Jumbotrons, which can show live action and instant replays, are common features in stadiums and facilities.

The first color display was installed at Arrowhead Stadium in Kansas City, Missouri, at a cost of $1 million in 1972. In 1986 Sony introduced its Jumbotron. Today's systems utilize light-emitting diodes (LEDs), which have bright colors and can also last up to 50,000 hours. New technological advances are expected for displays, including organic LED (OLED) and field emissive displays (FED), which have excellent resolution and are also cheaper to manufacture (Pihos, 2001).

Similar to the sound system in an aerobics room, the sound system utilized for large stadiums and arenas has to produce enough sound at an appropriate level of quality with as little noise interference as possible. The sound system at the National Stadium in the National Sports Complex in Malaysia, which was completed in 1998 at a cost of $220 million (U.S.), included 190 amplifiers, 220 loudspeakers, and 700 ceiling speakers (Whelan, 2001). The **front-of-the-house** loudspeakers had to be suspended from the membrane roof, which had only one access point. The distance from the control room to these loudspeakers was almost 1 mile (1.6 kilometers). To improve sound to the lower bowl, 64 additional loudspeakers were installed under the second tier (Whelan, 2001). The system also was installed with eight horns attached to eight amplifiers and battery backup units in case of an emergency.

The system was connected through fiber optic cables to help transmit the converted analog audio signal to the preferable digital form. These cables were fed into the control room, which housed a 16-channel, eight-bus mixing console. Since sound in the stadium changes based on **ambient sound** created by the fans, the system included automation that kept the broadcast sound at a predetermined level above the noise created by the fans. As this example highlights, sound systems can be very complex, and a qualified sound technician is critical for ensuring sound quality.

Sound Control

Recreation activity sounds are caused by normal facility use and are unavoidable. Mechanical sounds, on the other hand, are the sounds produced by the machinery on which the facility operates and hence are avoidable; they can be controlled if properly planned for in the design phase. Recreation activity sounds consist of both **airborne sound** and **structure-borne sound,** each with different transmission mechanisms that lead to different control strategies. Airborne sounds are primarily the sounds caused by facility users, such as those from voices, music, whistles, and cheers; structure-borne sounds, or impact sounds, are those caused primarily by direct impact with some part of the facility's structure. A basketball player's foot hitting the floor while the player is cutting to the basket creates both air- and structure-borne sounds. The airborne sound is the sound of the screech of the player's sneaker, while the structure-borne sound comes from the direct contact of the player's foot with the floor.

Structure-borne sound is much more difficult to control given the fact that it vibrates and is transmitted to the air. Consider a bouncing basketball as an example. The sound caused by the basketball vibrates off the floor and is transmitted to the air, where it spreads in the form of a dull thud. Additional structure-borne sounds can come from mechanical systems, the plumbing system, electromechanical systems (HVAC), and external factors such as traffic or construction. If a building has single-pane glass windows, external sound will be freely transmitted inside. However, thermal windows will significantly reduce a sound path into the building.

Noise control can be achieved through sound absorption, which involves decreasing echoes and reverberation within a space through the control of airborne sound transmission with doors, ceiling tiles, and so on, as well as through the control of impact or structure-borne sounds. Airborne sounds travel through the air with relative ease but are effectively muted by solid barriers. Because airborne sounds travel through the air as compression waves, they will reflect off of hard surfaces such as concrete or wood but can be absorbed by resilient material such as fiberglass insulation or acoustic tile. A solid partition, if it provides complete separation with no "leaks," can also effectively isolate airborne sound (Whitney and Foulkes, 1994). This is especially critical for adjacent areas such as offices next to a gym.

Broadcasting

While many professional sport teams make money from ticket sales, many also make a large percentage of their revenue from television broadcasts. Most facilities cannot just install a camera and expect to produce images that can be broadcast on national television. A camera is only the beginning of the process. A facility needs to have appropriate lighting that allows athletes to see the action well but at the same time allows those watching at home to see it without numerous shadows or dark areas. For proper placement of a camera, room has to be made on the sidelines for mobile camera vehicles; overhead for aerial cameras on guide wires attached to scoreboards or goals/baskets; and in the stands, where seats in front of the camera will need to be "killed" so fans will not be standing up and blocking the view. Some of the facility requirements for broadcasting an event include these:

- Place for a mobile control room weighing about 14 tons
- Room for camera vehicles
- Place for a cable tender vehicle
- Room for an electrical generator vehicle
- Space for possible additional vehicles such as aerial antenna trucks and mobile videotape vehicles
- Location to place possibly miles of cables
- Location for camera stands that can support up to 600 pounds (272 kilograms)
- Electrical power source to supply a three-phase 50-hertz, 200- or 300-amp supply
- Rigging or poles to support additional lighting requirements
- Appropriate wall covering/coloring that provides a nice broadcast background
- Proper acoustical design of the structure to properly absorb and reverberate sounds (*Film and Broadcasting*, n.d.).

Data Network

The data network is used to deliver data effectively throughout a facility. The data system covers everything from phone lines to the data required to control the scoreboard. With more and more building systems being controlled by computers, a seamless integration of computer systems, ranging from ticketing and security to HVAC and water control systems, must exist. A primary focus is on computer-related data, whether for a ticketing operation or just internal e-mail. Data security is a paramount concern for any data network. Hackers can potentially break into the system and steal season ticket holder credit card information or send malicious e-mails to those on the network. While some safety can be developed through installation of firewall software, designed to prevent hackers from getting into the system, internal controls need to be added since current or former employees are often as likely a source of a data attack.

Significant savings can be realized if computer network concerns are addressed during the building of a facility compared to renovation work. Existing facilities often need to put holes in walls to embed the data lines (fiber or coaxial) so that wires are not exposed. To avoid costly wall repairs, some facilities in special cases have used external wiring that is placed on the ground or near the ceiling and then along the wall. All these headaches and costs can be eliminated when a new facility is designed and provided with appropriate data lines.

Personal Transportation Systems

Personal transportation systems include elevators, escalators, and people movers. There are two types of transportation systems: vertical and horizontal. An elevator is a vertical system; a horizontal system moves people across a floor (e.g., people movers or trams at airports). Vertical transportation systems are visible at every sport facility. The Americans with Disabilities Act has forced facilities to make available more vertical transportation sys-

tems for persons who are disabled. People who are elderly and other customers may also appreciate vertical transportation systems, and these represent a good customer service option. While horizontal systems are not found typically at sport facilities, some sport complexes with multiple venues install such systems to decrease movement time.

Exterior Systems

Exterior systems are designed to provide strength for the building structure and to provide ancillary building amenities. Thus, a roof protects the contents of the building and ensures that the building will not face structural problems due to water damage. A landscaping system provides aesthetic and environmental benefits. Transportation and parking systems are also discussed here.

Roofs

There are four basic types of overhead spectator protection, classified according to the amount of coverage they provide. Small sun canopies provide minimal protection as they are not supported by interior columns, which could interfere with the sight lines. These canopies offer protection for the upper rows and are often viewed as more ornamental than functional. Such roofs are often used at sportsplexes to provide some shade.

Courtesy of the Kansas City Royals.

Kauffman Stadium, home to the Kansas City Royals, has a sun canopy roof, which provides minimal protection from the sun but doesn't interfere with sight lines.

Full roof canopies, high above the playing surface and crowd, cover most of the facility. These roofs normally have an opening in the middle where sunlight and the elements can enter. One of the biggest problems with this type of system is that as the sun travels across the sky it creates a major headache for televised events. Light areas and shadows tend to change during the course of an event and make photography more difficult. Full roof canopies are often seen at major international soccer venues.

Domes have gained popularity throughout the world in the past 20 years. These roofs cover the entire seating bowl and are supported at the perimeter so that no internal columns are needed. They allow a facility manager to control the temperature and lighting. The major drawback is that many fans and players prefer to have some sun exposure, even in winter conditions.

Retractable roofs have gained in popularity over the past 10 years through innovative designs that allow relatively quick closure. Retractable roofs enable a facility to be open on nice days and can close in about a half-hour when inclement weather threatens an event (Mancia, 2003).

For every $1 of damage a roof sustains, an estimated $10 worth of damage occurs in the structure below the roof (Borsenik and Stutts, 1997). There are several roofing systems that can protect a building: overlapping layers of roofing felt, coal tar pitch with gravel, elastomers (which when cured look like vulcanized rubber), thermoplastic roofing that softens when heated and hardens when cooled, fiberglass-reinforced roofing, and steel or aluminum roofing. Each roof has its own benefits and disadvantages. Some roofs work better in cooler weather and others work best in hot climates. A building designer/architect can help identify the best material to use in the construction of a roof.

Another concern with a roof is the weight that has to be carried. For example, a 1-inch (2.5-centimeter) puddle of water in a 100-square-foot (9.3-square-meter) area on a roof can weigh 520 pounds (236 kilograms). That weight significantly increases when the water is in the form of snow. A number of roofs have collapsed due to excessive snow, metal fatigue, or both. The roof of the Hartford Coliseum collapsed in 1978 several hours after a Hartford Whalers game.

As with other systems discussed throughout this chapter, it is imperative not only to install an effective roof system but to maintain it properly after installation. The roof is one of the most important systems in terms of the need for proper maintenance. One maintenance strategy is to check all downspouts to make sure they are not clogged. Clogged gutters can cause deterioration in wood; and during the winter, frozen water can cause cracks or other problems. Roofs should be inspected on a regular basis, but always at least once in the spring to identify concerns that could be addressed during summertime. A roof requires both an external inspection, to see if parts are falling down or whether there are uneven wear points, and an internal inspection for leaks, rusting, peeling paint, musty odors, discolored ceiling tiles, and warped wood.

Building and Grounds

Other external components that need to be regularly inspected and maintained include the building facade, which can deteriorate significantly in urban areas from factors like car emissions, acid rain, and sea salt. Windows, doors, signs, parking areas, and sidewalks all need to be properly maintained and supervised.

Most **landscaping** is coordinated with professionals who are experts in soil, climate, water, and horticultural issues to help a facility manager make the right decisions. While visual appeal is critical, safety is also important. For example, some ornamental plants have prickly leaves. A landscape architect would never plant cactus or similar prickly plants, for example, in an area where children may play.

But landscaping is for more than just visual appeal. Landscaping can generate cost savings by reducing maintenance-related expenditures. Strategies include the following:

- Utilizing plants that do not grow much after they are planted
- Using plants grown specifically for disease and insect resistance or drought tolerance
- Using perennials in planting beds to minimize grass maintenance
- Planting small shrubs close to each other to minimize the need for weeding
- Installing an automatic irrigation system to reduce water and manpower costs (Borsenik and Stutts, 1997)

Transportation Systems

Not every facility has a transportation system. Most facilities have several vehicles for moving items from one location to another. For example, small three-wheel or four-wheel carts similar to golf carts are used by maintenance workers to move from one location to another or for tasks such as trash removal. If any vehicles are in poor shape, the facility may be liable. Thus, if the brakes on a car are poor and are not repaired, the facility may be liable if as a result an employee is injured or a patron is hit by the vehicle.

Bigger events can require bigger vehicles. The Atlanta Olympics used a large number of buses to transport athletes from events to other events or to the athletes' village. However, the entire system was plagued by overworked drivers who did not know routes, were often late, or were even commandeered by irate athletes. As one official stated, some of the drivers might not have had any training in driving buses (Sullivan, 1996).

Parking and Public Transportation System

Numerous parking concerns need to be addressed, from drunk drivers to auditing of the parking attendants to avoid fraud. Additional concerns can include handicapped parking spaces, aggressive drivers, rough terrain, managing cars and people parked on multiple levels, and criminal misconduct. Different event goers have different parking habits as shown below. This type of information may prove useful for determining the appropriate number of parking attendants, identifying crowd management issues, and understanding how to manage and market parking areas more effectively.

Safety

Crime statistics provide a basis upon which facility managers can be put on notice that criminal acts are foreseeable and that they can be sued should such acts occur. Fights, assaults, robberies, underage drinking, and illegally scalping tickets are just some of the criminal activities presenting liability challenges. Cases claiming liability on the part of facilities for the criminal acts of third parties often allege such charges as poor lighting, missing or broken light bulbs, weak locks, no access control, poorly trained guards, or poor management policies. A 1996 report indicated that approximately 7% to 9% of simple assaults throughout the United States occurred in parking facilities or near parking lots. Furthermore, 8% of all violent crimes, 6% of all rapes/sexual assaults, and 7% of total assaults occurred in parking lots or garages (Abbott and Fried, 1998).

Parking lots and garages are critical for sport facilities, as only 5% of fans attending games utilize public transportation while another 5% take leased buses. Estimates show that football fans use their cars more intensively, averaging 3.5 passengers per vehicle, while baseball fans traditionally travel with 2.5 passengers per vehicle (Abbott and Fried, 1998). Risk management strategies for ensuring safe parking for fans are listed on page 146.

One landmark case concerning liability for conduct that spilled out of a sport facility and led to violence in a parking lot was the Bishop case (*Bishop v. Fair Lanes Georgia Bowling*, 1986). According to the case, two groups were using adjoining

Parking Habits of Attendees

Baseball fans: park, see the game, and leave

Football fans: make a day of it; park before the game to tailgate (unless the game starts at or before noon)

Baby boomer concert goers: arrive right before the event

Country music fans: arrive early, conduct themselves in an orderly fashion, and follow parking rules

Rock fans: tend to linger after an event; parking problems can persist well after an event

From "Outside the arena, parking is the name of the game", 1997.

Risk Management Strategies for Ensuring Safe Parking

Based on the potential liability associated with unsafe parking lots, facility managers need to answer the following questions:

1. Are statistics maintained on the frequency and type of criminal activity occurring around (within a half-mile of) the parking facility?

2. Has a thorough security audit been completed, including a review of security policies, and have any findings been acted upon?

3. Do both security and nonsecurity personnel understand and apply proper security measures?

4. What can reasonably be done to prevent criminal behavior?

5. Has a long-range goal been established for promoting security and crime prevention?

6. Is a public relations program in place to inform patrons and employees about security concerns?

7. What does it cost to incorporate additional security versus the harm that may be caused to possible victims? (Abbott and Fried, 1998)

bowling lanes and one of the groups engaged in harassing behavior over a significant amount of time. The other group complained to the bowling alley management, which took no action. In fact, the management continued to serve alcohol to the group that was engaging in harassment even though they were already intoxicated. After the 2:30 a.m. closing, the two groups were the last people to leave the facility. The intoxicated group, which had been the aggressor all evening long, attacked the other group in the parking lot. According to the court's conclusion, a jury could reasonably find that the bowling alley should have been aware of potential physical altercations between the patrons before the altercation occurred and would therefore be negligent for taking no action and failing to make its premises safe for invitees.

Notice is the key requirement for proving that something was foreseeable. In a suit stemming from a brawl during a 1980 AC/DC rock concert, the concert promoter claimed that there had been no notice because no unruly behavior, fighting, or drinking had been observed that would indicate a potential problem. Even though the arena had no prior problems, the court concluded that the promoter was on notice because a police officer had investigated prior tour stops and was informed of various problems. The officer also knew that the band had attracted a very rowdy, drunk, and drug-using crowd in past concerts (*Comastro v. Village of Rosemont*, 1984).

Alcohol management is another key component of a parking security risk management plan (see chapter 15). Arrests at sport events often revolve around alcohol abuse or intoxicated behavior (Abbott and Fried, 1998). Risk management strategies designed to reduce alcohol-related injuries include controlling tailgate parties and creating a designated driver program for intoxicated fans (Ammon, 1993). However, designing a safer parking area should be the first step

Environmental Parking Design

The use of architectural design to provide greater flexibility in protecting patrons is rapidly catching on throughout the world. **Crime prevention through environmental design (CPTED)** is a step that can be taken to reduce criminal activities (Gordon and Brill, 1996). This approach entails design modifications to a facility that make it safer. For example, concrete stairways in parking facilities are effective hiding places for criminals. Crime prevention through environmental design would change stairwells to include large windows throughout, making it harder for criminals to hide and allowing individuals on the street to see activity inside the stairwell.

Combined Interior/Exterior Systems

Other systems such as security, pest control, and waste management are both interior and exterior systems and are important for ensuring effective utilization and management of the entire facility.

Security Systems

The Atlanta Olympic Games had what was considered a top of the line security system. However, prior to the opening ceremonies, which President Clinton attended, a person was stopped with a gun inside the facility. The intruder had entered the facility using a security company uniform. Even though there were armed guards and an X-ray system to identify hazardous items, the intruder was able to get in. When asked how the intruder had penetrated the elaborate system, a spokesperson replied, "He came early" (Sullivan, 1996). To help prevent security breaches, a security plan needs to be developed; and to help implement a security plan, security systems are needed (chapter 15 deals in more detail with security concerns).

Security Devices

A security system relies on a number of devices. If a facility is going to be monitored, humans can only see so much even if there are hundreds of guards. To maintain an appropriate monitoring system, a facility may have **closed-circuit television (CCTV)** cameras and a monitoring station. Some sport facilities have over 100 CCTV cameras scanning both the interior and exterior and recording all images in a digital format that takes up very little data storage space. Some systems are motion activated while others are integrated with computer systems to monitor crowd activities and signal an alarm if someone is moving the wrong way in a crowd (e.g., sneaking in through an exit). Typical devices that may be present in a security system can include the following:

- Magnetic door and window locks/switches
- Mechanical switches that lock and open doors and windows in case of electrical interruptions
- Electrical switches that lock and open doors and windows
- Pressure mats that trigger when weight is placed on them
- Vibration detectors that respond to movement in restricted areas
- Thermal switches that notice changes in temperature when a person enters a room
- Audio detectors that identify unusual noises
- Infrared detectors that are triggered when a beam is broken (Carlson and DiGiandomenico, 1992)

Alarms fall into two categories, life safety and property protection (Carlson and DiGiandomenico, 1992). Life safety systems, such as a fire alarm, are designed to provide early detection and prompt notification of a hazard. Property protection systems exist in areas housing valuables that may need additional protection. Thus, an athletic facility may have a life safety alarm system in locations where patrons and guests congregate, as well as a property protection system in locations where cash or other valuables are stored. Either system relies on an initiating/sensing circuit or sensing loop to detect the hazard and then triggers the appropriate alarms.

Routine Security

Every facility has routine security issues, from those involving the loading docks to those related to cash. The ticket office may need additional security to protect tellers or may require a drop safe so that money can be deposited safely every 15 minutes. Each facility needs to undertake a security audit to identify security-related concerns so that appropriate systems can be implemented.

The security issues in an arena relate to many types of breaches, from fans bringing in banned items to potential terrorist attacks. Security planning can take weeks or months prior to an event. Because of the diversity of security-related concerns, many facilities work very closely with law enforcement officials. Furthermore, every professional sport league has a security director who works with facilities and teams in the league to make sure that events are as safe as possible. The following are some system-related steps that can help improve a facility's security:

- Utilizing video, alarms on doors, and metal detectors at entrances and exits
- Utilizing security posts to assist troubled spectators
- Reviewing videos from CCTV cameras
- Having a security system control center where data are properly stored and secured

Security systems are not the only systems that are considered both interior and exterior systems.

Pest Control

One of the often overlooked facility concerns is pests. Pests represent a health concern. If a facility has a pest infestation and there are any cooking or food service areas within the building, there may be health code violations that could lead the health department to shut down the food service. Pests also represent a marketing concern. An unclean facility with bugs can repel facility users and lead to economic loss.

Pests can be a problem in both the interior and exterior systems. Interior pests can include rats, mice, ants, and cockroaches. Many types of sprays, electronic systems, and even other animals can be used to control pests. For example, the Houston Astrodome utilized cats to keep mice and rats out of the facility. Fans at a game would sometimes have a cat rub against their leg. Astrodome personnel brought the cats to veterinarians each year, and the cats served as a supplemental deterrent. External control is critical for preventing external pests from entering a facility. Solutions can be as simple as fencing or can be more complex, as with ground termite systems.

Waste Management

The unglamorous task of waste management is often contracted out to external trash removal companies. However, these companies often remove the trash only after it has been collected into major receptacles. Most facilities have their own employees or a janitorial service take care of trash. Trash removal has to be conducted daily to prevent odors or an unpleasant environment. Waste reduction is both an environmental concern and a potential cost reduction strategy. The first key to a waste reduction program is to obtain administrator approval. Management may not consider the value of recycling. For example, during a survey of fans at a professional tennis event, one of the most frequently cited potential improvements was the use of recycling containers for soda and beer cans. Management may not customarily think of recycling as a marketing tool, but patrons several years after the survey were very positive about the new recycling program.

Certain recyclable materials may be frequently seen in the trash, but if it is too hard to separate them, they may not be the best materials to recycle. It may be possible to eliminate this problem by developing user-friendly storage and collection locations (Hennesey, 2001).

Summary

Discussion of the construction process in chapter 6 highlighted how complex the building process can be given the different types of building materials and other construction elements. Among the most important elements in a facility, and often the most expensive on a percentage basis, are the systems built in or added on. Everything from HVAC to energy and plumbing systems needs to be installed and maintained in an appropriate manner. A facility cannot be built with a mere collection of systems, but needs to integrate all the systems effectively to minimize costs and maximize benefits. An HVAC system needs to be connected to the electrical system to monitor air temperature and save the most energy when the facility is not in use. The key to the systems is that they are designed to help maintain a safe and comfortable facility. When any system goes down, the entire facility is affected. Facility users demand that systems work—for example, that lights not go off during an event and toilets not fail to flush—or that they be repaired very quickly. The next two chapters deal with facility operations and maintenance, which are critical to maintaining the building systems.

DISCUSSION QUESTIONS AND ACTIVITIES

1. Give five reasons why an HVAC system is important for an arena.

2. What would be the best fire suppression system for an arena versus a health club?

3. Visit a large facility in your town or city and ask to examine the HVAC system, and write a report describing the system.

4. Visit a large facility and examine the types of lighting systems used, such as indirect lights, direct lights, and ambient lighting.

5. Examine the type of pest management system used in your dorm or classroom and evaluate its effectiveness.

6. Visit your campus gym and examine the number of intake and exhaust areas. Try to calculate the number of air exchanges per hour needed to meet the ACSM recommendations. (For instructions on how to do this, see "Behind the Scenes: Calculating Air Exchange" on page 132.)

Facility Operations

CHAPTER OBJECTIVES

After completing this chapter you will be able to do the following:

- Appreciate some of the nuances associated with managing the operations of sport facilities
- Understand the steps in the changeover process
- Analyze the management requirements for key components of sport facilities such as weight rooms and gymnasiums
- Appreciate how an attractive and playable grass field is created
- Know the tasks involved in creating and maintaining proper soil and good ground appearance
- Characterize the components of an effective field maintenance program
- Appreciate some of the concerns unique to baseball and football fields

Chapter 3 dealt with effective managerial strategies for a facility. It is critical as well to understand how to apply theory and strategies to the day-to-day operations of a sport facility. Scheduling, for example, is one of the major tasks for a facility manager. Whether one is attracting events or just accommodating current programs, scheduling can become difficult. Several groups may want to use a gym at the same time. Who will get priority? Will priority be based on politics or revenue generation? What are the goals and objectives for the facility? These are just a few of the questions that management needs to deal with in order to make operations decisions.

In indoor facilities, various concerns are associated with scheduling, cleaning, floor maintenance, and ancillary areas such as rest rooms. Management also needs to analyze how to transform a facility from one event to another. **Changeover** management requires significant time, money, and energy. All aspects of everyday management and maintenance must also be addressed. Outdoor facilities have their own unique issues, weather being among the most important. It is not uncommon to see a nationally televised football game being played in the mud. Could the mud have been prevented? What steps can be taken to make sure a facility is in reasonably playable condition? Much is involved in preparing a field for an event, from removing snow and painting lines to mowing the lawn in a uniform manner.

This chapter covers some of the basics of scheduling and changeover management and then considers traditional sport facility-related components such as weight rooms, locker rooms, and gymnasiums. Attention is given to specific aspects that need to be managed as well as issues such as general maintenance. The chapter also looks at outdoor facilities from a managerial perspective and outlines

With indoor facilities, check-in desks allow staff to monitor who is using the facility.

the steps required to produce a playable and safe outdoor surface. Important issues in this context are the types of grass used in playing fields and how to maintain them properly, from mowing and fertilizing to providing for proper field drainage. Significant attention is paid to developing a field maintenance program. The chapter ends with an analysis of unique sport concerns such as synthetic surfaces, dirt management, and safety.

Space Management

Space management examines how a facility will be used. A facility that sits vacant wastes space as well as resources. On the other hand, a facility that is overused can deteriorate rapidly. Management has to balance between the extremes of overuse and underuse.

Most facilities have a reservation system whereby someone who wants to use the facility completes a reservation form indicating the desired date, time, and space. In a college, the physical education department often has first choice, followed by the athletic department, intramural and recreational sports, student groups, and lastly community groups. Facility usage and scheduling are often dictated by political pressure or money. A particular group may have fewer facility users than other groups but receive the best time due to political pressure. Title IX is shifting the priorities and scheduling practices at many high schools and colleges. Whereas historically the men's football and basketball teams were given the best facilities and times, women's teams are now receiving more equal treatment.

Managing Multiple Venues

The management process is even more demanding when one is overseeing several facilities. Most colleges have several athletic or recreational facilities that require significant managerial oversight. Facilities can be located miles apart—for example, the university boathouse, golf course, bowling alley, recreation center, stadium, arena, and fields. Because of tight budgets and in many cases neglected repairs, facility managers often have an uphill battle. A successful facility manager at the college level needs to be an expert in organizing and consolidating resources. Each day a number of events may be taking place in stadiums, arenas, gyms, and playing fields. The manager must be able to change gears at a moment's notice to handle a variety of events.

To effectively manage the space in multiple facilities, a senior manager needs to appoint a management team. A facility management team, typically reporting to one director, can help manage multiple facilities more effectively. In this case each facility may have its own manager; or there may be a manager for fields, for example, and managers for maintenance and other trades positions. It is often more effective to have team members that can apply their trade to a group of facilities than for each facility to have its own specialists. At a single facility, a repairperson might have to do plumbing, electrical, and maintenance work in order to justify his or her position. In contrast, a plumber who is a member of a team that manages multiple venues may take care of all the plumbing fixtures in the various facilities. Thus the management team becomes more intimately involved with the overall functioning of the facilities, and this type of decentralized system helps to ensure that the facilities are operating properly.

Managing Changeover

It can be interesting to watch the changeover process in a facility. Changeover refers to the process of converting a facility from one activity to another. Changeover at a high school gym can be as simple as putting basketballs away and rolling out dodge balls. More is involved in changing from badminton to volleyball because of the differing nets, standards, and equipment. It becomes important for a facility manager to explore all options when scheduling in order to group similar events together to reduce the time and costs associated with changeovers.

The process becomes more complicated when two events use completely different surfaces. In multisport facilities such as baseball and football stadiums it is necessary to move bleachers, remove pitching mounds, and extend fields to change over from baseball to football. However, since the seasons overlap for only a limited time period, the demand for changing over is limited. In contrast, the need to change over from hockey to basketball, or vice versa, occurs over an extended period of time because the seasons overlap significantly.

Changeover management is one of the more complex assignments for maintenance crews. The most complex version entails changing over from an event on ice to any other event. Some facilities can melt the ice so that the floor can be laid on the hard cement. However, this is a very expensive proposition. Madison Square Garden thaws and removes the ice only once during the entire New York Rangers' season—for the Westminster Kennel Club Dog Show, because the dogs are sensitive to the ice. Thus, when a basketball game is to be played, the court is normally installed over the ice.

A basketball floor cannot be placed right over ice without damaging both the floor and the ice. An intermediary surface is used to protect the ice; the different types of floor covers include plywood, pressed paper sheets, laminated wood with foam core, polyethylene shell with a foam core, and thermo-formed urethane foam sheets with fiberglass to reduce expansion and contraction (Townsend, 2003).

The changeover process typically begins as soon as an event ends. Whereas changing over used to take all night, it now can take just a few hours. The First Union Center in Philadelphia is managed by Global Spectrum, which introduced a quick-change process. The center is home to the Philadelphia Flyers, 76ers, and Wings (lacrosse) and hosts over 400 events each year. Global Spectrum uses a 47-member crew that includes 25 to 30 changeover employees, six carpenters, six ice crew members, two Zamboni drivers, two electricians, and one telephone technician (Richman, 2001).

Changeovers require a great deal of planning, and facilities are being designed with changeovers in mind. For example, the Staples Center in Los Angeles averages 130 changeovers each year. The fastest changeover from a hockey surface to a bas-

ketball surface was accomplished in 1 hour and 50 minutes. On average, most arenas use 35 to 60 staff members for a changeover, with the greatest amount of time being spent on removal of seating areas (Bisson, 2001).

Specialized Components in Sport Facilities

Some sport facility components, such as locker rooms, do not need to be scheduled or changed; but they still need to be properly managed. Management still needs to schedule employees to work in these areas. Also, time needs to be spent getting areas ready for daily use, from basic cleaning to making sure that the weights in a weight room are in place. This section discusses areas that require additional managerial oversight: weight rooms, locker rooms, and gymnasiums.

Weight Rooms

Weight rooms are among the most difficult facility components to manage due to constant use and abuse. Weight rooms must be kept clean and safe because of liability concerns. Other issues for weight rooms include maintaining the equipment and developing a positive environment for users.

In order to maintain a proper level of safety and cleanliness, it is essential for the facility manager to create and implement a customized preventive maintenance program. An effective preventive maintenance program incorporates daily, weekly, monthly, and yearly cleanings and repairs (Dahlgren, 2000b). The majority of the daily chores involve cleaning of equipment. As odors and perspiration can accumulate quickly, the walls and equipment and sitting/resting areas should be cleaned daily with general household cleaning agents; the floors should be vacuumed daily; and facility users should be given access to cleaners (soap solution or a mild antibacterial disinfectant) to allow them to wipe down the equipment. For vinyl parts of the apparatus it is best to use an antibacterial diluted to a 10% solution (Dahlgren, 2000b). It is also very important each week to lubricate all machine joints using lightweight (30-weight) motor oil and to clean them first to avoid lubricant buildup (Dahlgren, 2000b).

Although employees can fix many simple maintenance problems, at least one employee should take certifying courses provided by machine manufacturers to learn how to fix the machines. Managers may also keep spare parts in the facility to avoid long time delays waiting for parts. In some cases there are simple ways to head off repair problems, such as switching one bike for another when one is used more frequently than the other (Dahlgren, 2000b).

Because of the abundance of odors and moisture in the air, a manager should change heating, ventilation, and air conditioning (HVAC) unit filters fairly often (every 1-2 months). Care should be taken to avoid moisture damage in weight rooms tucked in the middle of a larger building. Fans, dehumidifiers, and air fresheners can help improve air quality and user enjoyment and can prevent rust, mildew, and bacteria buildup.

Supervision

The weight room's location can affect the ability to provide proper supervision. With weights and machines blocking one's view, it is often difficult to supervise the weight room and monitor conduct. Improved supervision can be accomplished by moving employees around, reconfiguring the room setup, or even installing a closed-circuit TV system. A check-in desk is an effective tool for monitoring who enters the weight room and monitoring patrons using the room. Some health clubs have a security access point at the check-in desk, which helps make patrons feel that the club is in some sense exclusive and is concerned about crime and inappropriate conduct.

Improving the Feel

Weight rooms have been transformed into warm and inviting places. Facilities have expanded through the use of open areas, a large amount of glass to let light in, television set banks, and central attractions such as climbing walls. Although most owners cannot create large facilities without significant cash, it is usually possible to create a much better environment in the space that already exists.

For example, flooring can come in a variety of colors and patterns and can be used to create unique designs in the weight room. A way to do this is to use one color for workout stations and another color for pathways (Sherman, 1997). The walls also can be painted various colors to generate a more relaxed atmosphere. However, too many

colors can become overwhelming, confusing, and "noisy" and can decrease lighting effectiveness. Indirect lighting or up-lighting can help create a better and brighter environment. The downside to this approach is that more light fixtures are needed, compared to fluorescent lighting, to adequately light the room.

Repainting and replacing old padding on machines can give equipment a renewed look. The old paint must be sandblasted off the machine; then the machine is repainted and new padding is added. Using nontraditional or school colors when repainting the machines can give the room a personal feel (Sherman, 1997).

Locker Rooms

Players of all ages and levels carry waves of emotions into the locker room after the game and can quickly create a hazardous environment for others. Athletes allow their skin to come in contact with many different surfaces within the locker room. Due to the moist conditions in this area, bacteria are easily bred and then spread to others (Turner and Hauser, 1994). Care should be taken to clean all surfaces in a locker room at least daily, depending on the use.

Another critical concern is the threat of slipping on water in areas where there are sinks or showers and in changing areas. The following strategies can create a safer environment in the locker rooms:

- Control traffic flow in the locker room by creating both wet and dry areas.
- Reduce the moisture level with a strong HVAC system to help stop the spread of bacteria and keep the floor dry.
- Move outlets at least 6 feet (2 meters) away from any water source or install **ground fault circuit interrupters (GFCIs)** to reduce the threat of electrocution.
- Kill bacteria using a quaternary ammonium solution once a week and a mild phosphoric acid solution once a month.
- Avoid full-length lockers in the middle of a room to keep sight lines open for supervision. Other options are slant-topped lockers or lockers that are flush with the wall (Turner and Hauser, 1994).

One of the important concerns in any locker room is the floor. The floor will help determine the room's look, feel, and safety. Since slipping is such a major concern, the floor needs to be constructed with slip-resistant materials or painted with non-skid paint. The following are materials used for most locker room floors:

- Ceramic tile provides both durability and a clean look and is primarily used in the wet areas of locker rooms. However, tile can easily become very slippery, and the grout between tiles is hard to clean and can house bacteria.

- Carpet, while not common, is slip resistant and has a nice look; but water-soaked carpeting can create a musty smell.

- Epoxy quartz floors are created when several layers of clear or colored epoxy are put down with a topcoat of sealer. This type of flooring is slip resistant and resilient but harder to maintain than other types of floors and not very attractive.

- Coated concrete is basic concrete topped by paint or a thick sealer. It is fairly slip resistant but not very aesthetic.

- Similar to the rubber floors used in weight rooms, rubber shower floors are slip resistant but are harder to maintain than other types of flooring (Cohen, 1994a).

Gymnasium

Whether managing a 15,000-seat multiple sport arena or a high school gym used just for basketball, there are certain standard maintenance steps (see tips for maintaining a gymnasium below).

A properly maintained gym not only reduces the risk of injury to athletes and spectators, but also increases the aesthetic appeal and extends the building's life. Decent lights, a floor with some give, and the proper equipment may be all that is absolutely necessary. However, most gym users want more. Athletes want a well-finished surface free of defects, a good HVAC system so air can circulate, and appropriate lighting.

Key areas that one should examine when analyzing maintenance needs for a gym include the floor (hardwood or synthetic), bleachers, dividers, basketball goals, padding, dashers, and the glass. These are discussed in the following sections.

Flooring

The primary surfaces used in gymnasiums are wood and synthetic surfaces. Wood floors may be maple or other wood options in a variety of grades depending on the amount of money spent. Wood needs to be properly maintained.

The drive to create a floor finish that is able to bend without cracking has created two types of finishes that have varied effects: oil based and water based. The floorboard must bend in order to withstand multipurpose usage and improper cleaning by janitorial staffs (Cohen, 1998).

- Oil-based wood floor finishes utilize vegetable oils and are modified to create a urethane. The urethane is applied to the floor wet and can be damaged in the drying process (Cohen, 1998). As the urethane dries, chemicals are released into the air that are harmful to both humans and the environment. As the liquid portion of the urethane

Tips for Maintaining a Gymnasium

- Small dents in the floor can be removed by covering the dent with a damp cloth and then pressing on the cloth with an electric iron.
- Any repairs should be discussed with the floor manufacturer before they are undertaken to make sure the repair will not void any warranty.
- Gum stuck to various surfaces can be removed by freezing the gum with dry ice and then removing the gum with a putty knife. Gum can also be removed by applying peanut butter to the area.
- Urethane floors can repaired by pouring/painting a new layer of urethane over the entire floor.
- Masonite should be placed under the wheels of movable bleacher systems to avoid damage to the underlying floor.

From Cohen, 2000.

Behind the Scenes: Fixing the Floors

While most schools replace only one gym at a time, sometimes a better deal can be made if several gyms are repaired at the same time. This scenario occurred when the Fairfax, Virginia, Public School District replaced four gym floors. The gyms had various surfaces, such as poured urethane, wood, and vinyl tiles, that were all changed over to maple wood. The gyms were of various sizes ranging from 4,800 to 28,000 square feet (445-2,600 square meters). The gyms were to be used daily by the students for classes and athletics, and some were also open to the general public.

The schools installed Taraflex Sport M flooring, which is 6.7 millimeters (0.26 inches) in thickness and covered with a resistant stain to reduce friction burns, prevent bacteria growth, and minimize maintenance costs. The multilayered floor utilizes a 100% pure vinyl wear layer with reinforced fiberglass and a closed-cell foam backing underneath that helps reduce stress on athletes' joints when they jump ("Fairfax County School," 2003).

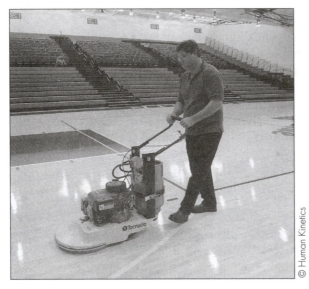

© Human Kinetics

Hardwood floors must be properly maintained, as replacing them is very expensive.

evaporates, it leaves a hard resin on the floor. These types of finishes tend to be higher gloss and not as wear resistant, but more flexible than other finishes (Cohen, 1998). Oil-based urethanes are the most common type of floor finish for gym floors.

• Water-based finishes have a clear color (unlike the oil-based finishes, which are amber colored) and are generally not as thick or glossy (Cohen, 1998). This means that in order to achieve a higher gloss, more coats must be applied. Unlike oil-based products, water-based finishes do not give off harmful vapors as they dry. Also, water-based products act more like an adhesive when they are applied. This can be bad if there are separations between some of the floorboards. The finish can get

between the boards and glue the boards together when it dries (Cohen, 1998). Using a simple surface prep solution to fill the cracks before applying the finish can avert this problem.

Under normal circumstance a 3/4-inch (1.9-centimeter)-thick tongue-and-groove solid maple floor can last from 40 to 80 years (Brickman, 1997). The floor's life span is affected by

• the events held on the floor,
• the moisture level in the gym,
• how frequently the floor is cleaned,
• whether mats are used to wipe feet before people enter,
• the quality and frequency of finish recoating (completed every year or every other year),
• the quality and frequency of sanding and refinishing (complete sanding and refinishing needed every 10-20 years), and
• the frequency of minor and major catastrophes such as floods (Brickman, 1997).

The cost to completely sand and finish a typical gym floor is around $12,000 to $16,000, while the cost of a new gym floor averages around $60,000. Thus, it is a worthwhile investment to properly manage and maintain a wood floor.

Synthetic materials include nylon turf, rubber, poured urethane, and ethylene propylene diene monomer (EPDM) granules in a urethane binder. Each floor system has unique issues that need to be addressed from a management perspective such as seams, cleaning, and repairs. Exposed seams can present a tripping hazard. Also, some surfaces that have a granular finish are very hard to clean, making it necessary to use special machines or leaf blowers.

Bleachers

There are guidelines and standards for both indoor and outdoor bleachers, as well as various techniques used for repair and maintenance.

Most gyms are built with telescoping bleachers that are easily taken in and out when necessary. In contrast, arenas are normally built with fixed seating that may include mold-injected plastic seats. Access is a key concern for bleachers. Aisles placed in the middle of the bleachers are the most effective means of access (Scandrett, 1998). A double-loaded bleacher allows aisle access to all its sections. Rows should be spaced about 24 inches (61 centimeters) apart, although a 26- to 28-inch (66- to 71-centimeter) space is most desirable to make passage between rows easier (Scandrett, 1998). Usually bleachers rise between 11 and 16 inches (28-41 centimeters) from one row to the next to help create acceptable sight lines for the crowd (Scandrett, 1998).

Although only 4 feet (1.2 meters) of space between the face of the bleachers and the court is mandated in some facilities (more than 10 feet [3 meters] is mandated in others), it is much safer to significantly exceed this minimum amount. If a scorer's table and player benches are in front of the bleachers as well, there should be a minimum of 10 feet from the out-of-bounds line to the front of the bleachers to give 4 feet of circulation space for fans and 6 clear feet (1.8 meters) for the athletes, coaches, and staff (Scandrett, 1998).

It is imperative to refer to building codes before installing or modifying bleachers. Some of the **uniform building code (UBC)** regulations that may apply are the following:

- No more than 16 rows are allowed if they are accessible only from either the top or the bottom.
- Aisles are required only when the bleachers are more than 11 rows high.
- There should be no more than 20 seats between aisles.
- Cutouts for wheelchairs can be provided in various spots along the first row of telescoping bleachers to accommodate wheelchairs. Platforms can be built overlooking the top

rows to provide seating that complies with the Americans with Disabilities Act. For a facility that seats over 500 people, six wheelchair-accessible seats are required, with an additional wheelchair location required for every additional 100 spectators over the initial 500 (Scandrett, 1998).

Everyday bleacher maintenance can be as simple as sweeping the bleachers and underneath the structures before closing them. While walking underneath open bleachers it is easy for a worker to look for signs of structural damage such as bent metal cross-braces or chipped paint that indicates fatigue cracks (Steinbach, 2000). Small repairs may be as simple as bending parts back in shape by hand. Moving parts can be lubricated with a lithium-based grease that is dabbed onto the structure using a small paintbrush (Steinbach, 2000).

Gym Components

Several other components within a typical gym present legal, managerial, or maintenance challenges. The components covered in this section include gym dividers, basketball goals, wall padding, dasher boards, and glass panels.

Divider curtains are frequently found in gyms where multiple activities will take place and require some separation. The separation is needed to prevent people from tripping over balls or other objects that might travel from one activity area to another. The curtains can also help create separate and distinct areas so multiple events can occur without the need to use more than one facility. A metal pole or weights at the bottom help keep the curtain straight and taut, but care needs to be taken to make sure that no one is hit by the curtain when it is going up or down. Hanging curtains tend to tear near the bottom. These tears can easily be remedied in place using a portable carpet-stitching machine or by resealing with a strong epoxy. One can patch holes by using epoxy to affix spare pieces of vinyl fabric to both sides of the hole (Steinbach, 2000).

Basketball goals can be fixed, dropped from the ceiling, or swung out from the walls. All nuts, bolts, wires, and gears need to be examined for wear and tear. Goals can be shattered and rims can be broken, and these items are hard to repair. Every facility with basketball goals should store an extra backboard and rim set in case equipment breaks. Minor repairs and maintenance issues include welding of new net hooks to keep

Just as equipment must be in good order for indoor facilities, outdoor facilities also must be maintained. Padding around goalposts should be checked for rips and tears, too.

© Human Kinetics

the net in place, repainting a chipping or peeling rim, and reattaching padding to the underside of the backboard.

Wall padding, used to protect players from injury when they run into walls or doors behind the basketball goals, can take significant punishment. Facilities often have torn, missing, or ripped pads. Damaged pads can be refurbished in-house. Pads can be removed from the wall, and the inside padding can be removed to patch the vinyl. After the padding (and maybe even the vinyl cover) is replaced and secured with contact cement, the vinyl can be rewrapped and stapled using industrial staples (Steinbach, 2000). Small tears can be repaired by cutting and using epoxy to glue a small piece of vinyl to cover the hole.

Dasher boards are used for events such as in-line hockey, indoor soccer, and arena football. Dasher boards need to be inspected to make sure they are not broken, splintering, or improperly secured. The majority of damage to these boards comes from the vehicles used in the arena (Zambonis, forklifts, etc.). Bad reinstallation can also damage the boards (Steinbach, 2000). Aluminum- or steel-backed dashers can be bent back into shape by heating the studs first to soften them. Scratches in glass dasher boards can be removed using light automotive polish, allowing it to dry, then removing it with a buffer. When cleaning other marks off the glass the recommendation is to use only products designed for Plexiglas, as other cleaners can weaken the glass (Steinbach, 2000). Several spare glass panels and plywood dasher boards should be kept in storage to be used if a board breaks.

The facility manager must make sure that all components within a gym or an internal facility are in good shape for the intended purpose. Pre-event inspections can help reduce the chance of injury and identify problems that can be fixed through routine maintenance. The same applies to external sport facilities.

Establishing Grass Fields

Fields can be covered by natural grass or artificial/synthetic turf. Grass fields can be established either by sodding (covering the ground with rolls of pre-grown grass) or by seeding. **Seeding** is the preferred method because of its relatively low cost and reduced labor requirements. A poor-quality surface is often created when a facility manager does not know about the various types of seeding available. Both spectators and athletes can be greatly disappointed if a venue looks rough and uncared for. A poor field can also be expensive. In 2002-2003, for example, Giants Stadium in East Rutherford, New Jersey, was in such poor condition that $120,000 had to be spent to put a new field down before the playoffs. This was the second field installed during that season, which created a significant expense because another field was going to be installed later that year. Based on the problems with the natural grass surface, the New Jersey Sport and Exposition Authority was considering synthetic turf ("Giants Stadium," 2002).

The process of establishing and maintaining an athletic playing field can be daunting. It is easy to

Proper maintenance of grass fields is necessary to ensure a safe playing area.

© Empics

avoid difficulties, however, with proper research regarding types of grass, species of grass, varieties of grass, seeding rates, and seed quality. The proper choice of **turfgrass,** either cool season or warm season, depends on the facility's location. Cool-season turfgrass, as the name suggests, is best suited for areas that are subject to low temperatures during the winter months. The optimum growing temperature is between 60° and 75° F. Warm-season turfgrass, on the other hand, is less hearty and will die if exposed to freezing temperatures for an extended time.

The optimal growing temperature for warm-season turfgrass is 80° to 95° F (Rogers and Stier, 1995). Not surprisingly, warm-season turfgrass is best suited for southern regions. The swath of land in the United States that begins in southern New Jersey and continues in a southwest direction to New Mexico is known as the transition zone because in this area, both warm-season and cool-season turfgrass can grow although neither is very well suited for the climate. Thus, facilities in the transition zone often experience trouble maintaining athletic fields.

Cool-Season Turfgrass

Three basic types of cool-season turfgrass are used for playing fields—Kentucky bluegrass (Poa pratensis L.), perennial ryegrass (Lolium perenne L.), and tall fescue (Festuca arundinacea Schreb) (Rogers and Stier, 1995). Kentucky bluegrass can reproduce itself because of its underground lateral stems called rhizomes, which allow it to

spread over a large area. A drawback to Kentucky bluegrass, however, is its slow growth and thus its inability to provide facility managers with a "quick fix."

Perennial ryegrass, on the other hand, germinates very fast and is therefore an ideal turfgrass when facility managers require a quick fix. But it is a bunch-type turfgrass and has trouble recuperating from excessive traffic. Perennial ryegrass and Kentucky bluegrass work well together in that their respective benefits and drawbacks complement each other.

Tall fescue, a turfgrass characterized by coarse, wide leaf blades, is by far the most wear tolerant of the three turfgrasses but is a slow-growing, bunch-type grass. Certain cool-season turfgrasses are not wear tolerant or are intolerant in relation to the cutting heights necessary for playing field maintenance and hence should not be used. These grasses include rough bluegrass, annual bluegrass, annual ryegrass, creeping bentgrass, colonial bentgrass, fine leaf fescues, centipede grass, bahia grass, and St. Augustine grass (Rogers and Stier, 1995).

Warm-Season Turfgrass

Bermuda grass and zoysia grass are the most frequently used warm-season turfgrasses, with Bermuda grass most commonly used for fields where soccer and football are played. The seeds produced by these warm-season grasses are sterile, so the grass is established by sprigs or sod. Warm-season grasses grow both by rhizomes and by stolons,

Behind the Scenes: Grass a Golf Course Manager Can Love

© Human Kinetics

Technology is constantly affecting turfgrasses and the manner in which they function in the sport industry. A new type of grass called seashore paspalum may provide some strong benefits to golf courses. This grass, originally from South Africa, has deep roots and is salt water tolerant. Because of the deep roots it does not require as much water as other grasses. Furthermore, because this type of grass can thrive in salt water, salt—which can kill weeds without the use of any other chemicals—can be used as a herbicide. One golf course in the United States spent over $300,000 a year on water, but after switching to the new grass was able to cut water bills by over 80% (Foust, 2002).

which are aboveground lateral stems, making them very wear tolerant and able to recuperate quickly.

The resilience of the warm-season turfgrasses, coupled with the various weaknesses of cool-season turfgrasses, make warm-season grasses the preferred turfgrass for athletic fields. Because the warm-season grasses do not flourish in colder weather but instead lie dormant and then recuperate with warmer weather, facility managers often overseed a playing field with both types so that regardless of the conditions there is ample green grass on the field. Some universities, such as Michigan State University, have also begun experimenting with turfgrass in an attempt to breed a grass that will flourish in both cold and warm conditions (Rogers and Stier, 1995).

Seeding Rates

Once the facility manager has chosen the most appropriate species and varieties for the playing fields, it is imperative to order the proper amount of seeds. Seed for various species differ in size. Table 8.1 provides the necessary information for determining how much of each type of seed is needed. Deviance from these guidelines will result in either a turf that is too thin or one that is too dense, making maintenance difficult.

Seeds should be spread at a rate of 6 to 12 seeds per square inch using a broadcast spreader. The

Table 8.1 Seeding Rates

Type of grass	Approximate number of seeds per pound	Seeding rate (lb/1,000 ft²)
Kentucky bluegrass	1,000,000-2,200,000	1-2
Perennial ryegrass	200,000	5-10
Tall fescue	200,000	5-10
Bermuda grass	2,000,000	1-2
Zoysia grass	1,000,000	2-3

From Roger and Stier, 1995.

broadcast spreader throws the seeds in all directions, resulting in uniform distribution.

Seed Quality

It is important to examine seed quality, including the percentage of each turfgrass and variety in the bag, the test date, and the purity percentage. The test date is important because germination declines with time. Therefore, a bag of seed with an old test date will yield less than newer seed. The purity percentage gives the percentage of weed seed in the bag. A weed seed percentage over 0.5% is unacceptable.

Regardless of the grass type planted, the key to a successful grass field is the couple inches of soil beneath the grass. One important component of grass field health is drainage.

Drainage

Whether for a little league or a major league game, players want to use the field even after it has rained. Apart from the root zone structure of a field, a quality drainage system increases the chances that fields will be playable after rain. Although the various systems are similar (underground piping and catch basins), the way they are set up depends on which sports are using the fields. It is imperative for the facility manager to carefully plan the type of system that will be used before building the field. To change or modify a drainage system after construction is very costly (Watson, 1998).

Football Fields

The first step in creating a good drainage system for a football field is to form a crown in the middle of the field that slopes down toward the sidelines. Standard football field crowns are about 18 inches (46 centimeters) above the ground level at the sidelines. If the football field is a combination field for football and soccer (flat field), a more moderate approach of about 8 to 10 inches (20-25 centimeters) is needed (Watson, 1998). Drainage can be

The crown of the football field helps maintain proper drainage.

enhanced by means of an internal (piping) drainage system installed about 15 to 18 inches (38-46 centimeters) below the surface and that flows from the middle of the field to the sidelines (Watson, 1998). There should then be pipes on the sidelines to take the water away from the field.

Baseball Fields

For drainage of surface water from a baseball infield, the highest point is always the pitcher's mound. The infield should grade down 4 inches (10 centimeters) toward each base, and then from each base another 4 inches toward the outer edges of the infield. The highest point of the outfield should be where it meets the infield. From this point there is a 10-inch (25-centimeter) drop toward the fence at a 0% to 2% grade (Watson, 1998).

Water Removal

Several techniques can be used to remove standing water from a field. If the standing water is due to blocked drainage pipes, the drainage system needs to be cleaned. Simply cleaning clogged catch basins may or may not be all that is needed. If the water still does not drain, the problem could be a compaction problem or a faulty drainage system. In either case one must remove the water if play is to begin or continue. Water can be removed by using Turface or other compounds that absorb water and leave behind a granular residue that breaks up into the soil. Other techniques include using hand sponges, sponges attached to poles, sponges attached to feet, hand or motorized pumps, and squeegees to move the water to another area.

Field drainage is just one component within a field maintenance program. Fields do not keep themselves in good condition. Similar to the situation with people's lawns, significant care and attention need to be given to make sure grass is growing correctly. The watering, weeding, fertilizing, mowing, painting, and aeration procedures must be carefully managed to avoid destroying the field.

Maintaining Grass Fields

Every field is different and requires a customized maintenance program. Players and spectators notice when a field has holes, has not been mowed, or is lacking painted lines. These may be relatively minor issues when people are looking for any grassy area in which to play. However, when there is a choice of fields or when safety is a priority, a well-maintained field is critical. Factors to be analyzed when one is examining field maintenance concerns include financial and human resources, field layout (northeast vs. south), types of soils and grasses, use of fields (intensity and frequency), and the sport or sports being played on the field. The first two variables are hard to control. If there is not enough money or time to maintain a field optimally, or if space is not sufficient, those who run the facility will be forced to make do.

Soil

Soil-based fields are constructed using native-type soil materials, which are able to hold higher water and nutrient levels. Unfortunately, soil-based fields are the most susceptible to compaction; still, when they are well aerated they are very good for all **root zone** types (Depew and Guise, 1997).

Sand-modified fields are native-based fields to which sand has been added on-site through top-dressing and aeration. As more sand is added, the resistance to compaction is also increased. A field is not considered sand modified until the amount of sand is in a 60% (sand) to 40% (native soil) ratio. Apart from the higher level of sand, there are not many noticeable changes in the root zone's properties until the sand volume is about 80% (Depew and Guise, 1997).

Fields with sand-based root zones are high-end fields as judged by cost and performance potential. Sand-based fields should have high drainage and aeration rates but low water retention rates (Depew and Guise, 1997). By building this type of field over a layer of coarse gravel, the facility can help slow water movement so the root zone has more time to retain draining water.

The latest trend in natural fields is to add artificial substances. The addition of synthetic materials to the root zones of fields can enhance aeration and drainage properties and help stabilize the soil (Depew and Guise, 1997). However, if the roots do not bond or intertwine with the material, this approach is ineffective.

The three basic components of soils are sand, silt, and clay. The proportions of these components found in soil control the factors that constitute field playability: infiltration rate, percolation, and degree of compaction (Mrock, 1999). The **infiltration rate** of soil is the rate at which water is absorbed from the surface into the soil. **Percolation** is the amount of time it takes for water to pass through the soil and the turfgrass roots. **Compaction** refers to the way in which the individual particles in the soil fit together. In a good growing environment, particles are packed together loosely enough to create pore space for air and water. If the air and water cannot pass through the soil, the roots will be deprived of two of the ingredients that are vital for growth and will die.

The faster the infiltration rate, the more quickly field surfaces will be ready to be played on, even in rainy weather (Mrock, 1999). On the other hand, a slow percolation rate can create the false impression of a dry field. Although the field surface may appear dry, the soil underneath the surface is still wet and in this softened state is more prone to compaction. A facility manager can determine the percolation rate by taking core samples every half-hour from various sections of the field once infiltration has occurred (Mrock, 1999).

Both infiltration and percolation rates can be improved through processes known as aeration and topdressing. The next section explains aeration. **Topdressing** is the spreading of new soil over the existing soil in order to create permanent pore space for the soil over time. Topdressing is often used in combination with aeration and overseeding to generate an effective environment for new grass growth.

Aeration and Aerators

Aeration is the process of opening channels in the soil so that air, water, and nutrients can flow through the soil and compaction is avoided (Landry, 1995). The areas that are subject to the most traffic (in front of soccer goals, between football hash marks) will suffer the greatest amount of compaction (Landry, 1995). A soil probe or stick or even a shovel can be used to test the compaction level. The more difficult it is to sink the device into the ground, the greater the compaction level. Compaction can be reduced through three aeration techniques.

• Core aerators are vertical-action aerators. Their piston-like action drives hollow metal tines into the ground. Upon entering the soil, the tine scoops out a hole, and as it exits the ground it deposits the soil core on the surface. The core can be broken up with field use or metal drag nets (Steinbach, 2001a). This is the most effective type of aerating but also the most time-consuming.

• Circular or drum aerators are simply rolling drums with spikes. The spikes penetrate the ground as the drum is rolled over the surface. This is a time-efficient method of aerating fields, but penetration or compacting the soil this way can also cause damage. Unlike what happens with core aeration, nothing is removed from the ground, which makes circular aeration more common during playing seasons.

• Slicer or slicing aerators provide the least compaction relief but also create the least amount of surface disruption (Steinbach, 2001a). Slicers use triangular shaped knives to cut thin slits into the ground while traveling at relatively high speeds.

Turfgrass Maintenance

It is not enough to have good grass seed, perfect soil, and the proper blend of nutrients in the soil. A turf needs to be continuously maintained through such means as addition of chemical fertilizers, weed-killing treatments, and appropriate watering and mowing schedules. Mowing, fertilizing, and pest control account for the greatest amount of time and money spent on a lawn; other steps involved in turfgrass maintenance include the following:

• Leaf removal
• Edging
• Weed control (pre-emergent, post-emergent)
• Core aeration
• Mechanical slit-seeding
• Lime (if necessary)
• Dethatching dead grass (if necessary) (Lewis, 1999)

Mowing

Mowing is an important maintenance function that managers must perform to keep a field's appearance and playability at its best. An overzealous mowing schedule or a few short cuts can have devastating effects on the field. A neglected field can quickly overgrow and can suffer significantly

from extreme growth and cut cycles when mowing is too infrequent.

Mowers Two different types of mowers are used on sport fields: reel mowers and rotary. Both types come in the walk-behind, riding, and pull-behind varieties. A reel mower uses a rolling cylinder to scissor grass along a stationary bed knife (Steinbach, 2001a). The most popular form of reel mower today is the triplex. This is a riding mower that offsets three reels (two in front of the tractor and one underneath) so that the reels always reach the grass before the tractor's wheels flatten it (Steinbach, 2001a). Reel mower blades should be sharpened at least twice a week, if not after every use.

Rotary mowers, the most common form of mower, are similar to home mowers. Rotary mowers are able to cut grass at much more varying lengths than reel mowers are (Steinbach, 2001a). They are also more time efficient as they can cut well while traveling at higher speeds and the blades do not need to be sharpened as frequently.

Proper mower maintenance requires checking and maintaining all fluid (oil, hydro fluid, and water) levels, filters, belts, and tire pressure. Another key maintenance issue is cleaning the equipment when moving from one field or facility to another. Turf diseases can be carried from one field to another if infected grass clippings are not washed off the mower (Trotter, 1996).

Cutting Heights Although cutting height varies from field to field depending on grass types and growing rates, a general cutting height for most fields can be determined. It is vital that the grass not be cut too short, as this can severely reduce its life span. When the blade is cut short, the plant tries to send stored food to the blade to regenerate growth. Once it has started feeding the leaf to create aboveground repair or growth, it tries to balance itself by feeding the roots to generate belowground growth (Trusty and Trusty, 1995). Since the effort is placed on strengthening the roots, the blades do not grow as well.

The cool-season grasses—bluegrass, perennial ryegrass, and turf-type tall fescue—have a suggested cutting range of 2 to 3 inches (5-7.6 centimeters) (Trusty and Trusty, 1995). Warm-season grasses have much lower cutting heights. A normal height for a warm-season field is anywhere from 3/4 to 1½ inches (1.9-3.8 centimeters). See maintenance timetables for cool-season and warm-season turf care on page 164.

Maintenance Timetables for Cool-Season and Warm-Season Turf Care

Cool-Season Turf Care

January/ February	If the ground is not frozen or covered with snow, this is the best time to repair drainage problems and low spots by adding more soil underneath the turf. Equipment can also be repaired for the upcoming season.
March/April	This is a good time to test the soil (test every 1-3 years). This is also the best time to aerify fields. In the North it is also the ideal time to start applying weed grass controls. If seeding, the pre-emergents should not be used until the seeds have germinated. At this point, the facility manager should be ready to apply the first fertilizer treatment for the year. A fertilizer should be selected that suits the field's needs based on prior soil-testing results.
May/June	Identifying broadleaf weeds and selecting an effective herbicide are very important. Late June is a good time to apply fertilizer with a higher potassium base. This helps get the grass ready for the summer months. As the summer months approach, it is useful to irrigate the fields frequently. Fields should once again be aerated.
July/August	If problems with diseases or insects occur it may be wise to use fungicides and insecticides to help reduce the problems. If the field manager plans on using this time to overseed the fields, he/she should be ready to apply more fertilizer at a rate of 1/2 lb (0.2 kg) of nitrogen per 1,000 ft^2 (93 m^2).
September	If financially feasible, another dose of fertilizer allows the field to continue growing and recover from the excessive usage.
October	In some areas there may be a need for more broadleaf weed controls as winter annuals start to germinate.
November/ December	If the facility manager notices damage to the field at this time, it should be fixed immediately.

Warm-Season Turf Care

January	During this time fields can be dethatched, and drainage systems can be repaired. The soil should be tested and fertilizer applied to any areas that will be overseeded.
February/ March	This is a period when turfgrasses begin to grow again, so it is important to fertilize the field with a balanced fertilizer (25-3-10). Insecticides should be applied to fields in the South. Once the turf is actively growing, it is time to aerify again.
April/May	Fertilizer and weed control need to be reapplied.
June-August	These months tend to require applying nitrogen at 1 lb (0.4 kg) per 1,000 ft^2.
September/ October	Reduce the amount of fertilizer to 1/2 lb (0.2 kg) per 1,000 ft^2 while increasing the amount of potassium in the applications.
November/ December	Fertilization and aerification are not recommended for turfgrass that is dormant.

From Horman, 1993.

Fertilizer

Television commercials often show beautiful lawns with families at play. Sport fans also relish the opportunity to see a freshly cut outfield. These images may make one wonder how such lawns are achieved. More lawns seem to have problems than not. For example, many fields in the South have fire ant hills. The key to avoiding problems is proper care. Everything has to be analyzed, from the base soil composition to the fertilizer used to the techniques of cutting and chemically treating the grass.

Keys to a great lawn include applying the proper amount of fertilizer and mowing the lawn at the appropriate times with a sharp blade. Fertilizer can improve grass longevity by 40% to 50% when proper amounts are applied nine times a year rather than five. One study showed that longevity also improved by 20% to 40% when the lawn was mowed twice a week rather than once a week (Martin, 2002).

Pests

Most facility managers at one time or another face the problem of pests, although the species and the severity of the problem vary from region to region. The challenge is how to get rid of the pest while limiting the potential associated safety and political hazards (Dahlgren, 2000a). In some areas, insects such as white grubs and mole crickets get in under the soil and eat the grass's root system. Even when pesticides are used, white grubs are usually responsible for destroying about 10% of fields each year (Dahlgren, 2000a). Turf managers have started to change the way they attack insects. Instead of using insecticides, managers are using pesticides that alter the insect's metabolism. If there still is an insect problem, then birds and other animals that feed on these types of insects will be attracted to the fields. Then the issue is no longer how to get rid of the insects, but how to get rid of the insects and the animals (Dahlgren, 2000a). As individual pest control problems can vary, there is no one best approach to eliminating insects.

Field Preparation

If a field is being used for football, soccer, lacrosse, or similar sports, it needs to be lined. Painting lines on the grass using stakes and strings as a guide for the roller is usually the best method. The following are some tips for painting sidelines or logos:

- Cut the area of the grass that will be painted a little lower than the other grass sections. Thus, if the regular playing length is 2 1/2 to 3 inches (6.4-7.6 centimeters), the area that will be painted should be mowed to 1 to 1 1/4 inches (2.5-3 centimeters) high for best appearance.

- The first field painting each year should be done slowly with diluted paint. The same line should be painted from the opposite direction with a less diluted paint mixture.

- Subsequent paintings can be accomplished on one sweep with a two-head sprayer.

- When painting multiple colors, it is best to paint the area white first, have it dry, and then paint other colors on top, as the white will serve as a good base.

- These steps do not cover coloring dirt areas such as the batter's box or the first or third base line, which is accomplished with a dry line marker using a white powder in a 2- or 4-inch (5-or 10-centimeter) band ("Designer Fields," 1998).

Other field preparation issues include weeding, spraying, and snow removal. Weeding is hard to undertake by hand but may be necessary if the field is to look its best. The process is more difficult when the weeds are intertwined with the grass. Some facilities utilize weed and feed granules that fertilize the grass and at the same time kill weeds. Spraying can be a good alternative if the proper chemicals are used.

A facility manager or employee without proper licensure cannot undertake the spraying of certain chemicals. For example, laws dictate what chemicals can be sprayed if certain trees are located even a mile away from the field. Other rules indicate whether spraying can occur on a given day based on the weather conditions. For example, spraying must be postponed if it is raining or windy. Because of complex laws relating to when certain chemicals can be sprayed and where, some facilities outsource the chemical spraying and treatment to professional contractors.

Field preparation can also entail such activities as snow removal. How will snow be removed and where will it be moved? How can snow be moved without damaging the turf? Will the vehicle used to move the snow damage the field? What will happen with the painted portion of the field, and can paint be applied in the wintertime? A facility manager needs to prepare for snow removal contingencies, including snowstorms, well before the weather changes; in fact, the best approach focuses on preparation. Having a snow blower does little good if there is no gas or electricity to operate it. Care should be taken not to remove snow too early, which may cause more work in removing it later. However, failing to remove a minimal amount of accumulation can possibly lead to statutory violations or legal liability.

Additional Outdoor Concerns

Grass fields are only one of the concerns with outdoor facilities. Other field-related issues have to do with synthetic surfaces, infield dirt areas, baseball and softball fields, outdoor bleachers, and safety.

Synthetic Surfaces

Synthetic surfaces can range from Astroturf grasslike surfaces to Mondo tracks. (Mondo tracks is a brand name for a poured product.) Because of the nature of tracks and the amount of work initially needed to install one, repairing is usually not a simple process. For patching small tears in a latex surface, a facility manager can get a patch kit of rubber granules and glue from the manufacturer and trowel it into place (Cohen, 2000). Most other repairs, including those for different surfaces, should be left to a professional or the manufacturer.

Full synthetic surfaces are being used at all levels of competition (Popke, 2000). The original Astroturf fields were easy to install and were versatile. The synthetic fields could be installed over concrete and were easy to roll out and put away. The first application of the synthetic surface was installed at the Houston Astrodome when the grass was not able to grow. The original design was modified over the years, but several major concerns remained, including loose seams, turf toe injuries, turf burn injuries, and the hard playing surface based on a hard undersurface.

Over the years, additional systems were developed to address some of these concerns. Brands include AstroPlay by Southwest Recreational Industries, Sofsport by Hummer, and FieldTurf by FieldTurf. AstroPlay is a combination of rubber and nylon fibers mixed with longer polyolefin strands to help reduce compaction and increase drainage and resiliency. Sofsport is a sand- and rubber-filled system that is installed over a 10-millimeter (0.39-inch) rubber pad for added support and durability. It houses more synthetic strands than other synthetic surfaces (Popke, 2000). FieldTurf's design is similar to that of Sofsport, but without the rubber padding on the bottom. Regardless of the surface used, the key to a surface is actually what is underneath. Most fields need a layer of gravel under the field to assist with drainage. The gravel's density and compaction need to meet preestablished standards for drainage and strength.

Infield Dirt

"Dirt" playing areas need as much care as fields do. Baseball players do not want a bumpy infield, as it can cause a bad hop and irregular bounces and can present a hazard for those sliding into bases. To minimize these problems, numerous techniques are used to make sure the infield is in proper shape (see primary rules for infield care on page 167). The starting point is analyzing the material that composes the infield. Infields can include lava rock, agri-lime, Stabilizer red, stone dust, crushed brick, Turface blends, pumice, heavy clay, heavy sand, native soils, and infield blends (Perry, 2002a).

Whatever material is used for the infield, the surface will become hard over time, and different techniques need to be used to make the ground playable. This is especially true if there is too much clay in the field; with only a small amount of clay, the ground is easier to work with. Hardened clay can be as tough as rock when dried in the sun for an extended period. The typical technique used to make surfaces playable includes scoring and dragging. **Scoring** entails various techniques to break up the ground. Heavy equipment or tools with nails or claws are often used to penetrate the field 3 to 6 inches (7.6-15 centimeters). The more common technique is to use smaller equipment that turns over only the top 1 or 2 inches (2.5-5 centimeters) ("scarifying"). **Dragging** involves using screens, rakes, or other devices to smooth the field. The techniques need to be

Primary Rules for Infield Care

- Water the infield before working the dirt, as the water loosens the surface.
- The top 1 to 1.5 inches (2.5-3.8 centimeters) of the infield should be scarified (broken apart).
- The ground should be dragged, broomed, and leveled back to a clod-free, smooth surface.
- Rewater the field to prevent wind-blown dirt or erosion damage.

From Perry, 2002a.

frequently changed so that there is no rippling or any washboard effect from constant dragging in the same direction (Steinbach, 2002). Raking the buildup by the baseline back into the infield can also eliminate lips that can cause bad hops. After dragging the dirt, the field groomer should apply light moisture to the dirt to help keep dust down (Steinbach, 2002).

Baseball and Softball Fields

Baseball and softball fields provide some of the greatest challenges to field managers because of the multiple types of surfaces. Certain areas take more of a beating during games and regularly require extensive attention on an almost daily basis. As with most fields, a regular routine should include daily as well as pre- and postgame maintenance.

The pitcher's mound and batting boxes are the most seriously abused part of any baseball or softball field. Every play that occurs in the game is initiated from these locations. In addition, the motions and techniques that pitchers and batters use to throw and bat the ball are constantly digging up these areas. The first step in protecting the pitcher's safety is to construct a quality mound. The mound can be constructed in many ways, with new materials including mound blocks, packing clay, poly-blend soils, two-tiered pitching rubbers, and subsurface pads.

A regulation-sized pitching mound in baseball is 18 feet (5.5 meters) in diameter with the rubber set 10 feet 6 inches (3.2 meters) from the home plate side of the circle. Using a leveling transient to determine the height, the top of the pitching mound should be 10 inches (25 centimeters) above the height of home plate (Perry, 1997). The pitching mound itself should be set 60 feet 6 inches (18.4 meters) from the apex of home plate and should sit near the front of a level area that is 5 feet (1.5 meters) by 34 inches (86 centimeters). From

6 inches (15 centimeters) in front of the rubber, the mound should slope toward home plate at a rate of 1 inch (2.5 centimeters) per foot. The underbelly of the mound should be made from hard-packed clay blocks to a height of 4 inches (10 centimeters) and then filled in with a mixture of soils that will help keep the clay moisture free (Perry, 1997). In contrast to baseball, the mound in softball is level, but the same basic underbelly should be developed.

The two areas that need the most attention around the plate are the right-handed batter's box and the catcher's area. Using clay blocks or a subsurface pad about 1 to 1 1/2 inches (2.5-3.8 centimeters) below the surface will help solidify the area. This lessens the amount of damage that occurs during a game. To prevent damage, artificial covering pads are now being used during pregame batting practice (Perry, 1997). Pads or mats help eliminate some of the damage done to the batter's box on a daily basis. When damage occurs, the fix is simply a matter of removing the covering dirt down to the clay blocks and repacking the area to the desired shape.

The issues on baselines and base paths and areas around the bases are similar. A broom or hose can help move infield dirt to prevent high lips. The dirt about 10 feet (3 meters) around the base should be softened to help cushion the blow a player sustains when sliding into the base (Perry, 1997).

Outdoor Bleachers

In 2001 the Consumer Product Safety Commission issued new guidelines on how to retrofit bleachers to increase spectator safety (LaRue, 2002). The standards were developed after it was reported that 19,000 people visit emergency rooms every year from bleacher- or grandstand-related injuries. Injuries occur when people slip or

Facility Focus: Rose Bowl

Courtesy of the Pasadena P.D.

In 1897 the city of Pasadena, California, purchased 10 acres of land. In 1921 the city decided to build a stadium with the south end left open. This gave the structure a horseshoe-like shape. The stadium was designed to fit as many people as possible as close to the action as possible. When first built the stadium sat 57,000 people. The stadium was given the name Rose Bowl by a police officer named Harlan W. Hall. The Rose Bowl was officially dedicated on January 1, 1923. The south end of the stadium, which had previously been open, was closed in 1929. This gave the structure its now famous sight line-enhancing elliptical shape. The closing of the south end brought the seating capacity up to 76,000 people (History, 2004b).

Today the seating capacity of the Rose Bowl is 92,542 people. The stadium has approximately 77 rows of seats. It measures 880 feet (268 meters) from the north to south rims and 695 feet (211 meters) from the east to west rims. The circumference of the rim is 2,430 feet (740 meters), while the circumference inside at field level is approximately 1,350 feet (411 meters). The turfed area inside the bowl measures 79,156 square feet (7,350 square meters). The fence around the Rose Bowl is 1 mile (1.6 kilometers) in circumference. The dimensions of the playing field for football are 53 yards (48 meters) (width) × 100 yards (91 meters) (length) and for soccer are 70 yards (64 meters) (width) × 120 yards (110 meters) (length). The stadium itself is approximately 830 feet (253 meters) above sea level. The Rose Bowl press box is the highest point of the stadium at 100 feet (30.5 meters) above ground level. The first PSLs (personal seat licenses) ever sold were sold to build the Rose Bowl. A total of 210 individuals and corporations purchased what were then referred to as "seat subscriptions" to finance the building of the $272,198 Rose Bowl Stadium ("General Information," 2004).

trip, fall off bleachers, or fall between boards. The primary concerns with bleachers are gaps between seat boards and footboards, guardrails that are not high enough, bleachers that are structurally unsafe, and aisles that are affected by weather conditions (LaRue, 2002).

Many of the same techniques used for maintaining indoor bleachers can be utilized for outdoor structures. The most important step is to set up a schedule of regular inspections. The Consumer Product Safety Commission guidelines suggest conducting inspections no less than four times per year, but if the bleachers are in constant use it may be wise to conduct more frequent inspections (LaRue, 2002). All manufacturer's guidelines for inspections need to be followed. Inspections also need to be documented (with date and signature) for the maintenance program as well as to help with litigation. If problems are found, the bleachers should be closed until a structural engineer or construction professional has remedied the problems (LaRue, 2002).

Safety Concerns

Outdoor facilities can represent potential hazards, especially when children are involved. Playgrounds are notorious for hazards such as inadequate matting or fall protection, pinch points, and choking hazards. In a 1992 study, 31% of inspected playgrounds had surfaces made of cement, packed dirt, or asphalt. In 2002 the number was down to 4.5% (Popke, 2003). Playgrounds also had equipment too high off the ground, swinging hazards, and even wood-based products with possible carcinogens. Thus, playgrounds need to be vigilantly analyzed and maintained to ensure that they do not represent a threat to users. Between 1990 and 2000, over 147 playground-related deaths were reported. However, as the numbers here indicate, injuries have declined significantly; and much of that success is due to aggressive educational programs for playground managers, parents, and children on how to be safer. Similar aggressive educational campaigns need to be undertaken for all other outdoor areas to prevent problems and injuries.

Another child-based concern involves "attractive nuisance." **Attractive nuisance** refers to the concept of legal liability for a part of the facility that an operator knew or should have known was dangerous and that an operator knew or should have known a child would want to go to. An outdoor facility that has a pond, for example, has an attractive nuisance. Facility managers should know that children may want to play around a pond and can fall in and drown. Thus, any facility with a pond must properly secure it so that children cannot enter the area without authorization.

Summary

Indoor sport facilities present various unique concerns typically not found in facilities like office buildings. A sport facility manager must deal with equipment that can cause significant injury, such as weights that could fall on a patron's foot. While a general facility has moving parts such as photocopiers, fax machines, and people movers, sport facility equipment can be much more dangerous, and appropriate precautions need to be taken. Sport facility components such as floors and bleachers need to be maintained more frequently than office flooring and seating areas.

While a traditional office building probably has landscaping, the scope of the environment and the focus on grass turf with sport facilities make turf planting and maintenance one of the top priorities for a sport facility manager. Planting the right seeds, having the right soil, and mowing the fields at the appropriate times are only part of the process of maintaining a well-manicured field. Facility managers must determine the amount of time and money they want to spend to make their fields look the best they can. The key is to develop a strategy and then to follow it.

DISCUSSION QUESTIONS AND ACTIVITIES

1. What steps can be taken to make sure a field is in the best condition before an event?

2. What steps can be taken to make sure a gym or grandstands are in the best condition before an event?

3. What would be the best grass type to plant in your region?

4. Walk through a gym or physical education facility on your campus and examine what could have been built or installed better or what changes you might recommend to make the facility better.

Facility Maintenance

CHAPTER OBJECTIVES

After completing this chapter you will be able to do the following:

- Describe various techniques used to help present a safe, clean, and functional facility
- Develop a maintenance plan for a facility and its components
- Appreciate how benchmarking affects a maintenance program
- Understand how to conduct a maintenance audit
- Design a maintenance department and strategies to keep a facility clean
- Know the basics of facility repair management

Think for a moment about a house. Once a house is built and all the amenities are in place, does a family live in the house forever without fixing or changing it? Of course the answer is no. They will constantly examine the house and work to make it their home. They may want to redo a bathroom after a couple years, add a deck, or convert a bedroom to an office. A home owner must purchase supplies such as light bulbs, toilet paper, and cleaning agents on a regular basis and constantly maintain the property. The exterior needs to be cleaned, plants need to be pruned, lawns need to be mowed, salt needs to be added to water softeners, and air filter screens need to be replaced or cleaned. In the living spaces, dishes need to be washed, toilets need to be plunged, walls need to be repainted, and other maintenance and repair concerns need to be addressed.

A large sport facility also must be constantly maintained and repaired. Some stadiums and arenas have hundreds of bathroom stalls. Constant work is needed to keep locks operating, seats attached, paper seat cover dispensers stocked, and toilet paper dispensers stocked and operating; it is an ongoing task to maintain sufficient water flow, keep toilets unclogged, and even remove graffiti. The maintenance issues can become even more complex in concession preparation areas and boiler/chilling mechanical areas.

Maintenance is the key to operating a safe and clean facility. Operation and maintenance activities normally account for 5% to 15% of a facility's total expenditure (Applied Management Engineering, 1991). However, the human resource time and effort are hard to calculate. The repair center at a major stadium can receive several hundred phone calls during a game for everything from spills to broken door handles. With everything going on in a facility, maintenance can often be pushed aside. The result can be an ugly and unsafe facility. The cost is even greater when routine maintenance is ignored and what could have been a minor repair becomes a major replacement costing thousands of dollars. Think about never changing the transmission fluid in a car. While it might take 20 minutes and $40 to complete the fluid change, failure to change and monitor the fluid could lead to a $2,000 transmission replacement bill.

The hallmark of any maintenance effort is implementation of a comprehensive maintenance and repair (M&R) plan. Such a plan typically starts with an understanding of what needs to be maintained or repaired, and this can start with an **audit.** An audit can identify the biggest concerns and the areas needing the greatest amount of time or money. An audit might lead to the conclusion that a maintenance department should be developed. Of course, maintenance is not always the answer, since sometimes items need to be repaired or replaced. But whether the need is for maintenance or repair, any effort must be tracked through the process called benchmarking, which helps determine if the M&R program is working correctly. Special care needs to be taken regarding certain sport-specific issues such as maintaining gym floors, as discussed in chapter 8. Lastly, the push for environmentally friendly buildings has put pressure on facility managers to maintain their facilities in a more responsible manner.

Maintenance and Repair Program

While some facilities attempt to limit spending on maintenance, the financial impact of such a decision can be disastrous. Some expenses can be minimized, but other expenses that could have been reduced through normal maintenance can in fact increase significantly without regular maintenance. Maintaining a home heating, ventilation, and air conditioning (HVAC) system may cost $500 a year, but failing to maintain it and then having to replace it earlier than would otherwise be necessary could costs thousands of dollars. In a public assembly facility, the replacement cost could be in the millions of dollars.

Underfunding maintenance can also lead to building code violations, structural failure, safety/health failure, lower productivity, excessive repair costs, service failures, premature loss, higher absenteeism, and other social costs (poor morale, increased pollution, and harm to employee recruitment/retention efforts) (Cotts and Lee, 1992). Thus, proper maintenance department funding can produce both tangible and intangible benefits for a facility.

The specific keys to an effective M&R system are daily housekeeping, prompt response to needed repairs, installation and execution of a mainte-

nance schedule to prevent premature failures, and completion of major repairs based on the lowest life-cycle costs. Other components include identifying improvement projects, lowering energy usage and costs, identifying ways to reduce operating costs, performing accurate cost estimates for future growth, accurately tracking maintenance work costs, properly scheduling necessary work, maintaining historical data, and monitoring the progress of all M&R efforts (Cotts and Lee, 1992).

An effective M&R system entails planning and programming, budgeting, staffing, supervising, and evaluating. This section discusses the components of an M&R system and steps in a maintenance and repair program are outlined on page 173.

Planning and Programming

In planning and programming, a facility examines basic data, plans, existing policies, procedures, and standards to establish maintenance policies. This phase examines what equipment and systems currently exist and how to keep the various elements operating effectively. The facility management team analyzes the work that will be performed and the **benchmarking** standards or other criteria it wishes to meet. Thus, goal setting is a major component within this phase.

Besides examining current equipment and facility needs, this phase examines future needs. Part of the planning process also entails tracking industry developments to determine if more efficient equipment is available. For example, if a refrigerator is working fine but costs $2,000 a year just for electrical usage, the planning process may involve exploring more cost-effective machines. While the evaluation phase deals with whether goals can be reached, the maintenance staff needs to know if there are more cost-effective solutions. If $2,000 per year is a reasonable cost and newer machines do not save money, then the equipment should not be replaced.

The planning process classifies work into six basic scheduling categories:

- Inspect and repair only when absolutely necessary
- **Cyclical repairs,** for example replacing the roof every 20 years
- **Preventive maintenance,** which is maintaining the equipment or facility according to preestablished standards (e.g., oiling

Steps in a Maintenance and Repair Program

Planning and Programming
Inventory of the facility
Categorizing work to be done
Developing appropriate standards
Analyzing the facility deficiencies
Prioritizing work by activity, class, or deficiencies
Developing short- and long-term plans

Budgeting
Setting the tone for all M&R work developed from the work plan
Analyzing the impact of capital budget on M&R
Developing a comparison with prior budgets
Developing an impact analysis if funds are cut
Identifying and eliminating ways money is overspent on M&R
Organizing all materials and inventory to save money
Allocating budgeted funds to resolve problems
Managing contracting strategies

Staffing
Developing an organizational model of M&R department
Creating clear lines of responsibility and authority
Hiring employees with technical competencies
Training workers to accomplish tasks and improve skills
Managing both in-house and outsourced workers

Supervising
Providing leadership and monitoring workers
Managing the work flow
Providing rapid responses to crises
Analyzing the condition of repaired equipment
Controlling budgets and financing
Managing the facility information system (FIS)
Ensuring accountability
Ensuring that proper documentation is kept and managed
Utilizing a quality control plan
Administering a tenant relations program
Coordinating activities with potential unions

Evaluating
Evaluating pre-repair and post-repair condition for quality
Comparing results with historical data
Examining customer/tenant feedback
Evaluating employee performance against set standards

From Cotts and Lee, 1992.

motors every 100 hours of use); preventive maintenance can be referred to as routine maintenance since the equipment is regularly maintained to prevent problems

- **Breakdown maintenance,** for example when a light bulb burns out or a machine stops running
- Repair projects, ranging from replacing a broken window to making major repairs
- General housekeeping and janitorial services (Cotts and Lee, 1992)

Preventive maintenance is defined as the pre-breakdown work performed on a facility's equipment and systems to eliminate problems, malfunctions, or breakdowns or to keep failures within predetermined limits (Lewis, 1999). Thus, preventive maintenance is undertaken after a cost–benefit analysis has shown that more money will be saved through prevention than through replacement of failed systems or equipment. For example, water needs to be moved through the plumbing system to make sure pipes do not become corroded or scaled (scaling involves the buildup of minerals such as calcium carbonate that slows water movement in pipes and reduces water pressure).

Routine maintenance refers to the day-to-day work required to make sure a facility stays open. Routine maintenance is required to check that toilet paper dispensers are not broken, toilets are not failing to flush, or that faucets are not dripping. An employee may have to check fixtures before or after each game, or both before and after, to identify anything that is not working.

Major repairs are hard to classify, as a $10,000 repair might be considered minor at one facility and a $100 repair considered major at another. As a general rule, however, any significant project outside the normally budgeted M&R scope would probably be considered major.

Maintenance plans can be supplemented with additional procedures such as alterations and janitorial care, which do not necessarily maintain the facility or equipment but enhance its operation. An **alteration** is a change that allows a facility, system, or piece of equipment to perform a function different from the one it was originally designed for. A bathroom can be altered to include a changing table for a baby as a convenience to parents. An improvement increases the functional or productive performance of a facility, system, or piece of equipment (Lewis, 1999).

Janitorial care refers to cleanliness and to providing a facility with needed cleaning agents and supplies. The industry term used to describe this function is housekeeping. Housekeeping entails various activities from sweeping and mopping floors and cleaning bathrooms to replacing toilet paper or removing trash. Housekeeping includes janitorial, ground maintenance, and operating services. Janitorial services primarily refers to cleaning, dusting, waxing, and furnishing of expendable supplies.

Budgeting

In the budgeting phase, policies are examined, prioritized, and then submitted for budgetary approval. If there are insufficient funds, then all items that are delayed need to be prioritized so they can be completed at some later point. Ordinary, less costly alteration and construction projects are usually excluded. Managers utilize historical comparisons, benchmarking standards, past budgets, and other techniques to help establish an M&R budget. The budget needs to be realistic and needs to highlight the primary tasks that must be completed immediately. In one analysis of school repair needs in Florida, a school district had 7,100 backlogged safety repairs; 1,800 of the repairs had been on the list for over three years, and 67 safety concerns had been on the list for over a decade ("Repair Backlog," 2003). Either these projects were very low priority or were too expensive and beyond the scope of any budget developed over the 10 years.

Budgeting is the primary reason why maintenance programs and plans are often not implemented. However, if senior executives can be shown the **return on investment (ROI)** from effective maintenance programs, they are likely to be more receptive to allocating necessary funds to support an M&R program.

Staffing

The M&R program should be overseen by a manager who will be in charge of all M&R activities, including tracking those activities to make sure that work is accomplished properly and in a timely manner. Staffing entails hiring and managing the right employees to perform the work required by the M&R program. One of the hurdles often encountered in this regard is unionized workforces.

Conflict may arise if individuals do not want to undertake any extra work not called for in the collective bargaining agreement.

The heart of staffing an M&R program is to have the right people doing the right job at the right time. This is much more difficult than it sounds. While routine maintenance can be planned and is easy to organize with computer maintenance programs, the daily routine is often interrupted by emergencies. Thus, significant time is spent trying to organize workers to help them accomplish routine tasks as well as respond to emergencies.

Supervision and Evaluation

In addition to appropriately budgeting and spending the department resources, supervising the M&R program requires the manager to prioritize projects, execute the work plan, and analyze the facility's general condition. The focus at this point is on the actual work. It is easy to schedule someone to work at a given spot or to perform a given task. It is much more difficult to make sure that the work is actually accomplished, and accomplished correctly. Supervision requires constant monitoring. Timing is also a major concern. Projects cannot be undertaken if they will conflict with ongoing events. Unless there is an emergency, repairs are not done on a basketball floor during a game. The repairs could be major, but it is preferable to attend to them before and after events. The goal is to minimize the need to shut down the facility or cancel an event.

Controlling is necessary in various contexts, from the budget to expenditures to crisis situations. It may be, for example, that a project is budgeted for $20,000 but that after some initial work, management discovers the presence of a hidden problem such as dry rot that will double the cost. This type of situation is not unusual for those involved in facility repairs. In fact, most repair projects run over budget because it is often impossible to determine the true condition of a facility, system, or component without actually getting into it and examining it. This is one reason some contractors in the trade areas (electrical, plumbing, security, etc.) refuse to give a solid quote until they have examined a system after doing some initial work. Controlling can focus on choosing the right workers who will do the job at the least expensive rate while still providing quality work.

Successful controlling can often produce a budgetary windfall, which can free some funds for repairs on the prioritized list. This can be accomplished by close monitoring of time and expenses for various projects and tracking of activity to see how quickly the work can be done. For example, the time required to change a facility over from hockey to basketball can be tracked and the process modified to save time and money. After a number of changeovers and revisions it might be possible to reduce the process from four to three hours, which with 20 employees doing the job at night might save hundreds or even thousands of dollars.

Evaluation entails examining whether the M&R program has been successful. Work orders can be reviewed to determine the amount of time spent on various projects and where the greatest expenses occurred (Cotts and Lee, 1992). Another focus is on performance evaluation for employees. For example, a facility manager can plant trash in strategic places to see if the cleaning crew will find and remove it. If the cleaning crew is doing a cursory cleaning rather than a complete cleaning, corrective steps need to be taken. Through utilizing a comprehensive M&R program, a facility can hopefully provide a clean and safe facility at the most reasonable cost.

Maintenance Audits

Maintenance audits provide the framework and discipline to systematically review, analyze, and recommend performance-related improvements for facility mechanisms (Applied Management Engineering, 1991). Audits help provide the working plan that shows what areas need improvement, what corrective actions will rectify potential problems, and how to monitor the outcome of any given action.

As shown on page 176, a maintenance audit starts with establishing priorities. Then an audit schedule is developed. After a schedule is developed, the audit parameters are defined and organized. Either before or after this step, an audit team needs to be established. Some argue that an audit team should be developed at the very beginning of the process to make sure that all issues are covered. Others argue for establishing the audit team after upper management has defined what it wants from the audit process. This could save time in

Audit Process

1. Establish priorities. Do certain systems need to be analyzed first? Senior management may establish large priorities for a future audit review team.

2. Establish an audit schedule. A time frame has to be established to determine whether maintenance will be examined on an annual, monthly, or other basis, as this time frame dictates what resources are needed and when.

3. Organize and define the audit. Through acquiring and organizing the required data, the various affected units or managers will understand the audit's scope, and a proposed statement of scope can be developed.

4. Select an audit team. Those who will be affected by the process need to have input into and involvement in the process.

5. Perform the audit. Once the scope, parameters, and team are defined, the audit plan is developed with practicality in mind to ensure that it can be implemented.

6. Prepare the report. Once the audit is completed, a detailed report highlights the findings.

7. Take action. Management needs to critically analyze the audit report and institute plans and procedures to implement the findings. One of the critical points is for management to allocate funds to help accomplish the desired results.

8. Follow up. Has the process been successful? Will the maintenance plan save money and extend the useful life of facility assets?

From Kaiser and Applied Management Engineering, 1991.

that the audit team will not reach decisions that are contrary to the directive established by upper management.

The audit team sets some parameters, but primarily performs the audit. The audit examines what occurred from mainly an objective point of view. Subjective issues such as how someone changed light bulbs are not as important as whether all the broken bulbs were replaced in a timely manner. After the audit is completed, a formal report needs to be presented to upper management. Upper management is then asked to take action. After the audit, action such as corrective maintenance must be taken. Thereafter a follow-up report is made to reexamine the process and determine what additional steps may be required.

One of the key elements within any maintenance auditing system is measuring effectiveness. Effectiveness can be measured through productivity (how productive is time spent on given projects?), performance (do the employees work well?), work quality (is the work satisfactory?), and priority (is time being spent on the right projects?) (Applied Management Engineering, 1991). Key elements in determining how efficiently and effectively a program is operating are outlined on page 177.

After a thorough facility audit, the maintenance department will need to handle all the various concerns identified in the audit. While one person can take care of a small building, a larger facility needs a large staff of trained tradespeople in such disciplines as plumbing, electricity, and carpentry.

Maintenance Department

While some facilities may not technically call a department the "maintenance department," all facilities have at least one person responsible for maintenance-related issues. Typically a maintenance department is responsible for the following activities:

- Preventive/Routine (daily, weekly, monthly, quarterly, and yearly) maintenance

- Ordering, processing, storing, and utilizing parts, inventory, and supplies

- Maintaining appropriate records on everything from energy usage to requested and completed repairs

- Monitoring energy management programs

Key Elements of a Maintenance Audit

1. Organization. What policies, procedures, personnel, and organizational structure are being used to assist in implementing the maintenance goals and objectives?

2. Workload identification. What equipment is available in the facility's inventory and what is the equipment's general condition? What maintenance system is currently being utilized, how are work requests processed, and how is inventory ordered? Is preventive maintenance undertaken, and how is routine and recurring work handled as well as all resulting documentation?

3. Work plan. What priority is given to which projects? For example, when will alterations and improvements be undertaken compared with emergency repairs or cyclical activities? Specific policies need to be developed for backlogged work, and budgets need to be developed for all backlogged work.

4. Work accomplishment. Have all the necessary supplies and parts been available for required maintenance work? Are the employees properly trained and equipped to perform necessary maintenance or repairs? Are employees properly supervised and provided with necessary resources such as transportation vehicles to quickly respond and reach their assigned location?

5. Appraisal. Is a management information system (MIS) in place, such as a computerized maintenance management system? Are performance, productivity, priority, and work quality measured and analyzed? Are all records for the facility and all equipment properly stored and analyzed?

From Kaiser and Applied Management Engineering, 1991.

- Minor rehabilitation work such as light painting or repairs
- Assisting in purchasing large capital assets or facilities, or making other major decisions (Borsenik and Stutts, 1997)

These categories could be supplemented by many additional activities. For example, the maintenance department at an ice rink may be responsible for securing goals, monitoring and repairing the ice surface, fixing dasher boards and replacing glass, and other specific activities associated with the ice-cooling system. Smaller facilities also need to utilize their maintenance department differently, perhaps by utilizing these individuals to work on construction, move management, janitorial functions, and administrative duties.

Facility Repair Management

While the goal of maintenance is to keep systems and equipment running, repairs are immediate expenses necessary to make a system or piece of equipment operable, and repairs are done at the expense of previously scheduled maintenance. For example, a facility may have scheduled $10,000 to maintain a roof, but if the roof leaks too much it may be necessary to make a repair costing $20,000 that was not previously budgeted. This process is completely different from what happens in a marketing department, which can create a budget at the start of the year and then adhere to it since marketing involves few true emergencies. A facility maintenance department has to respond to emergencies daily. Since it is hard to determine when an emergency might occur, there always is a struggle to allocate money, time, personnel, and other resources.

Whatever the maintenance or repair, it involves a process, and that process must be managed. The process can be as simple as someone's seeing a problem and fixing it or as complicated as having to go through a major bureaucratic exercise just to change a light bulb. A typical process for a repair project at a large facility, with the division in the facility responsible for the work indicated in parentheses, is outlined 178.

The list illustrates that making repairs is a process. Any process can run into trouble or bottlenecks. If someone is absent, will the work orders be dealt with or will they stay on the person's desk until he or she returns? As a process, the maintenance program can be managed so that work is completed more promptly and inexpensively. The process can be streamlined if the form passes

Repair Process

Someone sees a problem and calls it in to the repair department help desk

Receive call (help desk)

Create work order (help desk)

Authorize work order (management)

Define scope (planning)

Obtain necessary documentation such as warranties or blueprints (planning)

Determine which trades, parts, and materials are required (planning)

Determine cost estimates (planning)

Obtain approval (accounting)

Schedule resources (management)

Purchase parts and hire labor (accounting)

Perform work (maintenance)

Complete work and close work order (help desk)

Close work order (accounting)

Update all files, warranties, and blueprints (help desk and planning)

Conduct quality assessment (management)

Update benchmarking standards and measurements (management)

From Noferi, 2003.

directly from one person to the relevant worker or can be completed online. These are both ways in which an existing process can be modified. It is often possible to streamline processes through comparing an existing program with other programs by means of benchmarking and monitoring the repair process.

Benchmarking

Maintenance can be a complicated issue for a facility; benchmarking makes it simpler. Benchmarking is the process of comparing what one facility does to an industry standard. It measures performance of a facility's systems and components against the optimum performance expected from the systems and components. It is in essence a baseline comparison. For example, industry data may show that a motor used under given conditions typically lasts 10 years with utilization of a particular maintenance plan. If a facility buys that motor, they could expect it to last 10 years if they adhere to the maintenance plan. Thus, industry standards and best practices are used to help facilities maximize the return on their system investments.

The key to benchmarking is a critical physical analysis and review of the facility with respect to architectural, mechanical, electrical, plumbing, fire protection, energy usage, telephone/data, security, structural, environmental, facility operations, and related systems (Simons, 2002). There is a significant relationship between a facility's operation and the facility's physical condition. To make sure the facility is in good physical condition the operational plans need to be monitored to ensure that operations, policies, and preventive maintenance procedures are calibrated and working together to maximize system effectiveness.

Monitoring Repairs

Besides benchmarking, numerous facility monitoring programs exist to optimize facility maintenance. As seen in the analysis performed by OR&L in chapter 3 (page 51), some companies focus on providing better maintenance and janitorial services by offering computer analysis of current procedures. Thus, through benchmarking and use of computers a facility manager can more efficiently and effectively manage a facility's operations.

Behind the Scenes: Benchmarking Standards

Benchmarking numbers help a facility determine how effective its maintenance is compared with other facilities. Some pertinent statistics from the International Facility Managers Association (IFMA) benchmarking survey are the following:

- The mean cost per square foot for cleaning rest rooms, offices, work areas, and common areas is $1.29.
- Maintenance departments on average respond 14% of the time to emergencies in six minutes or less versus 18% within 30 minutes.
- The amount of space per employee declined from 471 square feet (44 square meters) per person in 1997 to 407 square feet (38 square meters) in 2001 ("IFMA Surveys," 2001).

The systems used to manage maintenance and cleaning are referred to as **computerized maintenance management systems (CMMS).** These programs are designed to streamline the maintenance system by processing critical information and providing solutions to help maintain systems and decrease life-cycle costs. They can produce work order printouts, maintenance history, material inventory, and financial analyses, improve monitoring and inventory management systems, and track utility usage.

A CMMS catalogs all the assets within a facility and their maintenance or monitoring schedules. Utilizing this type of system, facility operations and maintenance staff know when a machine has reached 1,000 hours of service and when it may need to be serviced according to manufacturer specifications. Following these strict guidelines enables a piece of equipment or the facility itself to last longer and decreases the need for major repairs. Guidelines for maintaining automobiles are a familiar example. Cars purchased today come with manuals that indicate what services are needed at specific time or mileage intervals. At 3,000 miles, very little work may be required, perhaps an oil change. At 50,000 miles, 20 different items may need to be checked, repaired, replaced, or monitored. If the time line or mileage milestone points are not followed, problems may develop and the car may break down before it should, costing the car owner a significant amount of money.

As any car owner will tell you, one reason for not following the maintenance schedule is a lack of time. People may be too busy to bring the car to a repair shop. Another reason may be money. If a maintenance check costs $100 and the owner does not want to spend the money, the sched-ule becomes irrelevant. All facilities and their equipment have maintenance schedules, but the schedules are not followed for various reasons. Some facilities do not have enough employees to accomplish all the required work. In other cases, staff do not know in what order work should be done, so less important items may receive attention before more important items. A CMMS can provide appropriate reminders and develop calendars that maintenance staff can follow, hopefully reducing future expenses and making the facility and equipment last longer.

Some companies have been reluctant to spend money on CMMS. These companies may be reluctant to change from the older card-based type of system for tracking maintenance projects. Others may not think that the benefits justify the cost of installing a CMMS. This mind-set has to do with the fact that these systems produce "soft dollar" savings; more executives are looking for "hard dollar" savings such as those achieved by terminating an employee. The "soft dollar" savings come from

- minimizing lost productivity,
- fewer operational interruptions,
- optimized labor costs,
- reduction in size of maintenance staff or their hours,
- reduction in number of emergencies that need to be handled,
- decreased overtime pay for off-hour nuisance alarm calls,
- decreased personnel time needed for manual machine inspections (called "rounds and readings"),

© Gil Fried

Yale Field, home to the Northeastern League's New Haven County Cutters, was originally built in 1927. However, the land for the field had a history that went back much earlier. In 1882, Yale University purchased an apple orchard and a farm. By 1902 the Yale Bulldogs were playing baseball on that piece of land. In 1927, Yale began construction of a new half-million-dollar stadium. It was built to resemble Yankee Stadium with its concrete arches.

Construction was finished that same year; the first baseball game took place in 1928 between the New Haven Professionals and the Yale Bulldogs (the New Haven Professionals beat the Bulldogs 12-0). For many years thereafter the field was the scene of collegiate baseball. Many professionals or soon-to-be-professionals such as Ted Williams, Jimmy Foxx, Yogi Berra, Lou Gehrig, and Jeff Bagwell made appearances. Also, former President George H. Bush played his entire college baseball career there as a Yale Bulldog (Healey, 2002-2004).

From the 1930s through the 1950s, Yale Field became a shrine to baseball. Besides Yale's own teams, some of the best teams in the major leagues, including the New York Yankees, the Boston Red Sox, the Brooklyn Dodgers, the Philadelphia Phillies, and the Boston Braves, played preseason exhibitions in New Haven (Beach, 1995). In 1990, Yale wanted to renovate the stadium. An enterprising group noticed that both major and minor league baseball were expanding and applied for an Eastern League expansion franchise. The franchise was granted, and in 1993 a $3 million renovation was undertaken. After the renovations, nothing of the old stadium remained except the original facade with its distinctive arches and the "Green Monster." The New Haven Ravens added a party pavilion and a couple of electric scoreboards during the renovation process. The Ravens played their first home game at Yale Field on April 14, 1994 and their last game there in 2003 before moving to New Hampshire. This left Yale Field without a professional baseball tenant until the New Haven County Cutters signed a lease in 2004 (Healey, 2002-2004). Besides undertaking regular maintenance efforts, the new team built several luxury boxes, removed the grandstands, and placed a protected children's playground where the grandstands had been located. The team was to take care of regular maintenance, according to a lease agreement with Yale that included specific maintenance standards.

- reduction in time required to prepare management reports (which can be performed instantaneously), and
- reduction in costs for internal staff (Buckley, 2003).

Costs can be reduced by enlisting technical staff from external sources. Through a service contract, a third party can monitor the facility's CMMS and immediately dispatch repair persons when the program identifies a problem. This is similar to "just in time" inventory management systems in which a supplier and manufacturer know at the same time that a part is needed (Buckley, 2003). Hard dollar savings can result from eliminating costs by selling a facility or terminating an employee, meaning that remaining employees assume more work.

Basic Maintenance

Facility maintenance is not just about planning, budgeting, and auditing. Obviously at a certain point the work needs to be accomplished. Tradespeople, from carpenters to electricians, and general maintenance employees must be informed about the work to be done and given the resources (parts and tools). Maintenance work focuses primarily on floors and on equipment and surfaces that can pose a safety hazard, as well as ensuring that procedures do not harm the environment.

Floor Maintenance

A shiny gym floor is probably a well-maintained floor. Workers in facilities spend significant time and energy mopping floors, using the right finishing materials, and regularly inspecting and maintaining floors. There is no one best way to take care of a flooring surface since there are so many different types of surfaces. A locker room floor raises water-related slipping and mold concerns; a poured urethane or tile gym floor must be treated differently than a wood floor.

If a floor faces excessive and early finish wear, the problem could be the result of improper maintenance, which can lead to an increased coefficient of friction level (more slippery surface). Steps to help reduce this problem are placing mats at entrances to reduce dust and regularly mopping the floor with an approved floor cleaner.

A peeling or bubbling finish on a maple wood floor typically means that the floor was not properly screened or cleaned between coats or that substances such as soap were not properly removed between coats. If the problem is inherent in the topcoat, the topcoat can be screened and repainted. However, if the problem exists in lower layers, all coats need to be sanded and then refinished. Finish roughness is often due to contamination in the drying process and requires following the same procedures as for peeling (Cohen, 1998).

The typical maintenance requirements for daily cleaning of a wood gym floor include the following:

- Sweeping with a properly treated dust mop (possibly several times a day if there is excessive activity or if dirt and other objects are being brought into the gym)
- Immediately cleaning any spills

- Using an approved floor cleaner to remove marks such as heel marks
- Checking the HVAC system to make sure it is functioning properly, as too much humidity can cause wood warp and other problems
- Inspecting the floor for any tightening or shrinkage and making sure expansion voids are clear so that the wood can expand ("MFMA Maintenance Tips," 2003)

Besides wear and tear and other conditions necessitating maintenance, floors can suffer water damage. Overexposure to water can cause wood flooring to swell or buckle, creating a possible tripping hazard. Problems can become acute when liquid leaks are not detected for an extended period. Wood flooring that has been exposed to liquids for several days normally cannot be saved. If the exposure has been shorter, the maintenance staff should try to dry the wood as quickly as possible. This could involve pulling up some of the boards, using a wet/dry vacuum to suction any remaining water, and placing fans or heaters on the floor to help speed drying (Hamm, 1998).

The following lists the steps required to renovate a gym floor.

- Any colored court marking lines are removed with a paint peeler.
- Stripping of the floor begins at one end using polyurethane peeler, which will cause the old finish to blister. After it blisters, the old finish is scraped away with a putty knife.
- After the finish has been removed from a large section of the floor, stripping begins. Stripping is done with a single-brush floor machine utilizing a steel wire brush.
- After the entire floor has been stripped, all the old finish needs to be appropriately disposed of according to EPA guidelines.
- The floor is thoroughly swept or vacuumed.
- An 80-grit steel wool pad is put under the wire brush, and the entire floor is disked (sanded) in the direction opposite to the way the floorboards run. This process normally utilizes several steel wool disks.
- The floor is swept in the same direction the floorboards run to remove all sanding dust.
- The floor is re-disked using 100-grit disks in the same direction the floorboards run. This

step entails light sanding and removes any swirls created by the 80-grit disks.

- The floor is swept and then a dry vacuum is used to remove any last dust particles. Care should be taken to make sure that dust is removed from cracks and joints. Before any final cleaning of the floor, all raised areas such as window sills and bleachers need to be dusted. The floor should then be mopped several times with a damp mop containing cleanup solvent.

- The floor should dry for 24 to 48 hours before the first coat of sealant is applied.

- Sealant is poured into an application pan, and a lambswool applicator is dipped into the pan. Care should be taken to make sure the sealant is not dripping. The sealant is applied across the wood grain in a U-shaped motion. One person applies the sealant while another person feathers it (smoothes it out). The feathering process follows the grain of the wood.

- The seal should dry overnight, and then a number 2 steel wool pad is attached to the single-brush floor machine. The machine is worked with the grain over the entire floor, and the floor is then mopped with damp towels dipped in solvent. The floor should dry for 30 minutes before the second sealant coat is added.

- After the second coat dries, game lines can be added before application of the final finish.

- After the lines are added, the floor is wiped with the solvent at least 30 minutes before the finish is applied. The finish is applied in the same manner as the sealant: cross-grain application, with-grain smoothing, and sanding between the first and second coats of finish. The final coat should be allowed to dry for 72 hours, and the floor should not be subjected to heavy wear for at least one week ("Basics," 1980).

Maintenance and Safety

Maintenance concerns can be prompted by reports from athletes or patrons of conditions such as poor lighting or slippery surfaces. Someone who has been injured may inform a facility manager that he or she slipped on a puddle caused by a leaking faucet, which will start the maintenance or repair process. The failure to properly maintain a drinking fountain can lead to spilled water, which can create a slipping hazard—similarly with a leaking ketchup or mustard dispenser. Leaking showerheads or sinks in a locker room also create a dangerous environment.

Failing to replace light bulbs can lead to various problems. A parking garage or lot with low lighting or broken bulbs may be an ideal environment for criminal misconduct. This is why lights need to be constantly monitored. Nonfunctioning lights in a gym or inadequate lighting on a playing field can contribute to player injury.

Other safety concerns include rough edges on bleachers, broken cement in walkways, loose floorboards, missing floor tiles, and a host of other concerns that must be addressed. It is also important to take special care in maintaining safety equipment as shown in the Behind the Scenes on page 183.

Green Buildings

Green buildings were briefly covered in chapter 6. Green buildings require special care. For example, a trend in Europe is to plant grass on rooftops to help insulate buildings. This raises the issue of how to maintain the grass. It may be impossible to bring a mower onto a slanted roof, but goats can be put on the roof to eat the grass as a way to keep it short. This type of concern is often referred to as sustainability.

The word "sustainability" is not new to the field of facility management, but it is one that many managers still do not use when designing facilities. **Sustainability** is a holistic approach to protecting the environment by incorporating design practices and materials that use energy most efficiently (Heikkinen, 2001). The theory is that the less energy we use, the less damage we cause to the environment while producing energy. In the past, facility managers have been nervous about taking this approach to their buildings because the up-front building costs are greater. As this practice has gained more momentum, costs have been reduced, and a properly designed sustainable building does not have to cost more. Although green facilities are best planned for when a building is being designed, many conservation projects are being launched to modify and maintain existing facilities as green buildings.

Behind the Scenes: Extending the Netting

© AP/World Wide Photos

Apart from regular checking of safety equipment, such equipment may also need to be modified to provide additional protection. Netting at hockey games is an example. The unfortunate death of a teenage fan in Columbus, Ohio, in 2002 spurred a new directive by the NHL to make the facilities safer (Steinbach, 2003). The new netting cost $0.55 to $0.90 per square foot, versus $0.30 to $0.40 for the existing netting, due to the stronger materials that need to be dipped in fireproofing compounds. The NHL mandated that the netting width be at least 118 feet (36 meters), which stretches from the point at which the rink's side boards become rounded at the corner (radius point) around the goal to the other radius point. The nets are supposed to be at least 20 feet (6 meters) high; the Colorado Avalanche extended their netting to over 100 feet (30.5 meters) high (Steinbach, 2003). Similar trends may be seen in baseball; some facilities are increasing the size of the nets behind home plate in order to provide additional protection for fans on the sidelines. Providing additional screening for baseball fans is not a novel idea, as most Japanese ballparks already screen the entire lower bowl area. Some baseball teams are starting to address safety concerns by adding screening in front of dugouts to protect players. No matter how much screening there is, it must be in good shape. If there is a hole in a screen and a ball or puck travels through the hole and hits someone, there will almost always be automatic liability for failing to provide a truly safe environment.

There are two main factors that help create a more sustainable environment: the design or layout of the building, and the materials used in the construction. A maintenance program can be combined with any remodeling or rebuilding efforts to design new or existing facilities so that they use better materials and are more efficient. For example, an old wood fence may need to be replaced. The wood may have been treated with arsenic to avoid decay and insect infestation, but such wood is bad for the environment. A green approach would be to use treated wood that minimizes the impact on nature.

When looking into building or renovating a "green" arena, a facility manager should consider many issues before choosing to go forward. Considerations include not only the cost, but also life safety factors, life cycle of the materials in the building, operating costs, and the effects of the manufacturing processes behind the products being used. An arena can become more sustainable through use of the following:

• Gray water. Water that has been previously used to wash hands, clothes, or dishes or for bathing, as well as collected rainwater, is called gray water. Through creation of a system that not only collects the water but also filters and redistributes it, water can be reused in bathrooms, for irrigation of the grounds, and for fire extinguishing (Yaeger, 1998).

• Natural light. Using windows in certain areas of the facility will reduce the amount of energy needed to light those areas. One must be careful when using an abundance of natural light so that it does not hinder the ability of the arena to host functions like concerts and televised games.

- Lighting. Using fluorescent or high-intensity discharge lighting to light a facility is the most cost- and energy-efficient option. Another effective tool for reducing lighting costs is to analyze every event separately to determine how much lighting is actually needed; this will avoid wasting electricity (Yaeger, 1998).

Through a maintenance program, many of these steps can be developed and implemented. For example, the maintenance department can be supplied with fluorescent bulbs instead of standard light bulbs. Instead of draining fluid into a sewer system, hazardous liquids need to be properly disposed of, not just to protect the environment but also to avoid breaking the law. Similarly, cleaning agents used to maintain the facility need to be properly disposed of and monitored.

Summary

A clean facility is like a clean home: an inviting place to be. It takes time, energy, and resources to keep a house clean and functioning well, and the scale is much greater for a sport facility (imagine thousands of people using your bathroom every day). A well-developed and well-funded program enables a facility to keep sufficient supplies to remain attractive to users and patrons.

However, a facility that looks good but does not have a good maintenance program will not survive. Equipment and structures that are not taken care of will stop functioning. To avoid this, a facility needs to allocate appropriate funds, develop and staff a maintenance department and program, and evaluate the results. An audit can help determine what needs to be done and then serve as a tool to evaluate the maintenance program's success, especially against well-established benchmarks. Special care should be taken in maintaining floors and specialty equipment and devices, as well as in striving for an ecological focus.

DISCUSSION QUESTIONS AND ACTIVITIES

1. Why is maintenance so important?

2. What are some of the key issues that one needs to examine when implementing a facility maintenance program?

3. Interview a maintenance department worker and a custodian at your university or college to see what they do on the job and how they do it. Also ask them what the best and worst aspects of their jobs are.

PART IV

Facility Administration

TEN

Marketing and Sales

CHAPTER OBJECTIVES

After completing this chapter you will be able to do the following:

- Appreciate how the 4 Ps interact to help market a facility
- Understand how to effectively market facility and sport experiences
- Know how to sell products from signage to sponsorship packages
- Appreciate the impact that marketing has on a facility's profitability and long-term viability

A facility should be designed for marketing success. A facility should be able to sell itself. A major trend in the 1990s was the concept of a destination location. A destination location is a place where everyone wants to go to be seen and to experience the festivities. How can a facility become such a destination? Through marketing. **Marketing** is the concept of packaging a product and services in the right way, at the right price, and in the right environment to encourage individuals to buy.

Every facility needs to have a unique marketing approach to sell what goes on within the facility. If there are health clubs in the same general area, why would a person want to join one versus another? Would there be a difference in price, quality, perceived value, ancillary services, or accommodations? These types of issues need to be analyzed in developing a facility to take advantage of marketing opportunities. If the health club is going to cater to affluent clientele, it must be located close to that demographic segment, must be built to the highest quality level with materials such as marble and other fine finishings, and must offer exclusive services such as day spa, manicures, and massages.

Whether a facility is engaged in public relations (free publicity) or advertising (paid publicity), the focus always is to encourage individuals to purchase a product. While a sales effort is required to get elected officials to support and "buy into" building a facility, most facility sales efforts focus on selling various products (which could be called assets), from tickets to naming rights.

This chapter examines the marketing elements critical for a successful sport facility, starting with the four Ps and then turning to marketing strategies, the marketing process, the ways in which a facility sells itself, and the selling of assets such as naming rights.

Marketing Concepts

Marketing focuses on getting a customer to purchase goods or services. Goods can be food, novelty items, or a parking space at a facility. A service can include the game, personal treatment such as an usher's walking someone to his or her seat, and the nostalgic feel of being in an old stadium or arena.

Marketing includes numerous functions such as advertising and selling, but these activities do not define marketing. Marketing attempts to bring buyers and sellers together so that they can conclude a transaction and both parties will leave the exchange satisfied. Thus, marketing is not successful if a customer buys a ticket to a game and then has a horrible time so that he or she will never go to another game again. This is referred to as buyer's remorse.

Marketing may be defined as a process of planning and executing the development, pricing, promotion, and distribution of ideas, goods, and services to create exchanges that will satisfy the objectives of everyone involved in the transaction (Zikmund and d'Amico, 1996).

Marketing a facility starts with examining what the facility has to sell. A facility has two types of products to sell—experiences and goods—referred to here as products or assets. While the term assets is used in the financial realm, the same term can be applied in marketing since an empty seat is a potential financial asset that could generate revenue and a marketer needs to be able to market that asset. The experience is the joy of attending a game or working out at a magnificent facility. It is hard to place a price on these experiences, but they are nonetheless very valuable to some. Goods can include foam cheese heads, hotdogs, game programs, and the facility itself.

Before undertaking the process of developing a marketing program, a facility needs to conduct a marketing inventory, which is an examination of all the various experiences and goods the facility can sell or give away. A facility also needs to know what is involved in marketing. Marketing is often examined in terms of positioning a product or service according to the **4 Ps:** product, place, price, and promotion. Some marketing experts add a fifth P to the list: public relations (Mullin, Hardy, and Sutton, 1993).

Product

Product is what the facility has to offer to its prospective customers, users, clients, or constituents. A product can be goods, a service, or an idea. The product can be the goods that are sold in facility concession stands or a health bar. Products can also include the facility itself, the teams that play in the facility, and the events held by and within the facility.

Unlike consumer goods such as soap, soft drinks, or motor oil, the products offered by sport facilities can change daily. Most sport facility customers are not comparing between two products (like two bars of soap) that may differ only in the packaging (the box). Sport facility customers are often comparing between significantly different products. A New York Mets game is different each night, whether in outcome, opponent, or atmosphere. One health club may offer swimming and racquetball while another club is more socially oriented or emphasizes weights and machines. Each club would market itself differently depending on the target market for the service or goods offered. The target market is determined through the market segmentation process discussed later, in the marketing process section.

Based on knowledge of who the consumers are, the product can be grown through product extensions that make it more desirable. Product extensions are additions that enhance or improve a product. Extensions in sport marketing include additions that do not change the basic nature of the product but make it more appealing. This concept is often referred to as the sizzle whereas the product itself is the steak (the **steak and sizzle**). For example, some people go to a football game to watch the game (the steak), but some may attend to enjoy the sizzle, which could include cheerleaders, dogs catching flying disks, drunk fans, mascots in the stands, and countless other sights and activities. Thus, someone who may not be as interested in the game could enjoy other activities and still have a good time.

Place

Place refers to where the product or service is sold or distributed. Place also refers to how the product reaches customers, how quickly it reaches them, and the condition the product is in when it finally reaches the customers. In the facility context, place can refer to how convenient the facility is to customers. A facility that is located next to several freeway on and off ramps is more convenient for fans and users than one that is not. If convenience is a major motivator for the given fans and users, the marketing effort can emphasize this aspect.

Another example of place marketing is concession sales. If all fans have to go to permanent concession stands, it may become difficult to sell items if the lines are very long. This has prompted facilities to utilize multiple sale points and roving hawkers. Providing a more convenient place to purchase items generates more sales.

Price

Price can include numerous variables. For example, there may be admission, reservation, rental, program, or concession fees. There are also numerous pricing points, such as per day usage, membership rates, equipment rental fees, and family versus individual rates. Price is always on trial in every marketplace, since price can be considered too high or too low at different times. If a ticket price is too high, people may not purchase a ticket. If a ticket is too cheap, then customers may perceive the ticket as lacking in value. Thus, price is a major concern from a marketing perspective. It should be noted that sport and other recreational facilities are competing against other entertainment venues, from theaters to bowling alleys to bars. If someone regards the ticket price for a sport event as high or has limited funds, he or she may decide to forgo a game and instead go with friends to a bar where beers are $1.00 versus $6.00 at a game. For others the price is not a concern since they want to attend a game almost regardless of the price. All this being said, marketing demands are not the only factors affecting price. Price is also dictated by contract provisions setting a minimum price, laws that specify taxes or charges, and most importantly financing. If a facility makes its money exclusively from ticket sales, then the ticket price has to cover the cost of opening the doors and putting on the show.

The cost of doing business in sport facilities has soared over the past 10 years. In the late 1980s the Miami Arena was built for $89 million. In the late 1990s the Staples Center in Los Angeles and the American Airlines Center in Dallas were built for over $450 million each. But stadiums and arenas are not the only facilities facing higher costs. All facilities face higher costs, from construction to payroll to insurance. All these costs lead to increased prices for customers. However, if costs decrease, very few facilities or teams pass the decrease on to the ultimate purchaser.

Price is affected by the concept of supply and demand. Supply and demand can create a higher value for a product if there is a small amount of the product and significant demand for it. This situation is often called a seller's market since sellers can ask what they want. The market for Super Bowl tickets is typically a seller's market. Since the supply is limited (only one game), scalpers can ask what they want for tickets. Because tickets to some championship events are scarce, the ticket may sell at the box office for one amount but be worth five times that amount the minute it is bought. Scalpers often engage in the supply side of the demand equation by purchasing tickets any way they can and then selling them at the market rate. But scalpers are not alone in their willingness to test the marketplace. Many professional and collegiate teams are now selling tickets on a per game basis, according to the opponent, game date, or significance of a given game. Such a strategy maximizes the demand for key games, with increased prices helping to generate additional revenue for the team instead of allowing the scalpers to benefit.

Each pricing strategy needs to be specifically formulated to maximize revenue while minimizing potential backlash. The law of diminishing returns states that as prices increase, more customers may shy away from purchasing. It may be that customers want tickets and that the supply is sufficient but the price is too high, which can cause regular ticket buyers to pass on buying the more expensive tickets. Thus, while the revenue per customer increases, the total revenue will at some point decline because fewer customers will purchase the product.

Promotion

Promotion refers to the process of informing people about the product, price, and place. If a

Behind the Scenes: Fan Cost Index

© Human Kinetics

It can be very expensive to bring a family to an event. Team Marketing Report of Chicago produces a Fan Cost Index, which analyzes the cost for a family of four to attend games played by professional teams. The index showed that the average price for a Major League Baseball game for a family of four in 2003 was $148.66. Comparisons in a given market could also be made. For example, in the Baltimore/Washington area, the average price for a family of four to go to various events (including game tickets, parking, concessions, a program, and a souvenir item) was as follows (Carter, 2003):

Team	Price
Washington Capitals (NHL)	$320
Washington Wizards (NBA)	$375
Baltimore Ravens (NFL)	$350
Baltimore Orioles (MLB)	$175
DC United (MLS)	$125
Baltimore Blast (NPSL)	$100

wonderful product is available at the right price and the right place, will it sell? What if the customers do not know about the quality of the item or its selling price? What if they want the product but cannot find it? These types of questions affect whether or not an item will sell. Promotion involves the effort required to market a product or service. The primary vehicles used to promote a service or product are advertising, publicity, and public relations.

Advertising

Advertising is a paid message designed to inform customers. Advertising can include television, radio, newspaper, magazine, and countless other media. Internet advertising has gained popularity over the past decade, but sometimes the ultimate customers do not get the message

due to clutter or noise in the communication channel. For example, do people really read or respond to pop-up ads, or do they feel violated by the unwelcome intrusion and purposely avoid doing business with the companies? Advertising can also incorporate such methods as point-of-purchase displays that place a product at the end of a grocery store aisle for extra visibility. Thus, a race car-shaped display, paid for by the product seller, can be positioned at the front of a store to maximize visibility and drive sales. Advertising can appear anywhere someone thinks a potential customer may be located. Elevators and urinals are two advertising locations that have been used more recently; the idea is that since people often spend close to a minute in these locations and are attempting not to make contact with others, these are great places for an advertising message.

Potential Marketing Tools for a Sport Facility

Publishing the marketing vision (using a slogan such as "Let's sell out the joint!")

Business cards and company letterhead

Brochures

Newsletters

Published surveys

Press packets with media credentials, a media guide, pictures, statistics, and so on

Signage, including logos

Personal history endorsements from athletes, coaches, or fans indicating why they love the facility

Coupons

Bumper and other stickers

Web sites

Customer awards

Employee of the month awards that encourage fans to see marquee employees such as vendors who use tricks or devices to get the crowd involved

Newspaper, television, and radio advertisements

Flyers

Posters

Bulletin boards

Word of mouth

Public service announcements

Press releases

Publicity

Publicity is a facility's window to the public. Publicity is referred to as "earned media" since it is unpaid and is disseminated based on its newsworthiness. Publicity is often derived through word of mouth, news releases, press conferences, editorial comments, and public service announcements (PSAs). (See the above list of potential marketing tools for a sport facility for other methods.) Each of these techniques is an added benefit that supports the marketing effort and does not cost any money. Word of mouth, for example, is invaluable. Happy customers tell others that they had a great experience, and this can often be the best promotion possible. On the other hand, if customers had a bad experience they will communicate their dissatisfaction. It is estimated that those who are happy with an experience will tell two people about it; if they are not happy, they will tell 10 people how bad the service or product was.

Publicity works by providing additional coverage. Some say it does not matter whether publicity is good or bad as long as it is publicity. This is not true. Positive publicity is great and can increase awareness and possibly patronage. Negative publicity can destroy a facility. If a news story documents health concerns at a facility, one can expect that a person concerned about exposure who has read or heard about the article will stay away from the facility. That is why "spin control" is such an important part of any promotion campaign.

As the press will either help or harm a facility, mastering the press is critical. For example, numerous facility spokespersons say "no comment" to a question by the press. This type of response can appear to be an admission of guilt, even if the facility did nothing wrong. If spokespersons say instead that they are looking into the matter and will contact the media immediately upon learning what happened, this type of response is not

The Charlton Athletic use signage and photos to create publicity and fan excitement.

newsworthy and will probably not lead to a negative story. Some of the other "secrets" for dealing with the media include understanding publishing deadlines, knowing how to contact key reporters, meeting with reporters before any problems arise so that reporters know the facility and facility management, being brief with the media, never trying to sell the media tickets to an event, and creating a contact list with the names and numbers of all the facility officials (Wilkinson, 1988).

If a facility plans to close one entrance gate for an event, it may be a good idea to communicate this decision to the general public to avoid any hard feelings. The facility may want to produce and post closing signs. The facility may also purchase advertisements in newspapers, on radio, or on TV. Another approach is to ask radio stations to play a PSA about the gate closure. Advertising and publicity, in other words, can promote this type of information.

Public Relations

Public relations is a blend of advertising and publicity. Public relations for a facility deals with trying to reach out to the public with a positive message. A health club may advertise that it is giving away memberships for free to the elderly to encourage their physical activity. By advertising on TV or radio, and possibly in the newspaper, and by trying to get a story in the paper, the health club is engaging in public relations. If seniors in fact come, they may bring others who are not qualified for the free membership to encourage them to join also. The purpose is to put forward a good public image and hopefully grow the customer base.

The Marketing Process

Everyone has heard the saying that the customer is always right. It is crucial to know who the customers are. The customers are the primary focus for any facility. Without members, a gym or health club would have a hard time staying open. A stadium or arena needs fans to generate income. Thus, facility managers need to focus on attracting fans or customers to their facilities. Some facilities—sportsplexes, for example—have multiple customers, such as spectators and participants. A sportsplex manager needs to develop multiple marketing approaches to attract these two different types of customers. No matter who is being courted as a customer, a facility manager needs to develop a strategy to reach the right people and get them to the facility. The right customers will hopefully be reached through the marketing process.

Identifying Customers

Market segmentation is the process of examining who will want to use or purchase a given product. Once the people who may want to purchase the product are identified, marketing efforts can be spent advertising or promoting the product to that group. This process is called positioning the product. All products need to be positioned in the mind of the consumer who will use or purchase the product. Sport is normally not a necessity. This creates a challenge for the marketer; it is not as easy to market sport as it is to market a necessity. For example, gas stations rarely advertise to encourage people to buy their primary product, gas, because just about everyone needs gas. Instead, gas stations advertise to encourage people to pick one gas station over another based on service attributes or lower prices. Since sport is not a necessity, a sport organization or facility has to position itself to fill a customer need in order to encourage participation or purchase.

Sport can fill the need for relaxation, pleasure, loyalty, art, and companionship. For example, Fenway Park in Boston is positioned as a sport experience. The field is historic. The "Green Monster" is very well known and has an aura all its own. The Boston Red Sox can market to "out-of-towners" the fact that they are engulfed in history when attending a game. However, this same positioning strategy cannot be used for season ticket holders since they are not as interested in history, but more in enjoyment or in seeing the team win. Thus, in sport facility marketing, numerous positioning efforts need to be undertaken simultaneously. Once a facility examines how it wants to position itself (i.e., its product), it can examine who the potential individuals are who may fit the newly positioned product. For a smaller facility such as a health club, if the product is a relaxing exercise environment that prohibits skimpy workout clothing, the product is ideally positioned to reach senior or less active segments of the market who might be turned off by revealing or seeing too much skin. This process can be accomplished through market segmentation.

Research

One of the keys to successful marketing is research. In order to successfully market a facility or event, one needs to analyze the event or facility along with the intended market. Thus, the first step requires the facility to examine itself—its strengths, weaknesses, opportunities, and threats (SWOT analysis). The first two elements, strengths and weaknesses, are internal issues; the later two, opportunities and threats, are external. Strengths can include a great facility, good employees, strong events/tenants, a supportive political environment, and possibly good access to transportation. Weaknesses could include the lack of good seating, poor tenant contracts, lack of star athletes on tenant teams, poor lines of sight, few advertisers, and related concerns. Opportunities can include the prospects of attracting new events, community

growth, lower potential taxes, a possible bond to finance building a new stadium, and related opportunities. Threats could include a new facility opening in the area, an economic downturn, a players' strike, or sponsors leaving a facility due to changed marketing strategies.

Although used for planning purposes, the SWOT analysis is just as important for marketing purposes. A facility needs to market its strengths, attack weaknesses, seize opportunities, and anticipate threats. Concerns and opportunities are identified through research. There are two types of data: primary and secondary. Primary data are obtained by the facility itself through surveys or other means. Secondary data are obtained through research and publications produced by second parties. Both primary and secondary data can help shape how a facility will market itself. Assume that a college is going to build a new fitness center for its students. The athletic director could possibly decide him- or herself what should be in the facility, but involvement of students, especially if they have to pay the bill, is critical. Thus, the primary data could come from surveys of students in the cafeteria and in the current athletic facility to see what they want. It may be determined after interviewing several hundred students that the students primarily want swimming, basketball, aerobics, weights, and a climbing wall. The college conducts some additional research (secondary research) and discovers that a recent study reviewed the problems with climbing walls. Based on both the primary and secondary information and the allowed budget, the facility is designed to meet all the major preferences of the students except for the climbing wall.

Positioning

A **market** is a group of actual or potential customers for a given product. These individuals have various attributes; the primary attributes are the ability to purchase a product such as a ticket to a game, willingness to buy the ticket, and the authority to make the purchase decision. Children may not fit into the ticket purchasing market segment because they do not have the money or authority to purchase a ticket. Nonetheless, children can have a major influence on someone who is in the market segment, such as a mother or father interested in taking the child to an event or facility. People who fit into the market segment need to be identifiable, significant in number, likely to respond to a marketing campaign, accessible, and measurable.

Methods of segmenting the market include demographic, psychographic, benefit, and geo-demographic segmentation. Demographics refers to variables associated with people who may want to purchase the product such as age, gender, race, nationality, residency (area the person lives in), and income level. Location, for instance, is a major concern for health clubs. Most health clubs do not anticipate drawing people who live 100 miles away, so marketing efforts should not be directed toward those individuals. Any market segment needs to have a certain size and have the ability to purchase the product. Some companies market exclusively to women with the idea that they may make more purchasing decisions in the house than men. A product that is marketed to children may be difficult to sell if children do not have a say in the purchase decision.

Psychographics refers to actions and thought processes on the part of individuals. Psychographics attempts to get into the customer's head to determine how he or she makes a decision. These decision factors can be used in marketing to motivate similar consumers to buy the product or service in the future. Why does someone buy beer at a stadium—to get drunk, enjoy time with friends, or is it a matter of succumbing to social pressure? These questions and their answers are very important. If the answers show that fans are drinking because it is considered the "appropriate" activity to engage in during an event, then the product marketing effort will be significantly different from marketing to those who just want to party. The latter group may purchase beer regardless of the cost. When profits from beer sales can reach 400% at a stadium, the marketing decision can be significant.

Benefit segmentation examines what benefit someone wants to receive from the product or service. If women want to work out without having men around, then they may want a health club for women only. An exclusive all-women's health club has a benefit that would be attractive to these consumers. If consumers express interest in a given benefit, marketers will find a way to reach and sell to these individuals if they represent a large enough group willing and eager to spend money.

Geo-demographic segmentation looks at customers and potential customers based on where they live or carry on their businesses. A team that wants to sell tickets to the wealthiest individuals in a community can identify the wealthiest neighborhoods, look up the zip codes, buy a mailing list that covers those zip codes, and then send the marketing materials to those individuals.

Regardless of the segment targeted, the marketing strategy needs to communicate a message that appeals to the potential buyer. In sport the buyer typically does not look for a single result such as a win or not having to spend too much time in the parking lot trying to get home. In sport a buyer is often looking for an experience.

Selling Experiences

Statistics show that the average family saves for two to three years for a trip to Disney World. The reason people save for so long is that the trip is a memorable experience and they want to have enough money to derive the utmost enjoyment from it (Coleman, 2000). Experience can include passive participation—just sitting in a seat—or active participation through involvement in a total experience. By marketing toward an active participant, a facility increases its chances of attracting new customers interested in receiving an enhanced experience. A total experience consists of a number of components—aesthetic, educational, escapist, and entertainment.

Aesthetic experiences have to do with immersing fans in an environment full of sights, sounds, smells, touch, and tastes. The focus is on the sensory thrill of being at an event (Coleman, 2000). The smell of popcorn or hotdogs is an excellent example, as people remember a facility by the smells and tastes they associate with the facility.

Food is only one element in the experience of a facility, game, or event. Everything from highbrow business meeting facilities to Internet access, cigar humidors, unusually comfortable seats, and hard-core cheering sections enhances the facility experience. These elements are offered since the facility is no longer just selling a team or event, but an experience.

Sporting events also include an educational element. Fans can see a memorabilia display and learn about the team or how the facility was built. This gives the fans a better feel for the facility in that it allows them to appreciate the hard work that went into building the facility.

Facility Focus: Marketing and Sales for Work Out World

Courtesy of Infinity Photography.

Work Out World (WOW!) is a family-owned and operated chain of fitness centers. WOW is always looking for ways to increase membership and keep current members. In October 2001, a WOW center opened in Freehold, New Jersey. The 25,000-square-foot (2,320-square-meter) center opened in a location that had previously housed a movie theatre. WOW Freehold offers fitness services including group fitness classes, strength and cardio equipment, one-on-one personal training, fitness testing, chiropractic services, free child care, and many others.

A unique feature of WOW Freehold—one that has increased female membership—is a private, ladies-only fitness area. Female members can access the ladies-only area directly from the locker room. There are also two private doors that lead into the regular fitness center. Two other special features that have attracted members to WOW Freehold are the physical therapy center and the cardiac fitness rehab center (McDonnell, 2004).

"WOWing" potential members is part of WOW's marketing strategy. The marketing plan includes a monthly direct mail program with a seven-day free pass. Internet users can receive a guest pass when they register online. Also, WOW markets itself with in-person promotions at local businesses, community events, corporate health fairs, and other events. Some of the marketing items WOW Freehold uses are coins, glasses, pizza boxes, and dollar bills. When you become a WOW member you are granted, among other benefits, access to all WOW fitness centers in New Jersey, four free personal training sessions, and ongoing monthly fitness evaluations and assessments. WOW also offers many programs to keep members happy and coming back. When members sign up they are given a guide book about the facility called *WOW Discovery*. They are also given e-mail coaching, which provides fitness information to help members reach their fitness goals. There is also a monthly newsletter, *WOW Squeeze*, that informs members about club happenings and contests (McDonnell, 2004).

The escapist realm involves immersing fans in the aesthetic and educational components. An escapist effect is achieved when fans actually participate in activities such as in-game promotions, go into batting cages, meet players, and do similar activities that involve them physically in the experience. The last component of the total experience is entertainment, which focuses on making the facility or event the most personal experience possible. To successfully sell an experience, each experience needs to be customized. For example, themed restaurants such as Hard Rock Cafe or Dan Marino's use the experience they offer to highlight a theme and a feeling that resonates through the activity of dining (Coleman, 2000). Other strategies include harmonizing impressions with positive cues (cleanliness, friendliness, fun), eliminating negative cues (dirt, bad smells, etc.), mixing in memorabilia, engaging a fan's senses, and training employees to support the impressions.

Food

While a sporting event in a facility is the main attraction, almost all fans will say that their food experience also influences the quality of the event.

Behind the Scenes: A Fun Guarantee

Courtesy of the Carolina Hurricanes.

While it is very difficult to guarantee a victory, even though some teams have offered such promotions, the facility can guarantee an enjoyable experience. This challenge was faced by the RBC Center, home for the Carolina Hurricanes and North Carolina State University basketball teams. Construction of the facility was started in 1997 and the center opened in 1999. In the 1997-1998 hockey season the Hurricanes had played at another facility and averaged less than 10,000 fans per game. After moving in 1999, the team started winning more games and doing better at the attendance gate. To make the fans feel better and enhance the game experience, the Hurricanes developed a contract with fans that included these promises:

- Better roadways to the arena
- Better parking areas with more paving, lining, and lighting
- Additional parking-related services such as free jump-starts for dead batteries
- Increased benefits for season ticket holders such as a ticket exchange program for unused tickets
- Improved communication with arena management
- Allowing fans to exchange tickets for "Canes Cash" vouchers for food and beverages (Deckard, 2001)

Did these strategies work better than some of the traditional giveaways such as hockey pucks, towels, and mugs? While the team had only 28 wins in 2004, they averaged 12,086 fans, with a total of just less than a half-million fans coming to RBC for games. Thus, it is hard to say that a single campaign such as a fan contract helped establish a core following that would attend games even during a poor season; but a fan contract combined with excellent service and innovative promotions can combine to generate a comprehensive experience.

In the past, fans were often content with a hotdog and beer. However, as times have changed, the palates of fans have also changed. Product evolution has been growing to match the growing fan sophistication. Fans' food preferences also vary by region (see a list of culinary curiosities around the United States on page 197). People want the food service to be clean and friendly, and they want their food fast but also want the highest quality level. Fans do not want long lines, untrained staff, inadequate numbers of staff behind the counter, confusing or misleading signs, and an insufficient number of service points (Galloway, 2001).

The outfield in Pacific Bell Park in San Francisco was designed so kids could reach the counters, and sold packages that resembled McDonald's Happy Meals with small entrees, fries, a soda, and a small toy (Finken, 2001). The baseball fans in St. Louis and Kansas City used to be able to buy a ticket behind home plate for $15, but now the cost is $120. However, people sitting in these seats get unlimited food and drinks.

Culinary Curiosities Around the United States

San Francisco: garlic fries

St. Louis: chili cheese fries

San Diego: fish tacos

Seattle: smoked salmon

Milwaukee: grilled bratwurst dipped in a secret sauce

New York: kosher deli products

Baltimore: crab cakes

New Orleans: anything Cajun or Creole

Chicago: Italian sausage with peppers

From Whiting, 1993.

Food and other concession items are closely analyzed by facility managers due to the high profit margin from these items. New items are constantly being added at different price points (i.e., $3.99, $4.50, $4.99, etc.) to see what the market will bear. A facility marketer needs to closely monitor food trends to maximize the potential food sales. Thus, if the population switches to special diets such as vegetarian or kosher cuisine, the facility needs to quickly adapt to the changes or face significant lost sales. However, while appetites may change, there is a constant need for liquid refreshments such as beer, soda, and water.

Incentives and Giveaways

Fans can also have their experience enhanced through incentive programs. Several companies currently produce swipe cards that allow a facility or team to provide added benefits to frequent fans. When fans enter the facility, they can swipe their membership cards and receive coupons or other discounts based on the number of games they have attended. These programs are often part of a customer relationship management program (McGlynn, 2001). The systems build fan support, but also serve to obtain valuable information about fans such as when they visit, what they purchase, and other psychographic elements.

The potential giveaways can be limitless. Examples include baseballs, T-shirts, autographed items, bobble-head dolls, bean-bag toys, collectible cards, free drinks and food, free tickets, school supplies, and countless other personal or household items. The Birmingham Barons, a minor league baseball team, worked with Roto-Rooter to give away special bathroom plungers that bore the Barons and Roto-Rooter logos and phone numbers. This innovative giveaway provided 1,500 homes with plungers and a phone number if the plunger was not able to clear the line (*Vertical Alliance's Sport Marketing Newsletter*, 2004).

Facility Marketing

In addition to selling and marketing an event, a sport facility must also sell itself in order to grow. A facility must market its tangible and intangible products and assets. Tangible assets can include its floor space, location, and seating configuration. Intangibles can include affiliation with an anchor tenant, being the only large facility in a location, and satisfying a city's need to have a "big-time" sport facility.

Significant effort needs to be devoted to marketing a facility not just for the end users or fans, but for those who will support the facility. Supporters can range from politicians to anchor tenants. Through aggressive marketing campaigns, several cities have been able to win an anchor team even though they may not have had the largest potential market. Such was the case with Tampa Bay, which spent years marketing its almost vacant stadium to various Major League Baseball (MLB) teams. Finally, after an aggressive marketing campaign, the city won the rights to a new MLB franchise that was awarded in 1995 and started playing in Tropicana Field in 1998. An enormous effort was made by many in trying to land the future baseball team for

Behind the Scenes: Giveaways and Safety

© Dale Garvey

While it is important to entertain the crowd, care has to be taken to make sure fans are not injured. There have been documented cases of individuals engaging in the dizzy bat promotions and getting injured when they later stumble to reach the finish line. Fans can also be injured in promotional events; a peanut vendor may throw a bag of nuts that hits someone in the head, and people can be injured when hotdogs or T-shirts are shot through air-pressurized cannons. In fact, Billy the Marlin, the Florida Marlins' mascot, along with the team, were sued by a fan who was hit in the eye by a fired rolled-up T-shirt. The fan sued the team for $250,000, and the jury, after deliberating for nearly two days, ruled in favor of the team ("Billy the Marlin," 2003).

Additionally, all special events should be carefully analyzed to examine their potential impact on safety. A ball giveaway can possibly arm an entire stadium with projectiles that people can throw at each other or the players. One of the craziest promotions—and one that went far out of control—was the Cleveland Indians' "10-Cent Beer Night" in 1974. Over 25,000 fans showed for the game, and many were drunk before they even reached the stadium. The team made money selling an estimated 60,000 cups of beer (10 ounces [0.3 liters] each). As early as the first inning, an explosion was heard in the stands. In the fourth inning, a nude man slid into second base. In the fifth inning, a father and son team jumped onto the field and mooned the crowd. With the game tied in the ninth inning, fans rushed the field and surrounded Texas Rangers slugger Jeff Burroughs, and punches were exchanged. Thousands of drunken fans poured onto the field and battled with police, players, and one another. Ultimately the game was called by the umpire, who himself was hit in the head with a chair (Hruby, 2002).

the new stadium. Everyone from the mayor to lay civic leaders had a role in marketing the city and community to anyone who could possibly influence the decision to help attract a professional baseball team to Tampa Bay.

Marketing New Facilities

In the case of a new sport facility, facility managers must undertake significant marketing efforts to win over those who will be crucial for the project's success. In the earliest stages, this type of marketing targets existing and potential investors. Investors need to be informed about any changes that could affect the project and their investment. Once a facility is planned or under construction, however, the marketing emphasis switches to those who will use and surround the facility. For example, local residents need to know what is going on and how the facility will affect them. Facility managers do not want to surprise residents with a completed plan, as this will almost always lead to backlash rather than support. Through press conferences, mailers, open houses, and other techniques, the local community can be educated about the facility.

Local politicians also need to be kept abreast of the facility's progress and plans. Marketing in this regard can include taking politicians on a tour of the facility. While such activity is common and is a useful tool for marketing a facility and generating support, it can also border on unethical behavior. If politicians are influenced by such activity and support a project purely for their own gain, there could be potential legal and political problems. Ethical marketing goes beyond just trying to build a facility and determining whether the decision makers can be bribed to build a certain facility in one county versus another. Ethical issues also affect who may get the facility naming rights, construction contract, and management contract, as well as whether beer or cigarette advertisements will be allowed in the facility. Any ethical breach can quickly lead to customer backlashes and voter distrust.

A central focus of a new facility's marketing campaign is developing the facility's identity. How should the community and external entities perceive the facility? Will the facility be known as a health club for serious weightlifters or one for older individuals interested in cardiovascular rehabilitation? No marketing effort can be undertaken until the facility can establish or remake its identity. A facility can use market segmentation to position the facility with the intended target market. This can be seen with Gold's Gym, which has heavily promoted shirts that show big muscles to highlight their emphasis on free weights and a gym to help people pump up their muscle mass. This strategy contrasts significantly with that of other gyms such as 24-Hour Fitness, which tries to highlight sexy people working on toned bodies with interval and machine workouts.

Attracting Anchor Tenants

Facilities also need to constantly market themselves to attract major tenants. A sport team at a stadium or arena is an anchor tenant. Facilities learn about potential new teams as tenants from new owners, those wishing to relocate a team, or leagues interested in expanding into new markets. For example, in 2000 New Haven and Bridgeport, Connecticut, were battling to win a new Arena Football League 2 (AFL2) franchise. The AFL had awarded a franchise to the area, and both markets were actively pursuing the team. New Haven won the bidding battle in part by offering to pay all the marketing expenses for the team. Bridgeport lost the bidding war but designed the arena it was building without a center scoreboard anyway in case the team ever decided to move from New Haven to Bridgeport, about 15 miles (24 kilometers) away. After only two seasons the New Haven Coliseum closed. The AFL2 team, having lost its home, attempted to negotiate with

Bridgeport to move the team. Those negotiations broke down and the team folded.

Current tenants can be kept happy if they are provided with lucrative contractual terms such as controlling a facility schedule or being allowed to keep all the revenue from parking or naming rights. There is no one method to keep a tenant or event happy. However, complying with the contractual terms and keeping the facility in good condition are keys to keeping both parties satisfied with the contractual relationship.

All this indicates that it is not enough just to land a major tenant for a sport facility. The facility needs to keep promoting and marketing itself to its current and future tenants or events. Once a primary tenant is landed, it is usually easier to attract other events and tenants, especially if the primary tenant is successful. Some markets are not strong sport markets. For example, minor league baseball and hockey have traditionally had a tough time succeeding in New Haven. A new team would be reluctant to consider coming to New Haven unless an established team or facility had already proven that the market can support the entity.

Attracting Events

A facility can make money only if activities are going on in the facility. With a large stadium or arena, revenue can be generated by attracting shows, concerts, conventions, theatrical productions, and sporting events. Small facilities may not be able to draw such events, but can hold special events such as fund-raisers, recitals, community plays, and other smaller events that generate revenue and increase exposure without incurring significant cost.

The first step in this type of marketing is determining what events should be brought in and what events should be excluded. An arena may be very interested in attracting a circus, for example, but may find the demographics or security concerns associated with a rock or rap concert undesirable. Other events may be rejected due to political pressure, among other factors. A facility on the campus of a religious school would probably be marketed to a significantly different group of potential events than a public facility. Once an acceptable event has been identified, the event needs to be booked.

Booking is the actual contracting of an act or event in the facility. The booking process secures specific space for a specific date and time for an agreed amount of compensation. Booking can only occur if the facility is available. A facility can also co-promote an event, but such a relationship is unusual. Scheduling refers to identifying and securing the specific dates and times for the event. All marketing efforts to attract additional events revolve around the scheduling needs of the anchor tenant. No matter how much a facility or event want to work together, if the space is being used by an anchor tenant such as a professional team, the event cannot proceed. Typically, facilities utilize diverse scheduling to provide the best mix of events. A facility will have a hard time marketing 15 concerts in a two-week period compared to different events that attract different crowds each night. Different events bring different spectators. A family event may generate more food sales while a hockey game could generate more beer sales. Booking leverages the scheduling process to maximize revenue.

A facility manager needs to identify the goals and objectives for a facility to make sure that the marketing and booking efforts comply with those goals and objectives. If a facility is in charge of bringing nightlife to a city, then more night events may be scheduled. However, the tenant often makes such decisions, especially if it is a professional sport team with a broadcasting agreement to air games at night. Competitive seasons and touring schedules also affect a facility manager's ability to attract certain events. Regardless of what it is, once the event is set, the facility manager and the marketing staff, along with the event's marketing staff, must coordinate their efforts to maximize ticket sales. These efforts will be directed not just at individual ticket holders, but often at groups, who represent the greatest opportunity to sell more tickets with the least amount of effort.

Developing Relationships

Part of the selling process entails developing relationships. Relationships need to be developed both with teams or acts and with promoters. A promotions company such as SFX manages numerous facilities and events and can help determine what events will play in what cities based on booking patterns and dates. This does not mean that a facility will be excluded from potential dates; but if a relationship is developed, event dates can be coordinated to help benefit all facilities. By developing strong relationships, hopefully a facility can sched-

ule competing events such as smaller circuses, for example, Cirque du Soleil versus Ringling Bros., which may play at different times of the year and appeal to different patrons.

Often smaller facilities also need to attract new members and retain existing members. In health clubs, especially, customer turnover is a constant concern. Some larger clubs are constantly advertising to attract new members but not marketing enough to existing customers. This creates a revolving door of clients and promotes little goodwill or loyalty. Facilities can minimize loss of patrons by developing relationships through surveying and interviewing fans or patrons to determine what they want from the facility and then providing, within limits, what the fans or patrons want. Thus, making patrons part of the process helps create a bond that can make them feel they are respected, which can lead to very loyal customers.

Facility managers need to cultivate numerous relationships. Having events sign a long-term contract is one of the primary goals for a booking specialist. If events sign only short-term contracts, the facility is constantly working to attract events. This is much less desirable than knowing that particular events will be coming every year. Some acts enter into a long-term contract to obtain a better price. A facility may charge an event 10% of the gross receipts if it is a one-time show. In contrast, if it is a well-known event and signs a 15-year agreement, the facility may charge only 5% of the gross receipts.

Sales

The purpose of facility marketing efforts typically focuses on selling items or experiences. It is not enough that people know about a facility; the goal is for them to go to the facility as a customer. This process involves identifying potential purchasers, communicating the value of going to the facility, and then closing the deal by having them buy. The sales process aims at completing the marketing process by having the customer decide that the price and timing are right to make a purchase. Many variables enter into closing the marketing process with a sale. Timing, standings, special events, giveaways, price options, and other variables can help finalize the sale.

For many the marketing process ends with selling a ticket, product, or membership, but most executives would disagree and would argue that the marketing process is only partially completed with the sale. After the sale, the marketing effort needs to continue to make sure that the customer has a good experience, as cognitive dissonance (buyer's remorse) can kill future buying from the same customer.

Commercial rights, such as sponsorship and signage, or naming and pouring, which will both be discussed later in this chapter, are all assets that can be sold by the facility to generate funds. Most facilities built in the past 20 years for professional or collegiate teams (and even some high schools) have sold naming rights, luxury suites, or other assets. Some assets, such as the naming rights for a facility or a sponsorship designation, are intangible. Other assets are real, such as tickets, luxury boxes, or even the old basketball floor at a famous arena.

Ticketing

Professional and collegiate sport teams generate revenue primarily from broadcast rights and ticket sales. Tickets are a consistent revenue source when a team has a die-hard following. Teams with a weak fan base have a harder time generating revenue from ticket sales. This has led to mini-season ticket and specialty game packages designed to attract infrequent fans. No matter how many tickets or what types of tickets are sold, facilities need to develop a ticket inventory and then sell the inventory. This requires computer-based systems that can communicate between various ticket-selling locations such as team stores and ticket outlets. With new computer-based systems, each ticket seller knows what tickets are available (ticket inventory) and can print tickets.

Ticket sales have changed with new marketing techniques. For example, years ago the only means to buy a ticket was to obtain a hard copy of a single game ticket. Now fans can buy tickets online (as discussed further on), purchase luxury suites that may not require tickets, or obtain personal seat licenses (PSLs). With a broad range of seating options available, a facility has to carefully examine pricing strategies and ticket delivery options.

Seat Pricing

Tickets have increased significantly in cost over the past 40 years. A seat at Dodger Stadium cost $3.50 per game in 1962 and had increased to $31.00 per game by 2000, a 785.7% increase. Major League Baseball tickets averaged $8.64 each in 1991 and had increased to $14.91 by 1999. Such increases pale in comparison to some other average ticket prices such as those in the NFL, which increased from $25.21 to $45.63; the NBA, which increased from $23.24 to $48.37; and the NHL, which increased from $32.75 to $45.70 during the same time ("NBA Ticket Prices," 1999). Baseball has been relatively inexpensive compared to other sports due to a larger ticket inventory based on more seats in a facility and a large number of games. In the NFL there are only a few games each year, and every game has potential playoff ramifications. The concept of supply and demand and the law of diminishing returns both affect the price for tickets.

Pricing, though, should not be examined in a vacuum. Many collegiate football programs charge significantly less for student tickets. This is designed to accomplish two primary missions. One is to reward the students who are helping to underwrite the athletic programs through increased tuition or fees. The second is to develop a strong following so that when the students become alumni they will remain dedicated fans willing to pay a higher price for tickets and hopefully donate back to the program at a later date. Similarly, professional teams often give free tickets to fans they want to attract to buy season packages or PSL/luxury seats. A small investment in free tickets can generate goodwill and larger future sales. It should be noted that free tickets to events may not necessarily be free if the tickets are taxed and the facility or team needs to pay a set tax per ticket.

Other parties can also dictate ticket prices. If the team or facility sets the ticket price, the process is called house scale. If a promoter indicates that tickets have to be sold at a given face value, this is called performance scale. Either option is usable at the box office, but ticket prices also must take into account any surcharges for Ticketron or other outlets and the various taxes that may need to be charged.

Ticketing Methods

The technological advancements of the Internet provide venues and ticket-selling organizations an innovative way to sell tickets. The goal is to make ticket purchasing fast and easy for consumers. Selling online has created a new opportunity to reach consumers and establish relationships. Tickets can be printed at home, and some European companies have developed systems that can send a ticket right to a fan's cell phone. The phone is then placed next to a scanner to open the turnstile.

The ticket companies Paciolan and Tickets.com entered into an agreement with VAST (Value Automated System Ticketing) in April 2001. VAST developed the "attendant free automated ticket and teller machine" (ATTM). The machine can dispense tickets as well as function as an ATM. The customer has the option of using a credit card or cash to purchase tickets. Machines have been installed inside and outside selected sport venues. The first such machine was installed in Pacific Bell Park, home of the San Francisco Giants, and was a main reason that the Giants won the box office of the year award at a major ticketing conference. Another system advantage is the opportunity to collect extra revenue by owning the ATM services rather than giving away ATM rights as part of a sponsorship package. Major League Baseball entered into a deal with Tickets.com in 2001 to increase the amount of marketing data MLB collects. Tickets.com handled the online ticket sales for 15 teams in 2001 (Herrick, 2001).

Another company, Ticketmaster, created a way for customers to print their own tickets, and by the end of 2001 the service was being used by over 100 venues. Tickets could be printed from the customer's home computer, and the venues utilize a system to read the barcode to validate the ticket. With this development, venues could also add more value to the ticket price by including extra items such as parking and concessions on the same barcoded ticket.

A new product that is being developed is the "virtual wristband," which allows fans to purchase tickets before the event goes on sale. This will help promoters get an idea of the demand for tickets and how they should be priced. The Internet is expected to be the dominant method of ticket selling in the future. In 1997, Ticketmaster's first year of selling tickets online, the company sold 1.1 million tickets. In just three years, that number jumped to 19.7 million tickets (Herrick, 2001).

Box Office As already mentioned, tickets can be sold in various forms. However, the regular paper ticket is still the primary means by which individuals attend an event or facility. Thus, one of the important managerial components for any facility with a ticketing revenue source is box office management. The box office represents the connection between the facility and the fans and needs to be managed appropriately to avoid upset clients, disappointed fans, and lost revenue. The box office is responsible for helping to determine what types of tickets will be sold for an event. Will there be general admission, along with all the problems associated with people pushing for the best seat they can find, or will the event have reserved seating? Can tickets be ordered over the phone and picked up at the will-call window? How will entry passes be distributed to the media? Are the box office attendants trained to answer questions beyond those about tickets? How many ticket booths will be used and where will they be located to ease congestion and reduce lines? Who will establish the appropriate ticket prices and the taxes charged on the tickets?

Resale and Scalping The San Francisco Giants developed a resale system whereby their season ticket holders resell tickets on the Internet. A season ticket holder can post unwanted tickets on the Giants' Web site, and people wishing to purchase tickets can buy them online. At the end of the year, season ticket holders will have fewer unused and unsold tickets and hopefully renew for next season. Other teams have developed similar systems to help cut out the middleman or scalper.

While scalpers are a reality in most cases, numerous laws restrict their activities. Some laws limit the premium that can be charged over the issue price; other laws limit where scalpers can sell tickets. A facility manager needs to work with local law enforcement to enforce the law but still allow legitimate fans the opportunity to sell extra tickets. The online exchanges developed by teams like the Giants allow ticket holders to sell tickets without risking arrest or losing the right to buy future tickets.

Luxury Seating

Luxury boxes and suites are often several hundred square feet of paradise. Offering scaled-down furniture to make the suites look larger, these mini high-tech centers provide luxury for those who can afford it. Besides containing normally 12 to 16 seats, the suites or boxes also offer televisions, fireplaces, pool tables, video games, and premier food services (Dorsey, 2001). Part of the appeal associated with the luxury suites is that they are a place to be and to be seen. With corporate America playing a major role in sport facilities, the amount of money spent on luxury suites and seating areas is one of the "cash cows" for sport facilities. Spectators at an arena or stadium may spend on average $7 to $8 per capita (per person) on food; the "per-capita" for those in a luxury suite averages around $30 (Dorsey, 1999). The cost associated with a luxury suite can range from $50,000 to over $350,000 annually. The 146 suites at the American Airlines Center in Dallas range in price from $150,000 to $250,000 for five-, seven-, or nine-year leases. The suites come with touch-screen monitors, TV monitors with live feed, wet bars, exclusive rest rooms, private concourses, VIP parking, and concierge service (Dorsey, 2001). The suites were an integral component of financing the facility. The initial construction price was projected at $230 million, but increased to $335 million due in part to major changes such as expanding the facility by 100,000 square feet (9,290 square meters), which increased the cost $17.5 million. Dallas was obligated to pay $125 million of the total construction costs from hotel and car rental taxes ("American Airlines Center," 2001).

Personal seat licenses (PSLs) were first introduced in the 1980s at the Palace of Auburn Hills, Detroit; the facility was built with more than 100 suites and a number of club seats. It is estimated that PSLs helped raise over $500 million for building stadiums and arenas in the 1990s (Hall, 2001). However, PSLs provide much more. It is estimated that, on average, a new facility is built such that about 16% of the seats are premium seats (Dorsey, 1999).

The major difference in luxury seating is not just the seat location, but how much each seat can earn. Assume that a typical premium seat can generate ticket revenue of $75 versus $25 for an average ticket. While the ticket income appears to be three times higher, the actual number is much greater with the $30 expenditure on food and beverages. This is only the tip of the proverbial iceberg, as the $75 ticket holder will probably also pay for a seat license and is more likely to renew ticket contracts, spend more on merchandise, and have a business relationship with the team or facility.

One concern with PSLs is that a seat is in fact an asset for the PSL holder. Several major court battles have been fought over the right to control PSLs during divorce cases, and at least one court held that a collegiate PSL was owned by the team, even though the couple had paid thousands of dollars to purchase the rights to buy the PSL seats. Similarly, what happens if the PSL holder runs into financial hardship? Does a team or facility have any mechanism to help sell the PSL for the fan, or will the fan stop paying and the seat go empty? The Denver Broncos actually sued some of their PSL holders for not paying their contractual obligations. While such a strategy may not be endearing to fans, the team gave the fans several chances to correct the problem, to no avail ("Broncos Sue," 2002).

Commercial Rights

One of the primary intangible benefits for a facility is the right to conduct activities in the facility, from the right to put a name on the facility to the right to sell drinks. Although commercial rights are primarily associated with large facilities at the collegiate and professional levels, a storm of controversy has erupted over the selling of rights at the high school level to put corporate names on buildings or sell only one brand of soda. Due to financial demands, state and federal government units have tested the market for selling naming rights to national monuments and state parks.

Naming Rights

Naming rights are somewhat controversial. A city or municipality may pay the bulk of the construction expense, and citizens should be recognized for their contributions. That is why so many older stadiums and arenas were named after people from the community as a tribute to their participation in a war. With the building boom of the 1990s, anchor tenants at large stadiums and arenas were asked to contribute funds to the building process. Many municipalities allowed the team to sell the naming rights and use those funds as part of the team's contribution to the construction effort. The name was an asset the municipality could have sold to reduce the public obligation; but in order to entice teams to stay, the municipalities were willing to transfer the asset to the teams. However, some facilities such as historic Lambeau Field in Green Bay and Soldier Field in Chicago have kept their names.

Another controversy associated with naming rights has to do with the strength of the sponsor. The Houston Astros' field was named after Enron, which became a disadvantage when the company collapsed. At the same time, other companies faced similar scandals, and these controversies significantly affected several facilities. Enron had agreed to a deal worth $100 million for 30 years. PSINet Stadium in Baltimore was part of a $105.5 million, 20-year deal before PSINet collapsed. Adelphia Coliseum in Nashville did not last long before the company went bankrupt. Mergers and bankruptcies can also affect naming rights. The TWA Dome in St. Louis was changed to Edward Jones Dome after TWA filed for bankruptcy; TWA had agreed to a 20-year, $36.7 million naming rights contract (Sieger and Patel, 2001).

Selling naming rights is a form of corporate sponsorship. North American companies were expected to spend $8.7 billion on sponsorship in 2000. Sponsors provide either cash or an in-kind asset such as advertising in an effort to improve the fortune of the company or product sponsoring the facility. Sponsorship is not philanthropy. The company doing the sponsorship is expecting something in return, whereas philanthropy is a one-way gift without any expectation. Because there exists an expectation of receiving something of value in exchange for the sponsorship, the process is more like a business transaction than a gift. Thus, there are numerous tax implications associated with sponsorship.

Naming rights can range from several hundred thousand to millions of dollars (see table 10.1). The value of such deals is based on multiple variables, including the following:

- The length of the contract, which normally runs for 20 to 30 years
- The type of facility, type of events, anchor tenants or teams
- Whether the deal involves only cash or also a trade-out of services
- What tie-in marketing strategies and campaigns will be used (Sieger and Patel, 2001)

Some deals have focused just on local businesses in an effort to be civic minded. For example, the Heinz Company paid $57 million to name the new stadium in Pittsburgh, where Heinz is headquartered. The $57 million amount was appropriate because Heinz is known for its company slogan, 57 varieties.

The key to valuing any asset is usually what the market will bear. The market is often very fickle. During good economic times, naming rights and other assets are often easy to sell. However, during tough economic times they can be almost impossible to sell. Thus, the $57 million may seem gimmicky or appear to be an overpayment, but the facility and Heinz had specific strategies that justified assigning that value to the rights deal.

No matter what the strategy is, rights raise some serious financial issues. For example, an important commercial rights issue involves how the IRS will classify the sponsorship or advertising revenue. If the facility provides significant benefit to the sponsor, the money received from the sponsor may be taxed as unrelated business income. The unrelated business income tax is currently around 28%. The Ohio State University received over $1 million from advertisements on its football stadium goal posts from various sponsors. The IRS concluded that the activity of promoting the sponsors on the scoreboard did not support the university's educational mission and was not related to the nonprofit purpose of the university, so the university had to pay 28% of the $1 million as unrelated business income tax (Fried, Shapiro, and Deshriver, 2003).

One needs to evaluate many other issues when determining the price of sponsorship. For example, will the sponsor be a name sponsor for the facility or just have its name on several billboards? The price is often based on the number of impressions that can be expected. Table 10.2 lists some of the industry norms for costs associated with each impression received. An impression refers to how many people may be exposed to the message. If there are 1,000 people at a game, it is assumed that everyone would see an outfield sign at least once, which means there would be at least 1,000 impressions. It is assumed that through these impressions a fan may form an opinion to purchase a product.

Pouring Rights

Assets can also include the right to conduct business in the facility such as selling concessions or pouring rights, or facility management rights. Pouring rights are often paid by beer and soft drink companies to gain the exclusive right to sell their product in the facility. Dallas Cowboys owner Jerry Jones created a controversy when he signed Pepsi as the official soft drink for Texas Stadium, even though Coca-Cola was the official sponsor of the NFL. Based on this act, the NFL–Coca-Cola contract was not renewed, and some teams lost significant money when teams or facilities had entered into

Table 10.1 Largest Stadium Naming Rights Deals

Facility	Location	Deal value (millions of dollars)	Deal length (years)
Reliant Park	Houston	$300	30
FedEx Field	Virginia (D.C.)	$205	27
American Airlines Center	Dallas	$195	30
Philips Arena	Atlanta	$168	20
Invesco Field at Mile High	Denver	$120	20
PSINet Stadium	Baltimore	$105.5	20
Enron Field	Houston	$100	30
Staples Center	Los Angeles	$100	20
Gaylord Entertainment Center	Nashville	$80	20
Xcel Energy Arena	St. Paul	$75	25
Compaq Center at San Jose	San Jose	$72	18
Savvis Center	St. Louis	$70	20
Pepsi Center	Denver	$68	20
Bank One Ballpark	Phoenix	$66	30
Comerica Park	Detroit	$66	30
Edison International Field	Anaheim	$50	20
Pacific Bell Park	San Francisco	$50	24
Tropicana Field	St. Petersburg	$46	30
Air Canada Centre	Toronto	$45 (Canadian dollars)	15
MCI Center	Washington, D.C.	$44	13
American Airlines Arena	Miami	$42	20
Miller Park	Milwaukee	$41.2	20
Conseco Fieldhouse	Indianapolis	$40	20
CoreStates Center	Philadelphia	$40	29
First Union Center	Philadelphia	$40	31
Ford Stadium	Detroit	$40	40
Safeco Field	Seattle	$40	20

From "Stadium & arena sponsorship," 2002.

Table 10.2 Industry Cost Norms per Impression

Activity	Cost per impression
Public service announcements	$.0025-.05
Banners	$.0025-.05
Printing name on ticket	$.05
Logo on brochure	$.0025-.05
Sponsor ad	Varies
Coupon	$.05-.10
Sample products	$.075-.15

From Moler, 2001.

individual contracts (Sullivan, 1995). Companies are willing to purchase assets in the hope of selling more products. Ogden Facility Management helped build the Arrowhead Pond in Anaheim for the Mighty Ducks. The concession company was interested in being part of the facility since it had a contract giving it exclusive rights to manage the facility and sell concessions for 30 years (Fried, Shapiro, and Deshriver, 2003).

Since the number of drinks sold at an NFL stadium or other major facility is immense, it is worthwhile for the sponsor to buy pouring rights to generate a perceived sales volume but also to gain valuable marketing exposure from involvement with a professional team. Based on the success associated with pouring rights, a number of other rights have been sold; for example, a company may be the official hotdog or pretzel provider.

Advertising Sales

Selling advertising rights can be a major marketing hurdle. Advertising is easy to sell when the facility can prove a direct correlation between the advertisement and sales. If a given advertisement campaign in the facility helps generate sales, there may be a possible direct correlation that can be measured. If the impact can be measured and is greater than the advertising investment, then the advertising buy was worthwhile on a cost–benefit basis. However, advertising is often purchased for

strategic reasons, unrelated to cost–benefit analysis. If a company wants to preclude a competitor from advertising at a venue, it will pay more than the advertisement is really worth just to preempt the competitor.

Advertising is typically priced on the basis of the anticipated exposure. If a baseball team will bring in 2 million fans and will have 20 games broadcast on national television, the team can estimate what the perceived value of an outfield sign may be on a per exposure basis. Using such an analysis, a team that draws more fans or more broadcasts will typically charge more for signs, and signs will be more expensive based on where they are located. For example, left field signs are seen more on television when a primarily right-handed team is batting, since more balls will be hit to left than to right.

Facilities are always developing new means to generate advertising revenue. Some facilities are starting to use virtual advertising to increase revenue. This advertising can appear in the outfield or behind home plate at a baseball stadium. To those in the stadium the blue background is plain, but an advertisement can be imposed on the background during the broadcast. The same technology has been used in other sports such as football and tennis.

Summary

Some think that if they open a sport facility, people will come—as with the fictional baseball diamond in a cornfield. However, an imaginary baseball field does not correlate with the reality of a competitive entertainment marketplace. To start the marketing process a facility needs to determine what assets or products it has to sell. The 4 Ps help define the product and its attributes. The facility then needs to determine who the customers are and how to reach them. By developing a unique sport experience, a facility can more easily market itself, whether it is a new facility or a facility trying to attract new tenants or acts, or customers.

The marketing process moves to the sales area in which tickets, memberships, naming rights, luxury seats, and other assets need to be sold. The marketing process is not about selling a ticket or a single facility use, but about an experience. This requires the marketing effort to constantly enhance and modify the product to encourage additional consumption of the facility experience.

DISCUSSION QUESTIONS AND ACTIVITIES

1. How would you market a health club in the South versus the east or west coast?

2. What additional assets (both tangible and intangible assets) can a facility sell?

3. What can a small stadium do to market itself without spending a lot of money?

4. Develop a marketing plan for a local sport team (high school, college, professional). The class should divide into groups. Half of the groups should choose a team with a winning record, and the other half of the groups should choose a team with a losing record.

5. Interview the owner/manager of a sport facility who has had to close the facility, and analyze the reasons given for closing the facility.

Finance and Budgeting

After completing this chapter you will be able to do the following:

- Understand the basics of sport facility finance
- Know how to prepare and follow a budget
- Understand how new stadiums and arenas are funded
- Apply the concepts of basic time value of money and capital project analysis to various building options

Facilities cannot function without money. Money is needed to plan, build, open, operate, and maintain facilities. The problem is that there is often no guarantee that money will be available to keep a facility operating. Some facilities, such as government facilities, may appear to have deep public pockets. However, that appearance is misleading, as most public facilities have tighter budgets than private facilities. The major emphasis in this chapter is on determining what money is available for a facility and how to establish what funds are needed through the budgeting process.

The chapter starts by examining basic financial concepts such as revenue and expenses, used to determine where money comes from and what the primary expenses for a facility are. Financial analysis is then covered in terms of measuring financial progress through income statements, balance sheets, cash flow analysis, and reconciliation statements. The chapter then turns to the basics of budgeting, with a focus on reducing expenditures and increasing revenue generation in accordance with preestablished criteria. A key area within the budgeting process is the capital budget and deciding which new facility option makes the most financial sense. The chapter then examines how to finance building a facility and the various sources of such funds. The final section covers what is often unthinkable—what if the facility fails and has to be sold?

Financial Concepts

Finance can be considered a language unto itself. There are very specific financial terms that are not well known. This section presents some specific terms that are important to know to grasp the rest of the chapter.

It should be noted that accounting and finance are completely different fields. Accounting is the process of calculating how much money a facility may have. **Revenue,** money obtained by the facility from selling assets (see chapter 10), and **expenses,** payments made by the facility, need to be calculated to see if the facility has made money. This calculation process is very rigid. Generally accepted accounting principles (GAAP) categorize all revenues and expenses. Finance, on the other hand, utilizes the numbers obtained by the accountants to determine the facility's future direction. The analyses conducted by financial analysts focus on developing a roadmap for the future based on past financial information and projected financial performance. This process is called budgeting. Thus, a budget is a roadmap for the facility executives to help them reach the facility's goals.

A budget is not the only document produced by financial analysts. Various types of financial statements are designed to tell the story of the facility. An **income statement** highlights the profit earned from all sales minus the cost of producing the events, taxes, and other expenses. A **balance sheet** explains how much a facility is worth and is based on two primary terms, **assets** and **liabilities.** An asset is something of value such as land, naming rights, and concession items. The greater the assets, the more a facility is worth. Liabilities are debts that are owed to others. A facility may owe money to lenders who purchased bonds to help build the facility or to the gas company for gas used to heat water in the building. If a facility's debts are worth more than the facility's assets, then the facility has a negative cash value.

Assets and liabilities are further classified as current or long-term. Current assets and liabilities are assets that can be redeemed within a year and liabilities that need to be repaid within a year. Current assets include cash, stocks, and money market notes. Current liabilities include monthly bills and salary obligations. Long-term assets include a building, which has value and could be sold within a year but normally will not be sold within the year. Long-term liabilities include bond and mortgage debts.

Other financial statements examine the flow of cash in a facility or can be used to calculate how much money was made or lost during a given event through the process of reconciliation. These various documents are not analyzed in a vacuum. The documents are compared with information for prior years to determine if the budget was met, if the facility grew monetarily, or if the facility can be compared favorably with other similar facilities.

One of the important points to remember about financial analysis is that it is difficult to examine numbers from a single point in time. If a facility charged $10 for a ticket in 2000 and charges $10 for a ticket in 2005, the facility is in fact not getting $10 worth of value in 2005. According to the concept of the time value of money, money does not maintain its value over time. A dollar tomorrow is not worth as much as a dollar today. Due to inflation and the demands for money, to get the same dollar value as this year a fan might have to pay $1.05 next year. On the basis of this concept, budgets typically increase every year because the cost to accomplish what was undertaken this year is going to be greater next year.

Revenue and Expenses

Revenue represents funds coming into a facility, and expenses are funds leaving the facility (i.e., to pay bills). Revenue and expenses are listed on financial statements, such as the income statement, and can tell a story such as what it cost to open the facility for an event. If an arena cannot open without guaranteeing at least $5,000 in revenue to cover expenses, any event generating less than that amount will not break even and should not be booked unless profit is not a motive. For some events, the facility management may not have a choice; the expenses for a graduation ceremony at a college facility will obviously exceed the revenue, but the event needs to be run anyway.

A facility can generate revenue from numerous sources. Some sources, such as ticket sales, parking revenue, concession sales, sponsorship revenue, advertising revenue, and naming rights revenue, are discussed in chapter 10. Other revenue sources can be unique for each facility. A facility that has extra cash can put that money into a bank account or invest in securities. Extra cash can also be invested in buying additional assets that can generate more revenue. A health club could use extra cash to buy another club; the combination of the two clubs can then generate even more revenue.

One of the first steps in understanding revenue and expenses is to identify what they are for a given facility. Revenue and expenses for a typical facility are highlighted below.

Revenue streams at various facilities can be enhanced through unique marketing efforts and innovations; a health club, for example, may add game rooms, baby-sitting, a juice bar, and a pro shop. However, all new revenue-generating ideas also entail new expenses. The expenses can include construction work, inventory, new employees, and even the cost of time for planning and developing a new revenue stream. A budget can help indicate how the proposed revenue-generating idea will affect the facility's bottom line.

One concern in this process is how to define certain revenues and expenses. For example, tickets can be defined differently from one facility to another, and such differences can have major ramifications. For instance, luxury suite revenue is not counted as part of the revenue-sharing agreement between the NFL and its players' association, but regular ticket sales are included. Thus, teams charge a significant amount for the suites and then charge people sitting in the suites for individual tickets as well. Rent is a vague term because rent can be a flat fee or a percentage of gross ticket sales. But however they are defined, a complete picture of revenue and expenses is needed to properly budget for the future.

As described in chapter 9, benchmarking is the process of comparing one facility or business with another. It is often hard to determine what the primary revenues and expenses are for facilities. Since it is difficult to find such data for the sport industry, looking at data for the lodging industry (hotels, resorts, etc.) can shed light on typical expenses and particularly energy expenditures (see page 212). Analyzing these numbers can help a sport facility identify what efforts to make to reduce expenditures to meet industry norms.

Financial Analysis

All facilities require financial planning. Will the facility generate enough revenue to pay all the salaries, cover debt service, and turn a profit to justify staying open? How much should it charge

Public Stadium Revenue and Expenses

Revenue	Expenses
Premium seating	Debt service
Ticket revenue	Salaries
Naming rights	Equipment
Advertising	Maintenance
Personal seat licenses	Supplies
Parking revenue	Janitorial
Concession revenue	Insurance
Novelty revenue	Professional expenses (legal)
Tenant rent	Taxes
Government subsidies	Utilities
Various bonds	Contractual expenses
Ticket surcharges	Capital replacement fund (sinking fund)
Facility rental	
Special events income	

General and Energy Expenses for a Typical Lodging Facility

The following are general expenses a lodging facility may incur:

Category	Percentage
Payroll	43
Utilities/Mechanical	19
Other	13
Building—general	6
Grounds	5
Supplies	4
Painting and decorating	4
Waste removal	3
Furniture	3
Total	100

Various utilities expenses of a lodging facility are as follows:

Category	Percentage
Electricity	63
Fuel (gas, oil, coal)	23
Water/Sewage	9
Steam	5
Total	100

From F. Borsenki and A. Stutts, 1997, *The management of maintenance and engineering systems in the hospitality industry*, 4th ed. (New York, NY: John Wiley & Sons, Inc.). Copyright 1997. Reprinted with permission of John Wiley & Sons, Inc.

for tickets or memberships? These are the types of questions facility managers face. The questions and the answers lie in financial statements. The two primary types of financial statements are the income statement and the balance sheet.

The income statement and balance sheet are used for various managerial activities. First, they help show a facility's financial health. Income statements show how much money a facility generated. The balance sheet highlights how much the facility is worth when all the assets are added together and the liabilities are subtracted from the total. The numbers can also be compared with industry ratios to examine how the facility is doing financially relative to other facilities. This process of benchmarking is used as well in specific areas such as maintenance, marketing, and the legal area. For example, if a facility earns $10 per fan from concession sales but other facilities are averaging $15 per fan, the facility is failing to meet industry standards. Finally, the numbers can be used to educate stakeholders, from elected officials to investment advisors, stockholders, the public, and tenants or customers, to help budget for the future.

Income Statements

An income statement highlights the revenue and expenses generated over a given period of time, normally one year (see a sample income statement on page 213). Through accounting, all revenue and expenses are calculated and then inserted into the income statement to show whether the facility generated any profit. Assume, for example, that a concession company operates a single drink stand at a facility. The stand sells 1,000 drinks at $5.00 each at an event. After the event, the accounting process adds up all the money the stand took in and then calculates all the expenses to determine if there was a profit or loss. The cost associated with selling the drinks included 50 cents for each drink for the cup, ice, water, syrup, and lid. Another cost was 25 cents for the time to process each order. These are the costs of the goods sold. Other expenses include depreciation, which is an accounting term referring to decreasing the value of equipment and property over a fixed period of time (allowing a company to reinvest future money to buy new equipment). Such an expense is normally calculated at the end of the year on all the equipment and property the government allows to be depreciated. Selling expenses are associated with overall marketing efforts such as the thousands of dollars the concession company spent to gain the right to operate the stand. The last major expense faced by the concession company is taxes that need to be paid to the government. Other expenses that could be included on an income statement are interest owed on money borrowed to build a facility or to use as operational funds. The sample income statement shows the concession stand made a profit of $2,800 after all costs, depreciation, and taxes were accounted for.

Balance Sheets

A balance sheet lists the facility's assets and liabilities on a given day (see a sample balance sheet below). The balance sheet changes every day. The amount of money owed to the facility and the amounts owed by the facility are constantly changing. A balance sheet contains three categories: assets, liabilities, and owner's equity. Assets range from the land and building itself (real property) to any personal property such as televisions, computer systems, and ticketing machines. Assets also include moneys owed to the facility such as membership fees or refunds. Liabilities are all the financial obligations that the facility has on the given date. These could include such obligations as repayment of a bond used to finance the building of the facility and salary obligations that have yet to be paid. Owner's equity refers to the amount owed to investors from their investment in the facility. The assets for our concession example could include cash, inventory (cups, ice, lids, syrup, etc.), and serving carts. The liabilities could be accounts payable (what the concession company owes vendors for supplies) and salaries payable. Owner's equity is the value the owner has in the business. The sample balance sheet shows that the amount of money the owners owe others is relatively small; the owners have significant value in the business since they possess the assets rather than owing money to others for

Sample Income Statement

Sales	$5,000
Material costs	500
Labor costs	250
Gross profit	$4,250
Depreciation	150
Selling expenses	300
Profit before taxes	$3,800
Taxes	1,000
Profit after taxes	$2,800

Sample Balance Sheet

Assets		Liabilities	
Cash	$10,000	Accounts payable	$5,000
Inventory	4,000	Salaries owed	4,000
Carts	30,000	Current liabilities	9,000
Total current assets	44,000		
Depreciation	4,000	Owner's equity	39,000
Total assets	$48,000	Total liability	$48,000

them. In a balance sheet the assets always have to equal the liabilities.

Using Financial Analysis

Table 11.1 presents a comparison of two sport events held at the New Haven Coliseum in 1998 and 1999. The table indicates how financial numbers can be compared to examine revenue and expenses over various events, and suggests the importance of the data in the income statement for future planning. For example, the concession per cap (per cap refers to the average per person expenditure on a given item), was $2.37 and did not change over the analyzed period. However, since there were approximately 1,200 more fans in 1998, the total gross concession revenue was significantly higher that year. Since the average ticket price increased $2.40, though, the total gross ticket revenue did not decrease as much as it might have. However, the data may also indicate that increased ticket price scared a significant number of patrons away from attending the event.

As highlighted in table 11.1, the financial analysis after an event is important for both the team or act and the facility to ensure that all parties know the correct numbers. The process of determining the final numbers, often called **reconciliation,** brings a promoter or team representative together with the facility's financial parties to determine the exact expenses and revenue for an event. A sample football game report from a major university shows how the financial analysis for an event is completed (see page 215). The post-event financial analysis is conducted for most single events such as a game, an event, or a concert. Typically the promoter and the facility finance director review the revenue and expenses to determine the final amounts owed under the contract. Accuracy is critical during this analysis, since if a contract requires revenue to be split 60%/40%, for example, any unaccounted-for revenue or expenses can significantly affect either party.

The information developed through the reconciliation process can also be utilized in budgeting for future events. However, before examining budgets, it is important to understand that there is a lot of cash in most sport facilities. Accountants cannot provide accurate numbers to base decisions on if all the cash is not accounted for.

Table 11.1 Sport Event Comparison

Category	1998	1999
Attendance	4,437	3,219
Average ticket price	$13.38	$15.78
Gross ticket revenue	$59,346	$50,806
Rental income	$2,578	$9,715
Concession per cap	$2.37	$2.37
Concession gross	$10,525	$7,635
Concession income	$6,244	$-1,454
Novelty per cap	$3.10	$2.81
Novelty gross	$13,738	$9,050
Novelty income	$3,426	$2,489
Parking gross	$3,141	$2,013
Parking income	$2,826	$1,751
Total event income	$21,060	$15,084

Tracking Cash

One of the primary daily concerns associated with financial management for a facility is cash management. Facilities are often overflowing with cash. If 50,000 people spend $10 each on various concession and souvenir items, the total is $0.5 million. There is also cash from ticket sales and parking revenue. At the end of an event, there can easily be over $1 million in cash. Obviously this does not include all the credit card transactions, checks, or electronic fund transfers that might be used.

All cash transactions need to be properly recorded and verified to make sure that money is not lost from the time it is used to purchase an item until it is deposited in the bank. Numerous checks and balances are used to make sure cash is not lost. For example, a facility may have two people at each parking lot entrance. The attendants wear aprons that cover their pants pockets to prevent them from sliding cash into their pockets. One attendant processes transactions and the other counts the cars with a counter. At the end of the event, management attempts to reconcile

Post-Event Financial Analysis

Tickets available for selling

| 78,484 | Reserved seats | @ $15.00 |
| 0 | General admission | @ $7.00 or $3.00 (none available for this game) |

Ticket distribution

5,589	Returned/Unsold		
5,334	Sold by opponents	@ $11.00 =	$58,674.00
32	Issued to press		
360	Issued comp to opponents' staff	@ $5.50 =	$1,980.00
16,834	Issued to students	@ $2.75 =	$46,293.50
690	Sold to faculty/staff	@ $5.50 =	$3,795.00
49,645	Sold by host school	@ $11.00 =	$546,095.00
78,484	Gross sales		$656,837.50
Less cost of officials			($3,298.00)
Subtotal			$653,539.50
Less 15% for game expenses			($98,030.93)
Net sales to be shared			$555,508.57
50% of net sales to opponents			$277,754.28
Less cash retained by opponents 5,334 × $15.00			($80,010.00)
Amount due opponents			$197,744.28

the ending balances. Thus, if each car had to pay $5 to park and there is a total of $5,000 in cash, the counter should have tallied 1,000 cars. If the numbers do not match, the reason for the discrepancy has to be determined. More importantly over the long run, if the numbers do not match, the facility will never be able to develop accurate forecasts and budgets.

Budgeting

Revenue and expenses from a prior year can be used as the starting point to develop a budget. A budget is a roadmap for the future of a facility. Just as people look at a map to figure out how to get where they want to go, a facility manager looks at the budget as a way to reach financial success. After

examining a map, people sometimes take a route different from the one they had planned to take and get lost. After examining a budget, a facility manager may try to follow the proposed plan but find that numerous distractions make it difficult to achieve the intended financial goals. The results can be either negative or positive. Through financial analysis a facility manager can see how close the facility is to the budget. Such regular analysis can help the facility determine if it is necessary to cut costs, generate additional revenue, or even cancel events.

The budget is a tool used by management to utilize resources effectively to reach a predetermined goal. If a wealthy investor offers to pay $200,000 to develop an initial site and feasibility study, the budget will work around that sum. If no other moneys are available, then $200,000 is the maximum amount of money available for the study, and total expenses have to come to less than $200,000. If the feasibility study will cost $75,000, then all other elements need to be accomplished for under $125,000 or additional funds will need to be found.

People follow this same process when they buy a car, house, or any other major item. A person would not buy a car requiring $400 a month in payments if he or she earns $2,000 a month and already spends $1,800 a month on food, rent, and so on. The process of making this determination is guided by a budget. Budgets help guide the financial decisions of most facilities. A facility cannot buy a $1 million heating, ventilation, and air conditioning (HVAC) unit if the machine is not in the budget. If the existing HVAC system breaks, the maintenance/repair budget may have to be tapped, or the capital improvement component of the budget will need to be examined. If there are not enough funds in the budget, management will need to consider inserting a line item in the next year's budget or authorize an emergency expenditure that will possibly throw the entire budget out of sync. Similar to the way in which a major medical emergency can destroy a person's finances, an emergency can destroy the financial position of a facility.

Management needs to develop an operational budget that details the various expenses expected in operating a facility. Basic elements within such a budget include the following:

- Utility expenses such as gas, water, electricity
- Rental expenses such as lease obligations and landlord-related expenses
- Planning and design expenses such as consultation fees, computer-assisted design and drafting (CADD) expenses, photography, and printing
- Maintenance and repair expenses such as preventive maintenance (grounds, roof, electrical, HVAC, etc.), custodial, and repairs and alterations
- Future growth expenses such as new alterations, noncapital equipment, and grounds improvements
- Moving expenses such as direct support for moving from one facility to another
- Management expenses (Cotts and Lee, 1992)

Forecasting

The revenues and expenses a facility might face cannot be examined only after they have been earned or spent. A facility manager needs to know past numbers and the potential future numbers to properly forecast revenues and expenses and thus to build an accurate budget.

The **financial forecast** is a bridge to help move the financial plan to the budget. There is no one correct way to forecast the future. Some facilities utilize their sales staff to analyze future conditions, based on which customers have entered into long-term contracts, for example. If research shows that customers are not interested in a facility, then such data need to be analyzed in the financial planning process. A facility manager can plan more effectively when he or she knows that for the next 20 years a given team will play their home games at the facility or that a college or high school is a member of a given athletic conference. If a circus or other event is booked for only two years, the facility manager knows that the third year is not as certain. Other techniques for forecasting are more complicated, such as regression analysis, econometric modeling, the Delphi method, and moving averages, and are not covered in this text (Cotts and Lee, 1992).

The starting point for a budget is typically any prior budgets, which can serve as a roadmap. If the facility anticipates that revenue and expenses will increase 10% next year, a rough budget can be developed by just adding 10% to this year's budget. But this simplistic approach rarely works because the numbers are never cut-and-dry. Another option is called zero-based budgeting (ZBB), which requires a budget to be based on a competitive internal battle. All divisions within the facility prepare their budget as if they had never had a budget before and base their monetary request on what they perceive they can do to benefit the facility's goals and objectives. The divisions that management feels will enhance the facility's goals the most will receive the greatest proportions of the budget.

One technique entails developing an annual work plan highlighting capital costs (construction, repairs, equipment purchases, etc.), nondiscretionary annual costs (utilities, operations, custodial, moving, and maintenance), discretionary annual costs (alterations, repairs, maintenance), lease costs, overhead costs (salaries, office equipment, etc.), and the cost of space needed for future projects (Cotts and Lee, 1992). These figures are used for both mid- and long-range plans. A facility can establish what anticipated repairs may be forthcoming in various ways, ranging from facility inspections to computerized systems indicating that a given component is past its useful life. Thus, if a roof has a 20-year life and has been in place for 24 years, the facility should be budgeting for a new roof. The roof can fail at any time; it has lasted this long because of luck or exceptional maintenance.

The greatest cost in any facility is upkeep. Over the life of a facility, the salaries of those who work in the facility account for 92% of the life-cycle costs. The operating and maintenance costs account for 6%, and the actual design and construction accounts for only 2% of the life-cycle costs of a facility (Cotts and Lee, 1992).

Paying the Daily Bills

Budgeting and financial analysis occur on a daily basis. If a given event does not generate the expected revenue and that revenue was going to pay certain bills, then other revenue sources need to be tapped to pay those bills. Managers frequently have to juggle between current needs, such as bills that are currently due, and future revenue such as that from future events. Managers also have to balance cash flow and streams. If there is $1 million in the bank, should it be put into long-term investments, put into lower-paying short-term investments, or used for capital improvements that will pay bigger dividends down the road? Similarly, with bills, should they be paid immediately, should they be paid after 30 days, or should they be ignored? While it might be illegal to ignore a bill, many businesses follow this strategy and might pay only when threatened with a lawsuit.

Bill tracking is a critical skill for any facility manager. How much did the facility spend last year on energy versus this year? Is there any reason for the change, such as cooler weather or an increased cost for fuel? Similarly, are repair and maintenance costs increasing? Would outsourcing facility management save money, or would there be a potential problem with union employees if such a step were taken?

While bill tracking and analysis help determine if the budget is on track, the process is significantly different for the day-to-day management of a facil-

ity, as discussed so far, versus the situation in which a facility is being built. The operational budget can be fairly consistent, with the expenses such as payroll and inventory remaining relatively constant. In contrast, building a new facility requires a capital budget that will face numerous changes almost daily. The next section focuses on finances related to building new facilities, including capital cost considerations and capital budgeting decision making to help determine which construction option may be the best for a proposed facility.

Capital Cost Considerations

Capital costs are costs associated with long-term investments such as buildings or equipment that may last more than 10 years. Capital expenditures in the sport facility area relate primarily to building the sport facility. Since facilities are extremely expensive, most entities building sport facilities utilize capital budgeting to fund construction.

Capital budgeting entails determining the needed space for any given planned activity and determining whether existing facilities can fill those needs. It is not worthwhile to build a facility when other facilities exist that could serve the needs and are not fully utilized. After determining whether existing facilities can serve the planned needs, the capital budgeting process requires management to examine additional options for acquiring any additional needed space, whether by leasing, building, or redistributing space in existing facilities (Cotts and Lee, 1992). If management decides to renovate or construct a new facility, then capital funds will be needed. The decision is influenced by several factors, including the prevailing tax codes and the impact associated with depreciating assets. The budgeting process is also affected by the financial market, how easily cash can be raised, and the cost associated with raising the funds (interest rate, bond issuance costs, etc.).

One of the primary capital budgeting concerns faced by those trying to decide whether to build is the choice between building a new facility and leasing an existing facility. When leasing land, a developer signs a contract indicating that he or she will pay the agreed-upon amount over a certain time period. At the end of the time period, the landowner has the option of renewing the lease. If the lease is not renewed, the facility must relocate, and the cost of relocation can be very high. In addition to this expense, leasing does not generate any equity for the facility developer. Thus, no money is being saved for the next facility through equity enhancement. On the other hand, advantages of leasing are that it allows a developer to limit the amount of commitment to the project and that lease payments can be written off taxes as a business expense.

The major advantage of purchasing a facility is the ability to build equity and control the facility. In the future, when the facility wants to expand or relocate, the funds will be much easier to obtain because of the company's equity. There are two major difficulties with buying land. First, the upfront payment for the land can be so high that the developer may not be able to afford building according to the original plans. Another problem is the long-term loan. If the facility should incur financial difficulty, the owner may be forced to sell the land and building.

The capital budgeting process starts with acquiring appropriate information. The next step entails prioritizing projects. Prioritization occurs through various predetermined methods such as average rate of return, average payback period, annual return on investments, cash payback methods, discounted cash flow, net present value (NPV), internal rate of return (IRR), and the benefit–cost ratio (BCR) (Cotts and Lee, 1992). Table 11.2 shows projected profits and cash flows for three different projects. Based on this financial planning analysis, different capital budgeting options are available (see table 11.3). A discussion of these options follows.

Using the average rate of return (ARR) method, Project C would be the best choice since it produces the highest rate of return—115% versus 107% or 80%. Utilizing the average payback period (APP) method, Project C is once again the best choice

Table 11.2 Financial Planning Analysis

Net investment	Project A		Project B		Project C	
	$240,000		$150,000		$150,000	
Year	Profit	Cash flow	Profit	Cash flow	Profit	Cash flow
1	$40,000	$88,000	$60,000	$90,000	$20,000	$50,000
2	$60,000	$108,000	$60,000	$90,000	$40,000	$70,000
3	$140,000	$188,000	$60,000	$90,000	$80,000	$110,000
4	$200,000	$248,000	$60,000	$90,000	$120,000	$150,000
5	$200,000	$248,000	$60,000	$90,000	$170,000	$200,000
Totals	$640,000	$880,000	$300,000	$450,000	$430,000	$580,000
Averages	$128,000	$166,000	$60,000	$90,000	$86,000	$116,000

Reprinted, by permission, from D. Cotts and M. Lee, 1992, *The facility management handbook* (New York, NY: American Management Association).

Table 11.3 Capital Budgeting Options

Prioritization technique	Project A	Project B	Project C
Average rate of return (ARR)	106.6%	80%	114.5%
Average payback period (APP)	1.44 years	1.67 years	1.29 years
Net present value (NPV) × 2	$306,892	$141,694	$203,934
Internal rate of return (IRR)	50.9%	52.8%	51.0%

Cotts and Lee, 1992.

since it repays the initial investment in the shortest time period. However, with the actual payback analysis, Project B would be the best choice because it actually pay backs the initial investment in 1.67 years (note that profits are consistent throughout the five years) versus 2.23 years for Project A and 2.27 years for Project C.

The NPV analysis is based on a current cost of capital of 15%. Using the NPV approach, Project A has the highest present value and should be chosen. Using IRR, Project B has the best return. The ARR helps determine the rate of return in a percentage so that various projects can be compared with one another. Rate of return is calculated by dividing the net income (after taxes), commonly called profit, by the average cost of the investment. The average investment cost is calculated by subtracting the facility's salvage value from the construction cost and then dividing by 2. This formula is easy to use, is well known and respected, and considers the full time frame for the capital investment decision. Problems with ARR are that it is difficult to calculate profit, that the method ignores the time value of money, and that arbitrary time frames for a facility's existence may be required (Cotts and Lee, 1992). The formula is as follows:

average rate of return (%) =
profit / average investment

Using Project A, this is calculated by dividing $128,000 by ($240,000 / 2). The APP analyzes a capital decision based on how long on average it will take to repay the initial investment assuming an average cash flow rather than possibly a more specific rate of cash flow (such as the actual payback period). The net investment is divided by the average annual cash inflow to get the APP. The APP method is easy to use, analyzes cash flows, and can analyze risk. The drawbacks are that it does not consider time value of money, that cash flows can be very subjective, and that APP does not consider subsequent cash flows (which could drop or increase significantly) (Cotts and Lee, 1992). Many utilize the APP approach because it analyzes the actual time it takes to cover the initial investment in building the facility. This method is similar to the APP, but also considers the timing of cash flows.

Net present value (NPV) determines the dollar value of some future series of cash flows, discounted by the facility's cost of capital. This process examines the time value of money, which means that a dollar tomorrow is not worth as much as a dollar today. Thus, the initial capital investment is subtracted from the net present value of future cash flows to get the NPV. This process requires the use of time value of money tables and considers relevant cash flows. Thus, it is a well understood calculation, but it is also difficult for most individuals without some financial experience to use.

The IRR is the discount rate assuming an NPV of zero. The initial investment and future cash flows are analyzed to determine a project's value. This process analyzes cash flows and the time value of money, but is very difficult to calculate and hard for people to understand. A last evaluation technique for capital investments is the benefit–cost ratio (BCR). This calculation divides the value of a project by the cost. The cost may be fairly easy to calculate, but the benefits are both economic and subjective so they are harder to calculate. That is why the BCR is used only when an experienced staff of economists can help with the calculations.

While there are numerous tools to compare various projects, these tools are not accurate unless they all utilize the same basic numbers. If two separate formulas use different data for the same project, it will be impossible to compare the numbers. Thus, the capital budgeting process often utilizes a worksheet (see page 220) that highlights the basic costs anticipated with the capital project.

Once the analysis is complete and the numbers are finalized, management needs to choose which project meets the planned needs. Some projects will provide appropriate payback in a set number of years and will be chosen over other projects that might take a longer time to repay the initial investment. This process is referred to as the cost justification process, used when costs are the overriding concern. However, numerous projects do not meet the predefined criteria. Some projects are accepted because they produce the greatest reward regardless of price, limit or minimize risks, or rank higher on the priority list.

One of the key concerns associated with capital budgeting is that many managers stop at that point. They determine that a facility will cost $200 million to construct and realize that they can raise that amount of money, so they move forward with the project. However, as described earlier, the greatest cost in a facility is upkeep. If the capital budget is not integrated into the operational budget from day one, the facility will probably face some

Budget Worksheet for a New Facility

Pre-Project Expenses

Temporary offices: _____

Utilities: _____

Insurance: _____

Moving costs: _____

Temporary furnishings: _____

Consulting Expenses

Feasibility studies: _____

Legal fees: _____

Design fees: _____

Site investigations: _____

Marketing expenses: _____

Site-Related Expenses

Land location expenses: _____

Title search: _____

Site appraisals: _____

Site surveys: _____

Boring tests/Soil tests: _____

Zoning compliance: _____

Land costs: _____

Closing fees: _____

Finance fees: _____

Utilities to site: _____

Demolition expenses: _____

Development fees: _____

Miscellaneous assessment: _____

Professional fees: _____

Preconstruction Costs

Architectural/Engineering fees: _____

Models and drawings: _____

Interior design costs: _____

Consulting fees: _____

Copying expenses: _____

Bidding-related expenses: _____

Construction Expenses

Construction contract: _____

Contingency fund: _____

Project manager for owner: _____

Insurance: _____

FFE (furniture, fixtures, and equipment): _____

Site development: _____

Landscaping: _____

Excavation: _____

Parking: _____

Access roads: _____

Signage: _____

Security: _____

Lighting: _____

Irrigation: _____

Storage facility: _____

Miscellaneous fees: _____

Miscellaneous Expenses

Bidding expenses: _____

Interest on construction loans: _____

Construction contingency: _____

Moving expenses: _____

Utility expenses: _____

Start-up staff: _____

Staff training: _____

Operating expenses: _____

Maintenance expenses _____

Sinking funds: _____

Total Project Costs

Pre-project expenses: _____

Consulting expenses: _____

Site-related expenses: _____

Preconstruction expenses: _____

Construction expenses: _____

Miscellaneous expenses: _____

Grand total: _____

From Wiggins, 1993.

financial hardships. If the operational budget is established while the facility is being built and enough funds are set aside to help operate at least for the first year, the facility should be in a strong financial position.

After the decision has been made to build or lease a particular facility, the construction funds need to be secured. The next section highlights the various financing options available to build a new facility.

New Facility Financing

With costs escalating every fiscal year, it is becoming increasingly difficult to finance a major sport facility or complex using funds from only one individual or group, including public taxes. There are three major financing options: private financing, public (government) financing, and miscellaneous methods. Each option has distinct advantages and disadvantages.

Private Financing

Private financing can come from different sources, from stock and bonds issued by private companies to private funds. For example, the Miami Dolphins used to play in Joe Robbie Stadium (now Pro Player Park), which was built with private funds from the Robbie family. The Green Bay Packers are a publicly traded company that issued approximately $24 million worth of shares to help finance renovations to Lambeau Field. Other facilities, especially smaller ones, are often built with private funds, whether obtained from savings, bank loans, or inheritances. Other facilities have private backers or may be part of a business partnership. Still others are built with corporate funds—corporate gyms, for example.

Collateral Financing

New and developing enterprises sometimes face the uncertain and difficult process of obtaining capital to build or grow their business, and lenders will require some **collateral** or **equity**. Private equity can come from various sources. Equity represents the total value of personal money, stocks, and property (both real and personal). Money can include the actual cash that someone has on hand, stocks, bonds, and anything else that has value. Property is divided into two categories, real

and personal. Real property is land and anything secured to the ground, including buildings and houses. Personal property is anything that can be lifted and moved. This can include teams, businesses, equipment, and automobiles. The problem with collateral-based borrowing is that if the borrower fails to pay the loan he or she can lose the collateral. Houses are a familiar example. A house serves as the collateral for a home loan. If the borrower defaults, the lender can foreclose and sell the house to get its money back.

Private Investors

Strategic investors are established companies with similar products who are looking for growth and expansion opportunities. Because strategic investors may lack the experience and ability to expand their own company, investing in another company gives them a low-cost alternative that will improve their company's value. For example, a large consumer product company may enter into a strategic alliance with a small fitness equipment company. The larger company can provide facilities to manufacture a new product, while the small company can lend its fitness product expertise without having to rent facilities or buy equipment.

Another source of private financing is wealthy individual investors or venture capital groups. These investors have dedicated a certain amount of their investment toward private investment opportunities. Most people have heard about **venture capital (VC)** investors, especially in connection with the "dot com" boom and bust. A VC investor supplies significant cash at the start of a business (or possibly at times of crisis) in exchange for a large percentage of the business. Venture capital investment is a form of private equity investing. Private equity investing can have significant benefits, such as financial flexibility, stable costs, and managerial expertise from investors. On the other hand, venture capitalists demand a high rate of return (often over 40% profit per year) and often a seat on the board of directors.

Corporate Bonds

Corporate bonds are bonds that are issued and backed by the issuing corporations. Unlike most government bonds, corporate bonds are not tax-exempt. (Tax-exempt bonds provide income protection for investors in that the interest payments made by the bond issuer are not taxed when paid to the investor. Otherwise, investors would not receive the total expected return since between 20% to 40% of the interest payment would have to be paid as taxes. However, the downside of tax-exempt bonds is that they pay less interest than corporate or private bonds.)

Corporate bonds are issued when a corporation feels it can obtain a lower interest rate than if it borrowed from a bank and wants a longer repayment period. If a facility builder approaches a bank and is offered a loan of $100 million at 9% but could issue a bond paying 8%, the 1% difference could be worth tens of millions of dollars over the bond's life. The one major caveat is that there must be bond buyers interested in purchasing corporate bonds. This problem makes bond issuance an option only for the biggest corporations or for prominent professional teams.

Partnerships

Money can also come from other people or organizations working together to build a facility. For example, two or more people can join together to build or finance a facility; two or more government entities such as a school district and a parks department can join together to build playing fields to be used by both entities. In limited partnerships, partners put predetermined amounts of money or assets into the project. The obvious downfall is the great amount of risk that this type of arrangement involves. If a partnership fails, everyone involved in the partnership loses money. On the other hand, profits made by the facility are split among partners.

A strategic partnership occurs when a developer forms an alliance with another company that has congruent goals. This goes beyond a transfer of cash and entails strategic cooperation. A strategic partnership may be pursued when it promotes an effective means to enter the market. Another benefit with partners is geographic location. Partners can operate in several different areas and start franchises with facilities in the various areas. Health club owners in different areas have used partnerships as a means to merge their clubs into a larger entity and then attempt to expand. While such an option may appear attractive, there are numerous financial and legal concerns that can arise and that make strategic alliances less common in the realm of sport.

Partnerships are practical solutions to financial problems, but are not advised when it appears that the relationship is going to be very one-sided or when the partners do not have a good working relationship. It is also very important to be able to trust partners. One concern with partnerships is the liability of each partner for the actions of other partners. Thus, if one partner makes a mistake and subjects the partnership to liability, then all partners can be personally liable.

Public Offerings

Public offerings involve selling corporate shares to the public in the form of stock. Corporations can raise significant funds in this manner. A number of examples exist in the sport industry, primarily in horse racing, auto racing, and health clubs. Facilities and corporations need money to grow, and a public offering may represent the best way to grow and acquire or build additional facilities. But although a public offering might be a good way to raise a lot of money, it opens the facility to intense scrutiny, first from the Securities and Exchange Commission and state regulators and then from entities in the financing community such as brokerage houses. Another concern is that corporate financial records become public records through annual reports and various government filings. Corporations have another major concern: double taxation of revenue—first, when earned, and then when paid to stockholders as dividends. However, there are significant benefits to a facility's going public, such as access to more capital, prestige, and the ability to limit the shareholder's liability for action taken by the corporation.

Public Financing

Whether the money is their own or has come from others, facility developers need enough cash to buy land, build a facility, and then operate the facility. These same funds are needed if a government entity builds a sport facility. The major difference is that government entities can raise money by other means. For example, as highlighted in chapter 5, government entities can acquire land through eminent domain. Even though this process costs money, it is often easier than other ways of acquiring property. The question becomes one of how the government entity will pay for the land. Funds can come from increased tax revenue, bonds, certificates of participation, or a combination of these. Increasing taxes has been used as a means to finance facilities such as the Alamodome. Even

Facility Focus: PNC Park

© Pittsburgh Post Gazette

In early 1999 an $803 million package was funded to build PNC Park (home of the Pittsburgh Pirates of Major League Baseball), build Heinz Field (home of the NFL Pittsburgh Steelers), retire the debt on Three Rivers Stadium and also destroy the stadium, expand the convention center, and construct a new Pittsburgh Development Center. The projects totaled over $1 billion in financing. Out of necessity, the $1 billion was raised through a strategy that tapped into the existing 1% county sales tax. The Regional Asset District contributes $13.4 million annually to finance $170 million in bonds for the project. The county hotel tax contributes $8 million annually to finance $99 million in bonds. A 5% surcharge on Pirates and Steelers tickets raises $3 million annually to finance $22 million in bonds. A 1% wage tax is levied on players who do not live in the city and contributed $7 million to the project. The state of Pennsylvania contributed $300 million in matching funds. Funds totaling $36 million of the project came from interest earnings; $28 million was tapped from a fund for federal infrastructure improvements; $11 million came from parking revenues for leasing the convention center garage; $45 million was given to the project from a Pittsburgh Investment Capital fund. The Pirates and the Steelers contributed $85 million combined. The Pirates are also expected to cover operating costs (utilities and maintenance) as long as the team receives the revenues from concessions and advertising. Lastly, on August 6, 1998, Pittsburgh-based PNC Bank Corp announced that it had purchased the right to name the new Pirates ballpark "PNC Park" when it opened in 2001. Under the deal, PNC Bank, a financial services company, will pay approximately $1.5 million a year through the 2020 baseball season for the naming rights (Gearhard and Schuler, 2001).

though a bond was issued for the Alamodome, the bond was secured by an increased sales tax. Lenders were eager to purchase the bonds since they were backed by a steady revenue stream that would guarantee repayment.

Over the past decade, most sport facilities have been financed through tax-exempt bonds. **Bonds** are, in a manner of speaking, a promise that in a specific period of time the borrower will pay back the lender the amount of money borrowed along with a specific amount of interest. Government entities often issue bonds to pay for schools, roads, and other construction projects. Most municipalities and school districts, subject to certain restrictions and limitations, have the right to raise capital by issuing bonds. In order to issue a bond there must be legal authorization from either the voters or a legislative body. Obtaining

authorization can prove to be difficult, and at times impossible, because project opponents are more likely to show up for the vote than supporters are (Howard and Crompton, 1995).

In 2002 there were 111 major professional sport franchises in America, and 91.9% (102) had moved into new or significantly renovated stadiums in the 1990s. The total taxpayers' price tag for stadiums or arenas built from 1995 through 2000 has been estimated at over $9 billion (Fried, Shapiro, and Deshriver, 2003). Municipalities interested in luring a new team or keeping an existing team argue that tax dollars should help finance facility construction because entertainment dollars are brought in from outside the community, thus infusing "new" money into the local economy.

Teams are also helping to cover the building expenses. The average level of team contribution

Behind the Scenes: Anatomy of Various Stadium Deals

- The Colorado Rockies built their stadium with a 1%, six-county-area sales tax, with the team contributing $53 million and Coors Brewing scheduled to pay $1.5 million a year for naming rights. Under the 17-year lease, the city receives 20% of parking revenue on game days and 3% of the revenue from a brew pub. The team receives 100% of net concession revenue.

- The United Center in Chicago was built in 1994 at a cost of $175 million; 80% of the financing was with funds from private bank loans, and 20% was with funds from the building owners. United Center Joint Venture privately funded the entire project. United Airlines currently pays approximately $1.8 million a year in naming rights.

- The Baltimore Ravens have a financially lucrative stadium deal, with the team receiving revenue from seat licenses and 100% of the revenue from concessions, ads, suites, club seats, and naming rights—and the team pays no rent. Ticket, novelty, parking, sponsorship, and advertising revenues are split between the team and government.

© AP/World Wide Photos

- Portland's Rose Garden (shown here) was built using a complex blend of private and public funding, including a $46 million cash contribution from Portland Trailblazers owner Paul Allen. Three major banks loaned a total of $16 million to the pot. Lastly, nine insurance companies purchased $155 million in privately placed bonds paying 8.99% interest over 27 years.

The city of Portland paid $34.5 million for street, parking, and related improvements. These city-funded projects will be paid for by a ticket tax of 6.5%, which will pay off the city's contribution in six years and thereafter provide the city with a perpetual return on its investment.

- The Gateway project in Cleveland was financed through a tax-exempt county bond offering that raised 45% of the $152 million needed to build the Gund Arena. Liquor and cigarette taxes (sin taxes) covered another 42%, and private naming rights covered the remaining 13%. Bonds were sold to various investors, and the income stream used to repay the bonds came from state capital improvement funds and a countywide sin tax. The sin tax consisted of $3 per gallon of liquor, 16 cents per gallon of beer, and 4.5 cents per pack of cigarettes. These taxes were to be in place for 15 years (Fried, Shapiro, and Deshriver, 2003).

to a new NFL stadium is 29%, or $82 million of the typical construction cost for a football stadium. Even without any team contributions, some municipalities are willing to foot the entire price of a facility to become a "big-league" city. Besides increased economic activity and increased sales, income, and employment tax revenues from those attending games and working at the facilities, proponents argue that the facilities help promote community image (Fried, Shapiro, and Deshriver, 2003). Making the "big leagues" can be expensive and can subject the citizens to paying debt service on bonds for years to come, without the facility's ever generating a profit. One major study concluded that older arenas with little debt and numerous scheduled events (NBA, NHL, Ice Capades, family shows, circuses, etc.) tended to make the highest profit while new stadiums for outdoor sports were less profitable (Fried, Shapiro, and Deshriver, 2003).

Bonds

As highlighted by the examples presented in this chapter, the thrust of any government financing, whether complete or partial, is on issuing bonds. Unless the government or team has significant cash reserves, it will be necessary to borrow. A bond is a detailed IOU. While a stock certificate is proof of ownership and can be given to a facility owner, a bond does not represent ownership. A bond represents a debt owed by the facility builder, whether private or governmental. The money obtained from issuing the bonds is used to pay for facility acquisition and construction costs. Bonds are a debt instrument that requires repayment of principal and interest over many years. Most bonds are for 10, 20, or 30 years; if a facility is built with $100 million worth of bonds to be repaid over 30 years at 10% interest, the facility will eventually have paid the bondholders in the neighborhood of $300 million.

Bonds are rated based on the strength of the issuing company or municipality and on whether the entity has ever defaulted on prior bonds. General obligation bonds (GOBs) and other bonds are rated by independent companies such as Moody's and Standard & Poor's based on the issuer's ability to repay the loan. General obligation bonds are often highly rated since currently existing and future tax revenue sources can be tapped for bond repayment. Bond ratings can be influenced by a multitude of factors, including

- the ability to repay the loan with existing revenue streams;
- the strength, breadth, and reliability of the tax base;
- the historical performance of the revenue stream;
- the risk associated with the project;
- the underlying economic strength of the stadium or arena or the community;
- political volatility; and
- whether or not the project is economically viable (Fried, Shapiro, and Deshriver, 2003).

The higher the quality rating, the more likely the bond is to be issued and the lower the interest rate will be. To enhance the marketability of a bond issue, a government entity may purchase bond insurance to guarantee repayment. The strength of the tax base to repay the bond is one of the most important criteria for GOBs. A small city with a low tax base may suffer significantly if property values decrease or sales drop markedly. In contrast, a large city with thousands of properties can experience downturns in the economy and still have a large enough tax base that the damage can be minimal.

Municipal entities frequently issue various bonds to fund such buildings as schools, police stations, and sport facilities. The several types of municipal bonds include general obligation, special tax, revenue, and lease-backed financing bonds, as well as certificates of participation. Each bond type is typically distinguished based on what revenue source is being used to repay the bond. Municipal bonds are often issued to help build new facilities.

Certificates of participation (CPs) allow a municipality to form a corporation to purchase land or build a facility. The corporation then issues CPs to pay for the land or building. The government then leases the building back from the corporation, and the lease payments are used to repay the bonds. Since the bonds are issued by a corporation rather than the municipality, they are not backed by the full faith and credit of the municipality. Thus, they carry a greater risk than traditional bonds. However, during tough times when a municipality may not otherwise be able to borrow money, the CP may be the only way to build a facility.

General Obligation Bonds General obligation bonds are among the instruments most commonly used to fund public facilities. These bonds are often called full faith and credit obligations as the city, county, municipality, state, or other government unit pledges to repay the obligation with existing tax revenues or by levying new taxes (Fried, Shapiro, and Deshriver, 2003).

Revenue Bonds With a **revenue bond,** the tax revenue to support repayment may come from the project itself. For example, an entrance tax of $1.50 per ticket could be charged and all revenues from this tax would first be allocated to repaying the revenue bond. These bonds traditionally have a lower credit rating than other bonds because there are significant financial risks associated with limiting repayment requirements to one specific tax or revenue source. The repayment concern

225

arose in the 1998 NBA strike, for example. If games were canceled and admission revenue was lost, some bond issuers might not have had any of their anticipated revenue sources to repay bonds secured by attendance taxes. This left the option available for a bondholder to declare an arena builder (team or municipality) in default, and possibly foreclose on the property and have it sold to repay the bonds.

Tax-Backed Bonds A public entity can also target a specific tax to finance a bond. Cleveland utilized a "sin tax" on alcohol and tobacco sales to help finance Jacobs Field and Gund Arena. San Antonio utilized a sales tax-based bond issue to help finance building the Alamodome. Special tax bonds are repayable from a specific pledged source and are not backed by the full faith and credit of the issuing entity. Thus, if the specific revenue source is inadequate, there may not be enough tax revenue to repay the bondholders. Examples of specific funding sources include the following (Greenberg and Gray, 1996):

- Utility taxes. A utility tax is added to an electricity, water, or gas bill to help pay for the bond's debt service. In the 1990s, the San Francisco Giants were considering a move to San Jose, California. The proposed stadium was to be partially financed by a utility tax. Opponents of the stadium distributed light-switch covers to communicate the idea that every time people turned on the lights they would be paying for the proposed stadium. The stadium ballot measure was defeated.

- Car rental taxes or tourist development taxes. These taxes are designed primarily to tax "out-of-towners" who visit the city. This is a popular technique because it is easy to tell a voting population that out-of-towners will pay for the facility even if local residents really are the most frequent users of rental cars.

- Ticket surcharges. A ticket surcharge is an additional amount, such as $0.50 or $1.00 per ticket, that increases the ticket price by that amount. The funds go directly to repay the bonds. This option is popular with voters since the people who go to the event pay a larger share than others.

- Real estate taxes. All property owners pay real estate taxes unless they have a special dispensation authorizing them not to pay such taxes. A municipality may increase the real estate tax obligations to help fund building a new facility. The concept is that the facility can help increase property values, so property owners should help support the facility.

- Possessory interest taxes. A possessory interest tax is charged to whomever possesses control of the facility and is designed to tax the primary facility user. This type of tax is very popular with taxpayers.

- Excise tax. Excise taxes are a general tax added to various products and are often initiated in periods of financial need such as times of war or economic downturn.

- Non-tax fees such as permits. Non-tax fees are special expenses passed on to particular parties. For example, the permit costs for other developers in the city can be raised. Other city expenses that are normally charged to vendors and citizens can be raised, with the extra funds going to pay for the facility.

- Lottery and gaming revenue. A municipality can dedicate funds received from special lotteries or games to fund civic growth projects such as roads, schools, and stadiums. Some states have received significant windfalls when Native American-owned casinos opened in the state.

- General appropriations. General appropriations are funds that are set aside for various purposes. Through political dealing a municipality may convince the state legislature or federal government to give a "gift" appropriation to help pay facility construction expenses or to fund bond repayments. The San Antonio Alamodome was built as a bus stop in order to help secure a federal appropriation for interstate transportation. Thus, there are few parking spaces next to the facility, but there are numerous bus stops.

Repayment Sources

Whichever type of bond is issued, repayment will always be the key concern for investors. Other factors can also be important to a potential investor, such as whether the bond is tax-exempt, whether the government entity purchased bond repayment insurance, and whether **contractually obligated revenue (COR)** (or **contractually obligated income, COI**) is sufficient to repay the bond. Even with these variables, investors look toward a stable repayment source as an additional assurance that the bond will be paid.

Although these revenue sources or payment guarantees can often support significant repayment obligations, CORs can also provide a strong guarantee that a debt will be repaid. Contractually obligated revenues are any contract whereby a party agrees to pay a specific sum for a guaranteed number of years. Typical long-term contracts that form the basis of COR backing include premium seat, luxury box, naming rights, pouring rights, signage rights, and parking rights contracts (Fried, Shapiro, and Deshriver, 2003). Contractually obligated revenues have two primary functions. They can be used as a source of revenue to guarantee repayment of bonds or other loans. They also can be utilized as an independent funding source. If the bonds are all covered through other revenue streams, the team or facility may be able to sell the naming rights and use those funds to enhance its bottom line.

Contractually obligated revenue from prepaid membership can help secure a loan to build a facility. Similarly, when anchor tenants are found who are willing to sign a long-term lease, then the COR associated with that lease can help fund the borrowing required to build a facility.

Miscellaneous Funding

In addition to the standard funding options such as loans, bonds, or COR, there are numerous unique strategies to finance a facility. One of the easiest is to have someone donate a facility. Sometime a facility can be built with a gift. Some colleges, universities, communities, and schools will not even entertain the idea of building a facility unless funds have been donated for that purpose. North Dakota had a $50 million gift from a wealthy alumnus to fund a $100 million arena. The University of Houston had a wealthy alumnus donate the athletic and alumni center and baseball field. Other unique funding options include grants and user funding.

Grants

In a strategy that is similar to individual giving, organizations and individuals can also grant money for projects. Many foundations have large sums of money that they need to give away. The Ely Lilly Corporation is a large drug manufacturer based in Indianapolis. The Lilly Endowment has granted a significant amount of money to the city

The Major Taylor Velodrome in Indianapolis, Indiana, was built by grants from the Lilly Endowment.

to build sport facilities. The process typically starts when the foundation provides nonprofit organizations that are interested in receiving funds with some rough parameters for proposals to be submitted by a specified date. All the proposals are analyzed, and the foundation's board selects the ones they wish to fund entirely or partially. Most foundations receive numerous requests, so the grant process is highly competitive. However, if a nonprofit organization or school has an innovative idea that the board likes, it may award significant cash to help build a facility.

User Funding

There are numerous ways in which facility users can help finance a facility. One of the most frequently seen forms of user support is student fees. A university with 10,000 students may charge an activity fee of $100 per semester to fund a new recreational center. This would represent a $2 million contribution to the facility and could possibly fund debt repayment and operating expenses, depending on the facility's size. The hazards with such a strategy are that students can resent the fee, especially if they do not use the recreation center, and that revenue is hurt if enrollment declines.

Selling a Facility

One financial consideration that is often overlooked with a facility is the financial repercussions of selling or otherwise disposing of the property. At a certain point a facility may outlive its usefulness. There are various methods for disposing of a facility, including the following:

- Transfer the facility from one operating division to another at full book value
- Put the facility on the market as a sport facility and see if someone will pay the value of the facility based on its current usage
- Sell all the equipment and then put the building on the market for any potential use
- Sell the facility to whomever will buy it for any use
- Sell the facility to a lender or financial institution and then lease it back
- Demolish the facility and rebuild a new structure on the same site
- Donate the facility to charity (Cotts and Lee, 1992)

The **sales–lease-back strategy** is gaining popularity with many facility and equipment owners. Someone who owns a building that is worth $100,000 and has $50,000 in equity could sell the building to a lender for $100,000. After paying the $50,000 the former facility owner would have $50,000 to expand or grow the business. He or she would then make a lease payment of possibly $1,000 a month for 10 years and then could either repurchase the facility or enter into a new lease. This option allows the former facility owner to gain valuable cash and reduce income by paying tax-deductible rent.

Summary

Many people do not like to talk about finance because there are numerous terms and formulas that people may not understand. However, for facility managers to have any credibility, they need to have a strong grasp of finance and how to run a facility under a budget. A facility has identifiable revenues and expenses that one needs to determine in order to learn how to make more money or reduce costs. Once the dollar value of income and expenses, along with assets and liabilities, is calculated, management can plug these numbers into various financial tools such as income statements and balance sheets to determine how well the facility is doing financially.

Financial analysis is used as a tool to forecast the future and develop an operating budget that will help the facility reach its goals. If the forecasts or budgets are wrong, it is almost impossible for a facility to reach its goals. The budget process does not focus only on day-to-day concerns; it may include developing a capital project to renovate an existing facility or build a new one. Once a strategy has been chosen and a building type identified, the money needs to be raised from private, public, or other sources. However, the financial analysis should not end when a building is built, but should continue as long as the facility is operating. Financial analysis is also needed when the time comes to dispose of a facility.

DISCUSSION QUESTIONS AND ACTIVITIES

1. What should be the primary financial concerns for a large stadium versus a small fitness facility?

2. What bills relating to a facility are the most time sensitive and require fast repayment?

3. Research one of the recent major sport construction projects in a city such as Cleveland, Cincinnati, Denver, Baltimore, Pittsburgh, or San Francisco to see if the project was a financial success. Include your criteria for measuring financial success.

Human Resources

CHAPTER OBJECTIVES

After completing this chapter you will be able to do the following:

- Characterize various types of employees a facility manager may have to supervise
- Understand the basics of hiring, promoting, and terminating employees
- Know the basics of how to properly classify independent contractors to avoid litigation
- Understand some of the essentials of evaluating and training employees to maximize their contribution to the facility
- Appreciate the legal challenges that arise from managing employees

No facility can operate without employees. A typical professional football game at a major stadium may require 500 to 700 ushers and security personnel, 200 to 300 concessionaires, and numerous other people doing everything from rest room cleaning to field maintenance to parking management. Even small facilities need employees and contractors to manage the heating, ventilation, and air conditioning (HVAC) systems, clean the facility, market the facility, and perform countless other tasks.

There are numerous issues when working with employees. Important questions include the following:

- What types of employees are needed?
- What is the proper training for sport facility employees?
- Should the facility hire part-time or full-time employees?
- What should happen if employees do not show up for work?
- How should employers deal with workplace violence and sexual harassment?

These questions represent just some of the issues associated with hiring, managing, and terminating employees. This chapter covers basic human resource issues, including employment options and legal issues. The chapter starts with an overview of the types of jobs in sport facility management, the hiring process, and the decision about hiring an employee versus outsourcing the work. The next sections cover the processes of motivating and evaluating employees, as well as termination and training. The final section deals with the various legal issues that arise in the context of employment.

Sport Facility Jobs

Numerous jobs are associated with a sport facility, but every sport facility is different. A small health club in a strip mall may have very few facility management concerns and may not need any employees to work in facility management. A larger facility may have hundreds of employees. The need for specialized employees is magnified even more when the facility is unionized and employees are limited in what jobs they pursue. In some facilities, a unionized tradesperson may make more money than the facility manager. For example, if the **collective bargaining agreement (CBA)** requires a union member to replace any glass over dasher boards at a hockey rink, the union member must be at hockey games from start to finish. Typically the union member earns overtime wages for those hours. Some of the functions facility employees undertake include the following:

- Facility manager
- Box office managers and ticket takers
- Security
- Parking
- Architecture/Engineering
- Maintenance
- Scoreboard operator
- Audiovisual coordination
- Press box administrators
- Locker room attendants
- Grounds grew
- Garbage removal
- Customer relations
- Finance/Human resources
- Concessions
- Sponsorship sales

This is by no means an exhaustive list. Just in the concession area alone, for example, at a large arena different individuals are responsible for inventorying and ordering the food, delivering the food, preparing and cleaning the cooking areas, preparing the food, packaging the food, selling the food, and cleaning debris. In smaller facilities, the person in charge of the locker room may also be responsible for the equipment room and laundry facilities. Indeed, most employees at small facilities are trained to assume multiple responsibilities

and duties as might be required by the event or circumstances.

A small health club manager may have to assume numerous duties. Larger facilities have staffs of 15 to 25 full-time employees and possibly several hundred part-time employees working in concessions, crowd management, and janitorial services.

There are so many types of jobs in facility management that it would be impossible to cover them all. This section covers several facility-related positions and their typical duties.

Concessions Manager

Food and souvenirs are among the highest profit centers for a facility. A soda may cost 15 cents to serve, but can generate $3.00 in revenue. Even after all the costs are paid, there is the potential for a nice return on investment. For this reason a concession manager needs to constantly monitor concession operations so that they generate the greatest revenue possible while costs are kept down. The concession manager spends a significant amount of time on human resource-related issues (hiring, training, scheduling, and terminating employees) and inventory management (ordering, pricing, tracking, and disposing of supplies and products).

Box Office Manager

The box office manager is the critical link to selling tickets, from coordinating season tickets to managing the "will-call" window and game-day ticket sales. Box office managers work all year long, even if they are working for a football stadium where there may be only 10 home games a year. When a season ends, box office managers start working on the next year. They must develop marketing campaigns, ticket packages, customer mailers, and training for new salespeople and must coordinate external sales policies and procedures with companies such as Ticketmaster.

Facilities Engineer

The heart and soul of a building are housed in the inner workings such as plumbing, electrical, and sound and lighting systems. Without these back-house systems, the facility would not be able to operate. Within a large arena there are miles of electrical wires and plumbing. These systems can be very complex, with electrical, phone, visual, and data systems intertwined. Because of this complexity, most facilities have several tradespeople who work exclusively in particular areas, such as an electrician, a plumber, or a computer network engineer. These individuals are all managed by the facility engineer, who coordinates their work schedules, filters work orders, assigns repair and maintenance jobs, follows budgetary guidelines, and makes sure the facility is operating correctly before, during, and after an event.

Turf Operations Manager

While a number of positions are critical for both indoor and outdoor facilities, the position of turf manager is a very specialized outdoor position—one that might be appreciated by those who love to work outdoors. The key to the position is learning how to use pesticides to ensure the quality of grass fields. People may be accustomed to applying various weed killers at home, but the chemicals used on commercial fields are very strong and involve significant environmental concerns. Therefore, the government (both local and national) regulates pesticide applications. People wishing to apply these chemicals need to obtain a license, which requires both significant learning and training. Because of what it takes to obtain a license, those with a license are in great demand among employers, from park and recreation departments to colleges with a large number of fields or golf courses.

A turf manager, besides having to know how to properly spray the grounds, must know about soil composition, operation of heavy land-moving machinery, growing seasons, types of grass that work best on given fields, the effects of weather conditions, and ways to repair fields after a rainstorm. It is also necessary to have a strong underpinning in human resources to work with and manage assistants, as well as the ability to work with external contractors who may be utilized to apply chemicals or install a new drainage system. A typical turf manager job description is presented later in the chapter.

Employment Options

One of the first questions for any facility is whether or not the facility will need to hire employees at all. The facility owner, a third-party contractor, interns, volunteers, family members, or independent contractors can help run a facility. However, each category raises unique issues and concerns. Interns, for example, may need to be paid even if they are receiving university credit. If an intern is replacing an employee and is not receiving valuable skills as part of the career education process, the Fair Labor Standards Act requires him or her to be paid at least the minimum wage and possible overtime (Fried and Miller, 1998).

Turf managers need to know about soil composition, chemical application, growing seasons, field repair, and turf equipment.

© Empics

The basic employment options include employees, volunteers, interns, and independent contractors.

An employee is someone hired directly by the facility to perform a specific set of tasks. An employee can be a full-time employee working 40 or more hours per week. If the employee works overtime (anything over 40 hours per week) and is not an exempt managerial-level employee (either on salary or having managerial responsibilities), the facility must pay the person time and a half for all time over 40 hours. Because sport facilities are open long hours, overtime pay is a key concern.

Employees can also be classified as part-time employees. These employees often have other jobs but work nights or weekends for a facility. Since they are not full-time employees, the facility does not usually have to worry about overtime compensation or benefits such as health care.

Employees can be either unionized or non-unionized. As discussed later in this chapter, unions were formed to protect employee rights and working conditions. However, from a management perspective, the insertion of unions into the workplace can sometimes lead to a more difficult communication process between managers and employees.

Volunteers are often brought in to help run events such as a college football game. The alumni office may coordinate 200 alumni to help work as ushers. While this "free" labor is a great money saver, the facility still needs to provide appropriate training and support for these individuals. A facility manager needs to determine if the volunteers will be covered by workers' compensation insurance if they are injured. The facility can also be held liable for a volunteer's negligence, so all volunteers need to be properly trained. A simple decision to save money by having volunteers work a game can backfire if the volunteers are negligent and expose the facility to liability.

Interns are often used by sport facilities, teams, and college athletic departments to help run events and facilities. While some people see these individuals as free help, the situation is similar to that with volunteers: Liability could be attached to their actions, and if injured they should be covered by the facility's workers' compensation policy. While having an assistant may seem attractive, the time required to properly train an intern dictates that managers must commit significant time and resources to make the learning experience meaningful.

If the facility owner, employees, volunteers, and interns cannot do the job, a facility may hire independent contractors. **Independent contractors (ICs)** are experts trained in a given specialty—for example, engineers, umpires, and private security. A concession company has its own employees and hires these employees out to facilities; the company is considered an independent contractor. A benefit of outsourcing is that the facility can focus on its core competencies and let ICs who are experts in particular areas do those jobs. Another benefit has to do with situations of unsatisfactory performance. If a facility employee is not doing his or her job, the person will need to be disciplined or terminated, and these processes take can time. In contrast, if ICs do not perform their job they can be terminated immediately for breaching their contract to perform services.

Some facilities try to grow without employees by using ICs or outsourcing services to provide assistance when needed. Companies such as Contemporary Service Corporation and Staffpro are often hired by teams and facilities to provide security. These companies hire, recruit, and provide hundreds of part-time employees to work as ticket takers, ushers, and security personnel. The following section covers ICs in more detail since this type of relationship is common in sport facilities but often misunderstood.

Independent Contractors

A health club may employ trainers and instructors who assist members with their workouts. In many situations, the manager characterizes these individuals as "independent contractors" to avoid paying benefits and workers' compensation insurance. Although there are many other criteria, if a trainer controls his or her own schedule, uses his or her own equipment, and can work for other health clubs, it may be correct to classify the person as an IC.

In other cases, however, the worker is technically an employee rather than an IC. If the health club controls the trainer's conduct to the point that the trainer cannot be differentiated from other employees, the government and case law classify the trainer as an employee. This concern arises not only with trainers but also with production crews, riggers, ushers, and similar workers. Even if the employment contract refers to a worker as an independent contractor, this may not be legally accurate. A facility operator can face substantial fines and punishments if a worker is incorrectly classified (Fried and Miller, 1998).

To be safe, whenever there is even a shadow of doubt about a worker's status the worker should be classified as an employee rather than an IC.

Outsourcing Facility Management Functions

In August-September, 2001, the magazine *Facilities* surveyed its readers regarding the acceptance of outsourcing for facility management (FM) and the overall sense of satisfaction with providers of outsourcing services. Outsourced FM services can range from providing janitorial or security services to HVAC maintenance. By examining areas in which other facility managers have successfully used outsourcing or ICs, a facility manager can outsource janitorial or security services and focus his or her own employees on marketing or event administration. The survey's key findings included the following:

- Outsourcing FM was used by 98% of the respondents, who outsourced at least one FM function. Additionally, the average respondent reported outsourcing FM for four of nine specific FM functions.

- Despite the popularity of outsourcing, many facility managers are leery about using one provider for all of their needs. Almost 80% of the respondents reported that they were not likely to use a single provider, and more than two-thirds reported that they contracted separately for each service.

- Facility managers have a great deal of involvement in the decision to outsource various FM functions, with 25% of the facility managers making the final decision.

- Almost 70% of facility managers reported being "somewhat satisfied" with the services provided ("Happy Together," 2001).

As figure 12.1 shows, the main reason for outsourcing facility management is insufficient internal resources. Surprisingly, fewer venues decide

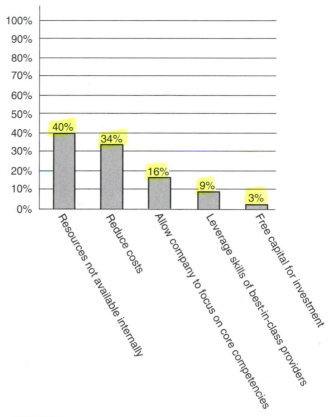

Figure 12.1 Primary reasons for outsourcing facility management.

From "Happy Together," 2001.

to outsource their facility management functions for strategic reasons such as freeing up capital for investment needs. Outsourcing is undertaken to save time or cover technological needs.

Figure 12.2 shows which facility management functions the venues were currently outsourcing; table 12.1 shows which facility management functions venues planned on outsourcing in the course of the next two years. Some functions (custodial/janitorial, landscaping/groundskeeping, HVAC/energy management, and security) that were currently being outsourced were likely to be outsourced by a smaller percentage of venues in the future. For example, 65% of the respondents currently outsourced the custodial/janitorial functions, yet only 60% anticipated outsourcing these functions within the next two years. These data indicate that venues either were unhappy with the services they had received or would be able to perform the functions themselves at some point in the future.

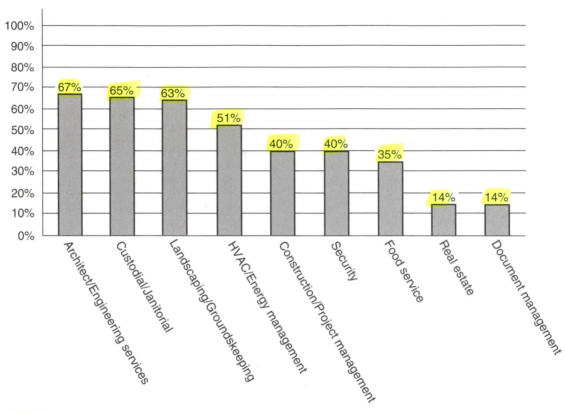

Figure 12.2 Facility management functions outsourced.
From "Happy Together," 2001.

Table 12.1 Likelihood of Outsourcing Facility Management Functions Within Next Two Years

	Very likely/Likely (%)	Not likely (%)
Architectural/Engineering services	72	15
Custodial/Janitorial	60	33
Landscaping	56	28
Construction/Project management	44	21
HVAC/Energy	38	33
Food service	38	37
Security	35	30
Real estate	21	56
Document management	19	56

Data from "Happy Together," 2001.

Figure 12.3 shows that almost half of the respondents planned on spending between $100,000 and $500,000 on outsourced facility management services. Almost half (47%) of the respondents conducted site visits, and another 43% occasionally made visits to other sites managed by those bidding for the facility management work. Almost all of the respondents (95%) reported that they required potential outsourcing firms to demonstrate their competency through the use of benchmarking data or references, or both, in addition to site visits.

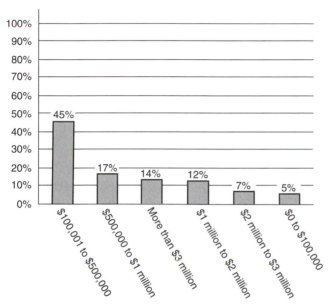

Figure 12.3   Expected amount to be spent on outsourcing facility management services.
From "Happy Together," 2001.

Managing the Provider

Once the outsourcing firm is chosen and the ICs are at the facility, the process is not over. The *Facilities* survey showed that approximately 83% of the respondents assessed the performance of their providers, with 57% reviewing the work on a regular basis. Facility managers were generally (98%) satisfied with the outsourced services ("Happy Together," 2001).

While the various types of workers discussed in this section play an important role in many facilities, the primary workers at a facility are people who need to be hired. The hiring process applies not only to employees, but also to volunteers and interns.

Hiring Process

If interns, ICs, or outsourcing are not used or are not sufficient to fulfill the employment needs, the facility will need to hire one or more people. The hiring process typically starts with a detailed job analysis of the activities involved in the proposed job. These activities are further defined and explained in a job description that specifies the skills, training, and results the position will encompass. A typical job description for a collegiate box office manager is shown below.

Sample Collegiate Box Office Manager Description

The XYZ Center, a 10,000-seat arena, and the GFH Stadium, a 25,000-seat stadium, on the campus of PDQ University are seeking a box office manager.

Responsibilities: The manager is responsible for ticket sales at the arena and at all other facilities on campus such as the ABC Theater. Ticketing responsibilities include ticketing for all intercollegiate events on campus. The position supervises a full-time staff of three and several student employees. Other responsibilities include daily deposits, sales reports, post-event settlements, and event creation for ticketing sales growth. The manager will also be responsible for working with event promoters to develop event setups in all the various venues and to provide daily ticket sales and cash accounting.

Qualifications: Strong knowledge base of box office management and operations including a high degree of independent judgment making and responsibility. Additional skills include a high-level command of ticketing procedures and application of ticketing policies to various situations, and the ability to contribute to the University's administration of its venues. Due to the nature of the position, the candidate will need to have a flexible schedule including evenings and weekends. The position requires at least five years of progressively responsible experience in a box office management capacity, preferably with a Division I-A school. The ideal candidate will have experience working with multiple venues and a thorough knowledge of Word, Access, Excel, and contemporary ticket software application.

Salary range: $38,818 to $48,920.

Job descriptions must indicate the exact training required and any degrees or certification that may be necessary. For people who will be using pesticides, for example, do they have the training and skills to work with those chemicals, as well as knowledge of any applicable statutes? Some positions in the facility management industry are certified positions. For example, the Ontario Recreation Facilities Association has developed the designation of Certified Ice Technician for those in the industry who complete a 90-hour program including theory and hands-on training in such areas as basic refrigeration, ice making, ice painting, ice maintenance, and equipment operations ("Certified Ice," 2001).

The hiring process varies in complexity according to what positions need to be filled. Low-level entry positions such as parking attendant or concession sales may be easier to fill since a larger number of people are qualified for such positions compared with a job as an HVAC specialist that may require licensure. Other variables affecting the hiring process include such issues as the region in the country, economic conditions, prevailing wage rate, and available benefits. High-end positions may require recruiting activities other than advertising in the local newspaper or using job placement agencies. However, because there are always many people seeking employment opportunities in the sport industry, normally a large number of individuals are regularly submitting resumes to work with teams or facilities.

Advertising a Position

Several steps need to be taken before advertising a position. A job analysis highlights the basic activities that are necessary to perform a specific job. A facility manager first needs to determine what activities need to be accomplished to reach the specific job goals, such as marketing the facility for a ticket sales position. The job analysis leads to the job description. The job description focuses on skills required to reach the job goals. The job description includes the required job responsibilities along with the nature of the job, such as whether someone will need to manage or supervise, as already noted. All duties and responsibilities identified in the job description should be "essential" for the job and listed in the advertisement to avoid any claim of discrimination. If the job does not require a college education, asking for only college graduates could be construed as an intent to discriminate.

The job description can be used as a basis for writing an advertisement. But while this strategy works well with a flyer that can be posted on a bulletin board, most advertisements use a limited space. Publications often charge for ads by the word or line. Thus, some facilities merely ask individuals interested in a position to visit the facility's Web site. In other cases, ads mention only the very basics associated with the position. This strategy may save money but in the long run can also create the need to process many applications from people who are not qualified, so the idea of saving a few dollars can in fact cost the facility much more in processing time and resources. Applicants are normally obtained through many avenues, from newspaper and Internet advertising to college placement offices and executive recruiters. The tendency in the sport industry is to produce a large number of applicants for almost every position. A classified advertisement for a facilities engineer is shown below, and an advertisement for a turf manager is shown on page 237.

Classified Advertisement for a Facilities Engineer

The FGH Field, located in downtown New Haven, is seeking a facilities engineer. The facilities engineer will report directly to the facility general manager. This position is responsible for energy and power plant management, operation of all HVAC, electrical, plumbing, mechanical equipment, artificial turf, and all preventive and regular facility maintenance. The qualified candidate should have experience in hiring, training, and supervising a maintenance staff; have a proven track record in energy and maintenance management; have worked with large professional sport facilities; and have at least five years experience and a BS degree in engineering or three years of hands-on electrical or systems experience in addition to the five years overall experience.

Classified Advertisement for a Turf Manager Position

The town of Sportsville is searching for a leader to direct the operations of the Park and Recreation Department's turf and grounds maintenance program. Responsibilities include all care and maintenance of athletic fields, other lawn areas, and shrub, recreational, and school areas. Requirements include a bachelor's degree in agronomy, landscape design, or turf management plus five years experience in turf and ground management including at least three years of supervisory experience. Applicants must possess the CT Custom Ground Applicator's Supervisory License or equivalent. The salary range for this position is $45,000-$68,000.

Screening Applicants

Management must process all the applicants and then interview enough people to be able to make a decision. It may be necessary to hire more employees than are actually needed in order to have a pool of people who are available and have been prescreened. For example, if 200 security staffers are needed for an event, it would probably be prudent to have 500 prequalified individuals who can be called upon to fill the needs for any given event. The extra candidates could be essential for some positions requiring background checks and formal training. Having a surplus is also more important for stadiums and arenas; since the work is often considered seasonal, a large percentage of those who would work in the facility have other jobs and need to coordinate their schedules.

Employee Management

Once an adequate number of employees are hired, the next phase of the employment process begins, which is employee management. The greatest expense for any facility is not the construction expense, but rather the salaries and expenses associated with employees. All employees need to be properly coordinated and managed to maximize their effectiveness. That is where innovative motivational techniques need to be implemented.

Once employees are evaluated and performance appraisals are completed, management needs to examine what techniques can help motivate an employee who is underperforming. For example, according to Maslow's hierarchy of needs, discussed in chapter 3, people at the bottom of the pyramid will not be as motivated with peripheral strategies, such as a new title or a bigger office, as they may be with more vacation time or a higher salary. Once management knows what will motivate an employee, it is much easier to manage the employee's movement up the pyramid based on concrete strategies rather than mere guessing. Various strategies for motivating employees are listed on page 238.

There is no one correct method to manage employees. What works at one facility will not necessarily work at another. Chapter 3 highlighted some of the primary managerial motivational and leadership strategies to help empower employees. However, it is not enough to utilize different ideas or campaigns to motivate people. Constant monitoring is also necessary. At times facility managers who may appear to be just relaxing and walking around may actually be evaluating employees. Managers sometimes conduct tests themselves or through the use of secret shoppers. Secret shoppers are hired by the facility to act like regular customers and evaluate their service experience. A manager or secret shopper might see a dirty napkin on the floor and observe whether any employee stops to pick it up. He or she can also observe how employees interact with customers to see whether they are friendly and courteous. These and other similar techniques help demonstrate whether managerial strategies, leadership skills, and various benefits actually succeed in changing behavior.

Regardless of the managerial techniques used, evaluation of employees is necessary in that it provides valuable information to managers. The next section addresses some of the issues associated with employee evaluations.

Employee Evaluation

Evaluations are used in every facility. Marketing efforts are regularly evaluated for their effectiveness. Benchmarking standards are used to evaluate the effectiveness of everything from maintenance efforts to the HVAC system. Just as all the mechanical and

Strategies for Motivating Employees

A plaque in the main hallway for employees of the month

Awards for employees in the front office, those working concessions, ushers, etc.

Recognition in game programs or on scoreboards

Exchanging jobs for a day with another employee or with a manager

Empowering employees to make decisions

Giving employees a specific amount of money to spend any way they want during the year to make customers happy

Providing a cash benefit for recruiting new employees

Allowing employees to engage in job rotation or job modifications such as flexible hours

Providing employees with better benefit options

administrative efforts of a facility are evaluated, the human capital must be evaluated. If an employee is not living up to the expectations specified in the job description, the employee needs to be motivated, retrained, or terminated.

Employee evaluation can take various forms, from on-the-job analysis to goal attainment. A ticket sales executive could be given the goal of selling 10,000 tickets in a specific price category in a given season. Selling 10,000 tickets means that the person has met the goal. Selling more means that he or she is entitled to additional benefits. If the person sells less than 10,000 tickets, he or she could be reprimanded, terminated, retrained, or managed differently. Other employees are often harder to evaluate since there may not be clear-cut criteria for evaluation. An usher would face a significantly different evaluation process than a ticket salesperson. Since an usher's job is not contingent on the number of people seated but rather the quality of service, the evaluation standard is subjective rather than objective. Ushers could be evaluated based on their efficiency, the number of compliments and complaints received, the quality of work performed, and related standards. Because the process can be highly subjective, it is imperative to perform such evaluations in an unbiased manner to prevent claims of discrimination or wrongful termination.

Worker productivity is always a thorny topic. One can look at quality rather than quantity, or vice versa. For example, what would be the best way to measure productivity in the maintenance department? Would it be better to evaluate an employee based on how well the equipment is working or based on how quickly the employee performs maintenance or repairs? One technique to measure effectiveness in the maintenance department is through work orders. New buildings have a large number of work orders when they open. The numbers then trail off for a number of years, and later, when the facility is older, the numbers start increasing again. However, a strong preventive maintenance program normally decreases the number of work orders. Thus, productivity is affected by external variables such as the building's age, as well as by policies and procedures.

One needs to take these types of factors into consideration when examining evaluation programs. If an employee is being evaluated based on criteria outside his or her control, the evaluation system will be perceived as biased and unfair. This could lead to significant distrust. One way to avoid such a problem is to determine the criteria for evaluation and job retention when an employee is hired. If concession workers know they will need to sell 100 sodas each game over a season, the variability of external factors can be somewhat reduced. Some games may be rained out; others will occur in hot weather, which will produce increased sales. Thus, sales could be averaged. However, if the team is losing every game, the evaluation criteria should be adjusted or the facility will lose all its employees because they do not meet preseason goals. The key concern in this example involves communication. The goals for employees must be clearly communicated; all employees should know what they are expected to accomplish and how each person's success will complement the work of other employees.

Termination

Employees who are not productive either can be terminated or may leave if they are not sufficiently motivated to do the job. Employees leave their jobs for a number of reasons, including personal reasons such as moving to a new area and opportunities to obtain a better job. Employees stay when they feel appreciated, when they get along with coworkers and managers, when management supports them, and when they feel they contribute to the facility's overall mission (Shenker, 2002). Specific reasons for losing employees include poor supervision, frequent supervisory changes, unclear or unreasonable expectations, lack of feedback, lack of rewards for quality work, poor pay, lack of advancement opportunities, company culture clash, and a host of others. The key for a facility manager is to communicate with employees to see what they are thinking about so that management can create a better work environment that may entice some disgruntled employees to stay. Communication is the key, since the lack of communication can often lead to employee unrest and ultimately the loss of good employees.

While some employees need to be retained, others need to be cut. Turnover can be a good means of bringing in fresh ideas and new approaches. Any change will cost money. These costs include hiring, retraining, severance pay, unemployment pay, position advertising, recruiting costs, applicant testing, background checks, signing bonuses, relocation fees, and possibly higher salaries. Indirect costs include lost business, staff time, lost productivity, delay as the new employee reaches an acceptable productivity level, and possibly a negative aura in the workplace from "bad vibes" or hurt feelings (Shenker, 2002).

One of the processes associated with evaluation is the grievance process. Most employees at sport facilities are employees at will, which means that they can be terminated for any reason or no reason whatsoever. This is true except in the case of union employees covered by a CBA. Thus, if the manager does not like the clothes an employee wears one day, he or she can technically terminate the employee. However, most employers utilize a grievance system to help maintain morale or to comply with a union's CBA. The typical grievance process involves several stages such as an initial warning, subsequent written warnings, and then potentially a termination. This process is called the **progressive disciplinary approach.** If a manager fails to provide an employee with a progressive process, the terminated employee can file a wrongful termination/discrimination suit. The chance that the former employee will win in such a suit is significantly decreased if the progressive disciplinary process was used and all the misdeeds documented.

If employees are not performing up to expectations they will need to be retrained (see later) or motivated in a more appropriate manner. This is the heart and soul of the management process. Employees are hired because they presumably have the appropriate and necessary skills and talent to perform the job. If they are not doing the job as well as expected, something needs to change. The employee may not live up to expectations because he or she does not care. In this case the only option is to terminate. There are two primary options for handling employees who are willing to work to improve their performance, which can be used singly or in combination: appropriate motivation so that the employee can achieve a higher level of success, and training to reach a higher skill level.

Training

Once employees have been hired, they need to be trained so they can accomplish the specific tasks that must be done at a given facility. Maintenance personnel who worked for five years at one facility may be lost at a different facility. For example, pipes may not be marked; electrical outlets may not be live; it may not be obvious what storage areas contain hazardous materials. Thus, new employees always need to be properly trained.

While it is preferable that training occur as soon as someone is hired, training is often done at a later date when a problem is identified. For example, if a special license is required to operate certain machinery, that training and testing may not be made available or paid for by the facility until an emergency arises. In some cases the thinking is that it would have been too costly to employ someone with the proper license. Training materials can consist of books, videos, and live lectures, among others. Numerous resources for training exist, such as industry-developed manuals published by the International Facility Managers Association, International Association of Assembly Managers (IAAM), Techniques for Effective Alcohol

Facility Focus: Connecticut Sportsplex

© Vincent Candelora

The Connecticut Sportsplex is New England's largest sport complex. Its five-field outdoor facility hosts baseball and softball tournaments every weekend (national, state, and sectional tournaments), in addition to weekday leagues. The sportsplex includes a 75,000-square-foot (6,965-square-meter) indoor dome facility that offers four multisport fields and a state-of-the-art artificial turf surface for indoor soccer, softball, field hockey, flag football, and other activities. It also includes a 25,000-square-foot (2,320-square-meter) field house that houses a 40-seat pub-style restaurant, an arcade, virtual golf simulators, batting cages, pool tables, air hockey, a basketball court, jungle gym, moon walk, party area, and an area for cheerleading and gymnastics. With all these amenities, the Connecticut Sportsplex needs a large number of employees to operate effectively.

Management (TEAM), and Building Owners and Managers Association (BOMA).

The IAAM's "train the trainer" program is designed to teach facility executives how to instruct their crowd management staff on proper techniques and strategies. Besides training manuals, numerous conferences and seminars can provide training. For example, the IAAM runs an annual conference on crowd management issues in which the latest tools and techniques are discussed. These conferences provide employees with a couple of days off work in a nice locale, but also invaluable assistance to help them with their job.

Legal Concerns

In addition to hiring, motivating, and terminating employees, the entire process of managing human resources requires close supervision to adhere to legal requirements. For example, reducing employee conflict seems to be a noble idea to make the workplace more harmonious. However, it is just as important to prevent future legal concerns as it is to enhance the workplace. If two employees have a strong dislike for each other, this makes for more than just a hostile environment. It can lead to workplace violence, discrimination claims, and even harassment claims, all of which can generate significant legal costs.

There are a multitude of federal regulations, such as the **Civil Rights Act of 1964** and the Americans with Disabilities Act (ADA), that apply if an employer has more than 15 employees. If a facility has only five employees, most civil rights and anti-discrimination laws are inapplicable. However, some laws, such as workers' compensation insurance coverage and Fair Labor Standards Act reporting requirements for minimum wage and overtime work, apply even there is only one employee.

Biased assignments for training programs can raise legal concerns such as discrimination claims. Such a claim represents just one of the many legal matters involved in the employment process. Legal issues associated with interns and ICs were discussed earlier in the chapter. Throughout the hiring process there are countless other legal traps. The following is a list of some basic legal issues that can come up within the employment process.

- Inappropriate application forms or questions
- Poor or inappropriate interview questions
- Improper classification of employees as at-will employees
- Lack of standardized documents
- Failing to review and update employment policies
- Failing to monitor, evaluate, and secure personnel files
- Failing to timely, honestly, and tactfully evaluate employees
- Failing to have appropriate evaluation criteria
- Improperly documenting evaluations and all other employment decisions
- Failing to provide a proper grievance process to try to resolve disputes
- Not providing proper notice for discipline and the opportunity to be heard
- Not acting promptly to terminate an employee who has engaged in egregious or violent conduct
- Not reviewing each termination and not making sure appropriate records are maintained
- Not considering all applicable local, state, and federal laws

A potpourri of federal and state laws also affect the employment law landscape. One of the most relevant laws is the **Fair Labor Standards Act (FLSA)**, which covers everything from minimum wage and overtime to teenage workers. Young employees are a major concern for sport facilities. As reported by the Department of Labor in 1997, the retail industry employs 51% of all teens, and the service industry (e.g., YMCAs, swimming pools, parks and recreation, ball parks, and amusement parks) employs 34% of all teens (Fried and Miller, 1998). Ignorance of the law is the most frequent reason for failure to comply with the FLSA. Numerous employers post the required FLSA poster, but employees fail to read or follow the information. In addition to prescribing hours that teens can work, the FLSA prohibits teenagers from 18 specified jobs. Facility managers should check with the experts before placing teen employees on lawn mowers or having them build or mend fences, work late at night, or operate mechanical amusement rides. Knowing and complying with the law also benefits an employer via increased employee morale, improved public relations, decreased insurance expenses, and a safer work environment.

In addition to FLSA, the **Occupational Safety and Health Administration (OSHA)** is a major legislative framework that affects sport facility managers; OSHA requires specific conduct to be undertaken to ensure a safe work environment. Safety steps are required, for example, to secure people to a building whenever they are working at elevations, such as on the rigging inside an arena. Thus, employees who may work in such positions need to be given safety harnesses and be trained in how to use them. The Occupational Safety and Health Administration also covers a host of other workplace-related safety concerns, from the noise level at concerts to wiping down countertops and benches to avoid contact with bloodborne pathogens.

Besides those listed earlier, there are other legal concerns that present unique challenges to sport facilities. Among the most major of these are unionization, ADA compliance, workers' compensation, and sexual harassment. It is important to note before discussing these challenges that one of the biggest traps for unsuspecting employers is the failure to purchase workers' compensation insurance. Workers' compensation insurance needs to be purchased only for employees, not ICs. In California, failure to purchase workers' compensation insurance can lead to a misdemeanor charge (six months in jail and $1,000 fine), criminal prosecution, and even an order suspending the use of employees.

Unions

Those studying employee motivation and management often overlook unionization. Sometimes students who are prospective managers feel that if they provide proper motivation and are best friends with their employees, they may be able to leverage that relationship to receive the most from employees. However, the realities of the workplace are very different. Many publicly owned, school, and college facilities have unionized workforces.

The primary function of a union is to negotiate and administer the CBA with the employer, which covers the conditions of employment for the union members. Unions have a significant impact on the employment environment. They reduce a manager's authority, reduce a manager's control over personnel policies, and reduce a manager's prerogative to make certain decisions without union involvement. At the same time, unions represent a significant benefit for employees through providing a unified voice, psychological satisfaction, strength in numbers, and economic benefits for its members (Fried and Miller, 1998). While it may appear that employees have a one-sided weapon against employers through unions, specific federal legislation provides both sides with tangible benefits.

There are both national and local unions. National unions establish rules under which local unions may be chartered and permitted to retain their membership in the national union. Such rules cover dues collection, initiation fees, union funds administration, and new member admission criteria. Local unions represent the direct interest of their constituency by monitoring management activities and making sure that the CBA is being followed. In addition, local unions help members rectify any unjust treatment or sponsor grievances claimed by local members.

Local unions operate through a business representative who negotiates the CBA and administers the agreement. When a union member has problems, he or she brings the problems to the attention of the union steward, who represents the union member's interest in his or her relations with immediate supervisors and other managers. Some stewards are paid by the employer solely to reconcile disputes involving union members in reference to work-related disputes. This creates several bureaucratic levels that can often make the employment process more difficult. For example, a manager may not be able to ask a union employee to clean a bathroom if that activity is not in the employee's job description. Thus, the manager may have to find a busy janitor to clean the bathroom while the other employee sits doing absolutely nothing except wait for work detailed in the job description. In some facilities it is difficult to ask an employee to do anything, even when it is in the person's job description, without going through a union supervisor.

Besides national and local, unions can be further classified as closed shops and open shops. Closed shops operate under a CBA wherein all employees as a condition of employment need to be union members. In open shops, both union and non-union employees can work for the employer even if the employer has a CBA with a union.

Both unions and employers are forbidden to require union membership. However, unions can secure from each employee a financial contribution to help pay for representation costs, and this contribution is typically the same as union dues paid by union members. In approximately 20 states, though, there are "right to work" laws that forbid unions from seeking financial contributions from non-union employees (Fried and Miller, 1998).

The laws related to unionization, union activities, retaliation, antitrust violations, and associated issues are very complex. It is critical for a unionized facility to hire a talented labor law specialist. A potential union will not be undertaking formation efforts without competent counsel. To face trained labor organizers without proper assistance is tantamount to committing business suicide. Many businesses fight to avoid unions by providing strong benefits. Happy employees often do not want unions since they do not want to lose these benefits. However, if an employer does not treat employees well, the employees may unionize to gain bargaining strength in numbers. Employees often unionize to obtain safer working conditions or other specific concessions. By addressing employee concerns, management can often avoid dealing with unions and thus avoid significant cost increases and a reduced ability to work with employees.

Americans with Disabilities Act

The ADA is covered in detail in chapter 13. However, it should be noted here that while facility access is a major concern under the ADA, the ADA can affect everything from advertising a position to terminating an employee. For example, it is illegal to ask someone if he or she has a disability. A facility manager can ask if someone can carry 50 pounds (22.7 kilograms), if the job requires carrying 50 pounds, but cannot ask if the person has any back problems. This does not mean that every potentially disabled person needs to be hired. Rather, it means that the employer cannot dismiss disabled applicants just because they are disabled, if they can do the job. On the other hand, the fact that a disabled applicant can do the job does not mean that the employer must hire that person. Another applicant who is more personable or better at establishing rapport can be hired instead. Thus, the ADA is very clearly designed to provide a level playing field for all potential employees.

Workers' Compensation

Some work environments produce significant and sometimes serious injuries. Construction, work with hazardous chemicals, firefighting, security, and punch press machine operation are among the activities that produce either frequent or in some cases life-threatening injuries. Typically, 6,000 to 7,000 individuals die in the workplace each year, and another 11 to 15 million are hurt in work-related accidents. That translates to 18 deaths and 36,000 injuries every day (Fried and Miller, 1998). The direct costs associated with these injuries totaled $65 billion in 1992, while the indirect costs, such as lost wages, totaled $171 billion. These losses cannot be completely avoided, but they can be reduced through safety education and equipment.

The purpose behind workers' compensation insurance is to have a no-fault safety net for every employer and employee. The no-fault system means that coverage begins immediately after the employee is injured and that the coverage is complete. In exchange for prompt and complete claims payment, the injured employee waives his or her right to sue the facility unless the facility management engaged in wrongful conduct such as failing to eliminate a known hazard.

Workers' compensation premiums are based on past claims associated with a given career and the prospect for injuries. Some facility-related jobs are highly dangerous, and the workers' compensation insurance premium may be 50% of every

OSHA Claim Percentages

Overexertion (27%)

Struck by an object (13%)

Fall on the same level (11%)

Bodily reaction—slip or twist (10%)

Struck against an object (7%)

Caught in or compressed by equipment or object (5%)

Fall to lower levels (5%)

Exposure to harmful substances or environments (5%)

Reprinted, by permission, from G. Fried and L. Miller, 1998, *Employment law* (Durham, NC: Carolina Academic Press).

dollar paid in salary. That would mean that if a construction/rigging worker earned $50,000 a year, the facility would have to pay $25,000 to purchase workers' compensation insurance just for that employee. The percentages for categories of OSHA claims in the 1990s are shown above and are listed in descending order of occurrence.

Besides having workers' compensation insurance, facility management should organize a safety committee composed of managers and various lower-level employees who consistently work in environments with hazardous conditions such as pools, food service, maintenance, weight room, and related program areas. The safety committee can be empowered to

- analyze safety concerns,
- provide suggestions for facility modifications or alterations,
- suggest potential safety precautions,
- help develop a safety manual and educational aids,
- help update the safety manual,
- help train other employees, and
- assume overall responsibility associated with safety matters.

Besides being an effective risk management tool, a safety committee also may be required by state law. In states with such laws, facility managers must do more than establish a safety committee; they are also required to act upon the committee's recommendations. Safety committees should

- meet at least once a month to discuss current issues,
- prepare minutes from all meetings,
- make periodic site inspections,
- review all incident and injury reports,
- review any safety complaints, and
- process any safety suggestions and recommendations (Fried and Miller, 1998).

While safety committees appear to be a win–win proposition for employees and employers, the primary concerns are the potential inadvertent forming of a union and the possibility that evidence can be generated that can torpedo an employer at a future trial.

Sexual Harassment

There are two types of sexual harassment. Quid pro quo refers to the situation in which an employer (supervisor, boss, or anyone with a position of authority over the employee) requires sexual activity or conduct as a condition of employment, future employment, future job advancement, or future salary increases. Many employees, managers, and employers understand that it is inappropriate to directly utilize sex as a vehicle for job advancement, but this still occurs. Examples still exist of employees, from secretaries to senior managers, who are forced to compromise their principles for their career. This difficult choice is the reason sexual harassment is such an important issue. Employees

should not have to choose between their dignity and their job (Fried and Miller, 1998).

Title VII of the Civil Rights Act of 1964 is violated by the second type of sexual harassment—conduct that creates a **hostile or offensive working environment.** The same law also covers other forms of discrimination based on race, religion, nationality, and sexual orientation. A different law, the Age Discrimination in Employment Act (ADEA), covers age-based discrimination. The Supreme Court has concluded that not all conduct that may appear to be sexual harassment is in fact sexual harassment. The conduct must be sufficiently severe or pervasive to alter the condition of the victim's employment and create an abusive or hostile working environment. Some courts have held that creation of a hostile work environment does not occur in instances in which an employer, upon learning of harassing conduct against an employee, takes prompt remedial action against the offending employee (Fried and Miller, 1998).

While sexual harassment is clearly a big problem, there are solutions. The key solution is to develop a sexual harassment education and compliance program. Such a program is contingent on adopting a sexual harassment policy (see sample on pages 245-246) signed and followed by all employees. Besides developing a less hostile environment, a facility manager needs to develop a response process for when sexual harassment occurs or is alleged. The facility manager needs to designate a representative who will be in charge of

 ## Behind the Scenes: Sexual Harassment

Examples of sexual harassment or potential sexual harassment due to a hostile work environment can be found in many sport facilities. In 1996, the Rose Bowl general manager was accused of sexual harassment by a former executive secretary. The suit claimed that the general manager told vulgar jokes, made sexual remarks about women, and constantly hugged her. While this type of conduct is unacceptable under any condition, the possible distrust and fear created by such conduct can destroy a facility. Another example is a case involving 25 women who worked as cleaning and janitorial staff members at a large stadium. Imagine that you are a foreign worker and your supervisor threatens to deport you or hurt your chance of staying in the country if you do not do what you are told. You are not asked to clean the supervisor's car or perform other tasks that are inappropriate, rather you must perform sexual favors to keep your job or avoid deportation. At this sport facility the cleaning supervisor grabbed the women, tried to take off their clothes, attempted to have sex with them, and threatened them with termination if they did not cooperate. The women filed a claim with the Equal Employment Opportunity Commission (EEOC). The EEOC and Astrodome USA worked out a settlement of over $500,000 to settle the claims (Fried and Miller, 1998).

Sample Sexual Harassment Policy

Fitness Center, Inc. (FCI) is committed to providing a workplace free of any and all sexual harassment. It is both against the law and FCI policy for any employee or nonemployee to sexually harass any coworkers, employees, or customers. FCI will strictly enforce this policy to the full extent of the law, and adherence to this policy is a mandatory condition of continued employment with FCI.

Sexual Harassment Defined

Sexual harassment is defined as any unwelcomed sexual advances or visual, verbal, or physical conduct of a sexual nature. Any conduct that creates an offensive and hostile work environment is sexual harassment. Furthermore, any sexual conduct that is coerced by a person in a position of apparent or actual power or authority is sexual harassment. Sexual harassment involves a wide variety of behaviors between members of the opposite sex as well as members of the same sex. It should be clear that some conduct that may be appropriate in a social setting, between friends, or even between individuals involved in a consensual relationship may not be appropriate in the workplace. Some prohibited conduct examples are described in this document. These represent only examples and are not an exhaustive list of conduct that is defined by FCI and the courts as sexual harassment.

- Physical harassment: unwanted physical contact of a sexual nature including, but not limited to, fondling, groping, suggestive touching, impeding or blocking movement, brushing up against a body, or any other activity that causes contact or the threat of unwanted contact
- Verbal harassment: excessive sexual jokes, innuendo, or suggestive comments; persistent and unwanted sexual advances; propositions or requests for companionship; any verbal offer of employment, advancement, or increased salary, or other benefits in exchange for sexual activity; threatened or actual employment reprisals, threats, demotions, or terminations after refusal of any sexual advances; and/or any graphic, lewd, or offensive comments about an individual's body or body parts.
- Nonverbal harassment: staring, leering, obscene gestures; displaying or distributing offensive or sexually suggestive objects, pictures, cartoons, drawings, or posters; making or airing suggestive or insulting sounds/noises; and/or writing and/or distributing offensive, suggestive, or obscene notes or letters.

This is not an exhaustive list of prohibited conduct. The term offensive or obscene refers to any conduct, activity, words, or sounds that an average person of normal sensitivity would find offensive or obscene.

Sexual Harassment Reporting Procedures

If you believe that you have been the subject of sexual harassment, immediately report the harassment to your supervisor, the Human Resources Department, or FCI's sexual harassment coordinator (Ms. Sally Smith). Do not report the conduct to the person who allegedly harassed you, but to anyone who is independent of or superior to the alleged harasser. Do not wait a significant period (more than one week) after the alleged harassment has occurred to report the incident. Such actions could jeopardize the ability to fully investigate a complaint or to find necessary witnesses. All complaints will be promptly investigated in a discreet manner. Information will be given to the complaining party only after a thorough investigation has been completed. Investigation will normally entail conferring with the parties involved and any potential witnesses disclosed by the complainant. FCI will take any and all necessary steps, including all forms of discipline, to stop the offensive or inappropriate conduct. The complainant will be informed of all findings uncovered through the investigation process and all actions taken as a result thereof. FCI takes every sexual harassment claim seriously and will resolve any and all complaints. No punitive action will ever be taken against a complainant who files a valid complaint. FCI will not tolerate any retaliation or

(continued)

(continued)

conduct of a retaliatory nature against any individual who has filed a valid complaint or who is a witness in any sexual harassment investigation. An individual who files a false and malicious sexual harassment claim will face severe disciplinary repercussions including, but not limited to, termination.

If FCI is unable to successfully resolve a complaint through the use of internal procedures, or if any employee who suffers sexual harassment is reluctant to utilize the internal procedures, such employee can file a complaint with any appropriate state or federal agency. The employee bulletin board contains a poster reiterating FCI's sexual harassment policy and describing appropriate contact agencies for filing claims. State or federal agencies will normally conduct an investigation and attempt to resolve the matter if a claim is filed with such a government entity. If evidence is found of sexual harassment, the matter can be brought to a public hearing. Possible remedies could include back pay, promotion, reinstatement, hiring, changes in FCI's policy and procedures, emotional distress damages, and possible fines.

FCI has never tolerated and will never tolerate, and the law specially prohibits, any retaliation against any employee for filing or otherwise participating in any hearing, proceeding, or investigation associated with a valid sexual harassment claim filed with any government agency or commission.

If you have any comments, questions, or concerns about sexual harassment, please contact FCI's sexual harassment coordinator.

I, _____ have read and understand all the above statements. I have had an opportunity to ask any questions I have concerning FCI's sexual harassment policy. In consideration for being hired or continuing my employment with FCI, I hereby agree to follow FCI's sexual harassment policy and will indemnify and hold FCI harmless for any and all liability and attorney fees if I engage in inappropriate conduct including, but not limited to, sexual harassment or retaliating against any individual who has filed a sexual harassment claim.

_____   _____
Signature   Date

Reprinted, by permission, from G. Fried and L. Miller, 1998, *Employment law*, (Durham, NC: Carolina Academic Press).

handling all sexual harassment claims. That person must be sympathetic and listen to any complaints. The representative then must investigate the claim, being mindful of personal and possibly civil rights, especially if the accused turns out to be innocent. If the accused has engaged in inappropriate conduct, the person must be disciplined according to the severity of the conduct, whether through a warning or immediate termination or various other options in between. The entire process must be documented, and all employees must understand that there cannot be retaliation against anyone involved in the process. The representative should also follow up with the alleged victim, government entities, and insurance companies as appropriate to make sure the matter is resolved and to minimize the possibility of similar incidents occurring again. The sample sexual harassment policy on pages 245-246 would provide a good start to any sexual abuse prevention program.

Summary

Among the numerous activities covered in this book, from building to marketing sport facilities, the activity that often takes the most time for a manager on a day-to-day basis is managing people. Think about how much time you spend in a typical week trying to patch problems involving friends, family members, and even those whom you do not like. A facility manager must be the referee in disputes involving other administrators, employees, patrons, external contractors, government officials, the media, and many others who can affect those working in a facility. Besides mediating disputes and helping to resolve conflicts, a manager has to serve as a mentor, priest, and psychologist at different times. In order to get people to do their jobs, managers need to undertake numerous roles, but this is just one component of human resource or personnel administration.

The other major element that necessitates significant managerial oversight comprises all the legal requirements related to hiring, training, promoting, and terminating employees. Issues from unionization to sexual harassment take a significant amount of a manager's time, and there is never a "down" time when it comes to legal concerns. The next chapter highlights some of the additional legal concerns that can affect a facility.

DISCUSSION QUESTIONS AND ACTIVITIES

1. What would you include in the job analysis and description for an usher, a concessionaire, and a facility manager?

2. Under what circumstances would it be advisable to outsource facility management functions?

3. How would you handle a sexual harassment complaint in a sport facility?

4. Develop specific policies and procedures you feel would be important to include in an employee manual.

THIRTEEN

Legal Responsibilities

CHAPTER OBJECTIVES

After completing this chapter you will be able to do the following:

- Understand the breadth of legal issues affecting sport facilities
- Apply basic tort and contract law principles to daily facility operations
- Appreciate how constitutional law and government regulations affect stadiums and arenas
- Learn how to apply risk management techniques to make facilities safer

The law is one of the more difficult topics to cover appropriately, and it is hard to do justice to the topic in one chapter. Thus, this chapter highlights some of the most important legal concerns facility managers face, primarily tort- and contract-related issues. These two issues are emphasized over others because facility managers face these concerns on a daily basis. Issues regarding constitutional and property law are seen less frequently, although their impact can be just as important as that of tort or contract disputes.

This chapter focuses on the main legal issues facing sport facilities. It starts with an overview of the law and then examines several key concerns that all facility managers should understand. Besides tort and contract law, special attention is given to property law issues such as zoning and eminent domain. Next the chapter looks at constitutional law, including First and Fourteenth Amendment freedoms related to public assembly facility management. Finally, government regulations such as the **Americans with Disabilities Act (ADA)** and smoking and alcohol regulations are discussed.

Basic Law

The law is an abstract concept. It is designed to provide guidance and directions for individuals and businesses. The law is designed to benefit society but can also hamper and confuse businesses. For example, some municipalities have outlawed scalping of tickets while other municipalities allow scalping to be conducted outside the facility, on public property, or only on private property, or to allow for resale without any ticket face price increase. Thus, what is legal in one area may be illegal elsewhere.

There are numerous legal issues that apply to sport facilities. Some laws are developed by legislative bodies and are called statutory laws. Tax laws, Occupational Safety and Health Administration (OSHA) legislation, health code regulations affecting concession operations, and legislation related to the tax deductibility of donations to athletic programs and the tax-free status of construction bonds are just some of the statutory concerns at the local, state, and federal level. Laws developed outside the legislative process can originate from administrative actions such as hearings and legislation or from federal and state constitutions; the latter may cover free speech, freedom of religion, due process rights, and the inspection of property such as locker rooms.

Laws are also developed through the court systems. These laws are called **common law.** For example, someone who is hit by a foul ball may file a claim of negligence (see next section), which is a claim that the team or facility deviated from a duty to protect the fans. Courts have refined this concept over the years. The courts have also developed another concept called assumption of risk, which is a defense that a team or facility can raise to counter a negligence claim.

Among the various types of laws that can affect a facility, the legal issues most frequently seen in these settings involve tort and contract law.

Tort Law

Tort law refers to a broad variety of claims based on damage to a person or property. There are both intentional and unintentional torts. An intentional tort against property includes theft of personal property. An intentional tort against a person can include assault, battery, false imprisonment, and defamation. If someone throws a punch that injures another person, the injured person can sue in civil court. Similarly, if someone makes a false statement about another person, the person with the injured reputation can bring a defamation claim.

Unintentional torts can occur to property through such instances as nuisance, for example when the noise or lights from a facility travel into a neighbor's house and cause the neighbor to lose the value/enjoyment of the property. This is in essence taking someone's property without compensation. Another unintentional tort is negligence, which refers to unintentional bodily or mental injury through failure to act in a reasonably prudent manner.

Negligence

There are four elements necessary for any **negligence** claim:

- Duty. Some of a facility manager's duties are to provide a safe facility, inspect the facility on a frequent basis, repair any dangerous conditions, provide proper supervision, and provide appropriate matching of opponents. One of the primary duties is to act as a reasonably prudent facility administrator would, which requires the manager to act similarly to the way other managers with the same amount of training, education, and experience would act in similar circumstances. There also is a duty to take steps to protect facility users when there is a known risk or threat to others that makes an injury foreseeable.

- Breach of duty. Facility managers are required to act upon their duty and exercise reasonable judgment to prevent a dangerous situation. If a facility manager has a duty to provide a safe facility but does not comply with appropriate fire code requirements, then the manager has breached his or her duty. The requirement to have a 4-foot-high (1.2 meters) fence around a pool's perimeter to keep children out might be a duty. If the fence is not present, the pool owner has breached a duty. When a breached duty is a statutory duty such as a required fence, the violation is considered negligence as a matter or law, or negligence "per se" in Latin.

- Proximate cause. Even if a duty was breached, that breach of duty may not be the direct cause of someone's injury. Proximate cause implies

Behind the Scenes: Foul Balls

© AP/World Wide Photos

One concern with stadiums and arenas is projectiles, such as foul balls and hockey pucks, leaving the playing area. The death of a young hockey fan in Columbus, Ohio, in 2003 started a new trend in examining safety at sport facilities. For example, stadiums normally have a screen behind home plate to protect fans. But how wide and tall should the screen be? Is the most dangerous part of the stands protected? Can additional protection be provided, such as the new screens being placed in front of dugouts to protect players? Can safety be incorporated throughout stadiums similar to the way Japanese parks screen the entire lower bowl to protect fans?

Some fans need more protection than others. In one rare case, Richie Ashburn, a slugger with the Philadelphia Phillies, really injured a fan. On August 17, 1957, he fouled a ball into the stands that hit a female fan. The fan was being treated and was put on a stretcher to exit the stands. As she was being moved, play resumed. On the very next pitch, Ashburn fouled the ball again, and guess who was hit by the ball? That's right, the woman on the stretcher. Thus, on two pitches, Ashburn hit the same fan twice (Nash and Zullo, 1992).

that an injury was the direct result of someone's breach of duty. For example, if a facility owes a duty to provide a safe environment but fails to clean the floor and remove a slipping hazard, the facility has breached a duty. If someone is injured on the slipping hazard, the facility may be found not guilty if there was an intervening act that broke the chain of causation. For example, if the person was injured not as a result of the slippery surface, but as a consequence of being pushed by someone else, then the person who did the pushing would probably be considered the direct cause of the injury. In one famous case, a person was drowning in a pool. During the rescue attempt the individual was being pulled out of the pool when his head slipped and slammed into the side of the pool. The court concluded that the proximate cause of the death was not drowning, but rather the botched rescue attempt since the swimmer died from his head trauma (Fried, 1999).

• Injury or damages. Any negligence claim will require someone to have been injured, whether physically or emotionally.

All four elements need to be present for a valid negligence claim. If one element is missing, then there cannot be a valid negligence claim. Other defenses include contributory/comparative negligence, assumption of risk, and immunity. Depending on the state, either comparative or contributory negligence can be raised as a defense. Such a defense basically claims that the injured party was somewhat or wholly responsible for injuring him- or herself. In a comparative negligence state the court examines each party's respective actions and can allocate damages accordingly. If the plaintiff contributed 40% to his or her own injuries and receives a $1 million verdict, then he or she would recover only $600,000. In contrast, a contributory negligence state allows the plaintiff's own negligence to act as a complete bar. Thus, in this example, the plaintiff who was 40% at fault would recover nothing.

Assumption of Risk

Assumption of risk means that the plaintiff knew about the risk of participating in a given activity,

Behind the Scenes: Fall Facts

Over 12,000 people die annually from slip and fall accidents. In addition, 17% of all disabling workplace injuries are caused by falls. And 26% of all deaths in public places are attributable to falls (Roderick and Quintana, 1996).

voluntarily assumed that risk, and then was injured. Under these conditions, the injured party should not recover any damages. One of the classic examples of assumption of risk entails foul balls at a baseball game. The courts have consistently held that spectators can see foul balls entering the stands and should assume that a ball can hit them if they do not sit behind a screen. A facility owner needs to provide enough screened seats for those who may request them, and the most dangerous part of the facility needs to be screened. Spectators can hypothetically ask to sit in a screened seat if they are concerned about being hit by a foul ball. If a person does not sit behind a screen (and if the most dangerous areas are screened) and is hit by a foul ball, then he or she is normally considered to have assumed the risk and cannot recover damages.

Immunity

Immunity is another major defense that can be used by government entities and some nonprofit agencies. For example, the state of Alabama has in its constitution a provision that the state cannot be sued for negligence. Thus, someone who is injured in a public high school gym cannot sue the school. In other states, the immunity protection is more limited and basically protects government entities from simple acts of negligence but allows suit if that entity acted in a willful, wanton, or reckless manner. Thus, a public facility could be liable if its staff knew about a very hazardous condition but did nothing to eliminate the hazard. Furthermore, some states allow the immunity defense to apply to public employees if they are acting in a discretionary manner. This refers to activities such as planning an event at a facility or scheduling security personnel. The states do not want public employees to be sued for every decision they make, so they are given immunity protection. However, even in these states, the courts are clear that immunity protection is not provided when the employee is engaged in ministerial conduct. Ministerial conduct refers to

mechanical execution of a directive. For example, it is a discretionary act when a supervisor develops a facility inspection and maintenance schedule. It is a ministerial act when the custodian follows the schedule. The supervisor can have immunity in the planning process, but the custodians will not have immunity for their ministerial act of failing to follow the schedule and inspect the facility in a timely manner. If someone is injured and the facility has breached a duty to provide a safe environment, the supervisor will probably be immune from liability, while the facility (as the employer) can still be liable for the custodian's conduct since he or she did not follow set regulations.

Risk Management and Insurance

Although injuries and accidents are always going to occur, there are various risk management strategies that can be used to minimize the potential for injuries and litigation.

Risk management focuses on two major issues: identifying risks and then eliminating or reducing those risks. Identifying risks involves a significant effort to examine current operations and then to systematically generate new strategies and techniques to reduce potential lawsuits. The **ECT approach** is one strategy to help implement a risk management system. The ECT approach is so named because every element ends with the letters "ect."

- Reflect. A facility manager needs to determine why he or she is interested in implementing a risk management program. Is the purpose to save money, reduce insurance obligation, run a safer facility, or a combination of these? Another part of the reflect stage is to rank potential concerns in order of magnitude and impact. For example, an earthquake is not a major concern on the east coast but could be one of the bigger concerns on the west coast.

Behind the Scenes: Ackler v. Odessa-Montour Central School District

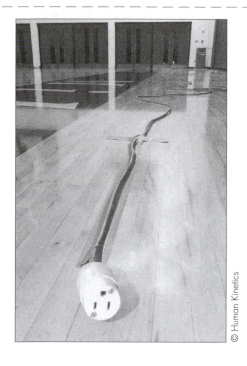

© Human Kinetics

Risk management can involve simple details such as tape on a floor that may be a tripping hazard or more complex issues such as insurance. The following case highlights a problem that may occur when temporary measures are taken in a facility and are not implemented properly.

A high school student in New York was injured when he fell on a gym floor. The student was trying out for the school's basketball team. He claimed that during a particular drill his foot hit a sticky substance, causing him to fall and injure his knee. The student sued the school, claiming that the school was negligent for creating a dangerous and defective condition. The dangerous condition had been created when a piece of tape placed on the floor to mark a volleyball boundary line had been improperly removed. After removal of the tape, a sticky residue remained, and the student tripped at the point where the residue would have been. The school district filed for summary judgment, which is an attempt to have the court rule on a case before it gets to a potential jury. But the court concluded that there were sufficient facts to warrant proceeding with the case, as the facts appeared to demonstrate that the school had acted negligently in handling and removing the tape (*Ackler v. Odessa-Montour Central School District*, 1997). This particular concern also arises in facilities where electrical cords are taped down to prevent a tripping hazard.

This case raises an important issue in that putting tape on a floor is not a negligent act in and of itself. The liability concern is the negligent maintenance, application, or removal of any flooring tape. Once a facility manager undertakes to make a facility safer, he or she has to implement the safety plan in a reasonable manner. Safety-conscious administrators sometimes place nonslip tape on a stair lip to provide extra traction, but over the years the tape can wear down or peel. It is common to see staircases with poor or missing no-slip taping. Customers do not necessarily notice the tape's condition, but expect it to be there. If they fall on an area where tape is missing, they may sue. To improve safety related to traction and vision, some facilities have installed permanent tread lips that illuminate in the dark.

• Deflect. A facility can possibly improve risk management efforts by deflecting liability onto others. This can be accomplished through purchasing insurance that will pay attorney fees and any damages if a claim is filed; inserting clauses in rental contracts that require the renter to have insurance, assume liability, and hold the facility harmless from any claims; and having participants (possibly parents) sign a waiver that they understand the risks of participating in the activity and will not sue the facility if they are injured while participating.

• Detect. A facility manager needs to learn how to identify potential concerns or retain individuals that are knowledgeable in risk management. For example, the National Fire Protection Association requires larger facilities to conduct annual life safety inspections. Such inspections are designed to identify numerous potential concerns.

• Inspect. It is not enough to identify risks and dangerous conditions; someone has to physically examine the facility and its policies to see if there are any hazards or if any area needs to be repaired.

Facility Focus: Martial Arts Studio Risk Audit

No matter what risk management strategies are undertaken, it is imperative that all the various risks that can expose a facility to any liability be analyzed and that specific steps be taken to minimize those risks. The appendix on page 335 is a risk management audit conducted at a martial arts studio in Connecticut. The audit shows the depth and detail required to reduce liability and provide a safe facility. A facility manager can prevent numerous problems by aggressively examining all legal issues, from facility safety concerns to valid contracts and insurance policies. One of the biggest legal concerns is patron safety, which is covered in chapter 15.

• Correct. Once an area or object or situation has been identified as hazardous, someone has to repair the hazard. This may require completing a work order or other means of communicating the needed repair to the appropriate individuals.

• Re-inspect. The mere fact that a work order has been completed does not mean that the repairs or required actions were undertaken, or were undertaken correctly to resolve the hazard. Thus, the area needs to be re-inspected to make sure it is safe.

• Reflect. After a set time such as a year, or after an event, the entire risk management process needs to be reevaluated to determine if it was effective and what steps can be taken to make it more effective in the future (Fried, 1999).

In addition to risk management strategies, there are numerous types of insurance policies that a facility manager needs to consider in addition to the traditional comprehensive general liability policies that cover basic business losses such as fire or liability for injuries on premises. Other necessary policies may include the following:

• Workers' compensation
• Automobile
• Business interruption
• Alcohol sales
• Employment practices liability insurance (EPLI)

There are also unique policies that can be purchased for a single event or for rare occurrences. Recent policies have been written to protect against such losses as natural disasters that in the past may not have been covered losses. For example, snow-removal insurance policies protect businesses if a snowstorm makes a business inaccessible for more than a set number of days (Yarborough, 1998). In 1995-1996, Logan International Airport purchased snow-removal insurance; the policy was written to activate after 44 inches (1 meter) of snow had fallen. The policy provided a $50,000 payment to the airport for every inch over 44 inches up to 84 inches (2 meters). Over 100 inches (2.5 meters) of snow fell that winter, and the administrators at Logan were considered geniuses since their $400,000 investment in the snow-removal insurance brought a $2 million return from the insurer. The insurance was necessary to help cover the costs associated with snow removal, lost parking, and lost concession revenue due to fewer passengers.

Such narrowly focused policies can be crafted to address or exclude specific circumstances. In the case of snow-removal insurance, the policy can specify what lost business will be covered, during which dates, whether snow removal is covered versus just lost business income, and which days will be specifically addressed as key business loss dates. For example, a football stadium may want snow-removal insurance only for Sundays when home games are played against opponents with a win–loss record over 70%. Any terms can be included in an insurance policy if it is negotiated and accepted as a valid contract.

Contracts

For most contracts, there is usually no need that they be in writing. A written **contract** merely provides evidence of what the contractual terms were. Some contracts, such as a contract for the sale of real estate or a contract that cannot be fulfilled within one year, need to be in writing. While it may not be necessary for a contract to be in writing to be legal, every contract needs to have four basic elements to be valid:

1. An agreement includes an offer and acceptance. If Mr. A offers to paint Ms. B's house for $1,000, there is an offer. If Ms. B says yes, there is an acceptance and the potential for a valid agreement. However, if Ms. B says she will pay only $800, the first offer is terminated and Ms. B has just made a counteroffer. The contractual terms in the agreement should be as specific as possible to avoid confusion. This can be very difficult in application. Sometimes individuals or entities enter into a memorandum of understanding. These simple contracts may provide basic terms, with a more detailed contract to follow. Memos of understanding have been used between a professional team and a city to build a stadium or arena. The memo is used to start the construction project, and then the complex and detailed contract can be completed at a later date.

2. **Consideration** is an exchange of value or promises. There is no requirement that any consideration have a minimum value as long as one party feels there is value. This point is important because without an exchange of value there cannot be a contract. Assume that a woman promises her grandson that she will give him $1 million. This is a gift that can be withdrawn without any repercussion, since there was not a contract. However, if the woman promises her grandson $1 million if he graduates from college, then a contract exists. The grandson does not have to stay in college or even go; in such a case, the woman would not be obliged to give him the money. However, if he chooses to attend college and also graduates, she owes the money. His staying in college was consideration for her promise to pay a certain sum.

3. Capacity represents the ability to enter into a contract. Some individuals cannot be legally bound to a contract because of their age, mental status, or mental state. Those under age 18 cannot be bound to a contract because it is presumed that they do not understand what they are agreeing to, no matter how mature they may be. Thus, although a facility should still ask minors (those under age 18) to sign a waiver to participate, the parents should also sign the waiver to make the contract legally binding. This does not mean that the minor cannot back out of the contract. It also does not necessarily mean that the parents have waived the minor's right to sue, because in certain states parents can waive their own rights, but not those of a minor. Persons who are insane or mentally deficient also cannot bind themselves through a contract, and any contract they enter into can be voidable. Lastly, those who are impaired through drugs or alcohol also do not have the capacity to enter into a contract.

4. Legality is the last element of a valid contract. Contracts must have a legal purpose. Thus, a court would not intervene to enforce a contract for selling or buying illegal drugs. Since the drugs are illegal, any contract regarding them is void from the outset and cannot be enforced in any court.

As already mentioned, all four elements to a contract need to be present. However, having a valid contract is not the end of contract law. The contract has to be performed. If all parties perform their contractual obligations, the transaction is completed. Contracts are entered into and completed every day. If someone pays to park in a sport facility, a contract is completed via the customer's paying the required amount and the facility's allowing the vehicle to park. However, a party that does not comply with its contractual obligations has breached the contract. For example, if a corporation signs a 20-year naming rights contract for a facility and cannot pay the required amount in a given year, the company has breached its contractual obligation. The facility can ignore the breach and try to settle the dispute, terminate the contract and look for another sponsor, assess damages under the contract, sue to enforce the contract, or take these actions in combination. If a contract is breached, the aggrieved party can sue to recover actual losses and possibly other damages.

There are numerous facility-related contracts, from simple ticket purchases or concession sales contracts (see a sample contract on pages 256-257) to complex lease agreements and bond issuance contracts. Lease provisions need to be carefully crafted. During the 2002 football season, county commissioners in Cincinnati were looking into suing the Bengals for breaching their lease obligations. The Bengals had lost six straight games during the start of the season, were 10-28 since having moved into the newly built stadium, and had only 7 of 19 home games sold out. A sentence in the lease stated that the sales tax increase used to fund the stadium was needed to "keep competitive and viable major league football and baseball teams in Cincinnati." Since the commissioners did not perceive the team as competitive, they were examining the option of suing the team for breach of contract for failing to field a competitive team ("County Probes," 2002).

Sample Facility Concession Contract

THIS AGREEMENT made this ___ day of _____, _____ by and between _____, a municipal corporation, having its main office _____, (hereinafter "Facility"), and Facility Operator, Inc., whose mailing address will be _____ (hereinafter "Operator").
WITNESSETH:

WHEREAS, the Facility is a multiuse sport facility; and,

WHEREAS, Operator is qualified and knowledgeable in the field of concession operation; and,

WHEREAS, the Facility desires that Operator provide concession service at the Facility during sporting events.

NOW, THEREFORE, the parties agree as follows:

1. Service to Be Provided. Operator shall, during the term of this Agreement and for and during the hours of operation herein below provided, provide concession items as mutually agreed upon by both parties.

2. Fees.

   a. Occupancy Fee. The Operator agrees to pay a concession fee of $_____ for permission to sell concessions at the Facility. This payment of $_____ must be received by _____ to be valid.

3. Term. This Agreement shall apply from the date hereof through December 31 _____. The Facility and Operator may by mutual agreement extend this Agreement for two successive one-year options, with modifications to this Agreement subject to the approval of both parties. Such renewal shall be in writing and signed by both parties.

4. Permits. Operator shall be responsible for obtaining all appropriate and necessary licenses and permits for the sale of its products. Appropriate and necessary permits and certificates for food service and from County Health Department must be obtained and exhibited prior to serving customers. Repeated health code violations or other poor performance leading to Health Department citation(s) shall result in this contract's termination.

5. Insurance. During the term hereof, Operator shall maintain in full force and effect bodily injury, property damage and comprehensive public liability insurance of not less than $1,000,000. Operator shall deliver to the Facility a certificate issued by the insurance carrier naming the Facility as an additional insured.

6. Indemnification. Each party shall indemnify and hold harmless the other and their respective successors, assigns, officers, directors, agents, affiliates, and employees from and against all costs, liabilities, damages, expenses, claims and demands whatsoever, including reasonable attorneys' fees, suffered by or asserted against the other party which result directly or indirectly from any negligent, willful, reckless or wrongful act or omission of the other party, its employees, representatives or agents, under this Agreement, or from any breach of its representations and warranties herein. If a claim arises, upon receiving notice or knowledge of any claim, event, or loss for which indemnity is sought hereunder, the indemnified party shall tender the matter to the defending party and cooperate with its defense as that party may reasonably request, and permit the defending party to defend, try, settle, arbitrate or appeal such matter as the defending party shall determine. After tender and acceptance of defense have occurred, the indemnitor shall not be responsible for further defense costs or further attorneys' fees.

7. Trash Removal. The Facility shall provide trash receptacles for Operator's operation at no additional cost or expense to Operator. It shall be the Operator's responsibility to empty trash receptacles at the end of each day, located inside each concession and eating area, and place outside the facility for final trash removal.

8. Uniforms. Operator's employees will use Operator's standard uniform designating them in a manner that sets them apart from security personnel.

9. Conduct. Courteous and polite behavior is required and expected of Operator's employees.

10. Applicable Laws. Operator shall observe all laws, ordinances and regulations applicable to its operation hereunder, and shall promptly pay when due, all sales, employment, income, and other required taxes.

11. Acts of God and Force Majeure. Neither party shall be liable for damages for its failure to perform due to contingencies beyond its reasonable control, including, but not limited to, war, fire, strikes, riots, storm, flood, earthquake, explosion, accidents, sabotage, public insurrection, public disorders, lockouts, labor disputes, labor shortages, or any other acts of God.

12. Attorneys' Fees. In any action to construe or enforce the terms and conditions of the Agreement, the prevailing party (as determined by a court of competent jurisdiction, if necessary) in such action and in any appeals taken therefrom, shall be entitled to recover all reasonable attorneys' fees and costs.

13. Waiver. Failure or delay on the part of either party to exercise any right, power, privilege, or remedy under this Agreement shall not constitute a waiver thereof.

14. Severability. The provisions of this Agreement shall be severable and the invalidity of any provision, or portion thereof, shall not affect the enforceability of the remaining provisions.

15. Authorized Signatures/Effectiveness. The persons signing this Agreement shall have all legal authority and power to bind Operator and Facility.

16. Entire Agreement. This Agreement constitutes the entire understanding between the parties and supersedes all previous agreements or negotiations, whether written or oral, and shall not be modified or amended except by written agreement duly executed by the parties.

17. Binding Agreement. This Agreement shall be binding upon and inure to the benefit of the parties, their heirs, successors and assigns.

18. Pricing and Signs. All display signage and advertising and promotion located in the Facility must be approved by Facility prior to display and shall not conflict with current Facility sponsors.

19. No Competition. During the term of this Agreement, the Facility agrees that it will not enter into an Agreement with any other entity permitting any concession operation at the Facility.

20. Security. The management staff at the Facility and the local police shall have keys to each concession location. The Facility is responsible for hiring, training, and managing the activity of all facility security personnel. Security personnel should make regularly scheduled visits to Operator's sites and help with securing money deposits after each event.

21. Default. In the event the Operator shall fail to comply with all the terms contained herein or fails to remain open for business at the times provided, or fails to abide by any of the terms and conditions thereof, the Facility may at its sole discretion provide written notice of any such breach/default.

In the event the facility gives written notice of any claimed breach/default the Operator shall be allowed 72 hours after hand-delivery receipt of such notice within which to cure the breach or breaches specified therein. If the breach(es) take longer than 24 hours to correct, the Operator will keep the facility Manager informed of the daily progress being made to correct the breach(es). No breach(es) will take longer than five (5) days to cure and if the breach(es) cannot be cured the Agreement will automatically terminate.

IN WITNESS THEREOF, the parties hereto sign this Agreement on the date below and hereby acknowledge acceptance of all the terms and conditions set forth herein.

_____   _____

Reprinted, by permission, from G. Fried, 1999, *Safe at first* (Durham, NC: Carolina Academic Press)

One of the important concerns associated with contracts is keeping them current. This is especially important for leases, as provisions written 20 years ago may not be applicable any longer. Significant bargaining and renegotiating often need to be undertaken when contracts such as leases expire. For example, it may not be worthwhile extending a lease if more favorable terms can be found. If there are numerous vacant buildings, some landlords may go into a reverse bidding war to offer the lowest price and best amenities to attract a tenant. Some of the strategies used when renegotiating a lease include the following:

- Finding a "walk-away" alternative facility that could serve the same purpose and would not be difficult to move to (if a landlord knows the facility cannot be replicated, then the landlord has all the bargaining power)
- Avoiding unfair escalation clauses that can significantly increase rent obligations
- Obtaining the right to audit the books to calculate operating expenses
- Changing the base year for future increases to the current year to avoid unfair increases
- Avoiding holdover clauses that charge large sums for staying just several days over the former lease ending date
- Eliminating any personal guarantees that will secure the lease obligations (Perry, 2002b)

Property Law

Sport facilities are affected by **property law** in various ways. A sport facility represents real property. Real property is any property attached to land. Personal property, in contrast, such as a car or lawnmower, can be moved. Numerous laws, regulations, and ordinances affect real property. For example, as discussed in chapter 4, zoning is a major consideration for any proposed facility. Local officials want to protect a neighborhood's integrity and may allow only residential property in a given area. However, if a community benefit can be derived from the facility, the zoning laws may be bent to allow a JCC or YMCA, for example, to be built in the neighborhood even though the existing zoning does not allow such a facility.

Other property issues previously discussed include the use of eminent domain by a municipality to take land for a public use. In one cir-

cumstance the city of Baltimore attempted to use eminent domain to try to keep a professional team from moving. The Baltimore Colts were interested in moving, and the city council voted to use eminent domain to keep the team. However, the team packed up its bags in the middle of the night and moved in its entirety in several trailers to Indianapolis. If the team was not in the city it could not be touched. Some legal authorities also felt that eminent domain would not work on a team since a team is not real property. However, the Colts did not want to stick around to see how the potential legal battle would end.

One of the biggest legal concerns associated with property law is the concept of nuisance. Nuisance is a type of tort in which a party's use of land interferes with others' uses. For example, if a facility has outdoor lighting or a sound system that allows light or sound to spill over into adjoining property, the property owners can ask that the lights and sound be reduced. If the facility does not act, the homeowners can bring a nuisance suit to force the lights and sound to be turned down. Thus, a facility that has its own property does not have unfettered use of the property if it violates a law or interferes with other property.

Constitutional Law

Constitutional law exists at the federal level and in all 50 states. Constitutional law applies only to state and federal actors, not to private facilities. The first question to ask when dealing with any constitutional law issue is whether or not a state or federal actor is involved. However, even in a private facility, state action can occur if a public entity, such as a college team, is using the facility for an official event. If a state employee, for example the coach, is forcing players to pray before a game with a private university opponent, there could be constitutional issues associated with the First Amendment's free exercise clause. The following sections cover several key constitutional issues associated with sport facilities.

First Amendment Freedoms

The First Amendment concerns rights such as freedom of religion, free exercise of religion, and freedom of speech. Issues related to freedom of religion and free exercise can arise when religious material is played over loudspeakers, a religious invocation is allowed before an event at a facility, or prayer is allowed in a locker room. In all these cases it may be argued that the state is providing support to or hindering a religion.

Freedom of speech issues occur more frequently in sport facilities but can be intertwined with religion-related issues. In one case, a fan brought a religiously oriented sign to a stadium and was expelled. This type of incident may be a blend of free speech and freedom of religion issues. The fan ended up settling the suit with the team, with no admission of any guilt or wrongdoing. Other cases involve free speech only, for example if a facility does not allow individuals to picket at the front entrance. Several cases have been raised by persons selling unofficial programs in front of stadiums and arenas. Courts are reluctant to impose a total ban against such activities and often impose what are referred to as reasonable time, place, and manner restrictions. Such restrictions allow a facility or municipality to regulate speech, not based on content but on other standard criteria. Thus, such restrictions are typically content neutral. Examples include noise ordinances that do not allow amplified sound after a certain time at night, requirements to obtain permits to assemble on public property, and precluding people from assembling at given areas or certain times. Such regulations are designed to prevent disruption to cities or facilities, but need to be enforced in such a way that they apply to all speech so that content is not an issue.

While the concept of content-neutral regulations is often used, other laws can override these regulations. For example, certain no-assembly rules may need to be enforced in front of a facility but may be relaxed if a union is calling a strike. This example suggests the complexity associated with free speech issues and the reason an attorney needs to be contacted before any attempt is made to regulate any speech. This is especially important if a facility is being leased to outside organizations. It is legal to lease a public facility to a religious organization, but if the facility is open to one group it must be made available to other groups regardless of their agenda or ideology. For example, if a facility is leased to a church group one week and a neo-nazi group wishes to rent it the next week, the neo-nazi group must be allowed to rent unless the facility is already booked or is unavailable for some other legitimate reason.

Fourteenth Amendment Protections

Equal protection is another major constitutional concern. Publicly owned sport facilities are state actors (act as agents of the state) pursuant to the Fourteenth Amendment and as such must provide equal protection under the law to all individuals working within the facility. This can apply not just to the players and field workers, but also to the press. One case highlighting this point was brought by a female reporter against the Yankees. The reporter was not allowed into the locker room and sued, claiming that the Yankees played in a public facility and thus she was owed equal protection under the law to be treated the same as male reporters (*Ludtke v. Kuhn*, 1978). On the basis of such cases, men's sports often allow both male and female reporters into the locker room to provide both genders with the same access opportunity. To avoid the issue, female sports do not let any reporters into the locker room. Often the press is allowed into the locker room only after everyone has showered, or athletes are interviewed only in a separate pressroom.

Government Regulations

Government regulations can affect a facility. Bleacher safety received a significant boost in 2002 when the Minnesota legislature passed legislation that conforms to the proposed Uniform Building Code (UBC) 2000. The regulations require bleachers over 55 inches (1.4 meters) high to have no more than 4 inches (10 centimeters) of spacing between the floor and seat boards. Telescoping grandstands in gymnasiums can have a spacing of up to 9 inches (23 centimeters). Guardrails also must have less than 4-inch spacing at the openings and must not be climbable. Guardrails can be protected using chain-link fencing. The mesh of the chain-link fencing must have a maximum 1 3/4-inch (4.4-centimeter) opening if it is reinforced with plastic or wooden slats, or otherwise a maximum 1 1/4-inch (3-centimeter) opening, to make the fence more difficult to climb. Guardrails should also be installed with vertical spacing bars every 4 inches to prevent children from falling through. Lastly, the regulations require that a building official or design professional certify that the bleachers meet the safety requirements ("Minnesota Leading," 2003). Other potential code concerns for grandstands and bleachers include aisle width, access to exits, and structural soundness.

Other government regulations affecting facilities include OSHA regulations and taxes. The OSHA regulations affect the work environment and are designed to make facilities as safe as possible for workers. Injuries happen frequently in sport facilities. For example, in the first three years during which the Bridgeport Arena at Harbor Yard was open, at least three employees were injured and lost fingertips while working with glass dasher boards used for hockey. All serious injuries need to be reported to either federal or state OSHA offices.

Tax-related issues can include income taxes for employees, collection of taxes on various items sold, collection of a ticket-related surcharge tax, and possibly property-related taxes. The New Haven Ravens approached the city of West Haven in 2002 to reduce the team's property tax obligation. The Ravens were the only team of the 130 teams in minor league baseball that had to pay property taxes. They paid $25,000 a year in property taxes for using the field (Zaretsky, 2002). The tax obligation was only one of the team's obligations. They also owed almost $80,000 for back overtime pay for officers who worked games. The Ravens were required to have three or four officers work the street in front of the stadium for every game, regardless of the number of spectators.

Clearly, government involvement in sport facilities has many facets. From zoning regulations to federal legislation affecting the environment, sport facilities constantly have to be aware of new regulations that can affect operations. Some important government regulations are discussed at the end of this section, but the most important law affecting sport facilities is addressed first. The ADA has had and will continue to have a greater impact on sport facilities than any other law ever passed by the federal government.

Compliance With ADA

In a watershed event for millions of Americans, the Americans with Disabilities Act was signed into law on January 26, 1992. The new law promised millions of Americans (over 50 million according to some estimates) the opportunity to obtain equality in facility usage and employment opportunities (Fried, 1999).

Nowhere can the ADA's effect be seen more prominently than in facilities. Sport and recreational facilities are especially prominent in relation to ADA coverage because of the publicity generated by such facilities and the number of people who attend events or engage in activities at facilities. Sport facilities have become the target for organizations such as Paralyzed Veterans of America, which has engaged in concerted efforts

Stadiums must provide adequate seating options for patrons who use wheelchairs.

© Empics

on behalf of its 17,000 members to challenge new sport facilities that do not meet ADA requirements. The group filed against several arenas claiming that although spaces were available for wheelchairs, these seats did not offer a clear view of the action when surrounding fans stood up. Regulations under the ADA require all wheelchair seats to be designed so that the wheelchair-using patron is not isolated and has the choice of various seats and ticket prices; and, in places where fans are expected to stand, facilities must provide a line of sight "comparable" to the view from seats provided to other spectators.

ADA Requirements for Sport Facilities

Title III of the ADA covers places of public accommodations and commercial facilities such as establishments serving food and drinks, entertainment facilities (movie theaters, concert halls, etc.), public gathering places (auditoriums, convention centers, stadiums, arenas, etc.), public transportation centers, places of recreation (parks, zoos, bowling alleys, etc.), places of education (private schools), and places of exercise or recreation (gymnasium, golf courses, etc.). The only exceptions from Title III coverage are private clubs and religious organizations.

Under the ADA, a place of public accommodation must remove all **architectural barriers** to access if such removal is "readily achievable." When an architectural barrier cannot be removed, the facility must provide alternative services. However, any new construction or facility alteration must comply with all ADA accessibility standards. New construction is required to be readily accessible and usable unless this is structurally impracticable.

The primary focus in analyzing sport facilities relates to the **public accommodation** requirements. Public accommodations may not discriminate against individuals with disabilities. Disabled individuals cannot be denied full and equal enjoyment of the "goods, services, facilities, privileges, advantages or accommodations" offered by all covered facilities. The ADA applies to covered facilities regardless of whether they are owned by the private, nonprofit, or government sector.

Disabilities Covered by ADA

The ADA employment provisions clarify what constitutes a disability under the ADA. Individuals covered by the ADA include those with significant physical or mental impairments, those with a record of an impairment, and those regarded as having an impairment. Persons with a record of disability are protected even though they may not currently suffer any impairment. Thus a cancer patient in remission is covered by the ADA. Furthermore, persons regarded by any other person as having an impairment are protected even if they have never had any impairment. For example, even though people with dwarfism might not consider themselves disabled, they are protected because other people might think they are. A person has a disability if he or she has a significant condition that substantially limits one or more "major life activities." Major life activities as defined by Department of Justice regulations include "functions such as caring for one's self, performing manual tasks, walking, seeing, hearing, speaking, breathing, learning and working" (28 CFR Section 41.31, 2004). To help determine significance, the following factors are examined: the length of time the condition has existed, the number and types of life activities affected, the extent to which the disability limits opportunities, and whether the condition is medically diagnosable.

Common examples of protected disabilities include AIDS (acquired immunodeficiency syndrome), paralysis, diabetes, arthritis, cancer, epilepsy, asthma, vision impairments, hearing impairments, speech impairments, learning disabilities, muscular dystrophy, heart disease, and manic depressive disorder. Conditions commonly regarded as impairments include dwarfism, albinism, cosmetic deformities, controlled diabetes, and visible burn injuries. The ADA specifically excludes homosexuals, bisexuals, transvestites, transsexuals, pyromaniacs, kleptomaniacs, and compulsive gamblers. Other conditions that are not covered by the ADA include colds, broken bones, appendicitis, hair color, hair type, and left-handedness (Fried and Miller, 1998).

Disabled individuals are not the only people protected by the ADA. The ADA prohibits discrimination against any individual or entity because the person has a known relationship or association with a person who is disabled. Thus, the roommate of a disabled participant cannot be excluded from attending. This does not mean the roommate can get into a stadium for free. But if the roommate and the disabled patron both have tickets, they should be allowed to sit together. These seats are often called companion seats.

Reasonable Accommodation

Reasonable accommodation refers to correcting both architectural and program-related barriers. An architectural barrier is a physical element of a building that impedes access for disabled individuals. Examples of architectural barriers include the following:

- Steps and curbs (rather than ramps)
- Unpaved parking areas
- Conventional doors (rather than automatic doors)
- Office layouts that do not allow a wheelchair to move through the space
- Deep pile carpeting, which is difficult for wheelchairs to traverse
- Mirrors, paper towel dispensers, and sinks that are positioned too high on a bathroom wall

All covered facilities must reasonably modify their policies, practices, and procedures to avoid discrimination. Modifications do not need to be undertaken if they would fundamentally alter the nature of the goods, services, facilities, privileges, advantages, or accommodations.

Prioritizing ADA Compliance   Facility operators when faced with possible access barriers often have to struggle with a prioritization process. In order to provide guidance, the Department of Justice has established priority suggestions for removing barriers, as follows:

- Removal of any and all barriers that would prevent a disabled individual from entering the facility
- Providing access to areas where goods and services are made available to the general public
- Providing access to rest rooms
- Removing all barriers to using the facility

Reasonable accommodation for ensuring equal communication can include a multitude of auxiliary communication aids such as qualified interpreters, transcription services, audio recordings, speech synthesizers, telecommunication devices for the deaf (TDDs), telephone handset amplifiers, video text displays, written material (including large print), note takers, assistive listening devices, closed caption decoders, and Brailled materials. Besides purchasing needed equipment, facilities must keep all equipment in accessible locations and in working condition.

Costs of Reasonable Accommodation   Public accommodations are required to remove barriers only when such removal is "readily achievable" (ADA Section 302(b)(2)(A)(iv)). "Readily achievable" means that the repairs or modifications can be made without significant difficulty or expense (301(9)). Several factors influence the expense associated with barrier removal, including the nature and cost of needed remedial action, the financial strength of the facility or organization that is required to provide the accommodation, and the relationship of the facility to the overall financial picture of the parent company.

Traditionally, landlords are responsible for facility repairs and modifications. Thus, landlords are typically responsible for financing required renovations or repairs. If a lease agreement specifically allows a tenant to renovate a facility, it will be the tenant's responsibility to pay for ADA-required modifications. If a lease is silent concerning responsibility for required repairs, the Department of Justice could force both the landlord and tenant to pay.

Penalty for Noncompliance

The ADA is enforced through several means. Private citizens can file their own ADA claim in federal court. Private claims are entitled only to injunctive relief and attorney fees. Thus, if a bowling alley does not provide reasonable accommodation, a patron can sue to force the facility to build a ramp so a wheelchair user could reach the lanes.

A private citizen can also file a claim with the attorney general. After receiving a complaint, the attorney general can then sue the facility owner and seek injunctive relief. The attorney general can also recover monetary damages and civil penalties.

Practical and Inexpensive ADA Solutions

Numerous ADA solutions can be implemented at little or no cost. While facility renovation costs and repairs are hard to reduce, it is much easier to implement program-wide attitude changes, which can significantly reduce the chance of incurring an ADA complaint.

To discover what potential ADA problems exist, a facility manager should perform a complete facility and program review. This involves six steps.

1. Designate one employee as the ADA expert. This "expert" will have to review literature in the field, become familiar with ADA regulations and specifications, and listen to the needs of employees and customers.

2. Conduct a comprehensive facility audit. All facility components should be analyzed and evaluated for accessibility. A written evaluation should be prepared to track needed repairs, facility evaluation dates, repair dates, repair costs, priorities, and so on. Such documentation is critical when one is facing an ADA investigation.

3. Evaluate policies, procedures, and facility practices. All policies, procedures, or practices that may affect individuals with disabilities need to be addressed. Waiters can be instructed to ask each party being served how he or she can accommodate any special needs that any patron may have. The key to any such effort is co-opting all employees into the process, with the idea that they should not be afraid to ask how they can help or what they can do. For example, a sporting goods store's normal practice may be to require a driver's license when accepting a personal check. If someone does not have a license, the sales clerk should not automatically reject the check. The sales clerk should ask for other pieces of identification or ask why the customer cannot produce a driver's license. Many disabled individuals do not have driver's licenses.

4. Acquire and maintain in readily usable fashion any necessary auxiliary aids such as interpreters, taped text, Braille text, and assistive listening devices.

5. Follow up to make sure the plans are acted upon.

6. Always check with the accountant to determine if accommodations can be used to receive a tax break.

Smoking and Alcohol

Government regulations, for example the recent bans on smoking in facilities, affect facilities and patrons. Numerous cities throughout the United States have adopted rules banning smoking at every type of location from arenas to bars. Regulations are already in place relating to smoking in restaurants, in office buildings, on beaches, and in numerous other locations. Stadiums and arenas have not escaped the scope of these regulations. For example, Chapter V of the San Francisco Municipal Code was amended by adding Article 19E, which prohibited smoking in places of employment and certain publicly owned sport arenas. A pertinent part of the ordinance is the following:

> "No owner, manager, or operator of a sport arena or stadium shall knowingly or intentionally permit, and no person on the premises shall engage in, the smoking of tobacco products in any enclosed or open space at a sport arena or stadium except in
>
> 1. concourses and ramps outside seating areas,
>
> 2. private suites and corridors to private suites, and
>
> 3. areas designated for parking.
>
> Any portion of a sport arena or stadium used as a bar or restaurant shall be subject to the provisions of this article governing bars and restaurants as places of employment."

The only way a facility could be found innocent of knowingly or intentionally allowing others to smoke would be if steps had been taken to prevent smoking. These steps include posting clear and prominent "No Smoking" signs at each entrance to the premises and requesting, when appropriate, that an individual refrain from smoking in an enclosed area. Reasonable actions do not include the physical ejection of an individual.

If a facility owner or manager fails to take these reasonable steps, he or she could be served with a notice from the Director of Public Health. The failure to comply with the notice within the specified time period could result in an action's being filed by the city attorney to enjoin or enforce the provisions of the article and to assess and recover civil penalties. The article also authorizes damages up to $500 a day for each day a violation occurs or is permitted to continue.

Alcohol regulations also need to be considered. The most universal regulations deal with the minimum age to purchase alcohol. However, regulations also affect alcohol advertising. Like their tobacco counterparts, alcoholic beverage manufacturers and advertisers are also regulated in numerous states. One such law in California regulates the type of advertising (signs, billboards, etc.) that can be purchased from on-site retail licensees. An on-site licensee is defined as the owner of either an outdoor stadium or a fully-enclosed arena with a fixed seating capacity in excess of 10,000 seats. The regulation (Business and Professional Code section 25503.6) limits advertising space and advertising time purchased for events at the stadium or arena. Alcoholic beverage manufacturers who participate in inducing a breach of the statute can face jail terms, a fine in an amount equal to the entire value of the advertising space or time involved in the contract plus $10,000, or both.

The regulatory provisions dictate what signs may be used in a stadium or arena. Signs cannot exceed 630 square inches (0.4 square meters) for interior use in premises where alcoholic beverages are sold for consumption on the premises. Facility owners need to be cognizant of this regulation, especially during special promotions where inflatable beer bottles or other such items are prominently displayed. The regulation (in section 25611.1) limits pictorial advertising—illuminated or mechanized—including, but not limited to, posters, placards, stickers, decals, shelf strips, wall panels, plaques, shadow boxes, mobiles, dummy bottles, bottle toppers, case wrappers, brand-identifying statuettes, tap markers, and table tents, which are not deemed to have "intrinsic or utilitarian value." Similar laws exist in other states and in Canada. Great Britain passed a law in 2002 that outlawed tobacco advertising and will make it illegal for even race cars to have tobacco advertising.

To help prevent problems with new laws affecting tobacco and alcohol usage, sales, and adver-tising, a facility manager can utilize a two-step contractual approach to minimize the potential effect of changing laws.

1. Every sponsorship contract should contain a clause requiring compliance with all applicable laws. The contract should specifically designate which party is responsible for ensuring that all signage complies with local, state, and federal regulations.

2. In order to further protect a facility's sponsorship and advertising income stream, all sponsorship contracts with tobacco- and alcohol-related manufacturers and distributors should contain escape clauses providing either party with the option of terminating the agreement based on the passage of new regulations or laws. Such an escape clause would allow facilities to attract tobacco and alcohol advertisers and at the same time limit their potential liability exposure.

Summary

Sport facilities can be dangerous according to the activities that occur within them. Even if a facility such as a gym is very safe, someone can still get injured in a freak basketball accident. It does not matter how safe the facility was if the injured person decides to sue to recover some of his or her losses. Thus, facility risk management may seem to be a losing battle in that no matter what managers may do, they always will have some legal exposure. Nonetheless, it is important to realize that through solid legal planning such as analyzing contracts, property law, and constitutional law and following government regulations, the potential for being sued or penalized is dramatically reduced.

DISCUSSION QUESTIONS AND ACTIVITIES

1. Walk through a sport facility and develop a list of the top 20 safety concerns you see in the facility. Give specific steps and suggestions to eliminate or reduce the risks.

2. In pairs (with one student the seller and the other the buyer), write up a contract to sell and buy a pen or some other small item. The idea is to see how detailed the contract can be and what elements each pair of students will insert into their contract.

3. Research a facility that was constructed in the past 10 years to find out what legal battles arose when the facility was being planned and what tax levy was being voted on, as well as any suits that arose when the facility was being built (for any project, normally a number of suits are filed by parties such as disgruntled voters, land rights advocates, and eminent domain opponents).

4. What is negligence and how can it affect a sport facility?

5. Why is it important to have a written contract?

PART V

Event and Activity Management

FOURTEEN

Facility Preparation

CHAPTER OBJECTIVES

After completing this chapter you will be able to do the following:

- Understand the various steps involved in obtaining an event for a facility
- Know the specific steps required to prepare a facility for an event
- Appreciate the multitude of issues that go into planning to prevent major disasters

The text so far has reviewed numerous issues and topics related to facility management. This chapter, as well as chapters 15 and 16, gather all the previously discussed information together so that the reader can see what is really involved in facility management—taking the reader through an actual planning process to bring an event to a facility. Since public assembly facilities (PAFs) exist to put on events for the public commensurate with their mission and goals, this part of the book deals with the heart and soul of PAFs.

The process of developing and attracting events is one of the most important components within any facility's marketing efforts. Numerous facilities compete to get the same event because of the potential impact a large event can have on the local tourism market. Once an event is secured for a facility, the real planning begins for everything from marketing to securing enough parking attendants to work the event.

Revisiting Planning

A facility manager needs to develop a business plan to provide direction for the facility. The plan should outline the challenges for the coming year and ways to meet those challenges while reflecting on performance and achievement for the previous year. The following key elements should be included in the business plan:

- Vision and values. This aspect relates to how the facility sees itself and how it wants to be perceived by others. It provides the framework for goals and expectations.

- Last year's accomplishments. Reviewing the previous year's business plan tells the facility what has been accomplished and how the new objectives should be formulated to repeat success or avoid the failures.

- Lessons learned. Understanding where mistakes were made in the previous year helps avoid the same errors and shows whether the expectations are too high or too low.

- Overall objective. This is the main goal the facility will focus on for the coming year or event.

- Key strategies. Five to six strategies are selected that will help the facility achieve the overall objective.

- Tactics. The strategies are broken down to outline ways to complete each key strategy, that is, specify how the work will get done.

- Performance measurements. Measurements are used to rate the facility's performance to ensure that the goals are being met successfully. Measurements should be both quantitative and qualitative (Hunter, 2001).

These goals and objectives should be monitored throughout the year and updated as needed. This process gives staff a clear picture of the business objectives and provides them with an understanding of what is expected from each employee to help accomplish the facility's goals.

Business plans can be developed for the long term (years out) or for the short term (monthly plans). The business plan should be reviewed at least quarterly to account for any unanticipated market changes. The plan should not exceed 20 pages because then it becomes too complex. Also, all levels of the organization should be involved in creating the plan so that employees feel their thoughts and ideas are being heard.

While many textbooks highlight the need for goals and objectives, most larger companies utilize more concrete policies and procedures rather than vague and abstract goals and objectives. Policies and procedures highlight what activities the facility approves and the steps needed to reach the intended outcomes. Thus, if the policy is to schedule three events per week, the procedures will include specific activities to help attract or create the events. Regardless of whether goals and objectives or policies and procedures are used, the key is for the facility to incorporate the business plan into an actionable strategy. Existing tenants and future event promoters under contract need to be involved in the planning process to make sure they are willing to work toward the same goals.

Attracting Events

A facility exists to host events. A vacant building serves no purpose and costs money in terms of upkeep, insurance, and even opportunity costs. Thus, facilities need to explore hosting events and teams that will help them achieve their goals. Some facilities with permanent tenants do not need to attract events. Other facilities must constantly compete with others to attract the best events, since the best events hopefully produce the greatest financial return on a facility's investment. Madison Square Garden, one of the most well-respected arenas in the world, hosts numerous events every year (such as Knicks and Rangers games) that will undoubtedly continue to be held. This limits the number of potentially available event dates. If dates are available, there probably are a large number of events that would be willing to play at the Garden because this would show that the event is in the big time. Madison Square Garden management is swamped with proposals for events and can choose which events they want to take based on the potential financial return or other variables.

In contrast, many smaller facilities are fighting for traveling acts such as the Ice Capades, circuses, or the Harlem Globetrotters. Facilities are often trying to win the rights to host such events as National Collegiate Athletic Association (NCAA) events and Amateur Athletic Union youth championships. Other small facilities such as health clubs also hold events. The primary tenants at a health club are the members who work out at the club. The club may also host an event such as a weightlifting tournament or a community-wide fund-raiser. Any such event should not conflict with existing usage unless the users are told in advance or are participants. Even if most existing users agree, there will always be some members who will object to losing their workout time.

The process of trying to win larger events is very competitive. Local chambers of commerce or convention and visitors bureaus often aggressively compete to win these events to increase the number of people staying in the host city and spending money to stimulate the local economy.

Organizational Structure

One of the first questions asked by a facility manager is who is sponsoring, underwriting, or bringing the event to the facility. This might seem like a simple question, but the answer can be highly political. The politics can stem from factors like the desire to raise money and the prestige of hosting the event. For example, a major NCAA championship would be a feather in the cap of anyone involved. It can happen that a large university has an arena and the city has a larger facility, and that the two fight over who should back the event and be the primary host.

No matter who takes the lead, some person or institution must resolve the political issues early on to prevent scandals or disruptions. At times it is impossible to prevent political fighting, while at other times a political leader such as a mayor or university president may step in to avoid the fighting and secure an event. Whoever facilitates bringing an event to a facility, the facility needs to have at least one person or a group to serve as the point person(s) to finalize the event's coming to the facility.

Some large facilities are able to dedicate one individual to attracting and booking events, while other facilities have a department that manages the process. Smaller facilities often rely on the manager to attract events. Others, especially public or non-profit facilities, may have to utilize either a paid or a volunteer group called a planning committee. In these cases the planning committee addresses any needs of the event, from the types of trophies to be awarded to how to attract potential volunteers. Just as it may be desirable for a building planning committee to involve opponents in the design

process, it is often worthwhile to bring marginal individuals or opponents into the event planning process to win their political support. It is important to obtain support especially if there are controversial regulations that could affect the event. For example, the Marlboro Grand Prix of New York, which was scheduled for 1992-1993, was canceled due to opposition, including a lawsuit alleging that New York City had failed to follow the required environmental reviews. There also was significant opposition to having a major tobacco company sponsor the event (Haven, 1992).

Bid Process

The **bid process** starts with either a mass mailing or an advertisement in publications such as *Sport Travel*, *NCAA News*, or *Athletic Business*. The announcement indicates that one or more facilities are needed for a given event on specified dates. The process normally occurs several years in advance, so bids may be solicited in 2005 for an event in 2007. The bid process for the Olympic Games usually starts more than 12 years in advance since there is an eight-year time lag from when a city is selected until the Games are held. A typical bid request asks for detailed information such as the following:

- A facility's size, such as seating capacity and parking capabilities
- The number of hotel rooms in the immediate area
- What other events have been held in the facility or the region
- The experience of employees and volunteers
- How the event will be integrated with other activities in the area

The bidding process may be dictated by a formal bid package. Assume that the United States Badminton Association (USBA) is searching for a host site for the national championships in three years. The USBA may send those who inquire about the event a package with forms that need to be completed. The forms may request the following types of information:

- Facility dimensions, locker rooms, spectator seating, lighting configuration, and so on
- Past events hosted at the site

- Transportation issues such as the closest airport and available public transportation
- Skills and background of the people who will manage the event
- Experience working with the media sources in the area
- Accommodations for fans and athletes
- Proposed budget for the event

The package also usually contains numerous specifications such as the playing court size, broadcasting requirements, number of seats that will be needed, and number of free passes that will need to be given to USBA board members.

A facility manager interested in bidding for the USBA event will review the submission guidelines, research the local community to find facilities and housing that comply with the bid, and complete the bid response. Time is also spent contacting the USBA for clarification, aligning political support, and finding sponsors. It can take weeks to months to gather all the necessary materials and information.

Bidding for an event can be a major undertaking requiring significant time and energy. It is not uncommon to spend months on a bid. The process also costs a considerable amount of money. For example, the bids to host an Olympic Games can cost millions and require numerous meetings, facility tours, site visits, attendance at conferences, advertising campaigns, and significant travel to meet with officials and sell the city. The process is more informal for other events when the planners know which facility they want to go to; they just call to see if the date is available. If the date is available, the parties merely need to agree on contractual terms.

A number of concerns will arise with any given bid. For example, an outdoor facility in the South will have to demonstrate that weather will not affect the event. This may give rise to ethical concerns about telling the truth in a bid response. It is rumored that Atlanta manipulated the weather analysis when bidding for the Olympic Games and that those who voted for Atlanta thought it was 5° to 10° cooler in the summer than it actually is. Other concerns might be the ability to effectively broadcast from a facility and the public transportation system that will help support the event. Each concern needs to be addressed to avoid the impression that the bid reviewers are being given incorrect information.

Before the expense of bidding is undertaken, it is criti-

© AP/World Wide Photos

Bidding for major events, like NCAA championship games, is usually worth the time, expense, and scheduling conflicts it entails.

cal for the bid committee to examine its existing schedule and the process of booking dates and times. Before a bid can be submitted, it needs to be cross-checked with the facility's schedule to prevent conflicts. However, even if there is a conflict, some events are just so attractive that the facility is willing to face the conflict in order to possibly win the bid. This could occur with a major event such as an NCAA championship—a facility might "bump" an existing event if it wins the bid. Of course, if a facility moves another event there may be some contractual penalties, but this is a concern that should be examined when submitting the bid. A typical large college or university may have several gyms and fields that can have many events running simultaneously. Do these events have precedence over potential future events? If the badminton club reserves a facility, has fulfilled all the related requirements, and then is kicked out of the gym two weeks before the big tournament by another event, there will be some major infighting and many upset patrons.

While it may be that one event has more participants than another, the failure to properly plan and to clarify reservations in a timely manner can upset people. In the badminton example, it could be that the mother of a badminton team member is the university's largest donor. One can imagine the phone call the university president would probably receive and the call that the president would make to the facility manager.

For purposes of this discussion, assume that there is no conflict between the proposed date for an event and the currently booked events. The facility manager will need to book or reserve the date for the event he or she is bidding on in case the bid is successful.

Personnel

An important aspect that needs to be covered is the key individuals backing the event. Have these individuals hosted similar events? Do they have the political clout and experience to make things work when there may be a large number of bureaucratic land mines?

With any bid process there are numerous individuals who will need to have their names lent to the process. It is always important for the facility to gather some big-name supporters, especially if the bid is very competitive. If the bid is for a small event the political muscle may not be needed.

The facility also must have enough people to work on the bid. An Olympic bid may require 5 to 10 people working for several years. Most bids for smaller events are completed by one individual, such as a facility manager, with the help of some volunteers or a combination of employees and volunteers. Even if only one person is writing the bid response, he or she needs to show that there will be appropriate support if the bid is won.

Administrative

Bid committees often put several city officials, local business leaders, local civic leaders, and former or current star athletes on the committee. For example, when Houston was trying to secure the 2012 Olympic Games the committee included a city employee who worked full-time on the bid for over three years, a city council member noted for his work in sport, and several athletes who were in sports from basketball to track and field.

Besides big names backing the bid, the bid reviewers also like to know the names of the support staff that will be used, from secretaries to lawyers, accountants, and even mechanical/structural engineers. Sometimes someone associated with the event wants to contact the accountant or another administrator, and providing these contact names, along with their phone numbers and e-mail addresses, is a helpful gesture.

Before holding an event it is vital to consider all possible employment and volunteer needs. Image, both external and internal, plays a major role in determining the patrons' view of a facility (Farmer, Mulrooney, and Ammon, 1996). It is imperative that facilities employ enough people to adequately serve patrons, whether they are full-time employees, part-time employees, volunteers, or a combination of these. Employees could be required for the following duties:

- Ushers
- Food service
- Novelties
- Ticket sales
- First aid
- Security
- Event staff
- Housekeeping
- Management

Before bidding on an event, evaluate how many staff you will need to properly run the event.

© Dale Garvey

Youth and families typically require more attention—looking for lost or separated children, being alert to mischievous adolescents, and continuous housekeeping are just a few of the "extra" activities involved when young people are present. Also, events that families and children attend are often high-energy, action-packed events (e.g., the circus, Disney On Ice, rock concerts), so the staff should be physically and mentally able to handle a high-energy crowd. Employees should be properly trained in people management—how to politely answer questions, give directions, and provide immediate assistance, as well as how to ensure a positive experience at the facility.

Management

Management policies, procedures, and protocols need to be in place to make sure the event and facility will run smoothly. For example, how will purchasing be completed? Is the process complex? Who signs the form and where are the forms located? What needs to be signed when the item is received? The answers are fairly simple for a small facility. However, a large public facility may have numerous bureaucratic levels that need to be understood and streamlined by management to make sure that the bid and the event planning processes are as smooth as possible.

One example of the ability to smooth the bureaucratic process is film/movie divisions in some city halls. These units are responsible for working with movie and film producers interested in shooting in the city. The staff help navigate potential problems relating to matters such as permits and the use of police to block traffic. If a producer who plans to do filming has to devote a lot of time, energy, and money to making the arrangements, the city may not appear as attractive. It becomes more attractive if one or more people are designated to streamline the process. Management can provide the same assistance to a potential event at a facility by designating one person who can make arrangements for such issues as security and crowd management and finalizing the menu from the concessionaire.

Financial

The financial component of a bid involves everything from what price to charge for renting the facility to how much revenue the event could generate. Financial projections associated with the rough budgets and expected income are affected by numerous variables. Thus, most events have multiple budgets that rely on a best-case, a most likely, and a worst-case planning scenario. A financial analysis for a proposed event is shown on page 275, and table 14.1 highlights what one of these budgets might look like for a college basketball game at a local gymnasium. This is a very simplistic model designed to show what a smaller facility might look at. Larger facilities often use complex modeling, algorithms, and computer programs to

Financial Analysis for Proposed Event

Seating capacity—2,000

Cost for bringing teams—$3,000

Marketing costs—$1,500

Ticket price—$4.00

Average spending on food based on past experience—$3.00

Average revenue from parking—$3.00 per car (normally 3-4 people in each car)

Table 14.1   Best- Through Worst-Case Scenario Analysis

Category	Best case	Most likely	Worst case
Tickets	1,800	1,500	1,000
Ticket revenue	$7,200	$6,000	$4,000
Food	$5,400	$4,500	$3,000
Parking	$1,800	$1,500	$1,000
Total revenue	$14,400	$12,000	$8,000

crunch numbers and develop appropriate projections.

On the basis of these numbers, it appears that the event is a good one to bring to the gym because there is a most-likely projection of $7,500 profit ($12,000 – $ 4,500 in expenses). Even in the worst-case scenario, the event will still make a profit of $3,500.

Legal

During the bid-writing process, the facility must address specific legal concerns. The pre-event legal concerns can be significant. The primary legal aspects that affect events include contract issues, risk management, and potential government or industry concerns.

Contracts

As discussed in chapter 13, there are four elements for a valid contract: agreement, consideration, capacity to enter into a contract, and necessity that the purpose of the contract be legal. Thus, if the facility is bidding for an event but does not win, there is no contract. In fact, the bid is an invitation to make an offer, and if the offer is

rejected a contract never existed since there was no acceptance. Thus, a facility responds to each facility usage request and indicates either that the form has been approved, the applicant must complete an additional contract, or the form has been denied and the bidder cannot use the facility.

Additional contract concerns that should be examined include **waivers,** especially waivers signed by children, renewable contracts, and future consideration. Children often sign waivers, or parents sign waivers to allow children to participate in an event. For example, a youth marathon would have a waiver requirement, and the event organizers would want the facility to get every participant and his or her parents to sign waivers agreeing not to sue if injured. It is essential to examine the law in the state where the event will be held to make sure that the waiver will be valid and to determine who has to sign the waiver.

Some contracts are entered into in a particular year and then kept open. These **open-term contracts** often allow an event to return to the same facility in the future. Frequently such contracts are forgotten and the terms are not fulfilled. In one case, a gym let a basketball league use the facility every year. During the first several years under the contract, the league complied with the contract and provided proof of insurance coverage. The contract was renewed on a regular basis without the league's being asked for proof of insurance. Several years after the league had stopped providing proof of insurance, someone was seriously injured at the gym during league play. That person sued, and during the litigation process it was discovered that since the league had not been asked for proof of insurance for several years it had stopped purchasing insurance. Thus the gym was the only deep pocket, and the protection that the gym had intended to obtain via the contractual requirement for insurance did not exist.

Consideration is required for new or revised contracts. The pre-event preparation process involves numerous changes to the initial contract terms as new issues arise. For example, the number of reserved seats or personnel needed to work an event can change quickly. It is imperative to specify who is authorized to modify the contract and whether any new consideration is required. If new consideration is required, then any modification will in fact become a new contract, and this can become cumbersome. To prevent this problem, most contracts provide for modification, in writing, signed by both parties.

Government and Industry Regulations

Many governmental concerns need to be addressed before an event. Permits are a major issue, as some activities may not be allowed in certain facilities or certain parts of the city. The police, fire, and emergency units within the local, regional, state, or federal government units that may have jurisdiction, or may have a say in the event or facility, need to be contacted. Some events not only require contact with a government agency but also require personnel to be at an event. For example, the Arena at Harbor Yard in Bridgeport, Connecticut, has a special room with double cement walls to store fireworks for indoor shows. The state fire marshal sends someone to the facility on the event day to do a test run. Thus, each time fireworks are used, they are fired twice: once in the morning and then at the event itself, with specified fire and safety officials present both times.

Risk Management

Risks abound during an event. People can fall, run into others, get hit by projectiles (foul balls,

pucks), and sustain numerous other injuries. Many injuries can be prevented if risk management principles are adopted and practiced before an event. Ultimate responsibility for event safety needs to be determined from the very beginning of the contractual process. The facility needs to have a precontract or pre-event walk-through to make sure the facility is safe. Special care needs to be taken to check playing surfaces, bleachers, equipment, and other components to ensure that they do not represent a risk to potential users. Once the facility has been examined, photographs can be taken to document the facility's true condition before the event started.

Insurance

Insurance must be examined from several different perspectives. A facility that is leasing space out to other users or to a tenant must make sure that a current policy for at least $1 million in liability protection has been purchased. The insurance contracts should be examined on a yearly basis to make sure they are still current and that there have not been any major changes in the coverage. The event or team using the facility needs to purchase an appropriate insurance policy regardless of whether the facility requires one or not. The failure to purchase insurance coverage leaves the event or team owner or promoter open to so much potential liability that it does not make sense to run the event without insurance. Nevertheless, countless events and games occur each year without insurance coverage, and countless facilities run events without coverage. While many will never face a suit, the few that do are devastated financially.

Marketing

As covered in chapter 10, a facility or event needs to identify the target audience for a potential event and determine whether there are enough individuals in the greater demographic area who may wish to attend. A circus draws a family type of crowd whereas a wrestling event draws a different type of crowd. Are there enough families in the area? Do the families have available time—for example, is the event during the school year or over a three-day weekend? Do the families have enough money to afford the event? What could be the potential per cap sales for concession items? These are the types of issues a marketer needs to examine to determine whether or not to hold an event.

Numerous ancillary activities can be offered by a facility to market an event. These activities are offered to make the bid more attractive, but can be so diverse that grouping services, perks, and attractions together can make the package more appealing. Family oriented facilities are one example. Some facilities have family bathrooms that several people can enter together. Other facilities separate the rowdy fans from the family groups and tell families when they are buying tickets that they are being offered seats in areas that prohibit swearing. Other special services or amenities include the following:

- Nursery or day care
- Picnic areas
- Swimming pools and hot tubs
- Special dining areas accommodating children
- Slides, playgrounds, inflatables, and other play structures
- Preferred family parking
- Special Americans with Disabilities Act (ADA) facilities that do more than what is required by law
- Special facility tours
- On-site banking, dry cleaners, and other such services
- Specified autograph areas
- Special post offices for events to get stamps canceled

Advertising and Promotion

The primary marketing concern is typically bringing individuals to the facility as users or spectators. How will the event be communicated to these individuals? Is there an advertising/promotions budget? Will that budget allow for television, newspaper, or radio advertising? Will word of mouth be successful? Is there a co-sponsor/promoter who can help draw a large crowd? There are numerous techniques to sell tickets. An event can use trade-outs whereby a newspaper may give $10,000 worth of advertising space for $13,000 worth of tickets. While this does not necessarily translate to ticket sales, it does put people in the seats and

generates significant exposure through contests and giveaways.

Sponsorship

One of the critical elements within any marketing effort is obtaining sponsorship. Sponsors can range from name sponsors to minor sponsors who provide trade-out or a minor cash payment. Name sponsors, as the term implies, pay a certain sum to be the primary sponsor of the event, and their name is used to promote the event. This exchange of value provides the sponsor with visible recognition or community support. Examples include companies that have put their names on stadiums/arenas and events such as bowl games or major golf tournaments. The focus is on whether someone will receive just a promotional plug or rights. Commercial rights refer to options such as naming rights. Owning a right gives someone control. In contrast, a sponsor may not have as much in the way of rights and may be relegated to secondary status unless it is granted exclusivity.

Booking and Scheduling

Once all the pieces for the bid are in place, the bid is submitted. After the bid is submitted, it may be weeks to months, and in the case of the Olympics, years, before a decision is reached. Most cities and facilities do not bid on only one event; rather they are constantly bidding on various events, and they win some and lose most of the events they are trying to win. However, if they do win an event, they need to book it into their schedule to avoid any disruptions. Booking is the process of contractually finalizing an event on the schedule. When all the forms or contracts are completed, the event is recorded in such a way that all parties know the who, what, where, when, and why. The process requires more than just completing paperwork. The facility or the event may have to contact the media, local hotels, local attractions, the police, security companies, concessionaires, and a host of other parties to make sure everyone is ready for the event.

Scheduling requires examining how events interact with one another to avoid potential conflicts. The term "booking and scheduling" is often used in the industry, but the scheduling should always come first, as an event should

Facility Focus: Disney's Wide World of Sports Complex

© AP/World Wide Photos

In 1997, Disney opened a sports complex designed to help attract more families to Disney World. Components of the sports complex include the following:

- A field house
- A baseball stadium
- A baseball quadraplex
- Two youth baseball fields
- A track and field complex
- A softball quadraplex
- An 11-court tennis complex
- Four sport fields.

The entire facility was designed for comfort and enjoyment; for example, the seats for the baseball stadium are 21 inches (53 centimeters) wide versus an average of 18 to 19 inches (46-48 centimeters) for most other stadiums in the United States. The facilities are so nice that several major events such as Pop Warner Little Scholars moved their football championships to Disney, which brought thousands of families and kids to Disney-owned hotels and the theme park ("Disney's Wide World," 1998).

not be booked if there is a scheduling conflict that cannot be corrected. In fact, the booking process may uncover some wonderful symmetry between existing events and the proposed event that may enhance the value of the event and the credibility of the bid. On a college campus, for example, if parents' day and homecoming day occur on the same date as a night event that has been bid, there may be a natural audience for the night event.

Event Preparation

Once the event is scheduled, contracted for, and planned, the process of preparation begins. The facility must be ready for every event. For example, if a pool will be used, the chemicals must be checked; the water temperature needs to be adjusted (which means that all the heaters must be functioning); the filters must be operating; all safety equipment needs to be in place; all life guards need to be trained and ready; and the facility must be clean. Similar concerns apply to all facilities, regardless of the size or the event. Are there enough supplies such as toilet paper? Are all building systems functioning properly? Is the equipment properly maintained? Is the field or playing surface in good shape? These types of issues must be examined during pre-event operations and addressed before and during the event.

Facilities

The facility must be examined on a regular basis, but especially before a major event. Will the structural integrity of the facility be compromised by the addition of the weight of thousands of fans? Can the facility process enough air to be at an appropriate temperature/humidity level while allowing enough air exchanges per hour? Getting a facility ready can be as simple as cleaning the floor or much more complex, involving activities such as mowing lawns, painting lines, and preparing the infield.

No matter what elements are required to prepare a facility for an event, the process needs to be carefully planned. In one track and field competition in the Midwest, it appeared that all the issues had been covered. However, when participants arrived, it was discovered that the long jump pit had not been loosened; after several rainstorms and compaction, the pit was hard as rock. The event had to be delayed while a rototiller was rented to loosen the sand. While these types of problems may appear minor, they are a major concern for participants who have paid money and want the best available facility. How can preparation of a portion of a facility fall through the cracks? Without checklists identifying everything needed to get the facility ready, it is very easy to make a mistake. In fact, for the event in question, the jumping pits had been forgotten because the

event administrator had been busy with five other facilities where ancillary events were going on and did not realize that the pits were in such poor condition. A checklist could have reminded the event administrator about the small details. The extensive event safety checklist on pages 280-285 includes many concerns a facility manager should be aware of before, during, and after an event. A shorter pregame checklist that can help remind a facility manager about critical details to attend to is shown on page 285.

Sanitation

Every event produces waste. The waste comes in the form of water or sanitation or garbage. The facility should be examined to determine if there are any problems with drains or the septic system. A typical exercise involves bringing as many volunteers or employees together as possible and having them simultaneously flush the toilets. This exercise is designed to test the water pressure and to simulate what will occur during a major event, especially during intermissions.

An interesting exercise is to go to a facility and count the trash cans. In stadiums and arenas, tons of trash are produced by the fans. Preparation needs to be made to address the trash receptacle needs, recycling needs, and post-event trash needs. A significant amount of trash will not make it into the trash cans. Thus, the event planning process needs to include making sure there are enough trash cans, enough cleaning people, and enough sanitation supplies such as trash bags and brooms.

Ancillary Accommodations

Ancillary accommodations can range from additional office space to dorm rooms for participants. These facilities need to be secured, managed, and monitored to make sure they are functioning correctly. Ancillary facilities include living quarters, parking areas, dining areas, medical and first aid stations, outdoor rest rooms, and postal facilities.

Each facility that will be used needs to be examined to make sure it is functional, clean, and not dangerous. Security may be an issue in some areas, whereas other areas may require greater vehicular access for emergency vehicles or mail trucks. All facility areas used in an event must meet the event requirements.

Event Safety Checklist

Specific Event Concerns

Date _____ Name _____ Title _____ Number _____

Pre-Event Protocol

Who is responsible for providing security measures? _____

If security is outsourced, are there indemnity and hold-harmless provisions in the contract
to protect the facility?   Y N

1. Have an adequate number of security personnel been reserved for the event?   Y N
2. Is all safety equipment in place, such as padding behind basketball baskets?   Y N
3. Are the playing surfaces ready for their intended usage?   Y N
4. Are ancillary facilities (bathrooms, locker rooms, parking lots, concession areas, etc.)
   inspected before the event to detect problems?   Y N
5. Do you have a regularly updated security plan?   Y N
6. Do you modify the security plan for different types of events?   Y N
7. Do you have any emergency communication procedure in place?   Y N
8. Will staff members and volunteers need CPR certification?   Y N
9. Will an on-site defibrillator be used, and who is trained to use it? _____
10. Are there enough trash receptacles, and are they emptied properly and in a timely
    fashion?   Y N
11. Are pictures taken of the facility before an event (both general areas and key
    problematic areas)?   Y N

Event Protocol

12. Is a command center established for larger events?   Y N
13. Is the command center staffed during larger events?   Y N
14. Are weather conditions tracked, especially if inclement weather or lightning is
    expected or reported in the vicinity?   Y N
15. Is adequate supervision provided throughout the event (before, during, and after)?   Y N
16. Is adequate supervision provided for participants, including officials?   Y N
17. Is adequate supervision provided for spectators?   Y N
18. Is there a system in place to track keys?   Y N
19. Is there a system in place to avoid/prevent theft of office equipment and other
    property?   Y N
20. Will identification systems (such as photo IDs) be used at the event?   Y N
21. Will doors be monitored and will some doors have limited access?   Y N
22. Will event staff wear identifiable clothing/hats?   Y N

    Will there also be plainclothes event staff members circulating among the crowd?   Y N

Post-Event Protocol

23.	Do you hold post-event safety meeting(s) to discuss what occurred?	Y	N
24.	Do you have a relatively injury-free record concerning reported patron injuries?	Y	N
25.	Do you respond to patron complaints about safety concerns in a timely manner?	Y	N
26.	Do you take pictures of the facility after the event?	Y	N
27.	Do you analyze all incident and injury reports after an event?	Y	N
28.	Do you properly store and preserve reports after an event?	Y	N

Food Safety

Who is responsible for providing food at the event? _____

	Is there an indemnity and hold-harmless agreement with the food provider?	Y	N
29.	Do you have training for food preparation employees?	Y	N
30.	Do you offer training on how to utilize kitchen/service equipment?	Y	N
31.	Are all employees who work with cutting or cooking equipment over the age of 18?	Y	N
32.	Do you regularly check all refrigeration units to ensure they meet manufacturer recommendations?	Y	N
33.	Do you clean and disinfect all countertops and preparation surfaces before food preparation?	Y	N
34.	Do you clean and disinfect all countertops and preparation surfaces after food has been prepared?	Y	N
35.	Do you regularly clean equipment after usage?	Y	N
36.	Do you maintain compliance with OSHA requirements?	Y	N
37.	Do you consider yourself always ready for a health department inspection?	Y	N
38.	Are cutlery and other possibly dangerous equipment left lying around?	Y	N
39.	Is special training provided for employees that will work with slicing and cutting equipment?	Y	N
40.	Is special training provided for employees that will work with frying/boiling equipment?	Y	N
41.	Are all employees trained in proper hygiene rule compliance such as hairnets and hand washing?	Y	N
42.	Do all employees follow hygiene rules?	Y	N

Patron Movement Safety

43.	Do you provide training for ushers and security personnel?	Y	N
44.	Do you document that individuals have been trained in safety-related matters?	Y	N
45.	Have supervisors received additional training to make sure they are properly trained to both lead and instruct subordinates?	Y	N
46.	Have patron safety workers been trained on personal search concerns?	Y	N
47.	Have patron safety workers been trained on identifying suspicious behavior?	Y	N
48.	Do you check for patron safety before the event starts?	Y	N
49.	Do you check for patron safety after the event ends?	Y	N

(continued)

(continued)

50. Do you comply with the National Fire Protection Association (NFPA) standard of one trained crowd manager for each 250 patrons?   Y   N
51. Do you have an emergency evacuation plan?   Y   N
52. Do you practice the emergency evacuation plan?   Y   N
53. Do you have a prewritten statement to be read over the public address system in case of an emergency?   Y   N
54. Do you provide special accommodations for the disabled?   Y   N
55. Do you regularly check aisles for patron congestion?   Y   N
56. If aisles are congested, how do you clear the aisles and then ensure they stay clear? _____

_____

57. Are policies and procedures in place to prevent passing patrons overhead?   Y   N
58. Are policies and procedures in place to prevent fan migration?   Y   N
59. Do you utilize a command center to track crowd activities?   Y   N
60. Do you videotape the crowd to help detect and document problems?   Y   N
61. Do you prevent patrons from bringing in potential projectiles such as fruits, bottles, banners on sticks, etc.?   Y   N
62. Do you utilize a ticket dispute resolution process when duplicate tickets are issued?   Y   N
63. Do you have a coordinated safety meeting before the event including medical and police officials?   Y   N
64. Do you have a coordinated safety meeting after the event including medical and police officials?   Y   N
65. Are monitors in place to track line movement entering the facility?   Y   N
66. Are monitors in place to track line movement entering the rest rooms?   Y   N

Parking Lot Safety

67. Is there a parking lot attendant for lots greater than 300 spaces?   Y   N
68. Do you utilize video monitoring of the parking area?   Y   N
69. Do you regularly change the angles of the cameras to avoid creating identifiable patterns?   Y   N
70. Do you record images in a storable/retrievable manner?   Y   N
71. Are fake cameras also used (but not too many)?   Y   N
72. Do you utilize a parking lot attendant?   Y   N
73. Is there adequate line of sight for any attendant to see the lot?   Y   N
74. Does the attendant regularly patrol the lot?   Y   N
75. How frequently is the parking lot patrolled before an event? _____
76. How frequently is the parking lot patrolled during an event? _____
77. How frequently is the parking lot patrolled after an event? _____
78. Are lighting concerns addressed by having the light strength (in foot-candles) measured on a regular basis?   Y   N
79. Are there police/emergency contact boxes at the far reaches of lots (if applicable)?   Y   N
80. Is there adequate signage directing people to the facility and other locations?   Y   N
81. Is there adequate safety signage and "park at your own risk" signage?   Y   N
82. Is external access limited by fences or other means?   Y   N

83. Is additional security provided when the parking lot is in a neighborhood with a high crime rate?   Y   N

84. Do you track crime in the parking lot?   Y   N

85. Do you track accidents in the parking lot?   Y   N

86. Do you respond and make any program changes in response to increased crime or accidents?   Y   N

87. Do you monitor intoxicated fans heading to their cars?   Y   N

88. Do you provide assistance if someone has car trouble?   Y   N

89. Are there adequate ADA-accessible handicapped parking areas and clear travel routes?   Y   N

90. Are there adequate bus parking and safe movement areas for those leaving buses or waiting for buses?   Y   N

Transportation Safety

If you utilize your own fleet of vehicles:

91. Are the vehicles regularly serviced?   Y   N

92. Are the brakes in good condition?   Y   N

93. Are drivers properly trained?   Y   N

94. Do drivers follow basic vehicular safety regulations?   Y   N

95. Are drivers' backgrounds checked to make sure they are properly licensed and without any serious vehicular violations?   Y   N

Alcohol Service Concerns

96. Do you provide TEAM or other training opportunities for employees?   Y   N

97. Do you have a policy to stop sales after a set time such as the seventh inning at a baseball game?   Y   N

98. Do your concession personnel check IDs?   Y   N

99. Are employees trained in checking IDs?   Y   N

100. Are employees trained in identifying fake IDs?   Y   N

101. Do you offer a family friendly area where alcohol is not served?   Y   N

102. Do you provide extra security/police when alcohol is sold, served, or allowed?   Y   N

103. Do you work with any government authority to handle underage drinkers?   Y   N

104. Is there an alcohol policy statement concerning the protocols for all alcohol-related activities?   Y   N

105. Is the alcohol policy communicated through various means such as the scoreboard and game programs?   Y   N

106. Are rental contracts clear concerning policies for selling/serving alcohol?   Y   N

Criminal Deterrence

107. Do you conduct background checks for employees who will have direct contact with patrons?   Y   N

108. Do you take videos or other evidence of conduct in common areas?   Y   N

109. Do you take videos or other evidence concerning the conduct of those coming into the facility?   Y   N

(continued)

(continued)

110. Do you take videos or other evidence concerning those entering sensitive areas? Y N
111. Do you investigate local crime statistics on a regular basis? Y N
112. Do you meet with police on a regular basis to discuss deterrence strategies? Y N
113. Do you utilize plainclothes detectives/security personnel and uniformed security personnel to help deter potential criminal misconduct? Y N
114. Are lights adequate to illuminate dark areas? Y N
115. Are shrubs trimmed to eliminate hiding areas? Y N
116. Are employees provided with ID cards? Y N
117. Are ID cards checked at entryways to sensitive areas? Y N
118. Do you post adequate signage such as "No Loitering," "Crime Watch," "Punishment Notice," and similar warning signs? Y N
119. Can your security personnel be identified by clothing, hats, or location positioning? Y N
120. Do you utilize a reporting system for individuals to report any misconduct? Y N
121. Do you utilize a reporting system for individuals to report any employee misconduct? Y N

Terrorism Deterrence

122. Do you have a written bomb scare statement available for PA announcers to use? Y N
123. Do you have regular meetings with law enforcement personnel to discuss the prospects of terrorist activities? Y N
124. Do you practice mock drills to simulate response to disasters? Y N
125. Do you have a written policy statement and protocol for dealing with terrorist-related concerns? Y N
126. Is the policy statement distributed to relevant employees? Y N
127. Is the policy statement distributed to local government officials? Y N
128. Do the procedures indicate how to protect critical systems such as people transportation, backup generators, ventilation systems, etc.? Y N
129. Are backup phone, walkie-talkie, and/or mobile phone systems available? Y N
130. Are specially trained event staff members constantly looking for suspicious behavior? Y N
131. Are strong communication links established with the media to help communicate concerns? Y N
132. Are packages checked before being allowed in the facility? Y N
133. Are policies in place to monitor such packages? Y N
134. Are event personnel trained in checking packages? Y N
135. Are employees trained on body search concerns? Y N
136. Are patrons informed in advance about search policies? Y N
137. Are policies in place to allow patrons to receive a refund if they do not wish to be searched? Y N
138. Do you have a relatively injury-free record for workers' compensation claims? Y N

("Relatively" means that less than 5% of the workforce file workers' compensation claims each year.)

Comments

_____

_____

Score # Y _____ # N _____

If 0-15 Ns, the facility's safety communication program should be very effective.

If 16-30 Ns, then there is probably room for some improvements/planning.

If more than 30 Ns, the facility's risk management plan probably needs to be carefully scrutinized.

I attest to the fact that the completed checklist is true and correct and signed by me on this _____ day of _____.

_____
Signature

Pregame Checklist

Is parking available for VIPs, athletes, officials, entertainers, and spectators?

Are security personnel in place both inside and outside the facility?

Are bathrooms clean and well stocked?

Are locker rooms well equipped and clean, with all team supplies properly secured to prevent theft?

Are the will-call windows and other ticketing operations staffed and opened in a timely manner?

Are all entrances properly marked, staffed, and conveniently located?

Are special accommodations made available to those who might need them and are employees trained to recognize when someone might need assistance?

Is there an appropriate amount of change for ticketing, parking, and concessions operators?

Is the field or floor cleared from the last event?

Has all the trash been removed so the facility does not look like a dump?

Did the grounds crew arrive on time and complete all their tasks?

Are all the security personnel accounted for and properly positioned?

Is the press box clean, equipped with phone/data lines, and monitored by security to prevent unauthorized access?

Has food been ordered and delivered to the pressroom or designated area for the press and officials?

Have the scoreboard and public address system been tested to make sure they are operating correctly?

Are all concession (food/novelty/programs) stands properly stocked and situated to maximize revenue?

Are service trays for roving vendors prepared and ready to circulate?

Are enough garbage cans in place?

Are flags raised and is all ceremonial material ready for activities such as first pitch or national anthems?

Have lights been turned on with enough time so they can reach maximum efficiency when needed?

Behind the Scenes: Emergencies at the Meadowlands

© Norman Owen Tomalin/Bruce Coleman, Inc.

The New York/New Jersey Meadowlands is one of the premiere sport facilities in the United States. Right off highway I-95, the facility is located on a major thoroughfare to the biggest city in the United States. Thus any emergency in surrounding cities (such as accidents, derailments, or energy blackouts) will affect the facility, and an emergency at the Meadowlands will also affect traffic into cities.

When an event is canceled, all roadway graphics must flash appropriate messages to passing vehicles. Signs need to be posted at each toll plaza; toll plazas need to be blocked; toll collectors and parking lot attendants need to distribute preprinted cancellation notices and instructions; and the Port Authority needs to be notified. Management must also stop all ticket sales. Fans must be told to get refunds from the place where they purchased their tickets; any financial settlements need to be reviewed; and extra phone operators need to be hired to handle calls from fans and the media. The event security office must make sure that there is a force of security personnel to monitor the Meadowlands' perimeter.

Timing is critical when an emergency or an event cancellation occurs. For example, if an event is canceled right before it starts, all employees still need to be paid for a minimum of four hours. Thus, employees need to be told about a cancellation at least two hours before they were supposed to report to the facility. Even with ample notice, a number of fans will still show up at the gates. They must be told that the event is canceled, but some may want to use rest rooms or phones. Some people can be let in to the facility for limited purposes, such as use of rest rooms, if the facility is safe. Otherwise, individuals should be directed to portable bathrooms on the perimeter.

The event cancellation notice can read as follows:

"Ladies and gentlemen, we regret that for reasons beyond our control, tonight's event has been canceled. For further information regarding these events and refund procedures, please look for announcements in tomorrow's newspaper or listen to local stations. Parking vouchers will be distributed to each driver at the plaza as you exit the parking lot" (Perkins, 1998).

Such a notice will not prevent fans from getting upset. Even with a notice, additional security and precautions are needed to prevent distraught fans from taking their frustrations out on the facility.

Emergency Planning

At any facility, an emergency action plan must be researched and developed before a disaster occurs. Since no one knows when a disaster may occur, a disaster plan must be developed before every event. In order for an emergency plan to be activated, managers must look into all potential threats and plan what actions would happen if they were to occur. A risk evaluation matrix can help establish this. The risk evaluation matrix is a chart that identifies the most realistic threats to a business and helps prioritize a response and backup plans. A group of emergency coordinators including management, human resources, information technology staff, and security should be appointed or assigned to develop the matrix. After the coordinators and matrix are in place, a recovery plan can be developed. A backup plan with backup personnel needs to be created in case any emergencies arise that alter the primary plan. The plans should be documented; and after the local fire and police personnel are informed about the plan, the plan is tested as a means to appropriately train personnel (Bassett, 2002).

Equipment and Warehousing

One of the often overlooked components of an event is making sure there are enough supplies and that the supplies are stored in an easily accessible location. It is difficult to store several thousand rolls of toilet paper in a convenient location. Thus, space needs to be set aside for storing supplies that will be used during the event and for items that need to be placed out of the way. For example, in an arena, significant storage space is required for extra chairs, dasher boards, portable floors, forklifts, trucks, carts, tractors, refrigeration units, mechanical equipment, spare parts, and a host of other items.

Communication and Technology Systems

While a significant amount of wiring is now included in buildings as they are being built, many smaller or older facilities are not properly wired for communication or technology needs. If a facility is wired, then all the connectors and junction boxes need to be examined to make sure that outlets and phone lines are working. Although the bid process for larger events may require proper wiring, most facilities wait to install any such wiring, if needed, until after they have won the bid because then they can justify the expenditure.

The sound system and scoreboard need to be tested before an event. Are any lights burned out? Are all speakers properly aligned? Does the PA announcer have a prewritten script for announcing emergencies? Can the system become overloaded? What backup system is in place if power is lost or there is an emergency? These are the types of questions that need to be researched and answered before an event.

Media

One of the primary concerns with the media is making sure they have access to the facility. Media kits and credentials should be developed for the invited press. Uninvited press also need to be considered, along with the steps that will be taken if uninvited media representatives attend the event. Every event should expect both invited and uninvited press.

A pressroom needs to be developed with appropriate communication outlets and computer hookup stations. There also should be an area for serving food to the press, since providing food for the press is an industry standard. There should be refrigeration, outlets for coffee makers,

© Empics

The media are an important component of sporting facilities. It's important to make sure the press box and press rooms are well organized and equipped with necessary outlets and computer hookup stations.

and possibly a sink to help serve the food and allow for easier cleanup.

Another pre-event concern is appropriate lighting. Lighting for still photographs is not too critical because of flash cameras. However, television broadcasts require very specific lighting that sometimes means it is necessary to purchase or rent additional lights. Also, some seats need to be "killed," or kept empty, due to camera platforms and line-of-sight requirements to get the best shots.

Box Office and Ticketing

Tickets can be distributed through phone sales, ticket windows, the Internet, ticket brokers, mail orders, or even kiosks or sales buses. While pre-event ticket sales are often part of the event marketing efforts, the facility also needs to be aware of various concerns affecting ticket distribution and sales on the day of the event. For example, what rules regulate scalping in and around the facility? Is there to be a "will-call" window, and which tickets will be placed there? What identification or other procedures are used to monitor ticket distribution at will-call windows? Will day-of-the-event tickets be sold and how? Will there be ticket lines in front of the ticket windows, and will these lines interfere with people entering the facility? These are the types of questions about ticket operations that arise before an event.

The answers to these questions depend on the municipality and the facility. For example, if there are numerous will-call tickets, it may be necessary to set up several will-call windows, perhaps outside the entrance gate to avoid overcrowding by the entrance. Screening that slows people down at the front gate may minimize lines at ticket windows since they all have to wait in line to be searched before entering the facility.

Security

The need to protect assets, money, participants, and fans is paramount for any event. A successful security plan must be developed months or years before an event. The threat of terrorist activities at the Olympics forces organizers to spend years developing security systems and a security force. Pre-event security issues are primarily associated with crowd management and can include the following:

- When will the event start? Crowds do not have as much time to drink before early events, whereas an evening weekend event can lead to more problems resulting from pre-event drinking.
- Will traffic patterns affect how crowds arrive?
- Will the event be on a holiday such as Easter, when a different crowd can be expected?
- Have there been prior problems with the event? Is the event a touring event that had problems at a prior stop?
- Are event participants known for getting a crowd riled, such as a rock band that encourages mosh pit activity and crowd surfing, even if such activities are not allowed in the facility?
- Will the crowd be large and will it exceed the facility's capacity?
- What experience does the event administrator or facility manager have?
- What experience does the security company have?
- What are the weather conditions, and what will happen if rain forces fans to scurry for cover?
- Can the will-call and press areas be moved away from the front entrance to avoid crowding?
- How will alcohol sales affect the audience?

Parking and Transportation

Before an event is scheduled, all parking options must be examined. For example, will individuals park on surface streets or in a garage? Will there be an impact on local traffic or neighborhoods? Some neighbors do not mind a major event since it is an opportunity to sell parking spaces in front of their house or on their property. Other residents may be annoyed about the traffic and complain to local officials.

Is the parking lot area fenced in? Is there a significant amount of crime in the neighborhood that may spill into the parking area? Will there be tailgate parties in the parking lot? When will people show up for tailgate parties? How many disabled parking spaces are there, and how many will be needed? Parking attendants will need to be hired and in place several hours before the event begins. Since traffic-related concerns frequently lead to disgruntled fans, a facility should emphasize proper signage and ease of movement to accelerate parking and exit strategies.

Buses and shuttles are often used to transfer spectators and participants from one area to another, particularly with large or remote parking lots to help people get from the parking lots to the facility. Buses and shuttles are often used to transport participants and officials from their hotels to a facility. At The Ohio State University, buses transporting both the home team and the opponents for football games drove down a fraternity- and sorority-lined street where the fans could cheer and boo the players. This created an event within an event and a significant amount of tradition. The trip also was a logistical challenge, since all cars had to be moved from the street, police escorts had to be in place, and crowd management strategies had to be implemented.

Concessions and Food Service

Numerous regulations must be followed in order for food to be served. The area of health and safety regulations is dictated by local, state, and federal governments; and if these regulations are violated, there are significant penalties. All food vendors need to have proper licensing from all pertinent regulatory agencies. For example, municipal health departments need to be contacted to make sure the concession areas comply with all local regulations. This may require compliance with fire, plumbing, electrical, and health-related codes and compliance protocols. For example, sinks are required whenever raw food is being handled, and local codes can dictate how far away the sink can be from the preparation area. Private businesses and venues are also governed by the Occupational Safety and Health Administration (OSHA) regulations and rules concerning children working with sharp objects and dangerous equipment pursuant to the Fair Labor Standards Act.

Issues that affect operating a concession area include the location of the stand, the spatial dimensions, the equipment being used, and the type of food served (Sherman, 1998). The location of a concession stand can be anything from a table to a permanent location within a venue. A table or temporary stand may be used in situations such as high schools, community centers, colleges, and even small venues. Tables and stands can be used to serve bottled drinks, prepackaged foods, and in some cases prepared sandwiches. On the other hand, venues that have built concessions into the physical structure have the opportunity to sell fresh and hot food more conveniently through the ability to utilize electrical outlets rather than the generators required for mobile carts.

Spatial dimensions of concession areas help determine the food served at a venue. Concession stands should have a sanitary prep area, a cooking area, and a warming area. Also, if there is any raw food preparation, there must be a sink for hand washing. In the larger stands, fire codes and the amount of power allocated to the area define the safe level of equipment usage. If the equipment that will be used requires a greater electrical load, different equipment or new wiring/transformers may be needed.

Planners should remember that concessions can make or break an event depending on the organization, location, and foods served (Sherman, 1998). Every organization has its own unique food-related issues. Whether regarding menus or training of employees, policies and procedures must be developed. Is the primary focus revenue generation or service? Is the organization more interested in ease and convenience or in complicated, expensive items that generate more income? For example, the revenue from luxury suite food is much greater on a per person basis than that from spending by average fans. Thus, the facility needs to determine where the emphasis will be for its concessions program.

Pacific Bell Park in San Francisco is one stadium where the concessions cater to the city's diversity. Tacos are just one of the many different cuisines offered.

Recent Food and Concession Trends Across North America

Foods and drinks directed to female purchasers, such as low-calorie or nonalcoholic drinks

Low-fat food for health-conscious fans

Bundling various food items such as a drink, a hamburger, and fries at one low price

Greater emphasis on marketing before the event so people know what types of foods are available in advance

Theatrics such as open kitchens where customers can see their food being cooked

From "Trends driving foodservice at sports and entertainment venues," 1997.

Additional concessions policy concerns include training employees to use hairnets, gloves, slicers, and other equipment. Alcohol management, from knowing when to cut off beer sales to how to spot fake IDs, also requires significant employee training.

Most employers do not promote the fact that they use inexperienced or cheap labor. Facilities often have numerous young employees who are eager to work at certain events. However, experts suggest asking employees under age 15 to work a maximum of 20 hours a week to avoid high turnover numbers (Emmons, 2001). There also are a number of state and federal laws that limit how many hours teenagers can work, how late they can work on school nights, and what types of jobs they can undertake.

Food-related concerns can also become policy-related concerns. For example, should condiments be provided in pumps, which are cheaper to purchase than other types of containers, but are messy and hard to clean? In contrast, packets, which are more expensive, are easier to store and manage but cause more wastage when people take too many, and can be a hazard when people drop them on the ground. Similarly, while it may be more convenient to offer only two drink sizes, statistics show that having four drink sizes generates the greatest profit level (Emmons, 2001).

The food preparation and service areas should be built based on the proposed menu (Emmons, 2001). When buying the equipment for a concession area, the facility manager should ask the salesperson for 50% off the list price. The facility should ask for references to see who else uses the equipment in order to find out if others have any trouble with the equipment. Care should be taken to make sure that the reference is not getting a kickback from the equipment seller (Emmons, 2001).

Food service locations should be designed for speed and flexibility. The more quickly food gets from the preparation area to the service/sales area, the lower the chances of having problems. Outdoor locations present unique challenges such as rodents and bugs. Therefore outdoor food areas are inspected more frequently than indoor facilities. Food kept outdoors needs to be covered, and the refrigerator has to be cold enough and the heater hot enough to comply with all applicable health codes.

Food-related concerns before an event often center around what food to sell. Every facility has a unique menu based on the type of facility, region, the local fans, and even the event itself. A health club, for example, typically offers a health-oriented menu because of its clientele. A ballpark in New York may have to offer more variety to handle the broad array of fans than a park in Kansas City or Pittsburgh that may have more traditional fare. Interesting recent food and concession trends in North America are listed above.

Before an event, the facility marketing staff needs to survey what foods may bring the best sales results with the least amount of work. All food items should be either packaged or interchangeable. Packaged products reduce preparation time, and items such as nachos can now be purchased in individual packets requiring only that the cheese be microwaved. Even if convenience food is used, the process should be examined to make sure that food is not wasted. For example, not every 50-pound bag of popcorn is the same; some types of kernels pop more thoroughly, which generates additional revenue (Cohen, 1994b). "Interchangeable foods" refers to crossover foods that can be used in several dishes. Ingredients become expensive and hard to store if they are not used for several different dishes. Thus, if lettuce cannot be used for multiple dishes served at the event, it should not be used since it is expensive and does not have a long shelf life.

Alcohol

If liquor will be served, proper procedures must be in place, including obtaining a liquor license. Employees need to be trained on how to know when a customer is visibly intoxicated and how to spot underage drinking; they should be able to tell when spectators bring in their own beverages and should be familiar with ejection policies. Two nationally recognized alcohol training organizations are Training for Intervention Procedures (TIPS) and Techniques for Effective Alcohol Management (TEAM). Having either of these organizations train alcohol servers and management will help create a more successful alcohol strategy and serve as a useful risk management tool for all events. Beer distributors can be a good source of additional help in developing an alcohol sales program. Their clout in the area can be used to help the facility through proper training, advertising, their knowledge of government regulations, and their extensive political contacts.

Emergency Services

In addition to analyzing safety concerns, the facility should examine its existing emergency plans. Emergency plans for many facilities are very old, incomplete, or just inaccurate. A facility cannot respond to an emergency if it does not have enough of the necessary emergency response equipment. A facility also needs to have properly trained individuals capable of implementing the emergency plan.

Prior to an event, the facility should examine local fire and police departments, as well as ambulance companies, to evaluate response times and the medical attention they can provide. Local emergency crews should be familiar with the venue in order to make an efficient response. Often an **emergency medical technician (EMT)** crew visits a site before an event to familiarize themselves with the location and to become knowledgeable about the quickest routes around the facility and to local

hospitals, as some roads may be blocked for the event. Major injuries that require transportation to a hospital should be taken to the closest hospital. All medical situations, regardless of their severity, should be recorded in either the security log or a medical log. There is the possibility of lawsuits with any medical injury, and documentation will be crucial to help defend against such claims. The documentation should focus on the injury, facts about the incident, witness statements, and the actions taken.

In the event of a major injury, communication is the key to getting a quick response. Facility staff (excluding concessions and other services) and security need to be able to communicate by two-way radios, walkie-talkies, or cell phones. Instructions for medical personnel and patrons should be posted to indicate medical stations, emergency phones, and emergency exits.

Medical Services

Prior to an event a medical response team must be in place. With the possibility of an accident, all levels of medical response should be included in the development of an emergency action plan. Starting with first responders, facility staff should be certified in first aid, CPR (cardiopulmonary resuscitation), and AEDs (defibrillators). A medical station should be set up in a common location, possibly next to the security command post. With first responders and a triage program in place, an event is ready for basic cuts, bruises, and minor injuries.

Summary

The process of competing to bring events to a facility can be cut-throat. Facilities with existing tenants and a solid reputation do not need to struggle the way smaller facilities do. The battle to land events is not unique to sport facilities; convention centers have to fight the same battles. Facilities can reduce the time and cost associated with the bidding process if they develop a template that responds to most informational matters requested in typical bid packets.

Once a bid is pursued, a facility needs to garner all the appropriate personnel, resources, and strategies to help win the bid. Once the bid is won, a facility needs to deliver on everything that was promised, from having appropriate personnel to ensuring marketing and financial success. A facility manager spends a majority of his or her time finalizing all the details before an event. The most important area that cannot be left to last-minute planning is security-related concerns as discussed in the next chapter.

DISCUSSION QUESTIONS AND ACTIVITIES

1. What would be the key steps to consider if you are thinking about renting your facility to a potential user for an event?

2. What would you recommend as a potential new concession item that might be the next big rage?

3. Develop a sample bid package specifying what you would want a health club to offer in order to host a bodybuilding competition.

4. Examine the bid process undertaken by the Salt Lake City Olympics organizing committee. What steps did they have to take to win the event? What ethical concerns arose from the event?

FIFTEEN

Implementing a Security Plan

CHAPTER OBJECTIVES

After completing this chapter you will be able to do the following:

- Appreciate that fans need a safe facility but often contribute to making the facility dangerous
- Apply specific security management strategies to make facilities and events safer
- Understand how crowd mentality can affect an individual's judgment about engaging in inappropriate conduct
- Describe the steps involved in implementing a crowd management program
- Understand how alcohol affects individuals and crowds
- Understand the steps that need to be followed in order to respond to a crisis

Fan-related "extracurricular" activities have been a part of athletic events for decades. In the 1970s, fans entered the field to congratulate Hank Aaron after he had hit his 715th home run. Morganna the Kissing Bandit tantalized audiences with her on-field shenanigans. Eventually such activities became less benign as fans rushed onto fields or courts to tear down goal posts or steal a memory such as a towel or chair. In the 21st century the antics became more sinister as fans actually attacked players, coaches, and referees.

As noted in chapter 2, the primary directive for any public assembly facility manager is safety. Safety applies to employees, participants, and guests and spectators. Employee safety is covered by requirements such as Occupational Safety and Health Administration (OSHA) regulations or provisions within a collective bargaining agreement. Participants are informed of concerns and asked to sign waivers and consent forms; and coaches, players, and officials are often provided significant protection by uniformed officers, for example. Guests and spectators are the group that often requires the greatest effort since they are the most unpredictable. No facility manager can anticipate how anyone or everyone will react. All it takes is one person to possibly set off a mob. This chapter addresses these types of concerns and provides solutions for dealing with crowd-related issues.

Through engaging in specific actions or developing appropriate plans and strategies for particular situations, a facility can prepare for the worst, so people know that if the worst occurs they are ready. The key topics covered in this chapter include the nature of security, the elements of a security program, entry/exit management, fan education, alcohol management, and responding to crisis situations.

What Is Security?

Security can include the process of safeguarding an item, person, or place. Facility management involves protecting all of these. Items that need to be secured can range from facility vehicles and scoreboards to playing equipment and even attached bleachers. A facility may have many valuable items that are needed to operate effectively. A typical larger spectator facility may have 200 to 500 televisions. The facility's operation depends on the security of such items.

People also need to be secured. Every large crowd presents different security concerns, from pickpockets to drunken brawlers. Smaller facilities have the same problems. How does a facility react to a fight in the parking lot over a parking space? How would a facility respond if a health club member stole something from someone else's locker? Numerous crowd-related problems have arisen in stadiums or arenas when jubilant or distraught fans took the law into their own hands.

- Detroit suffered significant criminal activities in the 1980s involving baseball fans.
- Soccer games in Europe are regularly impacted by hooligan activities both in and around soccer stadiums.
- After the 1986 World Series, rioting fans left one dead, 80 injured, 41 arrested, and more than $100,000 in damages.
- After the Cleveland Browns' last home game in 1995, the infamous "Dawg Pound" erupted as fans vandalized the facility by destroying bleachers to bring home souvenirs (Fried 2004b).
- A street reveler was killed at a Boston Red Sox celebration in 2004 when she was hit in the eye by a projectile filled with pepper spray that was designed to be a nonlethal weapon.

The final category of security needs entails the place or facility itself. Closed-circuit TVs (CCTVs) are frequently used in sport facilities to deter vandalism and graffiti. However, these cameras can also pick up criminal conduct on the part of employees. These devices represent just one technique used to protect a facility. Other techniques that can help secure a facility and its users include the use of security guards, bomb-sniffing dogs, turnstiles, pre-event screening, and metal detectors.

While crowd security is the security issue that is most commonly researched and publicized, issues such as that of workplace violence arise much more often. Thus, a facility manager also needs to examine security from a broader perspective. Additionally, facility managers are not doing their job if they prevent security problems inside the facility but fail to prevent violence in the areas outside the facility, such as the street or parking lot, where the results could be more serious. Through proper planning, many of the security and safety problems that have arisen over the years could have been prevented.

Regardless of the security-related concern being analyzed, a facility manager should utilize the ECT approach (see chapter 13). By identifying the various safety challenges—from keeping the crowd safe to dealing with criminals—a facility manager can develop appropriate strategies to combat potential problems before, during, and after an event.

Security Management

The key to proper security management is **foreseeability.** Cases brought against facilities often allege claims such as poor lighting, missing or broken light bulbs, weak locks, no access control, poorly trained guards, or poor management policies (Gordon and Brill, 1996). The civil cases reported to date primarily relate to crowd management and crowd supervision matters. One key case involving the failure to prevent a fan stampede was the 1983 case of *Bowes v. Cincinnati Riverfront Stadium,* which was brought after 11 fans were trampled to death at a Who concert. The court concluded that the facility was liable under negligence and other theories because it was foreseeable that injuries would occur with the chosen seating arrangement. The facility had utilized a **general seating** arrangement in which the first people into the facility had the first seat choice.

Notice is the key requirement for proving foreseeability. In a suit stemming from a brawl during a 1980 AC/DC concert, for example, the concert promoter claimed that there was no notice because no unruly behavior, fighting, or drinking had been observed that would indicate a potential problem. Even though the arena had no prior problems, the court concluded that the promoter was on notice because a police officer had investigated prior tour stops and was informed of various problems including drunk, rowdy, and drug-affected crowds at past concerts (Fried, 2004b).

When a facility manager is equipped with information concerning possible criminal conduct, a duty arises to provide proper warning and protection. Factors that courts examine when evaluating security precautions include the following:

- What is the nature of the facility (for example, is it a college facility that will attract a lot of single women who might need to be protected/escorted at night)?
- Do security personnel follow their assigned patrols?
- Are security records properly taken and stored?
- Does the facility utilize standard/customary security precautions?
- Does the facility manager have experience in crime prevention and security protocols?
- What is the facility's location? (Gordon and Brill, 1996)

Almost every facility will have some foreseeable security concerns. These can be as mundane as kids stuffing toilets with paper to flood a floor or as serious as union members sabotaging a facility during a strike. Proper security planning entails appropriately trained security personnel, an appropriately sized security force, understanding building safety requirements, utilizing the most appropriate security equipment, and security planning strategies. These elements are discussed in the following sections.

Security Staff Training

The best means of obtaining appropriate security personnel is to hire people with security training. Some states require security personnel to be trained and even licensed. Licensure is especially important if a security person will carry a weapon. Security personnel such as ushers and gate attendants should not carry arms, as this may create a greater risk than if they had no weapons. Because of concerns associated with weapon misuse and inappropriate training, many larger facilities need to have police or off-duty police on the premises.

Other facilities utilize private security companies and incorporate in the contract a requirement that all security personnel be appropriately trained.

Regardless of who is providing the facility security, all security personnel should be properly trained to accomplish their specific tasks. There is no one correct method to train security personnel. However, since security personnel are actively involved with patrons and employees, it is imperative that they have a significant amount of training in interpersonal communication and dispute resolution. They also need to be trained in the facility's policies and procedures. This is especially important for part-time security personnel who are working for four or five different facilities, each with different policies and procedures.

The need for training applies also to nonsecurity personnel. In fact, every employee or volunteer is in essence a security person. Receptionists are normally not considered security persons, but they represent the first line of defense and therefore also need to be properly trained. Maintenance staff may be a valuable source of information as they are often in a position to observe unusual activity (e.g., someone casing the facility). Thus, all employees and others such as volunteers working at the facility need training.

Training is often undertaken on the job. Security personnel frequently have a minimal amount of formal training but do have real-life experience. Nevertheless, a facility cannot rely on random life experiences but needs to have a formal education program. Thus, most facilities offer some type of training, whether it involves reading, classes, or

© AP/World Wide Photos

Visible security personnel are vital to any facility. However, these personnel must have formal training to be maximally effective.

hands-on learning. The four phases of training that security personnel should receive are orientation, site-specific, ongoing, and advanced training (Morris, 2004).

Orientation training occurs when a security person or any other employee is hired. The material covered can include administrative issues such as break times, clock-in/clock-out procedures, overtime schedules, and change of shifts. Orientation training that relates to security can cover workplace violence, the use of pepper spray, protective services policies, and assertiveness training.

Site-specific training focuses on how to handle specific security protocols, with detailed examples showing how forms are completed. This phase also includes on-the-job training. This phase can include stints working at security gates, entrances, command posts, and other strategic positions.

Ongoing training includes refresher training. Such training may focus on new technology or techniques. Many facilities use weekly meetings at which employees are updated on security concerns. Weekly training can be very informal, with people reviewing recent industry articles or news stories about upcoming events and security issues raised at other facilities.

Advanced training may include managerial courses and other programs that may lead to certification. Certification categories include certified facility manager (CFM), crime prevention specialist (CPS), and certified protection professional (CPP), among many others. These certificates are offered by various trade associations such as the IAAM.

Other training options include the following:

- Basic training, which focuses on providing information such as where supplies are located and what forms need to be completed to purchase items.

- Team exercises, which focus on having employees work together to accomplish a mutual goal.

- **Tabletop exercises,** which analyze how team members (including leaders) would respond in a crisis. Some facilities make a scale model of the facility to identify in 3-D where people should be situated and how people might move within the facility.

- Functional exercises can test equipment systems such as the emergency backup generator.

- In walk-through exercises, personnel act out what they would actually do if an emergency occurred.

- In simulation exercises, an attack or disaster is simulated in real time or at half-speed, and the results are analyzed to improve execution the next time the test is run or for when an emergency actually occurs.

It should be noted that no book can explain how to respond to 500 terrified fans trying to leave a small area through one exit. The panic, fear, and anxiety cannot be duplicated and need to be experienced in order for people to truly learn and apply security-related knowledge. Nevertheless, while safety and security drills such as fire or earthquake drills are "make-believe," they provide significant insight into how to manage emergency situations. As shown by the studies discussed later in the chapter, industry research, experience, and mock drills have given experts valuable information about how people exit buildings, a critical component of crowd management.

One component of the training process entails examining what other facilities are doing. For example, some facilities are using older women as frontline contacts during the inspection and crowd contact components of a crowd management plan. While some event guests may be rude and argumentative with younger security personnel, these same individuals may act differently in front of older women. Even if a fan was drunk, would he or she try to hit a grandmother? This idea along with the resulting implementation of senior ushers has been successful at several facilities in Europe and the United States.

Security Staff Size

The number of security personnel or police must be adequate to secure the facility. The force must match the needs of the event and the type of crowd that will be present. The Los Angeles Police Department put 4,000 officers on the streets during the 1984 Summer Olympic Games. The 1996 Summer Olympic Games utilized Atlanta's 1,550-member police force, volunteer security professionals from around the world, and over 11,000 soldiers to complete the security staff numbering nearly 20,000 (Fried, 2004b).

Having enough security personnel is critical for resolving any disturbance in a large crowd. The Rid-

Behind the Scenes: Soccer Hooliganism

Hooliganism in sport facilities emerged during the 1960s in Britain. It initially was an outgrowth of social, class, religious, regional, or racial antagonism. However, this flame was also fueled by poorly designed stadiums, inadequate fan segregation, insufficient crowd management policies and practices, and poor ticketing allocation and distribution systems (Goss, 2003). Some researchers feel that hooliganism is just a form of patriotism or loyalty taken to an extreme, while others feel that it is a portrayal of a class struggle and allows the poor and disenfranchised a means to act out as a group and have safety in numbers.

dick Bowe versus Andrew Golota fight at Madison Square Garden provides an example. The postfight melee, which started in the ring before spreading into the stands, resulted in 22 injuries and 16 arrests (McShane, 1996). Eighteen New York City police officers were assigned to patrol outside the arena; but the Garden and event promoter were responsible for internal security, which consisted of 70 security officers and 50 ushers. Some commentators claimed that the melee could have been prevented or would have been less serious if additional security forces composed of uniformed police officers had been used inside the arena.

There is no clear-cut standard for the number of security personnel needed to staff any event or facility. Among the potential industry standards for fire prevention and safety developed by the National Fire Protection Association (NFPA) is one that applies to the number of crowd management professionals. According to *NFPA Life Safety Handbook* (Cote and Harrington, 2003), there should be one trained crowd management professional for every 250 fans in any facility that accommodates over 250 people.

Some of those who commented on the incident in Madison Square Garden pointed to poor training on the part of the security force, arguing that if the security personnel had known their roles the dispute would not have gotten out of hand and would not have lasted as long. Clearly the number

of security personnel and the amount and quality of training are both critical. A trained crowd management professional must understand crowd management issues and concepts, which will be discussed later in the chapter.

Building Codes

Building codes serve as guidelines to help develop and construct safer facilities. As discussed in connection with facility design (chapter 5), building codes are adopted by government entities to make sure a facility is constructed in the safest manner possible. The codes outline "best practices" for building, but they also come into play after construction, since facilities may need to be modified to comply with changes in codes. Inspection by fire marshals may also indicate that a facility must make structural or policy modifications.

Just as the law changes over time, building codes change frequently as research and public sentiment dictate. For example, the current standard model for stairs requires 22 inches (56 centimeters) of space from side to side to provide room for a person to move. This formula led to the development of stairways that are 44 inches (1 meter) wide to allow two people to be on the same tread at the same time. However, these numbers do not take into consideration the various ways people move on steps. People usually do not require as much room going up stairs, but need more than 22 inches of space moving down stairs. This can be seen in the shift and sway of people on stairs. The issue of stair width came into play in the World Trade Center tragedy as people going down the stairways had to stop and turn to the side so firefighters with gear could go up (Newman, 2002). However, to date no standards relating to stair width have been changed, so a 44-inch-wide stairway meets code requirements.

Tragic events can also lead to new ways of examining building construction and renovation needs. In light of the World Trade Center attacks, changes in design were proposed for a new 7 World Trade Center. Proposals included using a concrete building core (vs. steel and drywall, which does not protect against flying debris), having fire stairwells at opposite ends of the building, pressurizing stairwells to prevent smoke from entering them when fire doors are opened, and developing fire-resistant corridors on lower floors ("Safety," 2003).

The NFPA regulations provide potential guidelines for sport facilities. The 2002 standards that apply to facilities used for gatherings of 50 or more people are as follows (the number of the rule in *NFPA Life Safety Handbook* is given in parentheses) (Cote and Harrington, 2003):

- Occupancy load (number of people in a given area) for a facility with less than 10,000 square feet (930 square meters) should be no more than one person every 5 square feet (0.46 square meters) (13.1.7.1).

- Facilities with more than 10,000 square feet shall not exceed one person for every 7 square feet (0.65 square meters) (13.1.7.1).

- Turnstiles are not allowed if they interfere with exiting (13.2.2.2.7).

- If there are more than 6,000 people in the facility there need to be at least three stairways, and if there are more than 9,000 people there need to be at least four exits (13.2.4.2).

- Festival seating is prohibited unless there are less than 250 seats, there is a life safety plan, an evaluation has been performed, there is lawn seating with a lot of room, and security has the ability to access people (13.2.5.4.1).

- Aisles between seats need to have at least 12 inches (30 centimeters) of clear space from the front of a seat to the back of the seat in front of it (13.2.5.5.2).

- There can be no more than 100 seats in any row (13.2.5.5.2).

- Openings on footboards can be no greater than 1/2 inch (1.2 centimeters) (13.2.5.5.6).

- Dead-end aisles cannot extend beyond 20 feet (6 meters) (13.2.5.6.2).

- Since the 18 inches (46 centimeters) of spacing per patron is minimal, there exists the likelihood that people will extend their bodies into aisles, which requires facilities to increase aisle widths (13.2.5.6.3).

- The minimum stair rise for aisles is 4 inches (10 centimeters), and the maximum rise is 8 inches (20 centimeters). High risers reduce movement speed especially when people are descending (13.2.5.6.6).

- Railings need to be provided for ramped aisles with a gradient exceeding 1 in 12, and aisle stairs also require railing. The railing should have a gap every three rows and a maximum gap not exceeding every five rows so that people can get to and from their seating without having to loop around too many steps (13.2.5.6.7).

- There should be contrasting material 1 to 2 inches (2.5-5 centimeters) wide on each tread nose (13.2.5.6.8).

- The travel distance to any exit cannot exceed 150 feet (46 meters), or 200 feet (61 meters) if the facility has fire suppression sprinklers (13.2.6).

- Railing needs to be greater than 36 inches (91 centimeters) in height if the foot of the aisle has a fall to the ground of more than 30 inches (76 centimeters). Cross-aisles should have railing equal to or greater than 26 inches (66 centimeters) in height if there are no seat backs for the seats in front of that cross-aisle (13.2.11.1.6).

- Fire alarms are needed for all facilities with more than 300 people (13.3.4.1).

- Life safety evaluations (these are complex written reports analyzing hundreds of potential concerns) need to be performed and a written assessment approved annually (13.4.1).

Technology

Proper training and adequate personnel are complemented by high-tech security mechanisms. The 1996 Summer Olympic Games utilized over 1,000 video cameras, technology that scanned handprints of people who wanted to access residential areas, and radio frequency fields that were programmed to scan an employee's identification card and allow access to an area only if the identification card was approved for that area.

Video security is increasingly deployed to monitor student sections as well as police arrest procedures (Fried, 2004b). Closed-circuit television systems have significantly advanced since the 1980s and are so refined today that they can take pictures from any part of the stadium and zoom in on any particular fan. This technology is changing rapidly; the photophone, for example, combines CCTV technology with the ability to transfer images anywhere for immediate access and assistance. A photo can be taken in a command center and sent digitally to an usher or security person. In the future, these systems might be expanded to include smell, hearing, and touch (Goss, 2003).

Technological advancements have also resulted in new products that would not have been considered years ago. **Biometric scanning** (scanning a person's hand or retina) and facial recognition programs and systems are also being deployed more frequently at large stadiums and events such as the Super Bowl. A doctor has recently developed a new weapon in crowd management: a scent-based defensive mechanism utilizing manufactured foul scents to help dispel a crowd. Using scents named Stench Soup, Burned Hair, and Bathroom Malodor, the idea would be to spray the foul-smelling material on an unruly crowd, which would then disperse to avoid the odor or the spray itself ("Give Em a Stench," 2003).

Other Security Strategies

Animals are being utilized more frequently in the crowd management area. The animals most commonly used are horses and dogs. Horse-mounted security details can quickly respond to incidents throughout a facility. Secondly, horses position officers above the crowd so it is easier for them to see. Lastly, when horses are backed into a crowd, fans start moving. It is one thing for a drunk fan to argue with a security officer; it is another thing for the fan to see the derriere of a large horse approaching. There is no way to negotiate with a horse, and if horses kick they can cause significant injury. This is why officers turn horses around in a crowd; it is a highly effective way to get people to move.

Dogs can be utilized for inspecting illegal or unauthorized items. Dogs can intimidate people, so they need to be on tight leashes. However, as with horses, it is hard to argue with a dog, and people tend to think twice about their actions with a dog around. This is true for untrained as well as trained dogs. Thus, facilities may want to let people know that bomb-sniffing dogs are being used for an event. People who see a dog with a handler will automatically assume that the dog is sniffing for bombs when in reality the dog has been trained only for working with the disabled.

In order to ensure adequate security, the facility administrators must also effectively coordinate the applied technology for all security matters with the local police, sheriff, or other law enforcement

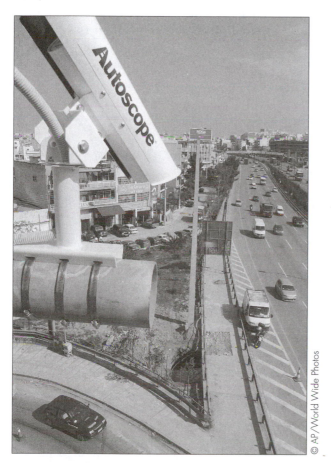

Cameras over highways were just one type of security device used at the 2004 Olympic Games in Athens, Greece.

entities. Pre-event cooperative meetings with all uniformed and nonuniformed security and law enforcement personnel are critical for event safety.

Security Planning

Security management cannot be successfully implemented without proper planning. Facility managers need to critically examine the risks they anticipate, as well as those they think can never happen, and then provide a secure environment in which the event can go forward. Planning focuses on identifying the various risks and types of incidents that are most likely to occur and that can cause the greatest harm to the facility. Since there are so many potential risks, it is important for the facility manager to have a list to help him or her identify them. An example of a security and crowd control checklist is shown on pages 300-304. Planning strategies to provide a more secure environment include the following:

- Provide additional security
- Provide refresher training courses (handling bomb threats, fire response, response procedures, baggage inspection, etc.)

- Check all employees to make sure they are in the proper location
- Coordinate with all appropriate government agencies
- Work with facility users to make sure that plans are in place and everyone knows who is responsible for what security issues
- Distribute keys appropriately to those who require access to critical areas
- Require ushers to watch the crowd rather than the game or event
- Require all security officials to wear appropriate identification markings such as badges or coats
- Track individuals who are photographing the facility or wandering around in a possibly inappropriate manner
- Develop internal communication through meetings, newsletters, and memos addressing security protocols and procedures
- Check the emergency response manual to ensure that it is accurate and up to date
- Conduct on-site mock drills to test response time and accuracy ("San Diego," 2001)

Emergency Action Plan Checklist

The following items should be completed in preparing for any event that a crowd might attend.

Event date:_____ Event time: _____ Primary facility used: _____

Secondary facility used: _____

Anticipated number of spectators: _____

Anticipated number of security personnel: _____

Anticipated spectator profile: _____

Number and type of associated events: _____

Spectator history from prior events: _____

Anticipated or known rivalries: _____

Competing events affecting the crowd: _____

Contact with police department: _____

Contact with fire department: _____

Contact with ambulance provider: _____

Facility's policies and procedure statement for security: _____

Describe the signage communication protocol:_____

Describe the audiovisual communication protocol: _____

If external security company is used, identify the contact: _____

Describe the steps taken before individuals arrive at the facility(ies):

_____

_____

Describe facility security protocols (door access, perimeter patrols, beverage policy, camera policy, pat-down procedures, etc.):

_____

_____

Describe policies for handling lost people (primarily children) or property:

_____

_____

Describe what first aid assistance will be available:

_____

_____

Describe what first aid training is required for each type of employee:

_____

_____

Describe what communication system will be used:

_____

_____

Describe how the exit routes will be communicated to patrons:

_____

_____

Describe parking configuration (geographic characteristics, parking lot, security areas, attendant location, police presence, etc.):

_____

_____

(continued)

(continued)

Describe protection strategies for VIPs, athletes, and officials:

_____

_____

Describe special circumstances affecting protection strategies:

_____

_____

Describe protection strategies for employees and spectators:

_____

_____

Describe special circumstances affecting protection strategies:

_____

_____

Describe specific steps taken to reduce criminal activity (vandalism, theft, stealing cars, locker room break-ins, crimes against women, workplace violence, etc.):

_____

_____

Describe strategies to use if/when a crowd rushes the field/court:

_____

_____

Describe strategies to use if/when a fight breaks out in the stands:

_____

_____

Describe strategies to use if/when a fight breaks out in other areas:

_____

_____

Describe strategies to use if/when a fight breaks out outside the facility:

_____

_____

Describe strategies to handle intoxicated fans:

_____

_____

Describe strategies to use if/when spectators need to be evacuated:

_____

_____

Describe strategies to use if/when a fire occurs:

_____

_____

Describe strategies to use if a bomb threat is reported or a bomb is found:

_____

_____

Describe strategies to use if/when a terrorist situation arises:

_____

_____

Describe strategies to use if/when hazardous materials are found:

_____

_____

Describe strategies to use if/when a tornado warning or watch is issued:

_____

_____

Describe strategies to use if/when a winter or lightning storm warning is issued/sounded:

_____

_____

Describe strategies to use if/when the facility is picketed by demonstrators:

_____

_____

(continued)

(continued)

Describe strategies to comply with all applicable fire code regulations:

_____

_____

Describe strategies to comply with all applicable NFPA regulations:

_____

_____

Describe strategies to comply with all applicable constitutional and legal rights:

_____

_____

Describe strategies to comply with all applicable OSHA code regulations:

_____

_____

Describe strategies implemented to reduce risks:

_____

_____

Describe how a command post will be established and manned:

_____

_____

Describe policies and procedures to be used by those in the command post:

_____

_____

Attach a copy of the "panic" statement to be used by the public address announcer and others.
Attach a copy of the insurance policy.
Attach copies of the contracts with independent vendors (such as security).
Attach phone list for all emergency personnel.
Describe strategies to document incidents and retain evidence:

_____

_____

The key to safety preparedness is to have a plan in place to deal with any contingency that may possibly arise. For example, various lists (from emergency phone numbers to asset lists) could be available to all pertinent officials, including insurance representatives. **Contingency planning** and business continuity planning refer to the need for plans to be developed and followed by all employees when a disaster occurs (Leibowitz, 2001).

The first step in properly managing inappropriate conduct entails developing, communicating, and enforcing written guidelines that set forth specific prohibited behaviors and the measures that can be taken when someone engages in these behaviors (Farmer, Mulrooney, and Ammon, 1996). Additional concerns that should be addressed by the security guidelines include proper seating arrangements, screening possible projectiles, reducing alcohol consumption, educating individuals about possible repercussions from illegal acts, and increasing police and security presence in and around sport facilities.

Miscellaneous Security Concerns

Facilities should refrain from using general seating whenever possible. General seating was the problem at the Who concert in Cincinnati and has been the problem at numerous international soccer matches. Stampedes at various soccer matches around the world led to the banning of standing-room-only seating at some World Cup events. Eliminating general seating can reduce the concentration of fans in certain areas, and fixed seating normally avoids the specter of fans fighting over seating assignments.

Projectiles such as snowballs and bottles need to be considered. Major League Baseball faced significant scrutiny when ball giveaways resulted in fans pelting the field and players. Similarly, bat giveaways also represent a significant concern. Any hard item meant as a giveaway promotion should be handed out after a game, or fans can be given a coupon to redeem the item at a later date (Fried, 2004b). Special attention has to be paid to checking individuals entering a facility to prevent the entry of bottles, cans, and fruit. Even something as seemingly innocuous as marshmallows can pose a problem. At the University of Wisconsin, the university president wanted to stop students from throwing batteries, coins, CO_2 cartridges, and other items at opposing players, so he suggested using marshmallows, which resulted in a huge cleanup problem (Fried, 2004a). In addition to not distributing any projectiles and preventing projectiles from entering a facility, managers must take special care to ensure that the facility is free of certain natural elements such as accumulated snow, which can lead to snowball fights.

Crowd Management

One of the biggest risks that any facility or event faces is patrons getting out of hand. A crowd can become violent for various reasons, such as a controversial call or a close game. In another scenario, crowds are passive throughout the event but quickly get out of hand when a tragedy occurs or

Angry fans can wreak havoc with beer bottles and other debris. These objects also pose a safety hazard for players, umpires, and the fans themselves.

when a small group decides to rush the field. Once the crowd starts moving, it may be impossible to break up without causing serious injury. **Crowd management** is the process of taking proactive steps before a crowd gets out of hand. Crowd control is what happens once the crowd has become unmanageable and police, dogs, sprays, or other solutions need to be used.

Movement Theory

A facility manager needs to know how and why people move—questions that are addressed by **movement theory.** There are three basic movement characteristics: density, speed, and flow. Density refers to the number of people in a given space. Speed refers to the distance covered by moving people in a given unit of time. Flow refers to the number of people that pass a given reference point in a given time frame. These elements come together in a formula to determine how quickly people can exit a facility:

$$\text{flow} = \text{speed} \times \text{density} \times \text{width}$$

For example, flow will be minimal if the exit-way width is minimal or the density is high. Speed is also dependent on density. If there is a lot of space between people they can move very quickly. However, if there is very little space between people, then no one can move quickly. This analysis can be expressed quantitatively. When the people den-

sity is 21 square feet (2 square meters) per person, people can move freely at the rate of 4.1 feet (1.2 meters) per second. If the density level increases, the movement rate decreases to a standstill at 2.1 to 2.6 square feet (0.20-0.25 square meters) per person (Society of Fire Protection Engineers [SFPE], 2002). Speed is significantly reduced on stairs, where even a fit person in low-density situations can average only 3.3 feet (1 meter) per second. This leads to an optimum flow condition in a 44-inch (1-meter)-wide stairway of descending one floor every 15 seconds (SFPE, 2002).

Critical density for pedestrians is less than 1.5 square feet (0.14 square meters) per person, which leaves basically no room between individuals. In such a situation, the crowd can involuntarily move a person as much as 10 feet (3 meters) laterally. The force can be so strong that it can be impossible to resist the combined force of people pushing in a given direction. This force can cause asphyxia or the collapse of steel support structures or railing. In fact, the pressure in several crowd rush disasters was so severe that it could bend 2-inch (5-centimeter)-diameter steel railing, which requires 1,100 pounds (500 kilograms) of pressure per square inch (SFPE, 2002). However, these numbers are never absolutes, because they are dependent on such variables as age, disabilities, clothing, and family groupings. Thus, in every facility the event staff must examine all exit ways, impediments to travel, and fan characteristics to help determine crowd movement concerns.

Good flow into and out of a stadium is important, especially for large events, such as the Super Bowl.

© AP/World Wide Photos

Based on the science of complexity, Scottish scientist Keith Still concluded that crowd movement is not random, but more like a pattern similar to how birds fly (Connor, 1998). According to computer models he developed, Still was able to show that fans exhibit a self-organizing movement pattern. The analysis was tested using an entryway with no barriers and then an entryway with a handrail in the middle. The first entryway had a flow rate of 150 fans per minute. Each patron had his or her own programming for reading and reacting to others and the environment. The second group, using the entryway with the railing, moved through the same size opening, but the number that were able to move through increased almost 30% to 190 people per minute (Connor, 1998). It was assumed that the difference was due in part to how people think and interact rather than the physical barriers. One of Still's conclusions was that in a crowd, a person loses his or her freedom of movement, and the geometry of the location has a greater impact than the fan's individual psychology.

Egress and Entry

Once it is understood how people move, the facility can establish specific steps to make it safer for patrons to move in and out of a facility. The reason it is important to analyze movement in and out is that when patrons are in their seats they do not pose as great a threat of surging as a crowd. However, when people are anxious to get into a facility or eager to exit, they can push and shove. This can lead to a struggle or to people's being pushed down and possibly trampled, as shown in the Camp Randall Stadium occurrence (page 308).

To get patrons into a facility, the facility needs to monitor and manipulate their movement in relation to the parking area. When people are parked far away from the entrance, it takes them longer to reach the facility, which can slow the rush toward the gate. Entrance areas need to be designed with screening locations, will-call windows, ticket taking locations, handicapped-accessible entryways, VIP/media entrances, and group entrances. Entrances can be spread out over several gates so everyone is not congregating in front of one entry point. While it may be impossible to move structural impediments to ease traffic flow, these structures need to be incorporated into the movement plan to serve as a barrier to block access to areas or help slow pedestrian movement. No matter what function

particular structures have, they need to be integrated into the crowd management plan.

Exit Procedures

In addition to knowing how people get in, managers need to calculate how individuals will leave. Not every patron knows where the nearest exit is located. Unlike the situation in an airplane, where the cabin crew points out the locations of all exits, most facilities do not have a communication and education effort pertaining to exit ways. Most people enter a large stadium or arena at the entrance closest to their car and leave at the exit closest to their seat. Fans often do not look at all the exiting options and locations. After a night club tragedy in Rhode Island in 2003 that killed over 100 people, Connecticut passed a law requiring all assemblies of over 100 individuals to be stopped at the beginning of an event for instruction on exiting the facility.

As well as patrons, employees need to know about exiting options. While patron safety may fall under general risk reduction duties or industry standards, employee exiting safety is covered by government statute: 29 CFR Part 1910 (2002) covers exit routes (egress), emergency action plans, and fire prevention plans for OSHA. Employers are allowed to follow the OSHA regulations or the similar NFPA section 101-2000 regulations. The regulations cover egress issues from design and construction requirements to maintenance and operational requirements as well as employee education.

As specified in Section 1910.36 of the OSHA statute, exit routes need to be permanent, made of construction materials with fire resistance ratings, have an adequate number of exits, and indicate the capacity, height, and width of exit routes. An exit route is an unobstructed path of exit travel within a workplace to a place of safety.

Evacuation Process

Evacuation time involves two major components: the delay time until the beginning of the start of the evacuation and the time needed to travel to a place away from danger. Both these elements focus on patron reaction and education. A sequence of events occurs in a disaster, and education helps patrons exit safely. Education is critical to address patron delay relative to starting an evacuation.

Facility Focus: Camp Randall Stadium

Camp Randall Stadium is home to the University of Wisconsin Badger football team. The stadium was built between 1895 and 1967, and in 1993 it seated 77,745 fans. There were 11,800 fans in the student section on October 30, 1993, when tragedy occurred. A crowd surged to the field at the end of the Michigan versus Wisconsin game, pinning a number of students against railings/fences, which collapsed under all the weight and resulted in numerous injuries. The following are highlights of some key security facts:

- On average, 65 security personnel worked each football game.
- On average, 125 to 180 ushers worked each game, and the security contract required 100.
- The security company provided 175 to 250 employees per game, with 200 employees for the Michigan game.
- The security company provided 19 security personnel for the student section (1 to 658 ratio).
- University regulations required four walking patrols (eight people), 45 beverage/container duty personnel, and 29 portal guards.
- The Madison police assigned nine supervisors to the event, four officers to the command booth, 67 officers at posts, five vehicular patrols, five squads, and a mounted patrol for the game.
- The police assigned 16 officers to work the area in and around the student section.
- The university conducted only physical inspection of fans; no pat-downs were conducted to prevent people from sneaking alcohol in.
- Track access near the student section was fenced in to allow athletes to leave the field.

Some very specific facts influenced the crowd behavior that fall day, including the following:

- There had been past incidents of fan misconduct (drinking, throwing, fan passing, scalping, etc.).
- The game was being played on Halloween day.
- It was daylight savings day—the time to change clocks.
- It was Parents' Day on campus.
- The weather was cold and dry.
- Wisconsin and Michigan were rival schools.
- The game had a morning start time, 11:30 a.m.
- The game was nationally televised.
- The student newspaper had run a full-page advertisement earlier in the week encouraging students to rush the field.

On the day of the game, the gates opened 1 1/2 hours prior to game time, and by 10:30 a.m. the student section was completely full. During the game between 800 and 2,000 fans migrated to the student section. Security and police attempted to clear the filled aisles but were unsuccessful. The following time line helps highlight the activities surrounding the crowd rush/surge toward the field.

Time	Comments
10:30 a.m.	At an hour before kickoff, student section appears full.
12:51 p.m.	Aisles in student section are still visible.

12:54 p.m.	Student section is packed, and students are throwing marshmallows.
12:55 p.m.	Students in costumes are seen celebrating a touchdown by throwing beach balls and toilet paper.
12:57 p.m.	Students point at field shouting "rush the field."
1:00 p.m.	Everything looks fine at field level.
1:02 p.m.	Michigan players start returning to locker room for halftime.
1:04 p.m.	Band plays during halftime.
1:36 p.m.	Students can still get through aisles to portals.
1:39 p.m.	View of aisles in part of student section is clear.
2:00 p.m.	Fans seen climbing up and down side of vometory entrance.
2:02 p.m.	Commotion occurs in stands when students try to impress cameraman.
2:05 p.m.	Police are seen on the field; the field fence and padding are visible and fans are moving freely in the area between the stands and the field fence.
2:08 p.m.	Band members start moving toward field.
2:12 p.m.	Fans are moving freely between field fence and first row.
2:17 p.m.	Body passing is seen in student section.
2:26 p.m.	Fourteen minutes before game ends, aisles in student section start to fill.
2:29 p.m.	Students chant "rush the field."
2:31 p.m.	Camera shows ecstatic fans.
2:32 p.m.	Security are seen freely opening and closing gate to allow people through.
2:36 p.m.	Fans start crowding around field fence.
2:37 p.m.	Fans start descending the bleachers.
2:38 p.m.	Police start forming ring around field and band starts moving to field.
2:39 p.m.	Badger mascot and cameraman near students are encouraging them. However, no movement is seen in student section.
2:40:50 p.m.	Fans from upper row start pushing with force, and fans are being pushed against red safety railing. Students count down final seconds on clock and yell "rush the field" and "storm the field."
2:40:52 p.m.	Red safety railing in student section collapses.
2:41:05 p.m.	With six seconds remaining, UW team takes a knee to end the game.
2:41:11 p.m.	Gates are closed as Michigan players start exiting the field.
2:41:50 p.m.	The top of the student section is almost completely empty as fans descend.
2:42:26 p.m.	Chain-link fence in student section comes down.
2:42:50 p.m.	Additional fencing collapses, and students stream across people underneath for another 50 seconds before they realize that people are being trampled.

As a result of the collapse and the crowd surge, 70 fans required hospitalization and four required extended hospitalization. Five hours after the rush, the university police established a command post, which operated until November 4, 1993. As a result of the injuries, 51 notices of claims were filed with the state, and 18 injured parties filed 15 lawsuits against the university and other defendants. The university and its employees were removed from the suits several years later based on sovereign immunity. This case shows that even if numerous steps are taken to make a facility safer for patrons, accidents and tragedies can occur and the results can be deadly (Fried, 2004a).

The delay refers to the time span from when a device or person detects the problem until movement begins. If the perception is that a disaster is imminent, crowd-related problems greatly increase. Thus, all efforts should be undertaken to ensure that the delay time is minimized through education of both patrons and event personnel. This can be accomplished by educating individuals about warning signs, sounds, sights, and symbols. Fire drills allow employees and patrons to hear a siren and put their knowledge to the test. However, facilities can also play sample siren sounds over the public address system to help teach patrons about the emergency communication system.

Research has also indicated that numerous employee-related issues affect exit time. For example, regardless of the employee training, facility-related issues such as smoke can slow down exiting by 0.2 to 0.4 meters (7.8-15.7 inches) per second. However, most emergency evacuations will be impacted by elements in a facility's control.

In a typical large assembly building, exit following a live directive (not a prerecorded message) with well-trained staff can take less than two minutes. Exit from the same facility following a nondirective voice message (prerecorded) or a warning system with visual displays, and a well-trained staff, can be accomplished in three minutes. However, in a facility with no trained staff or warning other than a fire alarm, evacuation can take more than six minutes.

Research shows that people in general are more cautious descending stairs than when they are going up. Statistics on use of handrails show that approximately 91% of unassisted patrons use handrails when walking up stairs whereas 94% utilize handrails when walking down. Devices used by disabled fans further affect evacuation time. Ambulatory devices such as electric wheelchairs, assisted manual chairs, crutches, and walking sticks can slow crowds down, as can assisted ambulants. While each type of device can affect movement rates on a horizontal surface, the impact can be even greater on stairs. As noted above, people are more confident going up stairs than going down. This confidence can be affected by an ambulatory device. All this points to the need to place special emphasis on how people leave a facility.

As indicated by the heading for this section, "Evacuation Process," exiting a facility should not be composed of random acts, but should be a process. Some observations not mentioned so far that relate to the process include the following:

- Panic is very infrequent even in fires as normal behavior patterns and route choices stay constant.
- People's behavior tends to be reasonable.
- People often ignore initial warning signals.
- When faced with little time to respond, people tend to exit by the most familiar route.
- People tend to evacuate as a group and with people they have emotional ties to.
- If a problem such as communication or wayfinding difficulties exists before an emergency, that problem will be exacerbated during an emergency (SFPE, 2002).

Fan Education

The best-trained and best-equipped security staff has very little value if fans do not know how to respond and care for their own safety. Education often focuses on ways to exit buildings, as just discussed, with facilities communicating information about exit procedures and about warning sounds that patrons should listen for.

Fan education should address other areas as well, such as crime prevention and general safety. The National Crime Prevention Council produced and distributed over 50,000 brochures and posters on crime prevention and general safety procedures for visitors and athletes at the 1996 Summer Olympic Games. Individuals need to be told that their conduct could lead to criminal liability and, often more importantly, that continued unacceptable conduct could force a team or program to cease operations (Fried, 2004b). Some individuals might only change their behavior if they know that failure to do so might force their team to forfeit the game. Coaches and referees have used this type of information effectively by announcing that the home team will forfeit a game if inappropriate conduct continues.

Another key aspect of fan education is alcohol awareness. Arrests at sport events often have to do with alcohol abuse or intoxication. Fans under the influence of alcohol sometimes throw items onto the field, which is not only disruptive but also dangerous. At a "Disco Demolition," alcohol helped turn an unwise promotion into a disaster.

Special precautions need to be deployed whenever alcohol is being served or consumed. Various sport facilities have designated certain areas as alcohol-free family areas or eliminated alcohol sales after a specified time. Also, alcohol servers are trained to refuse service to those who are visibly intoxicated.

Alcohol Policy

Sport events are unique in that the infusion of alcohol into the event can generate significant revenue but also significant risks. This is not true for most other types of events. A night at the symphony is usually not marred by brawls among drunken attendees. In contrast, people often expect to see several drunk and obnoxious fans when they attend sport events. Why is there such a difference in perceptions? It might be based on numerous issues, from the social status of attendees to the fact that alcohol seems to be an integral part of the sport experience but not of the symphony experience. In any case, the two primary problems related to alcohol at sporting events are aggression and impaired driving.

A 1982 study concluded that between 4% and 7% of fans at a sporting event consumed enough alcohol to be legally impaired. At a large stadium or arena, this could represent over a thousand people. The authors of the study also concluded that the severity of the problem was directly related to the length of the sporting event. If the event was relatively short, there was less likelihood that fans would be drunk, whereas at a doubleheader in baseball the likelihood was much greater that fans would drink more (Single and McKenzie, 1991). Canada has taken some specific steps to address this concern and reduce the risk of alcohol-related problems. Effective alcohol management techniques include the following:

- Developing alcohol-related regulations for specific sports representing the greatest likelihood of problems
- Providing "dry" areas where alcohol is not served or allowed
- Ensuring compliance with all age limits and laws to prevent underage alcohol sales
- Limiting each person to a maximum of two alcoholic beverages at any given purchase time

- Starting alcohol sales no more than one hour before the beginning of the event, and stopping at a specific time before the end of the event to give people less time to buy alcohol and some time to possibly sober up before leaving the facility and driving
- Providing various alternatives such as reduced-alcohol and nonalcoholic beverages
- Developing and promoting designated driver and other fan education programs with input from staff, fans, and local authorities
- Requiring all servers and managers to undertake TEAM (Techniques for Effective Alcohol Management) or SIP (Server Intervention Program) training, which has been successful in reducing alcohol-related problems and increasing overall income (these training programs focus on teaching servers how to identify appropriate IDs, already intoxicated fans, and other danger signs)
- Requiring each facility to have an adequate security staff, posting informational signs, providing alternative beverage options, and developing safe transportation strategies such as taxis and public transportation (Single and McKenzie, 1991)
- Separating alcohol sales from food sales so customers have to wait in two different lines
- Posting signage indicating when alcohol sales stop and how many drinks each patron can buy at one time
- Not selling bottles or cans
- Preventing alcohol sales in family areas
- Placing signage to indicate where beer cannot be consumed
- Security patrolling and looking for alcohol-related concerns
- Monitoring service areas and consumption areas with CCTV

Alcohol has played a significant role in fan-related violence. Drunken fans at a Chicago Cubs game stole a hat from a Los Angeles Dodgers pitcher, and the ensuing altercation brought 16 Dodgers into the stands. The players were suspended for 84 games and fined $72,000 for their part in the incident, but the fans were primarily to blame. In response to the incident, Wrigley Field changed its policy on when to stop selling beer, to the middle of the sixth inning rather than the top of the seventh inning ("Touched," 2000). The New York Yankees are even more strict; they have cut off all beer sales to the bleacher area.

Some of the policies and procedures applicable to alcohol management have originated, as with crowd management strategies, in Europe. In Scotland there has been a complete ban on alcohol sales at rugby and soccer matches since 1980 (Frosdick, 1998). Fédération Internationale de Football Amateur (FIFA) rules also prohibit both alcohol sales and possession at the World Cup and other FIFA-sponsored events.

Other Safety Concerns

Safety should not be analyzed only in terms of the spectators or facility users. The annual cost of violence in the workplace is estimated at $3 billion, stemming from 2 million physical attacks, 6.3 million threats, and 6.1 million harassment incidents ("Safeguarding Employees," 2001). In fact, in a nationwide study of security threats, many of the top 10 risks involved crime or violence in the workplace:

1. Workplace violence
2. Business interruption/Disaster recovery
3. Terrorism
4. Computer crime
5. Employee selection/screening concerns
6. Fraud/White collar crime
7. Unethical business conduct
8. General employee theft
9. Property crime (vandalism)
10. Drugs/Alcohol in the workplace ("Top Security Threats," 2002)

Crisis Management

Management needs to know how to deal with a crisis. This concern was the foundation for the discipline of **crisis management.** A crisis is any event that threatens people, tangible assets, or intangible assets. Crisis management refers to how to return to "normal" as soon as possible after a crisis occurs. If someone drowns at a pool, for example, how long will it take for the facility to investigate the

Sporting events after 9/11 were marked with increased security and memorial activities. Facilities also have to pay more for insurance.

situation, for the authorities to conduct an investigation, for any corrective actions to be taken, and then for users to be allowed to return?

Since 9/11, the need for security has grown at all large sport facilities. So has the cost, including everything from specialty security personnel and off-duty police officers to insurance. For example, in 2001 the Milwaukee Brewers paid $225,000 for property and liability insurance. The next year, after the 9/11 attacks, they purchased the same insurance policy for $2.25 million. The price had increased because sport facilities are among the prime potential spots for terrorist attacks given the large number of people in a small area (Ryan, 2002).

Crisis management focuses on identifying the multitude of concerns that can affect a facility. When analyzing the concerns, the facility manager should focus not just on attacks, but also on other activities that can result in damage. Having an event that offends community leaders or releasing sensitive data to the media exemplifies a crisis that can destroy a facility without an attack or natural disaster. Some of the areas managers should review to prevent a crisis include many that relate to communication:

- Press releases
- Marketing information
- Web-based materials
- Community outreach programs
- Public emergency response plans
- Sensitive material not destroyed through shredding

- Facility signage
- Building plans filed with public agencies
- Information provided to vendors, contractors, consultants, and the like
- Information produced in litigation or by expert witnesses, consultants, and so on (Baybutt, 2003)

Any one of these communication vehicles can backfire and turn a good idea into a disaster. All these items can be important tools for a facility, but sensitivity dictates that not all information should be disclosed. For example, a press release should never indicate the number of security personnel at a given site or all the techniques being employed to secure a site. When some information is withheld, it is more difficult for anyone planning to circumvent security to gain knowledge about how the event will be protected.

Crisis Planning

Facilities often start the crisis management process by building a crisis team that may include politicians, authorities, lawyers, the media, and others who can provide assistance. The crisis management team needs to examine and rank potential threats to prioritize response options. A threat matrix weighs the probability of a risk versus the potential magnitude of the results that would occur if the risk indeed happened. The facility needs to

develop specific plans of action through such means as defining the role of various departments, preparing training schedules to rehearse appropriate response strategies, and developing a proactive crisis response culture (Trest, 2003).

The number and types of crises that can occur are almost limitless. Numerous crises are man-made, such as terror attacks, legal disputes, employee misdeeds, and patron sabotage. Other potential crisis situations are natural—tornados, hurricanes, floods, lightning, earthquakes, and so on. Such crises can also be classified as internal, external, and even computer-based threats (see below).

Management can plan for each of these events or situations. Emergency plans need to be developed before a facility is ever open to the general public. Such a plan is as important as a budget or insurance policy. No fans or customers should be allowed into a facility that has not developed and written plans for, and trained employees in, proper crisis response. One of the typical emergencies that will occur at almost any facility is a heart attack. No matter how much time is spent in preventing other crises, heart attacks will happen. The question is how the facility will respond. If the facility has developed appropriate plans to handle medical emergencies, required employees to read the plan, and taught employees what to do, then employees should be able to provide appropriate assistance to prevent the attack from turning into a death.

Categories of Threats That Can Affect A Facility

Internal Threats	External Threats	Information Technology Threats
Drug/Alcohol usage	Civil unrest	System failure
Labor disputes	Tornado	Viruses
Low employee morale	Espionage	Power failure
Legal disputes	Missed deliveries	Hardware failure
Loss of workforce	Fire	Software malfunction
Employee injuries	Flooding	Service provider problems
Patron injuries	Government regulations	Lost files
Workplace violence	Terrorism	Corrupt files
Succession planning	Environmental hazard	Sabotage
White collar crime	Poor media image	
Patron injury	Weather concerns	
Low inventory	Low supplies	

Employees also need to be trained on the location and usage of equipment such as **automatic external defibrillators (AEDs)**.

Emergency Action Plan

The International Association of Assembly Managers (IAAM) established a Center for Venue Management Studies, which produced a guide called *Safety and Security Protocols, Best Practices Planning Guide for Security at Arenas, Stadiums, and Amphitheaters.* The protocols were designed to address concerns such as fire, medical, power, bomb, and terrorist emergencies (Fried, 2004b).

These protocols describe specific elements within an emergency action plan. The first component of the plan entails choosing a team that will handle the emergency. These individuals can range from police and fire personnel to facility managers, security providers, and state officials. These persons should have a vested interest in the project so that they are fully committed to it and can help attract personal and institutional support.

Management can help the team by undertaking a **vulnerability analysis** to identify what events are most likely to occur. Vulnerability can encompass historical incidents (fires, earthquakes, tornados, etc.); geographic, technological, and human conditions; physical elements; and regulatory requirements. The various vulnerabilities need to be ranked based on probability after an analysis of the potential human, property, or business impact.

The team should first identify the plan components, which are traditionally broken down into the categories of regulatory, human, building, and business components. The regulatory component applies to the governmental agencies that may dictate how emergencies need to be handled. From a local fire department to OSHA officials or the Department of Homeland Security, the facility needs to know what emergency prevention, response, and recovery concerns must be addressed.

Regarding the human components, the facility must examine the staff, tenants, artists/athletes, patrons, sponsors, media, and anyone else that may be in the facility and how they may respond to an emergency. Based on the populations using the facility, the emergency plan may need to be customized. The building component of the plan examines how the building would respond in an emergency, specifically with respect to the following elements:

- Building structure (resistance to fire, wind, water, etc.)
- Fire element (detection, containment, and suppression systems)
- Notification systems (alarm, power, and public address systems)
- Ingress and egress points (opening width, load capacity, signage, lighting, traction, etc.)
- Building security (access control, surveillance equipment, alarms, etc.)
- Transportation systems (vehicles, elevators, escalators, etc.)
- Emergency systems (smoke control, emergency power, fire control room, etc.)
- Heating, ventilation, and air conditioning (secure intake, zone controls, quality management, etc.) (Fried, 2004b)

The business component examines the potential impact an emergency may have on a business's ability to keep functioning. This requires analysis of financial implications, marketing implications, communication concerns and techniques, inventory control, records management, insurance assessment, and potential contract or legal ramifications. Plans also need to be made in case an emergency occurs and the event will need to utilize a different facility.

Once the planning team has studied the basic components, each component should be critically analyzed to determine what steps can be taken to prevent a disaster.

- Some actions may prevent the risk from occurring; what are they?
- Early detection of risks in their infancy can prevent a small incident from becoming a major issue.
- Once an emergency has been identified, appropriate officials and key constituents need to be contacted.
- Strategies must be developed for possibly evacuating or relocating patrons, if such action is the most appropriate step to take.
- Control and mitigation systems are designed to identify and eliminate the cause of an

emergency and help protect against the effects of the emergency.

- Documenting emergency efforts before, during, and after an emergency is critical for litigation and for managements use to change policies and procedures in light of results.
- After an emergency the facility must try to return to normal.
- Especially with sport facilities, perception can become reality; if patrons feel a facility is not safe, they will avoid it.

With this knowledge base, an **emergency response management team (ERMT)** can be formed. The team members should have the authority, knowledge, and decision-making capabilities to implement the emergency plan. The following are some of the key elements the plan should address:

- Emergency power for lighting and public address systems
- Distribution of the emergency plan to personnel
- The ability to contact ERMT members at all hours
- Proper firefighting equipment such as fire extinguishers and sprinkler systems
- Proper signage
- Adequate doorways and corridors for ingress and egress
- Prepared and recorded evacuation messages
- Ability to record phone calls when a bomb threat is made
- Public address systems that broadcast inside and outside a facility
- Cellular phones to communicate with other employees and ERMT members

Once the analysis is performed, the next step is coming up with a plan. Part of this plan should include securing necessary documentation and equipment in the event of a crisis. Documentation that would be critical in preparing for or responding to a crisis include property contracts, operational records, accounting/tax records, current personnel records, client records, critical reports, necessary manuals, and any specially developed

software that cannot be easily reproduced (Carlisle, 2003).

While there is no one perfect plan, the following minimum requirements for an emergency action plan are recommended by OSHA:

- Procedures for reporting a fire or other emergency
- Procedures for emergency evacuation and exit route assignments
- Procedures to be followed by employees who will be left to operate critical equipment before they are forced to evacuate
- Procedure to account for all employees (and patrons)
- Procedures to be followed by employees performing rescue and medical duties

The Occupational Safety and Health Administration also recommends plans for specific types of emergencies. For example, the minimum requirements for a fire prevention plan include the following:

- A list of all major fire hazards
- Proper storage and handling procedures for hazardous materials
- Potential ignition sources and how to control them
- An inventory of all the fire prevention equipment and where it is stored
- Procedures for accumulating, storing, and disposing of combustible materials
- Procedure for regular maintenance of safeguards on equipment that generate heat
- The names or job titles of those responsible for maintaining heat-generating equipment or controlling fuel source hazards (29 CFR Part 1910, 2002)

Even with all this analysis, the plan will not be effective unless it is implemented in a controlled environment. This is where training and rehearsals are critical to ensure that the emergency is handled appropriately. Crisis training can be as simple as a fire drill or as complex as having hundreds of volunteers pretend to be injured in a terrorist attack.

Finally, implementing a crisis management plan requires funding. Senior managers often do not find the dollar value in crisis management to

Managing Sport Facilities

warrant significant expenditures on a possibly remote occurrence. In fact, 24% of companies do not initiate a crisis management program due to a lack of funds, while 37% of those who have a plan need more money to effectively implement it ("Gartner: Businesses," 2003). Clearly a plan will not be successful unless the facility can find the funds to implement the plan. Often the best means to obtain the funds is to garner support from government officials and facility owners through an aggressive educational campaign.

Continuity Management

One of the often overlooked components of any crisis management plan is continuity management. In any business, **continuity management** focuses on how to keep the business operating even if a disaster occurs. For example, if the roof of an arena collapses, facility managers cannot just pack their bags and leave since there may be valid contractual obligations. The facility manager can establish a relationship with another venue such that if an emergency occurs at either facility, the other facility is made available, if possible, to assist in continuity. Thus, if a roof collapses, the facility manager could call the other facility and shift events there.

Some of the elements inherent in a continuity management program include risk management, disaster recovery, supply chain management (with vendors), health and safety management, knowledge management, emergency management, security protocols, and crisis communication and public relations (Smith, 2003). All these elements need to be integrated together so that when an emergency happens, the facility is prepared to keep going. No one element is more important than another; but without money, a facility will have a difficult time staying open. While it is often difficult to put money away for an emergency, a "rainy day" fund is critical even if the facility has insurance, since bills will need to be paid now and not several months down the road when the insurance issues are settled.

Summary

Safety is the most important element for any facility. No one wants to go to an event or a facility if there is the threat of a terrorist attack or even the risk of serious injury. However, there are so many potential safety concerns that patrons and employees are constantly exposed to risks. The extent to which such risks may in fact become a hazard are controlled by the facility management. Even if there is a possibility of a crowd surge that could injure fans, facility management can take specific steps such as redesigning seating arrangements and using more security personnel to reduce the risk of serious injuries. Through appropriate safety planning, most facilities can be reasonably safe and can survive most serious incidents.

DISCUSSION QUESTIONS AND ACTIVITIES

1. What is the best way to deal with a hostile crowd?

2. How should a facility deal with canceling an event several hours before the event is to be held?

3. Research a major crowd management problem that occurred in the United States and determine what was done right/wrong to handle the problem.

4. Research a major sport facility disaster anywhere in the world and determine what was done right/wrong to handle the problem.

5. Try to complete the following threat matrix based on the likelihood of occurrence of the incident or situation and the magnitude or seriousness of the potential damage.

316

		Risk of occurrence		
Seriousness of injury/damage		Likely	Possible	Unlikely
	Minor			
	Medium			
	Significant			

Place each of the following threats on the matrix in the area where you think it should go:

A: A bad case of athlete's foot is reported in the locker room.

B: A player has been stealing from other players.

C: A hailstorm hits during a tournament.

D: Cars are broken into in the parking lot during an event.

E: A person breaks his or her leg during an event.

F: A spectator slips on the sidewalk and is injured.

SIXTEEN

Event Management in the Facility

CHAPTER OBJECTIVES

After completing this chapter you will be able to do the following:

- Recognize how quickly something can go wrong at an event and how to come up with solutions
- Develop strategies to make even unhappy patrons into future customers by providing quality service
- Understand the importance of concessions to a facility's bottom line
- Appreciate how even the small details included in or missing from the planning process can affect the event
- Learn what is involved in analyzing an event after it is over
- Understand survey techniques to determine what is needed to improve an event or facility
- Understand why the planning process for future events starts immediately after an event ends

Chapter 14 highlighted the importance of preparing for an event, including elements such as the bid and selection process, facility scheduling, developing policies and procedures, checking the facility for safety, and marketing the event. An inattentive employee or a careless fan can disrupt all these steps in one minute. For example, the facility can develop risk management protocols and train employees to pick up trash or clean spills as soon as they happen, but these procedures and training are worthless when an employee fails to act as instructed. Frequently employees know what they are supposed to do but procrastinate or become caught up in other tasks. As an example, suppose that to save time and money a facility has switched from pump-dispensed condiments to little plastic packets. A fan takes several packets of ketchup and drops one on the floor. No one picks it up, and before long there's a mess. This may generate the feeling among fans that the facility is not well kept up and can also represent a slipping hazard. It is not that the facility is irresponsible or has failed to plan. Rather, facilities need to reevaluate themselves constantly according to what happens during use. Based on this fact scenario, a facility may feel that the condiment area is the riskiest slip location and use non-skid paint or install metal grates to make it safer and more attractive.

The focus of this chapter is on implementation and follow-up. Everything learned and considered in the planning process needs to be acted upon. The hotdogs ordered in anticipation of the event need to be located in a convenient storage and cooking location, cooked, stored, served, and then reordered. The topics this chapter covers are event analysis, post-event surveys, marketing for the future, and facility analysis. These topics are covered in relationship to what occurs during an event, immediately after the event, and at some later time.

Most people after an event go home and do not think about the event. A facility manager does not have this option. The facility manager needs to prepare for the next event, which could be several hours away. He or she must again be ready to deal with issues such as trash removal, changing merchandise in the concession areas, or changing over a floor from basketball to hockey. The issues are the same after an event as they are during the planning and running of an event.

For example, during the planning process, all insurance options need to be examined. During the event, the event must be monitored to make sure nothing violates the terms of the insurance agreement. If the policy requires someone to inspect the facility during the event, for example, that responsibility must be assigned to someone. After the event, management needs to determine if any claims were raised—and later, whether the insurance company handled the claims, how the claims were handled, and if the policy provided appropriate coverage.

Event Analysis

Policies and procedures developed before an event necessitate monitoring during the event to ensure that they are being followed. The checklists presented in chapter 14 contain items relating to security, concessions, parking, scoreboards, and other concerns. During the event all these items need to be revisited. While concessionaires might have had enough cash and change before the event started, they may run out of small bills and must be able to communicate with someone that they need change. They probably cannot leave their station, so a manager or other employee will need to bring the change to them. Financial analysis is needed to track where the change is going and to make

sure all money movement is properly recorded so that final settlements can be calculated at the end of the event.

It is during an event that management has the best opportunity to praise or to note the performance of employees. Although an employee responsible for acquiring sponsorship revenue will be judged before an event begins, concessionaires and ushers, as well as security, operations, and mechanical workers—among numerous others—can be evaluated in their work environment to determine if they are performing their duties.

Thus, managers cannot just sit back when the event begins and think the worst is behind them. The event or facility manager must ensure that all the right steps are being taken by subordinates and front-line personnel. For example, a disaster plan has been developed, but how would everyone act when a disaster really occurred? Would people move as rehearsed? At such times, management earns its stripes by being able to lead effectively given the information, resources, and time available.

Checking the Contract

One of the issues that must be carefully analyzed during and after an event is compliance with any contract, lease, or rental terms and conditions. For example, a facility rental agreement may require a tenant to comply with all applicable local laws and regulations. What happens if the municipality where the facility is located has a noise ordinance that prohibits a facility from generating loud noise after 9:00 p.m.? Hopefully management would have known about the law, but often managers are unaware of laws that could impact the event. If management does not know about the law and problems arise during the event, they have two options—comply with the contract terms or violate the ordinance and risk problems with government, the landlord, and possibly the public.

Another contractual concern is the number of employees. Lease and event contracts often require a minimum number of employees to work in areas such as concessions, entry management, security, and box offices. Numbers can also be established based on management research in areas such as ticket sales, type of event, anticipated crowd, the day of the week, the time the event begins, and whether other events are being run on the same date. If the contract calls for 700 ushers, how can management ensure that a sufficient number of ushers are present and doing what they are supposed to do? What if too many ushers show up for the event? What if only 600 show up? Under such conditions, managers have a difficult choice to make. They can cancel the event and violate the contract, or they can proceed with the event, knowing in this case also that they are violating the contract, but try to use other managers and concession workers as an ad hoc staff. If too many ushers show up, they can be placed around the facility for training purposes and be paid for their time.

This concern has significant ramifications in terms of liability, but also can show whether or not management can accomplish the job. If the manager has trouble meeting contractual requirements, this can lead to trouble renegotiating the contract or lease at a later date.

If there is a dispute between the facility and the event, and the parties cannot resolve issues in the contract, both parties should first try alternative dispute resolution such as mediation or arbitration. The contract should have a mediation or arbitration clause or both. Mediation can allow the parties to work out the dispute and hopefully come to a conclusion that will be mutually beneficial and then allow the relationship to grow. If mediation is not successful, the parties can go to arbitration to resolve the dispute. If the dispute is more adversarial and cannot be resolved through arbitration, litigation is the next option.

Evaluating the Employees

A performance appraisal for employees and subcontractors is one of the most important post-event activities. Did the employees do what they were supposed to do? Did they provide quality services? Did the salespeople sell tickets or merchandise aggressively? Did the ushers perform their job well and with a positive attitude? It is difficult to evaluate an employee unless there are objective criteria such as the number of tickets sold or the number of complaints handled during a given event. Most positions only have subjective performance criteria such as whether the usher acted appropriately and watched the crowd rather than the event. But even if evaluating employees is difficult, it has to be done. The most effective method is to have their immediate supervisors evaluate them based on preestablished criteria discussed with the employees when they are hired or promoted.

Another employment evaluation concern is liability for acts of others who are not directly employed by the facility. If third-party vendors provide ushers, security, and concessionaire services, can the facility be liable for their conduct? The answer may be yes.

For example, if the vendor discriminates in hiring, the facility could be liable for such discrimination even though the facility did not engage in any discrimination. Why? The facility should have examined the employment practices of the vendor before assigning that vendor the contract (Fried and Miller, 1998). Every contract with third-party vendors should be carefully written to establish standards for success and compliance with lease terms, but also the third-party vendor should indemnify and hold the facility harmless for any negligence and legal violations caused by the third-party vendor or any of its employees. The facility manager should take time during an event to evaluate the vendor and its employees to ensure that the vendor's employment practices reflect well on the facility.

Evaluating the Financial Success

After an event, the facility manager must evaluate its financial success. Rental and lease contracts often require payment of a given amount before an event to guarantee that the facility owner will be able to cover expenses. A facility knows in advance the cost of opening the facility to the public and will charge at least that amount as a pre-event payment in case gate receipts are low. Thus, if it costs $5,000 to open the facility, the facility owner would ask for at least this amount.

Management must carefully examine the financial viability of an event as it is going on. If concession sales are not doing well due to low turnout or weather, can the manager change prices or offer a new item to generate revenue? For example, on hot days, facilities often sell more bottled water than traditional drinks. In the opening weekend of the 2001 pro football season, stadiums posted significant sales for bottled water—40,000 units were sold at the Buffalo Bills' Ralph Wilson Stadium and 20,000 bottles were sold at the Baltimore Ravens' PSINet Stadium (Muret, 2001). By vigilantly monitoring sales throughout an event and over a season, a facility manager can identify new strategies to help increase sales.

If the rental agreement calls for revenues to be shared, are there any problems with calculating the revenue after the event? For example, would press passes count against the attendance totals? While the agreement may cover such issues, the post-event evaluation is designed to determine whether the agreement can even be enforced or whether provisions need to be changed for the future.

The post-event evaluation may show that an event should not be allowed back in the facility even if it was financially successful. For example, an ultimate street fighting event may have been booked in a facility and held with great apprehension. The media may be critical. Local officials may even try to ban the sport from coming back to the municipality. These reactions need to be critically reviewed to determine whether an event should be accepted again, even if it was a financial success.

The major task in post-event financial analysis is balancing the books. For each employee responsible for generating revenue, are all revenues accounted for? A ticket booth attendant might have been given 1,000 tickets to sell at $5 each. If the attendant has 400 tickets remaining after the event, then he or she sold 600 tickets and should have $3,000. If the person has only $2,500, then management needs to investigate why there is a $500 discrepancy.

Facility lease agreements often contain provisions for allocating income derived from ticket sales and concession revenue. Since the facility normally collects the money, the event producer or team relies on the facility to provide accurate and detailed records. Chapter 11 includes a sample reconciliation from a major football game. If a promoter collects the money, the facility should be careful to obtain all moneys owed before the event leaves town to avoid a possible collection problem. Facilities have lost significant amounts of money when a promoter left without paying bills; in cases like this, the facility may never see its share. Similarly, a problem arises when the facility, after paying all the suppliers, vendors, and employees, does not have enough money to pay the amount it owes the event. If this occurs, the facility may have to borrow money, try to renegotiate the debt, or, in extreme cases, file for bankruptcy.

If an event or facility is not successful, the final decision for management may be to close. Closing may generate contractual issues such as breach of contract. Many new facilities are constructed with provisions that the anchor tenant or team must use the facility for 20 to 30 years. If the team leaves earlier, it must pay a penalty. Similarly, if a fitness center located in a shopping mall has a 10-year lease and decides to terminate the lease after five years, it will be responsible for another five years' rent. Normally it is incumbent on the landlord to find another tenant, if possible, to mitigate the damages. However, if the landlord tries and does not find another tenant, then the original tenant will be responsible for all the owed rent.

A facility that is closing often puts on a sale to help pay any outstanding debts or generate money to help pay for moving elsewhere. The number of items that could be sold is almost limitless. Key assets that are often sold include vehicles, televisions, food preparation items, concession items, and mechanical equipment. When the New Haven Coliseum closed in 2002, the city hosted an auction that included the following items:

Item	Price
Popcorn cart	$450
Hotdog warmers	$175
Zamboni	$6,000
Basketball hoops set	$1,400
Concession stands	$20,000
Scoreboard	$50,000

From Carter, 2002.

Evaluating Liability

After an event, management needs to review all incident reports to determine if there is a likelihood of litigation. Most insurance policies require notification within 24 hours after an event for any incident that could possibly lead to a claim. Thus, any injury resulting in an ambulance ride or a visit to a hospital should be documented and the information shared with the insurance company. All facts should be documented, the area where the injury occurred should be photographed, and everyone in the area should be interviewed. The insurance company may want to be involved in this process. Furthermore, depending on the type of injury and who was injured, government officials such as Occupational Safety and Health Administration (OSHA) investigators may want to review the accident scene.

Risk management issues covered in the lease contract need to be analyzed before the event. For example, was the proper **certificate of insurance** issued with the requisite amount of coverage? Was the facility named as an **additional insured?** Does the policy cover attorney fees and costs? While a contract may require these provisions, the policy needs to be examined to make sure the proper coverage was purchased and is in place for the event. Also, are waiver forms available for participants and are all necessary signs in place to educate spectators? These simple steps are regularly discussed before an event, but sometimes forgotten when the event is held. Thus, all employees need to make sure all risk management strategies are implemented during the event.

Another insurance-related task after the event is reviewing the number of claims associated with a particular type of event or facility. If there are very few injuries, then the claims experience would be low and the premium cost should decrease in the future. However, above a certain number of claims, the insurance rates will increase.

During and after the event, management should also look at the relationship with the insurance company. Some insurance companies provide personnel to work events as risk managers. If an insurance company takes proactive steps to make an event and facility safer, this is a strong indication that the company is dedicated to protecting its investment and maximizing safety.

Post-Event Surveys

Post-event evaluation is another key management task. Did all the strategies work? Were employees successful at their assigned tasks? Did the mechanical systems work as intended? Did the marketing campaign bring enough sponsors or ticket sales? Did the event make or lose money? Did the event generate goodwill in the community? These types of questions are paramount for any manager. If the facility did not live up to expectations, tenants can be upset, owners can be furious, and patrons can decide to not attend again. One bad facility experience is often enough to dissuade people from attending a future event at that facility. If a patron spends several hours in the parking lot trying to leave after an event, can that patron be persuaded to attend another event? If the parking issue is not corrected, the patron will be hesitant to come back

or will want there to be other options for reaching the venue such as a shuttle service.

If a facility is having a problem with parking but management does not know about it, management cannot do anything to make the facility experience better. Management needs to know about problems and then take action. If there is a problem, management needs to be up-front. It is essential to let people know that the post-event surveying process has uncovered a problem and then to indicate what specific steps are being taken to solve the problem.

Customer Satisfaction

Post-event surveying is often undertaken to determine the degree of customer satisfaction. But even during an event, management often is forced to examine the little things. For example, if a foul ball lands in the stands, was anyone hit? If so, what condition is the person in? Did a kid get stomped on during the battle for the ball? Did an elderly fan get pushed by a drunken fan who was trying to get the ball? Was someone's food or beverage spilled in the process? Is the ball a memorable ball that should be retrieved? By paying attention to these small but often overlooked issues, management can take advantage of opportunities to develop relationships. Relationship building is just as important for spectators and facility users as it is for employees. If a fan loses his or her food or otherwise is not having a good experience, can management do anything to make it better? The fan can be offered other food, a coupon for a free ticket, or possibly even an opportunity to meet a player. People who receive this kind of attention

What can a facility manager do to enhance a fan's experience?

can become lifelong supporters and will communicate their positive feelings to others.

In a Major League Baseball game in 2004 a 4-year-old boy was about to catch his first foul ball when a man sitting behind him took the ball away after the ball landed on the ground. While the man jumped up with ecstasy, the little boy was crying. The scoreboard showed both the man and the boy and fans started shouting at the man to give the boy the ball. The man refused to give the ball to the child. Team officials went out of their way to comfort the child. A star player gave the boy a game-used bat. At the end of the day the youngster received significant media attention, several pieces of memorabilia, and some free game tickets ("Boy will get foul ball from man who knocked him aside", 2004). Such reaction turned a very negative experience into a lifelong memory that can make the boy a great future baseball fan.

Every effort should be made to discover what people are thinking. It is well documented that happy customers will tell one or two others about their experience. In contrast, dissatisfied customers will tell 8 to 10 others about their poor experience (Zikmund and d'Amico, 1996). However, many dissatisfied customers never mention their feelings to the facility management for fear of retribution, a perceived lack of interest, or a lack of time. Management has to remove obstacles to allow customers to freely indicate their concerns as well as their praise.

A critical task for management is surveying spectators and facility users. Information is most easily obtained from written, phone, or focus group questioning or from surveys. Surveying is undertaken to plan for the future. It is impossible to plan without proper information. One common strategy is to survey season ticket holders since their names are already in a database and they represent the most frequent facility users. Fans are often sent a survey and offered a discount or premium item for responding. A suggestion box is another way to allow people to give good and bad feedback.

A sample customer satisfaction survey is shown on page 325. There is no one correct survey instrument. The key is to determine what information the facility wants from the survey before writing the questions. The facility also needs to determine how to distribute the survey to obtain a well-rounded sample representing the broad array of patrons who may be at the facility.

On-Site Surveys

Another way to obtain valuable information is for facility managers to shop the facility themselves. The manager should drive to the facility from different directions to see firsthand what traffic issues exist. The manager should also be a "regular" fan and buy a ticket, go through the parking lot, enter through the front gate after waiting in the crowd, observe security and directional signage, obtain directions to the seat, buy concessions, use the bathrooms, try to complain about service, fake an injury, pretend to be intoxicated, get lost in the parking lot after an event, and engage in countless other activities to test the employees. All this said, often this strategy is not possible because most employees would recognize the manager. In these cases a "secret shopper" can be more effective in the information retrieval process during an event.

Once an evaluation is completed, it should be written down and shared with others in order to gain their perspective. If action needs to be taken, management needs to see what changes are necessary and what can be done to accomplish those changes. Some changes may be easy to make with a minimal financial expenditure or with minor modifications in policies and procedures. Other changes can be very costly or will take a significant amount of time to complete. Thus, the facility manager needs to know his or her budget and time restrictions before undertaking any renovations or repairs.

Marketing for the Future

The post-event time is not just for evaluating the planning and execution of the event, but also should be used to market the next event. If a sponsor provided money or services, how was the sponsor acknowledged? Was there an official thank-you in a publication? Was someone within the sponsor company personally thanked? Significant value can come from post-event recognition and marketing. It is recommended that a thank-you note be sent to each sponsor and all major participants in the event. Following up with sponsors communicates to them that the event or facility is genuinely appreciative.

If information about the event's success is included, the relationship can be strengthened for the following year. For example, if attendance

Sample Customer Satisfaction Survey

What is your zip code? _____

Is this the first event you have attended at this facility?   Y   N

How did you hear about the event? _____

Did you enjoy the event?   Y   N

Did you purchase tickets?   Y   N

Where did you get the tickets from? _____

Did you drive to the facility?   Y   N

How was the traffic coming to the facility?   Good   Bad   Okay

How was parking?   Good   Bad   Okay

Did you use the rest rooms?   Y   N

Were the rest rooms clean?   Y   N

Were there enough supplies such as toilet paper and towels?   Y   N

Did you purchase any food?   Y   N

Was the food served quickly?   Y   N

Was the food tasty?   Y   N

How much do you think you spent on food at the event? _____

Did you purchase any concession items?   Y   N

   What did you buy? _____

   Were you satisfied with the quality of the item you purchased?   Y   N

   How much did you spend in total on concession items? _____

What could the facility have done to make the event better? _____

_____

_____

_____

Other suggestions/comments:

_____

_____

_____

_____

_____

_____

If you would like to be added to our mailing list please write your name, address, phone number, and e-mail address below.

_____

_____

increased 20% over the prior year, this information could be critical to a sponsor and should be communicated. Other items that can be sent include newspaper clippings, event photos, signed photos of a star athlete standing next to the sponsor's sign, a thank-you plaque, sample tickets, and video of the event showing signage location and appearances on broadcasts. These and a host of other items can help show sponsors that they made a wise decision. Such information should also be sent to organizations that were solicited for sponsorship and who appeared somewhat interested but declined sponsorship. A potential sponsor who realizes that the event or facility was a good investment may try to set aside funds the next year to become a sponsor.

Marketing Efforts and Costs

Marketing during an event can take several different forms. The discussion of "sizzle" in chapter 10 highlighted the need for in-game promotions and related activities to enhance the event and market toward getting fans to return at a future date. It is hoped that making the experience enjoyable will encourage fans to return for another enjoyable experience.

Once patrons are at the facility they will have a good time, an unpleasant experience, or a neutral experience. The facility can affect this, but to a limited degree. If the home team loses, the fan may have had a great experience with every element of the facility and the event except for the outcome of the game. Fans may have a bad experience if they are annoyed or injured by another fan or hurt by a foul ball. These types of incidents are ones that the facility has little or no control over. Many other sources of dissatisfaction, though, are under the facility's control. Fans who get food poisoning at an event are going to be dissatisfied. Fans who get lost because the parking signage is inadequate or because of long traffic delays near the facility will be upset. They will have "buyer's remorse" (cognitive dissonance), and a facility cannot survive with upset customers. With regard to marketing, a fitness facility may market itself as a place for hard bodies, and a young person may join to meet other singles. If the new member discovers that the singles at the facility are mostly over 70 years old, he or she may be unlikely to continue or renew the membership. Thus information about customer

satisfaction, which needs to be obtained through surveys as highlighted earlier, will significantly affect marketing plans.

Marketing is also affected by price considerations. If the concession items are too expensive, sales may not be as strong as they could be. However, a marketing-oriented approach using visual cues on scoreboards, announcements over the loudspeaker, and information in event programs, combined with olfactory stimuli such as the smell of popcorn pumped into the stands, might help generate more sales. Thus, even if the price is high, patrons' other senses may override logic and encourage them to purchase a concession item.

Mistakes are also an opportunity. If a fan purchases a ticket that is inaccurate or already taken (which is very unusual), how does the facility respond? Operationally an employee may check both tickets and discover any error, confusion, or counterfeiting. After the operational component is completed, what will the employee do? The solution is to give the person already in the seat the right to remain if his or her ticket is accurate. The second fan can be given a similar seat or even an upgrade as a thank-you for his or her understanding. Such a simple gesture can possibly win a longtime customer. This is the hallmark of marketing an experience. If the experience is wonderful, the patron will become a valuable customer and move up the **marketing escalator** to become a more frequent purchaser. The marketing escalator represents a spectrum of facility users, from nonusers to frequent users. Most facilities focus their efforts on converting the casual users to frequent users.

After an event, managers need to analyze the entire marketing effort to determine what worked and what needs to be changed. Such an analysis can be complicated. If an event used only word of mouth to generate interest, it would be easy to determine whether or not the marketing effort worked. However, most events and facilities utilize multiple campaigns at the same time, and it is often difficult to determine which campaign worked. For example, a circus may utilize billboards, newspaper advertisements, supermarket giveaways, radio, and even televised commercials. It is not easy to decide which communication medium was most successful and should be used in the future or whether to continue using all the mediums.

Television and other media coverage, which can be publicity, needs to be monitored to ensure that no negative publicity is aired. Management should be careful with all media relations, but this concern is much greater after an accident or tragedy. The facility should have a designated person to handle press-related matters. Only one person should speak on behalf of the facility to the press. That person should be trained in how to deal with media inquiries. For example, if a question is asked and management does not have an answer, it is inappropriate to answer "no comment." Such a statement suggests implicitly that the facility has something to hide. Instead, the facility spokesperson should say something like "We do not have an answer yet to that very good question, but as soon as we conclude our investigation I will contact you to tell you the results." Such a statement is not newsworthy and will not be replayed on the evening news.

Facility Analysis

Operational planning issues abound during an event. What if the facility is too hot? Can the heating, ventilation, and air conditioning (HVAC) system be modified, and if yes, how? What happens if the lights go out, and how long will it take to bring them back to their required illumination level? What happens if the rink ice begins to thaw? These situations all have to do with the facility operations side of running an event or facility.

Operational analysis focuses on how the facility functioned during the event. Were there any problems with the facility? Were there any problems with the mechanical systems? Did the structural integrity of the facility become compromised by any activity during the event? Did the bathrooms work properly? What items were broken during the event and now need to be repaired? These are the types of questions that need to be answered after an event to make sure the facility is ready for the next event.

Operational issues inherent in any facility can range from sanitation problems to HVAC breakdowns. A facility and its management team will be judged by how they respond and how quickly they respond to a problem. It is anticipated that problems will occur at every facility and at every event. Facility users understand if the lights go out or if there is a problem with the blowers. However, if the problem is not corrected quickly, even understanding people can become irate. In order to ensure continuous operations with the fewest problems, the facility manager needs to have a maintenance staff in place that includes the various tradespeople who may be needed. In a smaller facility, the manager should have appropriate independent contractors available to come within a one-hour period. Normally a facility senior engineer helps direct several tradespeople in plumbing, electric, crafts, and other areas who are responsible for maintaining and repairing systems during an event.

To avoid a major tragedy such as the stands collapsing, the facility structure itself is the first concern. Thus, the facility structure needs to be reviewed not just before the event, but also during and after. Systems may be monitored for sounds, heat, pressure, or related potential clues that there may be a problem. Most larger facilities have a call center or an electronic monitoring system or both. A call center can receive several hundred phone calls during an event for problems like a broken toilet seat or a malfunctioning refrigerator at a concession stand. The call center dispatches appropriate personnel to make necessary inspections and corrections, if possible. An electronic monitoring system identifies when a problem occurs and automatically indicates where the problem is located and what steps could be taken to correct it. Some systems are so thorough that they can even identify whether the facility tradespeople can complete the work, and may contact outside vendors if the work needs to be outsourced to a third party.

A facility needs to be carefully examined after each event to make sure that no structural defects were caused by the event or the crowd. For example, a bleacher could have been broken or come unbolted. Structural problems could arise such as weakening of cement from years of use or possible misuse. While a roof does not collapse after most events, if it does, the results can be disastrous if anyone is in the facility. Some of the components that need to be inspected are the following:

- Facility envelope (annual inspection)
- Roof (annual inspection)
- Sprinkler system and sensors (quarterly inspection)
- Relamping (changing light bulbs) (as needed)
- Emergency generators (weekly inspection of all gauges, connections, batteries, fluid levels, etc., and monthly load testing)

- Trash chutes (quarterly inspection)
- Fire alarm system (annual inspection)
- Elevators (weekly inspection)
- Burglar alarm system (monthly inspection)
- Smoke detectors (semi-annual inspection)
- Irrigation system (biannual inspection)
- Site drains (quarterly inspection)
- Water heaters (annual inspection) (Lewis, 1999)

All aisles, rest rooms, stairwells, walkways, and food counters and related areas need to be cleaned immediately after an event. Cleaning of the food preparation area needs to be carefully reviewed. Failure to properly clean kitchen equipment can lead to numerous health code violations, but can also make future cleanup jobs that much more difficult.

Where does all the garbage go after everyone leaves? With recent innovations and technology, sport venues are integrating recycling into concession sales. Recycling containers for cups, paper, and bottles are appearing more and more often. Even though the costs of a recycling program are greater than those for traditional garbage removal, society changes and is becoming more environmentally concerned. In order for a recycling program to work, employees and signage should be placed near the containers to remind people, and announcements about the recycling program should be made throughout the game. Sport venues are also using recycled materials to make napkins, cups, and towels for use at a later time (Berg, 1992).

Special attention also should be given to general maintenance for things like broken seats, clogged drains, dripping faucets, and broken dispensers (both soap and condiments).

The lighting system should be checked to make sure all the lights worked well and to determine whether any lights need to be replaced or redirected. The HVAC system should be checked to make sure the heating/cooling units worked effectively and see whether any oiling, screen cleaning, or other services are required.

The playing surface should be examined. For example, outdoors, muddy areas may need to be drained or resodded; indoors, gym floors may be peeling. Checking the playing surface is especially important in cases in which the facility will be changed over from one event to another in mini-mal time. Skipping a problem because of time constraints can lead to bigger problems later on.

Equipment and Warehousing

All equipment not being used for the event needs to be properly stored so it does not get damaged. Seats, barricades, extra concession booths, and other similar types of items need to be moved before an event and properly stored to avoid getting damaged or creating a hazard. A potentially dangerous item such as a trampoline can represent an attractive nuisance and needs to be properly secured so that children cannot use it. If necessary, doors should be locked or a security person should be stationed in the area. Most storage areas can be properly monitored with a closed-circuit TV (CCTV) system, which saves the cost of a security person. Regardless of the strategy used, the storage area should be secured.

Special attention is usually warranted at championship-related events. Some events have a final awards ceremony that may require a platform. Platforms normally need to be stored away from the competition and then put in place at the end of the competition. There should be a clear and direct path for moving the platform. Trophies also represent a potential concern during an event. Steps must be taken to prevent damage and theft. Additionally, someone must be designated to present the trophies, and arrangements must be made to deliver them. If a team does not

Trophy set up and presentations present additional security and safety concerns for facility managers and staff.

win a game, it may be necessary to have arrangements for sending the trophies to another site.

After an event ends, the items utilized for that event may need to be stored until they are required for a future event. Madison Square Garden has numerous overlapping events. If the New York Rangers are playing on Friday night, the facility must find storage for all the novelty items, nets, dasher boards, and even the Zamboni so that the floor can be converted to a basketball surface and the concession stands stocked with primarily Knicks gear. This process is repeated the next day if a collegiate competition is scheduled. After an event it is also necessary to clean storage areas. Fire hazards can be created when storage areas are not properly cleaned. The accumulation of debris can represent a tripping hazard as well.

Storage areas are typically built into facilities, but they often are full or difficult to manage. Significant storage room is needed to ensure proper access to needed supplies. A regular spring cleaning can be a useful activity to help get rid of clutter that may reduce the amount of storage space in a facility.

Communication and Technology Systems

While internal wiring must be in place before an event, numerous concerns arise during an event. For example, what happens when an event is stopped by a power outage? Is there a backup generator? Is the communication system connected to the backup generator? Is the public address system connected? These types of concerns need to be monitored before and during the event.

If the event was broadcast, the camera crew should be contacted to see how the lighting worked and to determine if anything can be done to make the facility more camera friendly. Members of the press should be contacted to make sure their computer connections, phone lines, and seating area functioned appropriately. Since a facility needs media coverage for marketing purposes, it is incumbent on management to make sure that the media are treated well. If the media are given poor facilities, their coverage may reflect the poor conditions.

Facility Focus: Candlestick Park

© AP/World Wide Photos

Candlestick Park (more recently known as 3Com Park) is a well-known sport facility in San Francisco. San Francisco is known as a major earthquake area, and the facility is not far from the San Andreas fault. San Francisco has had a number of large earthquakes, including a major one in 1909 that destroyed a large part of the city. In a historic incident, an earthquake interrupted a 1989 World Series game between the San Francisco Giants and the Oakland A's. When the quake struck, the power was lost in large portions of the San Francisco area, including Candlestick Park, where the game was being played. The game was being nationally televised, and the chaos in the stands was shown across the country. Executives rushed to turn on the emergency generator, but it was out of gas. Furthermore, the public address system was not even connected to the generator. To communicate to the fans in the stands, police cars with loudspeakers were brought onto the field. However, the speakers were able to reach only the first several sections, and word of mouth was required to convey directions to those farther up in the stands.

Box Office and Ticketing

Tickets to an event are often sold in advance, but many people buy tickets at the gates. Does the box office have enough available cash? Are proper crowd management strategies in place to deal with the crowds? Have enough tickets been printed, or is there a computer system that automatically checks the seating inventory, indicates which seats are available, and prints tickets on the spot? These are only some of the questions that need to be considered when managing the box office. Most larger facilities utilize computer-based systems that streamline the process, but numerous ticketing concerns can occur during the event. For example, multiple tickets might have been sold for the same seat, or ticket takers might have accepted forged tickets. Other issues typically dealt with by the box office include providing armbands for people who can purchase alcohol and giving out special discount vouchers to buy items in the facility.

Another concern is the amount of cash that may be stored at the box office. Precautions need to be taken to make sure the money is secured. Some facilities regularly collect money from the concession areas, parking lot attendants, and others and then bring these funds to the ticket office to be counted and processed, either through a safe drop or an armored car pickup.

The box office's books need to be examined to determine if anyone is skimming money or failing to report all sales. The computer system needs to be reviewed to determine if there were any glitches such as double printing of tickets for the same seats. If the computer malfunctioned, then the program needs to be examined for programming glitches or hardware problems. Speed is of the essence, since tickets often must be printed for the next day, and the system cannot be down too long without causing major difficulties.

The event and facility also need to examine the relationship with any ticket brokers to determine how tickets sales are going. Are third-party vendors succeeding in selling tickets? Is the phone-based sales system working well? How many tickets are sold over the Internet, and how are those sales managed? Is the facility ready to handle people buying e-tickets? Those are just some of the questions that need to be examined not just after an event but also during the long-term planning process.

Event Security

Command posts must be staffed with properly trained personnel. Almost every larger facility faces security problems at each event. A facility must be prepared to handle security problems from pickpockets to auto thefts to lost children. Chapter 15 dealt with numerous security concerns that should be addressed to provide a safer facility. However, the proof is in the execution. No matter how well trained the personnel may be, facing a live emergency is different than any textbook analysis. While tabletop exercises and live drills help educate and train the staff, only a real disaster can provide the most comprehensive training.

Staff members should continuously monitor the CCTV system and scan the crowds to see what activities are occurring and whether it is necessary to send ushers or security personnel into any given area. If there is no CCTV system, security personnel rely upon their own observations. Security needs to be provided to monitor areas inside and also outside the facility, for example in parking areas or adjoining city streets where some fans may be celebrating.

After an event ends, the security personnel and ushers cannot leave the facility until all patrons have left. In one case during the 1990s, it was raining as the event ended and as an award ceremony took place. While fans remained in the stands awaiting the award ceremony, the security personnel were nowhere to be found. They had probably moved to out-of-the-way places in order to stay dry. This resulted in a situation in which several fans were injured. If the security personnel had been at their assigned stations the incident probably would never have happened.

Besides protecting fans, the security personnel protect players, officials, administrators, the media, mascots, cheerleaders, and others who are involved in producing the event. There are numerous examples of fans chasing after officials to challenge a call. Security companies have gone so far as to clothe police officers in officials' uniforms to serve as decoys while the real officials are leaving the facility.

Parking and Transportation

During an event the parking area must be monitored for criminal behavior. Break-ins are the primary concern, but sometimes cars are stolen from lots. Other concerns include tailgate parties that are continuing and hot or burning areas where barbeque grills have been used. Monitors also keep an eye on the parking lot in winter to see when it needs to be plowed so that people do not have difficulty leaving.

Another situation in lots is drunken fans trying to get to their vehicle. Sometimes intoxicated fans leave a game early because they are not feeling well. These fans can represent a concern to others. Several suits have been brought by patrons who were injured when a drunk fan fell on them as they walked to their cars (Fried, 1999).

Buses require fueling and parking spaces. These two concerns can create a tactical headache. Some buses do not have gas gauges. During the Atlanta Olympic Games in 1996, some drivers were not familiar with the operation of the buses they were driving and ran out of gas, stranding their passengers. Parking becomes a concern when marketing companies try to take prime parking spaces so that their trucks can serve as mobile billboards. Police may be required as well as tow trucks to move vehicles that could impede traffic or make it more difficult for buses to move or park.

After an event, the action moves to the parking area. Upset fans can take out their frustration on opposing fans or their vehicles. Intoxicated fans can cause problems by urinating on people or property, crashing vehicles, or falling down in the middle of a lot and disrupting traffic.

To help prevent these problems, an appropriate security detail needs to be stationed around the parking lot. Closed-circuit TV and gate monitoring can supplement the security detail. Care should be taken to help alleviate concerns associated with traffic delays and people cutting in and out of exit lines. Especially in hot weather or late at night, people can do stupid things to try to save one minute of driving time. Such actions can cause accidents as well as infuriate others and lead to fights.

After all the cars have left, there are normally several cars left in the lot with mechanical problems. There also is normally a significant amount of trash in the lot. Management has to have personnel or third-party providers clean the lot and examine the area for problems such as potholes, broken lights, and holes in security fences.

Concessions and Food Services

Concessions is one of the largest activities going on behind the scenes during an event. One reason is that concessions is often the biggest single profit center. Concessionaires strive to receive about 80% profit to cover their expenses. Thus, if an item costs $0.20, the goal is to sell it for $1.00 (Cohen, 1994b). Profit margins on specific foods are listed in table 16.1.

Drinks can be sold either in cans or as a mixture based on a syrup. A syrup-based soda generates more profit than cans or bottles. A 5-gallon bag-in-the-box (BIB) of fountain syrup should deliver 3,800 fluid ounces (112 liters) of soft drink and costs around $40. About 15 ounces (0.44 liters) of liquid is poured into a 20-ounce (0.6-liter) cup on top of ice. Including the cost of the cup, ice, and straw and lid, the total cost should be approximately $0.25. If the drink is sold for $1.50, then the profit is $1.25 per drink. In contrast, if a distributor sells cans or bottles for $0.50 each to the facility and the facility sells the drink to a fan for

Table 16.1 Concession Profit Margins

Food	Bulk cost	Sales price	Profit margin
Hotdogs	$0.30	$1.75-$2.50	80-83%
Popcorn	$0.18	$1.75-$2.00	90%
Nachos	$0.48	$2.50-$3.00	80-85%
Soda—syrup	$0.25	$3.00-$4.00	120-150%
Soda—bottle	$0.50	$4.00-$5.00	80-100%
Beer	$0.40	$5.00-$6.00	125-150%

From Cohen, 1994.

$1.50, the profit margin is reduced to only $1.00 per drink (Holtzman, 2001).

Other profits can be derived from premium food and novelty items. For example, the 2002 Major League Baseball All-Star Game generated $40 per head in revenue from concession and merchandising sales. The breakdown was $18 in retail sales, $13 from concessions, and $9 from premium dining ("All-Star Fans," 2002). A significant chunk of the revenue came from anything that bore the word "All-Star," such as caps, shirts, and balls. These financial results need to be continuously monitored during and after an event to ensure that the right products are being offered at the right prices.

Since management has to focus on profits, anything occurring during an event that can harm profits needs to be remedied. Long lines, warm beer, few options, dirty conditions, and poorly prepared products can all hurt profits for years to come. Management has to focus on providing customer satisfaction in the quickest time possible and at a relatively inexpensive price. Fans are accustomed to paying more for food at a ballpark or stadium than they would in other settings, but they demand high quality and quick service. Thus, consultants are often retained to show how the menu can be enhanced, how employees can be trained to be more effective, and how the facility can be laid out to maximize speed in placing and processing orders. Management should monitor when, where, how, and how often fans purchase foods. For example, because most sales occur early in an event rather than close to the end, more sales staff are needed earlier in an event.

After an event, the concession area needs to be thoroughly cleaned. Various government regulations cover the temperature required to clean certain food preparation equipment. Utensils normally need to be cleaned in extremely hot water. Employees must be trained on using cleaning equipment and avoiding injuries. Management should check that the equipment is working properly so that the concession area will be in working order at the beginning of the next event.

Food needs to be properly stored. Some foods can be refrigerated and some can be frozen; others cannot be stored for use at a later date and must be discarded. Leftover food can be eaten by employees, thrown out, or donated to a charity. Many soup kitchens are willing to take leftover food, and this is an option worth pursuing since it can result in

a tax deduction for charitable giving and also help develop positive public relations.

The concessions inventory is another post-event concern. A complete inventory needs to be made at each concession area to determine what drinks, snacks, and food items must be ordered. Is there enough room in the freezer? How long will it take to order more food? Is there enough room in the storage area to store all the necessary drinks, cups, plastic utensils, and condiments?

Medical Services

Medical issues can be delegated in part to external providers such as emergency medical technicians (EMTs) and the local fire department. However, not every medical issue is an emergency. Athletic trainers or other qualified individuals are needed to operate a triage unit at a facility. Does a bee sting require medical care? What if a fan is hit by a foul ball or hockey puck? What if someone is injured slipping on a walkway? Each injury and the effect on the person are different, and the event or facility must respond appropriately. The issues may be more difficult when participants or employees are injured.

> Will the team physician take over?
>
> What will the media say?
>
> Will the injured party sue?
>
> If an employee is injured, will there be an OSHA investigation? Is the facility safe?

Bloodborne pathogens are among the medical issues that must be addressed during an event. If someone has been injured and is bleeding, facility employees cannot just wipe up the blood and put it in the trash. Due to the threat of hepatitis B, human immunodeficiency virus (HIV), and other bloodborne-related illnesses, OSHA mandates that facilities implement a risk management plan to deal with blood spills (Vivian, Daugherty, and Dunn, 1994).

All facilities should have a designated OSHA compliance representative (either a manager or an employee). This representative needs to implement the following medical-related rules:

- Develop a written exposure control plan
- Develop a comprehensive precaution policy
- Properly train and educate employees
- Keep appropriate records

Behind the Scenes: An Opening to Remember

© AP/World Wide Photos

While one might assume that an experienced facility manager knows how to run a facility, screw-ups occur on a regular basis. On April 9, 1913, the Brooklyn Dodgers opened Ebbets Field, or at least they tried to. The owners forgot the keys to the front door, and fans had to wait in line for over an hour while an employee went home to get a spare key. Since the builders had forgotten to build a press box, the press had to watch the game from the grandstands. The owners even forgot the American flag that was supposed to be raised during the opening ceremonies (Nash and Zullo, 1992).

- Examine engineering- and work-related practices
- Purchase appropriate protective kits and equipment
- Purchase vaccines and exposure follow-up protocols
- Utilize appropriate labels and signs
- Develop and implement appropriate housekeeping practices and procedures (Vivian, Daugherty, and Dunn, 1994)

Besides having kits to handle spilled blood, a facility must have a standard first aid kit with splints, bandages, and wound cleaners. The kit should be replenished each time material is used. In addition, some states are starting to require sport facilities and even high schools to have defibrillators in each public facility.

Numerous insurance-related concerns arise with medical services and require careful attention. One that is crucial is proper documentation of every injury, all treatment received, and all ambulance usage. All photographs and incident reports should be immediately submitted to insurance companies to prevent rejection of a claim.

When someone has been injured, the management staff need to show compassion and concern. If a patron went to the hospital, did the facility send someone along to make sure he or she was all right? Did the facility cover the medical bills? Was the insurance company notified? Was an autographed item given to the fan in order to create positive feelings? Small gestures such as these may make someone think twice about suing.

Inventory of medical supplies must be checked in case small adhesive bandages, ice packs, Ace bandages, and so on were used for an event. Management should also evaluate how the athletic trainers, fire department personnel, and EMTs coordinated their services. Sometimes medical service providers do not cooperate with one another, and management needs to evaluate personnel to make sure that all those involved in medical care work as a team.

Summary

The planning process for hosting an event and then preparing the facility for the event are time-intensive activities, but the event itself can raise various concerns. Has the facility complied with all its contractual requirements? Are the employees doing their jobs? Will the event be a financial success? Will the event raise legal issues? These are just some of the questions the facility manager needs to ask and answer when evaluating an event.

The facility manager also needs to spend a significant amount of time analyzing future marketing opportunities based on the event's success and the patrons' experience. Through surveying, the facility should understand what patrons liked and did not like about a facility. The facility manager then needs to turn his or her focus toward the facility and evaluate whether or not the facility performed as it was supposed to. This review includes not only the facility structure but also specific elements such as ticket operations, transportation, and concessions.

DISCUSSION QUESTIONS AND ACTIVITIES

1. What are some of the key concerns that need to be analyzed during an event?

2. What is management's role during an event?

3. Contact a facility manager and try to follow the person during an event to see what he or she has to do as the event proceeds. Note in percentage form how the person's time is spent (e.g., 40% of the time spent is on personnel matters).

4. After an event, stay in the parking lot to see how people leave and how long it takes various people to leave. This exercise is designed to help you learn how to be a secret shopper and identify good and bad policies, procedures, and execution.

5. What do you think are the biggest concerns that need to be examined after an event?

Risk Management Audit

The following risk management review was conducted by an attorney or attorneys from Sabia & Hartley Law Firm in Hartford, Connecticut, under the express assumption that this report would be an official communication from an attorney to a client and as such covered by the attorney–client work product privilege. It should be noted that nothing in this audit should be construed as legal advice to any other facility and an attorney should always review any risk management strategy.

General Overview

The Martial Art Studio (hereafter "facility") is located at a major intersection in a strip mall with two major anchor tenants. The mall has several stores ranging from an electrical store to a fish store and a bakery. The mall is designed with a glass-enclosed and air-conditioned corridor between the actual storefront and the mall entrance. This enclosed area serves as a walking area for local seniors who want a workout but do not want to walk in the hot and humid New Haven weather. While these walkers do not necessarily pose a risk, there are risks that can be associated with their activities and the facility in question.

The facility is a martial arts studio specialized in karate. The owners are the chief instructors, and no other employees currently work at the facility. The business has been in operation since May 1, 1995. In 1998-99 the Martial Art Studio was officially incorporated as an LLC.

The following more specific details are based on a site visit on Monday, January 25, 1999 and Thursday, January 28, 1999 and a review of additional documentation provided by the owners.

Exterior

Parking appeared adequate with well over 150+ parking spaces for all mall visitors. The facility is just east of an anchor tenant (grocery store) with significant parking available. The parking lot has six (6) light poles within the parking area with each having four lights posted on poles between 25 and 30 feet aboveground. Most lights appeared to produce sufficient foot-candles, with three to four lights needing to be replaced due to low foot-candle dissemination. The parking lot also had three poles with two halogen bulbs on them, but the lights on the far north end of the parking lot were not turned on when I made my night inspection.

There was no indication of a security phone or security cameras around the parking lot or attached to the building if anyone needed assistance. While I was unable to determine the potential for criminal activity (the neighborhood is a typical middle class neighborhood with single-family residences), the Owner (hereafter "owner") informed me that his truck had been broken into and someone had tried to break into the facility's rear door. A sticker on one of the front doors to the mall indicated that the area is patrolled by Acme Patrol.

The sidewalk outside the mall entrance is a narrow walkway. There exist several wheelchair cutouts, which are fairly steep and possibly difficult for some mall users. Doors leading into the facility are glass doors with pull/push handles in their horizontal midplane. While several doors have handicap decals, they do not appear any wider than other doors nor are they electrically or push-button activated.

Suggestions for External Safety

1. Remind landlord whenever lights are not turned on and ask for a phone number to call at night if the lights are not on.
2. Suggest to the landlord adding a safety phone or security cameras to increase safety-related feelings of current and potential clients.

3. Post warning signs by the facility front door whenever any criminal activity has occurred that you are informed about.

4. Mention safety issues to classes, especially night classes, and ask men in the class to act as escorts for women wishing to go to their cars. You can also inform students that if they have any fears or concerns a facility agent will gladly walk anyone to their car.

5. Remind students about risk reduction techniques such as walking with the auto key ready to insert into the keyhole, checking for suspicious individuals, checking under the car and in rear seats, etc.

6. If criminal activity starts to increase, talk to the landlord about possibly installing a security cart or increasing constable/police patrols.

7. Be cautious concerning disabled patrons. If they have a hard time entering the facility, you should talk with the landlord about accommodation strategies. Both landlord and tenants are liable for any potential Americans with Disabilities Act (ADA) violations.

8. Find out how often Acme Patrol actually patrols and if they in fact are the landlord's official security company. Obtain a contact phone number and meet with them on a periodic basis to inform them of class times and any security-related concerns.

Entryway

To enter the facility, persons pass through the mall's glass entry doors, walk across a brick walkway, and pass through the facility's sole entrance, a glass door. The glass doors appeared to be in good condition and fairly visible to prevent someone from walking into them. However, at least one metal plating for the threshold to a door in front of the facility had some pitting, which could cause a heel to get stuck. There were no nonslip mats to remove any rainwater from the outside. The bricks can become slick when wet. The bricks are red-brown or maroon color, and water is hard to see on the bricks from certain angles. The bricks have mortar between them and are fairly uniform. However, some bricks have a height difference from other bricks, which can be negligible through 1/4 of an inch. Such a height discrepancy

is not significant. However, if the bricks ever shift or chip and a height discrepancy of 1/2 inch or more is created, then the tripping hazard could lead to liability. While the landlord would be the primary defendant, if the accident occurred in front of the facility the facility owner could also be sued. There were no significant warning signs posted in front of the facility's main entrance.

Suggestions For Entryway Safety

1. The landlord should be contacted to determine where nonslip mats are located and when they are placed by entryways. You should also have access to "Slippery when wet" or similar signs by the mall entrance and facility entrance whenever it rains and people track in water.

2. Make a point to tell people to walk carefully on rainy days.

3. Keep a mop handy in case some water accumulates during off hours and janitors are not around.

4. Monitor the brick to determine if any deterioration occurs and immediately notify management in writing (retain a copy for your records) when a problem occurs.

5. If someone complains about slipping in the corridor, fill out an incident report and take the time to examine the spot where they claimed to slip and what type of shoes they were wearing.

6. Post appropriate signs on your outer glass walls concerning specific facility rules, such as signs prohibiting eating or drinking and signs asking individuals not to warm up while waiting for their class in the corridor.

Facility Front Section

The facility front section includes several waiting benches, a mini-retail section, a single office, and some cubicles to store personal gear. While a mini-poster sets forth facility rules, the type is so small that it makes the poster less valuable as a warning mechanism. It should be stated that many of the policies are contained in additional materials and reinforced through the learning process, which leads to significant rule retention by students, but not necessarily by visitors/spectators.

- Foyer. The tile floor appeared to be in good condition and did not seem slippery. However, there was only a small nonslip mat if someone came from outside with wet shoes. Three wood benches appeared to be in good shape with no splinters or buckling. The screws/bolts were not tested for tightness.

- Office. On the first visit there appeared to be some baby supplies around. While it appeared that such items were for the owner's own child, there could be a workplace safety issue associated with a child's being injured or if inadequate supervision were provided for a child. There also could be ramifications if a child is injured and an insurance claim is raised against the carrier. The office has two window areas that are made with Plexiglas to reduce potential injuries. A first aid kit in the office had several types of bandages and gauzes. The kit also had some medicine and antiseptic solutions. Lastly, some unmarked lotion for "healing" purposes was also in the cabinet. The office had multiple wires running along the floor that presented a tripping hazard. The office should be cleaned to prevent tripping hazards such as boxes or dust bunnies.

- Sales area. Several types of products are made available, from protective equipment to uniforms and weapons.

Suggestions for Facility Front Section

1. Keep an open empty cash box on the sales counter after closing time to imply that no money is kept on the premises.

2. Check benches on a regular basis for any potential splintering, warping, or loosening of screws/bolts.

3. Purchase a larger nonslip entry mat and sign to put out whenever weather conditions warrant such warning.

4. Equipment sales should be reinforced with a sign indicating "Sold as is," especially with used equipment.

5. Make sure you have a sufficient first aid kit with necessary equipment such as splints, wrapping tape, etc.

6. Do not keep any drugs/unmarked lotions in the first aid kit, even aspirin or antacid tablets. Develop a policy not to provide any students with any drugs, even if they are very close friends.

7. Purchase and keep in an accessible location a blood cleanup kit with all the necessary disposal bags and cleaning solutions.

8. Clean the facility on a regular basis and keep boxes and supplies in the back closet if they are not used on a regular basis. All floor obstructions such as wires should be moved, put through walls, or covered by a walking tunnel or other protective device/technique.

Facility Workout Section

The facility workout area is composed of red carpeting throughout the floor area. Between the foyer area and the carpeting is a plastic strip approximately 2-3 feet wide running the length of the entryway that is used as a transition strip. This strip was not secured and was crumpled in certain places, which could lead to a tripping hazard. The carpet is cleaned on a regular basis with baking soda and related products to keep it smelling fresh and clean.

Two support poles were located in the middle of the workout area. These poles had sparring apparatus secured at a safe height above where any participant might come in contact with the poles. The poles were covered with black matting wrapped entirely around the pole. The ropes securing the matting appeared fairly tight with little give.

Rules were posted in both the foyer area and by a weapon rack area. The rules should be carefully scrutinized for accuracy on a regular basis.

A crash pad was leaning against one wall. Care should be exercised in moving and storing the crash pad so it does not interfere with workouts.

A phone was located on the office's rear wall in the workout area. There were no numbers posted by the phone.

One wall had several mirror sections which were approximately 5 feet tall and made out of what appeared to be glass. The owners indicated that the mirrors were specifically installed with thermal glue to prevent them from falling over if someone contacted them. However, the glass was not shatterproof.

Two fans were on to help circulate the air. It is unknown how frequently the mall air conditioning system helps to circulate the air. The air should be circulated 8 to 12 times per hour according to the American College of Sports Medicine's facility standard guide.

Suggestions for Facility Workout Section

1. The rules should be carefully scrutinized for accuracy and additional rules added as necessary such as "No touching weapons on the rack" or "All weapons brought into the facility need to be presented first to the instructor." The rules should also be uniformly enforced for both men and women.

2. A list of important safety numbers should be made and taped near and on the phone. A sign should also be posted on the phone indicating that the phone is for official use.

3. A sign should be posted on the office's external wall facing the workout area indicating that a first aid kit is located in the office.

4. The carpeting should be cleaned with an anti-fungal cleaning agent on a monthly basis.

5. The carpeting should be checked on a regular basis for rips, exposed seams, and ripples. The carpet should be pulled up whenever ripples occur and should be stretched to eliminate ripples.

6. Ropes securing pole padding should be checked on a monthly basis and tightened whenever necessary.

7. Every other month, handles on blocking mats should be checked to make sure they are not falling apart.

8. The carpet in front of the glass mirrors should be colored a different color, or a demarcation line should be added to help remind individuals to stay away from the glass.

9. The owner made an announcement that any equipment left on the floor can be taken by anyone else. This policy should also be in writing.

10. A photograph or video recording of the facility should be taken every month to help demonstrate the facility's general condition. These photos should be kept for several years.

Facility Rest Rooms

The rest rooms were fairly clean at the end of the day. While the trash cans appeared to be filling up, that would appear to be normal for a busy changing room. The rest room is located in the men's changing room. The women's changing room did not have a bathroom. The rest room was not ADA accessible. If any renovations are made to the existing facility, all renovations need to comply with the ADA. If the current setup for the rest rooms was in place prior to 1994, then no ADA issues currently exist. If, however, the rest rooms have been modified in any way since then, ADA-related liability could arise.

Piping under the sink was exposed. It is not known whether or not the piping becomes hot if hot water is run through the system.

Outside the men's changing room is a water cooler; it did not appear that the unit was too old or dirty. The water release mechanism should be regularly cleaned to prevent any diseases or contamination.

Suggestion for Facility Rest Rooms

Policies should be posted concerning individuals using the bathroom one at a time while others might be changing.

Administrative Issues

Various flyers were posted around the facility covering issues such as testing and class registration. Such flyers were not reviewed for accuracy.

Registration cards were not completed. They lacked emergency contact and phone numbers.

There currently are no employees.

The insurance policy the facility currently has is from Acme States Ins. Co., Ltd. based in Gibralter. An insurance industry acquaintance checked the company in the Best rating guides and could not find it listed, which is a concern. The policy has a $1 million limit, $2 million aggregate, and $5,000 medical. The insurance policy covers attorney fees and costs, but there is no indication as to who chooses the attorney. The policy does not cover competitions, but only injuries to students enrolled in classes. Property damage is not covered. The policy appeared to indicate that no coverage would be provided for selling items used by students at home or at another facility. The waiver required by the insurance company applies to only those enrolled in courses.

The policy specifically does not cover any advice given on dieting or injury care, ADA compliance, assaults and battery, communicable diseases, sexual abuse, or discrimination. Martial arts weapons are covered as long as they are used by an insured. An independent contractor teaching a course would not be covered unless they had a separate policy. There is a point of contact exclusion for free sparring. The owners are required to report any change in enrollment that affects enrollment, either positive or negative, more than ten (10) percent.

Suggestions for Administrative Issues

1. Brochures should contain a standard phrase such as "subject to final approval by management" to indicate that the owners have final say over testing, class schedule, registration, etc.

2. Have students complete all emergency information on their registration cards and have a master list for all students containing all pertinent contact information and any medical issues that might need to be relayed to EMT professionals.

3. The owners might want to offer volunteer workers some stock in the company so there is no question that a volunteer is not an employee, but rather is volunteering his/her time as a part owner. Volunteers are owed duties similar to those owed employees. However, a volunteer who is an owner cannot sue the facility, nor might some of the workplace safety laws apply.

4. The babysitter should be paid from personal funds such as a personal checking account rather than a business account. Otherwise she could be considered an employee and you would need to purchase workers' compensation insurance, etc.

5. There did not appear to be a sophisticated cash management system; however, polices should be in place to help prevent petty theft.

6. The Application for Testing should contain specific questions about an applicant's medical risk and an assurance from the test taker that he/she has doctor's approval to compete.

The form should also specify that test takers have to be both mentally and physically ready to take the test and to increase in belt level or are at risk for serious injury if they do not have both their mind and their body dedicated to advancement.

7. The Student Enrollment Agreement has several problems as listed below:

   A. The term "competent and qualified instructors" is vague and can mean different things to different people.

   B. The term "successful" should be inserted before the word "examination" to imply that a test taker will be promoted only after successfully taking the exam, not just taking the exam.

   C. Specify that the student has been cleared to participate by his/her doctor and has no outstanding medical conditions that were not reported to the owners.

   D. No guarantee on the equipment used or purchased.

   E. There is a significant inconsistency in that sometimes the form uses the word "student" and sometimes the word "member."

   F. Make sure to use gender-neutral language. Each instance of "he" should be followed by a slash and the word "she" (i.e., "he/she").

   G. The provision stating that civil codes do not apply is illegal, as a contract cannot affect a legal duty imposed by the state.

   H. There is a duplication of consumer rights provisions as they relate to cancellation.

   I. You should add a mediation/arbitration clause and a clause stating that any dispute would have to be brought in Connecticut, pursuant to Connecticut law. You should also include a provision that anyone who brings a claim about his/her enrollment and losses will have to pay the prevailing party's attorneys' fees and costs.

   J. You should examine similar contracts from local Connecticut businesses such as Bally's or 24 Hour Fitness to get a good idea of what elements they have covered.

Teaching Issues

The teachers appear to have received significant training by obtaining at least 8th-degree black belts. Instruction by the owner appeared to be lively, with a good student rapport. Safety instructions were reiterated on several occasions, and individuals without the proper equipment were prohibited from participating in sparring activities.

Some weapons, such as a bamboo stick, are fraying and are taped together. While fraying equipment utilized just for movement practice should not be a significant risk, such weapons should not be utilized for sparring if they will come in contact with other weapons or people.

The owner is taking a proactive approach to risk reduction and education by developing an instructor training manual, which is more thoroughly discussed with the suggestions below.

Suggestions for Teaching Issues

1. Provide specific rules for individuals such as whether or not glasses are allowed and whether, if glasses are allowed, thongs should be utilized to keep the glasses from falling off.

2. A sign should be posted specifically indicating the maximum class size allowed.

3. The chains on all weapons should be checked to make sure no links are broken or rusted.

4. All weapons should be tested before use; for example, poles should be taped on the ground to determine if they are broken or splintering.

5. Post a sign and make an announcement after each class asking anyone who has sustained an injury to immediately report it.

6. The following suggestions apply to the instructor training manual:

A. It should be clearly communicated that the manual does not specify or establish standards and that each school is different.

B. It should be clearly established that the teaching program is just an opportunity and that successfully completing the course does not guarantee employment or the opportunity to teach at Martial Art Studio.

C. The program being established might be considered a trade school-type program, which could raise some licensing issues. The educational program should be labeled an internship or apprentice program. The fee should be characterized as the cost for utilizing the facility during the internship/apprenticeship and for taking part in the lessons.

D. Carefully define terms such as "qualified instructor."

E. By developing an internship/apprentice program, the owners will open themselves up to significant employment law concerns such as affirmative action, equal employment opportunities, ADA, etc.

Conclusion

The Martial Art Studio was in overall excellent condition on the dates of my visits. While there are some changes, as specified above, that need to be made, the owner is very cooperative and enthusiastic about implementing risk management techniques and strategies. In fact, prior to completion of this report, some of the suggestions orally conveyed to the owners had already been adopted. The key areas for improvement include proper signage, keeping the facility clean, ensuring proper first aid supplies and policies, and purchasing reliable insurance coverage.

Glossary

additional insured—Another person or entity who will be covered by an insurance policy.

advertising—The use of paid sources to generate interest in a product or service.

aeration—Cutting or punching holes in the soil to help air, water, and nutrients filter down to the roots.

air exchange—Circulating air into a building from the outside and exhausting air from the building.

airborne sound—Sound made by people that travels through the air from their activities (such as yelling or stomping on the floor).

alteration—A change in a facility, system, or equipment to make it better or more responsive to people's needs.

ambient light—Naturally occurring light such as sunlight coming through a window.

ambient sound—Naturally occurring sound.

Americans with Disability Act (ADA)—Law that ensures equality for disabled Americans and includes equal rights to employment and access to facilities.

architectural barrier—Design barriers that prevent someone from fully enjoying a facility; such barriers need to be modified, if feasible, to comply with the ADA.

arena—An enclosed playing area with fixed seating capacity.

asset—Something that has value and can be converted quickly to cash.

assumption of risk—Defense to a negligence claim based on the injured person's knowing the risk of injury and voluntarily continuing even though it is dangerous.

attractive nuisance—A hazard that can attract and then injure a child.

audit—A detailed study designed to identify problems such as lost cash or poor management.

automatic external defibrillator (AED)—A device used to help resuscitate a person with a heart attack; can be operated by someone without significant training.

balance sheet—Highlights how much a facility or company is worth at a specific time by examining its assets, liabilities, and shareholder's equity (ownership value).

benchmarking—The process of establishing industry norms or standards by which a facility can compare its operations to make sure it is efficient; can be undertaken to review everything from ticket sales and concession revenue to maintenance standards.

bid process—Used by public entities to evaluate different vendors to determine which company can perform the required work at the best cost.

biometric scanning—References body parts from eyes to handprints to authenticate known individuals and to allow them to access the facility.

bloodborne pathogens—Diseases passed by blood.

blueprint—A technical drawing showing how a facility will be built.

bond—A promissory note stating that the issuer (whether a government or private corporation) will repay the loan with interest.

booking—The process of entering into a contract to secure a date and event for a facility.

breakdown maintenance—Maintenance undertaken as soon as an item breaks.

building area—The area five feet around the proposed building's exterior walls to provide enough room for building the facility.

building load capacity—How much weight the roof or rigging can support.

business plan—The road map for any facility that helps identify the product and market as well as the legal and financial outlook.

capital budgeting—Evaluating and determining long-term needs of the facility and whether new facilities need to be built or leased.

capital costs—Costs associated with long-term investments over many years.

capital planning—Examining and implementing programs that will help a facility and equipment last longer.

certificate of insurance—A form that shows that insurance coverage has been purchased.

changeover—The process of transforming a facility from one event surface such as basketball to another event surface such as ice hockey.

Civil Rights Act of 1964—Act that provided the framework for many key employment rights laws such as sexual harassment and discrimination under Title VII or gender equity under Title IX.

closed-circuit television (CCTV)—Self-contained video systems that record conduct to use as evidence or to investigate crimes.

collateral—Funds or assets used for securing a loan.

collective bargaining agreement (CBA)—The contractual agreement developed between an employer and a union that sets terms and conditions associated with the work environment.

commercial rights—Assets owned by a facility that can be sold, leased, or borrowed by others for a price; includes naming rights and pouring rights.

common law—Law developed and interpreted by the courts.

common space—Hallways, foyers, concourses, and general open areas for people to move around in.

compaction—Pressure on the soil that pushes sand and soil together.

computer-aided drafting (CAD)—Designing buildings on a computer for ease of operation and making changes.

computer-aided facility management (CAFM)—A software system that allows a facility manager to monitor needed repairs and adjust temperature and humidity controls.

computer management maintenance system (CMMS)—Monitors a facility and the equipment and systems in it to optimize their performance and minimize repair and replacement costs.

consideration—An exchange of value; required for a valid contract.

constituents—The individuals (such as patrons, athletes, and employees) who will use a facility.

contingency planning—Alternative plans used in response to the closing of a facility or the cancellation of a show.

continuity management—How a facility can continue operating after a disaster occurs.

contract—An agreement between at least two parties to complete a transaction.

contractually obligated revenue/income (COR/COI)—Money guaranteed by a contract that can be used in obtaining a loan.

core drilling—Drilling to see what lies underneath land such as rocks or water tables.

corporate bonds—Loans undertaken by a corporation for long-term purchases such as a new stadium; the new facility is used as collateral to secure repayment.

crime prevention through environmental design (CPTED)—Using architecture and landscaping to provide added protection against crime.

crisis management—How to respond to and prepare for a potential crisis.

crowd management—Specific steps or strategies taken to prevent a tragedy involving patrons; can include structural, signage, and personnel strategies.

customer—A person who purchases or receives services at a facility.

cyclical repairs—Repairs conducted at predetermined times, such as yearly or monthly.

demographics—Data about a given population such as age, gender, or income level.

design/build contract—Allows the future owner to provide the land and some control to the construction process, but the developer designs and builds the facility.

diffuse lighting—Lighting directed all over the facility to spread the light throughout the facility.

direct costs—Costs to build the facility; includes material and equipment costs and workers' fees.

direct lighting—Lighting that shoots down directly from a fixture on the area where light is intended to go.

displacement—The fact that some hotel rooms and diners would be present regardless of whether or not a facility is holding an event, which reduces the total economic impact of an event.

dragging—Going over the infield dirt with a screen to make sure it is smooth and without rocks and clumps of dirt.

economic impact—The net economic change in a community based on hosting an event.

ECT approach—Technique to help reduce the chance of injuries and lawsuits.

emergency medical technicians (EMT)—Emergency first aid and transportation to help injured patrons or athletes.

emergency response management team (ERMT)—Individuals dedicated to respond immediately to an emergency at a facility.

eminent domain—Ability of a government entity to purchase private land and convert it for public use.

energy audit—An attempt to find all uses for energy and help eliminate any waste.

equity—The total value of personal money, stocks, and property.

evacuation—The process of removing people from a facility in a safe manner.

expectancy theory of motivation—Managers will choose the option that will generate the outcome employees want.

expenses—Obligations that need to be paid, such as bills and salaries.

external constituents—A group of individuals who have an interest in the facility, such as stakeholders, lenders, and government entities.

facility management—The art and science of managing a facility to help meet the facility's objectives, goals, and mission.

Fair Labor Standards Act (FLSA)—Federal regulations for the workplace, such as minimum wage and overtime regulations.

feasibility study—Helps determine whether a project is worth pursuing from a marketing, legal, and community perspective.

financial forecast—An attempt to plan for future financial needs based on expected revenues and expenses.

foreseeability—The process of utilizing all the facts to know whether a specific event is likely to occur.

4 Ps—The four key elements of marketing, which are product, place, price, and promotion; some add an additional P, which is public relations.

front-of-the-house—An activity taking place in front of the audience, such as the game itself, versus back-of-the-house, which refers to areas used for staging and running the facility.

functional plan—A plan that helps define what the operational plan will try to accomplish; includes marketing or safety plans.

furniture, fixtures, and equipment (FFE)—Chairs, tables, televisions, paint on the walls, pictures hung on the walls, and other such items in a facility that help complete it.

Gemba Kaizen—A Japanese concept referring to knowing what is going on at the point of production.

general obligation bonds (GOBs)—Bonds backed by the full faith and credit of the issuing (borrowing) municipality that promises to repay the bonds with general tax revenue.

general seating—An event where there are no reserved seats and the first people into the facility have the first choice of where they will sit or stand.

glare—A point of light that affects a person's eyes.

grading—The process of smoothing over the land to build the foundation of a building.

green design—A facility built to be energy efficient; can lead to the LEED (Leadership in Energy and Environmental Design) certification.

ground fault circuit interrupters (GFCIs)—Help interrupt the flow of current to electrical outlets to avoid electrocution when water is in contact with an electrical appliance.

growth space—Unused space that could be used for future expansion needs and is attached to the existing facility.

grubbing—The process of removing brush, trees, and underbrush to clear the site to start building.

heat load—The number of people, the types of equipment in a facility, and the amount of heat they generate, such as heat from people's running and sweating.

heating, ventilation, and air conditioning (HVAC)—Allows cold and warm air to circulate within a facility.

horizontal space dividers—Separate areas through floors, ceilings, and floor heating systems.

hostile or offensive work environment—Sexual talk, actions, or photos that materially affect someone's ability to work.

immunity—Defendants who will not be responsible, even if they would otherwise be liable, since they are protected by the government or some other legal or statutory protection.

income statement—Highlights the revenue and expenses for the prior year and factors in taxes and interest payment to determine whether the facility earned a profit or loss.

independent contractor—A person who performs work for a facility but is not an employee of a facility; a facility cannot control a contractor's activities, resources, and assignments, whereas a facility can control these aspects of an employee.

indirect costs—Costs for a construction project including printing costs, attorney fees, and profit.

indirect lighting—Lighting that is directed against other objects, such as a wall or ceiling, so the light does not go directly into people's eyes.

induced effect—The ripple effect throughout an economy based on additional expenditures that filter throughout an economy.

infiltration rate—Rate water is absorbed into the soil.

internal constituents—Individuals inside the facility, such as employees, patrons, owners, and athletes, who could have an effect on the facility.

job analysis—Determining what activities need to be accomplished to reach a specific goal.

job description—Specific skills required for accomplishing the goals set forth in the job analysis.

landscaping—Using plants, dirt, water, and rocks to make the exterior of a facility more attractive.

liability—A financial obligation to pay someone; current liabilities are debts owed now such as salaries and utility bills; long-term liabilities typically refer to bonds or other borrowing instruments.

life-cycle costing—The total cost of a building or equipment over its life; includes initial construction, energy costs, maintenance, and repairs.

light intensity—How bright a light is; measured in foot-candles.

luxury boxes and suites—Sold for those wishing to attend games or events in the best environment or location.

management—The art of getting people and resources to work together efficiently to achieve the goals of the facility.

management by objective (MBO)—Managers and employees can work together to develop realistic and achievable objectives that make both parties happy.

market—A group of actual or potential customers who will be interested in the product.

marketing—The process of packaging a product or service and setting the right price, manner, and strategy to sell it.

marketing escalator—Theory that some people will not use a product while others will use it more frequently. The more often a person purchases the product, the faster that person moves up the escalator to become a frequent user.

Maslow's hierarchy of needs—Helps a manager identify what possibly will motivate an employee to perform better.

millwork—Customized finishes, such as wood, plastic, or metal.

mission—The overall ideal the facility wants to achieve; it focuses on general terms such as profitability, quality service, and workplace.

move management—Focuses on how a company can plan for and execute a full or partial move from one area or facility to another.

movement theory—The science of crowd movement; focuses on density, speed, and flow.

multiuse facility—Facility that can be used for different events.

naming rights—Allows a company to put its name on a building for a specific contractual amount.

needs assessment—Focuses on whether or not a community really needs a proposed facility.

negligence—The failure to act in a reasonable manner; that action is the proximate cause of someone's injuries.

objectives—Help people focus on reaching specific goals.

occupancy permit—A form completed by a government building inspector indicating that the finished building can be occupied and meets applicable building code requirements.

Occupational Safety and Health Administration (OSHA)—Establishes rules for workplace safety and investigates workplace accidents and hazards.

open-term contract—A contract that has no specific ending period and keeps renewing unless terminated by one of the parties.

operational plan—Highlights what specific steps are required for accomplishing either a strategic or a functional plan.

organizational flowchart—Highlights the line of command within a facility and indicates who reports to whom for direct supervisory responsibility.

outsourcing—The act of hiring an external party to manage the entire facility or parts thereof such as security, cleaning, or maintenance.

owner's representative—Acts on the owner's behalf to monitor the construction process and protect the owner's investment.

percolation—The amount of time it takes for water to pass through the soil to reach the roots.

personal seat licenses (PSLs)—A contractual right a person acquires for a fee that allows the person to purchase tickets for a specific seat; others cannot acquire tickets for that seat so long as the PSL contract is in effect.

personal transportation system—Vertical transportation such as elevators and escalators and horizontal transportation such as people movers.

personnel management—The process of managing or inspiring people to work together to achieve the goals of the facility.

place—The location in which a product is being sold or enjoyed.

planned approach—Forces a facility developer to examine what is needed and then develop a facility pursuant to some predetermined guidelines.

planning—The strategic process of identifying what the facility wants.

preventive maintenance—Undertaken on a predetermined basis to help prevent equipment and systems from breaking and to increase their longevity.

price—How much someone is charging for a given product.

product—The item (whether a service or goods) that is being marketed.

progressive disciplinary approach—The progression from a warning, written warning, formal complaints, and then termination; a manager can be more confident in terminating an employee knowing that the employee was given a chance to correct behavior on several occasions.

promotion—The activity being used to help sell a product.

property law—A variety of laws that affect the use of property from buying and selling property to how the property can be used.

proximate cause—Refers to the fact that a facility manager's actions are the direct cause of an injury versus an intervening incident that really caused the injury.

psychographics—The reason behind people's action to determine how or why they decided to purchase or not purchase a given product.

public accommodation—Facilities in which people congregate or attend events, such as theaters, arenas, and stadiums.

public assembly facility (PAF)—Any facility in which the public can enjoy an event, such as stadiums, arenas, theaters, convention centers, and performing arts centers.

public offering—Occurs when a stock is sold to the general public.

public relations—Uses free sources such as newspapers and word of mouth to help sell a product or service.

punch list—Itemizes all the repairs required for finishing the construction process of a new building.

reasonable accommodation—Repairs or reconstructions that need to be done in order to comply with ADA.

reconciliation—The process of calculating the total revenue and expenses for a given event.

redirected spending—Money that would have been spent on other activities in a community, (such as movies or bowling centers in a given area) if the money were not spent at the sport facility.

renovation—Taking an old facility and modernizing it.

request for bids (RFB)—A completed proposal in which the purchaser receives fixed bids in order to choose the most experienced company who has submitted the lowest bid to perform the proposed job.

request for proposals (RFP)—A request from external companies to suggest strategies to resolve a problem or develop a new program.

request for qualification (RFQ)—A request for different companies to prove they have the skill or experience to complete the proposed job.

restoration—Refurbishing a facility to its former appearance and replacing deteriorating and broken elements consistent with historical accuracy.

return on investment (ROI)—The financial return an investment generates.

revenue—Money received primarily from selling goods or services.

revenue bond—Utilizes revenue from specific sources (such as sales taxes or ticket surcharges) to repay the bond.

rigging—Trusses and beams to support items such as scoreboards and ropes from the ceiling and walls.

ripple effect—Similar to how water spreads in a ripple throughout a lake from when a stone is thrown into the water, a dollar spent in a community will likewise have an impact throughout the community.

risk management—The art of reducing the potential of someone's being injured by a hazard that could have been avoided or minimized.

root zone—The area around grass roots that needs to have the proper amount of water and minerals to keep the grass strong.

sales–lease-back strategy—Allows someone to sell an asset (equipment or building) to an investor who receives lease payments from the seller and the seller obtains a cash infusion.

sand modified fields—Fields use native soil combined with sand to help prevent compaction. To qualify as sand modified, the field needs to be at least 60% sand and 40% native soil.

scale model—A miniature model of the facility built to scale.

scoring—The process of breaking up the infield soil so that it is not hard or bumpy.

security—The safeguarding of an item, person, or place.

seeding—The process of spreading grass seeds to start a lawn instead of rolling out pregrown grass, which is called sodding.

site plan—A rendering of the facility with various subplans such as the master plan, grading plan, landscaping plan, and traffic plan.

soil testing—Tests to ensure soil is not contaminated.

soil-based fields—Native soils and materials that have a high water retention level.

space management—A focus on effectively organizing the space in a facility; scheduling, maintenance, and related concerns are often part of the process.

sport complex—A facility or group of facilities centrally located for ease of access and use.

sport facility—A facility in which sport activities are played or viewed.

sportsplex—A multiuse facility combining different activities on various fields or courts.

stadium—A large bowl or square- or rectangular-shaped playing area with spectator seating area that can have either a sideline or a full concrete grandstand.

stakeholder—Anyone who has an interest in the facility, such as neighbors, fans, or government officials.

steak and sizzle—The steak is the primary feature of a product, such as a football game, whereas the sizzle entails ancillary features of the product, such as cheerleaders or a halftime show.

strategic goal—Goal set by the highest-level managers to help run the facility and determine its future direction.

strategic plan—Focus on trying to achieve the facility's strategic goals; is often called the master plan.

structural load—The weight of the building and all the items in it.

structure-borne sound—Sounds made by the facility, such as exhaust fans or squeaky floors.

substructure—The entire building from the ground to the foundation, including the basement or underground parking structure.

superstructure—Everything above ground level, such as beams, frame, and structure.

support—The outside of the building, which helps support the building and protect it from the elements.

sustainability—Developing and running a facility that minimizes the impact on the environment and uses energy more efficiently.

swing space—Any space available to be used during renovations or alterations to an existing facility.

SWOT analysis—A focus on a facility's strengths, weaknesses, opportunities, and threats in order to plan for the future.

tabletop exercises—Safety training using models or maps and trainees indicating where they would go and what they would do during a real emergency.

tactical goals—Developed by midlevel managers to reach a strategic goal of a facility.

topdressing—Occurs through spreading additional soil over the existing soil.

tort law—A variety of claims against people for their actions (whether intentional or unintentional) toward another person or a person's property.

trespass—Light that spills over beyond the area intended, such as neighboring businesses or homes.

turfgrass—Grass on a playing field that is specifically planted to hold up to excessive use.

turnkey contract—A situation in which a construction company builds a facility with very little input from the owner and then turns over the complete facility to the new owner.

uniform building code (UBC)—Dictates approved standards for constructing a facility.

unintentional tort—Includes negligence and is not planned.

value-based engineering—Forces a developer to examine shortcuts that could save money but not compromise the looks or safety of a facility.

variance—A document from building inspectors or other government officials that states that a facility can be built in violation of established regulations.

venture capital (VC)—Initial funding from investors for a facility or company, but investors demand a significant return on the investment. The investment is risky because most new facilities and businesses normally do not generate enough funds to interest most investors.

vertical space dividers—Separate areas in a building through walls and columns.

vulnerability analysis—Examines situations in which the facility is most vulnerable; can include economic, natural, and manmade disasters.

waiver—A contract whereby someone agrees not to sue for a future claim the person might have if he or she were to be injured at a facility or event.

workers' compensation insurance—A no-fault system designed to provide coverage for any employee injured at work, regardless of who is responsible for causing the injury.

zoning—Laws designed to prevent unsightly or unorthodox buildings in a given neighborhood.

References

28 CFR Section 41.31. (2004, July 1 revision). ADA compliance under Part 41—Implementation of Executive Order 12250, non-discrimination on the basis of handicap in federally assisted programs.

29 CFR Part 1910. (2002, November 7). 67 FR 67950, *Federal Register*, Vol. 67, No. 217, Exit routes, emergency action plans, and fire prevention plans.

Abbott, J. and Fried, G. (1998). Asphalt jungle. *Cornell Hotel and Restaurant Administration Quarterly*, 40(2), 46–60.

Abbott, J. and Fried, G. (1998). Managing risks associated with parking structures. *Cornell Hotel and Restaurant Administration Quarterly*, 39(7).

Ackler v. Odessa-Montour Central School District, 663 N.Y.S.2d 352 (A.D. 1997).

"Advantage: Houston taxpayers." (1996, November 3). Houston Chronicle, 4c.

All-star fans post $40 per cap. (2002, July 16). *Venues Today* (e-mail newsletter).

American Airlines Center costs rise. (2001, July). *Stadia*, 5.

American College of Sports Medicine. (1992). *ACSM's health/fitness facility standards and guidelines*. Champaign, IL: Human Kinetics.

Americans With Disabilities Act, Public Law 101-336 July 26, 1990 104 STAT. 327, 42 USC 12132, SEC. 203. Enforcement.

Ammon, Jr., R. (1993). Risk and game management practices in selected municipal football facilities. Dissertation, University of Northern Colorado.

Amphitheater. (2002). Retrieved September 29, 2004 from http://depthome.brooklyn.cuny.edu/classics/gladiatr/amphthtr.htm.

Andelman, W. (1992, Winter). Profile: The economics of sports in the Tampa Bay area. Retrieved November 15, 2004 from http://www.andelman.com/articles/sportseconomics.html.

Applied Management Engineering, PC, and Kaiser, H. (1991). *Maintenance management audit*. Kingston, MA: R.S. Means Company.

Aramark acquires Ogden Entertainment. (2000, May/June). *Facility Manager*, 7.

Athens 2004. (2004). Retrieved November 9, 2004 from www.athens2004.com.

"Athens Challenge." (2001, May). Stadia, 17-18.

Aurandt, A. (2002). Games—in all seriousness. Retrieved September 29, 2004 from www.zianet.com/desertx/june98/game.html.

Balboni, B. Sr. (Ed.). (2001). RSMeans Square Foot Costs 2001. RSMeans Company, Inc. Kingston, MA.

Ballard, K., and King, J. (2002). Avoiding public recreation center planning pitfalls. Presentation at the 2002 Athletic Business Conference, Orlando, Florida.

Ballparks.com. National League teams and ballparks. (2002). Retrieved September 29, 2004 from www.ballparks.com/baseball/general/facts/national.htm.

Ballparks.com. (2004). Retrieved November 14, 2004 from www.ballparks.com/baseball/index.htm.

Basics of wood gym floor maintenance, the. (1980). St. Joseph, MO: Hillyard Floor Treatments.

Bassett, M. (2002, February 19). Emergency plans vital to cope with disasters. *Connecticut Post*, D1.

Baybutt, P. (2003, March). A real threat. *Contingency Planning & Management*, 10.

Beach, R. (1995, December). *Yale Alumni Magazine*. Retrieved September 29, 2004 from www.yalealumnimagazine.com/issues/95_12/baseball.html.

Beasley, K. (1997). *The Paralympic village: A barrier free city*. Lausanne, Switzerland: International Olympic Committee.

Beijing to spend 3.4 billion US dollars on Olympic facilities. (2002, March 29). *People Daily*. Retrieved December 19, 2002 from www.peopledaily.com.cn/200203/28/eng20020328_93035.shtml.

Bentil, K. (1989). *Fundamentals of the construction process*. Kingston, MA: R.S. Means Company.

Berg, R. (1992, September). Concessions going green. *Athletic Business*, 49-52.

Billy the Marlin wiggles off hook. (2003, January/February). *Facility Manager*, 6.

Bishop v. Fair Lanes Georgia Bowling, Inc., 803 F.2d 1548 (11th Cir. 1986).

Bisson, M. (2001, July). Turn it around. *Stadia*, 82.

Blanchard, K., and Johnson, S. (1986). The one minute manager. Berkeley, CA: Berkeley Publishing Company.

Blickstein, S. (1995). *Bowls of glory, fields of dreams: Great stadiums and ballparks of North America*. Encino, CA: Cherbo.

Borsenik, F., and Stutts, A. (1997). *The management of maintenance and engineering systems in the hospitality industry* (4th ed.). New York: Wiley.

Bowes v. Cincinnati Riverfront Stadium, Inc., 465 N.E.2d 904, 911 (Ohio Ct. App. 1983).

"Boy will get foul ball from man who knocked him aside." (2004, June 16). Retrieved on November 22, 2004 from http://www.cbs.sportsline.com/mlb/story/7425822.

Brailsford & Noyes. (2000). *Top ten project pitfalls.* Athletic-Business Conference Proceedings, Orlando, FL.

Breath of not-so-fresh air, a. (1999, March). *Athletic Business,* 10.

Brickman, H. (1997, November). Helping hardwood perform. *Athletic Business,* 67-72.

Bridges, F., and Roquemore, L. (1996). *Management for athletic/sport administration.* Decatur, GA: ESM Books.

Broncos sue 40 season ticket holders. (2002, June 24). Retrieved September 16, 2003 from http://benmaller.con/archives/benstakes/2002_06_23_benstakessarch.shtml#85194215.

Brooks, J., and Martinez, A. (2002, May). Direct, indirect costs. *Athletic Business,* 54.

Buckley, J. (2003, January). Calculating the true ROI of facility monitoring. *Contingency Planning & Management Online.* Retrieved March 12, 2003 from www.contingencyplanning.com/article_index.cfm?article=532.

By the numbers. (2003, May/June). Complete guide for selecting the right sports surface. *Recreation Management,* 19.

California Business and Professional Code Section 25503.6.

Carey, J. (1994, September 5). Arena Project Process. Memorandum to the Denton County Commissioners Court and the Lewisville City Council. Denton, TX.

Carlisle, V. (2003, March). All records are not created equal. *Contingency Planning & Management,* 20-24.

Carlson, R., and DiGiandomenico, R. (1992). *Understanding building automation systems.* Kingston, MA: R.S. Means Company.

Carter, A. (2002, September 20). The coliseum. *New Haven Register,* A1.

Carter, D. (2003). How much are you paying? *Baltimore Chronicle.* Retrieved August 4, 2004, from www.baltimorechronicle.com_sports_aug01.html.

Certified Ice Technician designation. (2001, September). *Stadia,* 38.

Chapin, T. (1997). Some ideas on stadium location. Retrieved April 5, 1997 from www.weber.u.washington.edu/~tmchapin/stadia/theory.html.

Charlotte Motor Speedway, estimated economic impact, AutoFair–September 15-18, 1994. (1994, November 3). Internal document.

Chelladurai, P. (1985). *Sport management: Macro perspectives.* London, Ontario: Sports Dynamics.

Circus Maximus, the. (2002). Retrieved September 29, 2004 from www.romeguide.it/MONUM/ARCHEOL/ccircus_maximus/circus.htm.

Cohen, A. (1994a, October). Don't give 'em the slip. *Athletic Business,* 53-56.

Cohen, A. (1994b, November). Food fight. *Athletic Business,* 45-48.

Cohen, A. (1998, November). The finish line. *Athletic Business,* 67-74.

Cohen, A. (2000, July). Feet first. *Athletic Business,* 54.

Cohen, A. (2001, November). Fabric fact & fiction. *Athletic Business,* 55-61.

Coleman, W. (2000, March-April). Let's go again! *Facility Manager,* 14-20.

Comastro v. Village of Rosemont, 461 N.E.2d 616 (1st. Dist. 1984)

Connor, P. (1998, August). Designer space. *International Magazine of Arena Construction and Management,* 26-30.

Conrad, C. (2000). Power meetings. Presentation at the 19th Annual Athletic Business Conference, Orlando, FL.

Context of the Games and the Olympic spirit, the. (2002). Retrieved June 13, 2002 from www.persus.tufts.edu/Olympics/spirit.html.

Cote, R. and Harrington, G. (Editors) (2003). *Life safety code handbook.* National Fire Protection Association, Quincy, MA.

Cotts, D., and Lee, M. (1992). *The facility management handbook.* New York: American Management Association.

County probes Bengals lease. (2002, October 17). Retrieved September 29, 2004 from www.findlaw.com/ap/s/2002/10-17-2002/20021017144506_077.html.

Dahlgren, S. (2000a, January). Fowl play. *Athletic Business,* 63-73.

Dahlgren, S. (2000b, July). Pumped-up prevention. *Athletic Business,* 71-78.

Davis, K. (1994). *Sport management, successful private sector business strategies.* Dubuque, IA: Brown.

Day, D. (1992, October-December). Feasibility studies. *Facility Manager,* 10-21.

Deckard, L. (2001, September 10). Arena, Hurricanes sign "contract with fans," set for ambassadors. *Amusement Business,* 10.

Depew, M., and Guise, S. (1997, May). In the root zone. *Athletic Business,* 67-71.

Designer fields: Stadium maintenance handbook. (1998). Cleveland: Pioneer.

Details, details. (1985, July). *Athletic Business,* 32-36.

Disney's Wide World of Sports Complex emerging as leading facility. (1998, October). *Facilities,* 15.

Dodds, D. (2003, November 7). Ralph Engelstad Arena: "Ralph" coins unveiled today. Retrieved March 26, 2004 from www.grandforks.com/mld/grandforks/news/7203070.htm.

Dohrmann, G. (2001, October 8). Face-off. *Sports Illustrated*, 44-49.

Domed stadiums of the world. (2002). Retrieved September 29, 2004 from www.ballparks.com/baseball/general/facts/domes.htm.

Donovan, H. (1994, January-February). Rigging the gig. *Facility Manager*, 16-18.

Dorsey, B. (1999, April/May). The premium-seat market: Reaching critical mass. *Facilities & Event Management*, 20.

Dorsey, B. (2001, May). In the lap of luxury. *Stadia*, 87-90.

Education laws and regulations. (2002). 606 CMR 38:00 School Construction. Retrieved September 29, 2004 from www.doe.mass.edu/lawsregs/603cmr38/603cmr38_1.html.

Elbo, R. (2000, May 31). Inside Japan's Kaizen power-houses. *Business World*, Volume XIII, No. 217.

Ellis, M. (2002). Can't tell the stadium without a scorecard. Retrieved September 29, 2004 from www.footballproject.com/story.php?storyid=102.

Elsberry, C. (2001, October 21). Arena by the numbers. *Connecticut Post*, 7.

Emmons, N. (2001, October 22). Holtzman tells attendees to develop concept, design around the menu. *Amusement Business*, 1.

Epidauro. (2002). Retrieved September 29, 2004 from www.arcaro.org/epidauro/

Fairfax County School District upgrades gym floors with Taraflex by Gerflor. (2003). Retrieved June 2, 2004 from www.gerflortaraflex.com/press/20030210.htm.

Farmer, P., Mulrooney, A., and Ammon, R. (1996). *Sport facility planning and management*. Morgantown, WV: Fitness Information Technology.

Film and broadcasting requirements in sports facilities. (1980s; n.d.). London, England: Sports Council.

Finken, Z. (2001, September). It's not all peanuts and cracker jack. *Recreation Management*, 20-23.

Fisher, J., and Martin, R. (1994). *Income property valuation*. Dearborn, MI: Dearborn Financial.

Foust, D. (2002, December 9). Even the greens will like these greens. *Business Week*, 84.

Fried, G. (1999). *Safe at first*. Durham, NC: Carolina Academic Press.

Fried, G. (2004a). Case study: Camp Randall. Proceedings from the Sport and Recreation Law Association (SRLA) Conference in Las Vegas, NV.

Fried, G. (2004b). Academy for Venue Safety and Security (AVSS) Manual. International Association of Assembly Managers, Dallas, TX.

Fried, G., and Miller, L. (1998). *Employment law*. Durham, NC: Carolina Academic Press.

Fried, G., Shapiro, S., and Deshriver, T. (2003). *Sport finance*. Champaign, IL: Human Kinetics.

Frosdick, S. (1998, August). Drink or dry. *International Magazine of Arena Construction and Management*, 20-24.

Gabrielsen, A., and Miles, C., eds. (1958). *Sports and recreation facilities for school and community*. Englewood Cliffs, NJ: Prentice-Hall, 43.

Galloway, D. (2001, November). Are fans being served? *Stadia*, 154-157.

Ganim goes to trial on corruption charges. (2003, January 6). Retrieved May 2, 2004 from www.nbc30.com/1871463/detail.html.

Gannon, M. (2002, February 1). Cheshire says pool builder in default. *New Haven Register*, B2.

Gartner: Businesses can't pay for disaster planning. (2003). Retrieved March 26, 2003 from, www.contingencyplanning.com/Information/NewsAlert/News-Alert-3.cfm.

Gearhard, G., and Schuler, R. (2001, August). Retrieved March 15, 2004 from www.ballparks.com/baseball/index.htm.

General information. (2004). Retrieved September 29, 2004 from www.rosebowlstadium.com/stadium/gen_info/gen_info.html.

Giants stadium resodded. (2002, December 31). *New York Times*, D4.

Give em a stench and they'll take afoot. (2003, January/February). *Facility Manager*, 7.

Gordon, C., and Brill, W. (1996, April). Crime prevention through environmental design in premises liability. National Institute of Justice research brief.

Goss, B. (2003, January/February). Hooliganism moves across the pond. *Facility Manager*, 32-35.

Greek theater. (2002). Retrieved June 14, 2002 from www.ebicom.net/~tct/ancient.htm.

Greenberg, M. and Gray, J. (1996). *The stadium game*. National Sports Law Institute of the Marquette University Law School. Milwaukee, WI.

Greusel, D. (1992, August). Building a shared vision. *Athletic Business*, 32-36.

Hall, B. (2001, November). Trading places. *Stadia*, 111-113.

Hamm, M.M. (1998, November 7). How to deal with damage after flood water leaves. *Houston Chronicle*, 5D.

Happy together. (2001, December). *Facilities Design and Management*, 13-16.

Haven, R. (1992, October 23). Cancellation of Marlboro Grand Prix of New York. New York: New York Public Interest Research Group.

Healey, P. (2002-2004). Yale Field. Retrieved September 29, 2004 from www.projectballpark.org/ne/yale.html.

Heikkinen, R. (2001, August). Sustainability in the building industry. *ASTM Standardization News*, 22-25.

Hennesey, K. (2001, May/June). It makes cents to recycle. *Facility Manager*, 40-45.

Herrick, J. (2001, July/August). Selling tickets at the speed of light. *Facility Manager*, 22-26.

Hewitt, S. (1998, September 3). Ballpark, college tie-in supported. *The Columbian*.

Heyman, B. (2003, December 10). Jets' stadium plan shows progress. *Journal News.* Retrieved September 29, 2004 from www.thejournalnews.com/newsroom/121003/c0110stadiumco.html.

History. (2004a). Retrieved September 29, 2004 from www.athens2004.com/athens2004/page/legacy?lang=en&cid=ec480812f7c39f00VgnVCMServer28130b0aRCRD.

History. (2004b). Retrieved September 29, 2004 from www.rosebowlstadium.com/stadium/history/history.html.

History of the Colosseum and Forum Romanum. (2002). Retrieved June 13, 2002 from www.iei.net/~tryan/h-colfer.htm.

Holtzman, M. (2001, December). Liquid cash. *Athletic Business,* 99-103.

Horman, W. (1993, January). A turf timetable. *Athletic Business,* 51-54.

Howard, D., and Crompton, J. (1995). *Financing sports.* Morgantown, WV: Fitness Information Technology.

Hruby, P. (2002, April 25). The 50 worst sports ideas ever. *Washington Times.* Retrieved April 26, 2002 from www.washtimes.com/sports/20020424-71647378.htm.

Hunter, B. (2001, July/August). The need for an annual business plan. *Facility Manager,* 42-43.

IAAM membership research needs study results. (2002). Unpublished survey by the IAAM, Coppell, TX.

IFMA surveys reveal security is top priority & office space is still shrinking. (2001, May). *Facilities Design and Management,* 9-10.

Immig, J., and Rish, S. (1997, March). Indoor air quality guidelines for Sydney Olympic facilities. Bondi Junction, Sydney, Australia: Green Games Watch 2000.

Introduction to property management services. (2001). Branford, CT: OR&L, Inc.

Jackson, B., and Menser, N. (2000). Olympic sporting facilities await athletes & spectators. *Engineers Australia,* Vol. 72, No. 8.

Johnson, A., and Sack, A. (1996, November). Assessing the value of sports facilities: The importance of noneconomic factors. *Economic Development Quarterly,* Vol. 10, No. 4, 369-381.

Jorgensen, P. (2001, December). Generation XXXL. *Stadia,* 18-20.

Judge rules on Grizzlies arena funds. (2001, July 16). Retrieved July 16, 2001 from http://news.findlaw.com/ap/s/2030/7-11-2001/20011071121175 3640.html.

Kasper Group, Inc. Bridgeport Regional Sports and Entertainment Complex. (2001). Conference handout at University of New Haven, May, 2001.

Kebric, R. (2000). *Roman people.* New York: McGraw-Hill.

Kick-off for 2002. (2001, January). *Stadia,* 15-16.

Korcek, M. (2001, September). Grass with class. *Recreation Management,* 48-50.

Kronish, E. (2002, May/June). Watch your step. *Recreation Management,* 20-25.

Landry, G. (1995, March). Aeration strategies to reduce compaction. *Sports Turf Managers Association,* 4-7.

LaRue, R. (2002, August/September). Safe in their seats. *Athletic Management,* 61-63.

Lay, K., and Lawson, W. (1996, November 3). Fact is, stadium a home run. *Houston Chronicle,* C1.

Leibowitz, J. (2001, July). When disaster strikes. *Facilities Design and Management,* 34-36.

Leonard, J.N. (1974). *Ancient America.* New York: Time-Life Books.

Lewis, B. (1999). *Facility manager's operation and maintenance handbook.* New York: McGraw-Hill.

Lewiston, City of. (1995). Arena Definition Schedule. Unpublished.

Lindstrom, C. (1993, September). Light up the night. *Athletic Business,* 47-51.

Loads of takers for shovelers at Stadium. (2002, December 7). *Connecticut Post,* D5.

Ludtke v. Kuhn, 461 F. Supp. 86 (1978, USDC, New York).

"Major corporate naming rights deals." (2002, March/April). *Facility Manager,* 29.

Make no small plans. . . . (2003). Retrieved September 15, 2003 from www.soldierfield.net/history.html.

Manchester, H. (1931). *Four centuries of sport in America: 1490-1890.* New York: Benjamin Bloom.

Mancia, D. (2003, January). Taking cover. *Stadia,* 27.

Maple Leaf Gardens history. (2002). Retrieved September 29, 2004 from www.angelfire.com/md/MattDurnford/gardens.html.

Martin, M. (2002, November). Good groundskeeping. *Recreation Management,* 23-27.

McCarron, C. (2001, April). Reuse, recycle, rebuild. *Athletic Business,* 55-62.

McDonnell, A. (2004, February). Wowing members with service and offerings. *Fitness Management,* 66.

McGlynn, J. (2001, November). Good relations. *Stadia,* 166-169.

McShane, L. (1996, July 13). Bowe's entourage blamed for brawl. SouthCoast Today. Retrieved November 22, 2004 from http://www.southcoasttoday.com/daily/07-96/07-13-96/c03sp077.htm.

MFMA maintenance tips. (2003, April). *Recreational Sports & Fitness,* 21.

Miniature golf on the roof at lunchtime a possibility with green roofing. (2002, January). *ASTM Standardization News,* 12.

Minnesota leading the way for bleacher safety standards. (2003, February). *Recreational Sports & Fitness,* 36.

Moler, C. (2001). Corporate sponsorship a golden opportunity. Presentation at the Athletic Business Conference, Orlando, FL.

Mooradian, D. (2001, July 23). American Airlines Center facts. *Amusement Business*, 23.

More than just a gym floor. (n.d.). Advertising piece from Sport-Tred, Sport Floors, Inc., Cartersville, GA.

Morris, R. (2004, February). Training your team. *Security Management*, 30-33.

Mrock, K. (1999, March). Turf wars. *Athletic Business*, 56-62.

Mullin, B., Hardy, J., and Sutton, B. (1993). *Sports marketing.* Champaign, IL: Human Kinetics.

Mundt, D. (1997, May). Laundry quandary. *Athletic Business*, 53-56.

Muret, D. (2001, September 17). Liquid flows freely during NFL openers. *Amusement Business*, 1, 13.

Nash, B., and Zullo, A. (1992). *Funtastic trivia and sticker book.* New York: Little Simon.

NBA ticket prices skyrocket. (1999, November 12). *Connecticut Post*, D9.

New York landmarks. (2002). Retrieved September 29, 2004 from www.new-york-new-york.com/madison-square-garden-new-york.htm.

Newman, M. (2002, October). Getting out alive. *Facilities Design and Management*, 20-24.

NFL stadium financing landscape, the. (2001). Retrieved December 26, 2001 from www.vikings.com/Stadium/StadiumLandscape.htm.

NFPA 101, Code for safety to life from fire in buildings and structures. (2002). Quincy, MA: National Fire Protection Association.

Noferi, C. (2003, February). Setting the eCRE standards. *Facilities Design and Management*, 16-19.

Operating budget. (2000). SMG–New Haven operating budget year ending 06/30/2000.

OR&L. (2003). Case study high school spending. Branford, CT.

Orlov, R. (2004). Anschutz Entertainment plans to build a 1,500 room hotel and entertainment center near Staples Center. Retrieved November 15, 2004 from http://www.hotel-online.com/News/PR2004_2nd/June04_StaplesHotel.html

Outside the arena, parking is the name of the game. (1997, October). *Parking Today*, 17-18.

Padres' park back on track. (2001, March). *Stadia*, 13.

Patton, J. (1999, April). Fitness in flux. *Athletic Business*, 51-56.

Perkins, L. (1998, November 9). Meadowland sports authority. Presentation at the International Crowd Management Conference, Charlotte, NC.

Perry, F. (1997, January). Smooth operators. *Athletic Business*, 55-61.

Perry, F. (2002a, March-April). Infield care requires a variety of techniques. *Sodasite*, 11.

Perry, P. (2002b, October). Renewal time. *Athletic Business*, 52-56.

Pihos, P. (2001, January). Past and present. *Stadia*, 71-72.

Pitzl, M. (1996, March 10). Tax protest a tea party: Stadium-levy foes rally support for petition drive. *Arizona Republic*, B1.

Popke, M. (2000, September). Taking root. *Athletic Business*, 53-62.

Popke, M. (2001, May). Mixing it up. *Athletic Business*, 45-52.

Popke, M. (2003, January). Playground confidential. *Athletic Business*, 9-10.

Ralph Engelstad Arena. (2004). Retrieved March 26, 2004 from http://theralph.com/new2/Arena_Info_Section/Arena_Info_Main.htm.

Real story of the ancient Olympic Games, the. (2002). Retrieved June 13, 2002 from http://upenn.edu/museum/Olympics/olympicpolitics.html.

Repair backlog in Broward County. (2003, September, 23). *Schoolhouse Beat* (e-mail newsletter).

Richman, I. (2001, November/December). Quick change artist. *Facility Manager*, 32-34.

Roderick, L., and Quintana, R. (1996, May). *Safety and ergonomics manual.* University of Texas at El Paso.

Rogers, J. (1994, December). Bright prospects. *Athletic Business*, 52-56.

Rogers, J. III, and Stier, J. (1995, May). Sowing seeds. *Athletic Business*, 49-56.

Ryan, K. (2004, March). A stadium in the park. *Recreation Management*, 52-53.

Ryan, P. (2002, July). Ready for anything. *Stadia*, 17-20.

Rynd, F. (1998, June 21). Personal interview at the University of Houston.

Safeguarding employees from workplace violence. (2001, July). *Facilities Design and Management*, 11.

Safety is top priority for new 7 World Trade Center. (2003, February). *Facilities Design and Management*, 8.

Sanders, P. (1998, April). The real cost of lighting. *Parking Today*, 14-17.

San Diego Convention Center adopts safety measures. (2001, November/December). *Facility Manager*, 12.

San Francisco Municipal Health Code (Article 19 A through E), Smoking Pollution Control Ordinance. (Added by Proposition P, 11/8/83).

Scandrett, D. (1998, December). Bleachers. *Athletic Business*, 86-91.

Schlossberg, D. (1983). *The baseball catalog.* Middle Village, NY: Jonathan David Publishers, Inc.

Schoenberg, D. (2001). Madison Square Garden turns 30. Retrieved October 16, 2001 from http://thegarden.com/cgi-bin2/msg?function=loadTemplate&file=about.html.

Schumacher, D. (2001, January). Keeping the score. *Stadia*, 29-31.

Shaping Houston's sports future. (1996, May 20). Houston, TX: Houston and Harris County Sports Facility Public Advisory Committee.

Shenker, J. (2002). Staff retention. Proceedings from the 2002 Athletic Business Conference, Orlando, FL.

Sherman, R. (1997, October). Strengthening weight rooms. *Athletic Business*, 74-80.

Sherman, R. (1998, April). Concessions and codes. *Athletic Business*, 63-67.

Sibold, S. (2002). The Olympic legacy. Retrieved December 19, 2002 from www.ovel.ucalgary.ca/oval_olympics/oly_olylegacy.asp.

Sieger, S., and Patel, J. (2001, July). Striking a deal. *Stadia*, 62-65.

Simons, R. (2002, July). Chartered territory. *Stadia*, 44-46.

Single, E., and McKenzie, D. (1991, December). The regulation of alcohol in sports events. Retrieved February 6, 2003 from www.ccsa.ca/docs/alcsports.htm.

SMG, Leisure management form merger of gigantic proportions. (2000, May/June). Facility Manager, 8.

Smith, D. (2003, March). BC culture shock. *Contingency Planning & Management*, 40-41.

Society of Fire Protection Engineers. (2002). *The SFPE handbook of fire protection engineering* (3rd ed.). Quincy, MA: National Fire Protection Association.

SODA. (1993). Member survey conducted by Sportsplex Operators and Developers Association, unpublished.

Sport disasters. (2003). Retrieved September 29, 2004 from http://print.factmonster.com/ipka/A0001453.html.

Stadium & arena sponsorship. (1998, June). *Facilities*, 46.

Stadium suit still alive. (1996, May 18). *Washington Post*, HO2.

Staples Center by the numbers. (2000, July-August). *Facility Manager*, 27.

Steinbach, P. (2000, May). Romper rooms. *Athletic Business*, 84-92.

Steinbach, P. (2001a, April). Ground control. *Athletic Business*, 89-97.

Steinbach, P. (2001b, May). Night games. *Athletic Business*, 61.

Steinbach, P. (2002, March). Dirty works. *Athletic Business*, 72-79.

Steinbach, P. (2003, January). Rethinking the rink. *Athletic Business*, 43-48.

Stinebaker, J. (1996, August 8). Stadium tax finds little poll support. *Houston Chronicle*, A1.

Sullivan, B. (1995, September 15). Dallas maverick. *Houston Chronicle*, B1.

Sullivan, B. (1996, July 25). In Atlanta, the bus stops here—or there. *Houston Chronicle*, A1.

Swimming pool guidelines. (1997). Alaska Department of Education.

Teicholz, E., and Noferi, C. (2002, January). Higher ED integrates CAFM better. *Facilities Design and Management*, 13-14.

Tepfer, D. (1999, November 7). 4 neighbors sue Fairfield U. to halt use of athletic fields. *Connecticut Post*, A21.

Top security threats. (2002). Pinkerton Service Corporation.

Touched by an Angeles. (2000, July-August). *Facility Manager*, 12.

Townsend, B. (2003, January/February). On dasher! *Facility Manager*, 18-21.

Trends driving foodservice at sports and entertainment venues. (1997, February). *Facilities*, 17.

Trest, G. (2003, February). Effective crisis management. *Today's Facility Manager*, 26-28, 41.

Trotter, B. (1996, January). The cutting edge. *Athletic Business*, 61-64.

Trusty, B., and Trusty, S. (1995, February). Mowing tips: Cutting heights, frequencies, & patterns. *Sports Turf Managers Association*, 1-3.

Turner, E., and Hauser, D. (1994, May). Safe and sanitary. *Athletic Business*, 61-64.

Understanding the hazard. (2000). New York: Factory Mutual Insurance Company.

Varouhakis, M. (2004, November 12). Final cost of Olympics soars to $11.6B. Retrieved November 12, 2004 from http://news.yahoo.com/news?tmpl+story&u=/ap/20041112/ap_on_sp_ol/oly_athens_cost.

Vertical Alliance's Sports Marketing Newsletter. (2004, July 29). Vol. 3, Issue 30.

Viklund, R. (1995, July). High-performance floors. *Athletic Business*, 41-44.

Vivian, J. Daugherty, D., and Dunn, R. (1994, March-April). Bloodborne pathogens. *Facility Manager*, 17-19.

Walker, M., and Stotlar, D. (1997). *Sport facility management*. Sudbury, MA: Jones and Bartlett.

Watson, J. (1998, January). Waterworks. *Athletic Business*, 59-64.

What is FM. (2002). Retrieved September 29, 2004 from www.ifma.org/whatsfm/.

Whelan, M. (2001, March). Down to the wire. *Stadia*, 85-87.

White, A., and Slade, L. (2001, September). Collegiate conversions. *Stadia*, 51-54.

Whiting, S. (1993, April 13). The gourmet bleachers. *San Francisco Chronicle*, B3.

Whitney, T., and Foulkes, T. (1994, December). Keep the noise down. *Athletic Business*, 57-60.

Wiggins, J. (1993, August). Building a budget. *Athletic Business*, 61-66.

Wilkinson, D. (1988). *The event management and marketing institute*. Toronto, Ontario, Canada.

Williams, J. (1996, November 6). County stadium referendum passes by narrow margin. *Houston Chronicle*, A1.

Williams, J. (1998, February 21). Authority tries today to resolve bidding war over ballpark cooling. *Houston Chronicle*, A25.

Williams, J. (1999, April 7). Enron to pay $100 million for naming rights. *Houston Chronicle*, A1.

Wrightson, Johnson, Haddon, and Williams. (2004). Retrieved April 12, 2004 from http://www.wjhw.com/aac.html.

Yaeger, C. (1998, November/December). Sydney 2000: The first green Olympics. *Facility Manager*, 17-21.

Yarborough, J. (1998, October 15). Let it snow. *American Way*, 78.

Zaretsky, M. (2002, October 2). Ravens seeking property tax break. *New Haven Register*, B3.

Zikmund, W., and d'Amico, M. (1996). *Basic marketing*. St. Paul, MN: West.

Index

Note: Page numbers followed by an italicized *t* indicate a table.

About the Author

Gil Fried, JD, is an associate professor at the University of New Haven in New Haven, Connecticut. He has taught sport facility management for more than 10 years and has written numerous articles, books, and book chapters on sport facility management issues. Fried speaks across the country on sport facility management issues ranging from how to build and finance facilities to risk management concerns. As an attorney, Fried has represented numerous sport facilities and has been the general counsel for more than 10 years for several different sport facility management associations. He has worked with the International Association of Assembly Managers (IAAM) and is developing the curriculum materials for the IAAM's Academy for Venue Safety and Security. Fried serves as counsel for the law firm of Sabia & Hartley (Hartford, CT) and director of risk management for OR&L Facility Management (Branford, CT).

*You'll find
other outstanding
sports resources at*

www.HumanKinetics.com

In the U.S. call

1-800-747-4457

Australia.. 08 8277 1555
Canada 1-800-465-7301
Europe..+44 (0) 113 255 5665
New Zealand... 0064 9 448 1207

 HUMAN KINETICS
The Information Leader in Physical Activity
P.O. Box 5076 • Champaign, IL 61825-5076 USA